The Longwood Reader

The Longwood Reader

Sixth Edition

Edward A. Dornan
Orange Coast College

J. Michael Finnegan
Orange Coast College

New York   San Francisco   Boston
London   Toronto   Sydney   Tokyo   Singapore   Madrid
Mexico City   Munich   Paris   Cape Town   Hong Kong   Montreal

Senior Sponsoring Editor: Virginia L. Blanford
Marketing Manager: Alexandra Smith
Senior Supplements Editor: Donna Campion
Production Manager: Ellen MacElree
Project Coordination, Text Design, and Electronic Page Makeup: Stratford
    Publishing Services
Cover Designer/Manager: Wendy Ann Fredericks
Cover Image: Top: © Dorling Kindersley and Bottom: © Stockbyte.
Manufacturing Manager: Mary Fischer
Printer and Binder: R.R. Donnelley and Sons Company
Cover Printer: Lehigh Press, Inc.

For permission to use copyrighted material, grateful acknowledgment is made
to the copyright holders on pp. 659–662, which are hereby made part of this
copyright page.

Library of Congress Cataloging-in-Publication Data

The Longwood reader / [edited by] Edward A. Dornan, J. Michael Finnegan.—
    6th ed.
        p. cm.
    ISBN 0-321-20960-7—ISBN 0-321-29058-5
      1. College readers. 2. English language—Rhetoric—Problems, exercises, etc.
    3. Report writing—Problems, exercises, etc. I. Dornan, Edward A.
    II. Finnegan, J. Michael.

    PE1417.L66   2006
    808'.0427—dc22   2005010495

Please visit our website at http://www.ablongman.com/dornan

ISBN 0-321-29060-7

    5 6 7 8 9 10—DOH—08 07

Contents

"The school seal has been pressed over a photograph of my mother at the age of thirty-seven. . . . She stares straight ahead as if she

our most base instincts let free, our nastiest fantasies realized . . . and
it all happens, fittingly enough, in the dark."

"In these stories, anything can happen, not because the world's a magical
place rich with wonder—as in folktales of yore—but because our world
is so utterly terrifying."

"I was in the fifth grade when Frankie died. . . . My whole class planned to
attend the funeral, since we knew him. My father thought going might give
me nightmares, but I insisted. I had never seen a dead person before. Most
of all, I wanted to be sure that the little creep would never touch me again."

"If we wouldn't let GM sell crack because it destroys our communities,
then why do we let them close factories? That, too, destroys our
communities."

"For many millenniums, Earth has been the home of a single intelligent
species. Humans are now engineering the second one."

"The polish man, usually a woman, is the joke's editor, charged with
burnishing the joke until it gleams."

"When we think about addiction to drugs or alcohol we frequently focus on negative aspects, ignoring the pleasures that accompany drinking or drug-taking."

"Gossip must be nearly as old as language itself. It was, I imagine, the earliest recreational use of the spoken word."

"The spoken word, like the written word, amounts to a nonsensical arrangement of sounds or letters without a consensus that assigns 'meaning.' . . . Words themselves are innocuous; it is the consensus that gives them true power."

"What is macho? That depends which side of the border you come from. . . . Take the newspaper descriptions of alleged mass murderer Ramon Salcido. That an insensitive, insanely jealous, hard-drinking, violent Latin male is referred to as macho makes Hispanics cringe."

"The creative person . . . is able to entertain and play with ideas that the average person may regard as silly, mistaken, or downright dangerous."

Thematic Contents

Current Issues

Family Life

Growing Up

Human Behavior

Language

Media

Men and Women

Minority Experiences

Personal Experiences

Politics and Government

Work

Pairs of Essays

Preface

The sixth edition of *The Longwood Reader* maintains the rhetorical arrangement of the first five editions but it also includes several unique chapters.

Unique Features

Chapter 3, Writing about Visual Images, is new to this edition. Chapter 3 emphasizes the significance of images students encounter on a daily basis, whether in popular media, fine art, or personal photographic records. Using a student essay as a model, it also provides the framework for the written analysis of visual imagery.

Chapter 4, Writing a Documented Essay, introduces students to research both online and offline. The chapter concentrates on the writing of a brief documented essay on a topic of current interest. It emphasizes the importance of critically evaluating sources and clearly distinguishing their work from the work of other writers. Chapter 4 also presents MLA documentation guidelines and suggestions for maintaining a documentation log while composing. Finally, the chapter includes a model essay that demonstrates the writing and documentation process.

Chapter 14, The Reflective Essay, continues to be a unique feature of *The Longwood Reader*. It presents seven artfully written essays for close examination. Through a sequence of unique tasks beginning with notebook entries and moving to a full essay, we hope to approximate the creative process many experienced writers describe. We also hope that completing the sequence will awaken the inexperienced writer's curiosity about the possibilities of self-exploration through writing.

Critical Reading

In chapters that concentrate on particular rhetorical modes, nine in all, we use student sample essays for illustration. We continue to follow each sample with a series of questions aimed at revealing the student writer's strategy. Our hope is that these sections, called Reviewing with the Writer's Eye, will engage students in a comprehensive analysis of each rhetorical mode. Moreover, the format encourages group discussion of the student samples much in the way that questions following professionally written essays encourage discussion.

Almost one-fourth of the essays are new to this edition of *The Longwood Reader*. While selecting these new pieces, we were guided by the same principle that guided our selections for past editions: the assumption that good reading influences good writing.

By "good reading" we mean the activity that engages a reader's imagination when he or she picks up a text. We mean the ability to question an author's ideas, to subject an author's argument to skeptical scrutiny, to use a pencil to note disagreements and counterpoints in a text's margins. By good reading we also mean the ability to read with a "critical eye," that is, to read with the ability to see an author's strategies: the way paragraphs are shaped, the way sentences create rhythm and impact, and the way images create feeling. Every writing course must then also be a course in reading with a second sight that sees beneath a text's skin to examine its bones and vital organs. Unfortunately, reading like a writer, reading with a critical eye, does not come naturally; students must acquire the ability.

Chapter 1 of *The Longwood Reader* prepares students to read with a critical eye. We explain the reader-writer contract: A reader must assume that a writer has created an understandable work; a writer must assume that a reader wants to understand the work. Together the reader and writer create meaning, relying on writing conventions to aid their effort. We explain the importance of reading to understand a writer's purpose, strategy, and style, a framework that establishes the pattern for the discussion questions that follow each essay. We also present the phases of critical reading and illustrate the practice of reading with a pencil in hand with paragraphs from Barbara Ehrenreich's "In Defense of Talk Shows" accompanied by student notes. We close the Introduction with an assignment that launches students into the process of reading critically.

Writing Process

Chapter 2, The Writing Process, features a student essay, one we use throughout the chapter to illustrate key concepts. In this chapter we define the essay, place essay writing in the college classroom context, and then discuss the composing process. The discussion begins with ways to find subjects and follows with an explanation of prewriting techniques that help writers explore their subjects.

We then offer methods for sorting and grouping information in rough form by using clusters or informal outlines. Next we explain the thesis statement—how to find one and shape it to serve as an essay's guiding principle. We go on to explain and illustrate formal planning with a clear sense of a reader in mind (a step many students resist). We then discuss essay structure in detail—a discussion that concentrates on strategies for writing introductions, discussions, and conclusions. We also present guidelines for maintaining unity, coherence, developing content.

Ten Tips for Revising Sentences follows. These are practical tips, ones we believe will not overwhelm student writers with technical detail but still provide them with enough direction to polish their essays.

Rhetorical Arrangement

We conclude The Writing Process with a detailed discussion of peer review sessions. Here we cover peer review responsibilities, which includes explanation and illustrations of effective ways of giving and receiving advice. We also present guidelines for reading and discussing a fellow student's essay.

We arranged Chapters 5 through 13 according to traditional writing methods, beginning with description and ending with argumentation. We believe there is a slight risk in teaching rhetorical modes. When misunderstood, they may generate "cookie-cutter" prose, but we believe the benefit of mastering rhetorical modes outweighs the risk. When students understand these common development patterns, they can examine them at work in professional essays, thus sharpening their critical reading skills. By way of caution, however, throughout *The Longwood Reader* we discuss essays as having a dominant mode. We point out that during the composing process writers respond primarily to their material by selecting paragraph and essay patterns that best suit their subject and purpose instead of trying to fit their material into preselected patterns.

Each chapter that concentrates on a rhetorical mode begins with a detailed discussion that explains the writing method, offers strategies for using the method, and presents a sample of student work, several paragraphs in length, that illustrates the method at work in college writing. Here we wish to emphasize "detailed," for *The Longwood Reader* offers a thorough, though economical, discussion of each rhetorical mode and uses a variety of examples to illustrate major concepts. In Chapter 6, Narration, for instance, you will find an explanation of narrative effect illustrated by a brief tale from Zen Buddhist lore. You will find advice on writing the opening, body, and climax of a narrative as well as a discussion of conflict, point of view, chronological and psychological time, and scene and summary. We use several examples to illustrate these concepts to help students understand them in the essays that comprise this chapter. In Chapter 7, Examples, you will find a detailed discussion of specific, typical, and hypothetical examples as well as the practice of mixing different types of examples in an essay. The discussion is amply illustrated by eight paragraph examples. We continue this practice throughout the text.

Seven chapters have five essays each, while Chapter 11, Persuasion and Argument, has six paired essays and Chapter 8, Process Analysis has three. Each professionally written essay is introduced with a brief biography of the author, brief comments to place the essay in context, and a prompt to initiate attentive reading. Each essay is followed by questions grouped under the headings Meaning and Purpose, Strategy, and Style. Two writing assignments follow the study questions, and each chapter closes with additional writing assignments, one designed to generate a response to a photograph, and the other to challenge students with a wide range of essay topics. Finally, there is also an ample manual available to support an intellectually rich classroom experience.

Reference Features

The Longwood Reader offers two important reference features. The Glossary defines rhetorical terms that appear throughout the text. When a term first appears, it is highlighted in bold type to signal its appearance in the Glossary. *The Longwood Reader* also offers a thematic table of contents for readers who wish to read several essays on a common subject and a list of paired readings for those who wish to read for similarities or differences in perspective and style.

Acknowledgments

We thank those colleagues from colleges and universities around the country who reviewed this edition of *The Longwood Reader:* Luis Contreras, Fresno City College; Holly Cullom, Portland Community College; Betty Freeland, University of Arkansas at Little Rock; Joseph S. Horobetz, Northern Virginia Community College; Kim Johnson, University of Louisville; Rebecca Phillips, West Virginia University-Parkersburg; SuEllen Shaw, Minnesota State University Moorhead; and Kristi Siegel, Mount Mary College.

Once again we thank those who advised us on previous editions: Karen S. Becker, Richland Community College; Katheleen L. Bell, University of Central Florida; Maggie Berdine, West Virginia University at Parkersburg; Michael Bobkoff, Westchester Community College; Judith M. Boschult, Phoenix College; Leigh Boyd, Temple College; Kathleen Byrd, South Puget Sound Community College; Henry Castillo, Temple College; Ragina Copeland, West Virginia University at Parkersburg; Patricia Creed, Temple College; Shirley Curtis, Polk Community College; Michel de Benedictis, Miami-Dade Community College; Charles Dodson, University of North Carolina-Wilmington; Jane Dugan, Cleveland State University; Janet Ever, County College of Morris; Jacqueline Goffe-McNish, Dutchess Community College; Judith Haberman, Phoenix College; Leslie Harris, Georgia State University; Iris Rose Hart, Santa Fe Community College; Elaine Sheridan Horne, Manchester Community College; Gloria Johnson, Broward Community College; Peggy Jolly, University of

Alabama-Birmingham; Robert A. Kelly, Macon College; Joseph LaBriola, Sinclair Community College; Russell R. Larson, Eastern Michigan University; Barry Maid, University of Arkansas-Little Rock; Thomas E. Martinez, Villanova University; Jerry McElveen, Richland College; Michael J. Meils, El Paso Community College; Gratia Murphy, Youngstown State University; Randy Oldaker, West Virginia University at Parkersburg; Judy Ann Pearce, Montgomery College; Ruth Peña, El Paso Community College; Rebecca Phillips, West Virginia University-Parkersburg; Andrea Porter, Mississippi State University; Beth Richards, University of Nebraska; Connie Rothwell, University of North Carolina-Charlotte; Gerald Schiffhorst, University of Central Florida; David E. Schwalm, Arizona State University; Carole M. Sherman, College of DuPage; Anne Slater, Frederick Community College; Ann Spurlock, Mississippi State University; Laurence J. Starczyk, Kent State University; Jo Koster Tarvers, Rutgers University; Donna Tobin, Bucks County Community College; Eugene Wright, University of North Texas; and Joseph Zeppetello, Marist College.

We also thank the professionals who have guided this edition through the development process at Longman Publishing.

We especially thank Virginia Blanford, our Sponsoring Editor, for her patience and insight and Joe Opiela, Senior Vice President, for his advice and guidance for all six editions of *The Longwood Reader.*

Edward A. Dornan
J. Michael Finnegan

The Longwood Reader

1

The Reading Process

There's a story that has become part of our campus's educational lore. At that time, student organizations were challenging campus authorities. A group of dissatisfied students began haggling with the faculty and administration over curriculum changes. Finally, months of negotiation ended in deadlock. Frustrated, the students called a rally. A representative from administration began to speak, offering the "official" view. Suddenly, a student leader leaped to the platform and grabbed the microphone. Veins pulsed in his neck; his face turned crimson; his eyes blazed with anger. Everyone became excited, ready for a fiery attack on the administration and faculty, but instead he shouted, "Words, Words, Words! I'm sick of words!" He dug into a bag and began tossing lecture notes, essay shreds, and pages torn from textbooks at the astonished crowd. "If words were feathers," he bellowed, "everyone on this campus would smother before anything changed." And then he stormed to the admissions office and promptly withdrew from his classes.

Or so the story goes.

A true story? Who knows for sure? It does, nevertheless, illustrate a common belief that words slow action. Indeed, taking direct action seems much easier than agonizing over a thoughtful, well-reasoned argument. But education relies primarily on words, written words—words *you* read and words *you* write. Reading and writing are sometimes slow, frustrating activities that at first glance may seem to oppose each other. On the contrary, though, reading and writing complement each other. The better reader you are, the better writer you can become.

Of course, you've been reading since grammar school. You might even spend some leisure time reading for pleasure, perhaps becoming engrossed in the psychological twists and turns of a popular thriller or enthralled by the intricate social weaving of a historical narrative. But you probably spend more time reading for information, gleaning facts from history, psychology, and science textbooks. While reading textbooks, you concentrate on a goal, which often has something to do with a midterm or final examination. In other words, you've learned efficient reading techniques. You've learned to approach a textbook as if it were a lake in which to trawl for facts and theories instead of bass or trout.

Certainly, reading in this way helps you to prepare for tests. It will also help after graduation when you face the heaps of memoranda, reports, and research that every profession generates. It won't, however, help you to become a better writer. For your writing to improve, you must learn to read like a writer. You can begin by learning to read with a "critical eye." The critical eye reveals a writer's purpose and strategies. It scrutinizes the way words work in sentences. The critical eye pierces a work's surface and reveals its bones and heart.

We offer the essays in this anthology as a means to help you to develop a critical eye. The essay is often described as a well-organized nonfiction composition in which the author concentrates on a single aspect of a subject. Usually, this kind of essay is written in formal English and designed to convey information. But essays as a group cover a much broader territory. They often rise to the level of artful prose and should be read with as much concentration as you would read a poem or short work of fiction. Artful essays are usually impressionistic or exploratory. They express personal feelings or attitudes based on a writer's experience and insights.

Because essays are so varied, these selections represent a great range, all the better, we believe, to help you sharpen your critical eye. They include works by modern essayists, such as George Orwell and E. B. White, as well as works by contemporary essayists, such as Gretel Ehrlich and Phyllis Rose. The essays are from varied sources: newspapers, magazines, academic and scientific journals, and nonfiction books. They cover many subjects: crime and violence, men and women, work and play, country and city life, even culture and customs. The collection embodies several styles, ranging from the newswriter's objective report to the poet's subjective expression. Some are serious. Some are playful. All are worth your attention.

To deepen your understanding of the essay, we have arranged *The Longwood Reader* by rhetorical patterns, that is, according to the dominant strategies writers use to organize the content of their essays. These are common strategies—description, narration, examples, comparison and contrast, cause and effect, process analysis, classification and division, definition, and persuasion and argument. Perhaps you already have a casual acquaintance with a few of these patterns. Good—but now you can get to know them intimately. *The Longwood Reader* examines them closely by beginning each chapter with a detailed explanation of a pattern and a student example of the pattern at work. As you study them, hold one idea in mind: You are reading like a writer; that is, reading to develop your writing skill—reading with a critical eye.

The Writer–Reader Contract

Pause for a moment. Imagine an essayist pushing back from a typewriter desk. The writer stretches and yawns before slipping a final manuscript into an envelope and sending it off for publication. You might think this is the critical moment—when the essay is completed and in the mail to the publisher.

But it isn't.

The critical moment comes when the work falls into a reader's hands—your hands. To begin reading an essay is the first act in a dynamic interaction—not between you and the writer, as you might guess, but between you and the essay itself.

This is not to deny that a relationship connects you and the writer. In fact, readers and writers are joined by an implicit agreement, a "contract." To meet the writer–reader contract, a writer agrees to create an understandable work; a reader agrees to try to understand the work.

Unfortunately, communicating in written language is often difficult. A writer cannot gaze over your shoulder and whisper into your ear to make understanding an essay any easier. Only the essay speaks to you. To fulfill the writer–reader contract, a writer employs principles known as "conventions" to help you understand the essay. Even if the essay is difficult, you must trust that the writer has kept the reader in mind during the writing. You must trust that the writer has seen the essay through *your* eyes. In other words, you must trust that the writer has used the conventions of essay writing to help you understand the work.

Generally, these conventions dictate that essays have a purpose, use clear strategies to achieve the purpose, and employ an appropriate style. Understanding these conventions will help you to decipher most nonfiction texts. Indeed, understanding the conventions will help to sharpen your critical eye.

Reading for Purpose

Writers know that readers expect a purpose to be at work behind a piece of writing. They tend to view purpose from two perspectives: the general purpose of the entire essay and the particular purpose of a paragraph or passage.

General Purpose

A general **purpose** gives an essay direction. It provides a destination. It keeps a reader on track. Some writers, especially when the primary intent is to convey information, state a general purpose: "My purpose is to explain the ways in which human beings have decorated their bodies through the ages: by tattooing, by scarring, and by reshaping bone structure." Other writers, especially those writing personal narration and description, do not state a general purpose as directly, thus encouraging the reader to become more deeply involved in interpretation. You must then formulate the general purpose in your own way: "The writer narrates an early childhood experience to show how important imaginative play is." When an essay is rich enough to invite interpretation, much like a careful reading of an intricate poem or short story, then all that you have heard, tasted, touched, smelled, seen, and thought, all your knowledge of people, books, music, art, culture, and language—literally everything you have lived through—is the raw material at your disposal. Drawing on that rich resource, you apply your knowledge to interpret the essayist's general purpose.

Particular Purpose

The particular purpose refers to what a writer intends in a single paragraph or short passage that helps to develop the general purpose.

Consider a short passage from Norman Mailer's *Fire on the Moon,* a work in which he concentrates on the U.S. space program. In this passage, astronauts Neil Armstrong and Buzz Aldrin have completed their historic moon walk on the Sea of Tranquility. The event takes place at the end of their first day on the moon.

> It was about three-thirty in the morning when the astronauts finally prepared for sleep. They pulled down the shades and Aldrin stretched out on the floor, his nose near the moon dust. Armstrong sat on the cover of the ascent engine, his back leaning against one of the walls, his legs supported in a strap he had tied around a vertical bar. In front of his face was the eyepiece of the telescope. The earth was in its field of view, and the earth "like a big blue eyeball" stared back at him. They could not sleep. Like the eye of a victim just murdered, the earth stared back at him.

One clear purpose is to describe the astronauts' preparations for sleep, but toward the end of the passage, Mailer compares the earth to a murder victim. Moreover, he suggests that Armstrong is haunted by the image of the earth "like the eye of a victim" staring at him. Is the comparison merely a dramatic flourish? We doubt it. The description will lead a sensitive reader to explore the deeper purpose in Mailer's comparison. Mailer does not spell out what the passage means. Instead, he invites the reader to interpret it. That puts the reader in an interesting spot, for just as Mailer has drawn on his knowledge and experience to create the image, readers must draw on theirs to interpret it, to find a meaning.

The meaning may vary from reader to reader, depending on each one's knowledge and experience. One reader might recall Edgar Allan Poe's macabre tale of murder, "The Tell-Tale Heart." In Poe's story the murder victim's eye—"a pale blue eye"—haunted the murderer, as the blue earth seems to haunt Armstrong. Does the image suggest, therefore, that the earth has been abandoned like a corpse by astronauts who seek other worlds?

Another reader might explore technological associations. At that point in history the Apollo II flight was our most advanced scientific achievement. But at what price? Aren't the human thirst for scientific achievement and the technology it generates sapping mother earth's natural resources? In a metaphorical sense, therefore, isn't technology killing the earth? And couldn't Mailer be using the moon landing to suggest that "ecological crime"? Who, then, are the perpetrators? Perhaps all humankind, represented by the astronaut who, Mailer suggests, feels accused by the "big blue eyeball" staring at him.

Not all essays invite a careful interpretation of purpose, but the many that do are rich in detail and express a personal vision.

Reading for Strategy

A **strategy** is composed of the various approaches, plans, or methods writers rely on to construct their essays. Any writer must develop a strategy to execute an essay's purpose.

Audience

A writer might first develop a sense of audience and a strategy for addressing them: To whom is the essay directed? How much will readers know about the subject? How much time are they likely to spend with the essay? Will they want a straightforward treatment of the subject or an exploration through richly textured prose? Answering questions such as these will give a writer a sense of the audience, a feel for the person sitting at a desk or in an easy chair reading the essay.

Structure

Having acquired a sense of the audience, the writer might next develop a strategy for the essay's structure, knowing that readers want essays to have clear organization. Usually, writers choose a dominant rhetorical pattern to organize their work. Rhetorical patterns are not formulas. They don't offer a magic recipe for success in writing. Moreover, professional writers seldom stick to any one pattern, choosing instead to use several within a dominant structure. We suggest that you look at rhetorical patterns as tools to guide your own writing and to provide effective ways to fulfill a reader's desire for structure.

To see how rhetorical patterns can work, imagine that you are a film critic and want to compare and contrast two movies. You pick thrillers and narrow your subject to plot structure. You decide to explain the similarities and differences in each director's way of hooking an audience, generating suspense, building to a climax, and constructing the resolution. Thorough knowledge of comparison-and-contrast patterns will help you to balance the similarities and differences in your analysis.

While composing your essay, however, you find yourself bringing the plot of a third movie into the discussion, one that represents still another structure. A warning light flashes in the back of your mind. You pause to think through what you're doing. Your knowledge of rhetorical patterns helps you to realize you're drifting into classification, which is a pattern different from comparison and contrast, perhaps one best avoided for this writing situation. You stop. You return to your original strategy or reconsider and in fact move to classification.

At still another stage, you drift into discussing the effects of thriller plots on an audience. It makes sense—an exciting plot does affect an audience, right? Of course it does. But you would be employing yet another rhetorical pattern, cause and effect. After some thought, though, you might decide to explore the effect on the audience, but you will do it in another section of your paper, and you will arrange it according to cause-and-effect technique.

Our point is quite simple: Knowledge of rhetorical patterns helps writers to organize their work. These aren't cookie-cutter patterns that writers press into the dough of their thought. They are effective strategies that writers use to organize their material and guide a reader through an essay. They also help writers to remain flexible, shifting smoothly from pattern to pattern according to the demands of the subject. The best way we know for you to build knowledge of rhetorical patterns is to examine how professional writers use them—that is, to read with a critical eye.

Reading for Style

People usually think of style as appearance. Imagine someone with a certain style walking across your campus. To what kinds of things are you referring when you speak of his or her "style"? Perhaps it's the leather jacket and silver studs; the hair dyed black and spiked; the defiant swagger; even the throaty voice, rasping across the quad—all these details, and more, create the "style" that this person generates.

Word Selection

Writing embodies many details that work together to generate a **style.** To identify a writer's style, you might begin by examining word selection. Are the words abstract or concrete? Do the words lull you into inattention, like the speech of a politician trying to obscure past transgressions, or do they catch your attention, like pebbles pinging against a window? Are the words common, found in everyone's vocabulary? Or are they scholarly, obscure words used by specialists? Or does the writer mix common with scholarly language?

Sentence Structure

You might also study a writer's sentences. Notice how the writer builds sentences and varies their structure. We have no simple rules for this technique. Writers learn a feel for sentences, the way potters develop a feel for clay. They shape them. They vary their length. They alter their rhythm to increase or slow the pace of reading for emphasis.

Figures of Speech

Writers use sentences to create **figures of speech,** the bits and pieces of colorful language sparkling through the essay. A writer might use figurative language to compare two things that are essentially different but alike in some way. With a crisp simile, Flannery

O'Connor compares a woman's determination to a truck: Mrs. Freeman's "forward expression was steady and driving like the advance of a heavy truck." In another memorable simile, Ralph Waldo Emerson offers a fresh way to see a child: "A sleeping child gives me the impression of a traveler in a very far country." With figurative language, writers not only help their readers to understand what is being said, but also add vigor to their prose.

Tone

Word choice, sentence variety, and figurative language combine to create another element of style: **tone.** Begin to think of tone as an expression of a writer's attitude, much as tone of voice may reflect a speaker's attitude. Imagine, for a moment, that you have given a speech. The next day you receive this note:

> That was an effective speech. You carefully covered the main points. We all thank you.

A straightforward compliment? We think so, don't you? But with a few word substitutions and additions and by altering emphasis, the tone changes dramatically:

> That was . . . *some* speech. You *lingered* on all the points— at least three times each. Thanks a lot.

The message no longer expresses appreciation. It now expresses snide criticism. In other words, the tone has changed.

Some kinds of writing are dominated by well-defined tones. News reporters seem to share a tone, an objective presentation of events—just the facts, please. Thriller and romance writers seem to favor a breathless, frenzied tone. Essayists, however, struggle to find the exact tone to fit the subject, audience, and attitude. The same writer may use one tone for one subject and another tone for another subject. The tone may be formal, informal, flippant, conversational, intimate, solemn, playful, or ironic. The tone may even reveal the writer's awe of the subject. Consider the opening lines from Richard Selzer's essay on skin:

> I sing of skin, layered fine as baklava, whose colors shame the dawn, at once the scabbard upon which is writ our only signature, and the instrument by which we are thrilled, protected, and kept constant in our natural place.

Selzer brings to his essay years of experience as a surgeon and medical school teacher. A reader with knowledge of Selzer's background might expect him to treat the skin in a matter-of-fact way, as merely a thin barrier that must be sliced through to reach the vital organs. But this is clearly not his attitude. He writes rhapsodically, "I sing of skin"; he makes a rich comparison, "layered fine as baklava"; and he claims its "colors shame the dawn." The sentence is a tribute to skin, and the tone expresses his sense of awe.

Style is difficult territory to explore, no doubt about it, but if you devote time to reading for style, you will achieve a *feel* for it. Study a writer's words, and you will learn to choose the right words. Study a writer's sentences and you will learn to shape your sentences. Study a writer's figurative language and you will soon be writing colorfully. Study a writer's tone and soon a voice will rise from your pages.

Critical Reading Phases

To read critically, you can't just sweep through an essay and then set it aside. You must read it several times, noting your responses and deepening your understanding during each phase.

Phase 1: Preview the Essay

Know the Writer. Whatever you learn about an author will help you to anticipate his or her biases. If the author is identified as a liberal politician and the subject is poverty, then you might anticipate an argument supporting government aid to the poor. If the author is an environmentalist and the subject is the greenhouse effect, then you might expect a plea to save the world's rain forests. Many periodicals and essay anthologies include information about an author, usually on the first page of the essay or in a section often titled "Notes on Contributors." In this collection, each essay is introduced by a headnote, which includes an author profile and brief comments on the essay. Read each profile with care; it will prepare you for your first reading of the essay.

Consider the Place and Year of Publication. Knowing where the essay was first published is necessary in establishing a writer's credentials. An essay titled "Bigfoot: Hoax or Hysteria?" would have more credibility if it were published in *Media, Culture, and Society* than it would if it were published in *The National Enquirer*. Why? *Media, Culture, and Society* is a highly respected periodical known for its analysis of the influence exerted by newspapers, television, and cinema on reader and viewer perceptions. In contrast, *The National Enquirer* is a popular tabloid known for its sensationalism. Knowing when an essay was first published will also give you clues about the social environment it was written in. Certainly, an essay on civil liberty written in 1960 is going to display different assumptions from one written in 2005.

Examine the Title. This seems obvious, right? Well, you would be surprised at how many readers mistakenly believe that an essay begins with its first line. It doesn't. It begins with a title.

A title can help you to anticipate what is to follow. It might announce the writer's subject, suggest the dominant rhetorical pattern, or hint at the writer's attitude. The title "A Hanging" lets you know you won't be going to a tea party. It makes sense to anticipate an essay about an execution, which will not be a pretty experience. The title "Cyclone! Rising to the Fall" is a little more ambiguous. Does "cyclone" refer to the destructive natural phenomenon? Or does it mean a roller coaster? Or could "Cyclone" be the name of a bronco? Anyway, you probably expect a description of a thrilling, or even frightening, experience, so get a tight grip on the book. "I Want a Wife" seems like a straightforward title. But if you know that a woman wrote the essay, you might expect an ironic tone.

Skim the Essay. Before you begin reading word for word, quickly skim the essay. Flip through it to estimate how long it will take to read critically. Begin by examining a few passages at random. Look for clues that reveal how difficult the reading might be. Are the paragraphs short or lengthy? Are the sentences simple or complex? Are the words from a specialized vocabulary or from common usage? Clues such as these will help you estimate how much time a thoughtful, critical reading will take.

Determine the Dominant Purpose of the Essay. Generally, essays can be categorized in one of four groups, according to purpose.

1. Narrative essays tell stories.
2. Descriptive essays depict experience.
3. Expository essays explain, inform, analyze, or interpret.
4. Argument essays address debatable issues.

By anticipating the dominant purpose of an essay, you'll be able to adjust your reading style accordingly. Narrative essays, for instance, are often indirect and require careful attention to specific detail. Argument essays, in contrast, are usually direct and require close analysis of evidence.

Phase 2: Read the Essay

Once you've skimmed the essay, you're ready to begin Phase 2 of the critical reading process. During this first reading your objective is to understand what the writer is saying. Read as steadily as possible, following the cues the writer uses to keep you on track.

Concentrate on the Essay. Set aside time to read the essay in one sitting. Avoid distractions, such as music, television programs, and ambient conversations. Don't rush, and do try to find something to enjoy in the essay—whether the writer's interesting experience, novel information, or even writing style. Stick to the reading, and avoid letting your mind drift to other pressing activities.

Mark the Essay.　　Read with a pencil in hand. Mark the stumbling blocks, circle words you don't know, and identify difficult or interesting passages. Use a code consistently, such as question marks when you're confused, stars for key points, and brackets to set off passages you might linger on during the next reading. If you are reluctant to write in your copy of the text, try photocopying the essay and use the copy as your primary text for a critical reading.

Record Your Thoughts.　　After the first reading, jot down your thoughts. You may have an objective response that concentrates on the essay's content, such as a series of questions the essay raises or a summary of the main point and supporting points as you remember them. Or you might have a subjective—that is, personal—response that captures your own point of view or a memory the essay has triggered.

Phase 3: Reread the Essay

After the first reading, you know what to anticipate for a second, more critical reading. Now you'll read with care, looking up unfamiliar words, pausing to reread any confusing passages, identifying the main point and subpoints in an expository or argument essay, or carefully tracing the sequence of events in a narrative or descriptive essay. Furthermore, during the second reading you'll check to see if your impressions from the first reading are accurate.

Annotate as You Read.　　During this more critical reading, make notes, either by hand or at the keyboard, that reflect your interaction with the essay. Use your own means of shorthand when annotating the essay; after all, these notes are for your eyes only.

By way of example, student-writer Anna Showalter annotated Barbara Ehrenreich's essay "In Defense of Talk Shows." Showalter learned that Ehrenreich is a political and social critic who writes essays on a diverse range of issues for such magazines as *Ms., The Nation, The Progressive,* and *The New York Times Magazine.* In 1995 *Time* magazine published "In Defense of Talk Shows" as an opinion piece.

For the first reading, Showalter used her private code to indicate trouble spots. During the second reading, she cleared up the trouble spots and wrote more detailed notes. The first two paragraphs of Ehrenreich's essay, along with Showalter's annotations, follow here. The entire essay is printed as part of an exercise at the end of this chapter.

❦ Barbara Ehrenreich ❦

*In Defense of Talk Shows

*How can they be defended?

Republican presidential appointee. Book of moral tales.

Show's very liberal—opposite of Bennett.

Moralistic! More like verbal mud wrestling.

**Keypoint: She takes talk shows seriously.*

These people and their problems aren't what they first seem to be.

Up until now, the targets of [Bill (*The Book of Virtues*) Bennett's] crusades have at least been plausible sources of evil. But the latest victims of his wrath—TV talk shows of the *Sally Jessy Raphael* variety—are in a whole different category from drugs and gangsta rap. As anyone who actually watches them knows, the talk shows are one of the most [excruciatingly moralistic forums] the culture has to offer. Disturbing and sometimes disgusting, yes, *but their very business is to preach the middle-class virtues of responsibility, reason, and self-control.

Take the case of Susan, recently featured on *Montel Williams* as an example of a woman being stalked by her ex-boyfriend. Turns out Susan is also stalking the boyfriend and—

*frisson? Are these
folks for real? Actors
or liars?*

here's the sexual frisson—has slept with him only days ago. In fact, Susan is neck deep in trouble without any help from the boyfriend: She's serving a year-long stretch of home incarceration for assaulting another woman, and home is the tiny trailer she shares with her nine-year-old daughter.

Phase 4: Evaluate the Essay

Evaluation isn't a simple matter of deciding if you like or dislike the essay. It requires a thoughtful response based on solid analysis and interpretation.

Analyze the Essay.   *Analysis* involves the separation of something into parts. For example, you can analyze the content of an argument essay by isolating its claims and supporting evidence to see if the writer's reasoning is sound. Or you might analyze the structure of a descriptive essay to see how the parts fit together in an organized pattern.

Interpret the Essay.   *Interpretation* involves pulling together details to figure out answers to key, often unstated, questions the essay raises. For example, it might be important to determine what audience is being addressed. In "In Defense of Talk Shows," for instance, Ehrenreich addresses a broad, educated audience. She expects her readers to know about the current political debate over popular media's effect on society.

An interpretation might also isolate a writer's unstated assumptions—that is, what a writer supposes to be true based on his or her beliefs or values. In her first paragraph, for instance, Ehrenreich assumes that members of the middle class share certain virtues. Furthermore, she assumes that talk-show producers realize they are preaching these "middle-class virtues." She even assumes that talk-show participants are who they represent themselves to be. If her assumptions are wrong, would it be fair to look at talk shows as pure entertainment, rather than as middle-class "morality plays"?

Sometimes you'll have to figure out a writer's main point in an essay. Some writers, especially when conveying information, state a main point directly, "Let me explain the ways in which humans have decorated their bodies through the ages: by tattooing, by scarring, and by reshaping bone structure." But other writers, especially those writing personal narrative or descriptive essays, don't state a point directly. You must then interpret the writer's main point yourself: "The writer narrates her childhood experiences to show the importance of imaginative play."

Ehrenreich seems to make her main point clear at the end of the first paragraph: to explain that the business of talk shows "is to preach the middle-class virtues of responsibility, reason, and self-control." But a complete reading of her essay reveals that she has a more complex purpose.

Analysis and interpretation, therefore, form the basis of any critical reading and help you develop and support your evaluation of whether an essay is effective or ineffective. They also help you support your own point of view if it differs from the author's.

Phase 5: Respond to the Essay

A careful critical reading of an essay will help you prepare for class discussion. But beyond that, there are three other common responses you can explore.

Respond to Prompts.   At the end of most essays in this anthology, you will find questions drafted to help in your analysis and interpretation of an essay. These questions are grouped into three categories: Meaning and Purpose, Strategy, and Style. Generally, instructors treat responses to these questions informally, assigning them to help you in the reading process rather than to test your formal writing skills.

In-Class Responses.   Sometimes an instructor will ask you to write a brief in-class response to a reading assignment without the aid of your textbook. Usually, these will be brief assignments and will ask you to demonstrate your understanding of what you've read. By having critically read the assignment, you'll be intellectually prepared to write a response, but you must also be prepared to arrange your thoughts in writing under pressure.

Formal Writing Assignments.   Formal writing assignments related to reading usually take one of two forms.

First, an assignment might ask you to write your own essay based on a critical reading of a text. Although a brief summary of the text's content might be part of such an assignment, its main thrust will be to present your analysis, interpretation, and, perhaps, evaluation of the text or a related subject.

The second kind of formal assignment calls for a personal response to a text. Here you'll be using the text as an entry into your own life. You might be asked, for instance, to transfer information from a text to your own experience or to draw parallels between your experience and the author's. No matter how the assignment is shaped, the focus will be on your experience, not on a critical analysis, interpretation, or evaluation of the text.

You will find suggested writing assignments, called Writing Tasks, following each essay in this anthology and at the end of each chapter. These assignments are intended to lead to your writing critical essays or personal essays.

Writing In-Class Responses to Reading

To write an in-class response to an essay, you should have a clear understanding of what your instructor wants you to do. If you are asked to summarize an essay, then you should state what the essay covers as objectively as you can. If you are asked to evaluate the essay, then you should offer your opinions related to the essay. Do not offer your opinions when you are asked to summarize an essay and do not merely summarize an essay when the instructor has asked for your opinions.

Develop a Three-Minute Outline

Before you begin to write, scratch out a brief outline of your response. Even though you might have only fifteen minutes to write your response, you should allow yourself three minutes to jot down your thoughts in logical order. A scratch outline such as this will keep you from straying during the writing process.

Follow Common Writing Practices

In responding to a written work, there are several practices you should follow, whether the assignment is to write in class or not:

1. In the first sentence, state the author, the title, and the author's purpose. Be sure to spell the author's name correctly and state the exact title.
2. After stating the author's full name in the opening sentence, use only the last name when referring to the author. Don't use Mr., Mrs., Dr., Ms., or any such designation with the last name.
3. Use specific references to the essay and attribute them to the author throughout your response. Try to use active verbs besides "says" when attributing something to an author, such as "argues," "claims," "maintains," "points out."
4. Use the historical present—that is, the present tense of verbs—throughout your response.
5. Close with a clincher—that is, a comment that echoes the opening.

What follows is a typical in-class assignment asking students to write a response to a reading assignment, in this case to Willard Gaylin's "What You See Is the Real You."

In 100 to 125 words, state Willard Gaylin's main purpose in "What You See Is the Real You" and trace his line of thought. You have 20 minutes to write your response. This is a closed-book assignment.

Now read one student's in-class response to the assignment and the margin comments that point out effective in-class writing practices.

Effective opening:
identifies author and
title, and responds

Willard Gaylin in "What You See Is the Real You" argues that what has become

directly to the
assignment.

Uses historical present.
After having stated full
name above, uses
author's last name
throughout.

Makes specific
references to Gaylin's
essay.

Closes with clincher.

known as the "inner" person doesn't exist. He maintains that only the "outer" person exists. Gaylin says that people are the sum total of what they do, not of what they think or feel.

Gaylin holds psychoanalysis responsible for people thinking that the inner person is the real person. He points out that the deep reasons for what people do don't matter. It's their actual behavior that matters. To illustrate his point, Gaylin says that a person who has an "evil" nature but resists doing evil deeds by doing "good" deeds is a good person, not an evil one, because he did good in the world.

Gaylin uses an analogy to make his point clear. He says that judging people by their thoughts and feelings, instead of by their outer behavior, would be like hanging on the wall an X-ray instead of a photograph of a person. A person is not what you don't see; a person is what you do see.

Allow Yourself Time to Proofread

Even in a fifteen- to twenty-minute in-class writing assignment, you should allow yourself time to proofread your response. Don't count on rewriting. Instead, scratch out unnecessary words, make additions in the margins or between lines, and correct any punctuation errors. Your instructor will not hold in-class writing to the same standard as out-of-class writing; nevertheless, you should be as precise and neat as time allows.

Reading Critically

The following is the entire text of Barbara Ehrenreich's "In Defense of Talk Shows." Approach the essay as you would any critical reading assignment. After this first reading, you'll find sample questions and writing assignments, just as you will throughout this book.

❦ Barbara Ehrenreich ❦

In Defense of Talk Shows

Up until now, the target of Bill (*The Book of Virtues*) Bennett's   1
crusades have at least been plausible sources of evil. But the latest
victim of his wrath—TV talk shows of the *Sally Jessy Raphael* variety—are in a whole different category from drugs and gangsta rap.
As anyone who actually watches them knows, the talk shows are
one of the most excruciatingly moralistic forums the culture has to
offer. Disturbing and sometimes disgusting, yes, but their very business is to preach the middle-class virtues of responsibility, reason
and self-control.

Take the case of Susan, recently featured on Montel Williams as   2
an example of a woman being stalked by her ex-boyfriend. Turns out
Susan is also stalking the boyfriend and—here's the sexual frisson—
has slept with him only days ago. In fact Susan is neck deep in trouble without any help from the boyfriend: She's serving a yearlong
stretch of home incarceration for assaulting another woman, and
home is the tiny trailer she shares with her nine-year-old daughter.

But no one is applauding this life spun out of control. Montel   3
scolds Susan roundly for neglecting her daughter and failing to confront her role in the mutual stalking. A therapist lectures her about
this unhealthy "obsessive kind of love." The studio audience jeers at
her every evasion. By the end Susan has lost her cocky charm and
dissolved into tears of shame.

The plot is always the same. People with problems—"husband   4
says she looks like a cow," "pressured to lose her virginity or else,"
"mate wants more sex than I do"—are introduced to rational methods of problem solving. People with moral failing—"boy crazy,"
"dresses like a tramp," "a hundred sex partners"—are introduced to
external standards of morality. The preaching—delivered alternately
by the studio audience, the host and the ever present guest
therapist—is relentless. "This is wrong to do this," Sally Jessy tells a
cheating husband. "Feel bad?" Geraldo asks the girl who stole her

best friend's boyfriend. "Any sense of remorse?" The expectation is that the sinner, so hectored, will see her way to reform. And indeed, a Sally Jessy update found "boy crazy," who'd been a guest only weeks ago, now dressed in schoolgirlish plaid and claiming her "attitude [had] changed"—thanks to the rough-and-ready therapy dispensed on the show.

All right, the subjects are often lurid and even bizarre. But there's   5
no part of the entertainment spectacle, from *Hard Copy* to *Jade,* that doesn't trade in the lurid and bizarre. At least in the talk shows, the moral is always loud and clear: Respect yourself, listen to others, stop beating on your wife. In fact it's hard to see how *The Bill Bennett Show,* if there were such a thing, could deliver a more pointed sermon. Or would he prefer to see the feckless Susan, for example; tarred and feathered by the studio audience instead of being merely booed and shamed?

There is something morally repulsive about the talks, but it's not   6
anything Bennett or his co-crusader Senator Joseph Lieberman has seen fit to mention. Watch for a few hours, and you get the claustrophobic sense of lives that have never seen the light of some external judgment, of people who have never before been listened to, and certainly never been taken seriously if they were. "What kind of people would let themselves be humiliated like this?" is often asked, sniffily, by the shows' detractors. And the answer, for the most part, is people who are so needy—of social support, of education, of material resources and self-esteem—that they mistake being the center of attention for being actually loved and respected.

What the talks are about, in large part is poverty and the distor-   7
tions it visits on the human spirit. You'll never find investment bankers bickering on *Rolonda,* or the host of *Gabrielle* recommending therapy to sobbing professors. With few exceptions the guests are drawn from trailer parks and tenements, from bleak streets and narrow, crowded rooms. Listen long enough, and you hear references to unpaid bills, to welfare, to twelve-hour workdays and double shifts. And this is the real shame of the talks: that they take lives bent out of shape by poverty and hold them up as entertaining exhibits. An announcement appearing between segments of *Montel* says it all: The show is looking for "pregnant women who sell their bodies to make ends meet."

This is class exploitation, pure and simple. What next— 8
"homeless people so hungry they eat their own scabs"? Or would the
next step be to pay people outright to submit to public humiliation?
For $50 would you confess to adultery in your wife's presence? For
$500 would you reveal your thirteen-year-old's girlish secrets on
Ricki Lake? If you were poor enough, you might.

It is easy enough for those who can afford spacious homes and 9
private therapy to sneer at their financial inferiors and label their
pathetic moments of stardom vulgar. But if I had a talk show, it
would feature a whole different cast of characters and category of
crimes than you'll ever find on the talks: "CEOs who rake in millions while their employees get downsized" would be an obvious
theme, along with "Senators who voted for welfare and Medicaid
cuts"—and, if he'll agree to appear, "well-fed Republicans who
dithered about talk shows while trailer-park residents slipped into
madness and despair."

Meaning and Purpose

1. What are your own ideas about the purpose of talk shows and where
   do your ideas come from? How do your ideas compare to Ehrenreich's?
2. Ehrenreich refers to Bill Bennett several times. Who is Bill Bennett
   and why does she frequently refer to him?
3. In paragraph 8, what does Ehrenreich mean by "class exploitation"?

Strategy

1. Do you think the first three paragraphs of Ehrenreich's essay are effective? Why?
2. In paragraph 4, Ehrenreich uses a series of quotations. What do you
   believe her strategy to be?

3. At the end of paragraph 1, Ehrenreich states what appears to be her main point. But in paragraph 8, she seems to shift to another main point. Write in a sentence what you believe to be Ehrenreich's main point.

Style

1. What is the tone of Ehrenreich's essay? Identify passages that are particularly effective in capturing her tone.
2. Does the title "In Defense of Talk Shows" reflect her intent in this essay? Is she defending talk shows? If not, what is she defending?

Writing Tasks

1. Critic and radio personality Ted Libbey writes, "In today's voyeuristic society, it's easy to get people's attention by showing them the seamy side of life. Reality-based television is the rage. It stars people . . . whose only claim to fame—of the 15-minute variety—is that they survived. Or didn't."

    Study Ehrenreich's essay to examine how she uses examples. Then write an essay agreeing with Libbey's observation. In your essay, explain what you believe to be a "voyeuristic society." Throughout the essay, use specific examples to support your position.
2. Write an essay that uses Ehrenreich's "In Defense of Talk Shows" to discuss another "lurid" and "bizarre" aspect of entertainment media.

    First, identify Ehrenreich's main purpose and summarize her argument. Then shift your focus by writing a transitional sentence, such as "Ehrenreich's view that talk shows are a form of class exploitation also applies to other forms of popular entertainment."

    The transitional sentence should lead you to a discussion of another exploitive spectacle, such as other television programming, music videos, talk radio, tabloids, or films. Like Ehrenreich, identify who is being exploited—the poor, minorities, a profession, a gender, or other social group—and how they are being exploited.

2

The Writing Process

The situation has changed. The writer–reader roles are reversed. You are no longer the reader. You are now the writer, in this case the essayist. The writer–reader contract still applies to the situation, but now you must meet the obligation you have to your reader, which is to compose an understandable work. You, in other words, will be using writing conventions to guide your reader, and your reader will rely on these conventions to decipher your essay. Bluntly, you, like every successful writer, must fulfill your half of the writer–reader contract: You must use what you have learned from reading with a critical eye.

Remember, essays are relatively brief nonfiction compositions. Essays concentrate on a single aspect of a topic. Effective essays always have a well-defined purpose, use clear strategies to achieve their purpose, and employ an appropriate style. Sometimes essays, especially in college writing, integrate research, but usually they tend to be personal, embodying a writer's voice and analyzing or interpreting a subject from a writer's personal perspective. Keep in mind, however, that even though an essay embodies a writer's perspective, it is not necessarily *about* the writer. Instead, essays gain their personal character from the individual writer's insights and values as manifested in the discussion.

Rhetorical Patterns

Although a writer might combine several rhetorical patterns in an essay (each discussed in a separate chapter in this text), one of nine common patterns will usually dominate the overall work, depending on the subject and the writer's approach.

1. *Description* captures the sense of an experience. Description renders what something looks like, its characteristics, the impressions it makes. (See Chapter 5.)
2. *Narration* relates events. Narration shows what happened, when and where it took place, who was involved, and why it happened. (See Chapter 6.)
3. *Examples* illustrate ideas. Examples offer typical cases and concrete instances to develop a point. (See Chapter 7.)

4. *Comparison and contrast* presents similarities and differences. Comparison relates how something is like something else. Contrast relates how something is different from something else. Combined, the pattern relates how two things are both alike and different. (See Chapter 8.)
5. *Cause and effect* identifies reasons and results. Cause and effect explores why something happened, what the consequences are, how something is related to something else. (See Chapter 9.)
6. *Process analysis* explains experience step by step. Process analysis shows how something happens, how it works, how it is made. (See Chapter 10.)
7. *Classification and division* establishes categories. Classification and division sorts things by their common components and characteristics. (See Chapter 11.)
8. *Definition* limits meaning. Definition explains what something is, what it means, how it is like and different from other members in its class. (See Chapter 12.)
9. *Persuasion and argument* convinces readers. Persuasion and argument attempts to move people to action or to convince them to change their opinions. (See Chapter 13.)

Writers use rhetorical patterns to help them make writing choices. Imagine, for a moment, that you have been assigned an essay on advertising. Once you decide on your essay's purpose, you will then decide which rhetorical pattern would best help to achieve the purpose; thus the pattern dominates the essay's development. For example, if your purpose is to relate consumer stories, you would choose narration. If your purpose is to reveal the subliminal messages in advertising images, you would choose description. If your purpose is to explain the similarities and differences between two advertising campaigns, you would choose comparison and contrast. Or if your purpose is to convince a reader that film directors should stop including "disguised" cigarette advertisements in movies, then you would choose argumentation. No matter which choice you make, your final essay will reflect the rhetorical conventions of the pattern you choose, thus helping the reader trace the development of the essay's central purpose.

College Essays

Once you decide on a dominant rhetorical pattern and are ready to write, you can employ another conventional essay strategy by structuring your essay in three main parts: an introduction, a discussion, and a conclusion. Often referred to as the thesis-support essay or the college essay, it is the most commonly used essay structure in academic writing, which doesn't mean that it is the only effective essay structure you can use. It is, however, the one we emphasize in this chapter.

Part 1: Introduction

Introductions are composed of one or more paragraphs, all designed to introduce an essay's central purpose—or, as we like to call it, your promise to your reader. An introduction should arouse curiosity, provide appropriate background information, and clarify any questions the reader might need to have answered to understand the central purpose. An introduction should also display the thesis, which is a clear, limited statement of the essay's general purpose. Think of the thesis statement as a direct promise to a reader put into specific language. It is a promise that clearly sets the course for the rest of the essay.

Part 2: Discussion

Discussions fulfill the promise made in the thesis. An essay's discussion should be several paragraphs long, substantially longer than the introduction, all organized by topic sentences that identify subpoints of the thesis statement. The topic sentences should also echo the thesis to show that the promise is being fulfilled and to rivet the reader's attention to the essay's central purpose.

Part 3: Conclusion

Conclusions bring an essay to a satisfactory close. At the very least, a conclusion should show that the promise made in the thesis statement has been fulfilled. One point to keep in mind: A conclusion should never apologize for covering the subject inadequately.

Typically, a college essay is between 500 and 1,500 words, but more appropriately, the length should be determined by the complexity of the subject and the amount of detailed discussion necessary to support the thesis.

Please don't get the wrong impression. Effective essays are not as mechanically contrived as our brief description might suggest—a fact that you can quickly substantiate by thumbing through several selections in this text. Our purpose here, before discussing the process involved in composing an essay, is to emphasize that writers employ a few common conventions to help them meet their part of the writer–reader contract. How well writers use those conventions depends on their skills.

A Student Essay for Study

Now, with this brief description in mind, study the following essay on one aspect of the topic *propaganda*. The student author, Lane Williams, has the following to say about his essay:

> For me composing an essay is a chaotic activity. Whenever I reread a final draft and it makes sense, I'm always surprised. The development of this essay was especially chaotic. I created it from my own ideas, class notes, and by looking at magazine and television advertisements.
>
> One major problem I had to overcome was to think about an essay in more complicated ways than I had been taught in high school where I learned to write five-paragraph essays. For this project I had too much information to fit into a simple five-paragraph structure, so I needed to work very hard at organization. But once I had all my material gathered, the central purpose emerged and the actual writing process began to organize itself. What is my purpose? I wanted to explain some ways advertisers use propaganda devices to trick us into spending our money. Clearly my essay had to define some important

terms, but overall I knew the rhetorical pattern would be dominated by examples.

Now study Williams's essay. After reading the essay through once, reread it along with the marginal notes, which point out some of the conventional strategies Williams uses.

Title uses an allusion to suggest essay will deal with advertising.

First sentence introduces the general subject: propaganda.

Who's Come a Long Way, Consumers?

To propagandize is to attempt to convince people of something by appealing to their emotion rather than to their reason. For good or evil, propaganda is everywhere in our lives. It helps shape our attitudes on thousands of subjects. Nowhere is propaganda more visible than in advertising. For example, why is investing in Fidelity Federal retirement account an investment in "the American way?" Or how can buying Betty Crocker cake mix confirm a sense of "motherhood"? Or how can a feeling of "freedom" be gained from smoking a Marlboro? Advertisers suggest there is a relationship between these products and the language they use to sell them. But in reality they are merely obvious attempts to trick consumers. Advertisers associate pleasing language with products to make consumers feel good about buying them. Such language is called glittering generalities, or virtue words. They tug at a consumer's emotion rather than at his or her reason. Besides glittering generalities, advertisers use several other propaganda techniques to trick consumers into buying their products.

Briefly mentions glittering generality, one propaganda technique.

Key word, "trick."

Thesis statement: Writer promises to explain propaganda techniques and show how they work.

Topic sentence presents one subpoint of thesis.

Bandwagon briefly defined.

Bandwagon is another technique advertisers use to trick consumers into buying their products. Through bandwagon, they urge people to buy a product because it is popular—that is, because everyone is doing it together. This call to "get on the bandwagon" appeals to the strong desire to join the crowd rather than be an outsider. A classic television advertisement for Plymouth's minivan uses bandwagon to motivate car buyers. The advertisement features a group of people working out in a gym. A message over the loudspeaker announces, "There is a Plymouth minivan parked in the street." The message is clear: If you want to be part of the crowd, buy a minivan. An early magazine advertisement for Cuervo Gold tequila also makes use of bandwagon. The advertisement features sixteen young party people either sitting on the edge or standing in an empty swimming pool. They are clearly enjoying themselves, each holding a margarita and toasting the viewer outside the advertisement. Clearly, a Cuervo Gold party is fun. The message is that the consumer can join the party. How? Quite obviously, buy Cuervo Gold . . . and hop on the bandwagon.

Example 1

Example 2

This brief paragraph links bandwagon discussion with next subpoint, testimonial.

The Cuervo Gold tequila advertisement also features a television personality—Dennis Miller. Miller stands in the group's center and also holds a Cuervo margarita. His presence adds prestige to the product, suggesting that if Cuervo Gold is good enough for a celebrity like Dennis Miller, it certainly is good enough for the average consumer. The technique of using a celebrity to sell a product is called testimonial, another method advertisers use to entice consumers.

Brief definition of testimonial.

Opening sentence sets up a more detailed discussion of testimonial.

Historically, testimonial has been a commonly used advertising ploy. Over a century ago, <u>Huckleberry Finn</u> author Mark Twain promoted Great Mark Cigars and heroic wild-west figure Buffalo Bill Cody promoted the Kickapoo Indian

Presents a catalogue of celebrities.

Series of brief examples

Medicine Company. Today, celebrities from film, sports, and even politics are lending (more accurately, "selling") the use of their names and images to represent a wide variety of products: Academy Award winner Robert De Niro for American Express; <u>Sex in the City</u> star Sarah Jessica Parker for Gap; champion golfer Tiger Woods for Buick; and even former member of the Senate and candidate for president Robert Dole for Viagra. Among the more clever uses of testimonial, Hanes, a hosiery manufacturer, featured former Jets quarterback Broadway Joe Namath wearing panty hose. What do celebrities know about the products they pitch? Probably very little, but advertisers bank on consumers being attracted to a product because a celebrity claims to use it. The appeal is to emotion, not to reason.

This paragraph begins with a clear topic sentence and defines "plain folks" with a brief comparison to testimonial.

Another device advertisers use to trick consumers is plain folks. In one way plain folks is like testimonial. Both involve someone standing up to praise a product, urging consumers to rely on his or her word, not on sound evidence, to make a product decision. But whereas testimonial features a respected celebrity, plain folks features someone "just like ourselves" to promote confidence in a product. Often plain folks takes the form of a dentist praising a toothpaste or a friendly neighbor recommending a brand of coffee or a Little League coach explaining that a detergent is powerful enough to remove grass stains. Of course what advertisers do not reveal is that these are all actors who are paid (just as celebrities are paid) to pitch the toothpaste, coffee, and detergent.

Examples of "common folks" who praise products.

An advertisement for Solgar Vitamin Supplements features a potent use of the

This opening sentence signals that the "plain folks" discussion will continue.

plain folks device. This advertisement features a young attractive working mother, who is obviously a single parent trying to make ends meet. In the middle of the advertisement, she stands behind her son, smiling with her arms wrapped around him in a protective embrace, and looks directly at the viewer. The son, about eight years old, is also smiling and holding on to his mother's arm. Both seem to be healthy and to care deeply for each other. Above the photograph is the phrase "First Things First," suggesting that loved ones come first. Below the photograph, the son is quoted as saying, "You're the most important thing to me, Mom. Please take care of yourself." Featured next to the comment is a bottle of Solgar Vitamins. Implicitly, the average working mother and son are testifying to the power of Solgar Vitamins to maintain their health and their loving relationship.

An extended example

Also at work in this Solgar advertisement and in most advertisements, for that matter, is another propaganda device called transfer. Through transfer advertisers attempt to lure consumers into buying their products by associating them with something consumers love, desire, or respect. No manufacturer uses transfer more effectively than Philip Morris, Inc. For decades Philip Morris has effectively transferred the desire for the rugged cowboy's outdoor life to smoking Marlboro cigarettes. Marlboro advertisements often feature images of cowboys herding cattle or riding horses across open spaces. More recently, Marlboro has concentrated less on cowboys at work and more on equipment these Marlboro men use: worn boots, spurs, lariats, saddles—each item designed to remind the reader of a life

Effective transition into next paragraph.

Briefly defines transfer.

Example 1

spent on open prairies with snow capped mountains in the background. And, in case the consumer misses the point, Marlboro advertisements usually include the slogan, "Come to Marlboro Country." How can consumers reach "Marlboro Country"? By lighting up a Marlboro cigarette, of course, thus completing the transfer.

Opening sentence connects with previous discussion of transfer.

Philip Morris also makes effective use of transfer in its Virginia Slims magazine campaign. Each advertisement features a beautiful woman staring boldly into the camera. Clearly, she is in charge of her life, the visual embodiment of an independent woman. In a box placed in the corner of these advertisements is a contrasting image, a photograph of a woman from an earlier historical period serving a man. An ironic slogan links the two images, "You've come a long way, baby" (ironic because "baby" echoes sexism). Without much analysis the advertiser's ploy here is clear. Philip Morris hopes to entice women into smoking Virginia Slims by transferring a desire for personal independence to its product.

Example 2 of transfer (echoes title)

Conclusion opens with a "question." Emphasizes critical thinking.

Do these propaganda ploys work? Can advertisers actually trick unwary consumers into buying their products? When subjected to critical examination, propaganda seems to be obvious, perhaps even ludicrous . . . certainly too clumsy to allow any manufacturer to pick a consumer's pocket. But the power of propaganda is emotional. Advertisers use propaganda techniques to operate beneath the level of intellect where images and concepts are not subjected to critical analysis. They work through suggestion, association, image. They seduce and their seductions have taken advertisers "a long way." Why else would they use these propaganda tactics to trick consumers year after year and decade after decade?

Echoes title "A long way."

Ends with a provocative question.

Williams's essay is effectively executed. He has established a strong purpose and expressed it in a clear thesis statement, which serves as his promise to the reader. He develops an ample discussion section by arranging his information around subpoints of the thesis statement, thus fulfilling his promise. And his conclusion successfully brings the essay to a close. In other words, Williams has met his part of the writer–reader contract.

Let's now examine the process that Williams and other writers follow to create their essays. We don't want to give you the impression that experienced writers sit down and write a perfect first draft—they don't. They struggle with subjects, shuffle rough notes, doodle with outlines—all in an effort to shape their material effectively into finished form. Generally, a finished essay unfolds according to a writer's unique composing methods, that is, the phases of the composing process that begin with finding a subject and end with a final draft.

Find a Subject

"What should I write about?" is an all-too-familiar question that often signals that a writer is blocked. If you find yourself asking this question, you must immediately turn the question to your advantage. Instead of "What should I write about?" ask, "How can I find a subject to write about?" The rephrased question gives you direction. You can stop chewing the pencil eraser and go to work.

Here's how to start.

Self-Initiated Assignments

Begin by keeping this writing principle firmly in mind: You will write your best essays on subjects you know and care about. We urge you, therefore, to examine your own experience for subjects. Look at your interests, your work, your values, your leisure activities. Watch the news, a film, or a television show for ideas. Browse through a newspaper or magazine for subject possibilities. Any of these sources can give you plenty to write about.

You must pursue this search actively. Engage yourself in the process by picking up a pencil and going to work. Try one of the following strategies:

1. *Create idea lists.* Time management experts urge busy people to keep lists of commitments—action lists. Action lists begin as random collections of upcoming events, commitments, or tasks. Once the list is complete, the list maker evaluates the entries, ranks them, and establishes a work schedule. The list provides the person with some clarity and direction for his or her activities.

   An idea list, like an action list, helps to bring your activity into focus. In this case the activity is writing. You can use an idea list to compile possible writing topics. Begin by setting a minimum time limit—perhaps thirty, forty, or sixty minutes—and stick to it. Your goal is to develop a *spontaneous* series of brief entries that capture your ideas and responses to them.

2. *Use a journal.* If you have kept a journal at any time in your life, browse through it for ideas. There is always a good chance that if an entry engages your interest, you can develop it into a full essay that will engage a reader's interest.

3. *Record from memory.* If a recent class discussion or lecture stimulated your curiosity or stirred a strong opinion that you hold, record the details you recall. Either the discussion or the lecture could inspire an essay.

4. *Browse through current reading material.* Glance through a newspaper or magazine until a subject catches your attention—perhaps merely a headline or an article title. Jot down your responses. A response to an article can make an effective essay, especially if the article ignites a strong value you hold.

5. *Consult with others.* Writers often find that discussing or brainstorming writing ideas with other people helps them to imagine their project. You might become part of a writing group that discusses writing ideas. You could also consult a

writing buddy—another student or a friend who is more experienced with writing than you are. You can also engage your instructor in a discussion to see whether a particular idea would work. Be sure to take notes or use a tape recorder. Don't risk letting good ideas slip away.

Instructor-Initiated Assignments

Often college writing is initiated by class assignments. At first you might think that an assignment makes the writing task simple, but it usually does not. In fact, an assigned task might be harder to complete than one that you generate yourself. It might create a sense of false security by leading you to skip the exploration process and plunge directly into the first draft.

As a way of defending yourself from this mistake, remember a second writing principle: An assignment is not a subject. You must create a subject from the assignment.

For example, consider Lane Williams's essay. He wrote it in response to the following assignment: "In four to five typed pages, discuss the role of propaganda in political or commercial communication." To an experienced writer, this assignment is much too large to be addressed successfully in a single essay. It must be placed in a more limited focus, reduced to a manageable subject. So instead of plunging into a first draft without exploring the assignment, he used the assignment wisely. Williams says,

> The assignment was just too broad to cover in a five-page essay. I would have to write about propaganda in politics and advertising. I immediately knew it had to be narrowed to manageable size so I decided to explore the assignment by writing an idea list. I knew if I listed enough of my interests I would eventually find something that would give me more direction.

Williams's idea list took the form of phrases capturing the flow of his thought. He put down whatever came to mind. Later he would judge the entries to see how they related.

Politicians and lying . . .
Campaign propaganda in the presidential race . . .
Local council members and land developers . . .
Advertisements and the consumer . . .
Why do people vote for politicians?
Why do people buy certain products?
How do advertisements get attention?
What propaganda techniques are effective in ads?
How can we protect ourselves from propaganda?
   In political decisions?
   In the marketplace?
I'm the victim of propaganda.
   In voting?
   In buying products?
What do advertisements reveal about consumers?
What does propaganda use reveal about politicians?
Propaganda undermines the democratic process.
Master propagandists—political "spin doctors."

Writing the list helped Williams place his subject in focus. Although no single entry represented a clear subject, he was able to combine several ideas to shape a general subject, the role of propaganda in advertising.

Use Prewriting Techniques

You, like all writers, must place your subject in focus and clarify your purpose—often a long and difficult process. The most effective way to start the process is by using prewriting techniques to discover what you know and do not know about the subject.

What is **prewriting** and how does it work?

Well, prewriting is easy to understand. But first, consider how some writers talk about the mind in relation to writing—a simplified view but one that will help you to understand the writing process.

When discussing how they compose their works, writers often talk of intuition and intellect. They associate intuition with creativity.

The creative part of the mind generates ideas, events, and metaphors—the raw material that makes fresh, interesting writing. In contrast, they associate intellect with criticism. The critical part of the mind judges content, organization, and logic—the refined evaluation that makes accurate, coherent writing. Intuition fuels the creative process; intellect guides the critical process. Through the creative process, writers *invent* their material; through the critical process, they evaluate and organize it for readers.

Both creative and critical abilities are necessary to write successfully. The creative process, however, is less self-conscious than the critical process. As a consequence, prewriting activities use the creative process while restraining the more self-conscious critical process.

Freewriting

Freewriting, or brainstorming, is valuable during any phase of the writing process. Freewriting is a method of free association for generating ideas. Freewriting can help you to frame a subject more accurately, generate material, clarify a purpose, and even develop a thesis. But perhaps its most important use is to start the actual writing process.

Once you have a subject, no matter how tentative, set aside some time for a writing session (as we advised you to do when compiling a memory list). While freewriting, abandon the urge to criticize yourself. Instead let the creative process take over, especially if you have a little voice in your head that automatically judges your writing efforts.

To direct the process, write your subject at the top of the page. Then go at it. Write down everything that comes to mind. Associate one idea to another. Don't judge your ideas or shut them out. Often the unexpected will present itself, ideas connecting to ideas in ways you could have never planned. Don't be concerned with the technical aspects of writing—grammar, punctuation, sentence structure, or logic. Merely enter the creative flow of your own thought, excluding the critical process. Remember—this draft is for your eyes only, not for your reader's. It is a rough map of your thought process, a chart of your mental meanderings, not a paper to be graded. About his freewriting process, Lane Williams says,

> Freewriting helps me gain perspective on my subject. The process releases a great deal of information I have somehow stored in my memory. By freewriting, that is, merely following the pattern of my thought, I gain access to that information. The hard part, of course, is sorting through all that I have written.

The examination of freewriting can be difficult. You will quickly discover that much of your freewriting will not help you to develop an effective essay, such as obvious observations, clichéd thinking, dead-end ideas, stalled musings, odd digressions, but other parts will be valuable—"hot" ideas that you can pursue. Evaluating the material in freewriting involves the intellect more directly; that is, now apply the critical eye to decide what material will help develop an effective paper and what will not.

While reading your prewritten draft, mark passages that seem to be hot leads for further exploration. Once you have the leads, you can use them to start another freewriting session to generate more new material.

Freewriting will also reveal what you do not know about a subject. This knowledge can direct your search to the library; to class notes; to discussions with relatives, friends, or teachers; or to any number of sources that will be helpful. All these activities will help to define a general purpose and generate material for your final essay.

Asking Questions

Frame questions about a subject, sometimes referred to as reporter's questions: Who? What? When? Where? Why? and sometimes How?

Of course, not every question will be appropriate for your particular subject, but using the ones that are can ignite an association chain that will help you to view your subject from different perspectives.

For example, the subject of rude behavior could be approached through the following questions:

What is rude behavior?
Who is rude?
Who is affected by rudeness?
Who can change rude behavior?
What causes rudeness?
What is my attitude toward rudeness?
When did I first become interested in rudeness?
Where have I seen rude behavior?
Why are people rude?
How can rude behavior be corrected?

Asking questions will get you started on most general assignments. Keep in mind, though, that you might have to tailor questions for more specialized assignments.

Sort and Group Information

The freewriting is complete. Now is the time to sort and group your ideas in a logical arrangement. Here, one of two common strategies will help—clustering and informal outlining.

Clustering

Clustering visually shows the relationships between ideas. Often freewriting appears to create a hodgepodge of unrelated material, but if you rearrange the material around the central purpose that emerges from the freewritten draft, then you can begin to see connections. In one sense, a cluster brings order to the creative chaos.

Begin a cluster in a simple fashion. Write what you have determined to be your essay's purpose in the center of the page. Draw a circle around the purpose. As you examine the prewritten draft, arrange major ideas around the central purpose in "orbits" connected by lines. Also circle the major ideas. As you discover (or develop) ideas related to the major ideas, create another orbiting system. All this is done in single words or brief phrases. Remember that you can always return to the prewritten draft to examine the full entry. Through this process, you are simply dividing and subdividing your roughly drafted material, becoming more specific as you isolate facts, opinions, examples, and specific details that could be used effectively to develop your purpose.

Here is a tip: Be prepared to create more than one cluster. Clustering, like freewriting, often generates even more material. We also suggest you develop your cluster on a large piece of drawing paper, or at least be prepared to tape several sheets of notebook paper together to accommodate all your material.

Lane Williams created a cluster from his prewritten material. Examine the part of it that is reproduced in Figure 2–1.

Informal Outlining

Another approach to sorting and grouping your material involves arranging the major ideas related to your purpose under broad headings in an informal outline, or "scratch" outline. The complexity of the outline depends on how you like to work. It might include only the broadest heading, or it might include broad headings followed by more specific points, even phrases that capture specific information.

You might create several drafts of a scratch outline, each becoming more specific. Gradually, drafts of scratch outlines might suggest your essay's final development pattern.

If you find yourself dissatisfied with your outlines, rather than spending a great deal of time rewriting them, photocopy them and then cut and paste the photocopies until you have one that satisfies you.

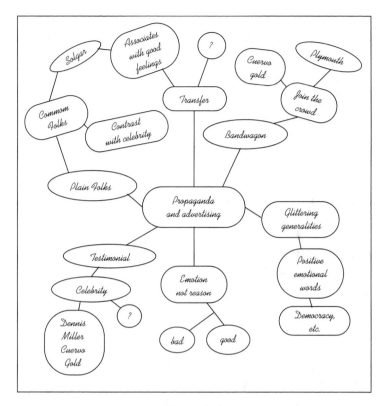

Figure 2–1

The example in Figure 2–2 shows part of the detailed scratch outline that Lane Williams developed from his cluster. About this outline Williams writes,

> I wasn't happy with just clustering. Eventually I have to develop a sense of my material as I imagine it will unfold in the essay. I'm not obsessed with detail or perfection at this stage of the writing process, but I do need to create a strong impression of how the development takes place. The cluster didn't give me

Propaganda and advertising
 What is it: appeals to emotion
 rather than reason.
 Use for good and bad causes.

Methods:
 ① *Glittering Generalities:* Positive words to
 stir strong values.
Develop {
a list of "Motherhood"
G. G. "Manhood"
 "American Way"

 ② *Bandwagon:* Invites consumers to
 join the crowd.
 Plymouth minivan — Health Club
 Cuervo Gold — Yuppie Crowd standing in an
 empty pool, drinking margaritas

 Link to Testimonial — Dennis Miller

 ③ *Testimonial:* Celebrities praise products
 Dennis Miller/Cuervo Gold — two methods
 working together.
 Develop extensive list of celebrities...
 include old Joe Namath ad for
 laughs.

Figure 2–2

the space to add the detail I wanted. For me, an informal outline is a strong preliminary plan that helps me to see where I
need to delete information or develop more information.

Craft a Thesis Statement

Always keep in mind that any essay you write unfolds through a
process. Although throughout this discussion we describe the writing process as if it follows a predictable pattern, in actual practice
you will find it does not always do so. An essay evolves, often chang-

ing its direction as you encounter new information and uncover new relationships in your material. Nevertheless, if there is a point at which an essay's final direction and shape become clear, it is the point at which you form a clear thesis statement.

A thesis statement embodies your essay's central purpose. It is the statement that all the following paragraphs support, argue for, or illustrate. The thesis statement should be broad enough to serve as an umbrella for the discussion that follows it while at the same time it should limit the discussion to a manageable size. In other words, the thesis statement marks the territory of the essay.

Pause for a moment to consider how useful a clearly stated thesis statement is for writers and readers.

For writers, a thesis statement articulates the central purpose and keeps the essay unified. Once you have a clear thesis statement, you will find it easier to make decisions about what to include and exclude. If you have trouble developing your thesis statement, then you know that you must seek more information to flesh out your content.

For readers, a thesis statement tells where the essay is headed. A clearly phrased thesis statement helps them to put your discussion paragraphs in perspective. Imagine the burden you place on a reader if you develop several paragraphs but fail to provide the perspective to understand their purpose. A thesis statement provides that perspective.

Limit the Thesis

What are the characteristics of an effective thesis statement?

An effective thesis statement, usually expressed in a single sentence, limits the central purpose of your essay. If you were writing about crime, for example, and tried to develop the thesis statement "Crime is destroying the social fabric of America," you would soon discover the impossibility of your task. This thesis statement is much too broad for a three- or four-page essay. At best, you could develop only a few general—very general— observations, all unsupported by much specific detail. This thesis statement could be limited, however. Writers limit their thesis statements in two ways.

Limit the Subject. As it now stands, the subject of the thesis statement is crime. But crime covers a large territory that includes murder, robbery, swindles, shoplifting, and so on. If the writer were to concentrate on one aspect of crime and modify the word *crime* to reflect that concentration, then the subject would be limited.

Violent crime is destroying the social fabric of America.
Gang crime is destroying the social fabric of America.
Crime *against children* is destroying the social fabric of America.

Limit the Predicate. These examples are still too broad, much too broad, for a brief essay, even though the subject is more narrow. Another way to limit a thesis is to limit the predicate part, in this example the part that reads "is destroying the social fabric of America."

The phrase "the social fabric of America" covers a great deal of territory, but if the writer were to write about his or her direct experience, the phrase might be narrowed to a city, town, or neighborhood.

Violent crime is destroying the social fabric of my
    neighborhood.
Gang crime is destroying the social fabric of my hometown.
Crime against children is destroying the social fabric of our
    local elementary schools.

These statements are now manageable. A writer could develop them from personal observation, police reports, and newspaper articles.

State a Thesis Precisely

An effective thesis statement is always stated precisely and lends itself to development. Vague language and overly general assertions misguide readers. Use precise language, not fuzzy words, to phrase your thesis statement.

Not: The study of people in prisons is fascinating.

But: Psychological studies of imprisoned murderers reveal that the death penalty is no deterrent to killers.

The second example, phrased precisely in specific language, leaves no room for the reader to be confused about the purpose of this paper.

Finally, an effective thesis statement makes a promise to the reader to fulfill the essay's purpose, a promise the writer must keep or risk writing an unsuccessful essay.

For example, consider the following three thesis statements:

If a thug has the firepower, holding up a mom-and-pop grocery store is a simple process.

The promise: To explain the easy process of robbing the innocent.

Although there were over 450 arrests in my neighborhood last year, crime can be categorized into three groups.

The promise: To classify local crime.

Some people think the political buzz phrase "law and order" has something to do with putting criminals behind bars, but in reality it has a racist definition.

The promise: To redefine the political phrase "law and order."

Lane Williams developed his thesis statement in several phases. He says,

> By the time I had finished freewriting and grouping my material, I had a pretty clear idea of my general purpose. I wanted to expose how some advertisers misguide consumers. After I developed more material by reviewing class notes and finding some typical advertisements, I decided it was time to formulate a more specific purpose, that is, a thesis statement that would keep me on track.

> I began with this statement: "The public needs to become aware of how advertisers deceive them." Sounds lame, doesn't it? At least

that's what I thought. Just too vague. I rephrased it: "The public needs to know how advertisers use propaganda to deceive them." I didn't like this either. What was I, the public guardian? Mr. District Attorney? The statement made me feel pretentious. But when I had written the word "propaganda," my mind started firing. The assignment called for a discussion of propaganda so the word had to be in my thesis. Moreover, the word stirred up my anger. I hate to be tricked by people, and bottom line, that's what advertisers do—they trick people. So now I was on to my thesis, which finally became "Advertisers use propaganda devices to trick consumers into buying their products." I wasn't sure this statement would be phrased this way in my final draft, but I knew it would help me arrange my paper—and announce what to expect to the reader.

Draft a Plan with a Reader in Mind

If you have not done so already, now is the time to imagine your reader. The reader you conceive in your imagination will influence choices you make about the content and vocabulary of your essay. If you were separately to report the events at an accident scene to a friend, your parents, a police officer, an insurance agent, or as a witness in court you would select different details and words for each occasion. In speech you make this adjustment quite easily. In writing you have to give this adjustment some thought. It is essential, therefore, that before you get too far into the writing process, you imagine who your reader will be so that you can determine how much he or she might already know about your subject, which will help you decide what to include and exclude.

For example, although Lane Williams was writing a paper for a critical thinking course, he decided his reader would be the "average consumer," one who did not know the meaning of propaganda and would not understand the way advertisers use it. This decision and the formulation of his thesis statement meant that he was ready to develop a more formal plan for his essay.

One method to plan your essay is to create a formal outline. Whereas an informal outline will help you to sort and group prewriting around ideas, a formal outline will help you to see the final arrangement of the material. A formal outline will include the thesis statement, the subpoints, and various levels of detail depending on the subject's complexity.

A formal outline can be written in topic or sentence form. The main items will be identified by Roman numerals, the first sublevel of items by capital letters, the second sublevel by Arabic numerals, the third sublevel by lowercase letters, the fourth sublevel by Arabic numerals enclosed in parentheses, and the fifth sublevel by lowercase letters enclosed in parentheses. All letters and numbers at the same level are indented to fall directly under one another.

I. _____

   A. _____

   B. _____

      1. _____

      2. _____

         a. _____

         b. _____

            (1) _____

            (2) _____

               (a) _____

               (b) _____

II. _____

You will rarely need all six levels, especially for college essays. But notice that each level is a division of the level above it. Therefore there must be two items at every level because, logically, a topic cannot be divided into one item. You cannot have an A without a B or a 1 without a 2, for example. Of course, there may be more than two items at any level.

Also keep in mind that all items at the same level must be expressed in parallel grammatical structure and the first word in each item must be capitalized. The following example is a formal topic outline for "Who's Come a Long Way, Consumers?"

Thesis: Advertisers use propaganda devices to trick consumers into buying their products.

   I. Propaganda appeals to emotion not reason
      A. Glittering generalities
      B. Advertisers and propaganda

  II. Bandwagon says join the crowd
      A. Plymouth minivan
      B. Cuervo Gold and bandwagon

 III. Testimonial features celebrities
      A. Cuervo Gold and Dennis Miller
      B. All-star list
         1. Michael Jackson for soft drink
         2. Michael Jordan for shoes
         3. June Allyson for diapers
         4. Martha Raye for denture cleaner
         5. Joe Namath for pantyhose

  IV. Plain folks features the common people
      A. Common folks list
         1. Dentist for toothpaste
         2. Neighbor for coffee
         3. Coach for detergent
      B. Solgar Vitamin Supplements

   V. Transfer associates with good feelings
      A. Marlboro cigarettes and the outdoors
         1. Cowboys
         2. Western gear
      B. Virginia Slims and female independence
         1. Today's woman
         2. Yesterday's woman

  VI. Advertising works

Developing a formal outline forces you to arrange your material for a reader. Throughout the process of constructing a formal outline, you will draw on the informal outline that you constructed earlier, your prewritten material, and any other material you collected. About his outlining process, Williams says,

> This is the first outline I have written. Before I finished I had my rough outline, prewriting, class notes, and the advertisements I planned to use as examples in a pile on my desk. I kept moving through the material, thinking how it should be arranged. I ended up with some surprises.
>
> For instance, I had planned to use glittering generalities as the topic for a discussion paragraph, but while outlining, I realized I didn't have enough material for a full discussion. As a result, I used it in the introduction.
>
> I decided to discuss transfer last because I thought my readers would be familiar with the Marlboro and Virginia Slims advertisements, and I also found them to be the most interesting.
>
> All in all, I discovered that writing a formal outline forced me to think through the actual essay before I started my first full draft. Looking back on the experience, I believe it saved me time overall.

Too often, beginning writers want to skip formal planning, yet it is an important part of the writing process, one that will force you to figure out the final arrangement of your material.

Write Parts of the Essay

At this point in the writing process you should be aware of your reader and the conventions you will use to guide your reader. In other words, you are consciously trying to meet the writer–reader contract by seeing and shaping your material with a critical eye.

To start, reread the final draft of Lane Williams's essay (pp. 30–34). Study how the material from his formal plan was developed into a full essay. Clearly, his initial strategy was to arrange his material in a traditional fashion—that is, to structure his essay with a clear introduction, discussion, and conclusion.

Write the Introduction

In a thesis-support essay the introduction presents the thesis statement. Actually, the term "presents" is not dramatic enough. Let's say that the introduction "showcases" a thesis statement, because to showcase is to display in a way the reader cannot miss. Remember that your thesis statement is your promise to the reader. Don't let the reader miss the promise.

Also remember that the introduction is your chance to grab the reader's interest, but too often student writers waste their introductions. They offer sweeping generalizations. They write aimless, dull comments. They end the sequence with an ill-phrased thesis statement. You should make your introductions do much more. Professional writers tend to use one of six strategies to begin their essays:

1. Relate a dramatic anecdote.
2. Expose a commonly held belief.
3. Present surprising facts and statistics.
4. Use a provocative quotation or question.
5. Create a dramatic narrative example.
6. Define a key term.

Any of these is an effective strategy to begin your essay—if it fits your purpose. That's the key to writing an effective introduction: It must be grounded in the essay's purpose and lead to the thesis statement.

Often introductions are only a paragraph long and end with the thesis statement. But an introduction can be one, two, three, or any number of paragraphs in length. We suggest that it be no longer than a fifth of the length of your entire essay, a reasonable length that should be determined by the complexity of your purpose.

Whatever approach you choose for your introduction, remember that it is an integral part of the essay. It should grow from your purpose, arouse a reader's interest, and showcase the thesis statement, usually by placing it in the closing sentences of the introduction.

Write the Discussion

The discussion develops and supports the thesis statement. Discussion paragraphs present the subpoints and supporting detail necessary to convince your reader that the thesis statement is reasonable. In other words, the discussion keeps the promise implied in the thesis.

To be effective, discussion paragraphs should follow three paragraph conventions: They should be unified, coherent, and well developed.

Keep Paragraphs Unified. Discussion paragraphs have **unity** when the information they present is clearly related to the main idea in the paragraph, which some writers shape in the form of a **topic sentence.** For example, consider the following paragraph from Olivia Vlahos's *Human Beginnings*. Vlahos opens with a clearly stated topic sentence, "Nearly all living creatures manage some form of communication," and follows with a series of examples, each clearly related to the topic sentence.

Topic sentence sets a direction.

Series of examples clearly relates to the main idea.

Nearly all living creatures manage some form of communication. The dance patterns of bees in their hive help to point the way to distant flower fields or announce successful foraging. Male stickleback fish regularly swim upside-down to indicate outrage in a courtship contest. Male deer and lemurs mark territorial ownership by rubbing their own body secretions on boundary stones or trees. Everyone has seen a frightened dog put his tail between his legs and run in panic. We, too, use gestures, expressions, postures, and movement to give our words point.

Keep in mind also that the main idea or topic sentence is one step in fulfilling your promise to the reader. It identifies one subpoint of the thesis and supports that subpoint. For example, Lane Williams begins this process in his first discussion paragraph. He clearly relates his opening topic sentence to his thesis statement, which maintains that advertisers use propaganda devices to trick consumers into buying their products.

Williams's topic sentence establishes the subpoint "bandwagon."

Brief definition of "bandwagon."

    Bandwagon is another technique advertisers use to trick consumers into buying their products. Through bandwagon, they urge people to buy a product because it is popular—that is, because everyone is doing it together. This call to "get on the bandwagon" appeals to the strong desire to join the crowd rather than be an outsider. A classic television advertisement for Plymouth's minivan uses bandwagon

Bandwagon example 1

to motivate car buyers. The advertisement features a group of people working out in a gym. A message over the loudspeaker announces, "There is a Plymouth minivan parked in the street." The message is clear: If you want to be part of the crowd, buy a minivan. A magazine advertisement

Bandwagon example 2

for Cuervo Gold tequila also makes use of bandwagon. The advertisement features sixteen young party people either sitting on the edge or standing in an empty swimming pool. They are clearly enjoying themselves, each holding a margarita and toasting the viewer outside the advertisement. Clearly, a Cuervo Gold party is fun. The message is that the consumer can join the party. How? Quite obviously, buy

Clincher

Cuervo Gold . . . and hop on the bandwagon.

While this paragraph is unified because the entire discussion relates to its topic sentence, it also adds to the overall unity of the essay because the topic sentence refers back to the thesis statement. Echoing the thesis statement in topic sentences is an effective strategy to use throughout an essay. The technique reminds the reader of your thesis and shows how the subpoints are connected.

Maintain Coherence. Guide your readers smoothly and logically from one sentence to another. Don't let them stray from the direction you establish in the paragraph's opening. If they do stray, you risk losing their attention. When a paragraph flows smoothly and logically, the paragraph is coherent; that is, the main idea advances from sentence to sentence in a well-constructed verbal web.

You can create **coherence** in your paragraphs in three conventional ways:

1. by repeating and rephrasing key words and concepts;
2. by using pronouns to refer to key nouns in previous sentences; and
3. by using transitional expressions that guide your reader through a paragraph.

Poet and novelist Erica Jong repeats a key word to create coherence in the following paragraph from "The Artist as Housewife." The paragraph's main idea deals with a poet's problem of creating a personal voice in her work. Jong then associates with *authenticity* in the second sentence. She then repeats or rephrases the key word *authenticity* throughout the paragraph.

Writer maintains coherence by effectively repeating "key word."

The main problem of the poet is to raise a voice. We can suffer all kinds of kinks and flaws in a poet's work except lack of <u>authenticity</u>. <u>Authenticity</u> is a difficult thing to define, but roughly it has to do with our sense of the poet as a mensch, a human being, an author (with the accent on authority). Poets arrive at <u>authenticity</u> in very different ways.

Each poet finds her own road by walking it—
sometimes backward, sometimes at a trot. To
achieve <u>authenticity</u> you have to know who
you are and approximately why. You have to
know yourself not only as defined by the
roles you play but also as a creature with an
inner life, a creature built around an inner
darkness. Because women are always encouraged to see themselves as role players and

Rephrases "key idea." helpers ("help-mate" as a synonym for "wife"
is illuminating here), rather than as separate
beings, they find it hard to grasp this
<u>authentic sense of self</u>. They have too many
easy cop-outs.

In the following paragraph, conservationist Cleveland Amory repeats a key noun—coyotes—and uses pronouns to refer back to it.

Coherence is created by   The <u>coyote's</u> only hope lies in his clever-
the effective use of key   ness. And stories of <u>coyotes</u> outwitting
nouns and their   hunters are legion. <u>Coyotes</u> will work in
pronouns.   teams, alternately resting and running to escape dogs set upon <u>them. They</u> have even
been known to jump on automobiles and flat
cars to escape dogs. And <u>they</u> have also successfully resisted bombing. Lewis Nordyke
reports that once when a favorite <u>coyote</u>
haunt in Texas became a practice range for
bombing, the <u>coyotes</u> left—temporarily. Soon
<u>they</u> were back to investigate and found that
the bombing kept people out. <u>They</u> decided
to stay. Meanwhile, <u>they</u> learned the bombing
schedule and avoided bombs.

Conscious and careful repetition of key words and ideas is a subtle
way to keep a paragraph coherent. A more direct strategy is to use tran-

sitional words and phrases. In "Who's Come a Long Way, Consumers?" Lane Williams uses overt transitions effectively in one paragraph.

Williams uses overt transitions to create coherence.

A recent advertisement for Solgar Vitamin Supplements features a potent use of the plain folks device. This advertisement features a young attractive working mother, who is obviously a single parent trying to make ends meet. <u>In the middle</u> of the advertisement, she stands behind her son, smiling with her arms wrapped around him in a protective embrace, and looks directly at the viewer. The son, about eight years old, is also smiling and holding on to his mother's arm. Both seem to be healthy and to care deeply for each other. <u>Above the photograph</u> is the phrase "First Things First," suggesting that loved ones come first. <u>Below the photograph,</u> the son is quoted as saying, "You're the most important thing to me, Mom. Please take care of yourself." <u>Featured next to</u> the comment is a bottle of Solgar Vitamins. Implicitly, the average working mother and son are testifying to the power of Solgar Vitamins to maintain their health and their loving relationship.

No matter what strategy you use to create coherence, remember that the purpose is to direct the reader's attention as he or she reads from sentence to sentence.

Paragraph Development.   Beginning writers often ask the question, how long should a paragraph be? Paragraph length depends on several considerations: the complexity of material, the rhetorical method, and the length of preceding and following paragraphs. But most important, a paragraph should be developed enough to do justice to the main idea.

Well-developed paragraphs might contain examples, definitions, comparisons, causes, effects, facts, statistics—all presented in enough detail to make a paragraph several hundred words long—or a paragraph might serve as a transition between subpoints of a thesis statement and be only a sentence or two long. When a paragraph becomes exceptionally long, writers will often separate the material into two or more paragraphs to ease the reading process, even though the information amplifies the main idea in a single subpoint. For example, Williams breaks up several exceptionally long paragraphs in "Who's Come a Long Way, Consumers?" as the following example illustrates:

Topic sentence introduces transfer.

First extended example of transfer.

Also at work in this Solgar advertisement and in most advertisements, for that matter, is another propaganda device called transfer. Through transfer advertisers attempt to lure consumers into buying their products by associating them with something consumers love, desire, or respect. No manufacturer uses transfer more effectively than Philip Morris, Inc. For over two decades Philip Morris has effectively transferred the desire for the rugged cowboy's outdoor life to smoking Marlboro cigarettes. Marlboro advertisements feature images of cowboys herding cattle or riding horses across open spaces. More recently, Marlboro has effectively transferred the desire for the rugged cowboy's outdoor life to smoking Marlboro cigarettes. Marlboro advertisements feature images of cowboys herding cattle or riding horses across open spaces. More recently, Marlboro has concentrated less on cowboys at work and more on equipment these Marlboro men use: worn boots, spurs, lariats, saddles— each item designed to remind the reader of a life spent on open prairies with snow-capped mountains in the background. And, in case the consumer misses the point, Marlboro advertisements usually include the slogan, "Come to Marlboro Country." How can consumers reach "Marlboro Country"? By lighting up a Marlboro cigarette, of course, thus completing the transfer.

Opening sentence continues the main idea from the previous paragraph.

Philip Morris also makes effective use of transfer in its Virginia Slims magazine campaign. Each advertisement features a beautiful woman staring boldly into the camera. Clearly, she is in charge of her life, the embodiment of the 1990s image of an independent woman. In a box placed in the corner of these advertisements is a contrasting image, a photograph of a woman from an earlier historical period serving a man. An ironic

Second extended example of transfer.

slogan links the two images, "You've come a long way, baby" (ironic because "baby" echoes sexism). Without much analysis the advertiser's ploy here is clear. Philip Morris hopes to entice women into smoking Virginia Slims by transferring a desire for personal independence to its product.

In the opening sentence, Williams sets up the transition from one paragraph to another by referring to the previous discussion of Solgar Vitamin Supplements. He then develops the main paragraph idea with a brief definition of the transfer device. He follows with the analysis to two extended examples to show transfer at work in advertisements. But since the examples are long, he breaks the paragraph into parts, yet both parts amplify a single main idea—that is, advertisers use the transfer device to trick consumers. Williams is careful to begin the second paragraph with an opening statement that clearly shows the discussion of transfer is continuing, even though he has begun a new paragraph.

While composing an essay, you might discover that you need more information to develop an effective paragraph. You can take three actions: First, you can return to your freewriting draft for an idea. Second, you can actually develop more freewriting. Third, you can consult outside sources for more information. The process of inventing and acquiring material continues until the final draft is complete.

Write the Conclusion

Too often beginning writers treat their conclusions in a perfunctory manner—a couple of general statements about the subject and a rapid "That's all, folks" to close. Experienced writers, in contrast, use a different strategy based on the simple principle that readers remember best what they read last. They therefore treat their conclusions as a challenge, one that demands skill and concentration. Generally, writers use one of four common strategies to close their essays:

1. Review the subpoints and restate the essay's thesis statement.
2. Recommend a course of action.
3. Offer a prediction based on the discussion.
4. Present an appropriate quotation or anecdote that leads a reader to reflect about the subject.

Keep in mind that a conclusion must flow logically from the essay. If it does not, it will merely seem tacked on.

Create a Title

Titles are not afterthoughts, a phrase hastily typed at the top of the page before rushing to class. A title actually begins the essay. Titles should suggest the general subject and serve as an invitation to read the essay.

The best time to compose a title is after you have written your essay. Only then will you know the complete content. The title should be brief but interesting and may be taken directly from the essay. Often, however, it will echo a thought that runs through the essay. About his title, "Who's Come a Long Way, Consumers?" Lane Williams says,

I usually have a hard time thinking of titles, but if I reread the essay or parts of it enough, a title will eventually come to mind . . . persistence, I guess, is my method.

The title "Who's Come a Long Way, Consumers?" is my way of reworking the Virginia Slims slogan. I hope it is read ironically, since my essay's purpose is to make unaware consumers conscious of ploys advertisers use to get their hard-earned cash.

So how should you proceed in composing a title? Well, we can offer no clear guidelines because the process involves more intuition than logic. But once you have a title follow this rule: Never underline or place quotation marks around your own title. Use quotation marks or underlining for other people's titles, not yours.

Edit and Revise Sentences

Once you have a well-structured essay in hand, you can begin the editing and revision process that will lead to the final draft. You might think each phase of the writing process refines the material for the final draft—and each does—but the final draft is the only part of the process your reader will see. We therefore suggest that you approach revision with care.

During the early phases of the composing process, we mentioned that you should imagine your reader. Now the reader becomes a major part of the process, as if he or she is sitting on your shoulder as you make revision decisions.

As you reread your essay with an eye toward revision, consider its style (see pp. 9–11). Style, as you probably recall, has to do with word selection, sentence length and variety, and tone. For college papers, we suggest you employ a plain style that communicates your purpose clearly and directly. You should write in Standard American English, which is taught in schools and used in mainstream magazines and newspapers. In most writing situations, Standard English is appropriate.

Standard American English can be formal or informal. Informal writing is characterized by common expressions taken from spoken

English and makes use of contractions such as "don't," "can't," "won't," and "could've," which are contractions of "do not," "cannot," "will not," and "could have." Formal written English seldom uses contractions and avoids other characteristics of informal writing, such as abbreviations and the personal point of view. About his style decision, Lane Williams says,

> I tried to conform to my instructor's view of English, which leans toward the formal. You may have noticed for instance that I avoided using some common abbreviations. I wrote out "television" and "advertisement" instead of using the more common "TV" and "ad." I also avoided using contractions, to create a more formal tone. I did, however, address my reader as "you" now and then and used the personal pronouns "we" and "our" several times, decisions some instructors might discourage.

At this point in the writing process, you are ready to edit and revise your sentences to make them more readable. Unfortunately, no one has invented a clear procedure to follow in editing and revising prose. Some writers revise as they carefully work their way through a rough draft; others swoop through the first draft and then revise during a second or third draft. Each writer, it seems, devises his or her own approach.

Two preliminary steps in revision do seem to be adopted by all writers. First, they must learn what makes sentences effective. Second, they must pick up a pencil (or sit at a keyboard) and go to work on their sentences. Toward that end, we offer the following ten editing tips for refining sentences. We suggest that you study the ten tips with care before revising the sentences in your rough draft.

Ten Tips for Revising Sentences

1. Eliminate clutter.
2. Select specific and concrete words.
3. Make passive sentences active.
4. Rewrite trite expressions.
5. Place modifiers with care.
6. Correct faulty pronoun reference.
7. Eliminate inconsistencies in sentences.
8. Complete incomplete sentences.

9. Eliminate sexist language.
10. Revise for parallelism.

You should revise sentences with an eye for effectiveness—that is, for clarity, conciseness, diction, and style. Reread the essay slowly, preferably out loud. The ear often detects problems that the eye misses. As you read, make improvements directly on the page.

Checklist for Revision

1. Eliminate Clutter

Your goal is to write in a simple, clear style. Your words should be easily understood, and your sentences should move with some speed. You must therefore cut clutter from your sentences.

Cut Empty Phrases.   Often one or two words can replace a phrase.

believes
Roland Barthes ~~is of the opinion~~ that culture can be

understood by reading the "signs" it generates.

Diet   *usually*
~~It is usually the case that diet~~ books ‸encourage the dieter's

fantasies about being slim.

Replace common empty phrases with shorter and clearer ways of saying the same thing.

Empty Phrase	*Replacements*
come to the realization	realize, see
of the opinion that	think, believe
in order to	to
present with	give
for the purpose of	for

in the nature of	like
concerning the matter of	about
prior to	before
subsequent to	after
during the course of	during
in the event that	if
in the amount of	for
regardless of the fact that	although
at this point in time	now
at that point in time	then
at any point in time	whenever
on the occasion of	when
in view of the fact that	as, since, because
for the reason that	because
make contact with	call
it is often the case that	often
the fact that	that
for the simple reason that	because
due to the fact that	because
on the occasion of	when, on
give consideration to	consider
make an adjustment	adjust
is of the opinion	believes
give encouragement to	encourage
make inquiry	ask
comes into conflict with	conflicts
give instruction to	instruct

Cut Unnecessary *There Are* and *There Is* Constructions.
The word *there* followed by a form of the plain verb *to be* is an exple-
tive, a word used to fill out a sentence. Rewrite such sentences so
that they are direct.

~~There were~~ two reasons. ~~for the disagreement.~~ *They disagreed for*

~~There is little~~ we can do for the rain forests. *Little*

Cut Intensifiers.   Cut words such as *very, really, quite, totally, completely, definitely,* and *so.* When speaking, people use them with vocal emphasis.

The ~~really terrible~~ storm ripped across the bay and ~~totally~~

destroyed business buildings and homes when it hit shore. The

result was ~~very~~ disastrous: ~~So much~~ wreckage, ~~so many~~ helpless

people, ~~so many~~ lost dreams. The sight was ~~really~~ heart breaking.

In writing, emphasis comes from using strong, specific words, not from vacant intensifiers.

Cut Pretentious Language.   Pretentious writing draws attention to itself. Pretentious vocabulary is unnecessarily complex, perhaps because the writer has thumbed through a thesaurus, replacing simple with difficult words. Always try to select simple, direct words.

Killed
The earthquake ~~struck with a malignant force that destroyed~~

~~the lives of~~ more than four thousand villagers.

playing   *friends show*
Children ~~frolicking~~ with ~~their companions exhibit~~ these fears.

Dogs make good pets.
~~Domesticated canines will contribute felicity to anyone's life.~~

Cut repetition and redundancy.   Repetition of key words is often necessary for parallel structure or for emphasis, but needless repetition leads to wordy sentences.

rattler
The Pacific ~~rattlesnake~~ is California's most dangerous snake.

Redundancy unnecessarily conveys the same meaning twice, as in the phrases "visible to the eye" and "large in size."

By probing the ~~factual truth deeply~~ *facts,* researchers found the solution.

Millions of ~~people who vote~~ *voters* support national health insurance.

Cut any of the following common redundancies from your writing:

advance forward	continue to go on
autobiography of her life	disappear from sight
basic fundamentals	factual truth
circle around	important essential
close proximity	refer back
combine together	repeat again
consensus of opinion	round in shape

2. Select Specific and Concrete Words

Definite, specific, and concrete language pulls the reader to the page. General, vague, and abstract language pushes the reader from the page. As an ad writer might phrase this thought: Vivid language gives an "up-close" feeling; vague language gives a "far-back" feeling.

Far Back
He was old when he gained success.

Up Close
He had turned gray and had seen his seventy-first birthday when he won the Nobel Prize.

Far Back
The police arrested him in an alley.

Up Close
Six police officers with drawn pistols captured him in an alley.

Far Back
At Bernard's the sales staff greets customers courteously.

Up Close
At Bernard's the sales staff greets customers with a smile.

Far Back
For me to write an essay takes patience.

Up Close
For me to write an essay takes hours of pacing and pencil chewing, at least a hundred pages covered with useless scribbling, and several pots of black coffee.

Revise Slang.   Slang can be colorful vocabulary that arises from the experience of a group of people with common interests, such as teenagers, rock stars, jazz musicians, actors, baseball fans, street gangs, surfers, skateboarders, even truck drivers. However, in college writing, you should generally revise your sentences to eliminate slang because it is imprecise and can be confusing.

>   *depressed*
> As a type, comedians are ~~bummed out~~ one moment and
> *elated*
> ~~flying~~ the next.
>
>   *criticized*
> The reviewers ~~ragged on~~ Kaufmann's poetry collection for being
>
> sentimental.

Revise Euphemisms.   A euphemism is a word or phrase substituted for another word that is harsh or blunt. The funeral industry substitutes "loved one" or "the deceased" for "corpse," "vault" for "coffin," and "final resting place" for "grave."

Although euphemisms might often be necessary for tactfulness, they more frequently distract us from the realities of experience. We have become accustomed to "low-income," "inner city," and "correctional facility" as substitutes for "poor," "slum" or "ghetto," and "jail."

If you find euphemistic phrasing when revising your sentences, rewrite the phrase in more specific language.

> His money problems
> ~~The deterioration of his economic status~~ began when he ~~became~~
> lost his job.
> ~~unemployed~~.
>
>   lying
> Military officials seem to believe that ~~misrepresenting the facts~~
>
> is acceptable. ~~behavior.~~

Replace Weak Verbs with Strong Verbs.   Use strong, accurate verbs. For example, consider something as simple as saying how a man "walked."

> The man *walked* down the street.

If you wanted to tell how the man walked, you might write,

> A man *walked quickly* down the street.

Or you might say he *walked rapidly*. But a strong, more accurate verb could do it better:

> A man *scurried* down the street.
> A man *strode* down the street.
> A man *swaggered* down the street.

When revising, check to see whether you can replace weak with strong verbs. Remember to select verbs that fit what you're saying; don't pick them because they sound fancy. For instance, you wouldn't be helping your prose much if you wrote, "A drunk perambulated down the street"—unless you wanted to get a laugh. Instead of *perambulate,* you would probably write *staggered.*

You might say that finding active verbs is easy to do for description, but what about using them in expository or argumentative writing? Well, it can be done. Read the following passage from C. M. Bowra's *Classical Greece:*

> The Greeks won their war with a famous ruse that military men and statesmen often *try to repeat* in other ways. They *gave* Troy a gift—a wooden horse with Greeks hidden inside. While the Trojans *slept,* the Greeks *crept* out and *opened* the city's gates to the rest of their army. Masters at last, the Greek soldiers *saw* Helen reunited with Menelaus, and everyone *started* for home. But one among them, the ingenious Odysseus who had *devised* the wooden horse trick, *found* the route 10 years long.

Verbs and verb phrases such as *won, gave, try to repeat, slept, crept, opened, saw, started, devised,* and *found* make this passage active. Whenever you can, use strong verbs to generate life in any writing you do.

Rewrite Hidden Verbs Disguised as Nouns.   In the following sentences, *was led, search,* and *perform* are not the real verbs. *Solved, replace,* and *analyze* are the real verbs, but they are hidden because they are disguised as nouns.

I ~~was led to the solution of~~ **solved** Travanian's identity.

Since John Simmons quit the committee, we must ~~search for a~~ **replace him.** ~~replacement~~.

To understand *The Deer Hunter* we must ~~perform an analysis~~ **analyze** of its imagery.

Avoid Overuse of *To Be* Verbs.   Revise sentences and passages that overuse forms of *to be*. Often they add clutter to your writing.

At sixty-three, Max Ernst
~~Max Ernst was sixty-three and~~ knew madness and death ~~were~~ lay

before him.

setting sun turned the
The ~~sun was setting. The~~ few clouds ~~that were~~ on the horizon

~~were~~ orange.

The
~~Hemingway's "The Killers" is a story that is dominated by the~~

feeling of impending violence. ╱ dominates Hemingway's
"The Killers."

3. Make Passive Sentences Active

Voice is the quality in verbs that shows whether a subject is the actor or is acted upon. "The arroyos were flooded by rain" is a passive sentence because the subject, "arroyos," is acted upon. In contrast, "Rain flooded the arroyos" is an active sentence because the subject, "rain," is the actor. Active sentences are more concise, direct, and forceful than passive sentences.

The tornado left death and despair.
~~Death and despair was left by the tornado.~~
Nelson Mandela's speeches captured the
~~The~~ Western world's attention. ~~was captured by Nelson~~

~~Mandel's speeches.~~

Generally you should eliminate passive sentences, but at times the passive voice might be necessary. Passive sentences are appropriate when the subject is ambiguous or when you wish to emphasize the receiver of an action.

The mysterious story was sent by e-mail.

The writer does not know who sent the story.

His self-esteem was damaged by years of severe criticism.

The writer wishes to emphasize the thing that received the action: "self-esteem."

4. Rewrite Trite Expressions

Trite expressions are phrases that have become stale from overuse. They include **clichés** (He ran around the neighborhood *like a chicken without a head*), wedded adjectives and nouns (They *made a lifelong commitment*), and overused phrases (We all know that *the rich get richer and the poor get poorer*).

Often trite expressions appear in rough drafts, especially if the writing has been rushed.

He was guilty beyond ~~a shadow of~~ doubt.

debt.
The company was sinking in ~~a sea of red ink.~~

In brief,
~~To make a long story short,~~ the widow married the banker.

The following is a list of common trite expressions. If they appear in your writing, revise them to make them more direct or fresh.

a crying shame	in the final analysis
a thinking person	in the nick of time
after all is said and done	last but not least
at this point in time	method in his madness
depths of despair	never a dull moment
drop in the bucket	none the worse for wear
face the music	pay the piper
flat as a pancake	quick as a flash
in this day and age	sadder but wiser

5. Place Modifiers with Care

A writer can confuse a reader by misplacing a modifier. When revising your sentences, be sure to place modifiers so that a reader will be certain which words they modify.

Correct Dangling Modifiers. A dangling modifier is a phrase or clause that is not clearly related to any word in a sentence. To correct a dangling modifier, revise the sentence to relate it clearly to a specific word.

As he ran
~~Running~~ through the meadow, his breathing made steamy clouds.

writer must keep a
To complete a screenplay, a daily schedule ~~must be kept.~~

the man spent   *his*
After six months in therapy, ~~the~~ psychiatrist pronounced him

cured.

I was
When a student at Reed, Ken Kesey was the student body's

favorite writer.

Place Modifiers Close to the Words They Modify. When a modifier or modifying phrase is placed away from the word it modifies, the result will be confusing.

in Hollywood restaurants
Many beginning actors wait on tables to support themselves, ~~in~~

~~Hollywood restaurants.~~

Aging athletes who exercise (occasionally) will hurt themselves.

Be particularly aware of where you place limiting modifiers, such as "only," "hardly," "just," "nearly," "almost," and "ever." These modifiers can function in many positions in a sentence, but they modify the expression that immediately follows them. As these limiting modifiers change position in a sentence, the meaning of the sentence also changes.

> I will go *only* if he asks me. [Otherwise I will not go.]
> *Only* I will go if he asks me. [The others will not go.]
> I will go if *only* he asks me. [Please ask!]
> I will go if he asks *only* me. [If he asks others, I will not go.]

Rewrite Faulty Split Infinitives.   An infinitive consists of "to" plus the simple form of a verb: "to dance," "to moan," "to study," and so on. Usually, a split infinitive can be revised effectively by placing the modifier more accurately.

Faulty
His inability to clearly explain the issues cost him the election.

Faulty Revision
His inability to explain the issues clearly cost him the election.

Good Revision
His inability to explain the issues in clear language cost him the election.

6. Correct Faulty Pronoun Reference

Pronoun reference is the relationship between a pronoun and its antecedent—that is, the word to which it refers. If a pronoun's reference word is unclear, the sentence will confuse or misinform a reader. Revise sentences so that a pronoun refers clearly to one antecedent.

After Duff had studied Shakespeare for a decade, he realized

Shakespeare
that ~~he~~ was a master psychologist.

Revise sentences that use "this," "that," or "it" to make a broad reference to an entire sentence rather than to a specific antecedent.

While ^(I was) watching *Friday the 13th* on television, my cat howled

and sprang onto my lap, ~~This~~ ^(, which) frightened me.

Revise sentences that use "it," "they," and "you" without specific an-
tecedents. In conversation these pronouns are often used to make
vague reference to people and situations in general. In writing, this
practice should be avoided.

During the "Six O'clock News," ~~it~~ ^(one reporter) gave a special report on
intelligence testing.

^(School policy does not)
~~They do not~~ allow soliciting on campus.

^(police officers)
In law enforcement, ~~you~~ must stay alert to a community's

^(they)   ^(they)
changing values. If ~~you~~ do not, ~~then you~~ will fail.

Using "you" to refer to "you the reader" is perfectly appropriate in all but
the most formal writing as long as the reference to the reader is clear.

If you major in accounting, then you should find a job easily.

Revise sentences with pronouns ending in "-self" and "-selves," used
in place of other personal pronouns.

^(me)
The philosophy professor tried to convince Robin and ~~myself~~

that Albert Camus was fundamentally an optimist.

Pronouns ending in "-self" and "-selves" should refer to words within
the sentence.

To stay calm, *I* talked to *myself.*

Nick Ufre and *Janet Lee* tricked *themselves.*

7. Eliminate Inconsistencies in Sentences

Revise sentences that make faulty shifts. Often faulty shifts take place in pronoun references.

you
If you stretch your muscles before a workout, ~~a runner~~ will not

face injury.

Faulty shifts in verb tenses can confuse time sequences.

mastered
The dancer rehearsed for six months, but finally ~~masters~~ the

movement and was ready to perform.

Faulty shifts in the mood of a verb can be confusing.

Study the causes of World War I, and then ~~you should~~ study

World War II.

A common inconsistency befalls a writer who shifts from active to passive voice, thus dropping from the sentence someone or something performing the action.

In the game of curling, a player slides a heavy stone over ice
a teammate sweeps
toward a target, and the ice in front of the stone ~~is swept~~ to

influence its path.

You should also revise sentences that have shifts between direct and indirect discourse. Direct discourse includes a direct quotation: Dr. Jones said, "Life, my friends, is boring." Indirect discourse rephrases a direct quotation and therefore does not require quotation marks: Dr. Jones had indicated that life is without interest.

Faulty shift
The judge said to pay the fine and "Never return to my court again."

Revised
The judge said to pay the fine and never return to his court again.

Revised
The judge said, "Pay the fine and never return to my court again."

8. Complete Incomplete Sentences

Some sentences are incomplete because they lack words a reader needs to understand them. Often comparisons are not complete. Revise your comparisons to make them clear and logical.

Dr. Casey treats students better/ **than other professors do.**

are
Mystery novels are easier to read than romance novels.

the wail of
The silence of the streets was more frightening than a siren.

In some sentence constructions, writers omit words that are understood. This practice is correct.

Correct
Two people control the city government: one is the mayor; the other, the mayor's wife.

But if omitted words do not fit consistently into the structure, the omission is faulty and the sentence must be revised.

I feel
In the woods I feel the peace of nature; now, the violence of the

city.

in
Humans have a strong belief and desire for love.

9. Eliminate Sexist Language

Changes are taking place in American English usage that reflect a growing awareness of sexism in U.S. society. These changes affect what some social critics describe as a masculine bias embedded in our language. One striking illustration of this bias appears among masculine and feminine word pairs. Generally, female forms are created from male forms:

actor	actress
heir	heiress
hero	heroine
host	hostess
prince	princess

Although you might have a difficult time eliminating words such as these, you can avoid other words and usages that might be construed as carrying a masculine bias.

You can choose to avoid singular, masculine pronouns (he, him, his) to refer to both men and women when the sex of the antecedent is unknown or when the antecedent consists of both males and females. One way to eliminate sexist language in this situation is to make the subject plural.

> *Managers*   *their*   *s*
> ~~Each manager~~ must post ~~his~~ schedule.

You can also avoid the generic use of man to refer to both men and women—"Man dominates the natural world"—by substituting humans or human beings, terms that are generally considered inclusive and less offensive.

Using recent coinages will also help you to avoid sounding biased. For instance, you can replace chairman, which in the recent past was used to refer to both men and women, with chairwoman when a woman holds the position and chairperson for either sex or when the person's sex is unknown.

At this time there is no comprehensive set of rules for avoiding the use of language that seems to carry a masculine bias.

However, you should become sensitive to the social issue. Whenever possible, you should avoid perpetuating a masculine bias in your own writing.

10. Revise for Parallelism

Maintain **parallel structure** by keeping similar ideas in the same grammatical form. In a pair or a series, you must make items parallel to avoid awkward shifts in construction. A noun must be matched with a noun, a verb with a verb, a phrase with a phrase, and a clause with a clause. Revise your sentences to make coordinate ideas parallel.

She loved reading Anne Tyler's novels and ~~the~~ poetry~~,~~ ~~of~~ *Anne Sexton's* ~~Anne Sexton.~~

His summer activities were ~~the dances~~ *dancing* at Hotspur's and sleeping until noon.

Words such as "by," "in," "to," "the," and "that" should usually be repeated when they apply to both elements in parallel construction.

By not developing their land and *by* ignoring tax-reporting requirements, the family found itself bankrupt.

Revise sentences to make compared and contrasted ideas parallel.

Ms. Lauko would prefer ~~to work~~ *working* on her physics project to playing chess.

Zen masters are materially poor, but they are rich~~,~~ *spiritually* ~~in spirit~~.

Revise correlative constructions to make them parallel. The ideas that are joined by correlative conjunctions, such as "either . . . or," "rather . . . than," and "not only . . . but also," should be parallel.

The law applies not only to people but also~~^to~~ corporations.

Cosmo is either dreaming about the future or ~~in a deep~~ *examining* ~~examination of~~ the past.

Proofread and Prepare the Final Draft

Proofread your edited and revised draft with care. Proofreading involves checking the punctuation and spelling, the "nitty gritty" details of writing. Once you have carefully proofread your essay, you're ready to prepare the copy you'll turn in.

Use Standard Manuscript Form

Following standard manuscript form is a courtesy to the reader. These standard guidelines, as set by the Modern Language Association, make a paper easy to read.

Materials.   For handwritten papers use 8½-by-11-inch lined white paper with neat edges, not pages torn from a spiral notebook. Use black or blue ink—not green or red—and write on one side only. Skip every other line to make reading and correcting easier.

For typewritten or computer-printed papers use 8½-by-11-inch white typing paper. Do not use onionskin because it is flimsy; do not use erasable bond because it smudges. Double-space between lines and use one side of the paper only.

Use a type style or font that is standard and easily readable— that is, not italic or cursive. For computer-printed manuscripts, use a letter-quality printer or a dot matrix printer in a letter-quality mode.

Unless otherwise directed, use a paper clip to hold the pages together. Many instructors do not like pages stapled together, and no instructor likes the upper left-hand corner to have been dog-eared to hold the pages in place.

Margins.   Leave margins of one inch on all sides of the paper to avoid a crowded appearance. On lined white paper, the vertical line indicates a proper left-hand margin. On most computers, justification of the right margin creates awkwardly spaced lines. Turn the right justification control off while formatting your paper on a computer.

Indention.   Indent the first line of every paragraph uniformly—one inch in a handwritten manuscript, five spaces in a typewritten one, one-half inch in a typeset one.

Paging.   Place the page number, in Arabic numerals (2, not II), without a period or parentheses, in the upper right-hand corner, one-half inch from the top of each page. You may omit the number on the first page, but if you choose to include it, center it at the bottom.

Identification.   Include your name, your instructor's name, the course title and number, the date, and any other information your instructor requests. Place that information on separate double-spaced lines, beginning in the upper left-hand corner of the first page. Place the line that your name is on, one inch from the top of the page. Also put your last name in the upper right-hand corner, with the page number: Bennett 3.

Title.   In handwritten papers on lined paper, place the title in the center of the first line and begin the first sentence two lines below it. In typed papers, double-space below the date and center your title on the page. Begin the first sentence two lines below it. Capitalize the first and last words, any word that follows a colon, and all other words except articles, conjunctions, and prepositions. Do not underline the title or place quotation marks around it. If the title of another work or a quotation is part of your title, however, underline or use quotation marks as appropriate.

Peer Review

Having other class members review your work can be helpful before completing a final draft. We all have blind spots, but when several sets of eyes examine our essays, the blind spots will usually be revealed.

Some writing instructors organize formal peer-review sessions; that is, they require their writers to submit early drafts of their essays for other class members to comment on. Often peer review such as this is done in established writers groups whose members work together throughout the semester. Other times, instructors re-form writers groups every few weeks to give everyone in class a chance to work together. In either case, writing instructors usually set aside some class time for the groups to complete their reviews. For these peer review sessions, instructors will generally provide review guidelines based on the particular requirements of the assignment, thus establishing clear directions for the evaluation process.

If your instructor does not require formal peer review, you and other classmates might wish to form an informal writers group to help revise early essay drafts. Or you may wish to merely work with another class member to review each other's work. But whether you work in a formal or in an informal writing group or in pairs, the goal will be the same: to see your work through another reader's eyes, for often an essay that may be perfectly clear to you will be confusing to a reader who has intellectual and emotional distance from the material.

Peer Review Responsibilities

You have two responsibilities during the peer review process: to receive advice and to give advice in a collegial manner.

Receiving Advice.   Writing isn't easy, and sometimes it's in the flawed piece of writing that writers place the most emotional energy. When someone criticizes it, then, quite naturally, the tendency is to become combative. The writer will defend each paragraph, each sentence, each word against what may be perceived as an attack. Of course, when writers look at responses to their work unemotionally, it is easy to see that reviewer comments are offered as suggestions for improvement, not challenges. So relax when receiving advice. Judge the observations by what you are trying to accomplish and how well your effort is executed.

Once your work has been reviewed, read all written responses with care. Although they may be brief, they may still be valuable. Moreover, you can follow up written responses to a draft by asking the reviewer questions to help clarify or amplify any written advice. Be sure to consider all oral responses and note the advice you feel will help improve your draft. If a group member asks you a question, answer, but don't feel that you have to justify the decisions you made during the writing process. Most important, don't become defensive. Always remember that your reviewers will be evaluating the effectiveness of a piece of writing, not your character.

While revising, should you incorporate suggestions? To do so is your decision. Sometimes the responses will conflict, often reflecting a reviewer's inexperience or misconceived information. Other times the responses will agree, giving you a clear direction for revision. Remember, only you can decide which responses are appropriate and which are inappropriate. The responsibility for a final draft is all yours, not your group's nor your partner's.

Giving Advice.   When reviewing another writer's work, keep in mind that your task is not to rewrite the draft but to respond as a reader and offer advice for improvement. It's up to the writer to write the next draft.

What kind of advice should you offer?

First, know the assignment. Each draft that you read will be written in response to a writing assignment. To respond intelligently, you must be familiar with the assignment. The chances are you will be writing an essay for the same assignment, but if not, then it's your job to know what the assignment calls for and keep the requirements in mind when reviewing a writer's early draft.

Second, apply your knowledge of writing strategies when giving advice. You will have studied essay strategies, both as we will present them in the following chapters and as your instructor will present them in class. These strategies will help you make accurate observations and give you a vocabulary to describe your observations in a way the writer will be able to understand.

Third, offer specific advice. Identify a draft's strengths and weaknesses as specifically as you can. Vague and general observations don't help a writer. For example, the following two responses represent the extremes. One is ineffective, and one is effective.

Ineffective Response

Good work. I like the way it reads, even though it isn't clear. Also good use of words. I like it. Keep it up.

Clearly, this is an ineffective response. Why? Perhaps the reviewer fears hurting the writer's feelings. Or perhaps he has not read the assignment the writer is responding to. Or perhaps he's just plain lazy. Who knows? Still this fact remains: The student offers only vague, "feel-good" responses that avoid giving specific advice to improve the writer's draft.

Effective Response

Discussion of paragraph 2 is particularly strong. Using a question as a topic sentence followed by an answer clearly sets the pattern that follows: "How many situation comedies currently run on television? Only three, but they are broadcast under 23 different titles." This paragraph opening is effective, but the three categories that follow overlap—you should fix them.

One problem though is unity. You seldom refer to your thesis in topic sentences. To fix it wouldn't take much. I suggest you add a key word to your thesis, such as "dysfunctional" and work it, or synonyms for it, into your topic sentences. For example, "The dysfunctional family lurks behind all the antics in *I Love Lucy.*" Just a suggestion. Take it or leave it, but you still need to improve unity one way or another.

Another strong point is your use of active verbs: "shrieked," "maul," "cavort," and so on. They all add specific detail—good.

This reviewer's response is effective. She identifies strengths and weaknesses in specific language. Where she can, she gives advice to help the writer revise. She does all this specifically and clearly.

Fourth, don't be distracted by surface errors when giving advice. Do not spend your time correcting grammar, punctuation, and mechanics. Tell the writer that the errors exist, but remember it's the writer's job to proofread carefully and correct surface errors. Instead, concentrate on the larger elements.

Five General Questions to Guide Peer Review

To stay on track, use the following five questions to guide your review:

1. Does the draft reflect the concepts presented in the assignment?
2. What is the dominant purpose and is the organization logical?
3. At what points is the draft confusing?
4. Is the draft adequately developed? Does it need more information or examples?
5. What is the draft's main strength? Weakness?

The first step in the review process is usually done in writing, then the reviewer will discuss the written review with the writer.

Five Guidelines to Discuss a Review

Always respond sensitively. Most beginning writers have no experience submitting their work for peer review. They might misconstrue genuine advice for criticism. To avoid sounding critical, make objectively descriptive comments instead of subjectively evaluative comments. Keep in mind that your responsibility is to help other writers, not to criticize them for their mistakes. When discussing your responses with a writer, keep in mind the following guidelines.

1. A review session should be a dialogue, not a debate.
2. Ask questions that might help you develop a clear understanding of the writer's goals.

3. Take notes while reading a draft and use them to discuss the draft's strengths and weaknesses. Emphasize the strengths, but remember the writer needs to know the weaknesses.
4. Make suggestions for improvement related to the writer's intent.
5. Close your response by summarizing ways the writer can improve the draft.

Remember, the emphasis is on improvement—both for the writer as a writer and for the reviewer as a reader.

3

Writing about Visual Images

Seeing Beneath the Surface

The Method

The word *image* comes from the Latin word *imago*, which means imitation, copy, or likeness. Today, visual images have become powerful influences on how people perceive experience.

Whether they come from journalism, political propaganda, advertising, or the art world, images are often believed to depict reality when, in fact, the opposite may be true. Visual images, whether created by renowned artists or obscure photographers—especially those images that become part of the public consciousness—seldom depict reality. More often, they are consciously designed constructions calculated to affect the viewer.

When you examine powerful imagery with a critical eye, begin the analytical process with this in mind: A photograph or painting is not "the real thing." It's a *constructed replica*. Your task is to subject the image to analysis and interpretation to reveal its deeper, perhaps emotional, significance.

During the actual planning and writing process of your essay, you'll need to be flexible. The rhetorical patterns you use—that is, the paragraph structures—will vary. No doubt you'll use description to capture the details of an image. You will probably also use examples of images to illustrate your thesis. You may even decide to compare and contrast images or to classify them. More than likely, you'll discover the pattern that works best for each paragraph during the writing process. You'll have to be intellectually nimble enough to adjust as you compose each draft.

Strategy

Interpreting visual images means you must go beneath the surface to articulate your understanding of what the images mean. Begin with your general response to an image. Then examine the parts, relating them to your general response. During this exploration process, you should note patterns and relationships among the key elements and determine how they work together as a whole. Although interpretations are always speculative, the goal is to explain the whole image by examining its parts.

The following example paragraph is taken from an essay that interpreted three photographs selected from a single edition of *The New York Times*. The photograph interpreted here is of Jacques Derrida, a noted French intellectual; it accompanied his obituary. Pat Maguire, the author of the essay, found the image to be "haunting."

> The photographic portrait of Jacques Derrida that accompanies his obituary is haunting. According to the article, Derrida is a significant intellectual force. The central figure in the photograph is Derrida himself. He sits at a table, leaning forward, one hand casually holding an open book. His head is turned toward the viewer, framed by his white hair and white shirt collar. His eyes are dark, perhaps even black. There are two other significant elements in this image. The first is a single lighted candle on the table. It seems to be the only source of light. The other is the black background. The only significant elements that can be seen against the background are Derrida himself, the book, and the lighted candle. At one level the portrait suggests that Derrida is like a medieval scholar, an appropriate portrait for a noted intellectual. But the image is affective at another level. His eyes, dark as black stones, are haunting. The visual confrontation seems to challenge the viewer to enter Derrida's world. Of course, the haunting question is whether Derrida is inviting the viewer into the world of knowledge or into the world of darkness that awaits us all.

Maguire's opening sentence presents his final point—that the Derrida image is "haunting." Throughout the rest of the paragraph, he weaves objective detail—the key elements of the image—with his personal analysis.

When interpreting an image, you must first gather reliable information. Observe the image carefully. What do you feel? What do you see? Take notes during this process. These notes will become the raw material for a written interpretation. You can begin the process by answering four questions, writing down your observations as you answer:

1. What does this image make me feel?
2. What are the elements in the image that work together to create that feeling?
3. What do I infer from or associate with these elements?
4. Based on my inferences or associations, what do I believe the image communicates?

The notes Pat Maguire took while examining the Derrida image—some of which were used in the analysis—document his progression through this questioning process:

Derrida Portrait

- Derrida's image stopped me cold when I turned to it in the Times. I felt like I had just walked through a door and he turned from reading to look at me. Then, I felt he was almost ghostly. When I realized it was part of an obituary, the image became haunting.
- Derrida is the central figure, gray hair, pale face, white shirt. He sits against a dark background—ghostlike.
- His eyes are very dark and piercing.
- Two other important elements. The book. The candle.
- The article reveals a lot. Derrida is a respected intellectual. It makes sense to have a portrait of him reading, but why the confrontational stare? Why isn't he looking at the book?
- The candle I associate with classic works of art, Georges de la Tour and Caravaggio. But the candle is only a prop, put there as a symbol. The photographer lit Derrida with a soft light outside the frame. If not, his face and body would be in shadow.
- Clearly, the photographer is presenting Derrida as a scholar, fitting for his obituary. But his figure speaks to me in other ways. It's ghostly. Confrontational. Challenging.

What elements will attract your attention as you carefully observe an image? That depends on you, of course—that is, on the knowledge and experience you bring to the photograph. Several people looking at the same image might come up with very different interpretations. What's essential is that you base *your* interpretation on a careful observation of detail and what *you* infer from the detail.

Structuring an Essay about Visual Images

When writing about visual images, we suggest that you follow the three-part college essay structure—the thesis-support structure—explained in Chapter 2 and emphasized throughout *The Longwood Reader.* Because there are several elements specific to writing about images, we offer the following review of the thesis-support essay with specific illustrations from essays that interpret visual images.

Writing an Introduction

In the introduction, you have three primary tasks to achieve:

1. Present the essay's thesis statement, which should make it clear that you will be interpreting images.
2. Give any background information readers might need to understand your thesis and put the context in perspective.
3. Identify the artist, or if the images are from a media source—such as a magazine or newspaper—name the source and the date of publication.

For example, the following introduction opened an essay that interpreted several photographs from the 2000 presidential election.

The 2000 election for President of the United States was hotly contested. The winner was finally determined by the Supreme Court, after the Justices stopped the state of Florida from counting ballots. Throughout the campaign, candidates Al Gore and George Bush gave hundreds of speeches explaining their beliefs, positions, and commitments. Today, the words are lost from memory but the campaign still remains in my mind's eye. Five photographs, all published in *The New York*

Times during the fall of 2000, capture the emotion of America's most contested election.

Besides writing an introduction that incorporates the thesis and appropriate background information, as this writer does, try to arouse reader curiosity and expectation about the discussion that will follow.

The following introduction is from Clarita Tan's "Imaginatively Chaotic Art" (see pages 139–142). Tan fulfills the basic elements of an effective introduction. She also increases reader curiosity through a series of quick impressions of the images she'll be discussing.

> The Fine Arts Gallery is featuring George McNeil, a figurative Abstract Expressionist who lived and worked his entire life in New York City. The ten canvases, drawn together from local collections, are stunning for their color and imagery. It is hard to separate color and imagery in McNeil's work. From pools of purple, orange, and yellow emerge massive faces, airplanes, bodies, and cryptic scrawls. The imagery magically emerges from the method McNeil uses to compose his canvases. The result is that the viewer's mind is pulled from the real world into an imaginatively chaotic world.

Writing Discussion Paragraphs

Effective discussion paragraphs develop the controlling idea in the thesis statement. Each paragraph should open with a topic sentence that provides the context for information that follows and echoes the central thought weaving through your analysis.

When writing about visual imagery, the primary pattern of development will be description. You won't merely be telling readers about an image, you will be showing them the image—at least the key elements of the image—in words (see Chapter 5). As you write, then, keep in mind that one of your goals is to re-create the dominant impression the image made on you.

As an example, the following paragraph from an essay titled "The Moppet Show" interprets a painting by Alexandra Nechita, a 12-year-old painter who had been receiving critical attention for her imagery and large canvases. Student-writer Maria Simms creates the dominant impression that Alexandra's work is psychologically darker than Alexandra understands it to be.

> In a taped interview, Alexandra describes her summer experience visiting her grandparents in Romania as "enchanting," but the imagery in "Summer in Europe" suggests a different tale, one much darker than the young artist realizes. There are two large abstract figures—Alexandra and her grandfather—dominating the painting. With one hand, Grandfather is offering Alexandra a sip of wine while with the other hand he is drawing her near. She leans back and seems to be pushing him away. Her face, washed in red, is flushed; her lips are not just tightly shut, but perpendicular lines suggest they are stitched together. Her body is gray and contrasts sharply with his deep-green body. Two shapes that seem to be rising from his head suggest horns, and in the interview, Alexandra talks about the "shadow," which faintly outlines his face. This is a very thoughtful and well-executed painting, especially for someone as young as Alexandra. But it is not a painting that suggests joy. It is a painting that suggests dark emotions a 12 year old might not understand intellectually but feels emotionally.

In the following paragraph, excerpted from a student essay that explores imagery in various advertisements, student-writer John Ramsey develops the dominant impression that captures the sexually charged energy in a jeans advertisement.

> In a recent advertisement published in *Esquire* magazine, Jordache uses sexually charged imagery to sell its products. The image features a stunningly attractive couple wearing jeans and a classic car. The setting is a garage in murky light. The male figure is resting his back against the trunk of a car in a sexually suggestive pose—legs spread, one hand on a hip and the other hand brushing his thigh, an open shirt revealing rippled abdominal muscles, his skin glistening with sweat. The female figure crouches catlike at his side, hugging one of his legs as tightly as her jeans hug her hips while she stares at the

viewer with a sultry expression. The caption reads "Wear Jordache!" but suggests "Wear Jordache and fulfill your sexual desires."

As part of an essay that concentrates on women artists, Rebecca Douglas included a paragraph-length interpretation of a satiric self-portrait by photo-artist Sasha Youngju Lee

> In "Media Frenzy/Vogue, 1994," Sasha Youngju Lee offers some scalding satiric commentary about being a woman in a male dominated culture. The work is a photographic replica of a *Vogue* magazine cover. The cover features a head and shoulders portrait of Lee with arms dangling at her side and eyes staring at the viewer. She holds an apple in her open mouth. The apple immediately calls to mind Eve in the garden, the first woman to be the victim of male projection and power. A closer look reveals that the apple appears to be stuffed in Lee's mouth, suggesting that the female voice has been muted since the days of "original sin." At an even deeper level, the image suggests a pig—a *suckling* pig—perhaps soon to be served up at a banquet. In the male-dominated world Lee envisions women as a "dish" to be served at a male banquet. Perhaps the most ironic element in the image is Lee's use of *Vogue*'s imprimatur, a label associated with women who want to look beautiful for men.

Douglas's opening sentence presents her final interpretation of Lee's image as a "scalding satiric commentary about being a woman in a male dominated culture." Throughout the paragraph she weaves objective detail—the key elements of the image—with her subjective analysis.

Writing a Conclusion

Concluding paragraphs should be brief but developed enough to give a sense of completion to the essay. A common practice is to use the conclusion to restate the thesis and give a brief summary of the essay's content.

Do patriotic images in campaign literature actually influence unwary voters? When asked if they do, most voters say they are aware of the visual manipulation—such as images of a decisive candidate sitting at an oversized desk, pen in hand, an American flag over his shoulder, a bust of Lincoln on his desk—but they report that such images have no influence on how they vote. This might be true in an intellectual sense, but the power of patriotic imagery is emotional, operating beneath a voter's awareness. The political consultants who craft the imagery understand the power of emotion, and they exploit it. Why else would they continue to surround their candidates with symbols that stir feelings of patriotism?

Beginning and ending a conclusion with a question can be an effective tactic to round off an essay. An opening question can remind readers of the thesis statement and lead them to consider the discussion. A closing question can be rhetorical—that is, a question that is designed to restate the obvious indirectly.

Background

By way of background, we suggest you read the following essays that concentrate on images: Clarita Tan's "Imaginatively Chaotic Art," page 139; John Kifner's "Good as a Gun," page 284; and John Barton's "Friendly Smile, Clenched Fist," page 403.

An Essay about Visual Images

In the following essay, student-writer Judy Chan concentrates on two works by Jan Vermeer, a seventeenth-century Dutch painter. Chan reveals the significance beneath the realistic surfaces of the paintings. Read the essay carefully, and note how Chan interweaves the key elements in the paintings with interpretations of them.

Studies in Tranquility

His eye for detail and light edge up to the supernatural—   1
Jan Vermeer, innkeeper, art dealer, father of fifteen children,

and, most importantly, 17th-century Dutch painter of exquisitely executed canvases. For art aficionados, the name "Vermeer" signifies perfectly rendered domestic images. For me—
and perhaps for you, too—his name also signifies tranquility,
especially as it is captured in two of his most admired works.

At first glance, Vermeer's paintings seem to be snapshots   2
of the family life in Delft, his native city. In many of Vermeer's works, sunlight pours through leaded glass windows to
reveal every element of his domestic settings. Often his figures are alone in meticulously detailed rooms decorated with
luxurious tapestries, maps hang on gold rods, books with
leather covers, elaborately carved tables and chairs, and black
and white checkerboard floors. His palette is soft, rich in
blues, yellows, ochers, siennas and deep reds—all pigments he
ground himself. Every feature, surface, and object is rendered
in minute, realistic detail, creating a sense that viewers are
seeing an accurate domestic portrait of life as it might have
been lived in Vermeer's time. But in two of his most respected
paintings, Vermeer does much more than create a realistic
rendering of seventeenth-century family life.

Unlike the detailed scenes of family life Vermeer is known   3
for, "Girl with a Pearl Earring" actually seems timeless, set
free from the details of seventeenth-century life so she can
carry a mysterious message to those who have studied her
through the centuries. The work features the shoulders and
face of a young woman illuminated against a dark, undefined
background, atypical in Vermeer's work. She is made even
more mysterious because of her exotic outfit she wears. It
features a blue turban trimmed with a gold sash that hangs
behind her head and a large silver or glass earring, once
thought to be a pearl, dangling from her earlobe. Her face is
open and innocent; her soft pink lips are slightly parted; her
cheeks are plump and pale; but it is her eyes that capture attention, the large brown eyes that are clear and reflective. She
looks out from the canvas as though her gaze has stretched
over 300 years to look into the viewer's eyes. This striking
young woman seems to be disconnected from time and space
yet her gaze is riveting, whispering that life can be tranquil,
at least where she resides in the peaceful land of Vermeer.

Vermeer's "Woman Holding a Balance" suggests that tran-   4
quility comes from residing in the space between the profane
world and the sacred world. The painting features a young
woman standing before a table, one hand gently resting on its

surface and the other delicately holding a jeweler's scale, her little finger cocked outward as if she were lifting a cup of tea to her lips. She wears a dark indigo jacket trimmed in white mink and a white linen hood that frames her face while her eyes, half-closed in contemplation, gaze at the painting's focal point—a collection of pearls. Strands of pearls lie curled on the table and spill from an open jewelry box. She is weighing pearls on the scales. To the left, light filters through a curtain, illuminating her face, her hands, and the pearls. Dark shadows fill the space behind and beneath the table. The scene is calm, serene, and rich in symbolism, for the pearls have a dual significance: They are associated with riches and with purity—that is, with the profane and the sacred, the worldly and the spiritual. The canvas itself reflects a dichotomy—it is balanced by shadow and light. Vermeer seems to be inviting viewers into this woman's world—so different from the

contemporary world we all experience—to find our own balance, if only momentarily.

    Looking at my favorite Vermeers is like looking through a   5
window into a room where time has stopped. Peace, tranquility, and balance—these are the feelings Vermeer has infused
in "Girl with a Pearl Earring" and "Woman Holding a Balance," feelings too often ignored in the hubbub of daily life.

Reviewing with a Writer's Eye

1. In your own words, state Judy Chan's thesis statement. Besides pre-
    senting the thesis, what else does Chan's introduction achieve?

2. What is the function of paragraph 2? Identify the dominant rhetorical pattern. What is the purpose of the last sentence of paragraph 2?
3. State the topic sentence of paragraph 3. Review the paragraph and identify specific details from Chan's interpretation.
4. State the topic sentence in paragraph 4. At what point in paragraph 4 does Chan shift from description to interpretation?
5. What strategy does Chan use for her conclusion? Does it close the essay effectively?
6. What is your overall impression of Chan's essay? Does she effectively develop her thesis? Does the essay move smoothly from paragraph to paragraph? Does she provide enough specific detail to support her interpretation?

Peer Review

Before evaluating essays that interpret visual imagery, review the principles established in the introduction to this chapter and Chapter 5. Also keep the following in mind:

1. The introduction, besides presenting the thesis statement, should provide any background information the reader might need to understand the discussion.
2. The writer will be "interpreting" the image—that is, exploring the meaning behind the surface of the image. You must ask: Does the writer support the interpretation with specific detail from the image itself?
3. Determine the rhetorical patterns the writer uses. Are they structured effectively?
4. Finally, identify the introduction, the discussion, and the conclusion of the essay. Is the thesis statement clearly stated? Do the topic sentences in the discussion relate to the thesis statement? Does the conclusion complete the discussion?

Writing Tasks

1. *Fine Art.* Select at least three works from an artist who appeals to you and whose images seem to have a deeper significance. Analyze the images to interpret each work's deeper meaning. Use your interpretation as the basis for an essay.

2. *Photography.* Visit your college library and browse through its collections of books that feature the works of well-known photographers. When you find a photographer you like, select several of his or her images for interpretation and use your interpretation as the basis for an essay.

3. *Advertisements.* Browse several glossy magazines, such as *Esquire, Vanity Fair, Vogue, Time, Newsweek* or *The New Yorker.* Identify several advertisements directed toward a particular consumer group. Analyze the images to determine the meaning of the nonverbal message and use your analysis as the basis for an essay.

4. *Mass Media.* Write an essay based on dramatic images published in the mass media, such as newspapers, news magazines, campaign literature, movie posters, or CD covers. Analyze the images and use your analysis as the basis for an essay.

5. *Text Images.* Select three images from those that appear throughout this book. Submit them to critical analysis and use the result of the analysis as the basis for an essay.

6. *Thematic Images.* Read John Kifner's "Good as a Gun" (p. 284), in which he asserts that images of modern war have been shaping American attitudes toward conflict for several generations. Using Kifner's approach, select images from a single area—such as sports, art, politics, advertising, family, poverty, or wealth—that have shaped public consciousness. Interpret the images and use your interpretation as the basis of an essay. As a way to begin, we recommend that you explore *The New York Times* or the Google online image bank.

4

Writing a Documented Essay

Investigating Current Issues

The Method

An effectively written documented essay usually has an argumentative edge—that is, it attempts to change or reinforce someone's opinion or to move someone to take action. It follows the same general principles as any effectively written essay in that it needs to have a clear thesis, detailed planning, logical organization, and full development. It also embodies the same principles that underlie successful arguments, that is, it should blend the ancient Greek concepts of *logos, pathos,* and *ethos,* all of which are detailed in Chapter 13, Persuasion and Argument.

The key difference between writing a documented and an undocumented essay is research and the documentation itself—that is, you conduct an information-gathering process to reveal your subject, and you identify the sources of your research in the final essay. Ideally, through research, your understanding of the subject will deepen and perhaps even undergo significant changes.

Research projects have a wide range of complexity. Some take many years and end in a full-length book; others take only a week or two and end in a brief paper. For our purposes, think of the research project addressed in this chapter as a limited investigation of a subject of current interest. The investigation will involve collecting and reviewing a variety of information sources, much like a reporter gathers raw material for an analytical article.

For example, Tanya Rose, the author of the sample paper that follows this discussion, decided to investigate an event that took place at a local college campus shortly after the September 11, 2001, terrorist assaults on the World Trade Center and the Pentagon.

Across the country people were emotionally traumatized, confused, and fearful of more attacks. Tensions were so high that once the terrorists were identified as Islamic, some people irrationally blamed all Muslims for the attack, many of whom became targets of physical and verbal abuse.

A handful of incidents involving professors took place at several colleges across the country, most notably at the University of New Mexico, the University of South Florida, and Orange Coast College,

California. It was the Orange Coast College incident involving Muslim students and Professor Kenneth Hearlson that became the focus of Rose's research.

Information Gathering

To present an informed and balanced discussion, your essay should reflect a comprehensive understanding of the issues. For this reason, you will need to use primary and secondary resources.

A *primary resource* is the actual material that you write about. Primary resources include a wide range of possibilities, such as original fiction and nonfiction, films, letters, journals, government documents, surveys, reports, interviews, audio- and videotapes, and even oral histories. Using primary sources puts you in direct contact with the raw material from which your paper will develop.

A *secondary source* is a response to or about your subject. Secondary resources include books, magazines, newspaper articles, pamphlets, and other works that examine, analyze, or report the facts.

To develop her argumentative essay on the incident at Orange Coast College, for example, Rose used both primary and secondary sources. One primary source was an audiotape of the class session under question. Secondary sources included newspaper articles, interviews, and official reports related to the primary source.

Researching on the Internet. In the not-so-distant past, researchers spent hours in libraries compiling bibliographies—that is, lists of written works about their subjects—from card catalogues and published indexes. Now, especially when researching a current issue, as this chapter addresses, you can use the Internet to streamline the information-gathering process.

If you are new to the Internet and want to access it from your own computer, you will need a modem, as well as the necessary software and services of a commercial Internet provider, such as America Online, EarthLink, or Microsoft Network.

The Internet itself is made up of tens of thousands of computers. Try to imagine them as separate universes of information. All these separate universes are connected electronically. And you, anytime day or night, can search through any of these universes while comfortably sitting at a keyboard anywhere in the world.

If your computer program connects automatically with the Internet, you can start researching as soon as you click on the software link. If it is not directly connected, you must type in the Internet address of the location you want to contact. You need not be an Internet expert to make it work, but understanding some basics about Internet address formats can save you time in the research process.

Using a Search Engine.

A *search engine* is a computer program that hunts for resources all over the Internet. After you enter one or more *keywords* about a subject, a search engine scans the Internet and ultimately presents you with a list of possible sources.

Most colleges have their own computer research labs, and their computers have access to search engines, such as Alta Vista, Google, Netscape, Lycos, WebCrawler, and Yahoo. If your college has a lab, it might be easier to get started by visiting it. To launch your research would simply be a matter of following the instructions on the campus system or asking a lab assistant for help.

Tanya Rose initiated her research by using Google. In the box identified by "search," Rose typed in "Academic Freedom and Hearlson." Immediately, a list with a brief description of each item appeared. After browsing the list, she identified several sources worth exploring. One, www.thefire.org, gave her even more leads to pursue.

Understanding Domain Names.

A *domain name* identifies one of the tens of thousands of computers that make up the Internet. A domain name consists of letters or words separated by the symbol "." (pronounced "dot"). For example, the domain name of Bookwire, an Internet source about books and publishing, is www.bookwire. com, which means that Bookwire is

- Part of the World Wide Web—the *www.*
- Identified by other computers by name—*Bookwire.*
- Operated by a commercial organization—*com.*

If Bookwire were not a commercial entity, the domain name for its Internet address would end in different letters, such as *gov, edu, mil, net,* or *org* (for *government, educational, military, Internet network,* or nonprofit *organization,* respectively).

The information included in a domain name is useful. It tells you in advance about an Internet source. For example, sources with *com, edu,* or *org*—domains dealing with commerce, education, and nonprofit institutions—will have different types of information with varying degrees of objectivity and authority. For instance, www.amazon.com will give you much different information about books than www.ucilibrary.edu. The former domain was created to sell books; the second, to provide information.

Domain names are necessary for identifying Internet sources, but they are not complete addresses. To connect to a particular Internet site, your computer needs to know what communication system that site uses. This is where a *URL* comes in.

Understanding URLs. A *URL,* which stands for *uniform resource locator,* is the complete address for a computer—that is, one of the information universes—located on the Internet. The URL for the computer at Bookwire, for example, is http://www.bookwire. com. In plain terms, this is the address you must key into your computer to locate and connect over the Internet with the computer at Bookwire.

A URL, then, includes the Internet computer's domain name, which follows what is called a *protocol*—that is, the symbol ":// " and letters indicating a particular computer communication format:

URL Protocol   Domain Name
http://www.   bookwire.com

The *http* protocol in this example indicates that the Bookwire computer uses *hypertext transfer protocol,* a World Wide Web communications format which allows you to jump electronically to and from different Internet information universes. A computer with another communications format would require a different URL protocol.

Searching the Web with Hypertext.   Often written as *www* and spoken of as *the Web,* the World Wide Web is the most popular means of navigating the Internet and its richest, most up-to-date resource, making it especially ideal for researching subjects of current interest.

The technological power of the Web would never have been possible without the development of *hypertext,* the unique and seemingly magical tool that distinguishes it from all other Internet systems.

Here's how hypertext works. It appears on a Web document page as a highlighted word or phrase. When you click on the phrase, you automatically travel to another section of a document or to a whole new document.

For example, during her initial search for information related to the Orange Coast College incident, Tanya Rose found www.thefire.org, a Website devoted to issues of academic freedom. On the home page—the opening page that serves as the entrance to a domain—was a list of sources highlighted in hypertext. By clicking on the hypertext "buttons," Rose had immediate access to a cache of secondary sources.

December 7, 2001
    In September without any regard for due process, Orange Coast College lawless administration punished a professor for expressing his views on the terrorist attacks. Now, despite evidence proving his innocence, OCC still does nothing to remedy the injustice it has created.

> Read *The New York Times* here.
> Read the *Los Angeles Times* here.
> Read *The Orange County Register* here.
> Read *Michelle Malkin* here.
> See transcript of *Hannity & Colmes,* Fox News, here.

Rose quickly skipped from document to document, developing a broad understanding of the issues associated with the Orange Coast incident and creating a bibliography as she skimmed the material.

Evaluating Sources

Many people naively believe that if something appears in print, it must be true. In fact, however, it might not be. You should *always* evaluate information sources to determine their value. Ask yourself these questions: What agenda does the person or group have? Does the source give complete and accurate information?

A critical attitude is particularly essential for anyone conducting effective research on the Internet, considering the vast number of people and organizations who use it to promote their own interests. Much of the information available over the Internet is commercial, which raises the obvious possibility that it's highly biased—presented to sell a product or at least to emphasize certain characteristics over others.

Keep this in mind: Because the Internet is democratic and essentially unrestricted, its content may not have been subjected to any information-filtering mechanisms, such as competition, academic review, financial and legal concerns, and even commonsense judgments about whether something is worth circulating.

A Reliability Checklist for Sources

Currency: Does the material appear to be current and is there any indication of how often it is updated?

Fairness: Does the material demonstrate not only the author's knowledge but also other viewpoints and relevant research? Is the tone reasonable and temperate?

Evidence: Does the Website give statistics, specific examples, or verifiable anecdotal evidence? Are they presented fairly? Is fact clearly distinguished from opinion?

Research: Is there evidence of credible research, such as a description of methodology or a bibliography? Are links to other sites with established credibility listed?

Credibility: Would the Website's content be credible in the non-Internet world? If so, why and with whom? If not, why?

Always remember, you can find on the Internet everyone with an idea, every group with a cause, everything and anything someone thinks is important, even if the person is a complete crackpot.

Strategy

Generally, you will find that the investigation of a current issue follows a common pattern:

Step 1. The overview process will initiate and focus your investigation.

Step 2. During the information-gathering process, you will identify a question you want answered.

Step 3. Eventually, when all the information is in, you will reach a conclusion—one the evidence will support.

Step 4. Once the investigation is complete, you will shape a thesis that organizes your argument.

Step 5. Finally, you will write the argument, integrating the evidence and documenting your sources.

For example, Tanya Rose began her investigation thinking her subject would be "academic freedom," but by the time she completed the overview of news articles, published opinion pieces, and letters to the editor, a clear question emerged: Did Orange Coast College treat Professor Hearlson fairly or unfairly?

The initial overview gave her plenty of leads for a more detailed investigation. For instance, she had learned that there was a formal report on the incident and that it was available to the public.

She also learned that Hearlson had received an official letter, which he described as a "letter of reprimand," but that the letter was unavailable unless he made it public.

Furthermore, she learned that the college had policies in place that were part of the record and officially state-approved course descriptions that are quasi-legal documents.

Perhaps most important, Rose learned that Hearlson taped each class session and made the tapes available in the college library for student review.

At this point, she realized that a thorough investigation would have to include interviews with key figures in the controversy—especially Professor Hearlson himself and the Vice-President of Instruction, Robert Dees.

To keep her investigation on target, Rose jotted down an "Investigation Task List":

- review published material in more detail for specific evidence, both pro and con;
- get and review the investigative report;
- get and review audiotapes of class sessions;
- interview Hearlson and Dees; and
- get the college's policy manual.

Rose gave herself two weeks to complete her research, thus completing the project's investigation phase. She would then be ready to analyze the evidence, define her position, and write the argument.

Take Notes Strategically

As you conduct your investigation, take notes about what you find and where you found it. The most effective way of taking notes, even in the computer age, is on 4″ × 6″ index cards. They are durable, easy to organize, and go wherever you go for easy reference.

Take notes with your question in mind. Generally, your notes will include a variety of information:

- *background information* that you need to understand the subject;
- *general ideas* related to your preliminary focus and question;
- *specific quotations* that support or oppose the issue;
- *explanatory information,* such as definitions of terms, biographical data, and any information your readers might need to place the issue in context;
- *quotations, examples, and anecdotes* that will illustrate and support your claims; and
- *questionable and controversial evidence* that you may want to include in your essay.

Remember, too, it is very important to identify your source on your note cards. The following note card example is from the American Association of University Professors.

> http://www.aaup.org/statements/redbook/1940stat.
> Academic Freedom
>   A basic precept of the 1940 Statement of Principles
> is that "teachers are entitled to freedom in the classroom
> in discussing their subject."

Write Effective Paragraphs

Paragraphs in a documented argument tend to use one of three strategies.

Summary.   Use summary to condense information in your own words and style. It is useful for broadly characterizing the general content of a variety of sources or for registering your own reactions.

> On September 18, 2001, four Muslim students
> filed formal complaints with the college and other or-
> ganizations. They claim that they felt endangered af-
> ter being singled out and accused of being terrorists
> by their professor during an Introduction to Govern-
> ment class. They also claim that they felt the profes-
> sor's hostile behavior caused other students in the
> class to act aggressively toward them during what was
> a time of great emotion and unrest across America.

Paraphrase.   Use paraphrase to clarify or simplify a source's content by recasting it in your own words. Whereas a summary condenses, a paraphrase is usually about the same length as the original source, but the words are your own.

> The concept of academic freedom seems difficult to
> explain. One professor close to the issue believes that
> academic freedom is an essential ingredient for any
> academic community to be legitimate. Freedom of

speech is fundamental for the protection of the rights of teachers in teaching and of the student in learning.

Direct Quotations.   Use quotation—that is, a presentation of the precise words from a source—when you sense that what's said can be used to strengthen your discussion.

Be sure to quote accurately, giving your reader only enough quoted material to convey the key part of the information. To keep the discussion flowing, blend single words, phrases, and sentences directly into your own writing as much as possible.

Be sure to clearly show the pertinence of the quotation. Don't just quote a source and expect a reader to connect it to your argument. You must connect it yourself, so that a reader will understand your point. In the following paragraph, for example, Rose makes sure her reader knows that she is disagreeing with the source:

> Alarmingly, USF President Judy Genshaft stead-fastly maintained that activities—including speech—outside the scope of his or her employment that "result in harm to the legitimate interests of the university are reason enough to fire a professor." In other words, she tries to make the case that not only can a professor's classroom activity lead to dismissal, but so can his or her personal views—whether or not they have anything to do with the university. Genshaft's position seems unreasonable. How can a professor's personal views as expressed on a television show cause any real harm to students? Genshaft's argument smacks of a kangaroo court's rationalization concocted to explain an unjust decision.

When quoting a passage of more than four lines, set off the quotation from the rest of the paper by putting it in block form. Indent the entire passage ten spaces (one inch) and double-space the lines. The first line of the passage should be indented an additional three spaces (or one-fourth inch) if it marks the beginning of a paragraph. Do not use quotation marks (unless they appear within the quotation itself).

For example, Rose uses block form to quote the following passage from the Website of the American Association of University Professors.

> The American Association of University Professors is a champion of academic freedom throughout American universities. The organization maintains the following:
>
> > Teachers are entitled to freedom in the classroom in discussing their subject, but they should be careful not to introduce into their teaching controversial matter, which has no relation to their subject. (1940)
>
> Clearly, the AAUP advocates free expression related to subject content of a class. But it does not condone the abuse of academic freedom, that is, the kind of free-ranging discussion—or attack, as Muslim students claimed—that Professor Hearlson initiated in his Introduction to Government class.

Acknowledge Sources

In documenting an argumentative essay, you must let readers know the sources of your information. You may use direct attribution integrated into the text: that is, you can identify the source of the quotation by key phrases that lead into the quotation. For example,

> In a recent lecture on academic freedom Professor Harold Alvarez of California State University, Fullerton, says . . .

You must also make in-text citations and list your sources in Works Cited in the back of your essay. The requirements both of in-text citations and of a Works Cited page are explained in A Brief Documentation Guide, at the end of this chapter.

A Documented Argumentative Essay

Tanya Rose's assignment was to investigate a controversial event that had taken place recently in her community.

A September 18, 2001, incident at Orange Coast College was still in the news, so she decided it would be ideal as the subject of her investigation for several reasons.

First, it caused a great deal of interest both locally and nationally. Second, she had access to the primary source of the event. And finally, she knew from a quick overview of her subject that there were plenty of secondary sources for her to research.

She spent two weeks completing the investigation. Then she evaluated the evidence and reached her own conclusion. Although she set out to research the issue of academic freedom as it related to the Hearlson incident, her research led her in another direction.

Orange Coast College: 9.18.01

On September 18, 2001, the week following terrorist assaults on the World Trade Center and the Pentagon, an alarming incident took place at our local community college. Several Muslim students at Orange Coast College complained that Professor Kenneth Hearlson verbally harassed them during a discussion in political science class.

In a formal complaint, Muslim students said that Hearlson pointed at them specifically, calling them "terrorists," "murderers," and "nazis" during a heated classroom debate. The students said they felt in danger after being singled out in a packed lecture hall. They also claimed they felt the professor's hostile behavior caused fellow students to become aggressive and threatening at a time of great emotional intensity in America. Because of the complaint, college officials placed Hearlson on paid leave from classroom duties and initiated an investigation (Lobdell; Fisher, "Muslim").

Almost immediately Hearlson charged Coast administrators with acting unfairly. He accused them of denying him academic freedom, maintaining that he was only exercising what the 1st Amendment to the Constitution provides--freedom of speech (O'Reilly). In response, the administration said the issue was not "academic freedom"; it was "alleged endangerment of students" (Dees).

Although, the press and much of the academic community might disagree (Greenhut; Remington), I believe that the

Coast administration acted reasonably and responsibly by temporarily relieving Hearlson from teaching duties and investigating his classroom behavior.

According to newspaper reports and letters, the triggering incident came when Hearlson pointed at Muslim students and said it was "you" who crashed planes into the World Trade Center (Smallwood). The situation became even more tense when he referred to an incident that took place the previous semester involving a radical Muslim group circulating flyers with pictures of a Nazi swastika drawn on top of the Star of David (Jaffe 7). He allegedly yelled at a female student dressed in traditional Muslim clothing, "They were wearing the same dress as you are, young lady." The female student responded by saying, "That doesn't mean every [Muslim] does that" (Jaffe 8). Indeed, by this point emotion was running high.

Later, one Muslim student complained about Hearlson's behavior in a letter to administrators,

> [Hearlson] made sure that every person in that class was turned against us and believed that we were behind the terrorist attack. Upon leaving for break, we were being looked at in a very aggressive manner, by all those people in the class. I feel due to his false and incriminating accusations . . . safety on this campus is no longer as assuring as it once was. (qtd. in Jaffe 3)

In response, administrators, believing the situation was explosive and could result in physical harm to students as well as to Hearlson if not quelled, placed the professor on paid leave until they fully investigated the allegations (Smallwood 12).

Hearlson denied that he singled out particular students for any personal attack. In a phone interview, he did say that he accused Muslims in general of hypocrisy for denouncing the attacks on September 11th while they were supporting attacks against Israel. He maintained, "It was done to start an educational discussion" (Hearlson, Interview).

During his leave, Hearlson continued to allege that the college was violating his First Amendment rights and general principles of academic freedom, which he claimed were the first steps toward dismissal. But when interviewed, Vice-President of Instruction Robert Dees maintained that the college neither intended to fire Hearlson nor to contradict the college's liberal policy regarding a professor's freedom to teach as he or she sees fit. College officials were simply trying to determine what had truly happened. He further maintained that the college "dealt with the event solely as a safety issue."

Moreover, in contrast to the public impression that Coast administration forced him to take a leave, Hearlson had actually volunteered to leave the classroom. Dees said,   9

> We told him the college stood behind him but that
> we had an obligation to look into all student com-
> plaints. We talked on the phone about the possibility of
> taking an administrative leave, and he was open to
> that because at that time, he was scared and was up-
> set about the fact that the students had gone to the
> press. He seemed grateful to be taking a break.

Dees claimed that initially Hearlson was so agitated and worried about his own and his family's safety that he wanted to protect himself by leaving the classroom.

Hearlson admitted as much when he was interviewed.   10
He said that he did agree to a leave of absence, "I was asked if I would take a leave and let this simmer down--for my protection--and I said okay." But Hearlson thought he had an agreement that he would be on leave for only a week or two. "That would have been fine," he said.

Two days after the incident, the college asked Geraldine   11
Jaffe, an attorney with the Orange County Department of Education, to carry out an independent investigation. Hearlson said he didn't know he was going to be investigated. Dees said it is typical college procedure to investigate complaints (Dees; Hearlson, Interview).

No one can fault the Coast administration's investigation.   12
It was very thorough. Over the course of 11 weeks, Jaffe methodically interviewed 26 witnesses, including Hearlson, 19 students, 3 district administrators, one of the college's professors, a course assistant, and an audiovisual technician who was present on the day in question (Carnett 2). Ten of the 19 students interviewed were those suggested by Hearlson and his attorney. The investigator also reviewed 49 e-mails from students enrolled in the class, and 30 letters (Carnett 2).

According to Dees, the investigation's aim was to resolve   13
the issue. Apparently, the college treated this event as it would any other issue of professional conduct. "We [the Orange Coast College administration] have an obligation to respond to complaints and that's all we were doing" (Dees).

During the period following the September 11th attack,   14
there were actually several related incidents at universities
that shed light on the behavior of the Orange Coast College administrators. In one high-profile case, university officials made
decisions quickly, rashly, and drew intense criticism nationally. The Orange Coast College situation, conversely, was quite
different in that it was handled carefully and mindfully from
the beginning.

The most notable example of post-September 11th assaults   15
on academic freedom is the attempted firing of a tenured
Palestinian-born computer-science professor at the University
of South Florida. Sami Al-Arian, a professor for 16 years, was
questioned during a September 26th episode of <u>The O'Reilly</u>
<u>Factor</u>. He was asked about his alleged connections to Islamic
extremist and terrorist groups ("Firing"). Following the interview, university officials said that the university received angry telephone calls and threats in response to his answers.

As a result, Al-Arian was banned from campus. Why? Offi-   16
cials said that on <u>The O'Reilly Factor</u>, he did not distinguish
his personal views and past activities from university policies
(Smallwood).

Academics have criticized the Al-Arian affair as a knee-   17
jerk reaction to the high emotion surrounding September 11th
and as a serious blow to academic freedom with direct First
Amendment implications (Powers).

Alarmingly, USF President Judy Genshaft steadfastly   18
maintained that activities--including speech--outside the scope
of his or her employment that "result in harm to the legitimate interests of the university are reason enough to fire a
professor." In other words, Genshaft tries to make the case
that not only can a professor's classroom activity lead to dismissal, but so can his or her personal views--whether or not
those views have anything to do with the university (Powers).
Genshaft's position seems unreasonable. How can a professor's
personal views as expressed on a television show cause any
real harm to students? The argument smacks of a kangaroo
court's rationalization concocted to explain an unjust decision.

In sharp contrast, the investigation at Orange Coast Col-   19
lege had everything to do with the immediate classroom environment and the safety of all involved, not with free-speech issues. Vice-President Dees repeatedly said the investigation was

only concerned with responding quickly and fairly to student complaints about one teacher's conduct.

But Hearlson supporters disagreed with Coast officials, ar-   20
guing that the investigation was a thinly veiled attempt to stop expression of controversial views. Of course, there is merit in the argument that someone feeling offended by the content of another's speech is not reason enough to ban the speech. But Dees points out that in the Coast situation, if students had merely said they were "offended," it would not have been enough to place Hearlson on paid leave (Dees). It was the formal complaint about a threatening classroom environment that caused concern--that is, Hearlson's allegedly being agitated and angry, yelling in accusatory tones over students who were trying to talk, and pointing and shaking his finger at specific students (Jaffe 10).

The Orange Coast College investigation of Professor Hearl-   21
son's classroom behavior is now closed, at least for college officials, but not for Hearlson.

Though Hearlson received an official letter that reminded   22
him of college policies about classroom behavior and safety, he continues to maintain that he was reprimanded when he should have been exonerated completely (Interview). He is now back on campus and teaching his full class assignment. According to the <u>Los Angeles Times,</u> he has lectured at length about his ordeal and has even openly criticized Coast officials for having conducted an investigation at all (Gottlieb). According to Dees, Hearlson is absolutely free to do that, though his classroom responsibility is still the same as it has always been--that is, "to teach students what they came to class to learn."

In the emotional environment following the September 11th   23
attacks, Coast administrators found themselves stuck between a rock and a hard place. Hearlson claims he has the right to express his beliefs in class, but administrators claim that they have an ethical and legal duty to investigate all student complaints about teacher misconduct.

Moreover, if Coast officials had ignored the student com-   24
plaints that said Hearlson's behavior was erratic, then they might have been putting students at risk by not addressing a potentially dangerous situation, perhaps even facing lawsuits because of their inaction.

The bottom line is that student complaints should be thor-   25
oughly investigated before action is taken against a professor.
And that is exactly what happened at Coast. Hearlson's
charge that administrators violated the principles of academic
freedom seems to be nothing more than a smoke screen for
irresponsible classroom behavior--that is, a diversion from a
more significant issue of professional irresponsibility.

It's unfortunate that student complaints only focused on   26
the September 18, 2001 class, thus limiting the investigation.
They should have focused on whether or not Hearlson was
meeting his contractual obligations to teach the subject, thus
widening the investigation. Two other taped classes let the
public peek into the classroom of a teacher who is so preoccupied with personal issues that he is not doing an adequate job
of teaching the subject matter.

The American Association of University Professors is a   27
champion of academic freedom throughout American universities. The organization maintains the following:

> Teachers are entitled to freedom in the classroom
> in discussing their subject, but they should be careful
> not to introduce into their teaching controversial mat-
> ter, which has no relation to their subject. (1940)

Clearly, the AAUP advocates free expression related to subject
content of a class. But it does not condone the abuse of academic freedom, that is, the kind of free-ranging discussion—or
attack, as Muslim students claimed—that Professor Hearlson
initiated in his Introduction to Government class.

The Hearlson tapes of classes previous to the September   28
18th session capture the professor yammering on about his
fundamentalist Christian experience, his friendship with
minorities, and the danger of radical Islam, none of which has
any direct relationship to the course he was teaching (Hearlson, Sept. 11; Sept. 4). The official course outline for Introduction to Government, Political Science 180, states that the
course involves the following:

> Introduction to the principles and problems of govern-
> ment with particular emphasis on the American sys-
> tem at all levels. The course satisfies the state univer-
> sity requirements in the Constitution of the U.S., State,
> and local governments.

If that description is accurate, I fail to see how Hearlson's aggressive focus on Muslim students and terrorist attacks fit into the approved curriculum. I can only speculate that Orange Coast College officials investigated the wrong issue.

Works Cited

Carnett, Jim. "OCCC Political Science Professor Hearlson to Return for Spring Classes," Orange Coast College Community Relations Office 11 December 2001.

"Course Outline for Introduction to Government, Political Science 180." Office of Instruction. Orange Coast College.

Dees, Robert. Telephone interview. 1 Feb. 2002.

"Firing Decision Could Affect USF President's Future." Associated Press (Tampa) 2 Feb. 2002.

Fisher, Marla Jo. "Muslim Students Complain." Orange County Register 16 Oct. 2001: B1+.

---. "Academic Freedoms Erode." Orange County Register 8 Nov. 2001: A1+.

Gottlieb, Jeff. "Contrary OCC Professor Back; Students Seem Oblivious to Bait." Los Angeles Times 29 Jan. 2002: Metro 3+.

Greenhut, Steven. "Freedom at Issue." Orange County Register 8 Nov. 2001: Commentary 1.

Hearlson, Ken. Telephone interview. 1 February 2002.

---. Audiotape. "September 4, 2001 Class." Orange Coast College Library, Costa Mesa, CA.

---. Audiotape. "September 11, 2001 Class." Orange Coast College Library, Costa Mesa, CA.

---. Audiotape. "September 18, 2001 Class." Orange Coast College Library, Costa Mesa, CA.

Jaffe, Geraldine. <u>Orange County Department of Education In-vestigative Report</u>. County of Orange, CA, 7 December 2001.

Lobdell, William. "College's Incendiary Topic Is Terror." <u>Los Angeles Times</u> 30 Sept. 2002: B1+.

Metzger, Jeffery. Personal Interview 3 Feb. 2002.

Powers, Scott. "Lightening Up; Palestinian Denies USF Charges." <u>The Orlando Sentinel</u> 15 Jan. 2002: B2.

Remington, Alan. "Jury Is Still Out on OCC Professor." Letter <u>Los Angeles Times</u> 21 Oct. 2001: B17.

Smallwood, Scott and Robin Wilson. "One Professor Cleared, Another Disciplined Over September 11 Remarks." <u>Chronicle of Higher Education</u> 11 Jan. 2002: 12.

<u>O'Reilly Factor</u>. FOX 12 Dec. 2001.

"1940 Statement of Principles on Academic Freedom and Tenure." American Association of University Professors 2 Feb. 2002: http://www.aaup.org/statements/redbook/1940stat.

Reviewing with a Writer's Eye

1. In your own words, state Rose's thesis.
2. Identify the kinds of evidence Rose uses to develop her thesis.
3. In a few sentences, describe Rose's intended reader.
4. With a total score of 100, what percentage of Rose's essay relies on research and what percentage relies on interpretation of the research?
5. Is Rose's essay structured effectively? Explain.
6. Identify paragraphs that refute Rose's thesis. Is her response to opposing ideas successful? Why? Why not?
7. In no more than 300 words, write a brief critique of Rose's essay as if you were writing it for her professor. Identify the strengths and weaknesses of her essay.

Peer Review

If you have been asked to read a batch of documented essays for fellow students, study the characteristics of an effective essay and documentation guidelines.

1. As stated in Chapter 13, an argumentative essay should have the following:
   a. a clear thesis or proposition;
   b. an orderly presentation of the evidence;
   c. a clear connection between the evidence and the thesis;
   d. a reasonable refutation of opposing evidence; and
   e. a conclusion emphasizing the thesis.
2. An argumentative essay should have an appropriate balance between research and interpretation.
3. An argumentative essay should avoid logical fallacies. (See pp. 526–529.)
4. A documented essay should have parenthetical citations that clearly direct readers to the Works Cited. (See pp. 122–125.)
5. Finally, a documented essay should effectively integrate quotations into its text and, like the entire research essay, the Works Cited page should be double spaced.

Writing Task

Write a documented essay with an argumentative edge that investigates a controversial event that took place recently in your community. Examine recent newspapers for such an event. It might be one that took place on your campus, in city government, or within the police department or courts. Be sure to select one that has two sides—that is, opposing points of view—and has had several weeks of coverage in the press.

Once you have selected the incident and have a subject related to it in mind, conduct an overview of it on the Internet to discover secondary sources. Then skim the sources to find a direction for further research.

Finally, launch a more in-depth investigation by composing an Investigation Task List. As you conduct your research, identify a question you want to answer.

A Brief Documentation Guide

To a large extent, the success of your documented essay depends on how effectively you use and credit information from other writers. As you integrate information into your essay, you must use standard documentation practices to acknowledge them accurately. Always identify sources, for the following reasons:

- to acknowledge quotations, except for common sayings or well-known quotations;
- to identify summarized and paraphrased content; and
- to credit lines of thinking you adopt and statistics you use.

Do not provide parenthetical citations for facts or common knowledge.

What follows is a brief documentation style guide from the Modern Language Association (MLA). It should provide you with enough examples to document an investigation of a current issue.

If, however, your research project is more wide-ranging than the one this chapter addresses, you should refer to the most current edition of the *MLA Handbook for Writers of Research Papers*. Use the copy in your library reference section, or purchase your own from the college bookstore or from the MLA itself by visiting www. mla.org.

The MLA recommends acknowledging sources in two ways: first, by briefly referencing them in parenthetical citations integrated into the essay's text; second, by fully referencing them in the Works Cited at the end of your essay.

Parenthetical Citations

The purpose of a parenthetical citation is to provide just enough information to direct a reader to a more detailed reference entry in the Works Cited. A parenthetical citation must always designate a specific entry alphabetically listed in the Works Cited. Usually, but not always, the author's last name and a page reference are enough to identify the source.

> Modern technological warfare is gradually changing the way we think about the enemy. Both heroic and vitriolic images are being replaced with sterile concepts as the long reach of our weapons no longer makes it necessary for us to respect or hate those we intend to kill (Keen 72).

In the Works Cited readers would find the reference identified in more detail:

> Keen, Sam. <u>Faces of the Enemy</u>. San Francisco: Harper & Row, 1988.

Page references in parenthetical citations never include *p.* or *pp.* If you are referencing several consecutive pages, join the page numbers with a hyphen; for example, (Keen 76–78).

When referencing two or more individual pages in one citation, use commas to separate them; for example, (Keen 78, 80, 86).

If the work you are referencing consists of only one page, list the page number in your Works Cited but do not include it in a parenthetical citation; for example, (Smith).

Keep parenthetical citations concise. You are required to give only enough information to guide readers to the specific source you have fully identified in your Works Cited. If you have integrated into your text any information that should be included in the parenthetical citation, such as an author's name, you do not have to include it in the citation.

> Wilson Bryan Key has taken the mystery from subliminal advertising discussions. He claims to have found subliminal messages in vodka ads (99).

To keep your essay as readable as possible, insert citations before a period or comma, as close to the borrowed material as possible. When quoting a source, keep the citation outside quotation marks.

> In her 1979 essay collection <u>The White Album</u>, Joan Didion sounds confused by random violence and personal terror (15–16), but by 1982 its meaning has

become clear to her, "I came to understand, in a way I had not understood before, the exact mechanism of terror" (Salvador 21).

If the borrowed material is set off from the text, the parenthetical citation follows the final punctuation.

> In contrast to great art works, Oates sees literary criticism as a refined form of communication between writer and reader. She writes,
>
>> If the greatest works of art sometimes strike us as austere and timeless, with their private music, as befits sacred things, criticism is always an entirely human dialogue, a conversation directed toward an audience. (2)

For a work alphabetized by title in the Works Cited, use the title or a shortened version of the title in the citation. To make tracing the reference easier, begin the citation with the word by which the work is alphabetized. If you are identifying a one-page article, omit the page reference.

> A debit card "looks like a credit card but works like a check" (Now It's the No Credit Card).

> The <u>Planning Commission Handbook</u> clearly states that land development is not the landowner's god-given right, but is a privilege granted by a public agency (31–32).

To acknowledge more than one source in a single citation, cite each work as you normally would, but separate the citations with a semicolon and a space.

> Whenever readers open a novel, they embark on an adventure in which they have a chance to become new if they can assume the imaginary role the writer thrusts at them and if they can reformulate themselves by discovering what had previously seemed to elude their consciousness (Gibson 265; Iser 294).

Whenever possible, draw your material from an original source, but at times you will need to rely on an indirect source for information. For instance, you may need to use someone's published account of what another person has said. When you do quote or paraphrase from an indirect source, you must indicate that you have done so in a citation by stating *qtd. in* ("quoted in") before the source.

> Poet Michael McClure claims Mailer had a strong belief that he would only be listened to if he were irreverent. When people asked Mailer to moderate his irreverence, he would say, "Hey, I <u>feel</u> irreverence, and there's truth in the irreverence" (qtd. in Manso 281).

The Works Cited Page

To present the works you have referenced throughout a documented essay, close your paper with your Works Cited. Type the words *Works Cited* on a new page, centered, one inch from the top. Begin the first alphabetized entry at the left margin, two lines below the title. Remember to cite the first author of each entry with the last name first; type subsequent authors' or editors' names in the same entry in normal order.

When you have more than one work by the same author, the name is not repeated; instead, type three hyphens followed by a period.

Include all the pertinent publishing information: author, title, place of publication, publisher, and date of publication. Double-space throughout the Works Cited, and indent the second and subsequent lines of an entry.

Book with One Author

Ralph, Edward. <u>The Truth About Facts</u>. New York: Viking-Penguin, 2001.

Two Books by the Same Author

Sacks, Oliver. <u>The Island of the Colorblind and Cycad Island</u>.
New York: Knopf, 1997.

---. <u>A Leg to Stand On</u>. New York: Touchstone-Simon & Schuster, 1984.

Book with More than One Author

Dunlap, Kathleen and Nora Lam. <u>Strategic Thought</u>. San Francisco: Jossy-Bass. 2002.

Signed Newspaper Article

Reisberg, Leo. "Green Power Firms Feel Ignored." <u>Los Angeles Times</u> 8 Feb. 2002: B1+.

(For newspaper articles, include the section and a + sign for articles continued on another page.)

Unsigned Newspaper Article

"A 2nd Day of Demonstrations in Venezuela." <u>New York Times</u> 9 Feb. 2002: A2.

(See note under Signed Newspaper Article.)

Letter to the Editor

Holle, Carol. "Honor the Flag." Letter. <u>Los Angeles Times</u> 8 Feb. 2002: B14.

Unsigned Editorial

"Bigger than Bioterror." <u>Orange County Register</u> 10 Feb. 2002: B13.

Signed Editorial

Katz, Tom. "Park Hits." <u>Irvine Town News</u> 14 March 2002: A22.

Article in a Magazine

Brogan, Katie. "Romancing the Writer." <u>Writing Fiction Today</u> Winter 2002: 40.

Regularly Published Material on CD-ROM

Johnson, Barbara. "Why Can't Women Go to Mars?" <u>Journal of Modern Issues</u> 23 (1988): 403–409. <u>Infotrac: Magazine Index Plus</u>. CD-ROM. Information Access. Feb. 1999.

"Mayors to Meet Over Gang Crime." <u>New York Times</u> 18 June 1998: B2+. <u>New York Times on Disc</u>. CD-ROM. UMI-Proquest. April 1999.

(If the CD-ROM source also appears in another version—such as a newspaper or magazine article—give all the information you would about such a source. Then provide the title of the database, underlined, in which that other form of the source is available. Follow that with the publication medium, vendor, and publication date of the CD-ROM, in that order, and separated by periods.)

Online Newspaper

"Beaches Becoming Unsafe, Says Council." <u>New York Times on the Web</u> 23 Nov. 2000. http://www.nytimes.com/ns98nov/dis9/front/html.

Web Sites and Web Pages

<u>Renaissance Poetry Project</u>. Ed. Janice Altram. Mar. 1997. Indiana U. 3 June 1998.

Foundation for Individual Rights. Co-Dir. Alan Charles Kors.
  Feb. 2002. http://www.thefire.org.

Audiotape

Hearlson, Ken. Audiotape. "Sept. 18, 2002 Class." Orange
  Coast Community College Library. Sept. 18, 2002.

Interview

Lagos, Francine. Personal interview. 28 Dec. 2002.

Lecture

Gass, Paul R. "Why Academic Freedom Matters." University of
  California. Irvine, CA. 5 Feb. 2002.

Television or Radio Program

L.A. to You. ABC, KABC. Los Angeles. 9 Feb. 2002.

Official Letter

City of Irvine. Letter to Harold Moss. Jan. 25 2002.

5

Description
Capturing Sensory Details

The Method

To describe is to picture in words—the people we meet, the places we visit, the conversations we hear, the infinite number of things we encounter. **Description,** like narration, is often associated with imaginative literature: children's tales, short stories, and novels. In fiction, narrative events provide a story's bones; description adds flesh to the skeletal structure, helping a reader to imagine the narrative events: "The wind rattled the windows . . . a tall figure wearing a cape emerged from the darkness . . . a pasty white face . . . black hair plastered like a swimmer's cap to his head . . . red lips curled in a sneer . . . the air smelling of rotting meat. . . ." For a descriptive passage to be effective, fiction writers know they must involve their readers' senses to create a reaction to the words. This requirement also applies to essayists who use description as a dominant essay pattern. They, too, must involve a reader's senses—that is, make their readers see, hear, smell, feel, and taste.

To see descriptive detail at work, consider the following passage. Two simple events take place: a wild stallion trying to trample a cowhand and the cowhand trying to escape. But before reading the passage, read a few of the descriptive details the writer uses to appeal to the reader's senses:

Sight

the stallion rearing back on its hind legs
hooves pawing the air
mane whipping its neck

Sound

clubbing the ground
throaty whinny echoing

Smell

dust filling his nostrils

Taste

dust coating his lips and teeth

Touch

hand grabbing the fence post
palm raked with slivers

Motion

the stallion rearing back
hooves pawing the air
its mane whipping

Now read the passage to see how the writer uses these and other descriptive details to create a sensuous picture of the action.

> The stallion reared back on its hind legs, its hooves pawing the air, its mane whipping around its neck. The wrangler rolled toward the fence, gasping for breath, dust filling his nostrils and coating his lips and teeth. The stallion's hooves clubbed the ground, and again it reared up, a whinny erupting from deep in its throat, echoing over the ranch, as the wrangler grabbed the bottom fence post, his hand raked by slivers, and scrambled from the corral before the hooves flashing sunlight pummeled him.

In this brief passage the descriptive details, not the events themselves, create the experience. Creative writers know that they must activate the senses or risk the chance that readers will become bored and set the work aside. You can take a page from the creative writer's notebook: Make your readers see, hear, smell, taste, touch, and sense movement in your descriptive passages.

Often, inexperienced writers believe that adjectives and adverbs make for sensuous writing, so they pile these descriptive words against their nouns and verbs, a practice that can make for slack prose.

> The shiny red Porsche drove quickly through the
> wet streets. Its massive engine echoed loudly from the
> tall buildings that formed vertical canyons along the
> asphalt streets. Then a shrill siren erupted as a mud-
> smeared patrol car sped rapidly after the out-of-
> control Porsche.

If you reread the wild stallion example, you'll see that the
writer uses only one adjective—"bottom," modifying "fence post,"
which functions as a compound noun, as does "hind legs." The
descriptive power in this passage is carried by concrete nouns, active verbs, and verb phrases. If you have written a descriptive passage with excessive adjectives and adverbs, you can always rewrite
it by restructuring adjectives into phrases and by finding accurate
verbs to eliminate adverbs. Rewriting this way will make your description more vigorous. For instance, read the rewritten version
of the Porsche example:

> The Porsche, sunlight glinting from its red paint,
> raced through the streets slick from rain. The engine's
> roar echoed from skyscrapers that formed canyons
> along the Porsche's path. Then a siren erupted in a
> shrill blast as a patrol car smeared in mud raced after
> the Porsche fishtailing out of control.

Now there are only three adjectives, *red, slick,* and *shrill.* The passage
reads more quickly, the verbs are more accurate, and the descriptive
detail is easier to visualize—an effective revision.

When description enhances an explanation, then adjectives and
adverbs work effectively. For example, read the following passage
from John Steinbeck's *The Log from the Sea of Cortez.* Steinbeck is providing his readers information about sea life that he and his companions collected.

> The reef was generally exposed as the tide went down, and
> on its flat top the tide pools were beautiful. We collected as
> widely and rapidly as possible, trying to take a cross section of
> the animals we saw. There were purple pendent gorgonians like
> lacy fans; a number of small spine-covered puffer fish which

bloat themselves when they are attacked, erecting the spines; and many starfish, including some purple and gold cushion stars. The club-spined sea urchins were numerous in their rock niches. They seemed to move about very little, for their niches always just fit them and have the marks of constant occupation. We took a number of slim green and brown starfish and the large slim five-rayed starfish with plates bordering the ambulacral grooves.

But if the primary purpose is to describe, not to explain, then reduce the adjectives and adverbs by recasting your sentences.

How much descriptive detail should you include? Use enough to picture the experience. Keep in mind that, in descriptive writing, your task is to create an impression of an experience, not to meticulously recreate the experience in words.

Strategies

When reading with a critical eye, study the techniques writers use to involve your senses. Remember that serious writers calculate each detail in a descriptive passage, shaping the words to touch a circuit in your imagination.

Objective and Subjective Description

Descriptive writing is either objective or subjective. In objective description, writers concentrate on the subject rather than on their personal reactions or feelings toward it. In objective description, the purpose is to create a literal picture of the subject.

Many college assignments require objective description. For instance, marine science reports often involve precise descriptions of weather patterns or sea currents. A history project might call for a detailed description of a battle. A psychology assignment might require an objective description of a personality type. Newspaper reports are also written with objective distance from events, giving readers only the factual details. Of course, complete objectivity is impossible to achieve. After all, a writer must select the subject and the words to describe the subject. Nevertheless, in objective description, writers try to keep their personal reactions out of their work. For example, in the following paragraph from *The Mountains of California,* naturalist John Muir objectively presents a panoramic view of the Sierra Nevada mountain range:

> The north half of the range is mostly covered with floods of lava, and dotted with volcanoes and craters, some of them recent and perfect in form, others in various stages of decay. The south half is composed of granite nearly from base to summit, while a considerable number of peaks, in the middle of the range, are capped with metamorphic slates, among which are Mounts Dana and Gibbs to the east of Yosemite Valley. Mount Whitney, the culminating point of the range near its southern extremity, lifts its helmet-shaped crest to a height of nearly 14,700 feet. Mount Shasta, a colossal volcanic cone, raises to a height of 14,440 feet at the northern extremity, and forms a noble landmark for all the surrounding region within a radius of a hundred miles. Residual masses of volcanic rocks occur throughout most of the granite southern portions also, and a considerable number of the old volcanoes on the flanks, especially along the eastern base of the range near Mono Lake and southward. But it is only to the northward that the entire range, from base to summit, is covered in lava.

For the most part, Muir keeps his objective distance from his subject. He presents a detailed overview of the range, including significant peaks, their heights, and the materials that compose the Sierra. He does give the reader a peek at his feelings by using the words "colossal" and "noble," but not to the extent that the passage becomes subjective.

In subjective description, writers emphasize their personal reactions to or feelings toward a subject to create an impressionistic picture. Their goal is to get their readers to share these reactions or feelings. Sometimes writers will appear to present their material objectively but then end the passage with a subjective response. Consider, for example, the following passage from Sue Hubbell's *A Country Year: Living the Questions*:

> I've been out in the back today checking beehives. When I leaned over one of them to direct a puff of smoke from my

bee smoker into the entrance to quiet the bees, a copperhead came wriggling out from under the hive. He had been frightened from his protected spot by the smoke and the commotion I was making, and when he found himself in the open, he panicked and slithered for the nearest hole he could find, which was the entrance to the next beehive. I don't know what went on inside, but he came out immediately, wearing a surprised look on his face. I hadn't known that a snake could look surprised, but this one did. Then, after pausing to study the matter more carefully, he glided off to the safety of the woods.

Hubbell not only presents the objective detail of the experience, she also offers her impression of the snake, one that stands in sharp contrast to objective facts—that is, snakes do not look surprised, but her snake does.

Peter Schjeldahl, in the opening paragraph of "Cyclone," writes at the extreme of subjective description. He creates as much descriptive detail about how he feels riding the Coney Island roller coaster as he does objective description of the actual experience.

The Cyclone is art, sex, God, the greatest. It is the most fun you can have without risking bad ethics. I rode the Cyclone seven times one afternoon last summer, and I am here to tell everybody that it is fun for fun's sake, the pure abstract heart of the human capacity for getting a kick out of anything. Yes, it may be anguishing initially. (I promise to tell the truth.) Terrifying, even, the first time or two the train is hauled upward with groans and creaks and with you in it. At the top then—where there is sudden strange quiet but for the fluttering of two tattered flags, and you have a poignantly brief view of Brooklyn, and of ships far out on the Atlantic—you may feel very lonely and that you have made a serious mistake, cursing yourself in the last gleam of the reflective consciousness you are about, abruptly, to leave up there between the flags like an abandoned thought-balloon. To keep yourself company by screaming may help, and no one is noticing: try it. After a couple of rides, panic abates, and after four or five, you aren't even frightened, exactly, but stimulated, blissed, sent. The squirt of adrenaline you will never cease to have at the top as the train lumbers, wobbling slightly, into the plunge, finally fuels just happy wonderment because you can't, and never will, believe what is going to happen.

Schjeldahl's paragraph is packed with highly charged language: The Cyclone is "art, sex, God, the greatest . . . fun for fun's sake . . . anguishing . . . terrifying." He also mixes objective detail with his impressions: the train is "hauled upward with groans and creaks . . . [a] sudden strange quiet but for the fluttering of two tattered flags . . . a brief view of Brooklyn and of ships far out on the Atlantic . . . the train lumbers, wobbling slightly, into the plunge." To write effective subjective description, writers carefully mix objective detail with their responses.

Dominant Impression

To create an effective description, you might think writers do nothing more than record all they perceive. They do much more. As a critical reader, keep in mind that descriptive writing is not a haphazard activity. With so much detail available for any description, writers must select descriptive details with care and shape them with precision to achieve a **dominant impression.**

Selecting detail to create a dominant impression is even more critical in subjective description than in objective description. Writers must not only select but also embellish descriptive details to create the impression they want. When describing a desert, a writer might want to show that the land is hostile: "the harsh sunlight reflecting from the bleached sand like needles plunging into the hiker's eyes." Describing a politician, a writer might want to show him to be untrustworthy: "his face heavily lined from years of calculating behind closed doors, his eyes skipping around the crowd like those of a criminal about to be exposed." Writers seldom directly state the dominant impression they wish to create; they suggest it.

Consider this passage from Gretel Ehrlich's "A Season of Portraits." Ehrlich, who is an essayist, a novelist, and a Wyoming rancher, describes the dry summer of 1988, when raging fires consumed much of Yellowstone National Park's forests. In this passage she concentrates on the wind, suggesting that it is a wind from hell, savage and ghostly, perhaps even isolating her as souls are isolated in a mythical underworld.

> A breeze stiffens. Gusts are clocked at forty-five, sixty, eighty-five miles per hour. Rainless thunderclouds crack above, shaking pine pollen down. *La bufera infernale*—that's what Dante calls winds that lashed at sinners in hell. I decide to go out in the infernal storm. "This is hell," a herder moving his sheep across the mountain says, grinning, then clears his parched throat and rides away. Wind carries me back and forth, twisting, punching me down.
>
> I'm alone here for much of the summer, these hot winds my only dancing partner. The sheep and their herder vanish over the ridge. I close my eyes, and the planet is auditory only: tree branches twist into tubas and saxes, are caught by large hands that press down valves, and everywhere on this ranch I hear feral music—ghostly tunes made not by animals gone wild but by grasses, sagebrush, and fence wire singing.

Once writers decide on a dominant impression and select the appropriate details to suggest it, they must arrange the details in an effective order. Often a structure will become visible during the writing and revision, one that will be unique for that passage. Ehrlich arranges the passage above in two parts: the world she sees and the world she hears, which are clearly separated when she writes, "I close my eyes." She continues by suggesting that the wind plays the branches of trees like musical instruments and creates ghostly music by rushing through grasses, sagebrush, fence wire. By shutting her eyes, and yours as a sensitive reader, she transforms the world into a mysterious place.

Arrangement of Details

Although you will find no strict formulas for arranging descriptive details, writers do, however, follow some general principles. In visual description, a writer will usually structure the details in the way that the eye would record them, that is, by spatial arrangement—from left to right, right to left, near to far, far to near, center outward. A writer might begin with a broad picture and narrow to the particulars, like a film opening with a panoramic view of a landscape or city and gradually moving into the scene, finally focusing on one specific image.

To describe a person, a writer might begin with a general descriptive statement: "She looked as if she had stepped from the pages of *Vogue,* a stylish woman," and then moved downward from head to toe, "Her hair was the color of straw and cropped short; her neck seemed carved from ivory. . . ." Or this writer might begin by describing an unusual physical feature and work from there: "Her nose didn't fit her stylish appearance: It was a bit long and bent slightly to the left, as if it had stopped a boxer's left cross. Otherwise, she was unflawed. . . ." As you read descriptive passages, keep in mind that writers have many ways in which to organize a description. Critical readers examine writers' varied ways of structuring descriptive details and applying the techniques.

Description in College Writing

Vivid description supplements all but the most scientifically objective papers, often bringing life to arguments, explanations, and narrations. For example, if you were to take a position against allowing cigarettes to be sold in public vending machines where underage teens can easily buy them, your essay's dominant purpose would be to argue a position, but you might supplement your argument with a vivid description of a lung cancer victim. Or if you wanted to explain the effects of proposed cutbacks in medical aid to the poor, your essay's dominant purpose would be cause and effect, but you might supplement the explanation with a dramatic description of the impact on one impoverished family. If you wanted to write a personal narrative of the events that led to a dramatic insight, you would no doubt use some description to bring alive the people and places in the story. Finally, you might find yourself relying on description to write college reports for such courses as marine biology and art history, in which descriptive accuracy will be an important part of the assignment.

Guidelines for Writing Description

1. Select a subject that lends itself to description and examine it closely to decide whether your description will be subjective or objective.
2. Establish the dominant purpose, whether it is a supporting passage in an explanation or argument essay or the dominant method of development in a descriptive report.
3. Develop an extended list of descriptive details, then select the appropriate details from the list and arrange them for effect.
4. Decide on an appropriate structure and then write your essay, using concrete language.
5. Revise your essay, making sure that the dominant purpose is clear.

A Student Essay Developed by Description

In her contemporary art history class, Clarita Tan wrote a descriptive report in response to the following class assignment:

> This assignment will require you to do minor background research and to attend a current art exhibit at a local gallery or museum. Select a contemporary artist currently being exhibited as your subject. Then review representative works on display and describe the artist's method of working.

Now examine Tan's essay. First, read it through once, noting descriptive techniques that Tan uses. Then study it in detail by responding to the questions that follow.

Imaginatively Chaotic Art

The Fine Arts Gallery is featuring George McNeil, a figura-　　1
tive Abstract Expressionist who lived and worked his entire

life in New York City. The ten canvases, drawn together from local collections, are stunning for their color and imagery. It is hard to separate color and imagery in McNeil's work. From pools of purple, orange, and yellow emerge massive faces, airplanes, bodies, and cryptic scrawls. The imagery magically emerges from the method McNeil uses to compose his canvases. The result is that the viewer's mind is pulled from the real world into an imaginatively chaotic world.

In the foyer the curator displayed a series of photographs showing McNeil at work. The first photograph shows him walking into his studio to begin his day. A muted gray light streams from a skylight and McNeil stands in the doorway. At first glance he looks like a retiree getting ready to putter in a garden. He wears heavy work boots, tattered, oversized jeans that ride on his hip bones, a chambray shirt open at the neck with a T-shirt underneath, and a watch cap against the morning chill. But unlike a gardener's work clothes stained with soil and grass, McNeil's are splattered with paint. In fact, his boots are so crusted with paint they look like art objects. 2

Two of McNeil's physical features are dramatically riveting: his massive hands, gnarled from arthritis, that hang at the ends of long arms and his riveting eyes, set in the eighty-five-year-old face, that sparkle mischievously as if they belong to a spirited ten year old possessed by a humorous demon. 3

The next three photographs capture the initial phase of his painting method. Like other abstract expressionists, such as Jackson Pollock who is noted for his drip and splatter paintings, McNeil begins by stapling his canvas to a plywood sheet and laying it on the studio floor. The first photograph in this sequence shows him in action. McNeil leans over the canvas, dripping paint from a Styrofoam cup taken from a nearby table covered with other Styrofoam cups running over with paint. The next photograph shows him aggressively slashing the air with a brush as if it were a weapon, paint arcing toward the canvas. The third photograph shows him whipping the brush back, lashing downward, a mischievous grin on his face, his eyes twinkling. 4

The final phase of his method is captured in the fifth photograph. The canvas is now raised upright on the plywood base, a practice that deviates from Pollock's and that of other Abstract Expressionists. Here McNeil stands with his back to 5

the camera and faces the massive canvas. He is hunched forward with an upraised brush held like a symphony conduc-
tor's baton, and I think of composer Paul Dukas's "Sorcerer's
Apprentice." Indeed McNeil is performing artistic sorcery, for
he is creating images that suggest themselves from the splattered configurations on the canvas.

The images themselves are startling to view, often suggesting the untainted imagination of a child who knows none
of the technical restraints of someone who is "trained" to
paint. Two images in two paintings affected me the most.
"Kennedy Airport" (1989, 78 × 64 inches) is awash in color
with patches of blues, reds, purples, yellows, whites, oranges,

6

and blacks. McNeil has created the feeling that the viewer is looking down from the sky at a flat surface. Nothing is to scale—a huge head dominates the upper left-hand corner and a smaller head, its mouth agape, fills the lower right-hand corner. In between floats a mysterious cartoonish world—a woman in high heels and net hose, two tiny airplanes, and many spirals and circles. All is aswirl, as if the images have been whipped into the sky by an infernal wind that has brought havoc to the airport.

"Diablo Duco" (1986, 78 × 64 inches) is as dramatic as "Kennedy Airport." It, too, is alive with clashing colors. The central figure is a lime green dancer, whose high-heeled feet touch the canvas bottom and tilted head touches the canvas top. The figure is an abstraction, the lips and eyes smeared on with thick layers of blue, red, and purple paint. The hair, a massive mop, shoots upward. It is painted in orange, red, and yellow that suggest flames. In the center of the dancer's body McNeil has painted what appears to be a small city. The dancer herself is surrounded by other dancing figures, all much smaller, but all equally bizarre, perhaps even devilish.   7

Every canvas in the show is powerful, offering a unique vision of contemporary life. But perhaps the most important element in the show is the opening photographs that reveal this artistic magician at work. Without an understanding of how his paintings evolve from colorful splatters and pools into chaotic figures, I would have merely been distracted by the question, "How does anyone think of these images?" No doubt this question is the wrong one to ask when responding to art.   8

Reviewing with a Writer's Eye

1. Review Tan's writing assignment (see p. 139). It is composed of two parts. After selecting a contemporary artist, Tan had to review representative works and describe the artist's working method. Does Tan's essay meet the assignment requirements? Which paragraphs address part 1 and which address part 2?

2. In paragraph 1, the introduction, Tan provides important background information and creates an impression of what her essay

will cover. She also implies a general impression of how she wishes her readers to see George McNeil's art. What is that impression?

3. Creating a dominant impression (see pp. 136–137) can be an effective strategy in descriptive writing. In Tan's description of George McNeil, what dominant impression is she trying to create? List four key sentences that help to create the impression.

4. The arrangement of details is important in descriptive passages (see pp. 137–138). How does Tan arrange details in paragraphs 5 and 6? How does she arrange details in paragraphs 7 and 8? Briefly explain why her approach is different in these two sets of paragraphs.

5. Tan meticulously describes McNeil in paragraphs 2 and 3. Why? Do you think that the detail is excessive? Should it be cut? In a few sentences, explain your observations.

6. To be effective, descriptive writing must appeal to a reader's senses (see pp. 130–133). Tan mainly appeals to the sense of sight. List a few phrases that appeal to other senses as well.

7. Identify two allusions (see the Glossary) that Tan makes in "Imaginatively Chaotic Art." What purpose do they serve?

8. Is Tan's essay primarily objective, primarily subjective, or a mixture of objective and subjective description (see pp. 133–136)? Find passages that support your conclusion.

9. Write a note to Clarita Tan that states your overall response to her essay and details its strengths and weaknesses.

Peer Review

You may be asked to write an essay about one of the readings that follow. Before you meet with your writing group, review this introduction. As you read your group papers, use these general principles of description to help guide your comments.

1. A description should involve a reader's senses of sight, sound, smell, touch, and taste as appropriate for the subject being described.

2. A description should have an appropriate balance between the objective and the subjective. Look for a writer's feelings about what is described as well as the details of the description.

3. Concrete details make a description come alive. A reader cannot feel an experience conveyed only with general statements.
4. Details should be presented within an overall structure, usually, but not necessarily, in some variation of a spatial arrangement.
5. Except for purely objective descriptions, the paper should communicate some dominant impression. Without a dominant impression, what is the purpose of the description?

Most of us share senses—sight, sound, smell, touch, taste—and we have feelings. Professional writers know that by evoking sensory experience and feelings in their readers' minds they will enrich the reading experience. Read the essays in the following section. See how the authors evoke the senses; analyze their selection of descriptive details; and examine how they shape descriptive passages to achieve a dominant impression. Take notes as you read, mark an interesting passage, underline a vivid phrase. When you write your own descriptive passages, apply the principles you've learned from reading as a writer. Don't be timid about using a professional writer's passage for a model. The techniques of effective description are universal—available for everyone to use. Professional writers are challenged by the demands of description; certainly you, while developing writing skills, should also feel challenged.

❦ Maxine Hong Kingston ❦

Maxine Hong Kingston was born and raised in a Chinese-American community in Stockton, California, where her parents ran a laundry. She grew up listening to stories about China from her parents and relatives, who were first-generation immigrants. She attended the University of California at Berkeley and has taught creative writing at the University of Hawaii. Her stories, essays, and poems have been published in Ms., The New Yorker, *and* American Heritage. The Woman Warrior: Memoirs of a Girlhood Among Ghosts, *Kingston's award-winning autobiography, describes her memories and retells the stories she heard as a child. Her second book,* China Men, *winner of the National Book Award, traces the lives of three generations of Chinese men in America. Her novel* Tripmaster Monkey *is a fable of a young Chinese-American writer. Her latest book,* The Fifth Book of Peace, *combines memoir, history, culture, fantasy, and reality.*

Photographs of My Parents

In this selection from The Woman Warrior, *Kingston looks at much more than photographs. Her searching descriptions of mundane objects reveal some of the deep differences between the culture she grew up in and the China her parents left. In writing of both the familiarity and the strangeness in the photographs of her parents, she reaches into the past to better understand the present.*

Try to visualize as vividly as you can the differences between the Chinese and the Chinese-American photographs that Kingston describes. Consider how these differences contribute to the essay's central meaning.

Once in a long while, four times so far for me, my mother brings out the metal tube that holds her medical diploma. On the tube are gold circles crossed with seven red lines each—"joy" ideographs in abstract. There are also little flowers that look like gears for a gold machine. According to the scraps of labels with Chinese and American addresses, stamps, and postmarks, the family airmailed the can from Hong Kong in 1950. It got crushed in the middle, and whoever tried to peel the labels off stopped because the red and gold paint came off too, leaving silver scratches that rust. Somebody tried to pry the end off before discovering that the tube pulls apart. When I open it, the smell of China flies out, a thousand-year-old bat flying heavy-headed out of the Chinese caverns where bats are as white as dust, a smell that comes from long ago, far back in the brain. Crates from Canton, Hong Kong, Singapore, and Taiwan have that smell too, only stronger because they are more recently come from the Chinese.

Inside the can are three scrolls, one inside another. The largest   2 says that in the twenty-third year of the National Republic, the To Keung School of Midwifery, where she has had two years of instruction and Hospital Practice, awards its Diploma to my mother, who has shown through oral and written examination her Proficiency in Midwifery, Pediatrics, Gynecology, "Medecine," "Surgary," Therapeutics, Ophthalmology, Bacteriology, Dermatology, Nursing and Bandage. This document has eight stamps on it: one, the school's English and Chinese names embossed together in a circle; one, as the Chinese enumerate, a stork and a big baby in lavender ink; one, the school's Chinese seal; one, an orangish paper stamp pasted in the border design; one, the red seal of Dr. Wu Pak-liang, M.D., Lyon, Berlin, president and "Ex-assistant étranger à la clinique chirugicale et d'accouchement de l'université de Lyon"; one, the red seal of Dean Woo Yin-kam, M.D.; one, my mother's seal, her chop mark larger than the president's and the dean's; and one, the number 1279 on the back. Dean Woo's signature is followed by "(Hackett)." I read in a history book that Hackett Medical College for Women at Canton was founded in the nineteenth century by European women doctors.

The school seal has been pressed over a photograph of my   3 mother at the age of thirty-seven. The diploma gives her age as twenty-seven. She looks younger than I do, her eyebrows are thicker, her lips fuller. Her naturally curly hair is parted on the left, one wavy wisp tendrilling off to the right. She wears a scholar's white gown, and she is not thinking about her appearance. She stares straight ahead as if she could see me and past me to her grandchildren and grandchildren's grandchildren. She has spacy eyes, as all people recently from Asia have. Her eyes do not focus on the camera. My mother is not smiling; Chinese do not smile for photographs. Their faces command relatives in foreign lands—"Send money"—and posterity forever—"Put food in front of this picture." My mother does not understand Chinese-American snapshots. "What are you laughing at?" she asks.

The second scroll is a long narrow photograph of the graduating   4
class with the school officials seated in front. I picked out my mother immediately. Her face is exactly her own, though forty years younger. She is so familiar, I can only tell whether or not she is pretty or happy or smart by comparing her to the other women. For this formal group picture she straightened her hair with oil to make a chinlength bob like the others'. On the other women, strangers, I can recognize a curled lip, a sidelong glance, pinched shoulders. My mother is not soft; the girl with the small nose and dimpled underlip is soft. My mother is not humorous, not like the girl at the end who lifts her mocking chin to pose like Girl Graduate. My mother does not have smiling eyes; the old woman teacher (Dean Woo?) in front crinkles happily, and the one faculty member in the western suit smiles westernly. Most of the graduates are girls whose faces have not yet formed; my mother's face will not change anymore, except to age. She is intelligent, alert, pretty. I can't tell if she's happy.

The graduates seem to have been looking elsewhere when they   5
pinned the rose, zinnia, or chrysanthemum on their precise black dresses. One thin girl wears hers in the middle of her chest. A few have a flower over a left or right nipple. My mother put hers, a chrysanthemum, below her left breast. Chinese dresses at that time were dartless, cut as if women did not have breasts; these young doctors, unaccustomed to decorations, may have seen their chests as black expanses with no reference points for flowers. Perhaps they couldn't shorten that far gaze that lasts only a few years after a Chinese emigrates. In this picture too my mother's eyes are big with what they held—reaches of oceans beyond China, land beyond oceans. Most emigrants learn the barbarians' directness—how to gather themselves and stare rudely into talking faces as if trying to catch lies. In America my mother has eyes as strong as boulders, never once skittering off a face, but she has not learned to place decorations and phonograph needles, nor has she stopped seeing land on the other side of the oceans. Now her eyes include the relatives in China, as they once included my father smiling and smiling

in his many western outfits, a different one for each photograph that he sent from America.

He and his friends took pictures of one another in bathing suits 6 at Coney Island beach, the salt wind from the Atlantic blowing their hair. He's the one in the middle with his arms about the necks of his buddies. They pose in the cockpit of a biplane, on a motorcycle, and on a lawn beside the "Keep Off the Grass" sign. They are always laughing. My father, white shirt sleeves rolled up, smiles in front of a wall of clean laundry. In the spring he wears a new straw hat, cocked at a Fred Astaire angle. He steps out, dancing down the stairs, one foot forward, one back, a hand in his pocket. He wrote to her about the American custom of stomping on straw hats come fall. "If you want to save your hat for next year," he said, "you have to put it away early, or else when you're riding the subway or walking along Fifth Avenue, any stranger can snatch it off your head and put his foot through it. That's the way they celebrate the change of seasons here." In the winter he wears a gray felt hat with his gray overcoat. He is sitting on a rock in Central Park. In one snapshot he is not smiling; someone took it when he was studying, blurred in the glare of the desk lamp.

There are no snapshots of my mother. In two small portraits, 7 however, there is a black thumbprint on her forehead, as if someone had inked in bangs, as if someone had marked her.

"Mother, did bangs come into fashion after you had the picture 8 taken?" One time she said yes. Another time when I asked, "Why do you have fingerprints on your forehead?" she said, "Your First Uncle did that." I disliked the unsureness in her voice.

The last scroll has columns of Chinese words. The only English 9 is "Department of Health, Canton," imprinted on my mother's face, the same photograph as on the diploma. I keep looking to see whether she was afraid. Year after year my father did not come home or send for her. Their two children had been dead for ten years. If he did not return soon, there would be no more children. ("They were three and two years old, a boy and a girl. They could talk already.") My father did send money regularly, though, and she had nobody to spend it on but herself. She bought good clothes and shoes. Then she decided to use the money for becoming a doctor. She did not leave for Canton immediately after the children died. In China there was time to complete feelings. As my father had done, my mother left the village by ship. There was a sea bird painted on the ship to protect it against shipwreck and winds. She was in luck. The following ship was boarded by river pirates, who kidnapped every passenger, even old ladies. "Sixty dollars for an old lady" was what the bandits used to say. "I sailed alone," she says, "to the capital of the entire province." She took a brown leather suitcase and a seabag stuffed with two quilts.

Meaning and Purpose

1. Have you ever looked through old photographs of your parents or grandparents? What feelings did you have when you looked at them? What questions did you ask? What do the photographs tell you about yourself?

2. What are the contrasts between Chinese and Chinese-American photographs and what do these contrasts suggest about the meaning of "Photographs of My Parents"?

3. In paragraph 3, Kingston writes that "the school seal has been pressed over a photograph of my mother"; in paragraph 7, Kingston describes a small portrait of her mother, "there is a black thumbprint on her forehead . . . as if someone had marked her"; and in paragraph 9, she reports that another photograph has the English words "Department of Health, Canton" printed over her face. How do these descriptive details work in the essay?

4. What does paragraph 6 reveal about Kingston's father?

5. Discuss the significance of flowers pinned awkwardly on the graduates' dresses.

6. In the first paragraph, what does the "thousand-year-old bat" signify?

Strategy

1. What is Kingston's general organizational strategy for description? Where are the three transition points at which Kingston moves from one section to another?

2. Identify some descriptions that involve the senses and some that evoke impressions or feelings. What kinds of figures of speech are they—metaphor, simile, personification, descriptive image?
3. Is this descriptive essay subjective or objective, and how do you know?
4. What impression does Kingston give of the metal tube in the first paragraph? How does her description prepare you for the rest of the essay?

Style

1. How would you describe the tone of the essay or the narrator's feelings about the contents of the metal tube?
2. Consider the metal tube to be a symbol for Kingston's mother. What qualities does it suggest about her?
3. Kingston uses some medical terms. Be sure you know their meanings: *ophthalmology, pediatrics, gynecology, dermatology, therapeutics* (paragraph 2).

Writing Tasks

1. Study Kingston's essay to see how she uses photographs to reveal bits and pieces of her parents' history. Then select photographs of two friends or relatives who have both similar and opposing character traits. Use the photographs to write a description that reveals their character traits without stating them directly.
2. Describe a significant possession of someone you know, and show how it characterizes the person.

❦ Joanna Greenfield ❦

*Joanna Greenfield grew up in Connecticut. Throughout her childhood
she dreamed of going to Africa to work with wild animals. After graduation from college, she traveled to Israel to work in a game reserve dedicated to biblical animals. "Hyena" is her first publication.*

Hyena

*Experienced though she was, Greenfield, a person who is wise in the
ways of animal behavior, let her guard drop once and, as a result,
suffered horribly. As you read this essay, notice how Greenfield
moves from describing action to describing background information
and then back to describing action.*

The van slowed, then stopped, for a hyena in the road. It was a   1
spotted hyena, the kind people think of when they hear the word
"hyena"—a dirty, matted creature, dripping with blood. It must have
made a good kill. The prey must have been large enough for the
hyena to thrust its whole head in, up to the blocklike shoulders.

This must be why the hyena has such a snake of a neck—so it can   2
delve deep into a dying animal and eat the best parts before thieves
chase it away. Hyenas always go first for the softest parts, like entrails,
although they have jaws stronger than a lion's, and can eat bones.

This hyena's belly bulged over its legs, and it sat in the road, as if   3
musing, making no attempt to clean off the blood. The slurs that human beings cast at the species fall as useless as gossip about Greek
gods. The hyena sat there despite all our encouragement to it to
move, and, long past the point when a lion would have slunk peev-
ishly away, we had to slither over a ditch to pass by.

As we drove away, I saw other hyenas stretched flat on the sa-   4
vanna. They were all dipped in blood, but every stain was different.
One could see which animal had gnawed at a leg, cheek pressed to
bloody flank, or which had held a piece to its chest and embraced it

151

there as it chewed. The prey animal, a wildebeest or a zebra, like one of the human shadows of Hiroshima, was left only in negative, fragmented about the savanna in ghostly prints of blood.

The deathbed was almost clean. A crowd of vultures pounced on and squabbled over pieces of skin ripped free when the hyenas pulled off their parts, and a few insects had already stripped clots of blood from the soaked grass. Nothing else was left.   5

Spotted hyenas are the sharks of the savanna, superpredators and astounding recyclers of garbage. They hunt in large, giggling groups, running alongside their prey and eating chunks of its flesh until it slows down through loss of blood, or shock, or sheer hopelessness, and then the hyenas grab for the stomach and pull the animal to a halt with its own entrails or let it stumble into the loops and whorls of its own body. They eat the prey whole and cough back, like owls, the indigestible parts, such as hair and hooves.   6

Hyenas in the wild can roam dozens of miles a day. They leave their young in small dens and trot or lope across the savanna, head down or held high and rear tucked under, until they've found a hare or a pregnant gazelle or a nicely rotted piece of flesh. But when the herds begin to migrate the hyenas leave their dens to follow them, and, passing over hills, through rifts and acacia stands, and along dry riverbeds, they reach the open plains of the Serengeti, where wildebeest beyond count mill and groan in clouds of dust.   7

I once saw a family of hyenas playing on an elephant skull. They rolled on their backs, biting gently at each other's legs. Two cubs squeezed under and then out of the elephant's mandible. A female turned on her side, paws in the air, and broke off a piece of the skull as if eating a biscuit in bed. Hyenas almost never kill humans—only now and then taking a piece from the cheek of a sleeping man, and that probably because some villages used to put out their dead for hyenas, flies, and any vultures in the area. As the man jumps up— perhaps he is a messenger between villages or someone searching for a bride—the hyena instantly, peaceably, retreats.   8

I had never wanted to work anywhere except in Africa, but after I graduated from college a wildlife-reserve director from Israel told   9 me that he needed someone to set up a breeding site for endangered animals and I decided to go. When I got there, I was told that the project had been postponed and was asked if I'd mind taking a job as a volunteer at another reserve, cleaning enclosures. The reserve was dedicated to Biblical animals, many of them predators from the Israeli wild—hyenas, wolves, foxes, and one unmated leopard—attackers of kibbutz livestock. It was something to do, with animals, so I trudged off every day in the hundred-and-fourteen-degree heat with half a sandwich and a water canteen. I was being groomed for the job I'd initially been offered, but for the moment I sifted maggots for the lizards and snakes, and cleaned the fox, cat, hyena, wolf, and leopard corrals.

As the days got hotter, my fellow-workers and I carried gallon   10
jugs of water in our wheelbarrows, poured it over our heads, and drank the rest until our stomachs were too full for food. It became a steady rhythm: sift dung, pour, drink, sift. We worked in pairs among the larger animals for safety, but toward the end of the month I was allowed to feed a young hyena and clean his cage. Efa had been taken from his parents as a cub because his mother rejected him. Also, he was a cross between a North African and an Israeli striped hyena, and nobody wanted him to confuse the gene pool further by mating. He was a beautiful animal. A mane trickled down sloped shoulders like a froth of leftover baby hair; he looked strangely help-less, as if weighed down by the tangled strands, and his back rounded to a dispirited slump. Even though he had a hyena's pos-ture, he was like a German shepherd, a little dirty, but graceful, and so strong he didn't seem to have any muscles. His stripes twisted a bit at the ends and shimmered over the coat like feathers at rest. With his bat face and massed shoulders, he would have been at home in the sky, poised in a great leap, or swooping for prey. But here he was given aged meat, and he often left even that to rot before he ate it.

He had been, they said, an adorable cub, crying "Maaaaaa!" to   11
Shlomi, the gentlest of the workers and the one who reared him, and he followed Shlomi everywhere. Then he grew too big to run loose, and he started biting at people, so they put him in a corral—a square of desert surrounded by an electrified fence with a large water basin perched in the center.

Efa was bored and lonely. He flipped the basin over every day, 12
attacking it as if it were prey. When we fed him in the morning, there
was nowhere to put his water. He knocked over everything, so we
had no choice: we had to put him in a holding cage outside his corral while we built a concrete pool that he couldn't move. This was
worse. Locked in a cage, he rebelled. He refused to eat, and every
box we gave him for shade was torn to pieces. After a few days, I
walked by and saw him standing defiant in the cage, his shade box
in splinters and his water overturned again. "Maaaaaaaa! Mmaaaaa!"
he croaked at me. I made a note to return and water him when I'd
finished with the others.

I stopped to talk to the leopard, who was in heat. This was my 13
first chance to get near her; when she was not hormonally sedated,
she lunged at passersby, swatting her claws through the chicken wire.

"You're so beautiful." 14

She purred, and rubbed against the mesh. The men said you 15
could stroke her like a house cat when she was in these moods. I
wanted to touch her, a leopard from the oases of Israel's last deserts,
but I stayed away, in case she changed her mind, and squatted out of
reach to talk to her. I didn't want to force her to defend herself.

It might have been the attention I gave the leopard, but Efa was 16
in a frenzy of "Mmmaaaaaaaaa"s when I returned to his cage. He
crouched like a baby, begging for something. I filled a water tray and
unlatched the door that opened into a corridor running between the
cage and the corral, then I closed it. If only I'd just squirted the hose
into the cage, but instead I unlatched the cage door and bent over to
put the dish down, talking to him. The mind, I found, is strange. It
shut off during the attack, while my body continued to act, without
thought or even sight. I don't remember him sinking his teeth into
my arm, though I heard a little grating noise as his teeth chewed
into the bone.

Everything was black and slow and exploding in my stomach. 17
Vision returned gradually, like an ancient black-and-white television
pulling dots and flashes to the center for a picture. I saw at a remove
the hyena inside my right arm, and my other arm banging him on
the head. My body, in the absence of a mind, had decided that this

was the best thing to do. And scream. Scream in a thin angry hysteria that didn't sound like me. Where was everyone? My mind was so calm and remote that I frightened myself, but my stomach twisted. I hit harder, remembering the others he'd nipped. He'd always let go.

Efa blinked and surged back, jerking me forward. I stumbled 18 out of my sandals into the sand, thinking, with fresh anxiety, I'll burn my feet. I tried to kick him between the legs, but it was awkward, and he was pulling me down by the arm, down and back into the cage. When I came back from Africa the first time, I took a class in self-defense so I'd feel safer with all the soldiers, guerrilla warriors, and policemen when I returned. I remembered the move I'd vowed to use on any attacker: a stab and grab at the jugular, to snap it inside the skin. But the hyena has callused skin on its throat, thick and rough, like eczema. I lost hope and felt the slowness of this death to be the worst insult. Hyenas don't kill fast, and I could end up in the sand watching my entrails get pulled through a cut in my stomach and eaten like spaghetti, with tugs and jerks. I started to get mad, an unfamiliar feeling creeping in to add an acid burn to the chill of my stomach. Another removal from myself. I never let myself get mad. I want peace. I tried to pinch his nostrils so he'd let go of my arm to breathe, but he shook his head, pulling me deeper into the cage.

I think it was then that he took out the first piece from my arm 19 and swallowed it without breathing, because a terror of movement settled in me at that moment and lasted for months. He moved up the arm, and all the time those black, blank eyes evaluated me, like a shark's, calm and almost friendly. By this time, my right arm was a mangled mess of flesh, pushed-out globs of fat, and flashes of bone two inches long, but my slow TV mind, watching, saw it as whole, just trapped in the hyena's mouth, in a tug-of-war like the one I used to play with my dogs—only it was my arm now instead of a sock. It didn't hurt. It never did.

The hyena looked up at me with those indescribable eyes and 20 surged back again, nearly pulling me onto his face. I remembered self-defense class and the first lesson: "Poke the cockroach in the eyes." All the women had squealed, except me. "Ooooh, I could never do that." Ha, I'd thought. Anyone who wants to kill me has no right to live. I'd poke him in the eyes.

I looked at those eyes with my fingers poised to jab. It was for my family and my friends that I stuck my finger in his eyes. I just wanted to stop watching myself get eaten, either be dead and at peace or be gone, but other lives were connected to mine. I'm not sure if I did more than touch them gently before he let go and whipped past me to cower against the door to the outside, the Negev desert.

Events like this teach you yourself. We all think we know what we would do, hero or coward, strong or weak. I expected strength, and the memory of my tin-whistle scream curdles my blood, but I am proud of the stupid thing I did next. He cowered and whimpered and essentially apologized, still with those blank, unmoving eyes, and I stood still for a second. My arm felt light and shrunken as if half of it were gone, but I didn't look. From the corridor, I had a choice of two doors: the one through which I'd entered, leading back to the desert, and the one opening onto the corral. I didn't think I could bend over him and unlatch the door to the desert. He'd just reach up and clamp onto my stomach. And I didn't want to open the door to the corral, or he'd drag me in and be able to attack the men if they ever came to help me. My body, still in control, made the good hand grab the bad elbow, and I beat him with my own arm, as if I had ripped it free to use as a club. "No!" I shouted. "No, no!" Lo lo lo, in Hebrew. I might even have said "Bad boy," but I hope not. It was the beating that damaged my hand permanently. I must have hit him hard enough to crush a ligament, because there is a lump on my hand to this day, five years later, but he didn't even blink. He came around behind me and grabbed my right leg, and again there was no pain—just the feeling that he and I were playing tug-of-war with my body—but I was afraid to pull too hard on the leg. He pulled the leg up, stretching me out in a line from the door, where I clung with the good hand to the mesh, like a dancer at the barre. It felt almost good, as if the whole thing were nearer to being over. In three moves I didn't feel, he took out most of the calf.

I opened the door to the desert and he ran out, with a quick shove that staggered me. I couldn't move the right leg, just crutched myself along on it into the Negev. He waited for me. The cold in my stomach was stabbing my breath away. The hyena and I were bonded now. Even if someone did come to help, there was still something left to finish between us. I was marked—his. I saw, in color, that he was going to knock me over, and I thought, in black-and-white, No, don't, you'll hurt my leg, I should keep it still.

A workman stood by a shed uphill, leaning on a tool in the sand. He watched me walk toward the office, with the hyena ahead and looking back at me. He was the only spectator I noticed, though I was told later, in the hospital, that some tourists, there to see the animals, were screaming for help, and three—or was it five?— soldiers had had their machine guns aimed at us throughout the whole thing. Israeli soldiers carry their arms everywhere when they're in uniform; but they must have been afraid to shoot. I don't know. Stories get told afterward. I didn't see anyone except the workman, looking on impassively, and the leopard, pacing inside her fence, roaring a little, with the peace of her heat gone as suddenly as it had appeared. 24

I am sure Efa crawled out to greet me with no intention to kill. He had cried to me like an infant in distress, hunched over and rounded. His ruff lay flat and soft and his tail hung down. He attacked me, I think, in a moment of thirst-induced delirium and loneliness. If he had wanted to eat or to attack, he could have taken my arm in a snap: one sharp jab and jerk, and the wrist would have been gone before I even noticed. If he had wanted to kill me, he could have leaped for my stomach as soon as he had pulled me down by the arm. 25

Cheetahs often catch hold of their prey's nose and run alongside it. As the victim stumbles and falls, or staggers, or tries to run, the cheetah holds tight, closing mouth and nostrils in one stapled hold, or—with larger prey—biting into the throat to cut off air. Leopards like to leap down from trees for a quick crack of the back. Lions improvise. Each has its own specialty. Some leap up from behind, like a terrestrial leopard; some try a daring front leap, risking hooves and horns to bite into neck or face. 26

Hyenas are far more efficient. They catch hold of flesh, not with small nips and throwing of weight but by smoothly and quickly transferring chunks of it from prey to throat. Food slips instantly from toothhold to stomach. Like human infants nursing, they seem 27 to swallow without pausing for breath, as if food and air travelled in separate channels. They are the only predators adapted to eating bone. Their dung is white with it.

I heard a story of a young boy in Nairobi who was watching over   28
a herd of goats and fell asleep leaning on his stick. A hyena appeared and opened the boy's stomach with one quick rip. For the hyena it might have been play, this trying on of assault. But he won, as he was bound to do. I was told that someone took the boy to a doctor and he died a while later. He could have lived; we don't need all our intestines, and the hyena had probably left enough behind. But maybe they didn't have the right antibiotics or sterile dressings. I would have liked to ask him what he saw in the hyena's eyes.

In the ambulance, the driver chatted for a bit, then said, "Don't   29
close your eyes. If you feel faint, tell me and I'll stop right away."

To do what, watch me? I didn't tell him that I'd been exhausted   30
for months—I'd got parasites in Africa—and always shut my eyes when I had the chance. I closed them now, and he asked me questions with an anxiety that warmed my heart. I love to be taken care of. It was good to be strapped down and bandaged, all decisions out of my hands after the hard ones, the life-and-death ones. It was also, I learned, a good thing to have the wounds hidden. Once they were open to the air, my stomach clenched with pain that made life temporarily not worth living. The arm, I finally noticed, was curled up on itself, like paper shrivelling inward in a fire, but heavy instead of too light.

We arrived at the hospital with a screech and a yank and a curse.   31
The doors were stuck, but the driver pushed, and ran me in. Then he left with a wave of farewell. I waited and waited. A doctor came in and plowed my arm in search of a vein with blood, going deep under the muscle, to attach a saline drip. My nails were white, like things soaked in formaldehyde, and I was freezing. Bled white, I was. Nothing left to fill a test tube.

I asked the doctor to talk with the reserve's veterinarian before   32
he did anything. Hyena bites are violently infectious. The animals' mouths are full of bacteria from rotten meat. He shrugged. But when Shlomi told him to wait for the vet he did. The vet told him

to clean the holes out and leave them open for now, because the infection could kill me.

"The infection will probably take the leg anyway," the doctor 33
told me. "The chances are fifty-fifty that we'll have to amputate."

I looked down once at the leg before they began cutting out the 34
dirtier shreds of flesh and paring the whole surface of the wound.
The holes were impossibly wide, more than twice the size of the
hyena's face. I know now that skin and muscle are stretched over
bone like canvas over a canoe. One thinks of skin as irrevocably
bonded to flesh, and all as one entity. But skin is attached to flesh
only with the lightest of bonds, and, once it has been ripped, the
body gives way naturally, pulling the flesh back to its scaffolding of
bone. The invisible woman, I thought, as the chill took me; I can see
right through my leg.

I couldn't see all of it because of my bad eyesight, and the leg was 35
still covered with blood-stuck sand, but it was strange the way the leg
went down normally, then cut in to the bone, along the bone, and then
out again to a normal ankle, except for a small gash on the side with fat
poking out. I couldn't yet see the other hole. It was lower down, starting halfway past the one I could see, and continuing around the back
of the leg to the other side, so almost the whole leg was girdled
around. I still don't know how blood got to that stranded wall of flesh.

The doctor worked on the leg for an hour, clipping pieces of 36
flesh out of the wounds with little scissor snips, as if my leg were a
piece of cloth that he was carefully tailoring with dull tools. I asked
for a larger dose of anesthetic, not because I felt any pain—I never
felt any, really—but because I could feel the scissors scissoring away
the flesh and I couldn't breathe. Between bouts of cutting, I kept jok-
ing, happy it was over, or might be over, and people crowded into
the room to watch. No sterilization? Who cares? I was alive. They
pumped saline into me so fast that my arm swelled and I had to go
to the bathroom. For the first time, I realized how my life had
changed. There is, after all, no simple dichotomy: intact and alive
versus torn and dead.

I had expected the hyena bite in Africa, not in Israel. I had ex- 37
pected the price I paid for Africa to be high. The need that had

driven me since I was eight years old had made me willing to risk anything, even death, to be in Africa watching animals. Anyone who works with animals expects to get hurt. You are a guest in their life—any intrusion is a threat to them. It is their separateness that makes them worthy of respect.

After the hospital, I went back to America for physical therapy and treatment of the parasites, which burned a path in my stomach for the next six months. Before I left, people from the reserve asked me to stand near Efa's cage. They wanted to know if his animosity was specific to me. He looked at me, again with those friendly blank eyes, and then rose up against the wire with a crash so loud that I thought he was breaking through. For one second, I saw his face coming toward me, mouth open, and I hopped back. They told me they were going to send him to a zoo where the keepers wouldn't have to go into the cage, but I heard later that a veterinarian came and put Efa to sleep. ("Forever asleep," the workers said.) Shlomi was there. 38

Back in America, too ill for school, I read about animals on my own. Then I went to graduate school, but I found the statistical and analytical approach to animals too reductive. So I gave it up. But I couldn't not return to Africa. Five years after the hyena bite, I went back. Without a job, or any scientific purpose, I backpacked between Tanzania and Kenya, seeing the savanna in short bursts of safaris and hired cars and matatu buses. 39

I had almost died, eaten alive, and I was glad to be alive. The scars had healed. Three long dents ran around the arm and the leg, blurred with spider tracks of canine punctures. The one war wound, the bump that grew where I hit the hyena, still hurt, but I was back in Africa. 40

Meaning and Purpose

1. In the introductory three paragraphs of this essay, Greenfield describes a hyena in such a way that we can later picture her personal

experience with a hyena. What are three qualities of a hyena mentioned in these paragraphs that help you to better understand what later happens to Greenfield?

2. Greenfield had wanted to go to Africa but instead worked in Israel. Why did she work in Israel?

3. Obviously, the relationship between Efa and Shlomi differs greatly from the relationship between Efa and Greenfield. Why do you think this is so?

4. How did the first lesson that Greenfield learned in a self-defense class help her to deal with Efa?

5. How can you tell from reading this essay that Greenfield does not blame Efa for the attack?

Strategy

1. In paragraph 6, what point does Greenfield make about wild creatures in general when she writes, "Spotted hyenas are the sharks of the savanna"? What do hyenas and sharks have in common?

2. How does Greenfield describe Efa's attack? How can you tell that the attack was sudden?

3. What is the importance of the term *dichotomy* in paragraph 36? Suggest an appropriate synonym.

4. In paragraph 27, why are hyenas called *efficient?*

5. As Greenfield also notes in paragraph 27, hyenas eat the bones of the animals that they have killed. How does this information add to the tension of Greenfield's experience?

Style

1. This essay interweaves two descriptions. What are those two descriptions, and how does one support or add understanding to the other one?

2. What would you say is the best description of the people in the vicinity, as conveyed in paragraph 24, when Efa was attacking Greenfield?

3. As used critically, the term *tone* often refers to an author's attitude towards her topic. What, in your opinion, is the tone of this essay?

4. Why is this essay titled simply "Hyena"?
5. In paragraph 22, why does Greenfield shout, "Lo, lo, lo!" to Efa?

Writing Tasks

1. Each of us has been in a tight spot, though let us hope in not as tight a spot as Greenfield found herself. Write an essay describing an incident in your life that caused you harm or could have caused you harm. Be sure to relate the details of the incident.
2. Many of us have pets that have reacted angrily, often with good reason. Write an essay describing an incident in your pet's life when the pet reacted in some unexpected ways, being sure to describe the incident so that your reader will be able to imagine it, to "see it" mentally.

❦ Marcus Laffey ❦

Marcus Laffey is the pen name of Edward Conlon who wrote "Cop Diary" when he wanted to remain anonymous as a cop on the beat in New York City. Conlon comes from a long line of NYC policemen, and even though he is Harvard educated he felt compelled to become a NYC policeman too. He published Blue Blood *under his own name, a portrait of his Irish-American family and his fascinating life as a policeman on the streets of New York. The book has won high critical acclaim.*

Cop Diary

Because of numerous police movies and television shows, many people have stereotyped police officers. As you read this essay, try to keep your own stereotypes of police officers in mind as you consider Laffey's commentary on what a real police officer does and thinks.

Over the past year, more than a hundred people have worn my handcuffs. Not long ago, in a self-defense class, I wore them myself. There was a jolt of dissonance, like the perverse unfamiliarity at hearing your own voice on tape. Is this me? They were cold, and the metal edge pressed keenly against the bone if I moved, even when they were loose. The catch of the steel teeth as the cuffs tighten is austere and final, and never so much so as when it emanates from the small of your back. I thought, Hey, these things work. And then, Good thing. Because their intransigent grip means that, once they're on the correct pair of hands, no one should get hurt. Barring an unexpected kick or a bite, the story's over: no one's going to lose any teeth or blood, we're both going safely to jail, and at least one of us is going home tonight.

The handcuffs are a tool of the trade and an emblem of it, as are the gun and the nightstick. People—especially children whose eye level is at my equipment belt—stare at them, sometimes with a fearful look, but more often with fascination. Since I hold them from the other end, I regard them differently, just as surgeons don't feel un-easy, as I do, at the sight of a scalpel or a syringe. Police work can look ugly, especially when it's done well: you might see a man walk-ing down the street, untroubled, untroubling, when two or ten cops rush up to him, shouting over sirens and screeching tires, with their guns drawn. You haven't seen the old man rocking on a stoop three blocks away with one eye swollen shut. You haven't heard his story, his description of the man being handcuffed: coat, color, height, the tattoo on his wrist.

The transformation from citizen to prisoner is terrible to behold,   3
regardless of its justice. Unlike my sister the teacher or my brother the lawyer, I take prisoners, and to exercise that authority is to in-voke a profound social trust. Each time a surgeon undertakes the re-sponsibility of cutting open a human being, it should be awesome and new, no matter how necessary the operation, no matter how rou-tine. A police officer who takes away someone's freedom bears a bur-den of at least equal gravity. Let me tell you, it's a pleasure sometimes.

I walk a beat in a neighborhood of New York City that is a by-   4
word for slum. Even if the reality of places like the South Bronx, Brownsville, and Bed-Stuy no longer matches the reputation, and maybe never did, these bad neighborhoods are still bad. Children still walk through three different brands of crack vials in the building lobbies. People still shit in the stairwells. Gunshots in the night may have become less common in my precinct, but many people, young and old, can still distinguish that hard, sharp crack—like a broom-stick snapped cleanly in half—from fireworks or a car backfiring.

The genuine surprise is how wholesome and ordinary this   5
neighborhood sometimes seems, with its daily round of parents' get-ting kids ready for school, going to work, wondering if a car or a coat will make it through another winter. Life in the projects and the ten-ements can be just the way it is in suburbia, except that it takes place on busier streets and in smaller rooms. Sometimes it's better, in the way that city life, when it's good, is better than life anywhere else. In the summer, you can walk through the projects beneath shady aisles of sycamore and maple, past well-tended gardens and playgrounds teeming with children. There will be families having cookouts, old

ladies reading Bibles on the benches, pensive pairs of men playing chess. Once, I went to the roof of a project and saw a hawk perched on the rail. Always, you can see Manhattan in the near distance, its towers and spires studded with lights, stately and slapdash, like the crazy geometry of rock crystal. There are many days when I feel sorry for people who work indoors.

The other revelation when I became a cop was how much peo- 6 ple like cops. In safe neighborhoods, a cop is part of the scenery. I used to notice cops the way I noticed mailboxes, which is to say only when I needed one. But in bad neighborhoods I notice people noticing me, and especially certain classes of people—older people, young kids, single women, people dressed for work or church. They look at me with positive appreciation and relief. I am proof that tonight, on this walk home, no one's going to start with them. Sometimes they express that appreciation. The exceptions are groups of young guys on the street (older, if they're unemployed). Sometimes they're just hanging out, sometimes they're planning something more ambitious, and you're a sign that this wild night's not going to happen—not as they hoped, not here. Sometimes they express themselves, too.

When I'm working, I wear a Kevlar vest, and I carry a nightstick, 7 pepper spray, a radio, a flashlight, two sets of handcuffs, and a gun with two extra fifteen-round magazines. A thick, leather-bound memo book has been squeezed into my back pocket, and leather gloves, rubber gloves, department forms, and binoculars are stuffed in various other pockets. When you chase someone in this outfit, it's like running in a suit of armor while carrying a bag of groceries. But I'm safe, and it's only very rarely that I feel otherwise. All the people I've fought with were trying to get away.

I walk around on patrol, keeping an eye out and talking to peo- 8 ple, until a job comes up on the radio. The radio is constant and chaotic, a montage of stray details, awful and comic facts:

"Respond to a woman cornered by a large rodent in her living 9 room."

" . . . supposed to be a one-year-old baby with its head split open." 10

"The perp is a male Hispanic, white T-shirt, bluejeans, possible 11 mustache, repeat, possible mustache."

The appeal of patrol is its spontaneity and variety, its respon- 12
siveness to the rhythms of the street: there will be long lulls and
then sudden convulsions as pickup jobs and radio runs propel you
into a foot pursuit, a dispute, or a birth. When the action's over, the
world can seem slow and small, drearily confined. And then you
have to do the paperwork.

When you arrest someone, it's like a blind date. You spend a few 13
hours with a stranger, a few feet apart, saying "Tell me about yourself." You ask, "How much do you weigh?" and "Are you a gang
member? Really! Which one?" And you hold hands, for a few minutes, as you take prints—each fingertip individually, then four fingers together, flat, and the thumb, flat, at the bottom of the card. A
lot of people try to help you by rolling the fingers themselves, which
usually smudges the print; sometimes that's their intent. Crackheads
often don't have usable prints: their fingers are burned smooth from
the red-hot glass pipe. Junkies, as they're coming down, can go into
a whole-body cramp, and have hands as stiff as lobster claws. Perps
collared for robbery or assault may have bruised, swollen, or bloody
fingers. You try to be gentle, and you wear latex gloves.

When you print a perp, you're close to him, and because you're 14
close you're vulnerable. You take off the cuffs and put your gun in a
locker. Once, I was printing a guy as he found out he was not getting
a summons but, instead, going through the system. He became en-
raged at the desk sergeant, screaming curses and threats, and I wondered if he'd make a run at him or, worse, at me. But I was holding
his hands and could feel that they were as limp and loose as if he lay
in a hot bath—as if his body were indifferent to the hatred in his
voice. So I went on printing as he went on shouting, each of us concentrating on the task at hand.

The paperwork involved in policing is famously wasteful or is a 15
necessary evil, sometimes both. Often, it reaches a nuanced complexity that is itself somehow sublime, like a martial art. If, for example, you arrested a man for hitting his girlfriend with a tire iron
and then found a crack vial in his pocket, the paperwork would
include a Domestic Incident Report (for follow-up visits by the
domestic-violence officer); a 61, or complaint, which describes the

offense, the perp, and the victim; and an aided card, which contains information on the victim and what medical attention she received. The 61 and the aided are assigned numbers from the Complaint Index and the Aided and Accident Index. The aided number goes on the 61, and both the complaint and the aided numbers go on the On-Line Booking Sheet. The O.L.B.S. provides more detailed information on the perp; it has to be handwritten, and then entered into the computer, which in turn generates an arrest number.

You would also have to type two vouchers—both of which have 16 serial numbers that must be entered on the 61 and on the O.L.B.S.— for the tire iron and the crack vial; affix a lead seal to the tire iron; and put the crack vial in a narcotics envelope in the presence of the desk officer, writing your name, your shield number, and the date across the seal. You also fill out a Request for Lab Exam (Controlled Substance and Marihuana) and attach it to the envelope. Next, you run a warrant check on the computer, take prints, and bring the perp up to the squad room to be debriefed by detectives, who ask if he knows of and is willing to tell about other crimes.

The prisoner is then searched again and delivered to Central 17 Booking, at Criminal Court. There he waits in a holding cell until he is arraigned before a judge. At C.B., you photograph the prisoner and have him examined by the Emergency Medical Service, interviewed by the Criminal Justice Agency for his bail application, and searched yet again. Only then is he in the system, and out of your hands. Next, you see an assistant district attorney and write up and swear to a document that is also called a complaint. The entire process, from the arrest to the signing of the complaint, usually takes around five hours—if nothing goes wrong.

There are arrests that cops hope and train for like athletes, and 18 in this felony Olympics, collars for homicides, pattern crimes, drugs by the kilo, and automatic weapons are considered gold medals. But the likelihood that things will go wrong with arrests seems to escalate with their importance: a baroque legal system, combined with the vagaries of chance, provides an inexhaustible source of misadventure. You feel like a diver on the platform who has just noticed that all the judges are Russian.

There was my rapist, a match for a pattern of sexual assaults on 19 elderly women. My partner and I responded to a report that a suspicious person was lurking in the stairwell of a project, one floor up from the latest attack. When the man saw us, he ran, shouting, "Help me! Get a video camera!" We wrestled with him for what seemed like ages; he was limber and strong and sweat-soaked, as slippery as a live fish, and was chewing on a rolled-up dollar bill filled with cocaine. He looked just like the police sketch, and also had distinctive green eyes, which victims had described. He had been staying on that floor with his girlfriend until he beat her up and she threw him out, on the same day as the last attack. He was the rapist, beyond a doubt.

At the precinct, he collapsed, and he told the paramedics he'd ingested three grams of cocaine. At the hospital, his heart rate was two hundred and twenty beats per minute, and he was made to drink an electrolyte solution and eat activated charcoal, which caused him to drool black. He was handcuffed to a cot in the E.R. while the midnight pageant of medical catastrophes was brought in. There was an E.D.P. (an emotionally disturbed person) who had bitten clean through his tongue, clipping into it a precise impression of his upper teeth. Another E.D.P., an enormous drunk picked up from the streets, was writhing and thrashing as a diminutive Filipina nurse tried to draw blood: "Now I prick you! Now I just prick you!" An old man threw up, and another prisoner-patient, handcuffed to the cot next to him, kindly handed him the closest receptacle he could find—a plastic pitcher half filled with urine, which splashed back as he vomited, and made him vomit more.

I'd worked almost twenty-four hours by the time we got back to the precinct, when a detective from Special Victims called to say that my perp had already been taken in for a lineup, a few days before, and had not been identified as the rapist. This meant that we had to let him go. I'd felt nothing toward my suspect throughout our ordeal, even when I fought with him, although I believed he had done hideous, brutal things. But now, suddenly, I hated him, because he was no longer a magnificent and malignant catch—he was just some random asshole who had stolen an entire day of my life.

A few days later, I saw him on the street, and he said hello. I didn't. A few days after that, he beat up his girlfriend again, then disappeared. The rapes stopped.

*   *   *

Now, after a few years on the job, I have my own war stories. On 23
weekends, I'll sit back, lift up my feet, and tell my girlfriend, "I took
a bullet out of a lady's living room. It must have been shot from Jersey. It went through the glass, and stopped on the sill. It landed there
like a sparrow." Or "I talked a runaway into coming home. She was
fourteen years old. All I had to do was tell her I'd lock up her
boyfriend's whole family if she didn't." At times, the point of the job
seems to be to make it home with an intact skin and a good story.
The stories are a benefit, like the dental plan.

And you need them, like your handcuffs or your vest, to control 24
events when you have to, and to cover your back. If you're a cop,
you need a quick tongue, to tell the victim, the perp, the crowd, the
sergeant, the D.A., the judge, and the jury what you're doing, what
you did, and why. Are you ready to make a statement? No? Then you
just did. You told me you weren't ready. "Police were unprepared to
answer," says the lead in the morning paper. Or the gossip in the
locker room, or the word on the street.

I also hear more than my share of stories. And so, aside from the 25
odd Christmas party or fund-raiser, I don't hang out with cops from
the precinct. My friends who are cops were friends of mine before I
went on the job. And most of the people I see regularly have nothing
at all to do with police work. The job has enough of me. For five
days a week, I stay off the streets unless I'm working them. And
when I'm not in uniform I'd just as soon not see blue.

But I also notice that when I'm out on weekends and there's an- 26
other cop there—at a wedding or a cookout or a club—I'll often
spend most of the time talking with him. There are things you've
done and places you've been that no one else has had to do or see in
quite the same way.

Meaning and Purpose

1. How does Laffey quickly establish that he is well qualified to write
   this essay?
2. How does Laffey quickly establish that he is not the stereotypical
   "brutal cop"?

3. Laffey says, in paragraph 3, that a police officer "who takes away someone's freedom bears a burden of at least equal gravity" to that of the surgeon who cuts open a human being, but Laffey adds, "Let me tell you, it's a pleasure sometimes." What can be pleasurable, according to this essay, about taking away someone's freedom?

4. What is Laffey describing in paragraph 7, when he says he sometimes feels like he is "running in a suit of armor while carrying a bag of groceries"?

5. What is Laffey describing, in paragraph 18, when he says that sometimes "You feel like a diver on the platform who has just noticed that all the judges are Russian"?

Strategy

1. In paragraphs 15 and 16, why does Laffey list and discuss all the forms that he must fill out? How does this strategy add to the complete picture of the working life of a cop?

2. In paragraph 13, why does Laffey describe arresting someone by saying that it's "like a blind date"?

3. What strategy does Laffey use in this essay to show that he believes police officers must do too much paperwork?

4. The last sentence of the essay, "The rapes stopped," hints that Laffey suspects something. What might he suspect? Why does he use an indirect strategy in this sentence?

Style

1. Laffey says, in paragraph 8, that his radio is "a montage of stray details." What does *montage* mean in that phrase? Suggest a synonym.

2. What does Laffey mean, in paragraph 13, when he says that someone is "collared" for a robbery? What does that term suggest to you?

3. In paragraph 18, Laffey says that we have "a baroque legal system." What does the term *baroque* mean? Suggest a synonym for how that word is used in this essay.

4. As is noted in paragraph 12, at some point after a period of excitement, a police officer can become "drearily confined." In one or two sentences, describe Laffey's idea of dreary confinement.

5. What does the word "emblem" mean as it is used to describe handcuffs in paragraph 2? In what two or three other ways can the term *emblem* be used in other contexts?

Writing Tasks

1. All of us have had calm days that were suddenly punctuated by a period of excitement. Write an essay that describes such a day in your life, starting with your description of the day's calm beginnings and then moving to your description of the day's period of excitement. If your choice of topic permits, end the essay by describing the calmness at the end of that day.

2. Sometimes we believe that we know a person fairly well, and then that person suddenly gets angry or sad or ecstatic, seemingly for no reason, surprising us until we understand what caused the unexpected mood change. Write a descriptive essay that relates an incident that happened to you or one of your friends and caused you or your friend to suddenly change from acting "normal" to behaving unpredictably. Be sure to describe what caused the change in the person.

❦ George Simpson ❦

Born in Virginia in 1950, George Simpson studied journalism at the University of North Carolina. He wrote for the Carolina Financial Times *in North Carolina and for the* News-Gazette *in Virginia before joining the staff at* Newsweek. *In 1978 he was appointed* Newsweek's *director of public affairs. For a series of articles about the football program at the University of North Carolina, he won the Sigma Delta Chi Best Feature Writing Award. He has contributed stories to* The New York Times, Sport, Glamour, *and other major publications.*

The War Room at Bellevue

In this essay, first published in New York *magazine in 1983, George Simpson uses objective description of events during one night at Bellevue Hospital to achieve immediacy. Arranging the emergency room scenes in strict (by-the-clock) chronological order creates the impression of a minute-by-minute account and contributes to the power of the description.*

Simpson describes the staff at the Bellevue trauma center speedily responding to emergencies with both efficiency and care. Notice how the staff members maintain commonplace relationships among themselves even amid the chaos.

Bellevue. The name conjures up images of an indoor war zone: 1
the wounded and bleeding lining the halls, screaming for help while
harried doctors in blood-stained smocks rush from stretcher to
stretcher, fighting a losing battle against exhaustion and the crushing
number of injured. "What's worse," says a longtime Bellevue nurse,
"is that we have this image of being a hospital only for. . . ." She
pauses, then lowers her voice; "for crazy people."

Though neither battlefield nor Bedlam is a valid image, there is 2
something extraordinary about the monstrous complex that spreads
for five blocks along First Avenue in Manhattan. It is said best by the
head nurse in Adult Emergency Service: "If you have any chance for

172

survival, you have it here." Survival—that is why they come. Why do injured cops drive by a half-dozen other hospitals to be treated at Bellevue? They've seen the Bellevue emergency team in action.

9:00 P.M. It is a Friday night in the Bellevue emergency room. 3
The after-work crush is over (those who've suffered through the day, only to come for help after the five-o'clock whistle has blown) and it is nearly silent except for the mutter of voices at the admitting desk, where administrative personnel discuss who will go for coffee. Across the spotless white-walled lobby, ten people sit quietly, passively, in pastel plastic chairs, waiting for word of relatives or to see doctors. In the past 24 hours, 300 people have come to the Bellevue Adult Emergency Service. Fewer than 10 percent were true emergencies. One man sleeps fitfully in the emergency ward while his heartbeat, respiration, and blood pressure are monitored by control consoles mounted over his bed. Each heartbeat trips a tiny bleep in the monitor, which attending nurses can hear across the ward. A half hour ago, doctors in the trauma room withdrew a six-inch stiletto blade from his back. When he is stabilized, the patient will be moved upstairs to the twelve-bed Surgical Intensive Care Unit.

9:05 P.M. An ambulance backs into the receiving bay, its red and 4
yellow lights flashing in and out of the lobby. A split second later, the glass doors burst open as a nurse and an attendant roll a mobile stretcher into the lobby. When the nurse screams, "Emergent!" the lobby explodes with activity as the way is cleared to the trauma room. Doctors appear from nowhere and transfer the bloodied body of a black man to the treatment table. Within seconds his clothes are stripped away, revealing a tiny stab wound in his left side. Three doctors and three nurses rush around the victim, each performing a task necessary to begin treatment. Intravenous needles are inserted into his arms and groin. A doctor draws blood for the lab, in case surgery is necessary. A nurse begins inserting a catheter into the victim's penis and continues to feed in tubing until the catheter reaches the bladder. Urine flows through the tube into a plastic bag. Doctors are glad not to see blood in the urine. Another nurse records pulse and blood pressure.

The victim is in good shape. He shivers slightly, although the 5
trauma room is exceedingly warm. His face is bloodied, but shows no major lacerations. A third nurse, her elbow propped on the treat-

ment table, asks the man a series of questions, trying to quickly outline his medical history. He answers abruptly. He is drunk. His left
side is swabbed with yellow disinfectant and a doctor injects a local
anesthetic. After a few seconds another doctor inserts his finger into
the wound. It sinks in all the way to the knuckle. He begins to rotate
his finger like a child trying to get a marble out of a milk bottle. The
patient screams bloody murder and tries to struggle free.

Meanwhile in the lobby, a security guard is ejecting a derelict who   6
has begun to drink from a bottle hidden in his coat pocket. "He's a regular, was in here just two days ago," says a nurse. "We checked him pretty
close then, so he's probably okay now. Can you believe those were clean
clothes we gave him?" The old man, blackened by filth, leaves quietly.

9:15 P.M. A young Hispanic man interrupts, saying his pregnant   7
girl friend, sitting outside in his car, is bleeding heavily from her
vagina. She is rushed into an examination room, treated behind
closed doors, and rolled into the observation ward, where, much
later in the night, a gynecologist will treat her in a special room—the
same one used to examine rape victims. Nearby, behind curtains, the
neurologist examines an old white woman to determine if her
headaches are due to head injury. They are not.

9:45 P.M. The trauma room has been cleared and cleaned merci-   8
lessly. The examination rooms are three-quarters full—another overdose, two asthmatics, a young woman with abdominal pains. In the
hallway, a derelict who has been sleeping it off urinates all over the
stretcher. He sleeps on while attendants change his clothes. An
ambulance—one of four that patrol Manhattan for Bellevue from
42nd Street to Houston, river to river—delivers a middle-aged white
woman and two cops, the three of them soaking wet. The woman
has escaped from the psychiatric floor of a nearby hospital and tried
to drown herself in the East River. The cops fished her out. She lies
on a stretcher shivering beneath white blankets. Her eyes stare at the
ceiling. She speaks clearly when an administrative worker begins
routine questioning. The cops are given hospital gowns and wait to
receive tetanus shots and gamma globulin—a hedge against infection from the befouled river water. They will hang around the E.R.
for another two hours, telling their story to as many as six other
policemen who show up to hear it. The woman is rolled into an

examination room, where a male nurse speaks gently: "They tell me you fell into the river." "No," says the woman, "I jumped. I have to commit suicide." "Why?" asks the nurse. "Because I'm insane and I can't help [it]. I have to die." The nurse gradually discovers the woman has a history of psychological problems. She is given dry bedclothes and placed under guard in the hallway. She lies on her side, staring at the wall.

The pace continues to increase. Several more overdose victims   9
arrive by ambulance. One, a young black woman, had done a striptease on the street just before passing out. A second black woman is semiconscious and spends the better part of her time at Bellevue alternately cursing it and pleading with the doctors. Attendants find a plastic bottle coated with methadone in the pocket of a Hispanic O.D. The treatment is routinely the same, and sooner or later involves vomiting. Just after doctors begin to treat the O.D., he vomits great quantities of wine and methadone in all directions. "Lovely business, huh?" laments one of the doctors. A young nurse confides that if there were other true emergencies, the overdose victims would be given lower priority. "You can't help thinking they did it to themselves," she says, "while the others are accident victims."

10:30 P.M. A policeman who twisted his knee struggling with an   10
"alleged perpetrator" is examined and released. By 10:30, the lobby is jammed with friends and relatives of patients in various stages of treatment and recovery. The attendant who also functions as a translator for Hispanic patients adds chairs to accommodate the overflow. The medical walk-in rate stays steady—between eight and ten patients waiting. A pair of derelicts, each with battered eyes, appear at the admitting desk. One has a dramatically swollen face laced with black stitches.

11:00 P.M. The husband of the attempted suicide arrives. He   11
thanks the police for saving his wife's life, then talks at length with doctors about her condition. She continues to stare into the void and does not react when her husband approaches her stretcher.

Meanwhile, patients arrive in the lobby at a steady pace. A   12
young G.I. on leave has lower-back pains; a Hispanic man complains of pain in his side; occasionally parents hurry through the adult E.R. carrying children into the pediatric E.R. A white woman of about 50 marches into the lobby from the walk-in entrance. Dried blood covers her right eyebrow and upper lip. She begins to perform.

"I was assaulted on 28th and Lexington, I was," she says grandly, "and I don't have to take it *anymore*. I was a bride 21 years ago, and, God, I was beautiful then." She has captured the attention of all present. "I was there when the boys came home—on Memorial Day—and I don't have to take this kind of treatment."

As midnight approaches, the nurses prepare for the shift change. 13 They must brief the incoming staff and make sure all reports are up-to-date. One young brunet says, "Christ, I'm gonna go home and take a shower—I smell like vomit."

11:50 P.M. The triage nurse is questioning an old black man about 14 chest pains, and a Hispanic woman is having an asthma attack, when an ambulance, its sirens screaming full tilt, roars into the receiving bay. There is a split-second pause as everyone drops what he or she is doing and looks up. Then all hell breaks loose. Doctors and nurses are suddenly sprinting full-out toward the trauma room. The glass doors burst open and the occupied stretcher is literally run past me. Cops follow. It is as if a comet has whooshed by. In the trauma room it all becomes clear. A half-dozen doctors and nurses surround the lifeless form of a Hispanic man with a shotgun hole in his neck the size of your fist. Blood pours from a second gaping wound in his chest. A respirator is slammed over his face, making his chest rise and fall as if he were breathing. "No pulse," reports one doctor. A nurse jumps on a stool and, leaning over the man, begins to pump his chest with her palms. "No blood pressure," screams another nurse. The ambulance driver appears shaken. "I never thought I'd get here in time," he stutters. More doctors from the trauma team upstairs arrive. Wrappings from syringes and gauze pads fly through the air. The victim's eyes are open yet devoid of life. His body takes on a yellow tinge. A male nurse winces at the gunshot wound. "This guy really pissed off somebody," he says. This is no ordinary shooting. It is an execution. IV's are jammed into the body in the groin and arms. One doctor has been plugging in an electrocardiograph and asks everyone to stop for a second so he can get a reading. "Forget it," shouts the doctor in charge. "No time." "Take it easy, Jimmy," someone yells at the head physician. It is apparent by now that the man is dead, but the doctors keep trying injections and finally they slit open the chest and reach inside almost up to their elbows. They feel the extent of the damage and suddenly it is all over. "I told 'em he was dead," says one nurse, withdrawing. "They didn't listen." The room is very still. The doctors are momentarily disgusted, then go on about their business. The room clears quickly. Finally there is only a male nurse and the still-warm body, now waxy-yellow, with huge ribs exposed on both sides of the chest and giant holes in both sides of the neck. The nurse speculates that this is yet another murder in a Hispanic political struggle that has brought many such victims to Bellevue. He marvels at the extent of the wounds and repeats, "This guy was really blown away."

Midnight. A hysterical woman is hustled through the lobby into an examination room. It is the dead man's wife, and she is nearly delirious. "I know he's dead, I know he's dead," she screams over and over. Within moments the lobby is filled with anxious relatives of the victim, waiting for word on his condition. The police are everywhere asking questions, but most people say they saw nothing. One young woman says she heard six shots, two louder than the other four. At some point, word is passed that the man is, in fact, dead. Another woman breaks down in hysterics; everywhere young Hispanics are crying and comforting each other. Plainclothes detectives make a quick examination of the body, check on the time of pronouncement of death, and begin to ask questions, but the bereaved are too stunned to talk. The rest of the uninvolved people in the lobby stare dumbly, their injuries suddenly paling in light of a death.   15

12:30 A.M. A black man appears at the admission desk and says he drank poison by mistake. He is told to have a seat. The ambulance brings in a young white woman, her head wrapped in white gauze. She is wailing terribly. A girlfriend stands over her, crying, and a boyfriend clutches the injured woman's hands, saying, "I'm here, don't worry, I'm here." The victim has fallen downstairs at a friend's house. Attendants park her stretcher against the wall to wait for an examination room to clear. There are eight examination rooms and only three doctors. Unless you are truly an emergency, you will wait. One doctor is stitching up the elbow of a drunk who's been punched out. The friends of the woman who fell down the stairs glance up at the doctors anxiously, wondering why their friend isn't being treated faster.   16

1:10 A.M. A car pulls into the bay and a young Hispanic asks if a shooting victim has been brought here. The security guard blurts   17 out, "He's dead." The young man is stunned. He peels his tires leaving the bay.

1:20 A.M. The young woman of the stairs is getting stitches in a small gash over her left eye when the same ambulance driver who brought in the gunshot victim delivers a man who has been stabbed in the back on East 3rd Street. Once again the trauma room goes from 0 to 60 in five seconds. The patient is drunk, which helps him endure the pain of having the catheter inserted through his penis into his bladder. Still he yells, "That hurts like a bastard," then adds sheepishly, "Excuse me, ladies." But he is not prepared for what comes next. An X-ray reveals a collapsed right lung. After just a shot of local anesthetic, the doctor slices open his side and inserts a long plastic tube. Internal bleeding had kept the lung pressed down and prevented it from reinflating. The tube releases the pressure. The ambulance driver says the cops grabbed the guy who ran the eight-inch blade into the victim's back. "That's not the one," says the man. "They got the wrong guy." A nurse reports that there is not much of the victim's type blood available at the hospital. One of the doctors says that's okay, he won't need surgery. Meanwhile blood pours from the man's knife wound and the tube in his side. As the nurses work, they chat about personal matters, yet they respond immediately to orders from either doctor. "How ya doin'?" the doctor asks the patient. "Okay," he says. His blood spatters on the floor. 18

So it goes into the morning hours. A Valium overdose, a woman who fainted, a man who went through the windshield of his car. More overdoses. More drunks with split eyebrows and chins. The doctors and nurses work without complaint. "This is nothing, about normal, I'd say," concludes the head nurse. "No big deal." 19

Meaning and Purpose

1. Have you ever been in a hospital emergency room? How would you describe the experience? Were you aware of the attitudes of the doctors and nurses? Of the people waiting with the patients? Do any of Simpson's descriptions compare with what you saw?

2. What do you believe to be Simpson's purpose in "The War Room at Bellevue"?
3. What impressions of the hospital and its staff grow from the description? What details give you that impression?
4. Although Simpson does not describe the city that surrounds the hospital, what impression of the city does he leave you with? Support your answer with details from the essay.
5. Why does Simpson capitalize "Bedlam" in paragraph 2? What are the denotation and connotation of the word?

Strategy

1. What is the structure of this descriptive essay?
2. Many internal workings of "The War Room at Bellevue" are constructed on a stimulus–response pattern—that is, an event takes place and people respond. You'll find a stimulus–response pattern in paragraph 4: It opens with the arrival of an ambulance; a patient is rolled into the lobby on a mobile stretcher; a nurse screams "Emergent!"; and the scene explodes with action. Find a stimulus–response pattern in other passages of the essay.
3. Often Simpson has to describe simultaneous events—that is, separate actions that take place at the same time. Find at least four overt transitions at the beginning of paragraphs that capture the sense of simultaneous action.
4. Simpson describes the Bellevue emergency room in the present tense. What is the effect of using this tense?
5. Comment on the spatial arrangement of some of the descriptions. Is it broad to narrow? Near to far? Center outward? Give examples.

Style

1. How would you describe the narrator of "The War Room at Bellevue"? Is the material presented objectively or subjectively?
2. What words and images help to create the sense of a battle in the first two paragraphs?

3. How does the tone of the final paragraph differ from the tone that Simpson creates through most of the essay?
4. Identify phrases that help to create the sense of sound in paragraph 3. Find words that create a dominant sense impression in one or two other paragraphs.

Writing Tasks

1. Describe a scene in which a great deal of action takes place—a sports event, a shopping mall, an intersection, a park, or a school yard. Keep your description objective, carefully selecting the details to create, without emotion or judgment, a dominant impression.
2. Compare the subjective description in "Once More to the Lake," which you'll find in Chapter 14, with the objective description in "The War Room at Bellevue." What words make the essays predominantly subjective or objective? What is the overall effectiveness of each strategy and its suitability to the subject? Could each essay be told from the other point of view?

❦ Gretel Ehrlich ❦

Journalist, poet, fiction writer, and documentary film maker, Gretel Ehrlich was born in California and studied at Bennington College, UCLA Film School, and the New School for Social Research. After a journey to Wyoming to make a documentary film, Ehrlich decided to live there, doing various kinds of ranch work including branding, sheep herding, and helping with the births of lambs and calves. Her many books include a collection of essays, The Solace of Open Spaces; Drinking Dry Clouds: Stories from Wyoming; Arctic Heat: A Poem Cycle *(with David Buckland); and* A Match to the Heart: One Woman's Story of Being Struck by Lightning, *in which the work below appears.*

Struck by Lightning

This essay, from a larger work, imitates an ancient mystical journal from death or near-death to rebirth. While describing all of the events that occur as a result of Ehrlich's being struck by lightning, the essay also stirs emotions far below the event's surface, entering the realm of thoughts of death and how it is possible to describe that which one has not yet endured.

As you read this essay, pay particular attention to how Ehrlich uses time as a device to bring the reader in and out of the experience, just as Ehrlich herself mentally traveled through those events. And note how she uses description to appeal to the image-making qualities of a reader's mind. You not only can mentally "see" many events in this essay, but you can also "feel" many of its parts.

Deep in an ocean. I am suspended motionless. The water is gray. 1 That's all there is, and before that? My arms are held out straight, cruciate, my head and legs hang limp. Nothing moves. Brown kelp lies flat in mud and fish are buried in liquid clouds of dust. There are no shadows or sounds. Should there be? I don't know if I am alive, but if not, how do I know I am dead? My body is leaden, heavier than gravity. Gravity is done with me. No more sinking and rising or bobbing in currents. There is a terrible feeling of oppression with no oppressor. I try to lodge my mind against some boundary, some reference point, but the continent of the body dissolves . . .

A single heartbeat stirs gray water. Blue trickles in, just a tiny stream. Then a long silence.   2

Another heartbeat. This one is louder, as if amplified. Sound takes a shape: it is a snowplow moving grayness aside like a heavy snowdrift. I can't tell if I'm moving, but more blue water flows in. Seaweed begins to undulate, then a whole kelp forest rises from the ocean floor. A fish swims past and looks at me. Another heartbeat drives through dead water, and another, until I am surrounded by blue.   3

Sun shines above all this. There is no pattern to the way its glint comes free and falls in long knives of light. My two beloved dogs appear. They flank me like tiny rockets, their fur pressed against my ribs. A leather harness holds us all together. The dogs climb toward light, pulling me upward at a slant from the sea.   4

I have been struck by lightning and I am alive.   5

Before electricity carved its blue path toward me, before the negative charge shot down from cloud to ground, before "streamers" jumped the positive charge back up from ground to cloud, before air expanded and contracted producing loud pressure pulses I could not hear because I was already dead, I had been walking.   6

When I started out on foot that August afternoon, the thunderstorm was blowing in fast. On the face of the mountain, a mile ahead, hard westerly gusts and sudden updrafts collided, pulling black clouds apart. Yet the storm looked harmless. When a distant thunderclap scared the dogs, I called them to my side and rubbed their ears: "Don't worry, you're okay as long as you're with me."   7

I woke in a pool of blood, lying on my stomach some distance from where I should have been, flung at an odd angle to one side of the dirt path. The whole sky had grown dark. Was it evening, and if so,   8 which one? How many minutes or hours had elapsed since I lost consciousness, and where were the dogs? I tried to call out to them but my voice didn't work. The muscles in my throat were paralyzed and I couldn't swallow. Were the dogs dead? Everything was terribly wrong: I had trouble seeing, talking, breathing, and I couldn't move my legs or right arm. Nothing remained in my memory—no sounds, flashes, smells, no warnings of any kind. Had I been shot in the back? Had I suffered a stroke or heart attack? These thoughts were dark pools in sand.

The sky was black. Was this a storm in the middle of the day or   9
was it night with a storm traveling through? When thunder exploded over me, I knew I had been hit by lightning.

The pain in my chest intensified and every muscle in my body   10
ached. I was quite sure I was dying. What was it one should do or think or know? I tried to recall the Buddhist instruction regarding dying—which position to lie in, which direction to face. Did the "Lion's position" taken by the Buddha mean lying on the left or the right? And which sutra to sing? Oh yes, the Heart Sutra . . . gaté, gaté, paragaté . . . form and formlessness. Paradox and cosmic jokes. Surviving after trying to die "properly" would be truly funny, but the chances of that seemed slim.

Other words drifted in: how the "gateless barrier" was the gate   11
through which one passes to reach enlightenment. Yet if there was no gate, how did one pass through? Above me, high on the hill, was the gate on the ranch that lead nowhere, a gate I had mused about often. Now its presence made me smile. Even when I thought I had no aspirations for enlightenment, too much effort in that direction was being expended. How could I learn to slide, yet remain aware?

To be struck by lightning: what a way to get enlightened. That   12
would be the joke if I survived. It seemed important to remember jokes. My thinking did not seem connected to the inert body that was in such terrible pain. Sweep the mind of weeds, I kept telling myself—that's what years of Buddhist practice had taught me. . . . But where were the dogs, the two precious ones I had watched being born and had raised in such intimacy and trust? I wanted them with me. I wanted them to save me again.

It started to rain. Every time a drop hit bare skin there was an   13
explosion of pain. Blood crusted my left eye. I touched my good

hand to my heart, which was beating wildly, erratically. My chest was numb, as if it had been sprayed with novocaine. No feeling of peace filled me. Death was a bleakness, a grayness about which it was impossible to be curious or relieved. I loved those dogs and hoped they weren't badly hurt. If I didn't die soon, how many days would pass before we were found, and when would the scavengers come? The sky was dark, or was that the way life flew out of the body, in a long tube with no light at the end? I lay on the cold ground waiting. The mountain was purple, and sage stirred against my face. I knew I had to give up all this, then my own body and all my thinking. Once more I lifted my head to look for the dogs but, unable to see them, I twisted myself until I faced east and tried to let go of all desire.

When my eyes opened again I knew I wasn't dead. Images from World War II movies filled my head: of wounded soldiers dragging themselves across a field, and if I could have laughed—that is, made my face work into a smile and get sounds to discharge from my throat—I would have. God, it would have been good to laugh. Instead, I considered my options: either lie there and wait for someone to find me—how many days or weeks would that take?—or somehow get back to the house. I calmly assessed what might be wrong with me—stroke, cerebral hemorrhage, gunshot wound—but it was bigger than I could understand. The instinct to survive does not rise from particulars; a deep but general misery rollercoasted me into action. I tried to propel myself on my elbows but my right arm didn't work. The wind had swung around and was blowing in from the east. It was still a dry storm with only sputtering rain, but when I raised myself up, lightning fingered the entire sky. 14

It is not true that lightning never strikes the same place twice. I had entered a shower of sparks and furious brightness and, worried that I might be struck again, watched as lightning touched down all around me. Years before, in the high country, I'd been hit by lightning: an electrical charge had rolled down an open meadow during a fearsome thunderstorm, surged up the legs of my horse, coursed through me, and bounced a big spark off the top of my head. To be struck again—and this time it was a direct hit—what did it mean? 15

The feeling had begun to come back into my legs and after many 16
awkward attempts, I stood. To walk meant lifting each leg up by the
thigh, moving it forward with my hands, setting it down. The earth felt
like a peach that had split open in the middle; one side moved up while
the other side moved down and my legs were out of rhythm. The
ground rolled the way it does during an earthquake and the sky was
tattered book pages waving in different directions. Was the ground
liquifying under me, or had the molecular composition of my body del-
iquesced? I struggled to piece together fragments. Then it occurred to
me that my brain was torn and that's where the blood had come from.

I walked. Sometimes my limbs held me, sometimes they didn't. I 17
don't know how many times I fell but it didn't matter because I was
making slow progress toward home.

Home—the ranch house—was about a quarter of a mile away. I 18
don't remember much about getting there. My concentration went
into making my legs work. The storm was strong. All the way across
the basin, lightning lifted parts of mountains and sky into yellow re-
fulgence and dropped them again, only to lift others. The inside of
my eyelids turned gold and I could see the dark outlines of things
through them. At the bottom of the hill I opened the door to my
pickup and blew the horn with the idea that someone might hear me.
No one came. My head had swollen to an indelicate shape. I tried to
swallow—I was so thirsty—but the muscles in my throat were still
paralyzed and I wondered when I would no longer be able to breathe.

Inside the house, sounds began to come out of me. I was doing 19
crazy things, ripping my hiking boots off because the bottoms of
my feet were burning, picking up the phone when I was finally able
to scream. One of those times, someone happened to be on the
line. I was screaming incoherently for help. My last conscious act
was to dial 911.

Dark again. Pressing against sore ribs, my dogs pulled me out of 20
the abyss, pulled and pulled. I smelled straw. My face was on tatami.
I opened my eyes, looked up, and saw neighbors. Had they come for
my funeral? The phone rang and I heard someone give directions to
the ambulance driver, who was lost. A "first responder," an EMT
from town who has a reputation with the girls, leaned down and

asked if he could "touch me" to see if there were any broken bones. What the hell, I thought. I was going to die anyway. Let him have his feel. But his touch was gentle and professional, and I was grateful.

I slipped back into unconsciousness and when I woke again two   21
EMTs were listening to my heart. I asked them to look for my dogs but they wouldn't leave me. Someone else in the room went outside and found Sam and Yaki curled up on the porch, frightened but alive. Now I could rest. I felt the medics jabbing needles into the top of my hands, trying unsuccessfully to get IVs started, then strapping me onto a backboard and carrying me out the front door of the house, down steps, into lightning and rain, into what was now a full-blown storm.

The ambulance rocked and slid, slamming my bruised body   22
against the metal rails of the gurney. Every muscle was in violent spasm and there was a place on my back near the heart that burned. I heard myself yell in pain. Finally the EMTs rolled up towels and blankets and wedged them against my arms, shoulders, hips, and knees so the jolt-ing of the vehicle wouldn't dislodge me. The ambulance slid down into ditches, struggled out, bumped from one deep rut to another. I asked to be taken to the hospital in Cody, but they said they were afraid my heart might stop again. As it was, the local hospital was thirty-five miles away, ten of them dirt, and the trip took more than an hour.

Our arrival seemed a portent of disaster—and an occasion for   23
comedy. I had been struck by lightning around five in the afternoon. It was now 9:00 P.M. Nothing at the hospital worked. Their one EKG machine was nonfunctional, and jokingly the nurses blamed it on me. "Honey, you've got too much electricity in your body," one of them told me. Needles were jammed into my hand—no one had gotten an IV going yet—and the doctor on call hadn't arrived, though half an hour had elapsed. The EMTs kept assuring me: "Don't worry, we won't leave you here." When another nurse, who was fill-ing out an admission form, asked me how tall I was, I answered: "Too short to be struck by lightning."

> "Electrical injury often results in ventricular fibrillation and   24
> injury to the medullary centers of the brain. Immediately af-
> ter electric shock patients are usually comatose, apneic, and
> in circulatory collapse. . . ."

When the doctor on call—the only doctor in town, waddled into   25
what they called the emergency room, my aura, he said, was yellow and gray—a soul in transition. I knew that he had gone to
medical school but had never completed a residency and had been
barred from ER or ICU work in the hospitals of Florida, where he
had lived previously. Yet I was lucky. Florida has many lightning
victims, and unlike the doctors I would see later, he at least recognized the symptoms of a lightning strike. The tally sheet read this
way: I had suffered a hit by lightning which caused ventricular
fibrillation—cardiac arrest—though luckily my heart started beating again. Violent contractions of muscles when one is hit often
causes the body to fly through the air: I was flung far and hit hard
on my left side, which may have caused my heart to start again,
but along with that fortuitous side effect, I sustained a concussion,
broken ribs, a possible broken jaw, and lacerations above the eye.
The paralysis below my waist and up through the chest and
throat—called kerauno-paralysis—is common in lightning strikes
and almost always temporary, but my right arm continued to be
almost useless. Fernlike burns—arborescent erythema—covered
my entire body. These occur when the electrical charge follows
tracings of moisture on the skin—rain or sweat—thus the spidery
red lines.

> "Rapid institution of fluid and electrolyte therapy is essential   26
> with guidelines being the patient's urine output, hemat-
> ocrit, osmolality, central venous pressure, and arterial blood
> gases. . . ."

The nurses loaded me onto a gurney. As they wheeled me down the   27
hall to my room, a front wheel fell off and I was slammed into
the wall. Once I was in bed, the deep muscle aches continued, as did
the chest pains. Later, friends came to visit. Neither doctor nor nurse
had cleaned the cuts on my head, so Laura, who had herded sheep
and cowboyed on all the ranches where I had lived and whose
wounds I had cleaned when my saddle horse dragged her across a
high mountain pasture, wiped blood and dirt from my face, arms,
and hands with a cool towel and spooned yogurt into my mouth.

I was the only patient in the hospital. During the night, sheet   28
lightning inlaid the walls with cool gold. I felt like an ancient, mum-
mified child who had been found on a rock ledge near our ranch:
bound tightly, unable to move, my dead face tipped backwards toward the moon.

In the morning, my regular doctor, Ben, called from Massachu-   29
setts, where he was vacationing, with this advice: "Get yourself out of
that hospital and go somewhere else, anywhere." I was too weak to
sign myself out, but Julie, the young woman who had a summer job on
our ranch, retrieved me in the afternoon. She helped me get dressed in
the cutoffs and torn T-shirt I had been wearing, but there were no
shoes, so, barefoot, I staggered into Ben's office, where a physician's assistant kindly cleansed the gashes in my head. Then I was taken home.

Another thunderstorm slammed against the mountains as I   30
limped up the path to the house. Sam and Yaki took one look at me
and ran. These dogs lived with me, slept with me, understood every
word I said, and I was too sick to find them, console them—even if
they would have let me.

The next day my husband, who had just come down from the   31
mountains where he worked in the summer, took me to another hospital. I passed out in the admissions office, was loaded onto a gurney,
and taken for a CAT scan. No one bothered to find out why I had
lost consciousness. Later, in the emergency unit, the doctor argued
that I might not have been struck by lightning at all, as if I had imagined the incident. "Maybe a meteor hit me," I said, a suggestion he
pondered seriously. After a blood panel and a brief neurological
exam, which I failed—I couldn't follow his finger with my eyes or
walk a straight line—he promptly released me.

"Patients should be monitored electrocardiographically for   32
at least 24 hours for significant arrhythmias which often
have delayed onset. . . ."

It was difficult to know what was worse: being in a hospital   33
where nothing worked and nobody cared, or being alone on an isolated ranch hundreds of miles from decent medical care.

In the morning I staggered into the kitchen. My husband, from   34
whom I had been separated for three months, had left at 4:00 A.M. to
buy cattle in another part of the state and would not be back for a
month. Alone again, it was impossible to do much for myself. In the
past I'd been bucked off, stiff and sore plenty of times but this felt
different: I had no sense of equilibrium. My head hurt, every muscle
in my body ached as if I had a triple dose of the flu, and my left eye
was swollen shut and turning black and blue. Something moved in
the middle of the kitchen floor. I was having difficulty seeing, but
then I did see: a rattlesnake lay coiled in front of the stove. I reeled
around and dove back into bed. Enough tests of character. I closed
my eyes and half-slept. Later, when Julie came to the house, she
found the snake and cut off its head with a shovel.

My only consolation was that the dogs came back. I had chest   35
pains and all day Sam lay with his head against my heart. I cleaned a
deep cut over Yaki's eye. It was half an inch deep but already healing.
I couldn't tell if the dogs were sick or well, I was too miserable to
know anything except that Death resided in the room: not as a human figure but as a dark fog rolling in, threatening to cover me; but
the dogs stayed close and while my promise to keep them safe during
a thunderstorm had proven fraudulent, their promise to keep me
alive held good.

Meaning and Purpose

1. If you had read this essay's first paragraph only what would you
   have imagined the rest of the essay to be about? What evidence do
   you have for your answer?
2. In paragraph 14, "Images from World War II movies" filled the author's head. Why do you suppose she would be mentally seeing
   such images?
3. What evidence is there to show that the author is interested in non-
   Western thought?
4. Why are paragraphs 24, 26, and 32 in quotation marks?

Strategy

1. Paragraph 2 begins with "A single heartbeat stirs gray water." Paragraph 3 begins with "Another heartbeat." What is the author descriptively emphasizing by this strategy?
2. What is the main purpose of the dogs in this essay? What do they illustrate?
3. In paragraph 25, Ehrlich says that the first doctor she saw had a poor professional medical background. Yet she was fortunate that that doctor was the first to see her. Why?
4. In paragraph 27, Ehrlich describes equipment and activities at the hospital. What do those descriptions tell you about the conditions at the hospital? Where else in the essay is evidence to strengthen your answer to this question? What is that evidence?

Style

1. What is humorous about the first sentence in paragraph 12?
2. Reread paragraph 15 and then read the definition of "rhetorical question" in this book's Glossary. Is the question in paragraph 15 a rhetorical question? Give a reason for your answer.
3. In paragraph 19, the author says "sounds began to come out of me." Why didn't she simply say, "I began to make sounds"?
4. Paragraph 22 has the phrase "ten of them dirt." To what does that phrase refer?

Writing Tasks

1. Write an essay that thoroughly describes someone whom you know well. In the first paragraph, of not fewer than 100 words, begin your description by detailing a characteristic of that person in such a way that you purposely mystify your essay's audience. For example, one student described her uncle, an automobile mechanic. Her first paragraph began, "No one in this neighborhood can hear a car being started on a cold morning without thinking about my uncle."

Then she went on to describe three cars briefly: One was an oil-burning clunker belonging to the next-door neighbor; one was a brand-new model that had blue smoke puffing from it every time its driver shifted gears; and one was an eight-year-old sedan that belonged to the elderly couple who lived across the street. It ran beautifully. Naturally, the elderly couple entrusted their car to the girl's uncle. After she pointed out that fact, the student described her uncle's other characteristics, habits, and physical features. Follow this strategy in your essay.

2. A small incident in a life can have an effect for a long time. The incident can be a happy one, a sad one, a thoughtful one, a reflective one, a cheerful one—almost any kind, in other words. If a small incident has strongly affected you, then describe that incident. Be sure to use details. Remember that you are trying to reinvent the incident in the reader's mind. To do that, use abstract words or broad-meaning words, such as "large," "pretty," "big," "great," and "nice" sparingly. When you use such words excessively, readers can only guess at what you saw. Be sure, therefore, to use specific and concrete words to help readers see in their mind's eye what you saw.

❦ Responding to Photographs ❦

Description

Woman Brushing Her Hair

Before children speak, they see. A child looks and recognizes before it can form words. At an early age we learn to respond to visual experience and interpret it. A smiling or scowling face, a closed or open hand, an erect or slumped body—all are gestures that invite our interpretation.

As we move through life, our interpretations of visual experiences become more complex. A young man walking down the street might go unnoticed. But add spiked hair, a leather coat, and torn jeans held up by a chain belt. Put a safety pin through one earlobe and thread an earring in his pierced nose, and this visual experience catches our attention. We examine the details of the young man's attire and perhaps draw conclusions about his character, lifestyle, personal values, or musical taste.

Photographs, unlike spontaneous visual experience, arrange details for a viewer. They are not, as is often assumed, a realistic record

192

of an experience, but an arranged and reproduced moment of experience. Whenever we look at a photograph we are being guided by the hand that held the camera. And whenever we look at a photograph we are being invited to respond to the image—to interpret it.

At first glance, "Woman Brushing Her Hair" seems to be a snapshot that captures a spontaneous moment in this woman's day. But on closer examination, the image seems to be carefully arranged, the hand of the photographer reaching to pull a response from the viewer.

With description as a dominant method of development, complete one of the following writing tasks. Before beginning your essay, reread the beginning of this chapter to familiarize yourself with the conventions of effective descriptive writing.

1. Write a "fly-on-the-wall" description, one that strictly reports the arrangement and content of "Woman Brushing Her Hair." After studying the contents of the photograph, decide on how you wish to arrange your description. Through your essay, be sure to follow the arrangement consistently.

2. Use "Woman Brushing Her Hair" as the basis of an *objective* description that creates a dominant impression of this woman's life. Like any writer, or photographer for that matter, you must select details, gestures, objects, arrangements that help to generate the dominant impression you wish to create. Remember, your task is not to describe everything in the photo, but to use material from the photo for your purpose.

3. Use "Woman Brushing Her Hair" as the basis of a *subjective* description that creates a dominant impression of this woman's life. As in assignment 2, you must select material from the photo that leads readers to a single impression, but because you are approaching the photograph subjectively, you may color the details with your feelings.

4. Select a photograph that engages your interest. Title the photograph, and then using it as the basis of your description, complete one of the writing tasks just outlined. Be sure to include the photograph as part of your final draft.

🌟 Additional Writing Tasks 🌟
Description

1. Recall a spot that you visited when younger, not far from your home. It should be a place you remember well but not one that you visit constantly. Once you have selected the spot, draw upon your strength of recollection: Visualize yourself in this place, seeing the physical features, hearing the sounds, and smelling the odors and aromas. Jot down your memories. What details do you recall and in what order of importance? Record your memories just as the place was at that time in your life. How would you tell what you saw if you were describing the scene for a stranger? Which details would create images in this stranger's mind? Try to write this part of the description from a child's perspective.

    Once you have described the place as you recall it, write a description of how the place appears now, after years have passed. This part of the description should be done from an adult's perspective. Perhaps the place has not held up under time's pressure. Perhaps your view of it has changed. Perhaps you colored this place with romantic illusions.

    Once the second rough description is completed, begin the first draft. Develop a structure that shifts between past and present, revealing both the child's and the adult's attitude.

2. Select several photographs that represent milestones in your life. Describe them as if you were a reporter relating the events that are taking place in the photo. Keep your description objective but vivid. Or, if you wish, use several magazine ads as the basis for a description. Here, too, describe the events in the advertisement objectively, merely reporting the image you see on the page, not interpreting it.

3. Describe an animal that you have encountered, perhaps a wild animal such as a coyote, wolf, deer, bear, or whale. Begin with a description of the animal from folklore, which will probably require a visit to the library. Then follow with a description of the animal as you experienced it. Seek a connection between the two elements in this description.

4. Do something slightly out of the ordinary, and describe the experience. Perhaps you will climb a tree and sit among the branches.

Maybe you will sit in a closed closet for half an hour. You might roller-skate, stand on your head, dance a waltz, lie on the grass and stare at the clouds—the possibilities are endless. Once you have had the experience, describe it in detail.

5. Select a physical event and describe it in detail: the fog rolling through the woods or city streets, a storm gathering in the distance and sweeping toward you, a cloudburst, wind roaring through the trees and rattling the windows, an earthquake. In your description, capture a sense of motion, sound, and smell, as well as visual detail.

6. Describe people at work in various settings:

> A supermarket
> A fast-food restaurant
> A newsstand
> A factory
> A car wash
> A pizza parlor

In your description, create a dominant impression.

6

Narration

Relating Events

The Method

Once upon a time is the phrase that begins countless childhood narratives. *To narrate* is to tell a story. Our lives are full of stories, some exciting, some dull. These stories might be as brief as an anecdote—"A funny thing happened to me today while dissecting a frog in biology." They might seem as simple as a fairy tale, such as "Little Red Riding Hood," or as complex as a novel, such as James Joyce's *Ulysses*.

Narratives are so common in human experience that some psychologists have claimed that their patterns are etched on the human psyche, that people actually *need* stories. Absurd? Well, it is difficult to imagine that some people might require stories in the same way as they require affection. One fact, though, is certain: Effective narratives embody a few known characteristics, and good writers keep this fact in mind when composing their stories.

The most common of these characteristics is the **narrative effect**, which you may conceive as the narrative purpose, or, as some writers call it, the "payoff." Readers want a payoff—a moral, an insight, a message, a point, or just good entertainment. Often the narrative effect will be subtle, nothing more than getting the reader to utter a soft "Aha!" Consider this narrative, a teaching tale from Zen Buddhist lore. At first glance, it might seem to lack a narrative effect.

> A man traveling across a field encountered a tiger. He fled, the tiger after him. Coming to a precipice, he caught hold of the root of a wild vine and swung himself down over the edge. The tiger sniffed at him from above. Trembling, the man looked down to where, far below, another tiger was waiting to eat him. Only the vine sustained him.
>
> Two mice, one white and one black, little by little started to gnaw away the vine. The man saw a luscious strawberry near him. Grasping the vine with one hand, he plucked the strawberry with the other. How sweet it tasted!

What is the payoff? This is a fair question that every reader has the right to ask. Clearly, the narrative effect the storyteller might wish to achieve is not spelled out; the story reveals no thesis. But it certainly has something to do with being involved in the present and, perhaps, not worrying about what can't be controlled. One student suggests that fear of the past (represented by the first tiger pacing above the traveler) or fear of the future (the second tiger pacing below the traveler) should not interfere with our enjoyment of the present (the strawberry). But what about the mice? They're a detail that needs to be considered in any interpretation. Soon they will gnaw through the vine, sending the man to his death. Perhaps the tale suggests that when death is imminent, life becomes inordinately sweet.

Why create a story to illustrate a point, you might ask, even one as brief as this Zen tale? Why not just hold up a finger, smile sagely, and directly state a purpose? "Do not let fear of the past or future interfere with your enjoyment of the moment" or "Enjoy life now, for death may be near." In other words, why all the mystery?

Not all narratives are packed with hidden meanings or intended to provoke emotional responses. Many are factual reports, such as news reports or police reports, which simply recount events as they unfold, but narrative essays often deal with subjects that go beyond the limits of a report. Like the treasures in many children's tales, the purpose in many narratives—especially works of imagination such as tales, short stories, and novels—is therefore buried. In this way, the narrative essay offers its readers the opportunity to experience anything the storyteller has experienced—love, anger, fear, hate, prejudice, outrage, confusion, hope, disappointment—all the emotional states that we encounter in life. The events, therefore, must be dramatized, not explained, thus recreating, rather than reporting, events: First you live through a string of related experiences, and then you get the meaning—well, maybe you get the meaning.

Strategies

Because of the nature of narrative essays, the relationship between you and the storyteller is complex. Storytellers will entice you to use your imagination to re-create the experience. You should join, not resist, a writer in this effort. If the effort fails, then you will not make the creative leap that allows a narrative essay to achieve its emotional effect. Even if the purpose behind a narrative essay seems murky after a first reading, trust that the writer who chooses narration as a dominant essay pattern will always keep an eye on the purpose, usually dramatizing rather than stating it.

Narrative Structure

Every storyteller knows that readers love narratives to be driven by conflict between opposing forces, such as two figures in the narrative pitted against each other in a battle of wills or a single figure in conflict with his or her own feelings. But just as important, they also know that readers crave order, a sense that the action has direction, movement. To meet this need, many narrative essays are divided into three parts:

1. The **orientation**. The beginning sentences in a short narrative or the opening paragraphs in a long narrative are designed to establish the situation, identify the key figures, and suggest the conflict. The narrative purpose may be suggested, but the outcome should not be revealed.
2. The **complication**. The narrative should move forward through a series of scenes that intensify the conflict and build to a climax. The climax is the narrative's point of highest drama and sets up the narrative effect, that is, the writer's purpose, which always lurks within the climactic moment.
3. The **resolution**. The issues in the narrative should be resolved before the story ends. The resolution may be brief, often suggesting rather than directly stating the effect the writer has tried to create. At times the resolution will be ambiguous, thus forcing readers to reinterpret the narrative events in light of the closing observation.

You will find that most effective narrative essays follow this loose pattern. You can usually count on a storyteller to establish a story's situation in the orientation by providing information that answers these questions: Who? What? Where? and When? They will suggest a **conflict** as well. Consider this opening from Martin Gansberg's "Thirty-Eight Who Saw Murder Didn't Call the Police."

> For more than half an hour thirty-eight respectable, law-abiding citizens in Queens watched a killer stalk and stab a woman in three separate attacks in Kew Gardens.
>
> Twice their chatter and the sudden glow of their bedroom lights interrupted him and frightened him off. Each time he returned, sought her out, and stabbed her again. Not one person telephoned the police during the assault; one witness called after the woman was dead.
>
> That was two weeks ago today.

Whom does the situation involve? A murder victim, the murderer, and, most important, the "thirty-eight respectable, law-abiding citizens" who didn't call the police. What does the situation involve? Crime in the streets. Where did it take place? An area in Queens, a New York City borough. When did it happen? Two weeks before the date of the newspaper narrative. And the conflict? Gansberg clearly suggests a conflict related to social obligation: the indifference of the thirty-eight bystanders who fail to meet their legal and moral responsibility.

Point of View

Also in the orientation section of narrative essays, writers establish the **point of view**—that is, they reveal who is telling the story. As generally used in narrative essays, point of view is easy to understand. Stories are told either by a participant in the events (first-person point of view) or by a nonparticipant (third-person point of view).

Most often readers associate stories with the first-person point of view, which seems to give narrative essays authenticity: "I swear this is true—I was there! I lived it!" Often the events have directly affected the first-person storyteller in some emotional or intellectual way. At other times, the storyteller acts as a spectator, reporting events that he or she saw others experience. In either case, first-person narratives usually are more subjective than third-person narratives. They embody the storyteller's attitudes throughout the essay, directly in overt statements or indirectly in style. Writers almost always establish the point of view in the first paragraph. Consider the opening paragraph in Flannery O'Connor's essay, "The King of Birds."

> When I was five, I had an experience that marked me for life. Pathé News sent a photographer from New York to Savannah to take a picture of a chicken of mine. This chicken, a buff Cochin Bantam, had the distinction of being able to walk either forward or backward. Her fame had spread through the press, and by the time she reached the attention of Pathé News, I suppose there was nowhere left for her to go—forward or backward. Shortly after that she died, as now seems fitting.

O'Connor's opening paragraph illustrates one more bit of advice we can give you in reading first-person narratives: watch for the storyteller's own perspective. Notice that O'Connor begins by relating the emotional effect of an event that took place when she was five, but the first and last sentences clearly indicate that she is writing from an adult's perspective, not a five-year-old's, thus adding complexity, perhaps even irony, to the tone.

A writer who uses the third-person point of view usually relates events as accurately, and sometimes objectively, as possible. As a nonparticipant, the third-person narrator develops the story from reports by others, much as a journalist collects information for a story. This approach doesn't mean that a third-person narration lacks power or drama. It merely means that the storyteller is not part of the action. Consider the opening paragraph in Maxine Hong Kingston's brief narrative "The Wild Man of the Green Swamp."

> For eight months in 1975, residents on the edge of Green Swamp, Florida, had been reporting to the police that they had seen a Wild Man. When they stepped toward him, he made strange noises as in a foreign language and ran back into the saw grass. At first, authorities said the Wild Man was a mass hallucination. Maneating animals lived in the swamp, and a human being could hardly find a place to

rest without sinking. Perhaps it was some kind of a bear the children had seen.

Kingston's point of view is clearly **objective**, even dispassionate. We don't want to leave you with the impression, though, that third-person narrations are always objective and dispassionate. Review the opening from Gansberg's "Thirty-Eight Who Saw Murder Didn't Call the Police," presented on page 201. Gansberg's attitude toward the "thirty-eight respectable, law-abiding citizens" who watched a killer stalk his victim is clearly **subjective** and very passionate.

Chronological and Psychological Time

Because narratives unfold in time, storytellers must arrange the events so that the connections between them are clear. As you begin to read a narrative, notice the writer's narrative arrangement: Are the events arranged according to **chronological time**, that is, in sequence as they happened, step by step? Or are they arranged according to **psychological time**, that is, the way in which events might be connected in memory, shifting back and forth in time while keeping a sense of forward movement?

The decision a writer makes about the arrangement of a narrative essay is often determined by the subject. A historical essay, such as a narrative about a battle, usually marches along in chronological time. But if the subject comes from personal experience, then the essay may be arranged in psychological time, beginning *in medias res* ("in the middle of things") with an event that comes near the end of the actual chronology. This opening event can be highly dramatic, designed to keep readers in suspense until the essay closes, when its purpose becomes clear.

Writers use *flashback* and *flashforward* to shift the narrative action from one time frame to another. Flashback skips to the past to dramatize a previous event that has some bearing on the present. Flashforward skips to the future to help create suspense by showing a consequence that might result from present events. Although writers use flashback and flashforward mainly in psychologically arranged narratives, they can also use them, but to a much lesser extent, in narratives dominated by chronological development to add depth and variety to the predictable, step-by-step arrangement of events.

Whichever arrangement the writer chooses, he or she is obliged to guide you through the story. While reading with a critical eye, you should therefore watch for transitions in time. They may be complete sentences designed to smooth your way from one event to another: "My social life began to crumble into pieces like a stale oatmeal cookie after we settled in Santa Fe." They may take the form of brief phrases: "Two weeks later," "Only one year ago," "Soon I was to learn." Or they may be single words that help a writer to cut through time: "Now, Then," "Before, Today." Identifying the transitional tactics will help you follow the most complex narrative.

Scene and Summary

While crafting a narrative essay, the storyteller has two methods to use in presenting the events: **scene** and **summary**. You'll recognize scene because it directly portrays an event on the page. Like a scene in film or drama, a narrative-essay scene is played before your eyes. Summary is a synopsis of an event. It relates the high points but leaves out much of the specific detail that a scene usually includes. Many narratives include both scene and summary, with summary serving as the glue that holds the scenes together. It might help if you think of scene and summary as showing and telling: scene shows, summary tells. Consider this scene from a student's narrative that shows the writer's battle with fear:

> I stood paralyzed on the dock, my hands clenched and my knees locked tight. Bobby was flailing at the water, trying to pull himself to the overturned boat. He shouted for help, his voice rising to a shrill pitch and carrying beyond the boathouse and into the empty woods.
>
> I wanted to plunge into the lake, but my body would not unlock, and the horrible, empty spot in my mind threatened me like a black pit I might fall into. It was the water and all it symbolized—darkness, suffocation, a murky death.

The narrator presents this dramatic moment as if it were taking place before your eyes. He is showing it to you. Now compare this scene to a summarized version:

> When my brother Bobby overturned the rowboat and fell into the lake, I panicked. You see, I had almost drowned once in this very lake. The experience left me with the deep, irrational fear that if I ever swam in it again, I would be swallowed up. Although I knew he needed help, fear of the water paralyzed me.

Here the writer tells about the event. This summary lacks the immediacy of the scenic version, yet it, too, is effective.

Writers often, but not always, use dialogue in scenes, which helps to dramatize an event. Usually, dialogue will reflect the give-and-take that takes place between two speakers and is integrated with action. For example,

> Raymond leaned forward, jabbing a finger into Chico's chest, "You will never see Ellen again," he said. "Never!"
> "You are wrong," Chico said, "We are going to be married."
> Raymond, his face frozen in an angry mask, stared at Chico, who was much smaller and looked frail. Then Raymond glanced around the crowded locker room where the rest of the team had stopped to watch. "If you live," Raymond said before storming out the door.

In summary, writers will sometimes add key snatches of dialogue to create authenticity while moving on to more dramatic scenes.

> When Raymond confronted Chico in the locker room, their teammates watched in dismay. They had never seen Raymond so angry when he told Chico that he would never see Ellen again. Chico remained calm and told Raymond that he was wrong and then revealed that he and Ellen were to be married. Raymond could not hide his anger and said, "If you live," before storming out the door.

Whether writers use scene, summary, or both depends on the effect they wish to create. Often narrative essayists present the dramatic moments in scenes and use summary to move from scene to scene, thus skipping through the less significant events.

Narration in College Writing

College writers sometimes work brief narrative passages into an essay with other dominant patterns. In such papers, narrative passages may be used to create an interesting opening or to illustrate a point. In either case the narrative must have a clear structural purpose to justify its use. More frequently, however, narratives based on personal experience are frequent assignments in college courses. In cultural anthropology or social psychology classes you might be assigned a narrative report that requires your own observations. In a history class you might be asked to write from imagination a narrative about a historical event from a historical figure's point of view. In an English class you might be assigned an informal narrative essay based on personal experience that brought some insight.

Guidelines for Narrative Writing

1. Select an experience that lends itself to narrative development, and identify the narrative effect that you wish to achieve.
2. Determine the point of view to use: first person for a narrative based on experience or third person for a narrative compiled from outside information.
3. In prewriting, limit the events in your narrative. Pick out the highlights, then enrich them with descriptive detail. Remember, not every event should be presented in a scene. By dramatizing the emotional peaks, you will sustain your reader's interest.

4. Compose your first draft.

Write an *orientation* that sets the situation, identifies the key figures, establishes the conflict, and arouses interest.

Structure the *complication* by arranging events in climactic order with the most dramatic and revealing event serving as the climax.

Create a *resolution* that reveals, directly or indirectly, the narrative effect, that is, the narrative purpose or "payoff."

5. Revise your first draft with an eye for scene and summary. If you use dialogue, examine it to see whether you should present it in scene or summary. Be sure that your narrative has a strong forward movement with enough descriptive detail to engage the reader's senses.

A Student Essay Developed by Narration

Richard McKnight wrote a narrative essay in response to the following freshman composition assignment.

In "A Hanging" [p. 587], George Orwell uses first-person narration to communicate ideas without stating them directly. His narrator might not know the meaning of the events himself, but the reader is able to interpret the meaning from the way Orwell presents them. Write a 750- to 1000-word narrative in which you make a point without explicitly stating it. Tell a story of an incident that illustrates your point, such as (1) how a social event, such as a stylish wedding, shows that people care too much about money and appearance; (2) how a charismatic speaker shows that people are easily persuaded to believe something; or (3) how a sports event shows that old age is not the end of active living.

It was clear that McKnight had to arrange the narration in a way that would lead his readers to the lesson, thus allowing them to draw their own conclusions from the experience.

Read McKnight's final draft, which follows. First, note the narrative techniques that he uses, then study it in detail by responding to the items in Reviewing with a Writer's Eye.

The Last Ride

I watched a gray-haired surfer sitting on the longest board   1
I had ever seen, waiting for a wave in Candle Cove. He was
40 yards beyond the edge of a reef that seemed to rise and
fall dangerously as the sea sucked to and from the shore. Connie stood nearby, a year-round lifeguard who patrolled the
beaches in a jeep during winter. I wondered why a man his
age was alone and riding such dangerous winter swells.

At Candle Cove a winter swell can sometimes rise to   2
twelve feet. Twelve feet is not a remarkable height for waves
at sandy beaches where they break slowly and leave plenty of
room for surfers to maneuver. But at the Cove waves break
quickly and crash over a reef crusted with razor-sharp barna-
cles. Surfers must race across a wave's face to clear the reef
and reach the sandy beach. Only the best surfers will risk being swept over the rocks, even for a spectacular ride. But
sometimes even the best do not make it safely to the beach.

Just two weeks earlier, a hot-shot from Hawaii paddled   3
out in the heavy surf that a Mexican storm had kicked up. He
sat on his board beyond the break and waited for the big
swells to roll in. Suddenly, he swung his board's nose toward
shore to catch the day's biggest wave. He seemed to do everything right: He quickly leaped to his feet, cut sharply left,
moved to the board's nose to gain speed as he shot ahead of
the curl—but not in time. The massive wave broke over his
shoulder and tossed him into the roiling foam. The breaking
wave's force snapped his board in half and swept him over
the reef. He survived, but barely. Lifeguards raced him to an
emergency ward where doctors hovered above his body for
two hours with needles and thread.

Now the old man was in that kind of danger but with one   4
difference—he was well past his prime, much too old to be riding in dangerous waters.

"Better call him in," I said. "He's going to get hurt."   5
"He won't come in," Connie said.   6
"You're in charge of the beach."   7
"Don't you know who he is?" she said.   8
I said I didn't. She asked if I had ever seen <u>Slippery When</u>   9
<u>Wet</u>. The film was made by an amateur photographer thirty
years earlier, had become a surfing classic in the late 1950s. I
told her I had. She said that when he was a young man, the

old surfer had been featured in it. She said he was shown riding long boards on waves over twenty-five feet high at Sunset Beach in Hawaii and that he was even shown riding shore break at this beach. I vaguely remembered him, but there were many surfers in the film agilely maneuvering their boards as they rode waves.

"He's a living legend," Connie said.   10

"A living legend should know when to quit."   11

"If it's in your blood, you don't quit."   12

"Look," I said, "the living legend's going to need an   13
ambulance."

The old surfer was paddling to catch a wave, the largest   14
since I had been watching. His arms dug three, four times into the water before the wave swept him up, the reef rising dangerously close. He sprang to his feet, arched his back, and turned the board left as he raced down the wave's face. The wave broke behind him and crashed over the reef. Taking short, choppy steps, he inched his way to the board's nose to gain more speed and crouched low, avoiding the curl as it cracked behind him. Suddenly he was out of sight. The wave had tossed forward, and the curl folded over his crouching body.

"He's tanked," I said, looking at the white water as it   15
washed over the reef. "Better get him."

"Wait," she said.   16

"Now!" I said, but didn't know why. I wasn't a lifeguard   17
or her boss.

She looked at me. "Show a little courage," she said. "He is."   18

She was right. Still bent low on the front of the board, the   19
old surfer shot out of the curl, well ahead of the white water. And then an image from the film came back to me: A young man, over thirty years younger than this man, riding waves at this same beach. He, too, was shot out of the curl and cleared the reef on a massive wave, bigger than this one, that was crashing behind him. In the film, the beach was crowded with cheering spectators. They had seen a ride beyond their belief, but that was when surfing was new and still viewed as an astounding feat.

Now, this time as an old man with only two people watch-   20
ing, he once again cleared the reef and guided his board toward shore. In shallow water he stepped from the board, and swung it up under his arm, striding toward the sand where we stood. He walked passed us, nodding to Connie, who smiled

at him. He looked ancient, his skin thick from years of sun,
his hair gray and thin, his face wrinkled, and his belly growing thick. Yet his blue eyes were full of life, full of future
rides. I knew that I, like that crowd in the film, had seen
something special, an astounding feat, not just for someone
with gray hair and wrinkled skin, but for anyone, young
or old.

Reviewing with a Writer's Eye

1. Narrative structure (see pp. 200–201) gives direction and movement to story events. The structure is fueled by conflict that gains
   the most energy at the narrative climax. Usually, narrative structure
   follows a loose pattern: orientation, complication, and resolution.
   Identify the paragraphs that make up the orientation, complication,
   and resolution of Richard McKnight's "The Last Ride." At what
   point does the climax occur?
2. Writers arrange narrative events chronologically, as they happen in
   real time, step by step, or psychologically, as they might be connected in memory (see pp. 203–204). McKnight's narrative is primarily arranged chronologically, but at two points he does use
   flashback. Identify where he uses flashback, and explain why.
3. What conflict (see p. 201) drives McKnight's narrative? Explain.
4. McKnight employs first-person point of view (see pp. 201–203),
   which he immediately establishes in the opening sentence. Rewrite
   the opening paragraph in third-person point of view. What technical problems did you have to solve? Is third-person as effective as
   first-person point of view?
5. In a passage composed of dialogue and description, paragraphs 4 through 18, McKnight mixes scene and summary (see
   pp. 204–206). What do you believe his purpose to be? In particular, what is his purpose in paragraph 9?
6. The narrator's perception of the old surfer changes as the events unfold. Describe that change. What role does memory play?
7. McKnight chooses to suggest, rather than explain, what he wants
   his readers to gain from "The Last Ride." Explain what you think is
   the narrative effect McKnight is trying create.

8. Imagine that you are reviewing "The Last Ride" as a peer reader. In a 150- to 200-word note, explain to McKnight your overall response to the essay and what you believe to be its strengths and/or weaknesses.

Peer Review

You may be asked to write an essay about one of the readings that follow. Before you meet with your writing group, review this introduction. As you read the group papers, use these general principles of narration to help guide your comments.

1. The situation should be clear, that is, the who, what, when, and where of the story.
2. Some sort of conflict should be suggested early. If there is no conflict, the paper may be flat and uninteresting.
3. The point of view (who is telling the story) should be clear.
4. People in the narrative should be carefully distinguished from one another.
5. The time sequence should be clear. Readers must be guided carefully through any changes in chronological order.
6. The narrative should have a purpose. Readers want a payoff.

What follows is a collection of narrative essays by professional writers. As you read them, keep in mind that you are reading as a writer who is learning the craft, not merely reading to gather information for a test.

❦ Rene Denfeld ❦

Rene Denfeld, author of The New Victorians: A Young Woman's Challenge to the Old Feminist Order *(1995) and* Kill the Body, the Head Will Fall: A Closer Look at Women, Violence, and Aggression, *took up boxing at age twenty-six. She was the first woman to win the Tacoma Golden Gloves tournament. Denfeld sees aggression as a "human condition, not confined to one sex."*

The Lady of the Ring

In the following essay, which first appeared in The New York Times Magazine *on August 24, 1997, Denfeld speaks of what boxing has taught her. As you read the essay, look for the key words and phrases that help you to understand her point of view.*

I started boxing as a lark, a fantasy. I saw myself becoming glistening, fit and tough—a woman fighter. I saw myself rising from the canvas and fighting back, delivering amazing combinations until my opponent fell among the ropes, vanquished.

My first week in the gym in a run-down neighborhood in Portland, Ore., squashed my fantasy as I began to understand the long, difficult training regimen ahead of me. But I fell in love with the sport: the sound of the timer and the guys talking; the flying, hissing jump ropes; the punishment of the heavy bags, and, above all, the relationships between the fighters and our trainer, Jess Sandoval.

When I first went into the gym, Jess was in his 70s and increasingly infirm. He had lost his own professional career when he shipped out during World War II, but taught the sport afterward. He was shy around me, his only female fighter. We were all drawn close to Jess, though, an uneasy group, grieving in advance for the frail, titular head of our family.

Most of the other fighters were Mexican immigrants like Jess. Sometimes, when they were away for a while, Jess would make sad remarks about prison. Still, their lives were not the easy, cheap simplifications about laziness and crime that many Americans believe about immigrants and illegal aliens. The younger ones seemed touchingly self-conscious despite their macho baggy pants and careful gang attire. Alberto worked at McDonald's and attended school. Bob supported his family by working as a janitor, while his wife sewed satin trunks for the fighters—$25 a pair.

Immigration got Ernesto, Jess told us grimly. But one day 5
Ernesto was back. He snuck in, Jess said, triumphant. I still think about how hard it must be for these young men, who are torn between a love for their native country (he changed flags, they said contemptuously of one Mexican fighter who trains under a gringo coach) and a longing to be wanted and appreciated right here.

I understand. As a woman in a boxing gym, I had changed flags, 6
too. I'm sure Jess never imagined training a woman, and I'm sure the other fighters never imagined having to spar with one. Ernesto would hit me as he would a man—hard enough to bruise my ribs, water my eyes, cut my lips and make my nose bleed. He had to, you see: if he didn't hit back, I would beat him. This is the dilemma I forced on these men. Hitting a woman? They think that only a bully, a wife beater, does that. But the prospect of being beaten by a woman? Only a sissy, a punk. And yet we found a way to manage. There in that safe place, we had an unspoken truce.

Sparring with men, I felt liberated from generations of fear, self- 7
doubt, finger-waving and genteel restrictions: Men aren't so tough, I found, once you get close enough. Perhaps women's fear has been misplaced, conferring a malignant power on those who neither deserve nor desire it.

In entering this world, I lost more than superficial fantasy and 8
gained more than physical self-confidence. My perceptions of the sexes have been altered, and this has affected nearly every aspect of my life. I feel differently when I walk down the street alone— stronger, less fearful. No longer do I assume that I am less capable of handling anger and conflict.

But the greatest challenge was to the male fighters. I imagined 9
their worries: What will she think of us when she realizes we are not as tough, as cold or as mean as women everywhere have been led to believe? Will she breathe a sigh of relief, or laugh in contempt?

A boxing gym is only one of many places where the myth of   10
male superiority in strength and aggressiveness remains unques-
tioned. But it is also a place where the myth can begin to unravel.
Just as I have always been strong, and never realized it, men have always been vulnerable and complicated.

Now the fighter of my dreams is replaced by myself, in honest   11
memory, leaning over the ropes at the Golden Gloves after having
won the title. My opponent was already receding, like a vapor behind me, while the men from the gym cheered in the audience, But
there was only me, and Jess, and I was kissing his face, in thanks.

Not long ago, Jess passed away. When I heard the news, I put   12
down the phone and cried, thinking, with surprise, I've lost my father. I had gone into a boxing gym to learn how to be tough. But I
also found affection, sincerity and caring—and the deep bond between athlete and coach. Boxing has, in the end, left me softer.

Meaning and Purpose

1. The first paragraph says that Denfeld started boxing "as a lark."
   What does she mean by that phrase?
2. Who is "the head of our family" in this essay? Why was he called
   "the head of our family"?
3. In paragraph 6, Denfeld says, "I had changed flags." What do you
   infer from that sentence?
4. What problems do the male boxers think they face when it comes
   to hitting a woman?
5. According to this essay, what were the greatest challenges that the
   male boxers faced?

Strategy

1. How do you know from reading the essay that Denfeld succeeded
   as a boxer?
2. In the essay, Denfeld said that she started boxing as "a fantasy." In
   your opinion, when did she discover that her "fantasy" was a reality?

3. What myth is discussed in this essay? Why is it called a "myth"?
4. In this essay, who is Denfeld's "fighter of my dreams"?
5. In this essay, who replaced Denfeld's "fighter of my dreams"?

Style

1. Look up the word *dilemma* in a reliable college-level dictionary. Which of its definitions is the most appropriate for the way *dilemma* is used in this essay (paragraph 6)? Suggest a synonym.
2. In this essay, who says, "Will she breathe a sigh of relief, or laugh in contempt?" (paragraph 9)? What is the purpose of that question?
3. Why does Denfeld describe gang attire as "careful" (paragraph 4)?
4. When Denfeld speaks of "entering this world" (paragraph 8), what world is she entering?
5. How can you tell that Jess was in either the Navy or the Merchant Marine during World War II?

Writing Tasks

1. In a narrative essay, tell about a time when you entered what was, for you, strange territory. For example, it could have been a club, another town or city, or a neighborhood quite different from your own. Describe your feelings while you were in that territory, and describe your feelings about it now, focusing on what you learned from having been in that territory.
2. Our first impression of a person often differs greatly from our later impression of that same person, after we have come to know her or him better. In a personal narrative, discuss a person who impressed you in one way when you first met that person and in quite another way when you came to know that person. Be sure to include enough details in your essay so that your reader will understand what made you change your mind about that person.

❦ Jeff Z. Klein ❦

Jeff Z. Klein lives in New York City and has been staff editor of The New York Times *since 1996. From 1990 through 1995 he was sports editor of* The Village Voice *and has written about sports for those two papers, as well as other publications, for over ten years. In 1995, he published* Mario Lemieux, *a biography for young readers, and the following year the short story, "Now I Can Die in Peace," in the fiction collection* Original Six. *He co-authored, with Karl-Eric Reif,* The Death of Hockey, *two editions of* The Hockey Compendium, *and* The Coolest Guys on Ice. *Klein has been a lifelong Buffalo Sabres hockey fan but claims that his peak moment in life was on June 14, 1994, when he drank champagne out of the Stanley Cup in the dressing room of the victorious New York Rangers.*

Watching My Back

This essay was first published in The New York Times Magazine. *In it, Jeff Z. Klein, one of the magazine's editors, narrates a series of events that led him to the realization that he loved his girlfriend even more after she took the initiative in a violent and potentially dangerous confrontation on the streets of Prague.*

Notice as you read how Klein goes through a series of minor insights that lead to his final enlightenment.

He charged at me, shouting something in Czech. It was the 1
middle of the night in Prague. My girlfriend and I were there for
New Year's, and as we strolled through a deserted business district,
two young men came bounding out of a pedestrian underpass.
Loud, menacing and drunk, one ran up and shoved me, then
missed with a liquor-slow karate kick. I shoved back. We squared
off, staring.

Here I should say that my girlfriend had just completed an ad- 2
vanced self-defense course. She was standing to my left. I couldn't
see her, but I could hear her firmly addressing the attacker—"Back

216

off! Go away!"—as she had been taught. I hadn't been in a punch-up since I was 10 and had no idea what to do in an actual fight. But I had seen her in class, whupping two heavily padded mock attackers. I knew what she could do.

As my assailant and I faced each other, another couple, a big   3
man and a woman, walked unaware onto the scene. My assailant suddenly went after the big guy, who simply threw him to the ground. That was plenty for me. "He's got it," I said to my girlfriend. "Let's go." We backed away, but after a few steps, she stopped and said: "Wait. We should go back. They may need our help." I wasn't keen on the idea, but back we went. We saw the big guy standing over the assailant, who was down and out. It was over. Everyone dispersed.

My girlfriend and I walked down into Wenceslas Square to an   4
all-night cash machine. "I've got your back," she assured me jokingly as I went into the bank. As we waited for a cab, I admitted that I was still pretty wired. "I'm not," she said. "I was ready to fight, but I'm fine now. Of course, I wasn't the one the guy tried to start a fight with."

Once we were back where we were staying, I asked my girlfriend   5
how she would have handled it if he had attacked her. "Let's say I'm the guy, and I try to kick you like this," I said.

She demonstrated, pantomiming a series of blocks and strikes.   6
"But something worries me," she said as I stood there, utterly blown away. "I'm afraid I'd make a mistake." I thought she meant she was afraid she would forget what to do in the heat of action. But that wasn't it.

"We're trained to start fighting as soon as an attacker throws a   7
punch and to keep going until he can't get up again," she said. "But you got out of it without fighting, even though, he actually came at you. So I'm worried that I'd start fighting and really hurt the guy— or maim him, or even kill him—when it could've ended without anyone getting hurt at all."

Now I was really blown away. Months earlier, while she was tak-   8
ing the basic self-defense course for women, she told me about a man who approached her on a train. "He was kind of creepy," she said, "but I figured it was O.K. because I knew I could beat him up."

At the time, I was impressed by how quickly she had absorbed the confidence that the course was supposed to impart, but I wasn't convinced. I was now. Fully.

I tried to fall asleep, but I couldn't. So I went to find her. There 9 she was, supercool, soaking her feet in the tub, reading "Bridget Jones's Diary."

The next night, we were out having a drink, still rehashing what 10 happened. "I've got to tell you something," I said. "I know this might sound weird, but do you know how attractive it is that you can do this?"

She looked somewhat astonished, because obviously she hadn't 11 learned how to fight to titillate me or anyone else. "I never thought of it in those terms," she said. "I just like knowing that in a situation like the one last night, I can be of help."

At that point, I resolved to take the men's course. It turned out, 12 several weeks later, that half the men were in the class precisely because their wives or girlfriends had taken it, and they were dazzled by how capable the women were. Since then I've taken a couple of other courses, both in the company of my girlfriend. Some of the mystery, I must admit, is gone, but I still love the way she moves, and I love the idea that she knows exactly what to do to defend herself.

The day after we got back to New York, she offered to do 13 some of my laundry. "I can't let you," I said. "It's too, I don't know, *traditional.*"

"Look," she said. "A few days ago, I was willing to beat some guy 14 up for you. So, come on, I can do your laundry."

I happened to be facing away from her as I spoke. "Do you really 15 think," I asked, "you would've done a better job beating up that guy than I would have?"

"Not a *better* job," she said. "But I would've been much less 16 likely to get hurt doing it. Especially if he wasn't drunk and had been thinking clearly."

I turned and looked at her. "I think you're right," I said, and I 17 leaned in to kiss her. It's nice to have a girlfriend who's got your back.

Meaning and Purpose

1. What is the difference in Klein's and his girlfriend's fighting experience when they're threatened on the street in Prague?
2. What two incidents during and immediately following the Prague confrontation give the readers a clue that there will be a reversal of sex roles in the essay?
3. What words would you use to describe Klein's girlfriend?
4. What is Klein's purpose in this essay?

Strategy

1. The essay begins with the description of the conflict between the narrator and a drunk on a street in Prague. Is this the central conflict of the narration? If not, what is? Explain.
2. The essay begins *in medias res* (see Chronological and Psychological Time in the Strategies section of this chapter). What effect does this create?
3. Besides throwing readers into the middle of things, what else does the opening paragraph accomplish?
4. Where in the essay does Klein break his straightforward, step-by-step chronology? What is his purpose for doing so?

Style

1. What is the significance of the essay's title? In what places does it directly connect to the essay?
2. For the most part, the essay is written in Standard English. Why does Klein use the slang term "blown away" in paragraph 8?
3. Explain what Klein means by the sentence, "Some of the mystery . . . is gone" (paragraph 12).

Writing Tasks

1. Klein's essay begins with a violent encounter that initiates a series of incidents leading him through a number of small discoveries about himself and his relationship with his girlfriend. This process culminates in a final discovery of increased love and appreciation. Write a narrative essay in which you show the events that led up to a discovery of your own. If appropriate, begin your essay *in medias res* with a scene that will pull your reader into your narrative.

2. Klein's title is repeated in slightly different words in paragraph 4 and again in the final sentence. Write a narrative essay in which you repeat your essay's title, thereby lending added significance to that title.

❦ May Akabogu-Collins ❦

May Akabogu-Collins emigrated to the United States from Nigeria, received her Ph.D. in economics from the University of Southern California, and has taught in a number of colleges since. She currently teaches in Southern California.

Coming to Black America

In this essay, May Akabogu-Collins narrates how, as a black immigrant to America, she came to terms with racial bigotry—both bigotry directed against her and her own bigotry directed against black Americans.

Pay close attention as you read to the variety of forms racism takes in Akabogu-Collins's American experience.

My sister, Agnes, was visiting from Harvard law school, and we were strolling the streets of Koreatown that summer of 1989. I was a doctoral student of economics at USC. Bored, we entered a video store and were excited to find "Coming to America." 1

"What do we need to rent a movie?" Agnes asked the cashier. 2

"Just a minute. I go ask," she replied, and she disappeared to the back. Just then, another clerk approached and said something in a thick accent. It sounded like: "Sorry, only Koreans." 3

Agnes and I wondered if we had misheard. Then the owner appeared, not looking thrilled to see us. "Credit card and driver license," she announced. Agnes heaved a sigh of relief and pulled out her wallet. After scrutinizing her American Express card and license for what seemed like a minute, the owner declared: "One hundred dollars cash deposit and you leave license here." 4

By this time Agnes and I had the scent: Only Koreans. 5

Growing up in Africa, my impression of the black American was of a lazy, uneducated, ghetto-dwelling, dependent, disruptive and accomplished criminal. Upon arriving in America in 1980, I was sur- 6 prised to find black American students on a college campus. *Racial preferences,* I thought, and distanced myself from them. But now, at least according to the Korean video clerk, I was one of them.

I'm not exactly sure where or how I got this stereotype of black 7 Americans, though I'm certain the movies had something to do with it. As did my parents. When I left Nigeria for grad school, my dad told me: If you look for racism in America, you'll find it. But prove to them that you are a tribal African, not one of those addle-brained former slaves. And do steer away from them; they're nothing but trouble.

When my mother came to visit, she made us cross the road 8 upon spotting a black man approaching. With her it wasn't just prejudice against black Americans. A real estate magnate in Nigeria, she would rent only to expatriates—Caucasians and non-black foreigners. "The black man has no respect for property," she claimed. And it didn't matter if he was the college or bank president.

In grad school, I collaborated in my own discrimination. A Ko- 9 rean classmate was equally surprised to find me—a black doctoral student. She had grown up in Korea to believe that black people were "lazy and dumb . . . only dance and crime." I concurred but with a slight modification: "only black Americans, not black Africans." I had assumed that to get respect in America, I needed to distinguish myself from those blacks.

Of course, some African Americans resent the self-righteous atti- 10 tude of some black Africans. Once, upon learning that I was a professor, one acquaintance responded with a touch of envy: "You Africans come here and grab the affirmative action jobs designed specifically for us. You people think you're better blacks."

Although we were raised in Africa to revere expatriates, my sister 11 and I were never made to believe that we were their intellectual inferiors. We attended the same schools as their children, excelling academically as well as athletically. There was no animosity or tension. So while I kept my distance from black campus groups in America, I had no self-consciousness among a predominantly white or Asian population.

But the Korean video store was a turning point. As a target of 12 old-fashioned explicit racism, for the first time I felt the rage and frustration of the black American. And, as I watched Koreatown go up in flames during the L.A. riots of 1992, I understood the motivation.

After grad school, I found myself the only black professor at a small college in Pennsylvania, where I was seen as a representative of a group rather than as an individual. I felt tacit pressure. Although I would rather have slept in on Martin Luther King Jr. Day, I felt obligated to attend campus events. Black History Month became my Armageddon. I was a walking laboratory—a field trip for African Studies students, something akin to an ornament. I resented that burden.

I had spent 15 years in America trying to prove I was a better black. By the time of the O.J. Simpson verdict, I was no longer proud of all that time and energy.

It was October 3, 1995. The all-white faculty had convened at the department lounge outside my office to watch the televised verdict: Not guilty, both counts! Almost simultaneously, I could hear my colleagues: *A travesty! Dumb jurors! Whaaaat!* I shed a few tears, said a little prayer for the repose of Nicole's soul and stepped into the lounge on my way to class. Silence greeted me. I had fully intended to join in the condemnation of the verdict and to share with my colleagues how Nicole's murder had convinced me to finally end my violent marriage. But then I read the expression on the pink faces: *You're black, therefore . . .* I quickly continued on to my classroom, where, once again, I confronted an all-white student body. *What did I think of the verdict?* They wanted to know. I sensed the hostility, canceled class and left campus for the day—and decided to move back to California.

When I arrived in America, the dynamics of black-white politics were unfamiliar. In a monetary theory course that first semester, I received the highest score on the midterm exam. The professor announced, as he handed back my exam: "You surprised me: I kept slowing down for you, thinking you were lost." A compliment, I thought. Not so, said a classmate. The professor had presumed you were dumb because you are black, she explained. I wasn't persuaded. But many years later, I began to understand how that was a plausible interpretation.

My dad had said, "If you look for racism . . ." I hadn't been look-   17
ing for it that first semester, so I may have missed it. Fifteen years
later, I still wasn't looking for it when I stepped into the faculty
lounge after the Simpson verdict. Yet, there it was.

Nevertheless, it would take me more years, and hours of watch-   18
ing "Oprah," to comprehend the black experience in America. As
Oprah interviewed proud and successful black American women—
Maya Angelou, Alice Walker, Toni Morrison, Condoleezza Rice—
who wore their blackness like empresses, I began to feel racial pride.
As I watched Oprah pay tribute on Martin Luther King Jr. Day, and
saw Coretta Scott King with her erect posture that commanded respect, I began to understand what a big deal the civil rights movement was. Then I could appreciate the need for a Black Student
Union on college campuses and the significance of Black History
Month.

Today, I'm a lot more secure in my blackness and much more   19
comfortable among black Americans. I prefer to be described as a
Negro woman, although I see myself, in the words of Alice Walker,
as "a womanist." Still, being black now feels more like a birthright
than a burden.

Meaning and Purpose

1. Why was May Akabogu-Collins surprised to find black American
   students on a college campus? What reason did she give herself to
   explain their presence?
2. Why, as a native Nigerian, was Akabogu-Collins prejudiced against
   American blacks?
3. The author calls the incident at the Korean video store a "turning
   point" (paragraph 12). What does she mean by that?
4. While she was in graduate school, one of Akabogu-Collins's professors
   said she surprised him: "I kept slowing down for you, thinking you
   were lost." What are two possible interpretations of his comment?

5. How and why did Akabogu-Collins's attitudes about Black History Month change between the times when she was a young professor just out of graduate school and now?

Strategy

1. Are the events in Akabogu-Collins's narrative arranged according to chronological or psychological time (see Chronological and Psychological Time in the Strategies section of this chapter)? Explain your answer.
2. The author begins her narrative with an anecdote. What is the purpose of this brief story?
3. What is the function of the second section of this essay, paragraphs 6–8?
4. Briefly describe the central conflict of the narrative.
5. How does Akabogu-Collins resolve the narration's conflict?

Style

1. In paragraph 5, Akabogu-Collins says that she "had the scent." Explain her metaphor.
2. The author says that while she was teaching in a small college in Pennsylvania, Black History Month became her "Armageddon." What does she mean by that?
3. If necessary, look up the following words: *scrutinizing* (paragraph 4); *animosity* (11); *tacit* (13).

Writing Tasks

1. Akabogu-Collins's essay describes her journey from ignorance to a kind of enlightenment about racial bigotry. Think about some incident in your own life that led you to a better understanding, epiphany, or enlightenment, and then construct a narrative essay that describes your progress toward that new understanding. Neither

the incident nor the understanding needs to be monumental. Then, like Akabogu-Collins, construct a narrative essay in which you arrange your events in psychological time, going back and forth in time to shed light on the present.

2. Write a narrative essay in which you describe some encounter(s) you have had with racial prejudice—or with some other form of prejudice or discrimination—that resulted in you or someone else being treated unfairly. If you write about your own experience, use the first-person point of view; if you write about someone else, use the third-person point of view. In either case, consider beginning your narrative with a dramatic anecdote that will immediately hook your reader, as Akabogu-Collins does in her essay.

❦ Ryan Boudinot ❦

Ryan Boudinot received his BA from Evergreen State College in Olympia, Washington, and his MFA from Bennington College in Bennington, Vermont. He lives in Seattle, Washington, and has published several short stories and a novel about selling ice cream.

The Littlest Hitler

In this narrative, the writer tells the story of all the things that went wrong when, at nine years old, he went to school on Halloween dressed as Adolph Hitler. Be careful to notice, as you read, the many emotional states the boy goes through and the things that caused him to react the ways he did.

Notice, too, the different ways the "littlest Hitler" becomes another victim of the original Hitler, who victimized millions.

Then there's the time I went as Hitler for Halloween. I had gotten the idea after watching World War II week on PBS. My dad helped me make the costume. I wore tan polyester pants and one of his khaki shirts, with sleeves so long they dragged on the floor unless I rolled them up. With some paints left over from when we made the pinewood derby car for YMCA Indian Guides, he painted a black swastika in a white circle on a red bandanna and tied it around my left arm. Using the Dippity-Do he put in his hair every morning, he gave my own hair that plastered, parted style that had made Hitler look as if he was always sweating. We clipped the sides off a fifty-cent mustache and adhered it to my upper lip with liquid latex. I tucked my pants into the black rubber boots I had to wear whenever I played outside and stood in front of the mirror. My dad laughed and said. "I guarantee it, Davy. You're going to be the scariest kid in fourth grade."

My school had discouraged trick-or-treating since the razor blade and thumbtack incidents of 1982. Instead, they held the Harvest Car-

227

nival, not officially called "Halloween" so as not to upset the churchy types. Everyone at school knew the carnival was for wimps. All week before Halloween the kids had been separating themselves into two camps, those who got to go trick-or-treating and those who didn't. My dad was going to take me to the carnival, since I, like everybody else, secretly wanted to go. Then we'd go trick-or-treating afterward.

There were problems with my costume as soon as I got on the 3 bus that morning. "Heil Hitlah!" the big kids in the back chanted until Mrs. Reese pulled over to reprimand them. We knew it was serious when she pulled over. The last pulling-over incident occurred when Carl Worthington cut off one of Ginger Lopez's pigtails with a pair of scissors stolen from the library.

"That isn't polite language appropriate for riding the bus!" Mrs. 4 Reese said. "Do you talk like that around the dinner table? I want you both in the front seats, and as soon as we get to school I'm marching you to Mr. Warneke's office."

"But I didn't do anything!" 5

I felt guilty for causing this ruckus. Everybody was looking at 6 me with these grim expressions. It's important, I suppose, to note that there wasn't a single Jewish person on the bus. Or in our school, for that matter. In fact, there was only one Jewish family in our town, the Friedlanders, and their kids didn't go to West Century Elementary because they were home-schooled freaks.

When I got to school Mrs. Thompson considered me for a mo- 7 ment in the doorway and seemed torn, both amused and disturbed at the implications of a fourth-grade Hitler. When she called roll I stood up sharply from my desk, did the salute I'd been practicing in front of the TV, and shouted, "Here!" Some people laughed.

After roll was taken we took out our spelling books, but Mrs. 8 Thompson had other ideas. "Some of you might have noticed we have a historical figure in our class today. While the rest of you dressed up as goblins and fairies and witches, it looks like Davy is the only one who chose to come as a real-life person."

"I'm a real-life person, too, Mrs. Thompson." 9

"And who would you be, Lisette?" 10

"I'm Anne Frank." 11

Mrs. Thompson put a hand to her lips. Clearly she didn't know 12
how to handle this. I'd never paid much attention to Lisette before.
She'd always been one of the smart, pretty girls everyone likes.
When I saw her rise from her desk with a lopsided Star of David
made of yellow construction paper pinned to her Austrian-looking
frock or whatever you call it, I felt the heat of her nine-year-old
loathing pounding me in the face.

"This is quite interesting," Mrs. Thompson said. "You both came 13
as figures from World War II. Maybe you can educate us about what
you did. Davy, if you could tell us what you know about Hitler."

I cleared my throat. "He was a really, really mean guy." 14

"What made him so mean?" 15

"Well, he made a war and killed a bunch of people and made 16
everybody think like him. He only ate vegetables, and his wife was
his niece. He kept his blood in jars. Somebody tried to kill him with
a suitcase and then he took some poison and died."

"What people did he kill?" 17

"Everybody. He didn't like Jesse Owens because he was Afro- 18
American."

"Yes, but mostly what kind of people did he have problems 19
with?"

"He killed all the Jews." 20

"Not all Jews, fortunately, but millions of them. Including Anne 21
Frank."

The classroom was riveted. I didn't know whether I was in 22
trouble or what. Lisette smirked at me when Mrs. Thompson said
her character's name, then walked to the front of the class to tell us
about her.

"Anne Frank lived in Holland during World War II. And when 23
the Nazis invaded she lived in someone's attic with her family and
some other people. She wrote in her diary every day and liked movie
stars. She wanted to grow up to write stories for a newspaper, but the
Nazis got her and her family and made them go to a concentration
camp and killed them. A concentration camp is a place where they
burn people in ovens. Then somebody found her diary and everybody liked it."

When Lisette was done everybody clapped. George Ford, who 24
sat in front of me and was dressed as Mr. T, turned around, lowered
his eyes, and shook his fist at me. "I pity the foo' who kills all the
Jews." Recess was a nightmare.

I was followed around the playground by Lisette's friends, who 25
were playing horse with a jump rope, berating me for Anne Frank's
death.

"How would you like it if you had to live in an attic and pee in a 26
bucket and couldn't walk around or talk all day and didn't have
much food to eat?"

It didn't take long for them to make me cry. The rule about re- 27
cess was you couldn't go back into the building until the bell, so I
had to wait before I could get out of my costume. I got knots in my
stomach thinking about the parade at the end of the day. Everybody
else seemed so happy in their costumes. And then Lisette started
passing around a piece of notebook paper that said "We're on Anne
Frank's Side," and all these people signed it. When my friend Charlie
got the paper he tore it up and said to the girls, "Leave Davy alone!
He just wanted to be a scary bad guy for Halloween and he didn't really kill anybody!"

"I should just go as someone else," I said, sitting beneath the 28
slide while some kids pelted it with pea gravel. This was Charlie's
and my fort for when we played GI Joe.

"They can kiss my grits." Charlie said. He was dressed as a 29
deadly galactic robot with silver spray-painted cardboard tubes for
arms and a pair of New Wave sunglasses. "This is a free country, ain't
it? Hey! Stop throwing those son-of-a-bitching rocks!"

"Charlie!"   30

"Oops. Playground monitor. Time for warp speed." Charlie 31
pulled on his thumb, made a clicking sound, and disappeared under
the tire tunnel.

Despite Charlie's moral support, I peeled my mustache off and 32
untied my armband as soon as I made it to the boys' room. There
were three fifth-graders crammed into a stall, going, "Oh, man!
There's corn in it!" None of them seemed to notice me whimpering
by the sink.

Mrs. Thompson gave me her gray-haired wig to wear for the parade. 33

"Here, Davy. You can be an old man. An old man who likes to wear khaki." 34

I knew Mrs. Thompson was trying to humor me and I resented her for it. Lisette, for whatever reason, maybe because her popularity in our classroom bordered on celebrity worship, got to lead the parade. I was stuck between Becky Lewis and her pathetic cat outfit and Doug Becker, dressed as a garden. His mom and dad were artists. Each carrot, radish, and potato had been crafted in meticulous papier-mâché, painted, lacquered, and halfway embedded in a wooden platform he wore around his waist. The platform represented a cross section, with brown corduroys painted with rocks and earthworms symbolizing dirt, and his fake-leaf-covered shirt playing the part of a trellis. For the third year in a row Doug ended up winning the costume contest. 35

By the time our parade made it to the middle school I was thoroughly demoralized. I had grown so weary of being asked, "What are you?" that I had taken to wearing the wig over my face and angrily answering, "I'm lint! I'm lint!" 36

Meaning and Purpose

1. Besides choosing to wear a Hitler costume, how does Davy distinguish himself in the first paragraph from most other nine-year-olds?
2. How does Mrs. Thompson, Davy's teacher, attempt to turn Davy and Lisette's costumes into a history lesson? How does this lesson further complicate Davy's life?
3. Why does Boudinot combine the two images he does in paragraph 32?
4. How would you describe Davy's emotions when he says "I'm lint! I'm lint!" at the end of the story?

Strategy

1. The first two paragraphs serve as the narrative's introduction. Describe what Boudinot does in those two opening paragraphs.
2. The second section of the narrative, paragraphs 3–7, establishes the story's initial conflict. What is that conflict? How does Davy feel about being at the center of the commotion?
3. How does the introduction of Lisette complicate the story's conflict?
4. Describe the function Charlie has in the narrative.
5. How does Boudinot resolve the narrative's conflict?

Style

1. What impression does Boudinot create by beginning his narrative with the words "Then there's the time . . ."?
2. In the first paragraph, Davy says that Hitler's hair made him look "as if he was always sweating." Why would Davy have that impression? Does Davy's observation favorably compare with the images you've seen of Hitler?
3. Look up the derivation of the word *ruckus* (paragraph 6) in a dictionary that includes word etymologies. How did the word come about? How appropriately is it used here?

Writing Tasks

1. In *The Littlest Hitler*, Ryan Boudinot writes a narration that follows a cause–effect pattern. That is, the story's opening scene creates the situation from which everything else in the story inevitably follows. Using Boudinot's story as a model, write a narrative essay in which you begin with a scene that naturally generates a series of events that follow. As Boudinot does, include only those details that heighten your story's interest and meaning.

2. Think of an event in your own experience that you found embarrassing or distressing, and write a narrative essay about it that follows
   chronological rather than psychological time (see the Strategies
   section of this chapter). Avoid a then-this-happened-then-that-
   happened format, and instead construct a series of scenes that advance your story, as Boudinot does in *The Littlest Hitler.*

❦ Gabrielle Hamilton ❦

Gabrielle Hamilton is her father's daughter in more ways than one. In her youth, her father, Jim Hamilton, would throw huge dinner parties at their home in rural New Jersey and would cook for up to a hundred guests at a time. She recalls that her father "... couldn't roast a leg of anything; he had to roast a whole animal." In 1988 he turned cooking pro and opened Hamilton's Grill Room in his hometown, a restaurant that has subsequently won numerous honors. Gabrielle has followed in her father's footsteps by opening her own restaurant in the East Village in New York City, where she is both chef and owner. At Prune (christened with her childhood nickname), she now turns out food that has also won numerous awards. Newsday has said her bill of fare is "truly her own and startlingly delicious."

Killing Dinner

In this little narrative, Gabrielle Hamilton describes a traumatic experience when she was seventeen years old. As you read, play close attention to how she distinguishes between her attitudes toward herself and her father during the event, when she was seventeen, and now, several years later, when she writes about the experience.

It's quite something to go barehanded up through a chicken's ass   1
and dislodge its warm guts. Startling, the first time, how fragilely
they are attached. I have since put countless suckling pigs—pink,
the same weight and size as a pet beagle—into slow ovens to roast
overnight so that their skin becomes crisp and their still forming
bones melt into the meat. I have butchered two-hundred-and-
twenty-pound sides of beef down to their primal cuts; carved the
tongues out of the heads of goats; fastened baby lambs with crooked
sets of teeth onto green applewood spits and set them by the four-
some over hot coals; and boned the saddles and legs of rabbits,
which, even skinned, look exactly like bunnies.

But when I killed my first chicken I was only seventeen and un-   2
accustomed. I had dropped out of school and was staying in the
basement of my father's house, in rural New Jersey, for very little
rent. That fall, I spent a lot of time sitting outside on the log pile at
dusk smoking hand-rolled cigarettes in my canvas jacket, watching
the garden decay and thinking about death and the inherent beauty
of the cycle of life. In my father's chicken coop, one bird was being
badly henpecked. My dad said we should kill it and spare it the slow
torture by its pen mates. I said I could do it. I said it was important
to confront the death of the animal you had the privilege of eating,
that it was cowardly to buy cellophane-wrapped packages of bone-
less, skinless breasts at the grocery store. My father said, "You can
kill the damned thing when I get home from work."

From a remote spot on the back kitchen steps, he told me how to   3
pull the chicken decisively out of the pen. I spoke to it philosophi-
cally about death, grasping it firmly yet calmly with what I hoped was
a soothing authority. Then he told me to take it by the legs and hold it
upside down. The chicken protested from deep inside its throat, close
to the heart, a violent, vehement, full-bodied cluck. The crowing was
almost an afterthought. To get it to stop, I started swinging it in full
arm circles, as my dad instructed me. I windmilled that bird around
and around the way I'd spun lettuce as a kid in the front yard, sending droplets of water out onto the gravel and pachysandra from the
old-fashioned wire-basket spinner my mom used.

He said this would disorient the bird—make it so dizzy that it   4
couldn't move—and that's when I should lay it down on the block
and chop its head off, with one machinelike whack. In my own way,
not like a machine at all, I laid it down on a tree stump, and while it
was trying to recover I clutched the hatchet and came down on its
neck. This first blow made a vague dent, barely breaking the skin. I
hurried to strike it again, but lost a few seconds in my grief and horror. The second blow hit the neck like a boat oar on a hay bale. I was
still holding its feet in one hand and trying to cut its head off with
the dull hatchet in my other when both the chicken and my father
became quite lucid, and not a little agitated. The chicken began to
thrash, its eyes open, as if chastising me for my false promises of a
merciful death. My dad yelled, "Kill it! Kill it! Aw, Gabs, kill the fuck-

ing thing!" from his bloodless perch. I kept coming down on the bird's throat—which was now broken but still issuing terrible clucks—stroke after miserable stroke, until I finally got its head off. I was blubbering through clenched teeth. My dad was animated with disgust at his dropout daughter—so morose and unfeminine, with the tips of her braids dyed aquamarine, and unable even to kill a chicken properly. As I released the bird, finally, and it ran around the yard, bloody and ragged but at least now silent, he screamed, "What kind of person are you?"

It was a solid minute before the chicken's nerves gave out and it   5
fell over motionless in some dead brown leaves. I wiped my snot on my sleeve, picked up the bird from the frozen ground, tied its feet, and hung it on a low tree branch to bleed it. The other chickens in their pen, silhouetted against the dusk, retreated inside to roost for the night. My dad closed the kitchen door and turned on the oven. I boiled a blue enamelled lobster pot full of water, and submerged the bird to loosen its feathers. Sitting out on the back steps in the yellow pool of light from the kitchen window, I plucked the feathers off the chicken, two and three at a time. Its viscera came out with an easy tug: a small palmful of livery, bloody jewels that I tossed out into the dark yard.

There are two things you should never do with your father: 6
learn how to drive, and learn how to kill a chicken. I'm not sure you should sit across from each other and eat the roasted bird in resentful silence, either, but we did that, too, and the meat vas disagreeably tough.

Meaning and Purpose

1. What is the difference between Gabrielle Hamilton's reason for killing the chicken and her father's reason? How does that difference comment on Hamilton's attitudes toward herself and her father?

2. How are Hamilton's musings while she sat on the woodpile and smoked similar to the reason she gives for wanting to kill the chicken?

3. For what reason do you think Hamilton attempted to kill the chicken in her "own way" instead of "with one machinelike whack," as her father had instructed (paragraph 4)?
4. Is the central conflict in this narrative between Hamilton and the chicken or between Hamilton and her father? Explain.
5. What is the significance of Hamilton's final comment that the chicken's "meat was disagreeably tough"?

Strategy

1. Why does Hamilton describe her extensive experience with butchering and cooking animals in the first paragraph?
2. Hamilton gives her readers some background in the second paragraph, before she actually starts her narrative in the third. Why is that background important for understanding what follows?
3. Why does Hamilton compare the chicken and her father in paragraph four ("both the chicken and my father became quite lucid")?
4. How does Hamilton connect the fifth paragraph with the first, bringing the story full circle before her conclusion?

Style

1. In paragraph 2, Hamilton says that she sat on a log pile "thinking about death and the inherent beauty of the cycle of life." How does that statement become ironic? What is the author's attitude toward her teenage self here?
2. Comment on the effectiveness of Hamilton's simile "like a boat oar on a hay bale" in paragraph 4.
3. If necessary, look up the following words in a dictionary: *fragilely, primal, saddles* (paragraph 1); *inherent* (2); *vehement, pachysandra* (3); *lucid, chastising, animated, morose* (4); *enameled, viscera, livery* (5).

Writing Tasks

1. The central conflict of Hamilton's essay involves the narrator having to prove herself to her father. Write a first-person narrative essay in which you describe how you had to prove yourself to someone in authority—for example, one or both of your parents, a teacher, a police officer, or a government official.
2. Hamilton begins her essay with a brief summary of her extensive experience as an adult in butchering and cooking animals, experience that contrasts with and comments on her adolescent inexperience, which is the subject of the rest of her essay. Write a narrative essay in which you begin with a description of yourself as an adult that comments on a childhood experience that is the focus of the rest of your essay.

❦ Responding to Photographs ❦

Narration

The Storyteller

Ancient cultures viewed storytellers as being touched with divine madness. These storytellers had tales that explained life's mysteries.

But times have changed

Astronauts have soared through space. The deepest rain forests and highest mountain peaks have been photographed. What mysteries need to be explained? What lessons need to be taught? What is the role of the storyteller in an age when movie and television production companies create visual stories by formula?

Is the photograph "The Storyteller" commenting on the role of storytellers today?

The Storyteller's outfit suggests that he indeed might be touched by divine madness. He wears ribbons, balloons, streamers, a whimsical laurel around his head, and a banner that identifies him.

Displayed on a wall are hundreds of photographs, many of African-American and Native-American leaders, perhaps each embodying a story of its own. Behind his head, slightly obscured, are the words of Martin Luther King, Jr., "I have a dream."

This storyteller stands in the classroom, but where are the students who might be eager to hear a meaningful story? He is looking and pointing outside the photographic frame, but at what or whom? From the viewer's perspective he is alone . . . or is he?

In a unified narrative respond to one of the following writing tasks. Before you begin the first draft, review effective narrative conventions described at the beginning of the chapter.

1. Create your own tale about the storyteller in this photograph. Begin by studying the photograph. Imagine how the storyteller feels in his attire. Imagine how he feels during his performance. Imagine what his life is like when he is not being a storyteller. What does he do? Where does he live? What do his friends think of his storytelling? Is he a fulfilled person? A happy person? A sad person?

    As you imagine the storyteller, list your observations. Once this exploratory phase of the assignment is complete, review your observations, and determine what dominant impression you wish to create.

    Finally, to start your first draft, you might begin this way: "Once upon a time an ordinary man who lived in our city decided to become a storyteller." Throughout your draft, integrate physical details from the photograph.

2. Imagine that the storyteller in the photograph is fully aware that ancient mysteries have been clarified scientifically. He is still compelled to tell tales, meaningful tales designed to give people insight into a society that some people see as growing more and more chaotic.

    For this task, tell how the storyteller became successful. Include in your narrative a summary of one tale that gave his listeners insight into contemporary life.

❦ *Additional Writing Tasks* ❦
Narration

1. All of us have had experiences that can be retold in narrative form. Often these experiences stay with us much longer than impersonal events that we have merely observed. For this writing task, select an incident from your early years that involves a simple action that you can recall clearly and vividly. The incident does not have to be exceptionally dramatic, but it should be interesting enough to move from the opening through the body to the climax—the major components of narrative. The incident may involve you alone or it may involve others as well. It must have enough action with connected events to be developed as a narration.

   Because this is to be an incident from your early years, you might begin by setting aside time to explore your past. Begin by spontaneously jotting down memories from your early past as a way to begin the selection procedure. Make a list by devoting no more than three or four sentences to each experience you recall. These three entries are from one student's memory list:

   > I remember walking home from school one June morning. Hot. Humid. A man with a Bible and wearing a black suit stopped me and asked, "Have you been saved, Sonny?" I was frightened.

   > When I was ten I visited my grandfather in the hospital. He was very ill, dying. I recalled all the wonderful and all the horrible fishing trips we took together.

   > Why was my dog shot? The killer was never found. I remember searching the faces of strangers for looks of guilt.

   Each writer, of course, will have his or her own memories: an automobile accident, a mystery, a sudden appearance, a victory, a defeat, a meeting with a famous person, and so on.

   Once you have compiled a list, select one of the memories, perhaps the one that stirs the most emotion in you when you recall it, and use it as the basis for your narration. Before starting your first draft, take at least an uninterrupted hour to compose a rough sketch of the incident, capturing the movement of events and the people. Then you will be prepared to start the first draft. Begin by arranging the material in dramatic order to serve as a loose outline.

2. Select an incident to narrate that you have not directly experienced yourself. The incident might come from what you have seen, heard, or read. Perhaps you will select an incident from a television show, film, short story, news article, or friend's experience. If you select a newspaper article as your source, you might want to retell it as though you had witnessed the incident. If you want to convey a friend's story, you might add observations of your own. If you select an incident from a film or short story, you might want to concentrate on an incident involving one character and rearrange the events to suit your purpose. Keep in mind, though, that your task is not to merely summarize the story line; your task is to select material for your own narrative.

7

Examples

Illustrating Ideas

The Method

Examples bring the vague and abstract down to earth. They clarify the historian's lectures. They make concrete the philosopher's abstractions. They electrify the politician's arguments. By using examples effectively, you will not only help your readers to understand your point, but also improve your chances of holding their attention because vivid, concrete examples can make your writing more interesting to read.

Examples are much used, even in everyday conversation. If someone claims that advertisers use fear of rejection to manipulate consumers, you might say, "Show me."

Examples such as these would follow: "What about those mouthwash commercials? One actually shows a salesman rejected because he has bad breath. And then after a quick rinse, Presto! he makes the sale, and the customer drives away smiling. And what about the commercial that shows a young female banker passed over for a promotion? A wiser, older colleague whispers in her ear. In the next scene she is scrubbing her head with the advertiser's shampoo, and the commercial closes with the smiling banker now managing her own department."

The speaker is using examples to clarify the general observation that advertisers use fear of rejection to manipulate consumers into buying their products. Writers use examples with the same intent—to illustrate a generalization, that is, to select one thing from many to represent the *whole*. In fact, the word *example* derives from the Latin *exemplum,* which means to "one thing selected from the many." Examples used to represent ideas are essential to clear communication because they give readers something concrete to visualize. It might be difficult for a reader to understand what social critic Jack Solomon means by this statement.

> No matter how you look at it, in the scant space of some forty years, television has revolutionized our lives. First introduced as a novelty alternative to radio, television has rapidly evolved into the most profound invention of the age. Nothing is immune from its influence.

For the sake of clarity, Solomon immediately provides several examples to illustrate his idea for the reader:

Politicians play for the cameras, and so do international terrorists. Physicians call news conferences, and judges host courtroom dramas. Television, through its hyping of the Olympic Games, has transformed sport into politics and politics into sport, treating everything from presidential elections to military conflicts as prime-time entertainment. What is not televised is hardly thought of at all in a world in which television creates reality as much as it records.

These examples add clarity to Solomon's statement. Without them the reader would have only a vague understanding of Solomon's point in this paragraph, which would amount to a slip in communication.

Strategies

Professional writers use three kinds of examples—specific, typical, and hypothetical—to support their ideas. They can be used in any combination and are often mixed within one paragraph.

Specific Examples

Specific examples capture an experience, event, incident, or fact. Banesh Hoffman, in "My Friend, Albert Einstein," uses a specific example (an **anecdote**) to support the general comment that the essence of Einstein's personality was simplicity.

He was one of the greatest scientists the world has ever known, yet if I had to convey the essence of Albert Einstein in a single word, I would choose *simplicity*. Perhaps an anecdote will help. Once, caught in a downpour, he took off his hat and held it under his coat. Asked why, he explained, with admirable logic, that the rain would damage the hat, but his hair would be none the worse for its wetting. This knack for going instinctively to the heart of the matter was the secret of his major scientific discoveries.

Hoffman selects this specific example with a clear purpose in mind. He wants to make concrete the generalization in the topic sentence. The example is vivid and interesting, capturing Einstein's essence.

Hoffman's specific example illustrating Einstein's simplicity is a short narrative, but writers often shape examples in other ways. Sometimes the writer will use several specific examples in one paragraph. A series of brief examples might function like verbal snapshots, freezing in time several events or experiences. In this paragraph, naturalist Jane van Lawick-Goodall uses seven short visual examples to illustrate social behavior among the chimpanzees she studied in Tanzania.

> While many details of their [the chimpanzees'] social behavior were hidden from me by the foliage, I did get occasional fascinating glimpses. I saw one female, newly arrived in a group, hurry up to a big male and hold her hand toward him. Almost regally he reached out, clasped her hand in his, drew it toward him, and kissed it with his lips. I saw two adult males embrace each other in greeting. I saw youngsters having wild games through treetops, chasing around after each other or jumping again and again, one after the other, from a branch to a springy bough below. I watched small infants dangling happily by themselves for minutes on end, patting at their toes with one hand, rotating gently from side to side. Once two tiny infants pulled on opposite ends of a twig in a gentle tug-of-war. Often during the heat of midday or after a long spell of feeding, I saw two or more adults grooming each other, carefully looking through the hair of their companions.

Sometimes writers will create a *list* or a *catalogue* of specific examples to illustrate their observations. In this paragraph from *The Distant Mirror,* historian Barbara Tuchman catalogues how people in fourteenth-century England might imagine the distant places they had heard of but never seen.

> Faraway lands, however—India, Persia, and beyond— were seen through a gauze of fabulous fairy tales revealing an occasional nugget of reality: forests so high they touch the

clouds, horned pygmies who move in herds and grow old in seven years, brahmins who kill themselves on funeral pyres, men with dogs' heads and six toes, "cyclopeans" with only one eye and one foot who move as fast as the wind, the "monoceros" which can be caught only when it sleeps in the lap of a virgin, Amazons whose tears are of silver, panthers who practice the caesarean operation with their own claws, trees whose leaves supply wool, snakes 300 feet long, snakes with precious stones for eyes, snakes who so love music that for prudence they stop up one ear with their tail.

Tuchman's and Goodall's paragraphs also illustrate another point: Examples can come from various sources. Tuchman finds her specific examples by researching historical documents; Goodall gets hers by observing chimpanzees in their natural habitat. Both writers use their examples for the same purpose, however: to illustrate a general observation.

Typical Examples

In contrast to specific examples, writers compose **typical examples** by generalizing from many experiences, events, incidents, or facts. Consider this paragraph from Jonathan Kozol's essay "The Human Cost of an Illiterate Society." Kozol uses a typical example to develop the point that illiterates, people who cannot read, lead a precarious existence, even when they are in the care of professionals who are trained to provide for their health. As you read Kozol's paragraph, keep in mind that this typical example represents the experience of many people, not that of one specific person.

Illiterates live, in more than literal ways, an uninsured existence. They cannot understand written details on a health insurance form. They cannot read the waivers that they sign preceding surgical procedures. Several women I have known in Boston have entered a slum hospital with the intention of obtaining a tubal ligation and have emerged a few days later after having been subjected to a hysterectomy. Unaware of their rights, incognizant of jargon, intimidated by the unfamiliar air of fear and atmosphere of ether that so many of us find oppressive in the confines even of the most attractive and expensive medical facilities, they have signed their names to documents they could not read and which nobody, in the hectic situation that prevails so often in those overcrowded hospitals that serve the urban poor, had even bothered to explain.

Kozol begins with a general statement that establishes the dangers illiterate patients face. He follows with two sentences of background: Illiterate patients cannot understand insurance forms or the legal documents that give away their rights during surgery. He then supports his general statement with an extended typical example, thus illustrating, even dramatizing, the result of being unable to read: Several illiterate Boston women signed papers permitting hysterectomies when they wanted tubal ligations.

Typical examples, as Kozol's illustrates, are composites of many experiences. They are not rooted in specific times but compiled after many observations over an extended period. In the next paragraph, cultural anthropologist Edward T. Hall uses typical examples developed after extended observation to illustrate how people react when their sense of space is violated:

> People are very sensitive to any intrusion into their spatial bubble. If someone stands too close to you, your first instinct is to back up. If that's not possible, you lean away and pull yourself in, tensing your muscles. If an intruder doesn't respond to these body signals, you may then try to protect yourself, using a briefcase, umbrella, or raincoat. Women—especially when traveling alone—often plant their pocketbook in such a way that no one can get very close to them. As a last resort, you may move to another spot and position yourself behind a desk or a chair that provides screening. Everyone tries to adjust the space around himself in a way that's comfortable for him; most often, he does this unconsciously.

Hypothetical Examples

Sometimes writers create **hypothetical examples** from their imagination. Hypothetical examples are similar to typical examples, usually composed from bits and pieces of experience or information. Often a writer will use a hypothetical example where something concrete is needed to tie down an abstraction and no *actual* example is available. In the opening paragraph of *The White Album,* essayist and novelist Joan Didion uses hypothetical examples to illustrate why stories are important in life.

> We tell ourselves stories in order to live. The princess is caged in the consulate. The man with the candy will lead the children into the sea. The naked woman on the ledge outside the window on the sixteenth floor is a victim of accidie, or the naked woman is an exhibitionist, and it would be "interesting" to know which. We tell ourselves that it makes some difference whether the naked woman is about to commit a mortal sin or is about to register a political protest or is about to be, the Aristophanic view, snatched back to the human condition by the fireman in priest's clothing just visible in the window behind her, the one smiling at the telephoto lens. We look for the sermon in the suicide, for the social or moral lesson in the murder of five. We interpret what we see, select the most workable of the multiple choices. We live entirely, especially if we are writers, by the imposition of a narrative line upon disparate images, by the "ideas" with which we have learned to freeze the shifting phantasmagoria which is our actual experience.

Didion has clearly drawn these brief examples from her imagination, yet they are effective because they make her observation more concrete. With these conjectures she hopes to stir her readers' interest by appealing to typical experiences they might have encountered in fairy tales and newspapers, the mysterious experiences for which many seek explanations.

Mixing Examples

When studying professional writing, you'll notice that writers use different strategies to develop their examples. You'll find specific, typical, and hypothetical examples mixed, and you'll notice that sometimes examples illustrating one point will be presented in several paragraphs. In this passage from *No House Calls,* Peter Gott, a practicing physician and medical columnist, develops his point in several paragraphs and mixes examples with explanation to reveal the scientific facts behind the commercial claims of mouthwash and disinfectant companies.

> With people's increasing knowledge about bacteria, it was inevitable that some companies would, with success, try to play upon the fear that we have all developed about "bacterial infection." For instance, Listerine and Lysol are currently being advertised to produce "clean breath" and a clean environment, respectively, as a result of their bacteria-killing properties. While it is true that these compounds do, in fact, kill bacteria, the consumer would do well to demand more precision in evaluating their claims.
>
> As an example, the mouth contains billions of harmless bacteria. Some forms of bad breath are caused by bacterial decomposition of food between teeth. Listerine—and many other mouthwashes—will kill millions of bacteria on contact, but only a tiny proportion of the *total*. Furthermore, as soon as the Listerine has been spit out, billions of bacteria are reintroduced into the mouth during breathing and eating. So while the consumer's mouth will feel "fresh," in fact the bacterial count rapidly rises to "pretreatment" levels; essentially, nothing has been accomplished.
>
> Lysol spray when applied to surfaces will kill some bacteria, but most of these are nonpathogens and would do us no harm anyway. Bacteria that cause venereal disease die quickly outside the body and would be unlikely to reside on public toilet seats long enough for the spray to make any difference. The Lysol spray will scent the air, however, and that seems to be the important consideration. Somehow, if we don't see or smell the germs, we assume they're all gone. The room must be safe. The evil has been repelled. We can take a shower.

Peter Gott's passage establishes an important principle to keep in mind: Every writer, whether a professional writer or a student writer, must develop an eye for examples. The most effective way we know of developing that eye is to read critically, that is, read as a writer reads. Study how professional writers shape their examples. Study how their examples relate to their generalizations. And study the kinds of examples they develop.

Examples in College Writing

Examples are so effective in clarifying an idea that you will probably use them in every college essay you write. The vivid, specifically written example brings to life the most abstract concept. Without examples an expository essay will lack vigor. In fact, turning in an essay without effectively using examples might indicate to your reader that your understanding of the subject is deficient, especially if you write a string of unsubstantiated generalizations.

Guidelines for Writing Examples

1. Select a subject that can be developed through examples, and determine whether you have enough information to develop examples.
2. Decide on a dominant purpose of the essay. Then use the dominant purpose to focus your prewriting to generate as many examples as you can.
3. Review your prewritten material, compose a thesis, and then select appropriate examples from your prewriting to develop it.
4. Decide on appropriate structure and arrange the examples to create the strongest effect. Vary the examples in length and type while keeping in mind the purpose they serve.
5. Revise your essay, making sure that the examples are adequately developed for your purpose.

A Student Essay Developed by Examples

Daniela Taylor wrote a personal experience essay about common behavior in response to this freshman composition assignment:

In an 800- to 1000-word essay, identify and discuss a common behavior that suggests changing social attitudes. Consider the following general subject areas as possibilities:

dress	speech
manners	dating practices
public displays	possessions
a sport	games
service	charity

Use examples as the dominant development mode, and base your discussion on personal experience and observation.

Taylor developed the examples from firsthand experience, a film she had seen on television, and a news article. She decided to concentrate on the general subject of manners, which she narrowed to a more specific subject: increasing discourtesy in public places.

Now examine Taylor's essay. Read it through once to see how she uses examples to develop her thought. Then study the entire essay in detail by responding to items in Reviewing with a Writer's Eye.

We Are Not Alone

Whatever happened to courtesy? I am referring to the everyday, run-of-the-mill courtesies people used to show each other, which now seem to have gone the way of helping the aged across busy intersections and quiet libraries. For example, last week as I came out of a grocery store, I saw a woman moving her groceries from a shopping cart to her trunk. That task completed, she shoved her shopping cart directly behind the car parked next to her. What was she thinking? Did she know that the driver of the other car would hit it if he failed to see it? Did she realize he would have to return her cart if he did see it? Did she care? The woman's behavior momentarily angered me and puzzled me. Sadly, however, my experience shows that this woman's discourteous behavior is not an isolated event. It seems that basic courtesy is rapidly being replaced by basic discourtesy. Everywhere I spend time in public—at school, at work, at shopping malls, in parks, in the-

1

aters, at sports events, at movies, and even on the highway—discourteous behavior seems to be increasing.

Nowhere has public discourtesy become more common than in traffic. I recall my early driving experience as being pleasurable. Other drivers would follow right-of-way guidelines, waiting their turn to make a left turn or cross through an intersection. Now this courteous attitude seems to be changing. Like me, you have probably experienced angry drivers in a rush, shouting and shaking their fists at you. Typically, these drivers may be well-mannered people, but they often go berserk behind the wheel of a car. Near campus lately, I have noticed something new taking place. After a left turn signal turns red, three, four, five, or even six drivers still rush through the intersection, delaying the cars that now have a green light. These drivers seem to share the same discourteous attitude, "I waited long enough for this left turn light to turn green, and now I'm going through even if it turns red again." Another recent trend is the spontaneous creation of illegal left turn lanes to the right of the legal left turn lane. Of course, dangerous drivers have always been on the road, but now others are compounding the danger because of their discourteous impatience. Sometimes discourtesy even erupts into anger. A recent survey of Southern California drivers, a place where commuters often spend two to three grueling hours a day in their cars, revealed that nearly 60% of those surveyed admitted giving chase to other motorists who had offended them. Usually these chases are abandoned as tempers cool, but sometimes the offended driver overtakes the offender and a battle of words, gestures, and even weapons ensues.

Last week I began to notice discourteous behavior that seems to have recently developed. Rollerbladers apparently find a challenge in weaving in and out of pedestrians strolling on public walkways. They seem to lack common courtesy, failing to keep in mind that a pedestrian walking at a much slower pace than their skating pace cannot always predict their movements. Their discourteous behavior can turn a relaxing afternoon stroll into a nerve-racking game of dodge the Rollerblader. The increase of cellular phones has given rise to another kind of public discourtesy. People no longer retreat to enclosed public phone booths to make private phone calls. They can now phone friends, loved ones, and business associates while standing in a crowd. Often their voices rise well above normal speaking range, thus disrupting the casual conversations of people who share the public space.

A recent Home Box Office showing of director Barry   4
Levinson's Good Morning, Vietnam, a 1987 film about the exploits of an Armed Forces Radio disc jockey in Saigon at the height of the Vietnam War, reminded me of how our culture freely and discourteously uses obscenity. Disc jockey Adrian Cronauer (played by Robin Williams) is teaching a group of Vietnamese how to use English in everyday situations. Cronauer bypasses all the conventional socially acceptable phrases and gets right to the nitty-gritty of American obscenity, teaching the Vietnamese which obscenities to use for which occasions. Political implications aside, I at first thought the scene was hilarious, perhaps the film's most memorable scene. But then I realized that beneath the obscene words and phrases, so incongruous and humorous in the mouths of non-English speakers, lies the very attitude that disturbs me, an attitude that seems to be saying, "I have a right to be as discourteous as I want, Mister!"

Now, over a decade later, I find the "Cronauer" attitude to   5
be increasing. In almost any public setting people appear to be determined to pepper their conversations with common obscenities that used to be reserved for locker-room conversations, scribbling on restroom walls, or moments of great frustration and anger. Recently, for example, a friend and I were standing in line to buy tickets for a popular movie. Several people behind us were speaking loudly and punctuating their observations with gutter language and uproarious laughter. The epithets in their rambling conversation, delivered by both young men and women, were directed toward actors, musical groups, members of the opposite sex, teachers, and each other when they disagreed. Behind me an older couple waited in line with their two children. They were clearly embarrassed, their faces turning red and their expressions pained, but the speakers seemed to be unaware of their embarrassment. I think such public use of generally unacceptable language reveals an aggressive, disrespectful attitude—perhaps the most extreme form of public discourtesy. It implicitly suggests that these teens feel free to say whatever they please without being sensitive to common social constraints. Should freedom of speech include the right to be publicly discourteous by spouting four-letter words no matter how uncomfortable it makes others who share the public space?

Why is public discourtesy increasing? I guess that more
and more people are focusing on themselves and forgetting
that their behavior might affect others around them. I know
at times I have, and you probably have too. Yet by merely remembering that we share public spaces with others, we might
help replace basic discourtesy with basic courtesy.

Reviewing with a Writer's Eye

1. Develop a scratch outline (see pp. 42–44) of Daniela Taylor's "We Are Not Alone." First, state the thesis statement in your own words. Then restate each topic sentence in your own words and identify the supporting examples for each topic sentence. How are paragraphs 4 and 5 related?

2. Taylor uses a variety of examples (see pp. 245–251). By paragraph, identify each type of example she uses. For instance, in the introductory paragraph, Taylor uses a specific example based on personal experience.

3. To guide her readers through the essay, Taylor uses overt transitions. Review paragraph 2, and identify the words and phrases that Taylor uses to keep readers on track.

4. Review Taylor's introduction and conclusion. How do they relate to each other?

5. Sometimes Taylor presents examples with very little comment, as she does in paragraph 3. Other times she responds to the examples, as she does in paragraphs 4 and 5. Review paragraphs 3, 4, and 5, and identify the examples and Taylor's responses to them. Why do you think she chooses to comment on some examples and not others?

6. Imagine that Taylor has asked you to read her essay to see whether the organization is effective and the examples are clearly distinguished. In response, write Taylor a note identifying any strengths and/or weaknesses you find in the organization and presentation of examples.

As you read the essays in the following section, you will see the variety of ways in which writers develop examples. Sometimes a writer will use a single extended example to develop a point. At other times a writer will combine short and extended examples, specific and typical examples, and will include personal observations and background information.

Sometimes examples will serve as the dominant development pattern, but like narration and description, examples also function in essays with other dominant patterns, such as comparison and contrast, cause and effect, classification, and argumentation. Always, however, writers use examples with one fundamental purpose in mind: *to make the general more specific and the abstract more concrete.*

Peer Review

You may be asked to write an essay about one of the readings that follow. Before you meet with your writing group, review this introduction. As you read the papers of your group, use these general principles of using examples to help guide your comments.

1. All examples should clearly relate to the general statements they illustrate.
2. The number of examples should be enough to validate the general statement but not so many that the reader feels overwhelmed and loses interest. There is no mathematical way to measure this balance, so rely on your own judgment as you read the paper.
3. The examples should be combined with explanations to guide the reader to the desired conclusion.

❦ Amy Tan ❦

Amy Tan was born in Oakland, California, in 1952, two and a half years after her parents emigrated to the United States from China. Her parents expected her to become a neurosurgeon, but instead she became a consultant to programs for disabled children and then a freelance writer. She visited China for the first time in 1987 and felt an instant cultural identity with her parents' homeland. Her first novel, The Joy Luck Club, *spent several weeks on American best-seller lists and earned much critical acclaim. It sensitively explores the relationships between young Chinese-American women and their immigrant mothers. Her second novel,* The Kitchen God's Wife, *further explores this theme. Tan has also written two books for children,* The Moon Lady *and* The Siamese Cat. *Her latest novel is* The Bonesetter's Daughter.

Mother Tongue

In the following essay, first published in Threepenny Review, *Tan describes how her use of English changes according to the needs of the circumstance and moment. During her exploration of language she also manages to paint an affectionate portrait of her mother and the relationship she has with her.*

Tan uses example after example to demonstrate her points. Notice how specific those examples are, how they aptly illustrate her generalizations, and how they lend interest to what she says.

I am not a scholar of English or literature. I cannot give you much more than personal opinions on the English language and its variations in this country or others.

I am a writer. And by that definition, I am someone who has always loved language. I am fascinated by language in daily life. I spend a great deal of my time thinking about the power of language—the way it can evoke an emotion, a visual image, a complex idea, or a simple truth. Language is the tool of my trade. And I use them all—all the Englishes I grew up with.

Recently, I was made keenly aware of the different Englishes I   3
do use. I was giving a talk to a large group of people, the same talk I had already given to half a dozen other groups. The nature of the talk was about my writing, my life, and my book, *The Joy Luck Club*. The talk was going along well enough, until I remembered one major difference that made the whole tale sound wrong. My mother was in the room. And it was perhaps the first time she had heard me give a lengthy speech, using the kind of English I have never used with her. I was saying things like, "The intersection of memory upon imagination" and "There is an aspect of my fiction that relates to thus-and-thus"—a speech filled with carefully wrought grammatical phrases, burdened, it suddenly seemed to me, with nominalized forms, past perfect tenses, conditional phrases, all the forms of standard English that I had learned in school and through books, the forms of English I did not use at home with my mother.

Just last week, I was walking down the street with my mother,   4
and I again found myself conscious of the English I was using, the English I do use with her. We were talking about the price of new and used furniture and I heard myself saying this: "Not waste money that way." My husband was with us as well, and he didn't notice any switch in my English. And then I realized why. It's because over the twenty years we've been together I've often used that same kind of English with him, and sometimes he even uses it with me. It has become our language of intimacy, a different sort of English that relates to family talk, the language I grew up with.

So you'll have some idea of what this family talk I heard sounds   5
like, I'll quote what my mother said during a recent conversation which I videotaped and then transcribed. During this conversation, my mother was talking about a political gangster in Shanghai who had the same last name as her family's, Du, and how the gangster in his early years wanted to be adopted by her family, which was rich by comparison. Later, the gangster became more powerful, far richer than my mother's family, and one day showed up at my mother's wedding to pay his respects. Here's what she said in part.

"Du Yusong having business like fruit stand. Like off the street   6
kind. He is Du like Du Zong—but not Tsung-ming Island people.
The local people call putong, the river east side, he belong to that
side local people. That man want to ask Du Zong father take him in
like become own family. Du Zong father wasn't look down on him,
but didn't take seriously, until that man big like become a mafia.
Now important person, very hard to inviting him. Chinese way,
came only to show respect, don't stay for dinner. Respect for making
big celebration, he shows up. Mean gives lots of respect. Chinese
custom. Chinese social life that way. If too important won't have to
stay too long. He come to my wedding. I didn't see, I heard it. I gone
to boy's side, they have YMCA dinner. Chinese age I was nineteen."

You should know that my mother's expressive command of En-   7
glish belies how much she actually understands. She reads the *Forbes*
report, listens to *Wall Street Week*, converses daily with her stockbroker, reads all of Shirley MacLaine's books with ease—all kinds of
things I can't begin to understand. Yet some of my friends tell me
they understand 50 percent of what my mother says. Some say they
understand 80 to 90 percent. Some say they understand none of it,
as if she were speaking pure Chinese. But to me, my mother's English is perfectly clear, perfectly natural. It's my mother tongue. Her
language, as I hear it, is vivid, direct, full of observation and imagery.
That was the language that helped shape the way I saw things, expressed things, made sense of the world.

Lately, I've been giving more thought to the kind of English my   8
mother speaks. Like others, I have described it to people as "broken"
or "fractured" English. But I wince when I say that. It has always
bothered me that I can think of no way to describe it other than
"broken," as if it were damaged and needed to be fixed, as if it
lacked a certain wholeness and soundness. I've heard other terms
used, "limited English," for example. But they seem just as bad, as if
everything is limited, including people's perceptions of the limited
English speaker.

I know this for a fact, because when I was growing up, my   9
mother's "limited" English limited *my* perception of her. I was
ashamed of her English. I believed that her English reflected the

quality of what she had to say. That is, because she expressed them imperfectly, her thoughts were imperfect. And I had plenty of empirical evidence to support me: the fact that people in department stores, at banks, and at restaurants did not take her seriously, did not give her good service, pretended not to understand her, or even acted as if they did not hear her.

My mother has long realized the limitations of her English as well. When I was fifteen, she used to have me call people on the phone to pretend I was she. In this guise, I was forced to ask for information or even to complain and yell at people who had been rude to her. One time it was a call to her stockbroker in New York. She had cashed out her small portfolio and it just so happened we were going to go to New York the next week, our very first trip outside California. I had to get on the phone and say in an adolescent voice that was not very convincing, "This is Mrs. Tan." 10

And my mother was standing in the back whispering loudly, "Why he don't send me check, already two weeks late. So mad he lie to me, losing me money." 11

And then I said in perfect English, "Yes, I'm getting rather concerned. You had agreed to send the check two weeks ago, but it hasn't arrived." 12

Then she began to talk more loudly. "What he want, I come to New York tell him front of his boss, you cheating me?" And I was trying to calm her down, make her be quiet, while telling the stockbroker, "I can't tolerate any more excuses. If I don't receive the check immediately, I am going to have to speak to your manager when I'm in New York next week." And sure enough, the following week there we were in front of this astonished stockbroker, and I was sitting there red-faced and quiet, and my mother, the real Mrs. Tan, was shouting at his boss in her impeccable broken English. 13

We used a similar routine just five days ago, for a situation that was far less humorous. My mother had gone to the hospital for an appointment, to find out about a benign brain tumor a CAT scan had revealed a month ago. She said she had spoken very good English, her best English, no mistakes. Still, she said, the hospital did not apologize when they said they had lost the CAT scan and she had come for nothing. She said they did not seem to have any sympathy 14 when she told them she was anxious to know the exact diagnosis, since her husband and son had both died of brain tumors. She said they would not give her any more information until the next time and she would have to make another appointment for that. So she said she would not leave until the doctor called her daughter. She wouldn't budge. And when the doctor finally called her daughter, me, who spoke in perfect English—lo and behold—we had assurances the CAT scan would be found, promises that a conference call on Monday would be held, and apologies for any suffering my mother had gone through for a most regrettable mistake.

I think my mother's English almost had an effect on limiting my   15
possibilities in life as well. Sociologists and linguists probably will tell you that a person's developing language skills are more influenced by peers. But I do think that the language spoken in the family, especially in immigrant families which are more insular, plays a large role in shaping the language of the child. And I believe that affected my results on achievement tests, IQ tests, and the SAT. While my English skills were never judged as poor, compared to math, English could not be considered my strong suit. In grade school I did moderately well, getting perhaps B's, sometimes B-pluses, in English and scoring perhaps in the sixtieth or seventieth percentile on achievement tests. But those scores were not good enough to override the opinion that my true abilities lay in math and science, because in those areas I achieved A's and scored in the ninetieth percentile or higher.

This was understandable. Math is precise; there is only one cor-   16
rect answer. Whereas, for me at least, the answers on English tests were always a judgment call, a matter of opinion and personal experience. Those tests were constructed around items like fill-in-the-blank sentence completion, such as, "Even though Tom was _____, Mary thought he was _____". And the correct answer always seemed to be the most bland combinations of thoughts, for example, "Even though Tom was shy, Mary thought he was charming," with the grammatical structure "even though" limiting the correct answer to some sort of semantic opposites, so you wouldn't get answers like, "Even though Tom was foolish, Mary thought he was ridiculous." Well, according to my mother, there were very few limitations as to

what Tom could have been and what Mary might have thought of him. So I never did well on tests like that.

The same was true with word analogies, pairs of words in which you were supposed to find some sort of logical, semantic relationship—for example, "*Sunset* is to *nightfall* as _____ is to _____." And here you would be presented with a list of four possible pairs, one of which showed the same kind of relationship: *red* is to *stoplight, bus* is to *arrival, chills* is to *fever, yawn* is to *boring.* Well, I could never think that way. I knew what the tests were asking, but I could not block out of my mind the images already created by the first pair, "*sunset* is to *nightfall*"—and I would see a burst of colors against a darkening sky, the moon rising, the lowering of a curtain of stars. And all the other pairs of words—red, bus, stoplight, boring—just threw up a mass of confusing images, making it impossible for me to sort out something as logical as saying: "A sunset precedes nightfall" is the same as "a chill precedes a fever." The only way I would have gotten that answer right would have been to imagine an associative situation, for example, my being disobedient and staying out past sunset, catching a chill at night, which turns into feverish pneumonia as punishment, which indeed did happen to me.

I have been thinking about all this lately, about my mother's English, about achievement tests. Because lately I've been asked, as a writer, why there are not more Asian Americans represented in American literature. Why are there few Asian Americans enrolled in creative writing programs? Why do so many Chinese students go into engineering? Well, these are broad sociological questions I can't begin to answer. But I have noticed in surveys—in fact, just last week—that Asian students, as a whole, always do significantly better on math achievement tests than in English. And this makes me think that there are other Asian-American students whose English spoken in the home might also be described as "broken" or "limited." And perhaps they also have teachers who are steering them away from writing and into math and science, which is what happened to me.

Fortunately, I happen to be rebellious in nature and enjoy the challenge of disproving assumptions made about me. I became an English major my first year in college, after being enrolled as premed. I started writing nonfiction as a freelancer the week after I was told by my former boss that writing was my worst skill and I should hone my talents toward account management.

But it wasn't until 1985 that I finally began to write fiction. And at first I wrote using what I thought to be wittily crafted sentences, sentences that would finally prove I had mastery over the English language. Here's an example from the first draft of a story that later made its way into *The Joy Luck Club,* but without this line: "That was my mental quandary in its nascent state." A terrible line, which I can barely pronounce. 20

Fortunately, for reasons I won't get into today, I later decided I should envision a reader for the stories I would write. And the reader I decided upon was my mother, because these were stories about mothers. So with this reader in mind—and in fact she did read my early drafts—I began to write stories using all the Englishes I grew up with: the English I spoke to my mother, which for lack of a better term might be described as "simple"; the English she used with me, which for lack of a better term might be described as "broken"; my translation of her Chinese, which could certainly be described as "watered down"; and what I imagined to be her translation of her Chinese if she could speak in perfect English, her internal language, and for that I sought to preserve the essence, but neither an English nor a Chinese structure. I wanted to capture what language ability tests can never reveal: her intent, her passion, her imagery, the rhythms of her speech and the nature of her thoughts. 21

Apart from what any critic had to say about my writing, I knew I had succeeded where it counted when my mother finished reading my book and gave me her verdict: "So easy to read." 22

Meaning and Purpose

1. What is Tan's thesis? Where does she state it?
2. Tan asserts that her mother's lack of command of standard English "belies how much she actually understands" (paragraph 7). How is this so?

3. Explain how her mother's "limited" English limited Tan's perception of her.
4. Explain how her mother's lack of English skills nearly limited some of the author's life possibilities.

Strategy

1. Tan uses anecdotes to illustrate her points, yet this is not a narrative essay. Why?
2. How effectively do Tan's examples illustrate her points?
3. Why does Tan distinctly break her essay at the end of paragraph 7 and again at the end of paragraph 17?

Style

1. In paragraph 7, Tan says that some of her friends claim to understand little of her mother's speech, while some others claim to understand none of it. Translate the transcription of her mother's language in paragraph 6. Can it be accurately described as an "expressive command of English" (paragraph 7)?
2. How many "Englishes" does Tan speak?
3. Tan says she eliminated the line "That was my mental quandary in its nascent state" from her novel *The Joy Luck Club* and labels the line "terrible." Why?
4. If necessary, look up the following in a good dictionary: *wrought, nominalized* (paragraph 3); *transcribed* (5); *belies* (7); *empirical* (9); *guise* (10); *impeccable* (13); *benign* (14); *insular* (15); *semantic* (16); *quandary, nascent* (20).

Writing Tasks

1. Using Amy Tan's essay as a model, write an essay in which you examine the various Englishes you use. What do you talk about when you speak with friends of the same sex? Of the opposite sex? With

both sexes? With your co-workers? With your parents? How does your language change? Make sure your examples are many and specific.

2. If you work in a job that has specialized jargon or if you play a sport or participate in any social activity that has its own slang, write an essay in which you categorize and explain that language.

❦ Brent Staples ❦

Brent Staples, born in 1951 in Chester, Pennsylvania, attended Widener University in his home town, where he received a B.A. in behavioral sciences. He then attended graduate school at the University of Chicago, earning a Ph.D. in psychology. He has been a writer and editor for the Chicago Sun-Times, *the* Chicago Reader, Chicago *magazine, and* Down Beat. *Since 1985 he has been on the editorial board of* The New York Times, *where he writes regularly on politics and culture. He has also been a regular contributor to* The New York Times Magazine, New York Woman, Ms., *and* Harper's. *His memoir,* Parallel Time: Growing Up in Black and White, *was the winner of the Anisfield-Wolf Book Award in 1991.*

Black Men and Public Space

"Black Men and Public Space" appeared in a slightly different form in the September 1986 issue of Ms. *magazine. The current version of the essay subsequently appeared in the December 1987 issue of* Harper's. *The essay is a provocative account of the ironic power and the real pain connected to being a young black man in our race-conscious society.*

As you read, pay close attention to the number and kinds of examples Staples uses to make his points vivid and alive.

My first victim was a woman—white, well dressed, probably in   1
her late twenties. I came upon her late one evening on a deserted
street in Hyde Park, a relatively affluent neighborhood in an otherwise mean, impoverished section of Chicago. As I swung onto the
avenue behind her, there seemed to be a discreet, uninflammatory
distance between us. Not so. She cast back a worried glance. To her,
the youngish black man—a broad six feet two inches with a beard
and billowing hair, both hands shoved into the pockets of a bulky
military jacket—seemed menacingly close. After a few more quick
glimpses, she picked up her pace and was soon running in earnest.
Within seconds she disappeared into a cross street.

That was more than a decade ago. I was twenty-two years old, a   2
graduate student newly arrived at the University of Chicago. It was
in the echo of that terrified woman's footfalls that I first began to
know the unwieldy inheritance I'd come into—the ability to alter
public space in ugly ways. It was clear that she thought herself the
quarry of a mugger, a rapist, or worse. Suffering a bout of insomnia,
however, I was stalking sleep, not defenseless wayfarers. As a softy
who is scarcely able to take a knife to a raw chicken—let alone hold
one to a person's throat—I was surprised, embarrassed, and dis-
mayed all at once. Her flight made me feel like an accomplice in
tyranny. It also made it clear that I was indistinguishable from the
muggers who occasionally seeped into the area from the surrounding
ghetto. That first encounter, and those that followed, signified that
a vast, unnerving gulf lay between night-time pedestrians—
particularly women—and me. And I soon gathered that being perceived as dangerous is a hazard in itself. I only needed to turn a corner into a dicey situation, or crowd some frightened, armed person
in a foyer somewhere, or make an errant move after being pulled
over by a policeman. Where fear and weapons meet—and they often
do in urban America—there is always the possibility of death.

In that first year, my first away from my hometown, I was to be-   3
come thoroughly familiar with the language of fear. At dark, shad-
owy intersections, I could cross in front of a car stopped at a traffic
light and elicit the *thunk, thunk, thunk, thunk* of the driver—black,
white, male, or female—hammering down the door locks. On less
traveled streets after dark, I grew accustomed to but never comfortable with people crossing to the other side of the street rather than
pass me. Then there were the standard unpleasantries with policemen, doormen, bouncers, cabdrivers, and others whose business it is
to screen out troublesome individuals before there is any nastiness.

I moved to New York nearly two years ago and I have remained   4
an avid night walker. In central Manhattan, the near-constant crowd
cover minimizes tense one-on-one street encounters. Elsewhere—in
SoHo, for example, where sidewalks are narrow and tightly spaced
buildings shut out the sky—things can get very taut indeed.

After dark, on the warrenlike streets of Brooklyn where I live, I of-   5
ten see women who fear the worst from me. They seem to have set

their faces on neutral, and with their purse straps strung across their chests bandolier-style, they forge ahead as though bracing themselves against being tackled. I understand, of course, that the danger they perceive is not a hallucination. Women are particularly vulnerable to street violence, and young black males are drastically overrepresented among the perpetrators of that violence. Yet these truths are no solace against the kind of alienation that comes of being ever the suspect, a fearsome entity with whom pedestrians avoid making eye contact.

It is not altogether clear to me how I reached the ripe old age of twenty-two without being conscious of the lethality nighttime pedestrians attributed to me. Perhaps it was because in Chester, Pennsylvania, the small, angry industrial town where I came of age in the 1960s, I was scarcely noticeable against a backdrop of gang warfare, street knifings, and murders. I grew up one of the good boys, had perhaps a half-dozen fistfights. In retrospect, my shyness of combat has clear sources. 6

As a boy, I saw countless tough guys locked away; I have since buried several, too. They were babies, really—a teenage cousin, a brother of twenty-two, a childhood friend in his mid-twenties—all gone down in episodes of bravado played out in the streets. I came to doubt the virtues of intimidation early on. I chose, perhaps unconsciously, to remain a shadow—timid, but a survivor. 7

The fearsomeness mistakenly attributed to me in public places often has a perilous flavor. The most frightening of these confusions occurred in the late 1970s and early 1980s, when I worked as a journalist in Chicago. One day, rushing into the office of a magazine I was writing for with a deadline story in hand, I was mistaken for a burglar. The office manager called security and, with an ad hoc posse, pursued me through the labyrinthine halls, nearly to my editor's door. I had no way of proving who I was. I could only move briskly toward the company of someone who knew me. 8

Another time I was on assignment for a local paper and killing time before an interview. I entered a jewelry store on the city's affluent Near North Side. The proprietor excused herself and returned with an enormous red Doberman pinscher straining at the end of a leash. She stood, the dog extended toward me, silent to my questions, her eyes bulging nearly out of her head. I took a cursory look around, nodded, and bade her good night. 9

Relatively speaking, however, I never fared as badly as another black male journalist. He went to nearby Waukegan, Illinois, a couple of summers ago to work on a story about a murderer who was born there. Mistaking the reporter for the killer, police officers hauled him from his car at gunpoint and but for his press credentials would probably have tried to book him. Such episodes are not uncommon. Black men trade tales like this all the time.

Over the years, I learned to smother the rage I felt at so often being taken for a criminal. Not to do so would surely have led to madness. I now take precautions to make myself less threatening. I move about with care, particularly late in the evening. I give a wide berth to nervous people on subway platforms during the wee hours, particularly when I have exchanged business clothes for jeans. If I happen to be entering a building behind some people who appear skittish, I may walk by, letting them clear the lobby before I return, so as not to seem to be following them. I have been calm and extremely congenial on those rare occasions when I've been pulled over by the police.

And on late-evening constitutionals I employ what has proved to be an excellent tension-reducing measure: I whistle melodies from Beethoven and Vivaldi and the more popular classical composers. Even steely New Yorkers hunching toward nighttime destinations seem to relax, and occasionally they even join in the tune. Virtually everybody seems to sense that a mugger wouldn't be warbling bright, sunny selections from Vivaldi's Four Seasons. It is my equivalent of the cowbell that hikers wear when they know they are in bear country.

Meaning and Purpose

1. Staples claims that he has the power "to alter public space in ugly ways" (paragraph 2). How and from where did he derive that power?
2. In what ways has this "ability to alter public space" affected Staples?

3. Does Staples suggest any solutions for the profound problems he describes in the essay?
4. Does Staples speak only for himself when he says in paragraph 11 that he "learned to smother [his] rage"? Explain.

Strategy

1. Staples begins his essay with an anecdote (see the term **anecdote** in the Glossary). Comment on the effectiveness of this introduction.
2. What is the function of paragraph 2?
3. Staples's claim that he has the "ability to alter public space in ugly ways" is rather abstract and vague. How does he make the term fully understandable to the reader?

Style

1. Is there a discrepancy between the language that Staples uses and the subject he describes? If there is, describe the effect that discrepancy creates.
2. In the first paragraph, Staples calls a woman who walked in front of him his "victim." Why is that designation ironic (see **irony** in the Glossary)? Is any real victim described in the essay?
3. Explain the analogy Staples uses in the final sentence.
4. If necessary, look up the following in a dictionary: *affluent, mean, impoverished, discreet* (paragraph 1); *unwieldy, quarry, dicey, foyer* (2); *taut* (4); *warrenlike, bandolier, forge, solace* (5); *bravado* (7); *ad hoc, labyrinthine* (8); *cursory* (9); *skittish* (11); *constitutionals, steely, warbling* (12).

Writing Tasks

1. Using Staples's essay as a model, write an essay that describes how you or someone else have altered public space—how you or someone else, in other words, have changed other people's behavior or

attitudes by merely being present. Make sure you use as many examples as you can to demonstrate your points.

2. Write an essay in which you argue for or against Staples's point of view. Whatever position you take, make sure your thesis is clear, and be sure to refer to Staples's points in your essay. Be sure, too, to use plenty of examples to illustrate the validity of your observations.'

❦ Caryl Rivers ❦

Caryl Rivers, born in 1937, is a graduate of Trinity College and Columbia University and a freelance writer who has taught journalism at Boston University. She has written a number of nonfiction books and several novels, including Beyond Sugar and Spice: How Girls and Women Develop Competence; For Better, for Worse, *a humorous account of her own married life with journalist Alan Lupo;* More Joy Than Rage: Crossing Generations With the New Feminism; Slick Spins and Fractured Facts: How Cultural Myths Distort the News; She Works/He Works: How Two-Income Families Are Happy, Healthy, and Thriving; *and* Camelot.

The Issue Isn't Sex, It's Violence

Grounded in feminism, Rivers casts a critical eye on the impact of social and political experience on women. In "The Issue Isn't Sex, It's Violence," a 1985 Boston Globe *article, Rivers identifies the legitimization of violence, not sex, as the social danger embedded in some rock lyrics. Notice how effectively she uses hypothetical examples to illustrate her discussion.*

After a grisly series of murders in California, possibly inspired by the lyrics of a rock song, we are hearing a familiar chorus: Don't blame rock and roll. It's all just adolescent rebellion. Kids will be kids. They love to rebel, and the more shocking the stuff, the better they like it. 1

There's some truth in this, of course. I loved to watch Elvis shake his torso when I was a teenager, and it was even more fun when Ed Sullivan wouldn't let the cameras show him below the waist. I snickered at the forbidden "Rock with Me, Annie" lyrics by a black Rhythm and Blues group, which were deliciously naughty. But I am sorry, rock fans, that is not the same thing as hearing lyrics about how a man is going to force a woman to perform oral sex on him at gunpoint in a little number called "Eat Me Alive." It is not in the 2

272

same league with a song about the delights of slipping into a woman's room while she is sleeping and murdering her, the theme of an AC/DC ballad that allegedly inspired the California slayer.

Make no mistake, it is not sex we are talking about here, but vio-   3
lence. Violence against women. Most rock songs are not violent—they are funky, sexy, rebellious and sometimes witty. Please do not mistake me for a Mrs. Grundy. If Prince wants to leap about wearing only a purple jock strap, fine. Let Mick Jagger unzip his fly as he gyrates, if he wants to. But when either one of them starts garroting, beating or sodomizing a woman in their number, that is another story.

I always find myself annoyed when "intellectual" men dismiss   4
violence against women with a yawn, as if it were beneath their dignity to notice. I wonder if the reaction would be the same if the violence were directed against someone other than women. How many people would yawn and say, "Oh, kids will be kids," if a rock group did a nifty little number called "Lynchin," in which stringing up and stomping on black people were set to music? Who would chuckle and say, "Oh, just a little adolescent rebellion" if a group of rockers went on MTV dressed as Nazis, desecrating synagogues and beating up Jews to the beat of twanging guitars?

I'll tell you what would happen. Prestigious dailies would thun-   5
der on editorial pages: senators would fall over each other to get denunciations into the *Congressional Record*. The president would appoint a commission to clean up the music business.

But violence against women is greeted by silence. It shouldn't be.   6

This does not mean censorship, or book (or record) burning. In   7
a society that protects free expression, we understand a lot of stuff will float up out of the sewer. Usually, we recognize the ugly stuff that advocates violence against any group as the garbage it is, and we consider its purveyors as moral lepers. We hold our nose and tolerate it, but we speak out against the values it proffers.

But images of violence against women are not staying on the   8
fringes of society. No longer are they found only in tattered, paper-covered books or in movie houses where winos snooze and the scent of urine fills the air. They are entering the mainstream at a rapid rate. This is happening at a time when the media, more and more, set the agenda for the public debate. They are a powerful legitimizing

force—especially television. Many people regard what they see on TV as the truth; Walter Cronkite once topped a poll as the most trusted man in America.

Now, with the advent of rock videos and all-music channels, rock music has grabbed a big chunk of legitimacy. American teenagers have instant access, in their living rooms, to the messages of rock, on the same vehicle that brought them "Sesame Street." Who can blame them if they believe that the images they see are accurate reflections of adult reality, approved by adults? After all, Big Bird used to give them lessons on the same little box. Adults, by their silence, sanction the images. Do we really want our kids to think that rape and violence are what sexuality is all about? 9

This is not a trivial issue. Violence against women is a major social problem, one that's more than a cerebral issue to me. I teach at Boston University, and one of my most promising young journalism students was raped and murdered. Two others told me of being raped. Recently, one female student was assaulted and beaten so badly she had $5,000 worth of medical bills and permanent damage to her back and eyes. 10

It's nearly impossible, of course, to make a cause-and-effect link between lyrics and images and acts of violence. But images have a tremendous power to create an atmosphere in which violence against certain people is sanctioned. Nazi propagandists knew that full well when they portrayed Jews as ugly, greedy and powerful. 11

The outcry over violence against women, particularly in a sexual context, is being legitimized in two ways: by the increasing movement of these images into the mainstream of the media in TV, films, magazines, albums, videos, and by the silence about it. 12

Violence, of course, is rampant in the media. But it is usually set in some kind of moral context. It's usually only the bad guys who commit violent acts against the innocent. When the good guys get violent, it's against those who deserve it. Dirty Harry blows away the scum, he doesn't walk up to a toddler and say, "Make my day." The A Team does not shoot up suburban shopping malls. 13

But in some rock songs, it's the "heroes" who commit the acts. The people we are programmed to identify with are the ones being violent, with women on the receiving end. In a society where rape 14 and assaults on women are endemic, this is no small problem, with millions of young boys watching on their TV screens and listening on their Walkmans.

I think something needs to be done. I'd like to see people in the industry respond to the problem. I'd love to see some women rock stars speak out against violence against women. I would like to see disc jockeys refuse air play to records and videos that contain such violence. At the very least, I want to see the end of the silence. I want journalists and parents and critics and performing artists to keep this issue alive in the public forum. I don't want people who are concerned about this issue labeled as bluenoses and book-burners and ignored.

And I wish it wasn't always just women who are speaking out. Men have as large a stake in the quality of our civilization as women do in the long run. Violence is a contagion that infects at random. Let's hear something, please, from the men.

Meaning and Purpose

1. In the first paragraph of this essay, Rivers says, "Don't blame rock and roll." Obviously, rock and roll isn't the only popular music we hear. What other popular music reflects her main point in this paragraph? Give two examples of music titles, along with the messages in their lyrics, to show that this is true.

2. Rivers notes in paragraph 4 that " 'intellectual' men dismiss violence against women with a yawn." Why does she put the word *intellectual* in quotes?

3. In paragraph 12, Rivers notes two ways in which violence against women is being legitimized, one of them being "the silence about it." How does being silent about violence against women "legitimize" that violence?

4. The author says in the last paragraph of the essay that "Violence . . . infects at random." How does that claim reinforce the main topic of the essay?

5. After reading this essay, what would you say is the author's most *immediate* purpose for having written it?

Strategy

1. Why does Rivers make it a point to tell her reader, in paragraph 14, that the "heroes" in popular music should be blamed in part for violence against women?
2. The British philosopher Stephen Toulmin says that a claim is a statement of belief or truth. In your words, what claim is made in paragraph 15?
3. Paragraph 6 ends with the sentence, "It shouldn't be." What "shouldn't be"? Is the author stating a claim or a fact? How can you tell?
4. Paragraph 5 deals with an effect, anything brought about by a cause or an agent. According to the author, what is the cause or agent that has led to this effect?
5. Although this essay discusses the effects of song lyrics on their listeners, Rivers says in paragraph 11 that it is "nearly impossible, of course, to make a cause-and-effect link between lyrics and images and acts of violence." How does this statement strengthen or weaken the examples that she gives to support her main point?

Style

1. Why does the author deliberately use the trite expression "Kids will be kids" in her opening paragraph?
2. In paragraph 8, what is meant by the phrase "fringes of society"?
3. How does the word *nifty,* in paragraph 4, seem particularly appropriate in its context?
4. A rhetorical question is a question that is not meant to be answered by its reader. Why, then, does the author end paragraph 9 with a rhetorical question?
5. In paragraph 4, why does the author suggests "Lynchin" as a song title, instead of the correctly spelled term "Lynching"?

Writing Tasks

1. Each of us has listened to the kind of music that the author refers to. Write an essay in which you mention three or more currently popular song titles and their lyrics that show that what the author

says is true today, not true today, or probably true today. Explain by using lyrics as examples of why your opinion is valid.

2. Using your knowledge of modern popular music, write an essay that shows by examples from lyrics, from the actions of performers, and from what takes place during performances themselves, whether on television or in person, how popular music endorses a movement or an opinion.

❦ David G. Meyers ❦

David G. Meyers is a social psychologist who teaches at Hope College in Holland, Michigan. His scientific writing has been supported by National Science Foundation grants and fellowships and recognized by the Gordon Allport Prize. His articles have appeared in more than three dozen periodicals, including American Scientist, American Psychologist, Psychological Science, Scientific American, Christian Century, *and* Skeptic, *where the following essay first appeared. He has also authored fifteen books:* The Pursuit of Happiness: Who is Happy—and Why *(1992),* The American Paradox: Spiritual Hunger in an Age of Plenty *(2000), and* Intuition: Its Powers and Perils *(2002) among his latest. Meyers, born in Seattle, is an all-weather bicyclist, an avid noontime basketball player, and a fan of his college's basketball teams.*

Do We Fear the Right Things?

In the following essay, David G. Meyers writes about a complex social/psychological phenomenon and makes it both understandable and interesting for the lay reader. He does this by using examples all of us are familiar with.

Examples clarify points by making them concrete for the reader. Notice as you read how Meyers illustrates each of his points with an example, more often with multiple examples.

"Most people reason dramatically, not quantitatively," said Oliver 1
Wendell Holmes. Even before the horror of 9/11, many Americans feared flying. "Every time I get off a plane, I view it as a failed suicide attempt," movie director Barry Sonnenfeld has said. With 9/11's four crashed airliners vividly in mind, and with threats of more terror to come, cancellations understandably have left airlines, travel agencies, and holiday hotels nose diving into the red. Airport security personnel are treating all approaching cars and even our elderly and children as potential threats. All told, we're preparing to spend $100

billion a year on Homeland security. Our society is understandably terrorized by terrorism.

Do our intuitive fears fit the facts? How closely do our percep-   2
tions of life's various risks correspond to actual risks?

Ironically, after 9/11 the terrorists continued killing us, in ways   3
unnoticed. In the ensuing months, Americans flew 20 percent less. "No way are we flying to Florida for vacation!" Instead, we drove many of those miles, which surely caused more additional highway deaths than occurred on those four ill-fated flights.

Consider: The National Safety Council reports that in the last   4
half of the 1990s Americans were, mile for mile, 37 times more likely to die in a vehicle crash than on a commercial flight. Commercial flying is so safe that our odds of dying on any flight have been less than the likelihood of our tossing heads 22 consecutive times in a row. When I fly to New York, the most dangerous part of my journey is my drive to the Grand Rapids airport.

Believe it or not, terrorists, perish the thought, could have taken   5
down 50 more planes with 60 passengers each in 2001 and—had we kept flying (speaking hypothetically)—we would still have finished 2001 safer in planes than on the road. Flying may be scary (531 people died on U.S. scheduled airlines in 2001). But driving the same distance should be many times scarier.

Why do we intuitively fear the wrong things? Why do so many   6
smokers (whose habit shortens their lives, on average, by about five years) fret before flying (which, averaged across people, shortens life by one day)? Why do we fear violent crime more than clogged arteries? Why do we fear terrorism more than accidents—which kill nearly as many per week in just the United States as did terrorism with its 2,527 worldwide deaths in all of the 1990s. Even with the horrific scale of 9/11, more Americans in 2001 died of food poisoning (which scares few) than terrorism (which scares many).

Psychological science has identified four influences on our intu-   7
itions about risk. First, we fear what our ancestral history has prepared us to fear. Human emotions were road tested in the Stone Age. Yesterday's risks prepare us to fear snakes, lizards, and spiders, although all three combined now kill virtually no one in developed

countries. Flying may be far safer than biking, but our biological past predisposes us to fear confinement and heights, and therefore flying.

Second, we fear what we cannot control. Skiing, by one estimate, poses 1000 times the health and injury risk of food preservatives. Yet many people gladly assume the risk of skiing, which they control, but avoid preservatives. Driving we control, flying we do not. "We are loathe to let others do unto us what we happily do to ourselves," noted risk analyst Chauncey Starr.

Third, we fear what is immediate. Teens are indifferent to smoking's toxicity because they live more for the present than the distant future. Much of the plane's threat is telescoped into the moments of takeoff and landing, while the dangers of driving are diffused across many moments to come, each trivially dangerous.

Fourth, we fear what is most readily available in memory. Horrific images of a DC-10 catapulting across the Sioux City runway, or the Concorde exploding in Paris, or of United Flight 175 slicing into the World Trade Center, form indelible memories. And availability in memory provides our intuitive rule for judging risks. Thousands of safe car trips (for most of those who have survived to read this) have extinguished our anxieties about driving.

In less familiar realms, vivid, memorable images dominate our fears. We can know that unprovoked great white shark attacks have claimed merely 67 lives worldwide since 1876. Yet, after watching *Jaws* and reading vivid accounts of Atlantic coastal shark attacks, we may feel chills when an underwater object brushes our leg. A thousand massively publicized anthrax victims would similarly rivet our attention more than yet another 20,000+ annual U.S. influenza fatalities, or another 30,000+ annual gun deaths.

As publicized Powerball lottery winners cause us to overestimate the infinitesimal odds of lottery success, so vivid airline casualties cause us to overestimate the infinitesimal odds of a lethal airline ticket. We comprehend Mario Grasso's winning $197 million in a 1999 Powerball lottery. We do not comprehend the 328 million losing tickets that provided the jackpot. We comprehend the 266 passengers and crew on those four fated flights. We do not comprehend the vast numbers of accident-free flights—16 million consecutive fatality-free takeoffs and landings during one stretch of the 1990s. Dramatic outcomes capture our attention, probabilities we hardly grasp. The result—we overvalue lottery tickets, overestimate flight risk, and underestimate the dangers of driving.

And smoking. Imagine, suggests mathematician Sam Saunders, 13 that cigarettes were harmless—except for a single cigarette in every 50,000 packs that is filled with dynamite instead of tobacco. There would be a trivial risk of having your head blown off, yet enough to produce more gruesome deaths daily than occurred at terrorists' hands on 9/11—surely enough to have cigarettes banned everywhere. Ironically, the lost lives from these dynamite-loaded cigarettes would be far less than from today's actual cigarettes, which annually kill some 3 million of the tobacco industry's best customers, the equivalent of 20 loaded jumbo jets daily. Yet rather than spend billions to prevent further carnage, as with Homeland security spending, our government subsidizes tobacco.

Because we fear too little those threats that will claim lives un- 14 dramatically, one by one (rather than in bunches), we will also spend hundreds of billions to save thousands instead of spending a few billion to save millions. A 2002 report by Deloitte Consulting and *Aviation Week* projected that the United States would spend between $93 and $138 billion during 2003 to deter potential terrorism.

Alternatively, $1.5 billion a year would be the U.S. share of a 15 global effort to cut world hunger in half by 2015, according to a 2001 study done for the U.S. Agency for International Development. Ten billion dollars a year would spare 29 million world citizens from developing AIDS by 2010, according to a joint report by representatives of the United Nations, the World Health Organization, and others. And a few tens of billions spent converting cars to hybrid engines and constructing renewable energy sources could help avert the anticipated future catastrophe of global warming via drought-fed wildfires, rain-fed floods, heat-fed tornadoes and hurricanes, and glacier-fed rising tides, which threaten to overrun lowland places such as Bangladesh, the Netherlands, and south Florida. While agonizing over missed signals of the 9/11 horror, are we missing the clearer indications of greater horrors to come? "Osama bin Laden can't destroy Western civilization," observed *New York Times* columnist Paul Krugman. "Carbon dioxide can."

The moral: It is perfectly normal to fear purposeful violence 16 from those who hate us. When terrorists strike again, likely where unexpected, we will all recoil in horror. But smart thinkers will also want to check their intuitive fears against the facts. To be prudent is to be mindful of the realities of how humans die. By so doing, we can take away the terrorists' most omnipresent weapon—exaggerated fear. If our fears cause us to live and spend in ways that fail to avert tomorrow's biggest dangers, then we surely do have something to fear from fear itself.

Meaning and Purpose

1. In the first paragraph, Meyers quotes Oliver Wendell Holmes: "Most people reason dramatically, not quantitatively." What does this mean in the context of Meyers's essay?
2. Meyers claims that after 9/11 terrorists continued to kill Americans in "unnoticed" ways (paragraph 3). Explain what he means by that.
3. What four psychological factors sometimes misguide people's intuitions about risk?
4. Explain why many people have a greater fear of airplane accidents than they do of car accidents, especially when they are in far greater danger in cars.
5. How does psychology at least partially explain why some people choose to smoke?

Strategy

1. Meyers presents his thesis in paragraph 2 in the form of two questions. What are the answers to those questions? Why would he put his thesis in the form of questions?

2. What effect does Meyers create by asking a series of questions in paragraph 6?
3. In paragraph 15 Meyers says that global warming, if ignored, could cause tides "which threaten to overrun lowland places such as Bangladesh, the Netherlands, and south Florida." For what strategic purpose would he list those countries in that particular order?

Style

1. In paragraph 1 Meyers claims that 9/11 and other terrorist threats have caused many travel businesses to "[nose-dive] into the red." Explain the peculiar aptness of that metaphor.
2. Meyers's final statement that "we surely do have something to fear from fear itself" is an inverted paraphrase of a famous line in a speech of President Franklin Delano Roosevelt. Find Roosevelt's actual quote in a book of famous quotations or on the Internet and comment on the effectiveness of Meyers's allusion.

Writing Tasks

1. In paragraphs 7–10 Meyers explains four influences that cause people to make inappropriate decisions about risk. Choose any two or three of these influences and write a paper in which you examine how those influences work in the risk-assessment judgments of people you observe firsthand. Make sure to refer back to Meyers's essay in your discussion, and also make sure to use multiple examples to illustrate your points, as Meyers does throughout his essay.
2. In paragraphs 13–15 Meyers alludes to some public policies that, he suggests, might be ill conceived and counterproductive because of the misjudgment of risks. Reread these passages carefully, choose one of the policies he alludes to, conduct some library and Internet research on your subject, and write a paper in which you take a position on the issue. Make sure to refer to Meyers's observations in your argument, and, like him, use plenty of examples to bolster your argument.

❦ John Kifner ❦

John Kifner writes on war and politics for The New York Times. *He has won several prestigious awards for his writing.*

Good as a Gun:
When Cameras Define a War

In this essay, first published in The New York Times, *November 3, 2003, John Kifner comments on a series of war photographs that have already shaped the thinking of many Americans and another series from Iraq that might do the same in the future. As you read the essay, pause and examine the photos carefully. Are they emotive? How? Do they reinforce your attitudes toward these wars or do they challenge your beliefs? How? Do any of the photos appear posed to you? If some do, how does that affect your response to them?*

    Note how Kifner illustrates his points with numerous examples.

Modern war has given us iconic images that both shape and reflect our views of conflict.   1

Consider, for example, the differences among some famous photographs burned into the nation's memory—the picture of the triumphant marines raising the flag over Iwo Jima toward the end of World War II and then a grim triptych from Vietnam: images of a police chief shooting a Vietcong prisoner in the head, a naked, screaming little girl burned by napalm running down a road, and a helicopter lifting off the roof of the American embassy, leaving Vietnamese allies behind as Saigon fell.   2

Last week began and ended with two startling images that seemed to portray the conflict in Iraq in very different ways and reflected the battle over what images will define this war.   3

For a brief, ugly moment, it seemed there might be an iconic image of a faltering American effort. It was a picture of the body of an   4

American soldier splayed out on a street in Mosul, accompanied by early—and now apparently erroneous—wire service accounts that a mob had slit the throats of two soldiers and mutilated their bodies.

"Bastards" was the one-word headline over the picture on the   5
front page of *The Daily News*; other newspapers gave similarly prominent coverage.

The iconic image on Iwo Jima inspired pride and passion.

Taken after a napalm attack, this image captured the suffering of the South Vietnamese.

The reason these two deaths so   6
resonated is that they immediately evoked another iconic image: an American soldier's body being dragged through the streets of Mogadishu after Army Rangers trying to capture a warlord were shot down in their Black Hawk helicopter, bringing an abrupt and embarrassing American withdrawal from Somalia. The syndicated cartoonist Jeff Danziger quickly produced a drawing showing two beleaguered G.I.s under fire in Iraq. "Well, at least we know this isn't Vietnam," says the first, and his comrade answers: "No. . . . It's SOMALIA."

Then newspaper front pages   7
and television news programs across the country were dominated by the image of President Bush in an army windbreaker, alternately teary-eyed and grinning, holding a Thanksgiving turkey on a platter, surrounded by cheering soldiers in a mess tent at Baghdad International Airport.

The president's stealthy, star-   8
tling trip to Iraq on a blacked-out

The photograph of a Vietcong prisoner being shot brought home the brutality of the war.

The evacuation of Saigon at the Vietnam war's end evoked terror facing those left behind.

Air Force One accompanied by only a handful of aides and a tiny press pool was intended, White House officials said, to boost the morale of troops, many of whom are disgruntled over their extended and increasingly dangerous deployment, and to emphasize his determination to, as he puts it, "stay the course."

But, in a sense, it was also a corrective to an earlier image artfully arranged by Mr. Bush's handlers: his swaggering arrival in a flight suit on an aircraft carrier outfitted with a banner reading "Mission Accomplished." Since the president declared major hostilities over on the flight deck that May 1, at least 287 service personnel have been killed in steadily mounting attacks—nearly twice as many as in the war itself. November has been the deadliest month, with more than 60 soldiers killed in hostile actions, more than in any other month.   9

The so-called *Top Gun* landing had clearly been designed as a tri-   10
umphal image that would play a prominent part in the president's re-election campaign. Instead, it now seems a symbol of the naïve, almost willful, optimism that has marked the administration's plan to overthrow Saddam Hussein and, in so doing, usher in a new era of democracy in the Middle East. Indeed, that footage will now almost inevitably figure in the campaign of whomever the Democrats finally nominate.

"You furnish the pictures and I'll furnish the war," the press lord   11
William Randolph Hearst is reputed to have telegraphed the artist

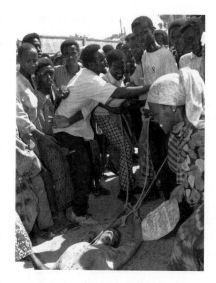

The image of a soldier's body helped lead to the United States' withdrawal from Somalia.

The image of a dead American conjured up the dangers of the occupation of Iraq.

Frederic Remington when he complained there was little action in Cuba. And, when the battleship *Maine* exploded in Havana's harbor on February 15, 1898, under circumstances that are still mysterious, killing some 250 officers, sailors, and marines, Mr. Hearst quickly put the blame on Spain. His *New York Journal* published a drawing on its front page showing a mine beneath the ship. "Maine is great thing. Arouse everybody," he telegraphed another of his subordinates as *The Journal* led the rest of the "yellow press" in pushing the country into war.

The sinking of the *Maine*—the Tonkin Gulf incident of its time— was an early example of how an image became an idea that drove action. In today's world of instant communication and 24-hour news cycles, one is constantly bombarded with successive, fleeting images competing for dominance. After the first Gulf War, a reluctant America was forced into a military relief effort by pictures and news footage of sick and starving Kurds who had fled into Turkey after they had been encouraged to revolt against Saddam Hussein and then abandoned. The success of that relief operation, along with images of famine in Somalia, then drew the United States into a similar relief operation that turned into a

12

President Bush's surprise visit to Iraq dominated news following Thanksgiving.

President Bush's aircraft carrier visit seems naïve.

disaster, leaving the memory of *Black Hawk Down*.

Those in charge, of course, seek   13
to control the image and thus the idea. When a young Marine corporal climbed up the statue of Saddam Hussein in Baghdad in April and put an American flag over its head, someone realized this was sending the wrong message—conquest—to the Iraqis. The flag was removed and troops were told not to fly American flags. The desired image was the footage of Iraqis smacking the fallen statue with their shoes— an Arab gesture of contempt— although, in truth, the statue was pulled over by a Marine tank.

But for all the efforts to con-   14
trol or create an image, it is most often reality, caught randomly in the lens of a photographer, that helps determine what we think. And the likelihood is, we have yet to see the defining image from Iraq. And we don't yet know whether the image of Mr. Bush in Baghdad will define his presidency.

Meaning and Purpose

1. Reread the first paragraph and then carefully study the image of the World War II American soldiers raising the flag at Iwo Jima. How ef-

fectively does it, as Kifner claims, inspire pride and patriotism? Does the image in any way reinforce the thoughts and feelings you have about World War II? If you are already familiar with the photo, did it in any way shape your thoughts and feelings about the war? Explain.

2. In what way does the photograph from Mogadishu (paragraph 6) shed light on the photo from Mosul (paragraph 4)?

3. What two reasons does Kifner give for the photos of President Bush serving Thanksgiving dinner to the troops in Iraq being taken? Could both reasons be valid? Do you tend to think one is more valid than the other? Why?

4. Which of the photos presented in the essay appear staged or posed? Do you think you would feel differently about any of the photos if you knew they were staged for political purposes? Explain.

Strategy

1. Kifner states a version of his thesis in the first paragraph and then restates and refines it in the final paragraph. Explain that refinement.

2. In what specific way does paragraph 2 clarify the essay's thesis?

3. Kifner's essay was first published in a newspaper and employs relatively short paragraphs to fit a newspaper's narrow column format. A typical academic essay generally needs more fully developed paragraphs to be effective. Reread the essay carefully, with paragraph organization in mind, and then go back and restructure the essay by combining some of the paragraphs. Make sure to do this using solid organizational principles.

Style

1. In paragraph 9 Kifner describes President Bush's arrival on an aircraft carrier as "swaggering." In the next paragraph he calls the incident a *Top Gun* landing. How do those terms connect, and what effect do they create?

2. If necessary, look up the following words in a dictionary: *iconic* (paragraph 1); *triptych* (2); *resonated* (6).

Writing Tasks

1. Make a list of photographs that are memorable to you, for whatever reasons. Examine those photos closely, choose two or three of them, and then write an essay in which you explain why those images are meaningful to you. You can attach copies of the photos to your essay if you wish, but write the essay as if you were not including them. That means you will have to supply your reader with a detailed description of each photo in the course of your discussion.
2. In his conclusion to "Good as a Gun: When Cameras Define a War," John Kifner says "we have yet to see the defining image from Iraq." Choose a series of photos from the war in Iraq that define for you the character of that war, and write an essay in which you explain just how those images define that war. Choose your photos from newspapers, magazines (print and/or online), or Kifner's essay.

❦ Responding to Photographs ❦

Examples

Style Is the Man

What is style? If we say a certain person has style, what exactly do we mean? Is it behavior? Clothing? Speech? Posture? Grooming? All of these? Some other things? Does everyone have style or do only a few?

Style might be hard to define precisely, but we know it when we see it, right? And most people would undoubtedly agree that the young man in the photograph "Style Is the Man" has it.

Style communicates. Before interacting with a person, we form impressions based on some elements at least of his or her personal style. We may be able to trace this impression to very specific things, or we may say we just have a feeling but are unable to specify particulars. A style may be created consciously and purposefully (perhaps to deceive), or it may simply grow out of the true values and accumulated experiences of the individual.

After reviewing the material at the beginning of this chapter, complete one of the following writing tasks.

1. Using specific examples from the photograph as your method of development, write a paper that characterizes the style portrayed by the young man. Begin with a short physical description of the man leading to a generalization about his style and the attitude and values it communicates to you. Then examine various items and aspects of his appearance, and discuss each as a specific example that led you to your interpretation of his message.

2. Write a paper combining typical and specific examples. Find three photographs of humans, each showing a different sense of style. These need not be as dramatic as the style illustrated in "Style Is the Man," though they may be. As in task 1, begin with a short description of the three photographs leading to a generalization about each style and what it communicates to you. In the discussion section of your paper, point to specific examples in each photograph that support your generalization, and then relate typical examples of the expected behavior, dress, and attitudes of a member of each style group. Include the photographs when you submit your final draft.

❦ Additional Writing Tasks ❦
Examples

1. Write an essay on one of the general statements listed here or on a general statement that you compose. Throughout your essay, use examples to illustrate your main idea or thesis. Your discussion should include a mixture of typical and specific examples. Remember that you are not bound by any of these statements; you may rewrite them to reflect your interests, or you may compose your own.
   a. People must assume responsibility for their actions.
   b. Success comes from 5 percent talent and 95 percent hard work.
   c. Vandals control the night in local neighborhoods.
   d. Teenagers can learn both positive and negative lessons about economic survival from part-time jobs.
   e. Graffiti scrawled on walls throughout the city carry psychological messages about human behavior.
   f. Books I have read have taught me a great deal about life.
   g. Bumper stickers reveal a person's values.
   h. Public obscenity is objectionable.
   i. Life in the fast lane leads to head-on collisions.
2. Write a full essay related to one of these situations. Be sure that examples serve as the dominant essay pattern of development.
   a. Some contemporary political figures have demonstrated courage in office. Using examples from recent history, write an essay illustrating how important political courage is.
   b. Society seems to require more and more cooperation among individuals and groups to function effectively. Write an essay illustrating how cooperation is needed for success.
   c. Although society seems to require more and more cooperation among individuals and groups, the values of the "rugged individualist" are still required for success. Write an essay illustrating how much "rugged individualism" helps in becoming successful.
   d. Often the better moments in life go unnoticed. Recollect some of your better moments, and write an essay making use of them to illustrate what they have taught you.

e. Magazine advertisers attempt to entice customers to buy products not by high quality but by associating the products with selected lifestyles. Write an essay illustrating that some magazine advertisements encourage consumers to buy products for the wrong reasons.

3. Read this paragraph from Jack Solomon's *The Signs of Our Time,* in which he generally concentrates on the messages that clothing communicates in American society.

> The complexity of the dress code in America, the astonishing range of styles that are available to us in our choice of clothing designs, directly reflects the cultural diversity of our country. Americans are differentiated by ethnic, regional, religious, and racial differences that are all expressed in the clothing they wear. Age differences, political differences, class differences, and differences in personal taste further divide us into finer and finer sub-cultures that maintain, and even assert, their sense of distinct identity through their characteristic clothing. From the severe black suits of the Amish to the safety-pinned T-shirts and chains of punk culture, Americans tell one another who they are through the articles of their dress.

Write an essay, with examples as the dominant method of development, illustrating Solomon's general observation that "Americans tell one another who they are through the articles of their dress."

8

Comparison and Contrast
Presenting Similarities and Differences

The Method

In conversation we often hear comments that could lead to **comparison and contrast:**

"I eat vegetables, fruits, grains, nuts, and dairy products. It is a lot healthier than a diet that includes red meat, fowl, and even fish."

"Strip away the rhetoric and compare their economic platforms; you will see few differences between Republicans and Democrats."

"The effects of marijuana are no more harmful than those of alcohol. In fact they may be less harmful."

No doubt in class discussions, at family gatherings, or during arguments at the local pizza parlor you have heard similar comments. How such comparisons are developed in conversation probably depends on the group's mood and analytical talent. Nevertheless, a fundamental principle is at work: We all make decisions by comparing and contrasting our options.

To compare is to point out similarities; to contrast is to point out differences. Poems and song lyrics are often similar in some ways: Both often rhyme; they are constructed on rhythmic patterns; sometimes they repeat key lines. They also have one major difference: Poems are written to be spoken; songs are written to be sung to music. Presenting similarities and differences is a common technique not only in conversation but also in all forms of writing, including essays, research papers, reports, and examinations.

Commonly, writers include informal comparisons that are merely incidental to the dominant essay pattern. Often such brief comparisons are implied rather than fully developed, merely suggesting a comparison. This paragraph opens an essay explaining the causes directing new trends in city planning.

In southern California, historically known for its suburban sprawl, city planning seems to have come full circle. Using the concept of the traditional village, planners are designing new urban villages that feature a main street and a mix of stores, offices, town halls, and parks. They are trying to re-create the traditional village by designing neighborhoods where thousands of residents can live and work, where they can walk to shopping and stroll to places of entertainment.

The writer, Jack Scott, does not intend to compare traditional with contemporary city design; he alludes to traditional design merely to place his reader in familiar territory.

When writers use comparison and contrast as a dominant essay pattern, they explore their subjects in detail, applying several principles to guide the composition. To sharpen your critical eye and read as a writer reads, be aware of these general principles.

Strategies

Professional writers know they need a basis for the comparison: Any subjects they choose to compare must belong to the same general category. If the subjects do not belong to that category, the writers have no logical reason to enumerate the similarities and differences. Usually, but not always, the general categories are obvious. For such a discussion, consider hammerhead sharks, great white sharks, chimpanzees, and dolphins.

Comparing and contrasting a hammerhead with a great white shark is clearly logical because although they are similar, they differ in several distinctive ways. But to compare and contrast a chimpanzee with a great white shark is clearly illogical. Yes, they belong to a category that we might call "living creatures," but do you see any other basis for a comparison? The chimpanzee is a mammal, the great white shark a fish. One lives on land, the other in the sea. One is a hunter, the other a forager. To compare and contrast them just would not make much sense.

To compare and contrast a dolphin and a great white shark, however, does make sense. Even though the dolphin is a mammal, it is a marine mammal. The dolphin and the great white shark are also shaped roughly alike, but with significant differences. Perhaps most important, both the dolphin and the great white shark are significant in sea lore. In fact, Hollywood films featuring a dolphin and a great white shark have been box-office hits, such as *Flipper* and *Jaws*.

What about comparing a dolphin and a chimpanzee? Although they are not obvious selections, both are categorized as mammals. A writer might ask whether their both being mammals makes them subjects worth comparing and contrasting. What else do they have in common? Close examination reveals that scientists are studying communication patterns of both chimpanzees and dolphins. Perhaps they are in the limited category of animals that communicate with human beings. Taking up this similarity, a writer might explore the possibility of comparing chimpanzees and dolphins.

Now we must consider an exception to the principle that subjects should belong to the same general category if they are to be logically compared. This figurative comparison is called **analogy.** Writers use analogy to explain something that is difficult to understand by describing it as if it were something familiar. A writer might choose to explain life by comparing it with a river, watching a situation comedy with taking a narcotic, or being in love with riding a roller coaster. Writers of analogy are interested only in using one subject to explain another; they are not out to explain the major similarities and differences of both subjects equally, as they would be when writing a typical comparison-and-contrast passage.

In this following paragraph, humorist James Thurber develops an analogy by comparing his editor Harold Ross to a skilled auto mechanic.

> Having a manuscript under Ross's scrutiny was like putting your car in the hands of a skilled mechanic, not an automotive engineer with a bachelor of science degree, but a guy who knows what makes a motor go, and sputter, and wheeze, and sometimes come to a dead stop; a man with an ear for the faintest body squeak as well as the loudest engine rattle. When you first gazed, appalled, upon an uncorrected proof of one of your stories or articles, each margin had a thicket of queries and complaints—one writer got a hundred and forty-four on one profile. It was as though you beheld the works of your car spread all over the garage floor, and the job of getting the thing together again and making it work seemed impossible. Then

you realized that Ross was trying to make your Model T or old Stutz Bearcat into a Cadillac or Rolls-Royce. He was at work with the tools of his unflagging perfectionism, and, after an exchange of growls or snarls, you set to work to join him in his enterprise.

Clearly, Thurber has stuck to the principle of analogy: He uses the familiar work of an auto mechanic to explain the unfamiliar work of a magazine editor.

Professional writers are always wary of confusing their readers. As you study comparison-and-contrast essays, notice how writers immediately orient their readers by informing them that a comparison and contrast follows.

Read the opening paragraph in Russell Baker's "From Song to Sound: Elvis and Bing." Baker quickly establishes that he will compare two eras and the popular singers who represent them.

> The grieving for Elvis Presley and the commercial exploitation of his death were still not ended when we heard of Bing Crosby's death the other day. Here is a generational puzzle. Those of an age to mourn Elvis must marvel that their elders could really have cared about Bing, just as the Crosby generation a few weeks ago wondered what all the to-do was about when Elvis died.

Baker's opening paragraph gives a clear idea that the essay is headed into comparison and contrast. Most professional writers do likewise, thus keeping their readers on the track.

Professional writers also use clear—and we stress that word—stylistic techniques to keep their readers from becoming confused. Sometimes they use parallel structure to balance the similarities and differences of their subjects. They also use such transitional words and phrases as *on the one hand, on the other hand, in contrast, like,* and *unlike,* words with which they delineate similarities and differences.

In a paragraph from an essay contrasting crows and ravens, Barry Lopez applies both transitional phrases and parallel structures.

> The raven is larger than the crow and has a beard of black feathers at his throat. He is careful to kill only what he needs.

Crows, on the other hand, will search out the great horned owl, kick and punch him awake, and then for roosting too close to their nests, they will kill him. They will come out of the sky on a fat, hot afternoon and slam into the head of a dozing rabbit and go away laughing. They will tear out a whole row of planted corn and eat only a few kernels. They will defecate on scarecrows and go home and sleep with 200,000 of their friends in an atmosphere of congratulation. Again, it is only a game; this should not be taken to mean that they are evil.

In his paragraph, Lopez concentrates primarily on the crow's destructive behavior, contrasting it sharply to the raven in the two sentences describing that black bird. Usually, writers will develop both subjects in more detail. They generally employ one of two organizational strategies when comparing and contrasting: **subject-by-subject** development or **point-by-point** development.

Subject-by-Subject Development

Developing a subject-by-subject comparison is quite simple: All the details of one side of the comparison or contrast are presented first, followed by all the details of the other side. Anthropologist Edward T. Hall uses subject-by-subject development to contrast Arab and American attitudes in a paragraph from *The Hidden Dimension.*

Another silent source of friction between Americans and Arabs is in an area that Americans treat very informally—the manners and rights of the road. In general, in the United States we tend to defer to the vehicle that is bigger, more powerful, faster, and heavily laden. While a pedestrian walking along a road may feel annoyed he will not think it unusual to step aside for a fast-moving automobile. He knows that because he is moving he does not have the right to the space around him that he has when he is standing still. It appears that the reverse is true with the Arabs who apparently *take on rights to space as they move.* For someone else to move into a space an Arab is also moving into is a violation of his rights. It is infuriating to an Arab to have someone else cut in front of him on the highway. It is the American's cavalier treatment of moving space that makes the Arab call him aggressive and pushy.

Hall contrasts these subjects in one paragraph, but sometimes a writer will divide the subjects into separate contrasting paragraphs, as Noel Perrin does in these two discussion paragraphs from his essay "The Two Faces of Vermont."

> On the one hand, it's to the interest of everyone in the tourist trade to keep Vermont (their motels, ski resorts, chambers of commerce, etc., excepted) as old-fashioned as possible. After all, it's weathered red barns with shingle roofs the tourists want to photograph, not concrete-block barns with sheet aluminum on top. Ideally, from the tourist point of view, there should be a man and two boys inside, milking by hand, not a lot of milking machinery pumping directly into a bulk tank. Out back, someone should be turning a grindstone to sharpen an ax—making a last stand, so to speak, against the chainsaw.
>
> On the other hand, the average farmer can hardly wait to modernize. He wants a bulk tank, a couple of arc lights, an automated silo, and a new aluminum roof. Or in a sense he wants these things. Actually, he may like last-stand farming as well as any tourist does, but he can't make a living at it. In my town it's often said that a generation ago a man could raise and educate three children on fifteen cows and still put a little money in the bank. Now his son can just barely keep going with 40 cows. With fifteen cows, hand-milking was possible, and conceivably even economic; with 40 you need all the machinery you can get. But the tourists don't want to hear it clank.

Point-by-Point Development

Subject-by-subject development is effective for an essay of a few paragraphs, but when an essay is longer, the reader might lose track of the information about the first subject while reading about the second. The point-by-point development solves this shortcoming by alternately presenting each point under consideration. Alison Lurie, in a paragraph from *The Language of Clothes,* uses the point-by-point method to compare and contrast boys' and girls' clothes.

> In early childhood girls' and boys' clothes are often identical in cut and fabric, as if in recognition of the fact that their bodies are much alike. But the T-shirts, pull-on slacks and zip jackets intended for boys are usually made in darker colors (especially forest green, navy, red and brown) and printed with designs involving sports, transportation and cute wild animals. Girls' clothes are made in paler colors (especially pink, yellow and green) and decorated with flowers and cute domestic animals. The suggestion is that the boy will play vigorously and travel over long distances; the girl will stay home and nurture plants and small mammals. Alternatively, these designs may symbolize their wearers: the boy is a cuddly bear or a smiling tiger, the girl a flower or a kitten. There is also a tendency for boys' clothes to be fullest at the shoulders and girls' at the hips, anticipating their adult figures. Boys' and men's garments also emphasize the shoulders with horizontal stripes, epaulets or yokes of contrasting color. Girls' and women's garments emphasize the hips and rear through the strategic placement of gathers and trimmings.

Lurie's strategy is quite simple. She organizes the discussion around three points: the different colors of girls' and boys' clothes, the different designs that decorate them, and the different cut. She presents the details point by point, carefully balancing one with the other.

Comparison and Contrast in College Writing

Generally, in college writing, you will compare the similarities and contrast the differences of subjects for one of two reasons: to describe two subjects to clarify them or to evaluate two subjects to determine which is better. For either reason, you must consider the outstanding features of each subject, and when the purpose is evaluation, you must carefully delineate both positive and negative aspects of the subjects.

Guidelines for Writing a Comparison-and-Contrast Essay

1. Select two subjects from the same general category to compare and contrast (unless, of course, you are developing an analogy).
2. With each subject as a focus, use prewriting techniques to generate a list of similarities and differences.
3. Establish your purpose and develop a thesis that does the following:

   • Names the subjects being compared and contrasted and
   • Clearly indicates whether the essay will compare, contrast, or both.

4. Select the points to be compared and contrasted, and decide which should be developed in a subject-by-subject arrangement and which should be developed in a point-by-point arrangement. Organize the paragraphs by placing the most dramatic point last in the sequence.
5. Revise your essay, making sure that you've used clear transitions to keep your reader on track as you move from one subject to the other.

A Student Essay Developed by Comparison and Contrast

For a freshman composition class, Jim Cartozian responded to the following assignment:

> Write an essay with comparison and contrast as the dominant development pattern on one of the following topics:
>
> | | |
> |---|---|
> | a. two athletes | d. two writers |
> | b. two film directors | e. two politicians |
> | c. two artists | f. two newscasters |

Cartozian selected item "d" and compared and contrasted writers Ernest Hemingway and William Faulkner. He had studied them in a

high school American literature course and recalled how different
the two writers seemed to be. He knew that he would have plenty of
material.

Two American Writers: Hemingway and Faulkner

If American writers Ernest Hemingway and William   1
Faulkner were to attend the same party, both would command
attention for different reasons. Hemingway, a big bear of a man,
seemed gregarious, and liked to hold the center of attention. He
was handsome, and some have said he prided himself on being
a lady's man. Faulkner, a frail, soft-spoken man, tended to be
reclusive. He would not seek the attention Hemingway seemed
to thrive on, but would probably find a mantel to lean on.
Speaking in a gentle, lilting voice, Faulkner would tell a story
about the rural South while holding the attention of everyone
within earshot. No two modern American writers have gained
as much worldwide critical recognition as Ernest Hemingway
and William Faulkner; moreover, no two are so obviously different while at the same time sharing significant similarities.

They each won the coveted Nobel Prize for literature, but   2
when the mild-mannered Faulkner won first, the boisterous
Hemingway is said to have lost his temper and then sulked.
Both were publishing at a young age, but Hemingway attracted popular attention early in his career while Faulkner
worked in near obscurity. Hemingway became America's first
modern literary media star. Magazines featured spreads of his
war exploits, his African safaris, and his bullfighting adventures. Faulkner, in contrast, was never a media celebrity. Instead, he seemed to embody the lifestyle of small-town Southern gentry, spending most of his quiet existence in Oxford,
Mississippi. Hemingway set his novels and stories in exotic lo-
cales like France, Spain, and Cuba; Faulkner set his works in
the South, in the mythical Yoknapatawpha County. Each dealt
with very different visions: Hemingway's work displays psychologically wounded characters struggling to establish a personal value code in an absurd world. Faulkner's work displays
characters who are victims of history, suffering because of the
sins of their ancestors, the men who wrenched the land from

Native Americans and enslaved Native Africans. In 1961 Hemingway died violently by his own hand; in 1962 Faulkner died peacefully.

The qualities that made such different men successful novelists are difficult to identify. No doubt their success came from determination and hard work, for both men were dedicated to their craft. But another quality—inspiration—must be figured into the equation. Inspiration that comes from pursuing the creative process is perhaps similar to the spiritual insight that comes from participating in a mystical practice, such as meditation, which is usually performed daily in psychological isolation. Most successful novelists pursue their creative inspiration by isolating themselves, too. Faulkner and Hemingway were no different. Both created special spaces to write in. When Faulkner wrote, he isolated himself in an upstairs bedroom located in the family house. Although Hemingway was more nomadic than Faulkner, he still created a "space apart" to write in no matter where he was living, the most famous one in the tower at his Cuban hacienda.

Too often spiritual insight and creative inspiration are thought to arrive like a bolt of lightning. But mystics claim insight comes from the relentless pursuit of routines. As writers, Faulkner and Hemingway ritually pursued their routines. Hemingway would rise at first light and spend the morning writing with a hand-sharpened pencil while standing at a high desk or bookcase top. Faulkner would also rise early, but he would sit at a desk and plunk away at an old typewriter. The routines seldom varied, but perhaps it was routine pursued with the fervor of a mystic that generated their inspiration and led to their recognition.

It is the creative process that unites Hemingway and Faulkner. Beneath Hemingway's distasteful <u>machismo</u> and existential sophistication was a sensitive and insightful artist who depicted the modern epoch full of all its horror and despair. Yet he continued to explore the value and capacity of the individual's faith in Self. Beneath Faulkner's deceptive regionalism and self-doubts was a socially committed artist who explored the impact of history's dark events on a culture and the individual psyche. Both were remarkable in their ability to connect with their readers—even readers who were born after those authors' deaths.

Reviewing with a Writer's Eye

1. One principle in writing a comparison essay is to be sure that the subjects belong to the same general category. List the categories that Ernest Hemingway and William Faulkner share.
2. Jim Cartozian's thesis statement comes at the end of paragraph 1. What principles of comparison does it embody?
3. Make two lists: one detailing how the authors are similar, the other detailing how they are different.
4. Why does Cartozian open with a specific comparison of the two authors? What effect does the comparison have?
5. Why doesn't Cartozian write a topic sentence for paragraph 2?
6. Identify examples of subject-by-subject and point-by-point development (see pp. 300–302).
7. In comparison essays, writers use parallel structure (see pp. 78–79) and overt transitions to keep writers from becoming confused. Identify examples of each technique.
8. What analogy (see pp. 298–299) does Cartozian develop? How does it function in the essay?
9. In a note, explain to Jim Cartozian the strengths and weaknesses of "Two American Writers: Hemingway and Faulkner." Pay particular attention to paragraphs 3 and 4. Do they drift too far from the assignment, or do they enrich Cartozian's essay? Briefly explain your response in your note.

Peer Review

You may be asked to write an essay about one of the readings that follow. Before you meet with your writing group, review the introduction. As you read the papers, use these general principles of comparison and contrast to help guide your comments.

1. Unless the paper is an analogy, the subjects should belong to the same general category.
2. The reader should be informed early in the paper that a comparison and contrast will follow.

3. The choice of point-by-point or subject-by-subject development (or a combination of both) should be appropriate to the content. A long paper with complex points of comparison and contrast usually requires a point-by-point method or a combination of both methods.
4. Clear transitions between subjects or points should guide the reader through the paper.

As you read the essays that follow, keep in mind that the most effective way to develop skill in comparison and contrast is to study the professionals. Analyze their choices. Ask yourself why a writer chooses point-by-point development over subject-by-subject for a particular passage. Notice how writers mix the two development patterns. Study the kinds of transitional techniques they use. This kind of careful reading—that is, reading with a critical eye—will prepare you to write your own comparisons.

❦ Richard Rodriguez ❦

Richard Rodriguez was born in San Francisco in 1944 to Mexican-American parents who spoke only Spanish at home. Rodriguez nonetheless mastered the English language and went on to study at Stanford, Columbia, and the University of California at Berkeley, where he earned a Ph.D. in English literature. He also received a Fulbright fellowship to study English literature in London. In spite of several offers to teach, Rodriguez made writing and journalism his profession. His books include Hunger of Memory, Mexico's Children, Days of Obligation: An Argument with My Mexican Father, Movements, *and his most recent,* Brown: The Last Discovery of America.

Los Otros, Mis Hermanos

This excerpt from Richard Rodriguez's 1982 autobiography, The Hunger of Memory, *portrays one of the conflicts that he felt growing up as a Hispanic in an Anglo culture. He concentrates here on his youthful sensitivity to language and how he identified his Spanish-speaking world with the comfort and security of family and the English-speaking world that surrounded him as alien and threatening.*

In the essay Rodriguez explains the different ways that language formed his identity. While you read, imagine as vividly as you can how he perceived people, and his relationship to them, in the way that they spoke. Notice the various ways he isolated in his mind the Spanish-speaking world from the English.

I grew up in a house where the only regular guests were my relations. For one day, enormous families of relatives would visit and there would be so many people that the noise and the bodies would spill out to the backyard and front porch. Then, for weeks, no one came by. (It was usually a salesman who rang the doorbell.) Our house stood apart. A gaudy yellow in a row of white bungalows. We were the people with the noisy dog. The people who raised pigeons and chickens. We were the foreigners on the block. A few neighbors smiled and waved. We waved back. But no one in the family knew the names of the old couple who lived next door; until I was seven years old, I did not know the names of the kids who lived across the street.

In public, my father and mother spoke a hesitant, accented, not always grammatical English. And they would have to strain—their bodies tense—to catch the sense of what was rapidly said by *los gringos*. At home they spoke Spanish. The language of their Mexican past sounded in counterpoint to the English of public society. The words would come quickly, with ease. Conveyed through those sounds was the pleasing, soothing, consoling reminder of being at home. 2

During those years when I was first conscious of hearing, my mother and father addressed me only in Spanish; in Spanish I learned to reply. By contrast, English (*inglés*), rarely heard in the house, was the language I came to associate with *gringos*. I learned my first words of English overhearing my parents speak to strangers. At five years of age, I knew just enough English for my mother to trust me on errands to stores one block away. No more. 3

I was a listening child, careful to hear the very different sounds of Spanish and English. Wide-eyed with hearing, I'd listen to sounds more than words. First, there were English (*gringo*) sounds. So many words were still unknown that when the butcher or the lady at the drugstore said something to me, exotic polysyllabic sounds would bloom in the midst of their sentences. Often, the speech of people in public seemed to me very loud, booming with confidence. The man behind the counter would literally ask, "What can I do for you?" But by being so firm and so clear, the sound of his voice said that he was a *gringo;* he belonged in public society. 4

I would also hear then the high nasal notes of middle-class American speech. The air stirred with sound. Sometimes, even now, when I have been traveling abroad for several weeks, I will hear what I heard as a boy. In hotel lobbies or airports, in Turkey or Brazil, some Americans will pass, and suddenly I will hear it again—the high sound of American voices. For a few seconds I will hear it with pleasure, for it is now the sound of my society—a reminder of home. But inevitably—already on the flight headed for home—the sound fades with repetition. I will be unable to hear it anymore. 5

When I was a boy, things were different. The accent of *los gringos*   6
was never pleasing nor was it hard to hear. Crowds at Safeway or at
bus stops would be noisy with sound. And I would be forced to edge
away from the chirping chatter above me.

I was unable to hear my own sounds, but I knew very well that   7
I spoke English poorly. My words could not stretch far enough to
form complete thoughts. And the words I did speak I didn't know
well enough to make into distinct sounds. (Listeners would usually
lower their heads, better to hear what I was trying to say.) But it
was one thing for me to speak English with difficulty. It was more
troubling for *me* to hear my parents speak in public; their high-
whining vowels and guttural consonants; their sentences that got
stuck with 'eh' and 'ah' sounds; the confused syntax; the hesitant
rhythm of sounds so different from the way *gringos* spoke. I'd notice, moreover, that my parents' voices were softer than those of
gringos we'd meet.

I am tempted now to say that none of this mattered. In adult-   8
hood I am embarrassed by childhood fears. And, in a way, it didn't
matter very much that my parents could not speak English with
ease. Their linguistic difficulties had no serious consequences. My
mother and father made themselves understood at the county hospital clinic and at government offices. And yet, in another way, it mattered very much—it was unsettling to hear my parents struggle with
English. Hearing them, I'd grow nervous, my clutching trust in their
protection and power weakened.

There were many times like the night at a brightly lit gasoline   9
station (a blaring white memory) when I stood uneasily, hearing my
father. He was talking to a teenaged attendant. I do not recall what
they were saying, but I cannot forget the sounds my father made as
he spoke. At one point his words slid together to form one word—
sounds as confused as the threads of blue and green oil in the puddle
next to my shoes. His voice rushed through what he had left to say.
And, toward the end, reached falsetto notes, appealing to his listener's understanding. I looked away to the lights of passing automobiles. I tried not to hear anymore. But I heard only too well the calm,
easy tones in the attendant's reply. Shortly afterward, walking toward
home with my father, I shivered when he put his hand on my shoul-

der. The very first chance that I got, I evaded his grasp and ran on ahead into the dark, skipping with feigned boyish exuberance.

But then there was Spanish. *Español:* my family's language. 10 *Español:* the language that seemed to me a private language. I'd hear strangers on the radio and in the Mexican Catholic church across town speaking in Spanish, but I couldn't really believe that Spanish was a public language, like English. Spanish speakers, rather, seemed related to me, for I sensed that we shared—through our language—the experience of feeling apart from *los gringos.* It was thus a ghetto Spanish that I heard and I spoke. Like those whose lives are bound by a barrio, I was reminded by Spanish of my separateness from *los otros, los gringos* in power. But more intensely than for most barrio children—because I did not live in a barrio— Spanish seemed to me the language of home. (Most days it was only at home that I'd hear it.) It became the language of joyful return.

A family member would say something to me and I would feel 11 myself specially recognized. My parents would say something to me and I would feel embraced by the sounds of their words. Those sounds said: *I am speaking with ease in Spanish. I am addressing you in words I never use with los gringos. I recognize you as someone special, close, like no one outside. You belong with us. In the family.*

(Ricardo.) 12

At the age of five, six, well past the time when most other chil- 13 dren no longer easily notice the difference between sounds uttered at home and words spoken in public, I had a different experience. I lived in a world magically compounded of sounds. I remained a child longer than most; I lingered too long, poised at the edge of language—often frightened by the sounds of *los gringos,* delighted by the sounds of Spanish at home. I shared with my family a language that was startlingly different from that used in the great city around us.

For me there were none of the gradations between public and 14 private society so normal to a maturing child. Outside the house was public society; inside the house was private. Just opening or closing the screen door behind me was an important experience. I'd rarely leave home all alone or without reluctance. Walking down the sidewalk, under the canopy of tall trees, I'd warily notice the— suddenly—silent neighborhood kids who stood warily watching me.

Nervously, I'd arrive at the grocery store to hear there the sounds of the *gringo*—foreign to me—reminding me that in this world so big, I was a foreigner. But then I'd return. Walking back toward our house, climbing the steps from the sidewalk, when the front door was open in summer, I'd hear voices beyond the screen door talking in Spanish. For a second or two, I'd stay, linger there, listening. Smiling, I'd hear my mother call out, saying in Spanish (words): "Is that you, Richard?" All the while her sounds would assure me: *You are home now; come closer; inside. With us.*

"*Sí,*" I'd reply.   15

Once more inside the house I would resume (assume) my place   16
in the family. The sounds would dim, grow harder to hear. Once more at home, I would grow less aware of that fact. It required, however, no more than the blurt of the doorbell to alert me to listen to sounds all over again. The house would turn instantly still while my mother went to the door. I'd hear her hard English sounds. I'd wait to hear her voice return to soft-sounding Spanish, which assured me, as surely as did the clicking tongue of the lock on the door, that the stranger was gone.

Plainly, it is not healthy to hear such sounds so often. It is not   17
healthy to distinguish public words from private sounds so easily. I remained cloistered by sounds, timid and shy in public, too dependent on voices at home. And yet it needs to be emphasized: I was an extremely happy child at home. I remember many nights when my father would come back from work, and I'd hear him call out to my mother in Spanish, sounding relieved. In Spanish, he'd sound light and free notes he never could manage in English. Some nights I'd jump up just at hearing his voice. With *mis hermanos* I would come running into the room where he was with my mother. Our laughing (so deep was the pleasure!) became screaming. Like others who know the pain of public alienation, we transformed the knowledge of our public separateness and made it consoling—the reminder of intimacy. Excited, we joined our voices in a celebration of sounds. *We are speaking now the way we never speak out in public. We are alone—together,* voices sounded, surrounded to tell me. Some nights, no one seemed willing to loosen the hold sounds had on us. At dinner, we invented new words. (Ours sounded Spanish, but made

sense only to us.) We pieced together new words by taking, say, an English verb and giving it Spanish endings. My mother's instructions at bedtime would be lacquered with mock-urgent tones. Or a word like *sí* would become, in several notes, able to convey added measures of feeling. Tongues explored the edges of words, especially the fat vowels. And we happily sounded that military drum roll, the twirling roar of the Spanish r. Family language: my family's sounds. The voices of my parents and sisters and brother. Their voices insisting: *You belong here. We are family members. Related. Special to one another. Listen!* Voices singing and sighing, rising, straining, then surging, teeming with pleasure that burst syllables into fragments of laughter. At times it seemed there was steady quiet only when, from another room, the rustling whispers of my parents faded and I moved closer to sleep.

Meaning and Purpose

1. What are Rodriguez's childhood feelings about Spanish and English? Use examples from the essay to illustrate your answer.
2. In paragraph 7 the author says that he felt differently about his own inability to speak fluent English and his parents' inability to do so. Why does he feel so differently? How strong are his feelings? Explain.
3. Rodriguez says in paragraph 8 that his parents' difficulties with English didn't matter in some ways but did in others. Explain this.
4. "I remained a child longer than most," says the author in paragraph 13. What does he mean by this? What does he consider the characteristics of childhood? How did language affect his slow development?

Strategy

1. Where and how does the author make clear what he intends to compare and contrast?
2. Paragraph 5 is an example. What function does it serve?

3. Paragraph 9 is also an example. What is its function?
4. Paragraph 15 consists of a short, single sentence. Why does Rodriguez separate it from the preceding paragraph?

Style

1. Examine the essay closely and point out some places where Rodriguez uses point-by-point development and where he uses subject-by-subject development. Why do you think he chose those methods when and where he did?
2. Rodriguez uses Spanish words and phrases to demonstrate "private" language. Are the meanings clear in context? What effect do they create even if you are unable to translate them?
3. What does the word *gringo* mean? What are its connotations? How does the author want the word to affect you? Explain.

Writing Tasks

1. If English is not your first language, write an essay in which you compare aspects of your native culture with those of American culture. If you are a native-born American but have encountered foreign cultures, compare some aspects of those cultures to your own. What were things you liked or disliked? Why?
2. Think about where you grew up. Did the place, the people, and your family affect the way you learned to think of yourself? How? Write an essay in which you enumerate and describe those things that formed your sense of identity.

✤ Bharati Mukherjee ✤

Novelist, short-story writer, essayist, and university professor, Bharati Mukherjee was born into a large, upper-middle-class family in Calcutta, India, in 1940. After earning a B.A. with honors from the University of Calcutta in 1959, she then studied at the University of Baroda, India, where she received an M.A. in English and Ancient Indian Culture in 1961. She moved to the United States that same year, after having been awarded a scholarship from the University of Iowa. She received an M.F.A. in Creative Writing there in 1963 and her Ph.D. in English and Comparative Literature in 1969. She has taught at many colleges and universities throughout Canada and the United States and is currently a Distinguished Professor of English at the University of California, Berkeley. She has published four books of nonfiction, two short-story collections, and five novels. Her latest novel is The Tree Bride, *a sequel to her 2002 novel,* Desirable Daughters.*

Two Ways to Belong in America

There was an unsuccessful effort by the U.S. Congress in the mid-1990s to enact legislation that would deny any government benefits to resident aliens, immigrants who live in the country legally, who work and pay taxes, but who are not citizens. The following essay, first published by The New York Times *in 1996, was written in response to those anti-immigrant proposals.*

As you read, notice the ways Mukherjee draws distinctions between herself and her sister and how those differences make comment on the larger issues of the immigrant experience.

This is a tale of two sisters from Calcutta, Mira and Bharati, who have lived in the United States for some 35 years, but who find themselves on different sides in the current debate over the status of immigrants. I am an American citizen and she is not. I am moved that thousands of long-term residents are finally taking the oath of citizenship. She is not. 1

Mira arrived in Detroit in 1960 to study child psychology and pre-school education. I followed her a year later to study creative writing at the University of Iowa. When we left India, we were almost identical in appearance and attitude. We dressed alike, in saris; we expressed identical views on politics, social issues, love, and marriage in the same Calcutta convent-school accent. We would endure our two years in America, secure our degrees, then return to India to marry the grooms of our father's choosing. 2

Instead, Mira married an Indian student in 1962 who was getting his business administration degree at Wayne State University. They soon acquired the labor certifications necessary for the green card of hassle-free residence and employment. 3

Mira still lives in Detroit, works in the Southfield, Mich., school system, and has become nationally recognized for her contributions in the fields of pre-school education and parent-teacher relationships. After 36 years as a legal immigrant in this country, she clings passionately to her Indian citizenship and hopes to go home to India when she retires. 4

In Iowa City in 1963, I married a fellow student, an American of Canadian parentage. Because of the accident of his North Dakota birth, I bypassed labor-certification requirements and the race-related "quota" system that favored the applicant's country of origin over his or her merit. I was prepared for (and even welcomed) the emotional strain that came with marrying outside my ethnic community. In 33 years of marriage, we have lived in every part of North America. By choosing a husband who was not my father's selection, I was opting for fluidity, self-invention, blue jeans and T-shirts, and renouncing 3,000 years (at least) of caste-observant, "pure culture" marriage in the Mukherjee family. My books have often been read as unapologetic (and in some quarters overenthusiastic) texts for cultural and psychological "mongrelization." It's a word I celebrate. 5

Mira and I have stayed sisterly close by phone. In our regular Sunday morning conversations, we are unguardedly affectionate. I am her only blood relative on this continent. We expect to see each other through the looming crises of aging and ill health without being asked. Long before Vice President Gore's "Citizenship U.S.A." drive, we'd had our polite arguments over the ethics of retaining an 6 overseas citizenship while expecting the permanent protection and economic benefits that come with living and working in America.

Like well-raised sisters, we never said what was really on our minds, but we probably pitied one another. She, for the lack of structure in my life, the erasure of Indianness, the absence of an unvarying daily core. I, for the narrowness of her perspective, her uninvolvement with the mythic depths or the superficial pop culture of this society. But, now, with the scapegoatings of "aliens" (documented or illegal) on the increase, and the targeting of long-term legal immigrants like Mira for new scrutiny and new self-consciousness, she and I find ourselves unable to maintain the same polite discretion. We were always unacknowledged adversaries, and we are now, more than ever, sisters. 7

"I feel used," Mira raged on the phone the other night. "I feel manipulated and discarded. This is such an unfair way to treat a person who was invited to stay and work here because of her talent. My employer went to the I.N.S. and petitioned for the labor certification. For over 30 years, I've invested my creativity and professional skills into the improvement of *this* country's pre-school system. I've obeyed all the rules, I've paid my taxes, I love my work, I love my students, I love the friends I've made. How dare America now change its rules in midstream? If America wants to make new rules curtailing benefits of legal immigrants, they should apply only to immigrants who arrive after those rules are already in place." 8

To my ears, it sounded like the description of a long-enduring, comfortable yet loveless marriage, without risk or recklessness. Have we the right to demand, and to expect, that we be loved? (That, to me, is the subtext of the arguments by immigration advocates.) My sister is an expatriate, professionally generous and creative, socially courteous and gracious, and that's as far as her Americanization can go. She is here to maintain an identity, not to transform it. 9

I asked her if she would follow the example of others who have decided to become citizens because of the anti-immigration bills in Congress. And here, she surprised me. "If America wants to play the manipulative game, I'll play it, too," she snapped. "I'll become a U.S. citizen for now, then change back to India when I'm ready to go home. I feel some kind of irrational attachment to India that I don't 10 to America. Until all this hysteria against legal immigrants, I was totally happy. Having my green card meant I could visit any place in the world I wanted to and then come back to a job that's satisfying and that I do very well."

In one family, from two sisters alike as peas in a pod, there could 11 not be a wider divergence of immigrant experience. America spoke to me—I married it—I embraced the demotion from expatriate aristocrat to immigrant nobody, surrendering those thousands of years of "pure culture," the saris, the delightfully accented English. She retained them all. Which of us is the freak?

Mira's voice, I realize, is the voice not just of the immigrant 12 South Asian community but of an immigrant community of the millions who have stayed rooted in one job, one city, one house, one ancestral culture, one cuisine, for the entirety of their productive years. She speaks for greater numbers than I possibly can. Only the fluency of her English and the anger, rather than fear, born of confidence from her education, differentiate her from the seamstresses, the domestics, the technicians, the shop owners, the millions of hardworking but effectively silenced documented immigrants as well as their less fortunate "illegal" brothers and sisters.

Nearly 20 years ago, when I was living in my husband's ancestral 13 homeland of Canada, I was always well-employed but never allowed to feel part of the local Quebec or larger Canadian society. Then, through a Green Paper that invited a national referendum on the unwanted side effects of "nontraditional" immigration, the Government officially turned against its immigrant communities, particularly those from South Asia.

I felt then the same sense of betrayal that Mira feels now. I 14 will never forget the pain of that sudden turning, and the casual racist outbursts the Green Paper elicited. That sense of betrayal had its desired effect and drove me, and thousands like me, from the country.

Mira and I differ, however, in the ways in which we hope to in- 15 teract with the country that we have chosen to live in. She is happier to live in America as expatriate Indian than as an immigrant American. I need to feel like a part of the community I have adopted (as I tried to feel in Canada as well). I need to put roots down, to vote and make the difference that I can. The price that the immigrant willingly pays, and that the exile avoids, is the trauma of self-transformation.

Meaning and Purpose

1. Describe the two sisters' relationship to one another.
2. Why does Mira resent the proposed law changes regarding immigrants?
3. How does Mira propose dealing with the looming change of status for U.S. immigrants?
4. Although the two sisters completely diverge in their immigrant experience, Bharati expresses sympathy for her sister's embitterment. Why?

Strategy

1. Bharati compares herself to her sister, Mira; that is, she points out their similarities. In what ways are they alike?
2. She also contrasts herself with her sister. In what ways are they different?
3. Does Bharati use primarily subject-by-subject development or point-by-point development? Why would she choose one method over the other?

Style

1. Mukherjee says that she celebrates the word "mongrelization" (paragraph 5). Why?
2. In paragraph 9, Mukherjee compares her sister's immigrant experience to a loveless marriage. How effective do you think that analogy is? Why?
3. If necessary, look up the following words in a dictionary: *saris* (paragraph 2); *certifications* (3); *mongrelization* (5); *looming* (6);

mythic, scrutiny (7); *curtailing* (8); *expatriate* (9); *divergence, demotion* (11); *cuisine* (12); *trauma* (15).

Writing Tasks

1. Have you ever lived or traveled extensively in another country, moved from one place to another, or changed schools? Write an essay in which you compare and contrast two different places. Make your points of comparison and contrast as specific as you can, and be careful to organize your essay using primarily point-by-point or subject-by-subject development.
2. Write an essay in which you accurately and fairly compare and contrast two different positions on immigration policy. Make sure to compose a thesis that holds your essay tightly together, and, if you can, incorporate some of Mukherjee's points into your argument.

❦ Deborah Tannen ❦

Deborah Tannen, born in 1945, earned her doctorate in sociolinguistics at the University of California, Berkeley, and now teaches at George-town University. Deeply interested in how differently men and women communicate, Tannen's publications include You Just Don't Under-stand; That's Not What I Meant! How Conversational Style Makes or Breaks Relationships; Gender and Conversational Interaction; Talking from 9 to 5: Women and Men in the Workplace: Lan-guage, Sex, and Power; *and* The Argument Culture: Moving from Debate to Dialogue.

Sex, Lies, and Conversation

This informative essay, from You Just Don't Understand, *published in 1991, points out some of the communication features that differen-tiate men and women when they engage in ordinary conversation. As you read, notice how clearly Tannen shifts her focus back and forth, from discussing the ways that men talk and listen to discussing the ways that women talk and listen.*

I was addressing a small gathering in a suburban Virginia living room—a women's group that had invited men to join them. Throughout the evening, one man had been particularly talkative, frequently offering ideas and anecdotes, while his wife sat silently beside him on the couch. Toward the end of the evening, I commented that women frequently complain that their husbands don't talk to them. This man quickly concurred. He gestured toward his wife and said, "She's the talker in our family." The room burst into laughter; the man looked puzzled and hurt. "It's true," he explained. "When I come home from work I have nothing to say. If she didn't keep the conversation going, we'd spend the whole evening in silence."

This episode crystallizes the irony that although American men tend to talk more than women in public situations, they often talk less at home. And this pattern is wreaking havoc with marriage.

The pattern was observed by political scientist Andrew Hacker   3
in the late '70s. Sociologist Catherine Kohler Riessman reports in her
new book *Divorce Talk* that most of the women she interviewed—but
only a few of the men—gave lack of communication as the reason
for their divorces. Given the current divorce rate of nearly 50 percent, that amounts to millions of cases in the United States every
year—a virtual epidemic of failed conversation.

In my own research, complaints from women about their hus-   4
bands most often focused not on tangible inequities such as having
given up the chance for a career to accompany a husband to his, or
doing far more than their share of daily life-support work like cleaning, cooking, social arrangements, and errands. Instead, they focused on communication: "He doesn't listen to me," "He doesn't talk
to me." I found, as Hacker observed years before, that most wives
want their husbands to be, first and foremost, conversational partners, but few husbands share this expectation of their wives.

In short, the image that best represents the current crisis is the   5
stereotypical cartoon scene of a man sitting at the breakfast table
with a newspaper held up in front of his face, while a woman glares
at the back of it, wanting to talk.

Lingustic Battle of the Sexes

How can women and men have such different impressions of   6
communication in marriage? Why the widespread imbalance in their
interests and expectations?

In the April issue of *American Psychologist,* Stanford University's   7
Eleanor Maccoby reports the results of her own and others' research
showing that children's development is most influenced by the social
structure of peer interactions. Boys and girls tend to play with children of their own gender, and their sex-separate groups have different organizational structures and interactive norms.

I believe these systematic differences in childhood socialization   8
make talk between women and men like cross-cultural communication, heir to all the attraction and pitfalls of that enticing but difficult
enterprise. My research on men's and women's conversations uncovered patterns similar to those described for children's groups.

For women, as for girls, intimacy is the fabric of relationships, and talk is the thread from which it is woven. Little girls create and maintain friendships by exchanging secrets; similarly, women regard conversation as the cornerstone of friendship. So a woman expects her husband to be a new and improved version of a best friend. What is important is not the individual subjects that are discussed but the sense of closeness, of a life shared, that emerges when people tell their thoughts, feelings, and impressions. 9

Bonds between boys can be as intense as girls', but they are based less on talking, more on doing things together. Since they don't assume talk is the cement that binds a relationship, men don't know what kind of talk women want, and they don't miss it when it isn't there. 10

Boys' groups are larger, more inclusive, and more hierarchical, so boys must struggle to avoid the subordinate position in the group. This may play a role in women's complaints that men don't listen to them. Some men really don't like to listen, because being the listener makes them feel one-down, like a child listening to adults or an employee to a boss. 11

But often when women tell men, "You aren't listening," and the men protest, "I am," the men are right. The impression of not listening results from misalignments in the mechanics of conversation. The misalignment begins as soon as a man and a woman take physical positions. This became clear when I studied videotapes made by psychologist Bruce Dorval of children and adults talking to their same-sex best friends. I found that at every age, the girls and women faced each other directly, their eyes anchored on each other's faces. At every age, the boys and men sat at angles to each other and looked elsewhere in the room, periodically glancing at each other. They were obviously attuned to each other, often mirroring each other's movements. But the tendency of men to face away can give women the impression they aren't listening even when they are. A young woman in college was frustrated: Whenever she told her boyfriend she wanted to talk to him, he would lie down on the floor, close his eyes, and put his arm over his face. This signaled to her, "He's taking a nap." But he insisted he was listening extra hard. Normally, he looks around the room, so he is 12 easily distracted. Lying down and covering his eyes helped him concentrate on what she was saying.

Analogous to the physical alignment that women and men take 13 in conversation is their topical alignment. The girls in my study tended to talk at length about one topic, but the boys tended to jump from topic to topic. The second-grade girls exchanged stories about people they knew. The second-grade boys teased, told jokes, noticed things in the room, and talked about finding games to play. The sixth-grade girls talked about problems with a mutual friend. The sixth-grade boys talked about 55 different topics, none of which extended over more than a few turns.

Listening to Body Language

Switching topics is another habit that gives women the impres- 14 sion men aren't listening, especially if they switch to a topic about themselves. But the evidence of the 10th-grade boys in my study indicates otherwise. The 10th-grade boys sprawled across their chairs with bodies parallel and eyes straight ahead, rarely looking at each other. They looked as if they were riding in a car, staring out the windshield. But they were talking about their feelings. One boy was upset because a girl had told him he had a drinking problem, and the other was feeling alienated from all his friends.

Now, when a girl told a friend about a problem, the friend re- 15 sponded by asking probing questions and expressing agreement and understanding. But the boys dismissed each other's problems. Todd assured Richard that his drinking was "no big problem" because "sometimes you're funny when you're off your butt." And when Todd said he felt left out, Richard responded, "Why should you? You know more people than me."

Women perceive such responses as belittling and unsupportive. 16 But the boys seemed satisfied with them. Whereas women reassure each other by implying, "You shouldn't feel bad because I've had similar experiences," men do so by implying, "You shouldn't feel bad because your problems aren't so bad."

There are even simpler reasons for women's impression that men 17 don't listen. Linguist Lynette Hirschman found that women make more listener-noise, such as "mhm," "uhuh," and "yeah," to show "I'm with you." Men, she found, more often give silent attention. Women who expect a stream of listener-noise interpret silent attention as no attention at all.

Women's conversational habits are as frustrating to men as men's   18 are to women. Men who expect silent attention interpret a stream of listener-noise as overreaction or impatience. Also, when women talk to each other in a close, comfortable setting, they often overlap, finish each other's sentences, and anticipate what the other is about to say. This practice, which I call "participatory listenership," is often perceived by men as interruption, intrusion, and lack of attention.

A parallel difference caused a man to complain about his wife,   19 "She just wants to talk about her own point of view. If I show her another view, she gets mad at me." When most women talk to each other, they assume a conversationalist's job is to express agreement and support. But many men see their conversational duty as pointing out the other side of an argument. This is heard as disloyalty by women, and refusal to offer the requisite support. It is not that women don't want to see other points of view, but that they prefer them phrased as suggestions and inquiries rather than as direct challenges.

In his book *Fighting for Life,* Walter Ong points out that men use   20 "agonistic" or warlike, oppositional formats to do almost anything; thus discussion becomes debate, and conversation a competitive sport. In contrast, women see conversation as a ritual means of establishing rapport. If Jane tells a problem and June says she has a similar one, they walk away feeling closer to each other. But this attempt at establishing rapport can backfire when used with men. Men take too literally women's ritual "troubles talk," just as women mistake men's ritual challenges for real attack.

The Sounds of Silence

These differences begin to clarify why women and men have   21 such different expectations about communication in marriage. For women, talk creates intimacy. Marriage is an orgy of closeness: you can tell your feelings and thoughts, and still be loved. Their greatest fear is being pushed away. But men live in a hierarchical world, where talk maintains independence and status. They are on guard to protect themselves from being put down and pushed around.

This explains the paradox of the talkative man who said of his   22
silent wife, "She's the talker." In the public setting of a guest lecture, he felt challenged to show his intelligence and display his understanding of the lecture. But at home, where he has nothing to prove and no one to defend against, he is free to remain silent. For his wife, being home means she is free from the worry that something she says might offend someone, or spark disagreement, or appear to be showing off; at home she is free to talk.

The communication problems that endanger marriage can't be   23
fixed by mechanical engineering. They require a new conceptual framework about the role of talk in human relationships. Many of the psychological explanations that have become second nature may not be helpful, because they tend to blame either women (for not being assertive enough) or men (for not being in touch with their feelings). A sociolinguistic approach by which male-female conversation is seen as cross-cultural communication allows us to understand the problem and forge solutions without blaming either party.

Once the problem is understood, improvement comes naturally,   24
as it did to the young woman and her boyfriend who seemed to go to sleep when she wanted to talk. Previously, she had accused him of not listening, and he had refused to change his behavior, since that would be admitting fault. But then she learned about and explained to him the differences in women's and men's habitual ways of aligning themselves in conversation. The next time she told him she wanted to talk, he began, as usual, by lying down and covering his eyes. When the familiar negative reaction bubbled up, she reassured herself that he really was listening. But then he sat up and looked at her. Thrilled, she asked why. He said, "You like me to look at you when we talk, so I'll try to do it." Once he saw their differences as cross-cultural rather than right and wrong, he independently altered his behavior.

Women who feel abandoned and deprived when their husbands   25
won't listen to or report daily news may be happy to discover their husbands trying to adapt once they understand the place of small talk in women's relationships. But if their husbands don't adapt, the

women may still be comforted that for men, this is not a failure of intimacy. Accepting the difference, the wives may look to their friends or family for that kind of talk. And husbands who can't provide it shouldn't feel their wives have made unreasonable demands. Some couples will still decide to divorce, but at least their decisions will be based on realistic expectations.

In these times of resurgent ethnic conflicts, the world desperately needs cross-cultural understanding. Like charity, successful cross-cultural communication should begin at home.   26

Meaning and Purpose

1. Tannen opens the essay with an episode that details the events of an evening. How does that device help to engage the reader?
2. A rhetorical question is a question that does not require a reply from its listener or its reader, but rather from the person who asked it. Why does Tannen open the second part of her essay with two rhetorical questions (paragraph 6)?
3. What are two important differences between the way women listen and the way men listen?
4. What are two important differences between the way men talk and the way women talk?
5. Why is it important to learn what Tannen teaches in this essay?

Strategy

1. Why does Tannen maintain that the "problem" must be understood? What problem does she mean?
2. Tannen discusses marriage in terms of communication. Why is that important to this essay?
3. In your opinion, who is the primary audience for this essay?
4. When Tannen discusses conversational habits, why does she refer to the studies of several scholars?

5. When Tannen compares and contrasts the various ways in which men and women communicate, what common features does she find?

Style

1. In paragraph 2, what does the term *crystallizes* mean?
2. Tannen remarks that "For women, as for girls, intimacy is the fabric of relationships" (paragraph 9). What does the term *fabric* suggest in that clause?
3. Tannen subtitles the last part of this essay "The Sounds of Silence." What is meant by that subtitle?
4. What does the phrase "physical alignment" (paragraph 13) mean in this essay?
5. Tannen uses the term *cross-cultural* several times in this essay. To what does the term refer?

Writing Tasks

1. Recall a conversation with a member of the opposite sex that led to a misunderstanding. Using information you gained from Tannen's essay, write a comparison-and-contrast essay in which you use the conversation to illustrate how men and women communicate differently.
2. In a cafeteria, a library, a shopping mall, a restaurant, or in another public place, observe a mixed-gender group of three or more people talking. Then, in the same area, observe another same-sex group of three or more people talking. In an essay, discuss the similarities and differences in the ways the members of the two groups interact conversationally.

❦ Teresa L. Ebert ❦
❦ Mas'ud Zavarzadeh ❦

Teresa Ebert received her Ph.D. from the University of Minnesota and is now an associate professor of English at the State University of New York at Albany. She currently teaches courses in Critical Theory, Marxism, Feminism, (Post)modernity, and Transnational Cultural Studies. She has written extensively on feminist issues and is the author of Ludic Feminism and After *(1995).*

Mas'ud Zavarzadeh is a professor of English at Syracuse University. He is the author of The Mythopoeic Reality: The Postwar American Nonfiction Novel, Seeing Films Politically, *and* Pun(k)deconstruction. *He has also published more than fifty essays in various scholarly journals.*

Our American Diet Divides Us

In much of their writing, both coauthors of this essay have often taken radical positions on issues in order to force their readers to consider common subjects from unusual perspectives. This short work is no exception. First published in the Los Angeles Times *in 2000, "Our American Diet" argues that popular weight reduction diets are political, that what Americans eat reflects their class or economic function in society.*

As you read, pay close attention to the various ways the authors contrast the Atkins and Ornish diets. And try to read with an open mind. The authors are attempting to get you to consider the commonplace subject of diets in an entirely new way.

Like everything else in social life, diets are determined not by what people desire but by the conditions of their class. This is quite an un-American thing to say, but people eat class and not food; food preferences are shaped by what one can afford to choose. 1

By class, we do not mean lifestyle, where one shops, what accent one has or what car one drives. These are signs of cultural prestige. They belong to social semiotics and not class. Class depends on 2 people's position in the social relations of production: Do they buy other people's labor and make a profit from it? Or do they sell their own labor in order to live?

The antagonism between the Atkins and Ornish diets and the politics that has divided their followers are class politics appearing as personal tastes in food, health and bodily aesthetics.   3

The Atkins diet is a proletarian diet: meat, eggs and other high-protein sources along with usually forbidden fats, especially butter and cream. This is "real food," according to Atkins, not upper-class "invented, fake food." In his recent *New Yorker* piece "On Impact," about recovering from a serious injury, Stephen King highlights the class culture of meat, writing that he and his wife "came from similar working-class backgrounds; we both ate meat." Meat is the food of the working people; a food of necessity for the class that relies on the raw energy of its body for subsistence.   4

The Atkins diet is a worker's diet that is highly satiating without requiring any special attention or calculation—unlike the elaborately complex Ornish plan, which is a full-time avocation in itself. All the Atkins' dieter needs to do is avoid nearly all carbohydrates and eat only "pure proteins" and "pure fats."   5

The Atkins diet books are written in a realistic style and shaped by what playwright Bertolt Brecht calls "coarse thinking"—thought that is highly suspicious of bourgeois indulgences and cultural elegance. When questioned about some of the inelegant consequences of his diet (such as bad breath from ketosis), cardiologist Robert Atkins laughs at the bourgeois mind-set that puts such refinements ahead of the strong, healthy body his audience needs to earn a living. He is contemptuous of the "sophisticated" bourgeois lifestyle that has made "low-fat, high-carbohydrate" diets dominant. This dominance, like the dominance of the bourgeoisie, is undeserved because, Atkins argues, this diet "hasn't … done a thing to take pounds off."   6

The low-fat, vegetarian Ornish diet, in contrast, is a diet for those with the time and leisure to play and experiment. It entails extensive lifestyle changes. Eating becomes a full-time leisure activity, requiring frequent "grazing" because with the low-fat, high-carbohydrate diet, according to internist Dean Ornish, "you get hungry sooner [and] feel full faster." Eating becomes a gaze into one's   7 soul: a meditation, a Zen moment in which a single bite becomes "exquisitely satisfying." It is an extended Proustian moment.

In its substance, the Ornish diet is elegant, colorful and highly pleasurable. The recipes, created by top gourmet chefs from places like Chez Panisse in Berkeley and Lutece in New York City, are instances of romancing food. 8

In Ornish's "amazing graze" of constant nibbling, each bite becomes "heaven." But all Atkins promises is an "amazing no-hunger weight loss." One diet offers assurances of continual sensual pleasure, the other a pledge for the absence of hunger. The diets perform what Marx and Engels regarded as the feature of advanced capitalism: society "splitting up into two great classes." 9

In spite of their innumerable surface variations, all diets repeat the two fundamental divisions of society into the classes of workers and owners. In eating food, we eat our class. 10

Meaning and Purpose

1. The authors' initial claim in this essay is that people themselves do not determine their own diets, but, rather, that those diets are determined by external forces ("the condition of their class"). How is this so? Why is this idea "un-American" (paragraph 1)?
2. What is the essay's thesis? Where do the authors state it?
3. How do the authors define class? How many social classes are there? Do the authors account for gradations within social classes?
4. In what way is the Ornish diet "a full-time avocation in itself" (paragraph 5)? What would a person need to successfully follow the Ornish diet?

Strategy

1. Paragraphs 1 and 2 serve as the essay's introduction. Explain what each does to lead into the authors' main argument.

2. Reread paragraph 3. What rhetorical function does it serve in the essay's overall organization?

3. The body of the essay, paragraphs 4–9, contrasts the Atkins and Ornish diets. Do the authors primarily use point-by-point or subject-by-subject development? For what purpose did they choose this method of development?

Style

1. In paragraph 2, the authors claim that the things that constitute one's "lifestyle" belong to "social semiotics." Explain what that last term means in the context that it's used.

2. In paragraph 7, the authors use the terms "a Zen moment" and "an extended Proustian moment" to describe eating the Ornish diet. What do these terms mean (look them up, if necessary)? How would you describe the tone of the final two sentences of paragraph 7?

3. Describe the word play in the first sentence of paragraph 9. What function does it serve? How does that word play connect with the final two sentences of the seventh paragraph?

Writing Tasks

1. Choose two diets or weight reduction programs other than the Atkins and Ornish diets and write a paper in which you compare and contrast them. If you have had any personal experience with more than one diet, use that personal knowledge as the core idea of your paper.

2. Compare and contrast two different people's attitudes toward food and how those attitudes are reflected in their eating behavior: their food choices, the peculiar ways they eat, how they handle their knives and forks, their choice of restaurants, etc. In the course of your paper, see if you can draw conclusions about your subjects' attitudes about the larger world as reflected in their eating habits.

❦ Jason Stella ❦

Jason Stella is a freelance journalist, actor, and playwright. His one-man show, Guide to Health and Strength, *played Off-Broadway to critical acclaim.*

Astroturf: How Manufactured "Grassroots" Movements Are Subverting Democracy

In this essay, Jason Stella describes how a number of various organizations pass themselves off as grassroots movements created to promote the common good, while they are actually public relations schemes designed to sway public opinion so as to promote their own financial self-interest.

Notice as you read how Stella carefully points out what these organizations really are as opposed to what they purport to be, distinguishing illusion from reality. Ask yourself what motivates this attempted corporate fraud.

She had only one name, Nayirah, when she came before the Congressional Human Rights Caucus on October 10, 1990. It was just after the Iraqi invasion of Kuwait, and Nayirah testified to having witnessed Iraqi soldiers tearing Kuwaiti infants from hospital incubators, leaving them to die on the floor. As she spoke, tears streamed down her face. 1

The videotape of her testimony circulated through every nook of American media, and then-president George Bush cited the incident frequently in building a case for military action. A country that polls had shown to be evenly split on intervention as late as December 1990 slowly became primed for war. When the Senate finally voted on its war resolution on January 12, it passed by five votes. And the number who said they voted because of the baby incubator incident? Six. 2

Nayirah had appeared under the auspices of an American grass-   3
roots organizing committee, Citizens for a Free Kuwait. She was part
of a larger mobilization, in which CFK provided American news organizations with color photographs of Kuwaitis of all ages who re-
portedly had been killed or tortured by Iraqis. CFK also distributed
videotapes that showed Iraqi soldiers apparently firing on unarmed
demonstrators, as witnesses related tales of horror. Their campaign
turned the Gulf War into a moral battle, a fight of good against evil
that stands today as the reason to oppose Saddam Hussein. It's the
genesis of the "Evil" in the Axis.

After the war, *Harper's* publisher John R. MacArthur visited CFK   4
while researching his book *Second Front: Censorship and Propaganda
in the Gulf War*. That's when he discovered a conspiracy, at the center
of which stood the Kuwaiti government and its PR firm, Hill &
Knowlton, which had created CFK from scratch.

Among the piles of war photos shown to MacArthur were depic-   5
tions of tortured Kuwaiti citizens who had apparently suffered gruesome deaths.

"But when I looked closely at the photographs," recalled Mac-   6
Arthur, "I saw that they were mannequins dressed up to look like
torture victims."

MacArthur dug further and found that the entire campaign itself   7
had been manufactured by Hill & Knowlton on behalf of the Kuwaiti
government, which had a lot invested in appearing the victim. Of
the $11.8 million raised by CFK, only $17,861 came from actual citizens. The rest was supplied by the Kuwaiti government.

Moreover, the supposedly anonymous young girl who had so   8
tearfully testified was actually the daughter of the Kuwaiti ambassa-
dor to the United States—not a hospital volunteer, as she had testified. She lived in the United States and the events she recounted had
not occurred. The Gulf War, it turns out, was waged not on a lie, but
rather on a mountain of them.

Enter Astroturf

In 1967, Monsanto Industries patented "monofilament ribbon   9
file product," and they saw that it was good. Said They, "A primary

object of this invention is to provide a synthetic product which simulates the physical characteristics and general appearance of natural turf." Then, baseball was played upon it, by the Astros in Houston, and They saw that it was good. And They named it, AstroTurf.

In 1995, *Campaigns & Elections* magazine defined a new brand   10
of Astroturf as "a grassroots program that involves the instant manufacturing of public support for a point of view in which either uninformed activists are recruited or means of deception are used to recruit them."

One of PR's most active recruiters has been Edward L. Bernays,   11
nephew of Sigmund Freud, and the most influential pioneer of modern public relations tactics.

To sell cigarettes as a symbol of women's liberation, he con-   12
vinced a group of women's rights marchers to hoist Lucky Strike cigarettes as symbolic "torches of freedom." Within months, sales of Lucky Strike were soaring as a new niche of nicotine addicts became "liberated."

Bernays would later find out that the practical application of his   13
own theories proved greatly effective for Joseph Goebbels, minister of propaganda for Hitler's Third Reich. As Bernays writes in his autobiography, "[Goebbels] was using my book, *Crystallizing Public Opinion*, as a basis for his destructive campaign against the Jews of Germany. This shocked me."

Today, such tactics are commonplace. The creation of illusory   14
grassroots groups is a time-tested process, one which is not exclusive to wartime propaganda. Corporations rely on Astroturf groups to rally support for or opposition to legislative measures that threaten to siphon cash from the corporate till.

To those seniors concerned about rising prescription drug costs,   15
Citizens for Better Medicine (CBM) might seem a worthy advocate for their cause. Billing itself as "a grassroots organization that is working to strengthen and improve Medicare," CBM is actually a front for the Pharmaceutical Research and Manufacturers of America (PhRMA), a trade group made up of the world's largest pharmaceutical firms.

Through CBM, PhRMA spent $65 million in the 1999–2000   16
election cycle on ads and direct mailings which featured the skeptical senior "Flo," who stressed the importance of "keeping big

government out of our medicine cabinets." Flo, a fictional character, was played by Diana Sowle, who is best known for playing Charlie Bucket's mother in the 1971 hit *Willy Wonka and the Chocolate Factory*.

CBM's ads talked about protecting seniors and their prescription   17
drug coverage. They were really about protecting industry's profits from commonsense reform. Through CBM's ads, seniors were invited to call Congress and oppose the very measures that would help them control the skyrocketing cost of life-saving prescription drugs.

Whether they manufacture consent for war or prey on the vul-   18
nerability of senior citizens, public relations firms are using Astro-turf and other veiled tactics to dupe the public into thinking that they are supporting a grassroots, nonprofit, or independent organiza-tion, when in fact they are unwittingly supporting the very causes, corporations, or policies they might otherwise wish to denounce. In so doing, they create for the public the illusion of active participation in the democratic process.

The overall PR strategy for manipulating and maintaining this il-   19
lusion is one of triangulation between three camps of traditionally liberal opposition: radicals, idealists, and realists. Speaking before the National Cattlemen's Beef Association, Ron Duchin, senior vice-president of the PR firm Mongoven, Biscoe, and Duchin, outlined his firm's basic divide-and-conquer strategy for defeating activist groups.

The first step is to isolate and marginalize the radicals. Radical ac-   20
tivists "want to change the system," and have "underlying socio/politi-cal motives—I would categorize their principal aims right now as social justice and political empowerment," Duchin said to his sympathetic au-dience. To isolate them, PR firms will try to create a perception in the public mind that people advocating fundamental solutions are extrem-ists, fear mongers, or social malcontents with anarchist aims.

After marginalizing the radicals, the next step, Duchin said, is to   21
identify and "educate" the "hard-to-deal-with" idealists—concerned and sympathetic members of the public—by convincing them that the changes advocated by the radicals would hurt people. Idealists, Duchin said, "have a vulnerable point. If they can be shown that their position in opposition to an industry or its products causes

harm to others and cannot be ethically justified, they are forced to change their position—thus, while a realist must be negotiated with, an idealist must be educated."

With the proper "educating," Duchin explained, idealists and re- 22 alists can be counted on to cut a deal with industry that can be touted as a "win-win" solution, but that actually serves what Duchin calls "the final policy solution."

"Realists are able to live with tradeoffs; willing to work within 23 the system; not interested in radical change."

If successful, this strategy should force the public to fear the rad- 24 icals, view the uneducated idealists as unrealistic, and view the realists as trusted leaders whose endorsement of the corporation or its product validates the corporation's claims.

In Bernays's 1928 book, *Propaganda,* he explains the full dimen- 25 sions of propaganda, PR, and Astroturf in tones that echo the covert darkness of the postwar era. "The conscious and intelligent manipulation of the organized habits and opinions of the masses is an important element in democratic society," he wrote. "Those who manipulate this unseen mechanism of society constitute an invisible government which is the true ruling power of our country."

And it was this ruling power that engineered consent for the Gulf 26 War. In the minds of Americans, the available facts did not seem to warrant military intervention. But when Nayirah's teary testimony paired with photos of dismembered mannequins entered the debate, fiction blurred fact, setting in motion a conflict that still exists today.

This kind of manipulation is nefarious because it turns good in- 27 tentions against their very ends. The danger of Astroturf comes not from its subversion of democracy, but in the way that it tricks us into subverting it ourselves.

Rugburn: Astroturf's Top Ten

Activistcash.com

Activistcash.com attempts to discredit activists by suggesting 28 that there is something disreputable about the money they have received from foundations. The site refers to activists as "nannies," "anti-choice zealots" and "hypocrites." Ironically, Activistcash.com makes no mention of its own funders, mainly the tobacco and alcohol industries.

National Smokers Alliance

As internal tobacco industry documents make clear, the NSA was invented by Big Tobacco in 1993 with the help of public relations giant Burson-Marsteller to counter antitobacco legislation.   29

The American Tort Reform Association

The ATRA claims to be comprised of the "average citizen," but is in fact a corporate front for the chemical, tobacco, pharmaceutical, and auto industries.   30

The Global Climate Coalition

Run by New York PR firm Ruder Finn, the GCC represents the big oil, gas, coal, and auto corporations. In 1997, the GCC distributed a video to hundreds of journalists claiming that increased levels of carbon dioxide would increase crop production and help end world hunger.   31

Contributions Watch

Posing as a "public interest" campaign reform organization, CW's hidden agenda is to dig up dirt at the state level for the corporate clients of its creator, the State Affairs Company (SAC), and the funder, Philip Morris. SAC and CW work to attack the political enemies of their clients, and to smear the "hidden, undisclosed consumerist agendas" of real public interest groups like Consumers Union, the Center for Science in the Public Interest, Ralph Nader's Public Interest Research Group, and Trial Lawyers for Public Justice.   32

Arctic Power

Working to promote oil drilling in the Arctic National Wildlife Refuge, AP bills itself as a "grassroots, non-profit citizens' organiza-   33 tion with 10,000 members." Its board members include representatives from the Alaska Oil & Gas Association, Resource Development Council, Alaska Miners Association, and Alaska Forest Association.

Environmental Conservation Organization

ECO is an anti-environmental umbrella outfit counting more than three hundred Wise Use groups as members. With a phone and fax network and a monthly newsletter, *eco-logic,* fronting as an eco-friendly publication, ECO promotes Wise Use efforts to stop the global warming treaty and to push founder Henry Lamb's conspiracy theories of a United Nations New World Order. [34]

New York Institute for Law and Society

Donald Trump funneled at least $118,000 to an anti-Mohawk ad campaign run by the Institute to block the St. Regis Tribal Council's plans for a Catskills Native American–run casino. Trump and his lobbyist Roger Stone were hit with a record $250,000 in fines for violating state lobby laws. [35]

Keep America Beautiful

A front for the packaging and waste-hauling industries, KAB lobbies against mandatory recycling laws, especially the passage of a national bottle bill in the United Stites. [36]

Consumer Alert

This Astroturf group calls global warming science "scare stories," and funds the Web site Globalwarming.org. Consumer Alert's networking project, the National Consumer Coalition, formed the so-called Cooler Heads Coalition (CHC), "to dispel the myths of global warming." Consumer Alert is funded by the Chemical Manufacturers Association, Chevron, Monsanto, Philip Morris, and other large corporations. [37]

Meaning and Purpose

1. Jason Stella compares the Gulf War of 1990 with the later Iraq War. How are the two similar?
2. How are the political ploys of PR (public relations) and Astroturf similar to the Nazi propaganda before and during World War II?
3. According to Stella, what are the public relations firms attempting to do with the political front organizations they have created?
4. What do all the "Astroturf's Top Ten" (paragraphs 28–37) have in common?

Strategy

1. Stella uses several different rhetorical patterns to develop his essay, but he uses comparison and contrast as his central and most basic structure. What two basic ideas does he contrast?
2. Consider the first three paragraphs of the essay as its opening unit and paragraphs 4–8 as its second structural unit. What is Stella's purpose in juxtaposing these two sections?
3. Why do you think Stella gives a brief identification of Diana Sowle, the actress who played Flo in the ads attacking the Clinton health care proposal in 1999–2000 (paragraph 16)?
4. Why do you think Stella simply lists what he calls the "Top Ten" Astroturf organizations at the end of the essay, with just a brief description of each?

Style

1. Stella uses the word *conspiracy* in paragraph 4. What exactly is the conspiracy he refers to? What impression does Stella create by using that word?
2. Stella uses the word *genesis* in paragraph 3. How does that word connect to what he says in paragraph 9?
3. Explain what you think Stella means by the phrase "the covert darkness of the postwar era" in paragraph 25.

4. Explain how well you think Stella's use of the word *nefarious* describes the situation he summarizes in paragraph 27.

Writing Tasks

1. In paragraph 18 of this essay, Jason Stella asserts that corporate Astroturf organizations "create for the public the illusion of active participation in the democratic process." Further, he concludes in paragraph 27 that the "danger of Astroturf comes not from its subversion of democracy, but in the way that it tricks us into subverting it ourselves." After you've done some Internet research on one or more Astroturf organizations, write an essay in which you draw your own conclusions about how nefarious these organizations really are.
2. Research one or more Astroturf organizations on the Internet, and write a comparison-and-contrast essay in which you show ways in which the organizations are different from what they purport to be.

❦ Responding to Photographs ❦

Comparison and Contrast

The New Warriors

For general purposes, think of photography as having two main uses: to record private experiences and to record public experiences. A photograph of private experience—a snapshot of a family outing, a portrait of a father, a candid photo of a child—is appreciated within a private context by those who have some direct connection with the recorded event or person.

A photograph that records public experience usually has nothing directly to do with us, its viewers, but we nevertheless bring meaning to it based on our experiences.

Both private and public photographs can evoke infinite associations from the viewer's own experience. But most public photographs have a second dimension. They create social or political associations that many people share. Often they suggest discontinuity in our common social experience. As an organizing principle, photographers create discontinuity through juxtaposition—that is, they oppose contrasting elements in their photographs.

342

Select one of the following writing assignments to explore the use of contrasting elements in photographs. Before you begin, reread the material at the beginning of this chapter to review strategies for developing contrasts.

1. "The New Warriors" is a public photograph that ironically explores the ideas on which the United States is predicated. By referring to details in "The New Warriors," examine its contrasting elements and determine what social or political message it embodies. Remember that you must select details from the photograph to support your contention, presenting them to readers as if they have not seen the image.

2. Select a private photograph from your or your family's collection. Be sure to find one that embodies contrasting elements. In a brief essay, examine the contrasting elements in the photograph. Keep in mind that since your readers have not been part of your family history, you must supply background information to create a context for the photograph.

❦ Additional Writing Tasks ❦
Comparison and Contrast

1. Using comparison and contrast as the dominant pattern, write an essay on one of these tasks or one that you compose for yourself. Keep in mind that you may modify any of the tasks to fit your interests.

   a. At the library, find two advertisements for the same product: one published in the 1950s and one published within the last year. Write an essay presenting the similarities and differences in these advertisements.

   b. Select two fairy tales that have similar patterns and characters, such as children journeying into a forest, an encounter with death, the appearance of a mysterious creature, a magical transformation. Identify at least three significant elements that the tales have in common and three significant elements that are different. Write an essay comparing and contrasting the similarities and differences in these two tales.

   c. Collect several advertisements for two brands of the same product type that direct their advertising campaigns toward men and women, such as Marlboro cigarettes (men) and Virginia Slims (women). After examining the advertisements, write an essay comparing and contrasting how these advertisements appeal to male consumers and how they appeal to female consumers.

   d. With accuracy and fairness, compare and contrast the arguments on both sides of a controversial issue, such as abortion, capital punishment, pornography, or gun control.

   e. Most people hold important social or political beliefs that are opposed by people close to them. Select a belief that you hold, and in an essay, contrast your attitude to the opposing attitude of one of your parents, a brother, a sister, or a close friend.

   f. Select two classes you have attended, two jobs you have held, or two vacations you have taken. Write a comparison-and-contrast essay discussing the similarities and differences of your subjects.

   g. Compare and contrast a past experience with a current experience. You might compare how you once viewed a holiday, such as Thanksgiving, Christmas, or Chanukah, with your view of it today. Or you might compare how you once viewed a special place, such as a vacation site, a fun zone, or even your bedroom, with your current view.

h.   Compare and contrast how two people from different cultures, economic situations, or age groups might perceive the same experience.

i.   Select two public figures with opposing views on one controversial issue. After familiarizing yourself with their positions, write an essay contrasting their attitudes.

j.   Select two campus groups that hold opposing social values. In an essay, compare and contrast their views and behavior.

2.   Write an essay with comparison and contrast as the dominant pattern on one of these general subjects or on a subject of your own choice. By the end of your essay, the reader should know why you prefer one thing to the other.

a.   Two people who embrace different lifestyles
b.   A national news program and a local news program
c.   Two methods for losing weight
d.   Female and male consumers
e.   Children's games yesterday and today
f.   Two characters from film or fiction
g.   A film created from a novel
h.   Watching a movie on television and watching it in a movie theater
i.   Coverage of a news event by television and by a newspaper
j.   Two classic films: horror, western, mystery, or romance

3.   Read this quotation from social critic Morton Hunt:

The record of man's inhumanity to man is horrifying, when one compiles it—enslavement, castration, torture, rape, mass slaughter in war after war. But who has compiled the record of man's kindness to man—the trillions of acts of gentleness and goodness, the helping hands, smiles, shared meals, kisses, gifts, healings, rescues? If we were no more than murderous predators, with a freakish lack of inhibition against slaughtering our own species, we would have been at a terrible competitive disadvantage compared with other animals; if this were the central truth of our nature, we would scarcely have survived, multiplied and become the dominant species on earth. Man does have an aggressive instinct, but it is not naturally or inevitably directed to killing his

Comparison and Contrast

own kind. He is a beast and perhaps at times the cruelest beast of all—but sometimes he is also the kindest beast of all. He is not all good and not perfectible, but he is not all bad and not wholly unchangeable or unimprovable. That is the only basis on which one can hope for him; but it is enough.

Hunt stresses humanity's dual nature. Write an essay with comparison and contrast as the dominant pattern that makes Hunt's general observation specific.

9

Cause and Effect
Identifying Reasons and Results

The Method

When you explain why something happened or the consequences of that happening, you are engaged in an intellectual activity that seems to be at the core of human curiosity—that is, the
search for **causes and effects**.

In their simplest form, cause-and-effect relationships appear as a
series of escalating events, one triggering another like a chain reaction. Consider the children's song in which a woman swallows a fly.
The lively fly causes her to swallow a spider to catch the fly. She then
swallows a bird to catch the spider, then a cat to catch the bird, then
a dog to catch the cat, then a goat, then a cow, and finally a horse.
The effect? She dies, of course.

In a more complex form, cause and effect are often at work in
thrillers and mysteries. A wealthy politician falls dead during a banquet. He had been in excellent health. There seems to be no clear
cause of death. Could he have been murdered in some mysterious
way? The question triggers the appearance of a supersleuth, who begins the investigation. The detective discovers clues, each of which
reveals a new suspect. After an exhaustive exploration of the many
reasons suspects had for wanting the victim dead, the murderer is
unmasked, the mysterious murder method is explained, and the
dark reasons for the murder are revealed.

Of course, mystery fans aren't consciously seeking cause or effect patterns. They're probably trying to beat the writer at his or her
own game by figuring out "Whodunit?" before the final scene. But
that question is not much different from "What caused it?"

If you think of causes as **reasons** and effects as **results**, you
might better understand cause-and-effect patterns. Like a detective you can begin with questions: Why did something happen?
What are the consequences of something's happening? When you
answer the Why, you are giving reasons, that is, causes. When you
answer the What, you are giving results, that is, effects. Professional writers observe this distinction when exploring the causes
or effects behind any event. Generally, the distinction keeps them
on the track.

Consider this question: "Why did the women's liberation movement bloom in the 1960s?" The question would lead a writer to seek reasons—that is, causes.

But the question "What were the consequences of the women's liberation movement on college campuses during the 1970s?" would lead a writer to seek results—that is, effects.

And the compound question "Why did the women's liberation movement falter in the 1980s, and what will be the consequences in the 1990s?" would lead a writer to explain the reasons and the results—that is, both causes and effects.

Strategies

When you begin analyzing the cause-and-effect relationships in a complex subject, you might feel somewhat like a detective unraveling a mystery. You must be prepared for the false starts and deceptive clues that will send you down the wrong path, but don't lose heart: You can learn by studying professional writers, who often approach cause-and-effect analysis from several angles, depending on the characteristics of their subjects. First, they may narrow their effort by concentrating only on the causes. Second, they may concentrate only on the effects. And third, they may choose to concentrate on both causes and effects. If you understand cause-and-effect development patterns and apply your knowledge critically as you read, you'll soon master the technique of analyzing cause-and-effect relationships in your own writing.

Identifying Causes

When effects are clear, writers will concentrate on causes. In 1948, Harry Truman upset Thomas Dewey, Governor of New York, for the presidency. Dewey was predicted to win by a landslide. In fact, one newspaper prematurely printed headlines announcing Dewey's victory. The political pundits were wrong: Truman won. A writer who asked, "Why did Truman win?" would not have to establish the result (Truman's victory), but he or she would concentrate on the reasons—that is, the causes—behind Truman's victory. Did his "underdog" image generate sympathy among voters? Did a last-minute whistlestop campaign through America's heartland swing the election his way? Was it a well-oiled Democratic machine that kept the party faithful in line? These and other causes would have to be explored in any analysis of the election.

In *Redoing America,* Robert Faltermayer discusses the interwoven character of American cities. In the following paragraph, Faltermayer concentrates on causes. He opens with the common assumption that the automobile has had a destructive effect on the "close knit fabric" of cities. He then presents the reasons for this phenomenon:

> The close knit fabric was blown apart by the automobile, and by the postwar middle-class exodus to suburbia which the mass-ownership of automobiles made possible. The automobile itself was not to blame for this development, nor was the desire for suburban living, which is obviously a genuine aspiration of many Americans. The fault lay in our failure, right up to the present time, to fashion new policies to minimize the disruptive effects of the automobile revolution. We have failed not only to tame the automobile itself, but to overhaul a property-tax system that tends to foster automotive-age sprawl and to institute coordinated planning in the politically fragmented suburbs that have caught the brunt of the postwar building boom.

In the opening sentence, Faltermayer establishes a relationship between automobiles and the changing character of cities and sprawling suburbs. In the next sentence he refines his focus by dismissing two possible causes: the automobile itself and the desire for suburban living. In the remainder of the paragraph he explains what he believes to be the true cause: the failure to fashion public policies that would have controlled the automobile and the building boom.

Identifying Effects

When writers select subjects with very clear causes, they will then concentrate on effects. For instance, drug merchants are expanding their operations into rural communities. Crack houses are springing up in small towns where drugs had previously been scarce. This fact has been substantiated by law-enforcement agencies across the nation. A writer who asked, "What are the consequences of increased drug use in rural communities?" would spend very little time establishing the existence of increased drug activity in small-town America because it is widely known. He or she would, however, concentrate on the effects this trend might have on rural communities. What, for instance, are the consequences for families? What will be the effects on undertrained and underbudgeted law-enforcement agencies, on social services, and on schools?

In this paragraph from *Anatomy of an Illness,* Norman Cousins uses this pattern. He quickly establishes the cause, a hypothetical injury, and then concentrates on exploring effects of pain suppressants on injured professional athletes.

> Professional athletes are sometimes severely disadvantaged by trainers whose job it is to keep them in action. The more famous the athlete, the greater the risk that he or she may be subjected to extreme medical measures when injury strikes. The star baseball pitcher whose arm is sore because of a torn muscle or tissue damage may need sustained rest more than anything else. But this team is battling for a place in the World Series; so the trainer or team doctor, called upon to work his magic, reaches for a strong dose of butazolidine or other powerful pain suppressants. Presto, the pain disappears! The pitcher takes his place on the mound and does superbly. That could be the last game, however, in which he is able to throw the ball with full strength. The drugs didn't repair the torn muscle or cause the damaged tissue to heal. What they did was to mask the pain, enabling the pitcher to throw hard, further damaging the torn muscle. Little wonder that so many star athletes are cut down in their prime, more the victims of overzealous treatment of their injuries than of the injuries themselves.

Cousins opens by establishing the direction the paragraph will take. He then states the cause of the effects that will follow—a hypothetical injury to a star baseball pitcher's throwing arm. Next, he develops the effects of the injury—under pressure to win, a trainer or team doctor prescribes a pain killer; the pitcher plays as if he had no injury; and the ultimate effect is a career cut short, not by injury but by the mistreatment of injury.

Identifying Causes and Effects

Writers are always cautious about assuming that readers know the causes or effects of an event, especially when exploring a complex subject that is not part of common knowledge. When such a subject is discussed, they usually explain both causes and effects. Often they will alternate causes and effects in one paragraph.

Victor C. Cline uses this pattern in a paragraph from "How TV Violence Damages Your Children."

> Much of the research that has led to the conclusion that TV and movie violence could cause aggressive behavior in some children has stemmed from the work in the area of imitative learning or modeling which, reduced to its simplest expression, might be termed "monkey see, monkey do." Research by Stanford psychologist Albert Bandura has shown that even brief exposure to novel aggressive behavior on a *one-time basis* can be repeated in free play by as high as 88 percent of the young children seeing it on TV. Dr. Bandura also demonstrated that even a single viewing of a novel aggressive act could be recalled and produced by children six months later, without any intervening exposure. Earlier studies have estimated that the average child between the ages of 5 and 15 will witness, during this 10-year period, the violent destruction of more than 13,400 fellow humans. This means that through several hours of TV-watching, a child may see more violence than the average adult experiences in a lifetime. Killing is as common as taking a walk, a gun more natural than an umbrella. Children are thus taught to take pride in force and violence and to feel ashamed of ordinary sympathy.

Cline's first sentence establishes that children learn aggressive behavior from television through modeling, or, as Cline phrases it, "monkey see, monkey do," In the second sentence he presents his first cause and first effect—even *brief exposure* to aggressive behavior (cause) can lead to children's repeating it in free play (effect). In the third sentence he presents the second cause and its effect: a *single viewing* of an aggressive act (cause) can be recalled by children six months later (effect). The next three sentences detail the violence a typical child might see over ten years, thus establishing a very dramatic cause. In his final sentence, Cline states the ultimate effect: Television teaches children to take pride in violence and to be ashamed of sympathy.

Rather than alternating causes and effects in individual paragraphs, writers will sometimes divide them into separate paragraphs. The following two paragraphs are from Frank Trippett's humorous essay "The Great American Cooling Machine." In the first paragraph, Trippett establishes that air conditioning has been overlooked as a major cause for change in U.S. society. In the second paragraph he presents three effects of air conditioning on society.

> Neither scholars nor pop sociologists have really got around to charting and diagnosing all the changes brought about by air conditioning. Professional observers have for years been preoccupied with the social implications of the automobile and television. Mere glancing analysis suggests that the car and TV, in their most decisive influences on American habits, have been powerfully aided and abetted by air conditioning. The car may have created all those shopping centers in the boondocks, but only air conditioning has made them attractive to mass clienteles. Similarly, the artificial cooling of the living room undoubtedly helped turn the typical American into a year-round TV addict. Without air conditioning, how many viewers would endure reruns (or even Johnny Carson) on one of those pestilential summer nights that used to send people out to collapse on the lawn or to sleep on the roof?
>
> Many of the side effects of air conditioning are far from being fully pinned down. It is a reasonable suspicion, though, that controlled climate, by inducing Congress to stay in Washington longer than it used to during the swelter season, thus presumably passing more laws, has contributed to bloated government. One can only speculate that the advent of the super-cooled bedroom may be linked to the carnal adventurism associated with the mid-century sexual revolution. Surely it is a

fact—if restaurant complaints about raised thermostats are to be believed—that air conditioning induces at least expense-account diners to eat and drink more; if so, it must be credited with adding to the national fat problem.

Identifying Immediate and Ultimate Causes and Effects

Careful writers usually distinguish between immediate and ultimate causes and effects, that is, the ones that are most apparent and those that underlie them. In the example above, Trippett, in his humorous way, presents the ultimate effects of air conditioning: bloated government, the sexual revolution, and the national fat problem. The depth to which a writer analyzes causes or effects depends upon the subject and the purpose. Exploring the ultimate causes or effects requires more effort than getting to the immediate ones because a writer must establish a foundation for the analysis.

In *The Seasons of a Man's Life,* Daniel J. Levenson studies the psychological development of men. In these two paragraphs, after establishing a solid foundation for his conclusions, he presents the ultimate effects of middle age on a man's relationships with young adults.

At around 40 a man is deeply involved in the Young/Old polarity. This developmental process has a powerful effect upon his relationships with his offspring and with young adults generally. When his own aging weighs heavily upon him, their exuberant vitality is more likely to arouse his envy and resentment than his delight and forbearance. He may be preoccupied with grievances against his own parents for damage, real or imagined, that they have inflicted upon him at different ages. These preoccupations make him less appreciative of the (often similar) grievances his offspring direct toward him.

If he feels he has lost or betrayed his own early Dream, he may find it hard to give his wholehearted support and blessing to the Dreams of young adults. When his offspring show signs of failure or confusion in pursuing their adult goals, he is afraid that their lives will turn out as badly as his own. Yet, when they do well, he may resent their success. Anxiety and guilt may undermine his efforts to be helpful and lead him instead to be nagging and vindictive.

Levenson's analysis probes deeply into the nagging relationship some middle-aged men might have with young adults. He exposes the ultimate cause and its effects—anxiety over aging, failure, and competition.

In this paragraph from *The Faces of the Enemy,* Sam Keen explores the ultimate cause of war, not the politicians who start wars or the generals who carry them out, but the "good people" who allow their leaders to act out community neuroses by waging war.

> The major responsibility for war lies not with villains and evil men but with reasonably good citizens. Any depth understanding of the social function of war leads to the conclusion that it was the "good" Germans who created the social ecology that nurtured the Nazis. Lincoln said, "War is much too important to be left to the generals." But the psychological truth is much more disturbing. The generals are the (largely unconscious) agents of a (largely unconscious) civilian population. The good people send out armies as symbolic representatives to act out their repressed shadows, denied hostilities, unspoken cruelties, unacceptable greed, unimagined lust for revenge against punitive parents and authorities, uncivil sexual sadism, denied animality, in a purifying blood ritual that confirms their claim to goodness before the approving eyes of history or God. Warfare is the political equivalent of the individual process of seeking "vindictive triumph," which Karen Horney described as the essence of neurosis.

Writers keep two cautions in mind when exploring cause-and-effect relationships; be aware of them. First, writers avoid confusing process patterns with cause-and-effect patterns. The analysis of a process usually stems from a question of How? not Why? or What? "*How* did Ronald Reagan get elected to the presidency?" sends a writer into process analysis. "*Why* was Ronald Reagan elected to the presidency?" sends a writer into an examination of the causes—that is, the reasons. "*What* were the consequences of Ronald Reagan's presidency?" sends a writer to examine the effects—that is, the results.

Second, they avoid the *post hoc, ergo propter hoc* fallacy, that is, the "after this, therefore because of this" or "false-cause" fallacy. Writers commit this fallacy (argument from a false inference) by jumping to conclusions based on insufficient information. That former President Ronald Reagan was elected when the electorate's average life expectancy was increasing does not mean that an older voting population will elect older presidents.

In a variation of the false-cause fallacy, an event is identified as triggering a series of events in a cause-and-effect chain reaction, or *causal chain*. This kind of reasoning was at work in the arguments of politicians who supported the U.S. military action in Vietnam during the 1960s and 1970s. They maintained that if North Vietnam was successful in its efforts to take over South Vietnam, then the nearby Southeast Asian countries would soon be taken over by Communist regimes one at a time, like a file of falling dominoes triggered by the first domino toppling into the second. History, of course, has shown that these events did not happen. But keep in mind that causes of complicated events are seldom simple or obvious and that predicting the future with cause-and-effect reasoning is a chancy business.

Cause and Effect in College Writing

Essays exploring cause-and-effect relationships are common in classrooms across campus. In a history class you might be asked to discuss the causes of racial discrimination following the Civil War. In an economics class you might be asked to explain the international effects of the massive U.S. budget deficit. In a psychology class you might be asked to discuss the causes of clinical depression and its effects or simply causes or effects.

Guidelines for Writing a Cause-and-Effect Essay

1. Select a subject that lends itself to the analysis of cause-and-effect relationships. Use prewriting techniques to develop a list of causes, effects, or both.

2. Group the causes and effects identified in your prewritten material. If appropriate, separate immediate causes from ultimate causes.

3. Decide on your approach to the subject—that is, if the causes are clear, then concentrate on the effects; if the effects are clear, then concentrate on the causes; or concentrate on both the causes and effects. Be sure to emphasize the most important causes or effects to avoid becoming distracted by the obvious or trivial. Determine which causes or effects should be developed in a single paragraph and which should be developed in two paragraphs.

4. With the general purpose of the essay in mind, write a tentative thesis that signals whether you will mainly emphasize causes, effects, or causes and effects. Write the first draft.

5. Revise your essay, avoiding the *post hoc, ergo propter hoc* fallacy.

A Student Essay Developed by Cause and Effect

Tom Kim wrote a cause-and-effect analysis in response to the following sociology assignment:

In a 900- to 1000-word essay, identify a campuswide problem and explain why it is taking place and what will result from it. Consider these possible subjects:

- Services needed by returning students
- Inadequate library support
- Lack of health professionals on campus
- Increase in student cheating
- Sexual harassment
- Tension among ethnic groups
- Lack of competitive sports
- Increase in part-time faculty

Kim decided to write on the increase in student cheating. It had become widespread, and school officials, professors, and students

were concerned about it. First read the essay, then reread it and respond to the items in Reviewing with a Writer's Eye.

Cheating: A Growing Campus Problem

Five years ago, according to student government records,   1
four students were officially charged with cheating. Each incident took place in a large lecture class: two in Psychology
100, one in Art History, and one in Economics. All four incidents seemed to be spontaneous acts that involved copying answers from another student's answer sheet and were committed "because the opportunity presented itself." Last year
206 cheating incidents were officially reported, a dramatic increase. Although most of these incidents took place in large
lecture courses, many of them took place in smaller classes
that require individual work. For example, a biology instructor
reported two students from different classes who turned in re-
markably similar projects. Two advanced psychology professors reported several students for turning in case studies
done by other students during previous semesters. Four English professors reported students who plagiarized material
from professional sources or submitted essays someone else
had written. Perhaps a way to approach the problem is to ask,
Why do students cheat? and What are the effects? Although
the reasons for cheating are not easy to identify, the effects of
cheating are clear.

The rise in cheating is often attributed to two immediate   2
causes. First, in these difficult economic times more and more
students are working more hours a week but not cutting back
on their course load. Currently, according to the campus
records office, over ninety percent of our student body works
at least twenty-five hours a week, but the average course load
has not decreased. This fact suggests that students are trying
to cram too much into their schedules. Once the semester is
underway, they discover they must take shortcuts or drop
classes. Cheating is an easy shortcut. A second reason students cheat may be because of pressure to attend graduate
school. Although most students can pass their courses through
their own efforts, a few believe they must earn "A"s to qualify
for graduate programs. These students feel that cheating will
give them the grade boost they need.

A third reason is more remote, thus much less obvious to a casual observer. Cheating may have increased because a subculture of cheating has developed—when a student's friends cheat, then it is easier to cheat. Students in this subculture exchange test information, science projects, essays, and research papers. This material gets reworked and recycled from semester to semester. Rather than keeping their exploits as cheaters secret, they celebrate them, often bragging about their prowess, thus fueling the process from semester to semester.

Although the causes of cheating are difficult to identify, its immediate effects can be seen around campus. Large lecture-class professors are taking new precautions. First, they are scrambling the questions on their tests, perhaps creating as many as five different tests for one class. Second, they are using more proctors to monitor the class during the examination. One professor had ten proctors roaming the lecture hall while students took the test. Finally, they are requiring students to "check in" to get copies of the test booklet. The proctors check their driver's licenses against the roster to be sure the enrolled student is actually taking the test. The ultimate result of this intense security could be the creation of a "Big Brother" atmosphere in some classes—yet it all seems necessary.

The effect of cheating in composition classes is less dramatic but equally significant. Many composition professors are assigning more in-class writing. Once the instructor becomes familiar with a student's writing ability, then spotting plagiarized or cribbed essays is easier. For instance, if a student consistently writes "C" papers in class, then begins to write "A" papers out of class, the instructor becomes suspicious. At this point, the instructor will usually meet in conference with the student to discuss the essay's subject and content. This discussion helps the instructor to determine if the student actually wrote the essay or had someone else write it. One English professor said she had not uncovered any cheating but believed her diligence deterred cheating.

Two other effects of cheating may ultimately damage students. The first is obvious. Students who cheat will eventually reach a point where they are unable to cheat and will lack the fundamental skills for success in upper-division classes. Some might say their failure is just retribution. How sad. Most students can be successful if they accept the challenge of education; those who cheat are hobbling themselves unnecessarily.

A second effect could possibly make serious students victims of cheaters. Students who actually struggle with course content may receive lower grades than those who cheat. This fact is discouraging, especially for those who know that some students achieved higher grades dishonestly. As a result, some students have quietly reported cheaters. This, of course, may make honest students feel as if they are betraying their classmates, thus disrupting their sense of collegiality.

The number of students reported to be cheating is a mere   7
fraction of the 15,673 enrolled students. But campus officials believe a great deal of unreported cheating takes place. As a consequence, a committee composed of students, faculty, and campus administration is investigating cheating to develop campus guidelines to combat it. Aside from creating a more formal process to determine if a student was actually cheating, the committee is also developing a strategy to educate the entire student body about cheating and its effects on campus life. The strategy will include information that all students will receive and a detailed honor system that all professors will present the first day of classes. What will be the result of the committee's work? That is hard to predict, but the effort has already heightened student and faculty awareness.

Reviewing with a Writer's Eye

1. Review Tom Kim's writing assignment (p. 357). Explain how he succeeds or fails to meet its requirements. Identify specific paragraphs of "Cheating: A Growing Campus Problem" that address particular aspects of the assignment.

2. Develop a detailed scratch outline of Kim's essay. Begin by restating the thesis statement in your own words. Then restate the topic sentences and subpoints (see pp. 358–360).

3. Identify the immediate causes and the ultimate causes of cheating. How does Kim distinguish them (see pp. 358–359)?

4. Identify the immediate effects and the ultimate effects of cheating. How does Kim distinguish them (see pp. 359–360)?

5. Indicate where Kim explains the causes and effects of cheating and where he illustrates with examples the causes and effects of cheating. Identify the key examples.

6. What is the campuswide outcome of cheating? Write a new one-paragraph introduction to "Cheating: A Growing Campus Problem" that concentrates on the campuswide outcome and ends with a thesis statement similar to Kim's.

7. Imagine that you're a member of Kim's peer-review group. He has asked you to review the structure of his essay, paying particular attention to transitions and responding to paragraphs 2 and 3. Write a brief note, no more than 150 words, detailing your responses.

Peer Review

You may be asked to write an essay about one of the readings that follow. Before you meet with your writing group, review this introduction. As you read the papers of your group members, use these general writing principles about cause and effect to help guide your comments.

1. The paper should not belabor the obvious; it should not present causes or effects that are already well known to most readers.

2. The causes that are discussed should clearly lead to the effects, and the effects discussed should clearly result from the causes.

3. The cause-and-effect relations should be based on sufficient information and logical reasoning.

As you will see while reading the essays that follow, professional writers frequently mix example and comparison-and-contrast patterns into essays dominated by cause and effect. Study these professionals for their craft. Examine how they construct their discussions. Separate the causes from the effects. And separate the immediate effects from the ultimate effects. Through this kind of critical reading, you will develop your own writing skills.

❦ Stephen King ❦

Stephen King was born in Portland, Maine, in 1947 and graduated from the University of Maine in 1970. Before finding enormous success with his writing, King worked in a knitting mill and as a janitor, laundry worker, and high school English teacher. Since then, he has become, arguably, the world's most successful writer of horror fiction. He has published short-story collections, screenplays, and nearly thirty novels that have sold over 20 million copies. Many of those novels—including Carrie, The Shining, *and* Pet Sematary—*have been made into movies. His short story "The Body," from the collection* Night Shift, *was produced as the film* Stand By Me. *His works include* Apt Pupil: A Novella in Different Seasons *and* Bag of Bones, *both published in 1998. King's original television miniseries,* Storm of the Century, *was broadcast in 1999. King also plays rhythm guitar for the Rock Bottom Remainders, a rock band composed entirely of professional writers. Amy Tan (see pp. 257–265) is a Remainderette—she sings backup vocals—with the same band. He co-wrote with Stewart O'Nan,* Faithful: Two Diehard Boston Red Sox Fans Chronicle the Historic 2004 Season, *and rejoiced when the Red Sox won the 2004 World Series.*

Why We Crave Horror Movies

In this essay, first published in Playboy *magazine, Stephen King speculates on the reasons why horror films have been so enormously popular over the years. He concludes that they not only entertain in a ghoulish way, but also serve an important psychological and social purpose.*

While you read, weigh the validity of King's conclusions against your own firsthand experience of horror films.

I think that we're all mentally ill; those of us outside the asy-   1
lums only hide it a little better—and maybe not all that much
better, after all. We've all known people who talk to themselves,
people who sometimes squinch their faces into horrible grimaces
when they believe no one is watching, people who have some hys-

terical fear—of snakes, the dark, the tight place, the long drop . . . and, of course, those final worms and grubs that are waiting so patiently underground.

When we pay our four or five bucks and seat ourselves at tenth-row center in a theater showing a horror movie, we are daring the nightmare.

2

Why? Some of the reasons are simple and obvious. To show that we can, that we are not afraid, that we can ride this roller coaster. Which is not to say that a really good horror movie may not surprise a scream out of us at some point, the way we may scream when the roller coaster twists through a complete 360 or plows through a lake at the bottom of the drop. And horror movies, like roller coasters, have always been the special province of the young; by the time one turns 40 or 50, one's appetite for double twists or 360-degree loops may be considerably depleted.

3

We also go to re-establish our feelings of essential normality; the horror movie is innately conservative, even reactionary. Freda Jackson as the horrible melting woman in *Die, Monster, Die!* confirms for us that no matter how far we may be removed from the beauty of a Robert Redford or a Diana Ross, we are still light-years from true ugliness.

4

And we go to have fun.

5

Ah, but this is where the ground starts to slope away, isn't it? Because this is a very peculiar sort of fun, indeed. The fun comes from seeing others menaced—sometimes killed. One critic has suggested that if pro football has become the voyeur's version of combat, then the horror film has become the modern version of the public lynching.

6

It is true that the mythic, "fairy-tale" horror film intends to take away the shades of gray. . . . It urges us to put away our more civilized and adult penchant for analysis and to become children again, seeing things in pure blacks and whites. It may be that horror movies provide psychic relief on this level because this invitation to lapse into simplicity, irrationality and even outright madness is extended so rarely. We are told we may allow our emotions a free rein . . . or no rein at all.

7

If we are all insane, then sanity becomes a matter of degree. If your insanity leads you to carve up women like Jack the Ripper or the

8

Cleveland Torso Murderer, we clap you away in the funny farm (but neither of those two amateur-night surgeons was ever caught, heh-heh-heh); if, on the other hand, your insanity leads you only to talk to yourself when you're under stress or to pick your nose on your morning bus, then you are left alone to go about your business . . . though it is doubtful that you will ever be invited to the best parties.

The potential lyncher is in almost all of us (excluding saints, past   9
and present; but then, most saints have been crazy in their own ways), and every now and then, he has to be let loose to scream and roll around in the grass. Our emotions and our fears form their own body, and we recognize that it demands its own exercise to maintain proper muscle tone. Certain of these emotional muscles are accepted—even exalted—in civilized society; they are, of course, the emotions that tend to maintain the status quo of civilization itself. Love, friendship, loyalty, kindness—these are all the emotions that we applaud, emotions that have been immortalized in the couplets of Hallmark cards and in the verses (I don't dare call it poetry) of Leonard Nimoy.

When we exhibit these emotions, society showers us with posi-   10
tive reinforcement; we learn this even before we get out of diapers. When, as children, we hug our rotten little puke of a sister and give her a kiss, all the aunts and uncles smile and twit and cry, "Isn't he the sweetest little thing?" Such coveted treats as chocolate-covered graham crackers often follow. But if we deliberately slam the rotten little puke of a sister's fingers in the door, sanctions follow—angry remonstrance from parents, aunts and uncles; instead of a chocolate-covered graham cracker, a spanking.

But anticivilization emotions don't go away, and they demand pe-   11
riodic exercise. We have such "sick" jokes as, "What's the difference between a truckload of bowling balls and a truckload of dead babies?" (You can't unload a truckload of bowling balls with a pitchfork . . . a joke, by the way, that I heard originally from a ten-year-old.) Such a joke may surprise a laugh or a grin out of us even as we recoil, a possibility that confirms the thesis: If we share a brotherhood of man, then we also share an insanity of man. None of which is intended as a defense of either the sick joke or insanity but merely as an explanation of why the best horror films, like the best fairy tales, manage to be reactionary, anarchistic, and revolutionary all at the same time.

The mythic horror movie, like the sick joke, has a dirty job to do. It deliberately appeals to all that is worst in us. It is morbidity unchained, our most base instincts let free, our nastiest fantasies realized . . . and it all happens, fittingly enough, in the dark. For those reasons, good liberals often shy away from horror films. For myself, I like to see the most aggressive of them—*Dawn of the Dead,* for instance—as lifting a trap door in the civilized forebrain and throwing a basket of raw meat to the hungry alligators swimming around in that subterranean river beneath.

Why bother? Because it keeps them from getting out, man. It keeps them down there and me up here. It was Lennon and McCartney who said that all you need is love, and I would agree with that.

As long as you keep the gators fed.

(12)

(13)

(14)

Meaning and Purpose

1. What is King's thesis? Is it explicitly stated or is it implied?
2. Is King serious when he claims in the opening sentence that "we're all mentally ill"? What exactly does he mean by this? Explain.
3. In paragraph 4 King asserts that horror movies are "innately conservative, even reactionary," and in paragraph 11 he claims them to be "reactionary, anarchistic, and revolutionary all at the same time." Explain what he means by these claims.
4. Why, according to King, are horror movies both a psychological and a social good?

Strategy

1. King grabs our attention with the opening sentence. Explain how the meaning of that sentence relates to the rest of the essay.
2. What does King claim are the immediate causes of the popularity of horror films? What is the ultimate cause? (See pp. 354–356.)
3. Explain how King organizes his essay around the immediate and ultimate causes for the popularity of horror films. How much time

and space does he spend on each? What effect does this organizational pattern have on the reader?

4. Why does King change from the first-person singular (I) in the first sentence to the first-person plural (we) in the second?

5. What evidence does King offer to support his claims about the reasons for the popularity of horror movies?

Style

1. Reread the essay, paying close attention to King's use of **concrete** language and **metaphor** (see Glossary). Point out passages in which King uses these devices and comment on their effectiveness. Try translating at least two of these passages into more common usage. Which version is more lively?

2. What is King's **tone** (see Glossary) in the essay? How does he establish that tone? Explain.

3. Closely examine the **analogy** (see Glossary) King uses in paragraph 3. What idea does it explain, and how effectively does it clarify that idea?

4. If necessary, look the following words up in a dictionary: *grimaces, hysterical* (paragraph 1); *province* (3); *voyeur* (6); *penchant, psychic* (7); *exalted* (9); *twit, sanctions, remonstrance* (10); *recoil, anarchistic* (11); *morbidity, subterranean* (12).

Writing Tasks

1. Write an essay in which you explain the reasons (causes) that you attend horror films regularly, attend them only occasionally, or never attend them at all. Use King's essay as a model, in that you organize your essay so that you spend more time on ultimate causes and relatively less time on immediate causes.

2. Write an essay that examines the validity or the invalidity of King's claims in "Why We Crave Horror Movies." Make sure that you include as much supportive evidence as you can to prove your thesis.

❦ Neal Gabler ❦

Neal Gabler, a media critic and historian, author of a history of Hollywood
(An Empire of Their Own: How the Jews Invented Hollywood), *a biography of Walter Winchell* (Winchell: Gossip, Power and the Culture of Celebrity), *and a study of U.S. popular culture* (Life the Movie: How Entertainment Conquered Reality), *believes that the evolution of popular theater, with its reliance on technology, has permeated our culture to the extent that entertainment is "the primary value of American life" and we now view life itself as entertainment.*

How Urban Myths Reveal Society's Fears

As you read this essay, first published in the Los Angeles Times *in 1995, notice how Neal Gabler compares urban myths with ancient myths, the stuff of folklore, to show how urban myths affect our ways of thinking.*

The story goes like this: During dinner at an opulent wedding re-   1
ception, the groom rises from the head table and shushes the crowd.
Everyone naturally assumes he is about to toast his bride and thank
his guests. Instead, he solemnly announces that there has been a
change of plan. He and his bride will be taking separate honeymoons
and, when they return, the marriage will be annulled. The reason for
this sudden turn of events, he says, is taped to the bottom of everyone's plate. The stunned guests quickly flip their dinnerware to discover a photo—of the bride *in flagrante delicto* with the best man.

At least that is the story that has been recently making the   2
rounds up and down the Eastern seaboard and as far west as
Chicago. Did this really happen? *A Washington Post* reporter who
tracked the story was told by one source that it happened at a New
Hampshire hotel. But then another source swears it happened in
Medford, Mass. Then again another suggests a banquet hall outside
Schenectady, N.Y. Meanwhile, a sophisticated couple in Manhattan
has heard it happened at the Pierre.

In short, the whole thing appears to be another urban myth, one   3
of those weird tales that periodically catch the public imagination.
Alligators swarming the sewers after people have flushed the baby
reptiles down the toilet. The baby-sitter who gets threatening phone
calls that turn out to be coming from inside the house. The woman
who turns out to have a nest of black-widow spiders in her beehive
hairdo. The man who falls asleep and awakens to find his kidney has
been removed. The rat that gets deep-fried and served by a fast-food
outlet. Or, in a variation, the mouse that has somehow drowned in a
closed Coca-Cola bottle.

These tales are preposterous, but in a mass society like ours,   4
where stories are usually manufactured by Hollywood, they just may
be the most genuine form of folklore we have. Like traditional folklore, they are narratives crafted by the collective consciousness. Like
traditional folklore, they give expression to the national mind. And
like traditional folklore, they blend the fantastic with the routine, if
only to demonstrate, in the words of University of Utah folklorist Jan
Harold Brunvand, the nation's leading expert on urban legends, "that
the prosaic contemporary scene is capable of producing shocking or
amazing occurrences."

Shocking and amazing, yes. But in these stories, anything can   5
happen not because the world is a magical place rich with wonder—
as in folk tales of yore—but because our world is so utterly terrifying. Here, nothing is reliable and no laws of morality govern. The alligators in the sewers presents an image of an urban hell inhabited by
beasts—an image that might have come directly from Hades and the
River Styx in Greek mythology. The baby-sitter and the man upstairs
exploits fears that we are not even safe in our own homes these days.
The spider in the hairdo says that even on our own persons, dangers
lurk. The man who loses his kidney plays to our fears of the night
and the real bogymen who prowl them. The mouse in the soda
warns us of the perils of an impersonal mass-production society.

As for the wedding-reception tale, which one hacker on the In-   6
ternet has dubbed "Wedding Revenge," it may address the greatest
terror of all: that love and commitment are chimerical and even
friendship is meaningless. These are timeless issues, but the sudden
promulgation of the tale suggests its special relevance in the age of

AIDS, when commitment means even more than it used to, and in the age of feminism, when some men are feeling increasingly threatened by women's freedom. Thus, the groom not only suffers betrayal and humiliation; his plight carries the hint of danger and emasculation, too. Surely, a legend for our time.

Of course, folklore and fairy tales have long subsisted on terror, and even the treacly cartoons of Walt Disney are actually, when you parse them, dark and complex expressions of fear—from Snow White racing through the treacherous forest to Pinnochio gobbled by the whale to Dumbo being separated from his mother. But these crystallize the fears of childhood, the fears one must overcome to make the difficult transition to adulthood. Thus, the haunted forest of the fairy tales is a trope for haunted adolescence; the witch or crone, a trope for the spent generation one must vanquish to claim one's place in the world, and the prince who comes to the rescue, a trope for the adult responsibilities that the heroine must now assume.

Though urban legends frequently originate with college students about to enter the real world, they are different from traditional fairy tales because their terrors are not really obstacles on the road to understanding, and they are different from folklore because they cannot even be interpreted as cautionary. In urban legends, obstacles aren't overcome, perhaps can't be overcome, and there is nothing we can do differently to avoid the consequences. The woman, not knowing any better, eats the fried rat. The baby-sitter is terrorized by the stranger hiding in the house. The black widow bites the woman with the beehive hairdo. The alligators prowl the sewers. The marriage in Wedding Revenge breaks up.

It is not just our fears, then, that these stories exploit. Like so much else in modern life—tabloids, exploitalk programs, real-life crime best-sellers—urban legends testify to an overwhelming condition of fear and to a sense of our own impotence within it. That is why there is no accommodation in these stories, no lesson or wisdom imparted. What there is, is the stark impression that our world is anomic. We live in a haunted forest of skyscrapers or of suburban lawns and ranch houses, but there is no one to exorcise the evil and no prince to break the spell.

Given the pressures of modern life, it isn't surprising that we   10
have created myths to express our malaise. But what is surprising is
how many people seem committed to these myths. The *Post* reporter
found people insisting they personally knew someone who had attended the doomed wedding reception. Others went further: They
maintained they had actually attended the reception—though no
such reception ever took place. Yet even those who didn't claim to
have been personally involved seemed to feel duty bound to assert
the tale's plausibility.

Why this insistence? Perhaps the short answer is that people want   11
to believe in a cosmology of dysfunction because it is the best way of explaining the inexplicable in our lives. A world in which alligators roam
sewers and wedding receptions end in shock is at once terrifying and
soothing—terrifying because these things happen, soothing because we
are absolved of any responsibility for them. It is just the way it is.

But there may be an additional reason why some people seem so   12
willing to suspend their disbelief in the face of logic. This one has
less to do with the content of these tales than with their creation.
However they start, urban legends rapidly enter a national conversation in which they are embellished, heightened, reconfigured. Everyone can participate—from the people who spread the tale on talk radio to the people who discuss it on the Internet to the people who
tell it to their neighbors. In effect, these legends are the product of a
giant campfire around which we trade tales of terror.

If this makes each of us a co-creator of the tales, it also provides   13
us with a certain pride of authorship. Like all authors, we don't want
to see the spell of our creation broken—especially when we have
formed a little community around it. It doesn't matter whether these
tales are true or not. What matters is that they plausibly reflect our
world, that they have been generated from the grass roots and that
we can pass them along.

In a way, then, these tales of powerlessness ultimately assert a   14
kind of authority. Urban legends permit us to become our own
Stephen Kings, terrorizing ourselves to confirm one of the few powers we still possess: the power to tell stories about our world.

Meaning and Purpose

1. "The story goes like this" seems an unusually friendly way to begin an essay. Why do you suppose Gabler opens the essay this way?
2. Reread paragraphs 7 and 8. What is one important difference between how traditional tales affected their audiences and how urban myths affect their audiences?
3. Reread paragraphs 9 and 10. How can urban myths exploit our fears, according to Gable?
4. What do Walt Disney cartoons, discussed in paragraph 7, have in common with urban myths?
5. Which one of the urban myths that Gabler discusses is, in your opinion, the most convincing? Why?

Strategy

1. How can any urban myth be said to be true? Why does Gabler say that we believe in them without checking their authenticity?
2. What strategies does Gabler use to show that urban myths do in fact cause us to fear parts of our own lives?
3. Using evidence from Gabler's essay, note why we need some kind of myths, be they folklore or urban myths.
4. What main strategy does Gabler employ in paragraph 9 to persuade the reader that myths "exploit" our fears?
5. How does Gabler imply that we can, in fact, overcome our fears?

Style

1. What does the word *opulent* mean, as it is used in the first sentence of this essay? Suggest an appropriate synonym.
2. Define the phrase *in flagrante delicto*, as it is used in the first paragraph. Why is this phrase in italics?
3. What are two current examples of "exploitalk programs" (paragraph 9) on television?
4. Why does Gabler talk about the fairy tales of our youth?

5. Of the several definitions of the word *terror* in a reliable college dictionary, which definition is the most appropriate definition in describing urban myths? Suggest an appropriate synonym.

Writing Tasks

1. We all experience what Gabler calls "the pressures of modern life" (paragraph 10). In a cause-and-effect essay, discuss two personal pressures that you now face and the effects of those personal pressures on your academic life.
2. Like all first-year college students, you had fears—fears about failing, fears about making new friends, fears about finding your way around campus, and so forth. Write an essay in which you discuss two of those fears, being sure that you discuss them from a personal point of view, and tell your audience how those fears affected you during your first few weeks of college life.

❦ Gina Greenlee ❦

Just four years after the events described in this essay, at the age of fourteen, Gina Greenlee became afflicted with wanderlust. At that time she spent the summer in Karishrue, Germany, her first time overseas. Three years later she packed up all her belongings and spent three weeks in the Caribbean. Since then she has traveled widely, visiting and living in such disparate places as Costa Rica, Singapore, Malaysia, Thailand, India, Greece, Turkey, Egypt, and much of the United States. In 2000, she took a four-month trip around the world. She is an artist and freelance writer who currently lives in Connecticut.

No Tears for Frankie

This essay was first published in The New York Times. *Although Gina Greenlee addresses only her own childhood experience with sexual harassment in the essay, that experience is poignant enough to have wide appeal for a national newspaper readership.*

As an adult, Greenlee looks back on a series of traumatic experiences that shaped her attitude towards a schoolmate's death. Notice how she carefully chooses both specific and general examples to explain her reaction to the boy's death.

I was in the fifth grade when Frankie died. It was 1971. My 1
whole class planned to attend the funeral, since we knew him. My
father thought going might give me nightmares, but I insisted. I had
never seen a dead person before. Most of all, I wanted to be sure that
the little creep would never touch me again.

Frankie lived in Lower Manhattan, where run-down tenements 2
along Avenues A, B and C were on the verge of becoming the crack
houses of the 80s. At the time, I lived nearby. Then in 1970 my family moved into an apartment in Co-op Village on Grand Street and
F.D.R. Drive. It was only three blocks—and a world—away from the

projects to a predominantly white middle-class community on the East River. Overnight at school, I became "that black girl who lives in the rich Jew buildings." Or at least that's what Frankie and my other African-American classmates thought I was. It became a familiar chant of theirs as I made my way through my old neighborhood to get to school.

Frankie and I were in the same grade, but I was 10 and he was 3 12 because he had been left back twice. He tormented all of the girls in our class. But Frankie relished singling me out . . . and he had done so since I first arrived from another school in third grade.

He never did any schoolwork. Instead, for the first three periods 4 Frankie's curriculum was mayhem; by fourth period he was usually in the principal's office; and by the fifth, he was back in class unremorseful and pumped to do it again. He only got worse in that working-class, urban-blight panacea, the after-school program. It was a nice idea: children whose parents were unavailable at 3 o'clock because they were working stayed after school to study, improve skills and tackle extra-credit projects. I spent those afternoons trying to stay alive.

Frankie and his crew would grab my breasts, genitals and but- 5 tocks when the teachers weren't looking. Their hands, quick as filthy street rats, darted across my private parts in assembly line, during dance rehearsals and yard processions. They would leave scrawled notes in my book bag that read, "I'm gonna beat you up after school," or "I'll get you in the stairwell."

One spring afternoon, I had made it through another harrowing 6 two hours after school, only to be cornered on the stairs by the whole nasty lot. They taunted me to walk down ahead of them. I managed each step as if it were my first, balancing myself on the chalk-blue shellacked handrail as I peered through the landing divider reminiscent of a wire cage, hoping to see another student, teacher, anyone. Frankie shoved me, and I tumbled one full flight, landing on my knees, my favorite brown plaid dress above my ears, easy pickings for the tiny vultures who cackled obscenities while snatching at my body, punching and kicking me. That day, I understood the depth of Frankie's perversity.

When I told a friend that our classroom emptied out at 3 p.m., 7 leaving me alone with Frankie's boys, without having to share another detail, she said, "Come to my house after school." I had enjoyed two afternoons of baking cookies and doll playing when I let slip that my parents thought I was in class. My friend's mother welcomed me to play at her home anytime as long as my parents knew. "Why were you at Amy's and not in the after-school program?" my father asked me later that night. I didn't tell him because I didn't think he could help me. His interventions would only inspire retaliations and spiral me deeper into the mess.

I did try to tell my teachers, but nobody believed me. They   8
chuckled and said, "Frankie just has a crush on you." That's what I told my father 15 years after the attacks, when he asked me if I had told my teachers. I guess in their world, 12-year-old boys don't sexually attack 10-year-old girls. What world did they come from, anyway? What world was I in, and how could I fix it so Frankie would disappear?

One morning when my teachers had stepped away from the   9
classroom, Frankie and his boys shoved me into the coat closet and held the door shut while I was alone with Frankie. It was dark. As he kept touching me, I tried to push him away and screamed to be let out. But Frankie's friends held steadfast until the teachers arrived; then they scrambled to their seats. None of the other kids said a word. But in front of them all, I told Frankie that I hated his guts and hoped he would die.

Quite accommodating, he lay in a casket later that year. I didn't   10
shed a tear. My heart was hardened, though. As usual, Frankie was up to no good—tampering with public property with the boys—when he got himself electrocuted. I was 10, and I was glad.

Meaning and Purpose

1. For what reasons did Greenlee insist on going to Frankie's funeral?
2. How did Greenlee become alienated from her fellow African-American classmates?
3. Why didn't Greenlee tell her father about her problems at school?

4. At the end of the essay, Greenlee says only that she was "glad" that Frankie had died. What other emotions do you think she felt? Why?

Strategy

1. Conventional morality tells us we should feel at least a degree of sorrow for the death of someone we know. But Greenlee uses her essay to explain and justify feeling "glad" for the death of Frankie. Does she make her case convincingly? Explain.
2. Greenlee cites typical examples of sexual harassment in paragraph 5. What is her purpose of using typical examples here?
3. She uses specific examples of harassment in paragraphs 6 and 9. Why does she use specific examples here?

Style

1. Look up the term "the projects" (paragraph 2) in a good dictionary. What is its meaning in context? Its derivation?
2. Explain what Greenlee means by "urban-blight panacea" in paragraph 4.
3. Greenlee's simile "quick as filthy street rats" (paragraph 5) describes two totally different things at the same time. What?
4. Why is Greenlee's description of a stairway landing divider as "reminiscent of a wire cage" (paragraph 6) particularly appropriate?

Writing Tasks

1. Greenlee portrays herself as an outsider to her school in a double sense: she first transferred from another school, and then she moved out of her black neighborhood to a white neighborhood but remained at that same school. These events are, at least partially, the

ultimate causes of the sexual harassment she describes. Using Greenlee's essay as a model, write an essay in which you analyze an experience you have had as an outsider, or the experience of another you have observed. Consider both the immediate and ultimate causes and/or effects of that experience.

2. Greenlee describes the causes of her sexual harassment at school and the effects those events had on her. Choose any event inside or outside your personal experience that has obvious causes and effects and write a paper that traces the development of those events. Any subject is fair game: being the member of any minority (ethnic, religious, sexual, etc.); the reluctance of many men to accept women as equals; the disintegration of a marriage or family; a candidate's success or loss of a national election. Anything.

❦ Michael Moore ❦

Born in 1954 in Flint, Michigan, Michael Moore is an author, award-winning documentary filmmaker, and provocateur. Both his books and films unapologetically attack what he considers corrupt corporate practices and opportunistic right-wing politicians. His films include Roger & Me, Bowling for Columbine, *and* Fahrenheit 911. *His books include* Dude, Where's My Country?, Downsize This!, *and* Adventures in a TV Nation.

Why Doesn't GM Sell Crack?

In this essay, Michael Moore challenges the widely held belief that the corporate pursuit of profits at any cost is both the right and obligation of business and that government has no right to regulate that pursuit. Pay attention to the way Moore establishes cause-and-effect relationships, what happens when business profits are unregulated, and what would happen if they were regulated.

People in the business world like to say, "Profit is supreme." They like chanting that. "Profit is king." That's another one they like to repeat. They don't like to say, "I'll pick up the check." That means less profit. Profit is what it's all about. When they say "the bottom line," they mean their *profit*. They like that bottom line to contain a number followed by a lot of zeroes.

If I had a nickel for every time I heard some guy in a suit tell me that "a company must do whatever is necessary to create the biggest profit possible," I would have a very big bottom line right now. Here's another popular mantra: "The responsibility of the CEO is to make his shareholders as much money as he can."

Are you enjoying this lesson in capitalism? I get it every time I fly on a plane. The bottom-line feeders have all seen *Roger & Me*, yet they often mistake the fuselage of a DC-9 for the Oxford Debating

Society. So I have to sit through lectures ad nauseam about the beauties of our free market system. Today the guy in the seat next to me is the owner of an American company that makes office supplies—in Taiwan. I ask the executive, "How much is 'enough'?"

"Enough what?" he replies.   4

How much is 'enough' profit?   5

He laughs and says, "There's no such thing as 'enough'!"   6

"So, General Motors made nearly $7 billion in profit last year—   7
but they could make $7.1 billion by closing a factory in Parma, Ohio, and moving it to Mexico—that would be okay?"

"Not only okay," he responds, "it is their duty to close that plant   8
and make the extra $.1 billion."

"Even if it destroys Parma, Ohio? Why can't $7 billion be   9
enough and spare the community? Why ruin thousands of families for the sake of $.1 billion? Do you think this is *moral*?"

"Moral?" he asks, as if this is the first time he's heard that word   10
since First Communion class. "This is not an issue of morality. It is purely a matter of economics. A company must be able to do whatever it wants to make a profit." Then he leans over as if to make a revelation I've never heard before.

"Profit, you know, is supreme."   11

So here's what I don't understand: if profit is supreme, why   12
doesn't a company like General Motors sell crack? Crack is a *very* profitable commodity. For every pound of cocaine that is transformed into crack, a dealer stands to make a profit of $45,000. The dealer profit on a two-thousand-pound car is less than $2,000. Crack is also safer to use than automobiles. Each year, 40,000 people die in car accidents. Crack, on the other hand, kills only a few hundred people a year. And it doesn't pollute.

So why doesn't GM sell crack? If profit is supreme, why not sell   13
crack?

GM doesn't sell crack because it is illegal. Why is it illegal? Be-   14
cause we, as a society, have determined that crack destroys people's lives. It ruins entire communities. It tears apart the very backbone of our country. That's why we wouldn't let a company like GM sell it, no matter what kind of profit they could make.

If we wouldn't let GM sell crack because it destroys our commu- 15
nities, then why do we let them close factories? *That, too,* destroys
our communities.

As my frequent-flier friend would say, "We can't prevent them 16
from closing factories because they have a right to do whatever they
want to in order to make a profit."

No, they don't. They don't have a "right" to do a lot of things: 17
sell child pornography, manufacture chemical weapons, or create
hazardous products that could conceivably make them a profit. We
can enact laws to prevent companies from doing anything to hurt us.

And downsizing is one of those things that is hurting us. I'm not 18
talking about legitimate layoffs, when a company is losing money
and simply doesn't have the cash reserves to pay its workers. I'm
talking about companies like GM, AT&T, and GE, which fire people
at a time when the company is making record profits in the billions
of dollars. Executives who do this are not scorned, picketed, or arrested—they are hailed as heroes! They make the covers of *Fortune*
and *Forbes*. They lecture at the Harvard Business School about their
success. They throw big campaign fund-raisers and sit next to the
President of the United States. They are the Masters of the Universe
simply because they make huge profits regardless of the consequences to our society.

Are we insane or what? Why do we allow this to happen? It is 19
wrong to make money off people's labor and then fire them after
you've made it. It is *immoral* for a CEO to make millions of dollars
when he has just destroyed the livelihood of 40,000 families. And it's
just plain *nuts* to allow American companies to move factories overseas at the expense of our own people.

When a company fires thousands of people, what happens to 20
the community? Crime goes up, suicide goes up, drug abuse, alco-
holism, spousal abuse, divorce—everything bad spirals dangerously
upward. The same thing happens with crack. Only crack is illegal,
and downsizing is not. If there was a crack house in your neighborhood, what would you do? You would try to get rid of it!

I think it's time we applied the same attitudes we have about 21
crack to corporate downsizing. It's simple: if it hurts our citizens, it

should be illegal. We live in a democracy. We enact laws based on what we believe is right and wrong. Murder? Wrong, so we pass a law making it illegal. Burglary? Wrong, and we attempt to prosecute those who commit it. Two really big hairy guys from Gingrich's office pummel me after they read this book? Five to ten in Sing Sing.

As a society, we have a right to protect ourselves from harm. As a democracy, we have a responsibility to legislate measures to protect us from harm. 22

Here's what I think we should do to protect ourselves: 23

1. Prohibit corporations from closing a profitable factory or business and moving it overseas. If they close a business and move it within the U.S., they must pay reparations to the community they are leaving behind. We've passed divorce laws that say that if a woman works hard to put her husband through school, and he later decides to leave her after he has become successful, he has a responsibility to compensate her for her sacrifices that allowed him to go on to acquire his wealth. The "marriage" between a company and a community should be no different. If a corporation packs up and leaves, it should have some serious alimony to pay.

2. Prohibit companies from pitting one state or city against another. We are all Americans. It is no victory for our society when one town wins at another's expense. Texas should not be able to raid Massachusetts for jobs. It is debilitating and, frankly, legal extortion.

3. Institute a 100 percent tax on any profits gained by shareholders when the company's stock goes up due to an announcement of firings. No one should be allowed to profit from such bad news.

4. Prohibit executives' salaries from being more than thirty times greater than an average employee's pay. When workers have to take a wage cut because of hard times, so, too, should the CEO. If a CEO fires a large number of employees, it should be illegal for him to collect a bonus that year.

5. Require boards of directors of publicly owned corporations to have representation from both workers and consumers. A company will run better if it has to listen to the people who have to build and/or use the products the company makes.

For those of you free-marketers who disagree with these modest   24
suggestions and may end up on a plane sitting next to me, screaming,
"You can't tell a business how it can operate!"—I have this to say: Oh,
yes, we can! We legally require companies to build safe products, to
ensure safe workplaces, to pay employees a minimum wage, to contribute to their Social Security, and to follow a host of other rules that
we, as a society, have deemed necessary for our well-being. And we
can legally require each of the steps I've outlined above.

GM can't sell crack. Soon, I predict, they and other companies   25
will not be able to sell us out. Just keep firing more workers, my
friends, and see what happens.

Meaning and Purpose

1. What value does Moore place higher than business profits?
2. Moore claims there are two reasons for companies to downsize—
    one legitimate, one not. What are the differences between the two?
3. What is the reason Moore's "frequent-flier friend" says government
    cannot prevent companies from closing down their factories (para-
    graph 16)? What is Moore's reason for saying that government not
    only has the right to do so, but has the moral obligation to do so?
4. What do you think Moore's purpose is in writing this essay?

Strategy

1. Moore uses typical examples in paragraphs 1–3 and a specific ex-
    ample in the form of an anecdote in paragraphs 3–11. What is the
    purpose of these examples?
2. Moore specifically compares and contrasts corporate downsizing
    and selling crack cocaine in paragraph 20. How are the two similar?
    How are they different?
3. What is the function of paragraph 22?

4. Considering everything Moore has to say in paragraphs 1–22, how logical are his five proposals for social reform in paragraph 23?

Style

1. Why does Moore italicize some words? What kind of tone does he create in doing so?
2. Moore's language is sometimes satirical and derisive. Pick out the words, phrases, or passages that you find less than neutral in tone. Is his language appropriate to his purpose? Why or why not?
3. If necessary, look up the meanings of the following words: *mantra* (paragraph 2); *fuselage, ad nauseam* (3); *debilitating, extortion* (23); *deemed* (24).

Writing Tasks

1. Write a cause-and-effect essay in which you argue against Michael Moore's position that government must regulate corporate downsizing. Do so by illustrating the deleterious effects that would result from such regulation.
2. Moore structures his argument around a syllogism—a form of deductive reasoning (see **deduction** and **syllogism** in the Glossary): Communities have the right to protect themselves by outlawing harmful behavior. Illegitimate corporate downsizing harms communities. Therefore, communities have the right to outlaw or regulate illegitimate corporate downsizing. Using Moore's essay as a model, construct your own cause-and-effect essay by structuring it around your own syllogism.

❦ Marshall Brain ❦

Marshall Brain is the founder of HowStuffWorks.com, a Web site that explains how just about anything you can think of works. He holds a bachelor's degree in electrical engineering from Rensselaer Polytechnic Institute and a master's degree in computer science from North Carolina State University. Before founding HowStuffWorks.com, he taught in the computer science department at NCSU and ran a software training and consulting company.

Relax, Wage Slaves—Robots Promise You an Endless Vacation

Marshall Brain begins with the premise that technology, especially robotic intelligence, will inevitably lead to profound changes in the American workplace and economy. Notice, as you read, the evidence he cites to substantiate his case.

Notice, too, how Brain creates smaller cause-and-effect relationships in the essay that help his larger cause-and-effect argument progress.

Vacation is true freedom. It's as close as we get to the "life, liberty and the pursuit of happiness" ideal of the Declaration of Independence.

What if you had that sort of freedom every day? We should be considering this possibility because we are now standing on the threshold of the robotic revolution. Primitive robots are already taking jobs all around us. The automated gas pumps and supermarket checkout lines are the leading edge of a robotic revolution in the workplace. And the revolution is about to accelerate rapidly.

Computer technology has been advancing steadily for the last 40 years, doubling speed and memory every 18 months in a process known as Moore's Law. If you simply extrapolate these trends, you find that desktop computers will have capabilities equal to that of the human brain by 2040 or so. As computing power finally reaches parity with the human brain and then begins to exceed it, robots will become more and more human in terms of intelligence, visual recognition and language processing.

For many millenniums, Earth has been the home of a single intelligent species. Humans are now engineering the second one. It will take only a handful of breakthroughs to open the floodgates of the robotic revolution, and intelligent robots will directly compete with humans for jobs. As time passes, the new species will get better and better, cheaper and cheaper. 4

Robots will start performing every essential task in the 2040 time frame. They will grow, package and transport all of the food we eat. Robots will build all of the housing we live in. Robots will manufacture and sell all consumer products. In 1903, when the Wright brothers' first rickety airplane took to the air, it was impossible to imagine that the B-52 bomber would be able to fly halfway around the world carrying 70,000 pounds of bombs just 50 years later. In the same way, it is impossible for us to imagine robots taking all the jobs in today's economy in 2050. Yet they will. Robots in the workforce are as inevitable as jet aircraft were. 5

With robots doing the work, we should all be on perpetual vacation. Unfortunately, in the structure of our current economy, that is not what will happen. 6

We may see massive unemployment, with robots taking so many jobs that millions of unemployed humans end up in government welfare dormitories. Or perhaps we will create mundane new jobs to replace the old ones. The third option is the revolutionary one: What if we let the robots have the jobs, while we all attain actual economic freedom for the first time in human history? 7

To achieve true economic freedom, we must break a fundamental doctrine in today's economy: the link between work and income. Robots will be doing all the work, so this link becomes meaningless. We need a new paradigm. 8

In the current paradigm, millions work to make the rich richer. For example, 3.5 million fast-food workers get minimum wage so 9 executives can make billions of dollars collectively. We see that same formula throughout today's economy. More and more money concentrates in the hands of the mega-rich.

With their wealth, the mega-rich buy candidates, lobbyists and   10
lawyers to amass immense economic power. So chief executives' salaries have risen by a factor of 10 since 1980. Dick Grasso, with his $140-million paycheck, is the most recent poster child for the phenomenon, but there are thousands of others: Ebbers, Anschutz, Gates, Case, etc. Meanwhile, the minimum wage has not changed since 1997, and workers' wages are stagnant.

Robots will turbocharge this concentration process unless we   11
stop it.

McDonald's is already deploying order-taking kiosks and burger-   12
flipping robots to thousands of restaurants. As this segment of the economy alone becomes robotic, it will leave 3 million fast-food workers unemployed while the corporate heads reap huge windfalls. The pattern will spread throughout our economy. Right now a large Wal-Mart store has 650 employees. A robotic Wal-Mart could drop that to 20 employees or less.

Instead of letting the mega-rich swim in an ocean of money cre-   13
ated by robotic productivity, we should tap that ocean to provide a swimming pool of money for each person. Give everyone a generous stipend—$25,000 or $30,000 per year, with the amount increasing along with robotic productivity. Let people live their lives in freedom while the robots do all the work.

The most common objection to this proposal is, "Without work,   14
people will have nothing to do." Here is the easiest rebuttal: If you, personally, received $25,000 per year, what would you do? If you are an artist, you would work on your art. If you are a writer, you would write. Inventors would invent, dancers would dance. Given true economic freedom, human creativity would explode.

We should redesign the economy to ignite this creative explo-   15
sion. The new paradigm should give each human an equal portion of the robotic output and let everyone share the fruits of this new species. Robots give us all the chance to achieve true economic freedom. We, the People, should seize that opportunity.

Meaning and Purpose

1. What does Brain claim will be the possible results of the robotic revolution?
2. What does Brain say is today's fundamental economic doctrine? What is the result of that doctrine?
3. What must we do, according to Brain, to alter or reverse current economic trends? How practical is his suggestion? Explain the reasons for your opinion.

Strategy

1. Where does Brain cite evidence to support his claim that "we are now standing on the threshold of the robotic revolution" (paragraph 2)? Is his evidence convincing?
2. What is the organizational function of paragraph 6?
3. What is the function of paragraph 11?
4. What evidence does Brain cite that the development of robotics is accelerating the trend of the rich getting richer at the expense of everyone else?

Style

1. In paragraph 2, where Brain says that "we are standing on the threshold of the robotic revolution," does the sense of this metaphor create a positive or negative tone? Or both? Or neither? Explain.
2. What effect does Brain's metaphor of "open[ing] the floodgates of the robotic revolution" (paragraph 4) create?
3. Brain uses the common metaphor "reap huge windfalls" in paragraph 12. Look up the word *windfall* and find its original or primary meaning. Is Brain's metaphor apt in the context in which he uses it? Explain.
4. Brain develops an extended metaphor in paragraph 13. Comment on its effectiveness.

5. Look up the following words in a dictionary: *extrapolate, parity* (paragraph 3); *millenniums* (4); *mundane* (7); *paradigm* (8); *turbocharge* (11).

Writing Tasks

1. Consider some experiences you have had with modern technology, and write an essay in which you trace how certain things happened (effects) as a result of your experiences (cause).
2. Do some library and Internet research in robotics, and then write an essay in which you agree or disagree with some or all aspects of Marshall Brain's point of view in "Relax, Wage Slaves—Robots Promise You an Endless Vacation." Make sure to acknowledge your sources, and bring Brian's essay into your argument as well.

❦ *Responding to Photographs* ❦
Cause and Effect

A Woman

Noted author Sharon Curtin has criticized American attitudes toward those who are growing old. In the following quotation she expresses her own feeling about aging and projects those feelings to others:

> I am afraid to grow old—we're all afraid. In fact, the fear of growing old is so great that every aged person is an insult and a threat to society. They remind us of our own death, that our body won't always remain smooth and responsive, but will someday betray us by aging, wrinkling, faltering, failing. The ideal way to age would be to grow slowly invisible, gradually disappearing, without causing worry or discomfort to the young. In some ways that does happen. Sitting in a small park across from a nursing home one day, I noticed that the young mothers and their children gathered on one side, and the old people from the home on the other. Whenever a youngster would run over to the "wrong" side, chasing a ball or just trying to cover all the available space, the old people would lean

forward and smile. But before any communication could be established, the mother would come over, murmuring embarrassed apologies, and take her child to the "young" side.

Curtin's reflections on aging find a haunting expression in "A Woman," which features an older woman with a photograph of herself when young. Drawing on Curtin's observations and elements in the photograph, compose an essay with cause and/or effect as the dominant development pattern. Before starting your project, review the material at the beginning of the chapter; then select one of the following writing tasks as the basis for your essay.

1. Begin with the assertion that aging is the subject of "A Woman." Review Curtin's reflection on aging, and also study the photograph, allowing its imagery to work on your imagination. Identify an emotion the photograph creates. Then relate the reasons the photograph has this effect.
2. Imagine that you are a psychologist who shares Curtin's belief about growing old in our society. The young woman in "A Woman" is your client. She is beautiful, and because of her beauty, she has a deep fear of growing old. She asks you what you believe the physical and social effects of growing old will be for her. You decide to be blunt and state your feelings as directly as possible, but you decide to do so in writing. First you describe her current beauty and relate the effects of her beauty on others. Then you describe her as she will appear fifty years in the future and what will result from growing old. You then give her positive advice on how to deal with the aging process, and then you predict the effects the advice will have on her twilight years if she follows it.

❦ *Additional Writing Tasks* ❦
Cause and Effect

1. Using cause and effect (or one of the two alone) as the dominant development pattern, write an essay explaining something that interests you. These general questions are offered as ways to get you started. Revise them in any way that reflects your interests, and then, in a well-developed essay, answer them, using the principles of cause and effect or one of the two.

   a. Why do works by some artists, filmmakers, poets, or novelists affect you?

   b. Why do people need "idols," such as singers, athletes, actors, and politicians?

   c. Why does a television series—police drama, situation comedy, talk show—succeed?

   d. What are the effects of music lyrics that some political activists believe are obscene and condone violence?

   e. What are the effects of stand-up comedians who deliver monologues that critics claim are racist and sexist?

   f. Why are stories that repeat familiar formulas successful?

   g. Is common sense an effective way to solve complex problems?

   h. Is routine the great deadener, or do we need it to organize experience?

   i. Is homelessness a "real" problem in America?

   j. Can government solve the national-deficit problem by printing more money?

   k. Should children be seen and not heard?

   l. What results can you expect from an education?

   m. Is deceit self-destructive?

   n. Should children be made to feel guilty as a way of controlling teenage recklessness?

   o. Why should a dieter avoid eating foods that are high in fat?

   p. What causes stress, and what are its temporary and lasting effects?

   q. What are the effects of a mental illness?

   r. Why does the destruction of symbols such as the American flag enrage some people?

   s. What would happen if everyone were given the college degree of his or her choice without completing course work?

2. Discuss one of these subjects in an essay using cause and effect (or one of the two) as the dominant pattern.

    a. Violence has always been a major element in action-oriented entertainment. In recent years, however, action-oriented children's television cartoons have become stripped of story line of any value and of characterization. The shows present unrelenting karate chopping and related mayhem and "us versus them" worlds with little or no complexity. Currently, some experts and a growing number of parents are beginning to worry about the possible harmful effects these shows might have upon children. In a cause-and-effect (or cause or effect alone) essay, explain the influence of action-oriented cartoons on children.

    b. David A. Goslin, Ph.D., of the American Institute for Research in Washington, D.C., which conducts behavioral and social science research, claims, "Choices do not make life easier; they make it more difficult, for all of us. As social scientists, we know that with an increase in choices, people tend to become more anxious."

        In your experience, is Dr. Goslin's comment valid? Write a cause-and-effect (or cause or effect alone) essay discussing his point of view. You might keep in mind that Americans can choose from more than 25,000 items shelved in their supermarkets. They can tune in more than fifty television channels. They can buy more than 11,000 magazines or periodicals. They are solicited by tens of thousands of special-interest groups. And now through the Internet Americans can expand their choices by linking up to a global marketplace while sitting in their living rooms. Some call this opportunity "freedom of choice," but social critics and experts are beginning to believe that the marketplace may have outsmarted itself by creating all these choices.

    c. In *The Tyranny of Malice,* Joseph H. Berke explains that "Envy is a state of exquisite tension, torment, and ill will provoked by an overwhelming sense of inferiority, impotence, and worthlessness. It begins in the eye of the beholder and is so painful to the mind that the envious person will go to almost any lengths to diminish, if not destroy, whatever or whoever may have aroused it." Basing a cause-and-effect (or cause or effect alone) essay on personal observation, discuss the sources of envy and how it might affect behavior.

d. "Think globally, act locally" was the rallying cry of environmental activism in the 1960s. This advice is as appropriate now as it was then. Just as the Greenpeace movement started more than three decades ago not with governments but at the grass roots, so today it is individuals who must occupy the front lines in protecting the environment. In a cause-and-effect (or cause or effect alone) essay, discuss individual or local-government actions that have resulted from environmental activism.

e. In "The Slaughterer," a short story by Isaac Bashevis Singer, Yoineh Meir wanted to be a rabbi. Instead, the religious authorities in his community made him the ritual slaughterer. Obediently, Meir learned the laws of slaughter as found in religious texts and followed the command of authority.

"Barely three months had passed since Yoineh Meir had become a slaughterer," Singer wrote, "but the time seemed to stretch endlessly. He felt as though he were immersed in blood and lymph. His ears were beset by the squawking of hens, the crowing of roosters, the gobbling of geese, the lowing of oxen, the mooing and bleating of calves and goats; wings fluttered, claws tapped on the floor. The bodies refused to know any justification or excuse—every body resisted in its own fashion, tried to escape, and seemed to argue with the Creator to its last breath."

Yoineh Meir's life ended in madness: "The killing of every beast, great or small, caused him as much pain as though he were cutting his own throat. Of all the punishments that could have been visited upon him, slaughtering was the worst."

Although Yoineh Meir is an extreme example, many people are forced to follow the dictates of authority against their better judgment. In an essay, describe a situation in which authority has been used to pressure an individual into action that seems contrary to his or her nature and discuss the related causes and effects.

10

Process Analysis

Explaining Step by Step

The Method

Are you, like many readers, fascinated by how things work? Are you attracted to writing that explains how to organize your life and time? You might want to understand how the stock market works or how Colombian drug producers smuggle cocaine into the United States. Perhaps your interests have to do with the mind—you might want to learn how psychotherapy works. Authors of essays or books explaining how things work use **process analysis**: They help us to better understand something by breaking it down into its components.

In some ways, process analysis comes close to narration and cause-and-effect analysis by attending to a sequence of related events. Narration, however, is meant to tell a story, and cause-and-effect analysis deals with the reasons for and results of an event or experience. In process analysis a writer examines the way in which something works. In short, narration concentrates on *what* happened; cause and effect, on *why* it happened; and process analysis, on *how* it happened.

Strategies

Careful writers distinguish between two kinds of process analysis: **directive** and **informative**. Directive process analysis explains *how* to do something. Directive process analysis is usually a practical kind of writing based on the assumption that someone will follow the directions to complete a task. Informative process analysis emphasizes *how* something works rather than *how* to do something. Informative process analysis might explain how the brain functions, how gravity holds human beings to the face of the earth, or how food is grown, processed, and merchandised, but an informative process analysis will not offer directions for completing a task.

Directive Process Analysis

Directive process analysis can range from brief instructions on a soup can label to a complicated plan for putting an astronaut on another planet. Keep in mind that directive process analysis has one clear purpose: to guide a reader to a predetermined goal by breaking down the steps required to get there. Consider this paragraph from Tom Cuthbertson's *Anybody's Bike Book,* setting out simple directions for checking bike tire pressure.

> There's a great *curb-edge* test you can do to make sure your tires are inflated just right. Rest the wheel on the edge of a curb or stair so the bike sticks out into the street or path, perpendicular to the curb or stair edge. Get the wheel so you can push down on it at about a 45 degree angle from above the bike. Push hard on the handlebars or seat, depending on which wheel you're testing. The curb should flare the tire a bit but shouldn't push right through the tire and clunk against the rim. You want the tire to have a little give when you ride over chuckholes and rocks, in other words, but you don't want it so soft that you bottom out. If you are a hot-shot who wants tires so hard that they don't have any give, you'll have to stick to riding on cleanswept Velodrome tracks, or watch very carefully for little sharp objects on the road. Or you'll have to get used to that sudden riding-on-the-rim feeling that follows the blowout of an overblown tire.

Cuthbertson's paragraph illustrates several characteristics of directive process analysis. First, he clearly establishes his purpose: to explain how to test bike tires for proper inflation. Second, he breaks the process down into simple steps and explains the final result: "The curb should flare the tire." Third, Cuthbertson addresses his reader directly by using the second-person pronoun *you,* a practice that many writers adopt in directive process analysis: "There's a great curb-edge test **you** can do to make sure **your** tires are inflated just right." A fourth frequent characteristic of directive process analysis alerts the reader to possible mistakes and their consequences. Notice that Cuthbertson states the consequences of overinflated bike tires.

Now consider this passage from *The New York Times Complete Manual of Home Repair.* Bernard Gladstone gives directions for building a fire. Notice that Gladstone's passage embodies most of the common characteristics of process analysis, but he chooses not to address the reader as "you." Instead he writes in the more impersonal passive voice, which seems to create a distance between the reader and the subject.

> Though "experts" differ as to the best technique to follow when building a fire, one generally accepted method consists of first laying a generous amount of crumpled newspaper on the hearth between the andirons. Kindling wood is then spread generously over this layer of newspaper and one of the thickest logs is placed across the back of the andirons. This should be as close to the back of the fireplace as possible, but not quite touching it. A second log is then placed an inch or so in front of this, and a few additional sticks of kindling are laid across these two. A third log is then placed on top to form a sort of pyramid with air space between all logs so that flames can lick freely up between them.
>
> A mistake frequently made is in building the fire too far forward so that the rear wall of the fireplace does not get properly heated. A heated back wall helps increase the draft and tends to suck smoke and flames rearward with less chance of sparks or smoke spurting out into the room.
>
> Another common mistake often made by the inexperienced firetender is to try to build a fire with only one or two logs, instead of using at least three. A single log is difficult to ignite properly, and even two logs do not provide an efficient bed with adequate fuel-burning capacity.
>
> Use of too many logs, on the other hand, is also a common fault and can prove hazardous. Building too big a fire can create more smoke and draft than the chimney can safely handle, increasing the possibility of sparks or smoke being thrown out into the room. For best results, the homeowner should start with three medium-size logs as described above, then add additional logs as needed if the fire is to be kept burning.

Like Cuthbertson, Gladstone opens by clearly stating his purpose; that is, to explain the steps necessary to build a fire in a fireplace. He then follows with a series of steps—six in all—that are clearly written and easy to follow. After devoting a paragraph to directions for building a fire he presents three common mistakes people make when building a fire and their consequences, with one brief paragraph devoted to each mistake. Although Gladstone's directions for building a fire are longer than Cuthbertson's for testing air pressure in a bike tire, both follow the same general pattern. They begin with a clear statement of purpose, then present the steps necessary to complete the process, and, as is often done in directive process analysis, they identify the common mistakes people make when following the procedure.

Informative Process Analysis

Instead of guiding a reader through a series of directions to complete a task as directive process analysis does, informative process analysis explains how something happens or how it works. In this paragraph from Caroline Sutton's *How Do They Do That?* she explains how stripes are put into striped toothpaste.

> Although it's intriguing to imagine the peppermint stripes neatly wound inside the tube, actually stripes don't go into the paste until it's on its way out. A small hollow tube, with slots running lengthwise, extends from the neck of the toothpaste tube back into the interior a short distance. When the toothpaste tube is filled, red paste—the striping material—is inserted first, thus filling the conical area around the hollow tube at the front. (It must not, however, reach beyond the point to which the hollow tube extends into the toothpaste tube.) The remainder of the dispenser is filled with the familiar white stuff. When you squeeze the toothpaste tube, pressure is applied to the white paste, which in turn presses on the red paste at the head of the tube. The red then passes through the slots and onto the white, which is moving through the inserted tube—and which emerges with five red stripes.

Sutton doesn't expect any of her readers to make a tube of striped toothpaste, but she does answer a common question, one that might have aroused your curiosity, too: "How do they get the stripes into the tube?"

An informative process analysis is usually arranged in chronological order and makes careful use of transitional techniques to guide a reader through the process. Sometimes the procedure is quite simple and easily organized in a step-by-step sequence. Often, however, the process is complex, such as a chemical reaction or human digestion, and challenges a writer's organizational skills, especially when the writer wishes to interrupt the explanation to add additional information or description.

For example, John McPhee in *Oranges* devotes a paragraph to describing the process that oranges undergo when made into concentrated juice. As you read McPhee's paragraph, notice that he interrupts to bring in related information—first to explain that oranges culled from the crop were once dumped in fields and eaten by cattle, thus accounting for the orangeade flavor of Florida milk, and later, to describe two kinds of juicing machines. Even though McPhee interrupts the process, he still guides the reader's attention with clear transitional techniques, especially phrases that create a sense of movement, such as, "As the fruit starts to move," "Moving up a conveyor belt," "When an orange tumbles in," and, finally, "As the jaws crush the outside."

As the fruit starts to move along a concentrate plant's assembly line, it is first culled. In what some citrus people remember as "the old fresh-fruit days," before the Second World War, about forty percent of all oranges grown in Florida were eliminated at packinghouses and dumped in fields. Florida milk tasted like orangeade. Now, with the exception of the split and rotten fruit, all of Florida's orange crop is used. Moving up a conveyor belt, oranges are scrubbed with detergent before they roll on into juicing machines. There are several kinds of juicing machines, and they are something to see. One is called the Brown Seven Hundred. Seven hundred oranges a minute go into it and are split and reamed on the same kind of rosettes that are in the centers of ordinary kitchen reamers. The rinds that come pelting out the bottom are integral halves, just like the rinds of oranges squeezed in a kitchen. Another machine is the Food Machinery Corporation's FMC In-line Extractor. It has a shining row of aluminum jaws, upper and lower, with shining aluminum teeth. When an orange tumbles in, the upper jaw comes crunching down on it while at the same time the orange is penetrated from below by a perforated steel tube. As the jaws crush the outside, the juice goes through the perforations in the tube and down into the plumbing of the concentrate plant. All in a second, the juice has been removed and the rind has been crushed and shredded beyond recognition.

Some processes defy chronological explanation because they take place simultaneously. Here a writer must present the material in parallel stages, as McPhee does in the last three sentences of his paragraph when he describes juicing, clearly indicating with transitional markings that two or more interlocked events are taking place at once.

In a paragraph from "The Spider and the Wasp," zoologist Alexander Petrunkevitch presents the procedure a female *Pepsis* wasp follows when paralyzing a tarantula before burying it with a wasp egg attached to its belly. The challenge Petrunkevitch faced was to show both the wasp's and the spider's simultaneous behavior.

> When the grave is finished, the wasp returns to the tarantula to complete her ghastly enterprise. First, she feels it all over once more with her antennae. Then her behavior becomes more aggressive. She bends her abdomen, protruding her sting, and searches for the soft membrane at the point where the spider's legs join its body—the only spot where she can penetrate the horny skeleton. From time to time, as the exasperated spider slowly shifts ground, the wasp turns on her back and slides along with the aid of her wings, trying to get under the tarantula for a shot at the vital spot. During all this maneuvering, which can last for several minutes, the tarantula makes no move to save itself. Finally the wasp corners it against some obstruction and grasps one of its legs in her powerful jaws. Now at last the harassed spider tries a desperate but vain defense. The two contestants roll over and over on the ground. It is a terrifying sight and the outcome is always the same. The wasp finally manages to thrust her sting into the soft spot and holds it there for a few seconds while she pumps in the poison. Almost immediately the tarantula falls paralyzed on its back. Its legs stop twitching; its heart stops beating. Yet it is not dead, as is shown by the fact that if taken from the wasp it can be restored to some sensitivity by being kept in a moist chamber for several months.

Often the success of a process analysis essay rests on clear information about the reader. The writer must estimate how much knowledge about the process the reader might already have and how much additional information must be included in the essay. If the writer's guess is wildly inaccurate, then he or she will include either too much information, which might send the reader into a fit of yawning, or too little, which may send the reader into an intellectual fog bank.

Process Analysis in College Writing

In the sciences and social sciences, process analysis is an important development pattern. In laboratory sciences you will often use directive process analysis to write reports that communicate the procedure in an experiment or research project. In courses such as geology, biology, cultural anthropology, and social psychology you will often use informative process analysis to describe such subjects as the formation of mountains, photosynthesis, initiation ceremonies, and socialization.

Guidelines for Writing Process Analysis

1. Select a subject that lends itself to either directive or informative process analysis. Be sure your subject is fresh—that is, avoid such common subjects as how to cook anything, how to put together anything, or how to find any place. Instead, look for the unusual, something from your own experience or research.

2. Decide whether your analysis will be primarily directive, informative, or a little of each. Develop a list of steps necessary to complete the process, or develop a list of key elements necessary to explain the process.

3. Use prewriting techniques to generate information necessary to understand and follow each element of the analysis. Then arrange your information in the proper order: for directive analysis, sequentially; for informative, chronologically.

4. Write your analysis. Carefully work in related information necessary to understand each step. Remember that a reader

will be expected to follow the procedure in directive analysis but only to understand the process in informative analysis.

5. Revise your analysis. Pay particular attention to the transitions. Be sure they accurately guide the reader, and be sure they clearly show the connection to related information and delineate simultaneous events.

A Student Essay Developed by Process Analysis

In his Introduction to Psychology class, John Barton responded to the following writing task.

In 550 to 600 words, write an overview of a supplemental analytic practice that attempts to show family relationships. Your essay should give a clear impression of what is involved in the process and how it proceeds. Select one of the following:

a. Transactional Analysis   d. Psychodrama
b. Photoanalysis   e. Hypnotherapy
c. Encounter Sessions   f. Cognitive Therapy

Barton selected item (b), photoanalysis, a subject that the lecturer had covered only briefly. First, read Barton's process analysis, then reread it and respond to the items in Reviewing with a Writer's Eye.

Friendly Smile, Clenched Fist

Although many critics of psychotherapy claim that the field is slow to change, some new techniques are developing. One is photoanalysis. No doubt you have heard that "A photograph is worth a thousand words." Well, photoanalysts would agree, but with a slight revision, "A <u>family photo album</u> is worth a thousand words." For example, a person might be aware that he has difficulty showing affection and expressing himself. After a session with a photoanalyst, usually a certified psychiatrist or psychologist, he could become aware that the difficulty is rooted in his family history. Instead of spending hours verbally exploring his family relationships, a client

1

working with a photoanalyst would examine a family photo album where the patterns of restraint might be documented in photographs.

Besides being trained as a therapist, a photoanalyst should also be sensitive to visual images and the nonverbal expression they embody. But analyzing photographs to uncover family themes is not simple. The analyst should use group photographs taken over a number of years. A single photograph may whet curiosity but is no more helpful in unearthing patterns of family relationship than a crystal ball. 2

Most analysts begin by spreading the photographs on a table. Then the analyst will study the faces to determine the general "tone" of the relationships. Are the subjects looking at each other or at the camera? Are their expressions happy? Or severe? Or angry? Often a child's first impression of the world comes from parents. Their expressions, captured in a series of photographs, may reveal their general perceptions. 3

Next, the analyst will study the body language of family members. Do they seem to interact with each other or do they seem emotionally isolated from each other? Are they touching? Perhaps one has an arm around another's shoulder or a hand on another's leg. Is the hand open or clenched? 4

Finally, the analyst will also examine family members' proximity to each other. If they are close enough to rub elbows, they probably enjoy a warm relationship. If they put distance between themselves to avoid touching, they may shun intimacy with each other. What if males and females are clearly separated? Does this distance suggest that men and women play traditional roles within the family? An analyst will notice who takes the dominant place in the photographs. Mother? Father? A grandparent? Perhaps the children. Whoever takes a dominant place in a series of photographs probably takes the dominant role at home as well. A parent who consistently gravitates toward one child in photographs might play favorites in family relationships. A person who always chooses to stand at the outside of the group might feel like an outsider. 5

Throughout a photoanalysis session, the analyst should avoid narrow interpretations of the photographs, but should offer observations for the client's response. After all, the client is the one with the direct experience and therefore should have the last word in interpreting any photograph. The photoanalyst must, however, point out that a friendly smile might 6 be masking the tension revealed by a clenched fist half hidden in a lap.

Reviewing with a Writer's Eye

1. Explain why John Barton's "Friendly Smile, Clenched Fist" is primarily either directive or informative process analysis (see p. 396).
2. What single sentence indicates Barton's general purpose?
3. List the steps a photoanalyst might follow.
4. Barton develops his essay mainly by asking questions. Why?
5. What purposes do paragraphs 2 and 6 serve?
6. In no more than 150 words, write Barton a detailed note that points out the strengths and weaknesses of his essay.

Peer Review

You may be asked to write an essay about one of the readings that follow. Before you meet with your writing group, review this introduction. As you read the papers of your group, use these general principles of process analysis to help guide your comments.

1. The paper's complexity and vocabulary should be appropriate for the intended audience.
2. A process analysis paper should proceed in clearly defined steps. In a directive paper, readers should be warned of possible missteps at appropriate places. In an informative paper, readers should be told of actions that take place simultaneously.
3. A reader's understanding of the process can be enhanced with careful use of transitional words and phrases.

In the professional examples that follow, you will find a variety of process analysis essays to study. Each is written for a different purpose. Yet each makes use of the fundamental strategies behind directive or informative process analysis. Study them with care to learn how professionals apply these strategies.

❦ Garry Trudeau ❦

Garry Trudeau, born in New York City in 1948, is most famous for his internationally acclaimed comic strip Doonesbury. *He attended Yale University and in 1970 was awarded a Master of Fine Arts degree from Yale's School of Art and Architecture.* Doonesbury *appears in newspapers nationwide and has been collected in numerous books. In 1975, Trudeau won the Pulitzer Prize for editorial cartooning. In 1977 he was nominated for an Academy Award for the animated film,* A Doonesbury Special.

Anatomy of a Joke

This short essay was first published August 1, 1993, in the opinion section of The New York Times. *In it, Trudeau traces in detail a single* Tonight Show *joke, from its inception to Jay Leno's delivery.*

As you read Trudeau's description, you might be surprised at the time, detail, and calculation that go into a seemingly impromptu and fleeting television joke. Consider why such meticulous and expensive attention would be given to something so inconsequential.

In the wake of last week's press "availabilities" of funnymen Dave Letterman, Jay Leno, Chevy Chase et al., there was much rim-shot critiquing, all of it missing the point.

The real jokes, the ones that count, occur not at press events but during those extraordinary little pieces called monologues. Despite the popular conception of the monologue as edgy and unpredictable, it is actually as formal and structured as anything found in traditional kabuki. The stakes are too high for it to be otherwise. Even the ad-libs, rejoinders, and recoveries are carefully scripted. While it may suit Leno's image to portray the "Tonight" show monologue as something that's banged out over late-night pizza with a few cronies, in fact each joke requires the concerted effort of a crack team of six highly disciplined comedy professionals. To illustrate how it works, let's follow an actual topical joke, told the night of Monday, July 26, as it makes its way through the pipeline.

The inspiration for a topical joke is literally torn from the head- 3
lines by a professional comedy news "clipper." Comedy news reading
is sometimes contracted out to consultants, but the big-budget
"Tonight" show has 12 of its own in-house clippers who peruse some
300 newspapers every day. Clippers know that the idea for the joke
must be contained in the headline or, at worst, the subhead. If the
idea is in the body text, then the general public has probably missed
it and won't grasp the reference the joke is built around. In this case,
the clipper has spied an item about flood relief.

A20 FRIDAY, JULY 23, 1993

House Delays Final Flood Aid Vote
$3 Billion Package Stalls in Dispute Over Budget Limits

The Washington Post

The news clip is then passed on to a comedy "engineer," whose 4
job is to decide what shape the joke should take. After analyzing the
headline, the engineer decides how many parts the joke should have,
the velocity of its build, whether it contains any red herrings (rare on
the "Tonight" show), and the dynamics of the payoff and under-
laughing. With Monday's joke, the engineer chose a simple interrogatory setup, which telegraphs to the often sleepy audience that
the next line contains a payoff. The finished sequencing is then sent
on to the "stylist."

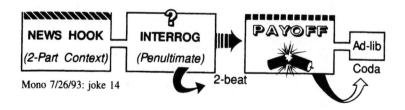

NEWS HOOK | INTERROG | PAYOFF | Ad-lib
(2-Part Context) | (Penultimate) | | Coda
Mono 7/26/93: joke 14 | 2-beat

The comedy stylist is the writer who actually fashions the raw 5
joke. The stylist is the prima donna of the team, the best paid, the

worst dressed—and never in the office. The stylist, who is typically a per diem session player, is faxed the original headline, the structural scheme, and a gross time count, and from those elements creates the rough draft for the joke. It's up to him to find the joke's "spring," that tiny component of universal truth that acts as the joke's fulcrum. In this case, the joke hinges on the public's resentment of Congress, a hoary but proven truism. The stylist then faxes his finished rough to the "polish man."

1./It looks like the House of Representatives is having trouble voting flood relief because they're worried about where to appropriate the money from.
2./Here's my question.
3./How come when the House votes itself a pay raise, they never worry about <u>that</u> appropriation?

The polish man, usually a woman, is the joke's editor, charged with burnishing the joke until it gleams. Obscure references, awkward phrasing, and puns are all removed, and any potentially offensive material is run by an outside anti-defamation consultant. Unlike the stylist, who usually works at his beach house, the polish man is always on the premises, available in the event of emergency rewrites. For Monday's joke, the polish man adds a "fall from the sky" coda that will allow Leno some physical business. The decision to use it, however, ultimately rests with the "timing coach."

The timing coach is responsible for timing out the phrasing and pauses, and bringing the 21-joke routine in under its seven-minute limit. Running over is a major no-no. During the Carson era, a timing coach, who asked not to be identified, signed off on a monologue that ran 13.5 seconds long, a deficit that came out of Barbra Streisand's guest segment. The coach was summarily sacked. Such errors are rare today, however, as the monologues are now digitalized on disk. A timer can modulate the phrasing pattern to within 0.01 of

@ too long   ⎣Senate⎦

It looks like the ~~House of Representatives~~ is

⎣passing, @ where? ⎦ ⎣for the midwest⎦

having trouble ~~voting~~ flood relief because ~~they're~~

⎣some Senators are⎦   ⎣is going to come⎦

worried about where ~~to appropriate~~ the money from.

⎣Now,⎦   ⎣Senate⎦

Here's my question: How come when the ~~House~~ votes

   big   ⎣wonder where⎦

itself a~~y~~ pay raise, they never ~~worry about~~ that

money's coming from?

~~appropriation?~~   <u>ad-libs:</u> Ever notice that?

It just seems to <u>fall</u> from the sky.

(6.3 sec. to pause) IT LOOKS LIKE . . . FLOOD RELIEF . . . WORRIED . . . MONEY IS GOING TO COME FROM. (.95 sec. beat) NOW, HERE'S MY QUESTION; (.6 second beat; 3.45 sec. to ad-lib) HOW COME . . . BIG PAY RAISE . . . WHERE <u>THAT</u> MONEY'S COMING FROM? (ad-lib under laugh; see menu).

---

a second, well beyond the performance sensitivity of any comic but Robin Williams.

The final joke is then e-mailed to the "talent," in this case Jay Leno. Leno dry-runs the joke in his office, adding spin and body movement, and locks in his ad-libs, including recovery lines in case the joke bombs. (Carson had such good recovery material that he used to commission intentionally bad jokes, but Leno has not yet reached that pinnacle of impeccability.) Once Leno approves the joke, it is transferred to a hard disk and laser-printed on cue cards with a special font to make it look hand-lettered. Finally, at exactly 5:30 P.M., California taping time, Leno walks on stage and reads it to 15 million people.

Meaning and Purpose

1. Now that you have read the essay, what significance does the title have for you?
2. Why are news headlines used as the bases for jokes in the *Tonight Show* monologue?
3. In paragraph 7, Trudeau says, "The timing coach is responsible for timing out the phrasing and pauses, and bringing in the 21-joke routine in under its seven-minute limit." Why are the subject, structure, and timing of a TV joke given such meticulous care?
4. What is the thesis of the essay? Where has Trudeau placed it?

Strategy

1. What is each stage of the joke process Trudeau describes?
2. Trudeau often disrupts the strict chronology of his process to give descriptions and explanations. Find two examples of this strategy. Why does he include these interruptions?
3. Trudeau is careful to use clear transitions. What transitions does he use to move the reader through each stage of the process? What other transitions does he use to clarify his ideas?
4. Why does Trudeau include visual illustrations? Do they help to clarify his ideas or not?

Style

1. Trudeau employs many colloquialisms in his essay (see **colloquial expressions** in Glossary). After finding several, determine why he uses them.
2. What specialized vocabulary does he use? Why?
3. Look up the following words in a dictionary: *anatomy* (title); *wake* (paragraph 1); *kabuki, cronies, pipeline* (2); *peruse* (3); *velocity, red herrings, dynamics, interrogatory* (4); *prima donna, per diem, gross, fulcrum, hoary* (5); *burnishing, anti-defamation, coda* (6); *summarily, digitalized, modulate* (7); *pinnacle, impeccability* (8).

Writing Tasks

1. Choose something in your own life that lends itself to an informative process analysis (see *Informative Process Analysis,* pp. 399–402). Then write a paper in which you clearly explain how, precisely, that thing in your life happens or how it works. Take care to carry the reader along with transitional expressions. Like Trudeau, include clarifying descriptions, explanations, and examples.

2. Trudeau traces the meticulous detail and care that goes into a single, fleeting TV joke. Consider why such care would be taken for such a seemingly trivial pursuit. What would the payoff be for such time, expense, and attention? Consider other pursuits that entail similar attention to detail: many medical procedures, many aspects of the space program, the creative process (art and writing, in particular), many legal matters, much neurotic and psychotic behavior. Write a paper in which you describe one or more processes that demand a meticulous attention to detail and result in a compensating payoff for that attention.

❦ Frank Gannon ❦

Frank Gannon, born in 1952, earned his bachelor's degree, magna cum laude, *and his master's degree from the University of Georgia. His works include* Yo Poe, Vanna Karenina, All About Man, *and a memoir,* Middle Irish: Discovering My Family and Myself. *His essays have appeared in* The Atlantic, Harper's, Gentlemen's Quarterly, *and* The New Yorker. *He remarks, "At first I was influenced by Yukio Mishima. Then Hemingway and Fitzgerald."*

Rat Patrol: A Saga

This selection was originally published in Harper's *Magazine in 1996 and appears in* The Best American Essays 1997. *The essay contains an anecdote, a short biographical account of an event in the author's life, as an important strategy to help clarify his reason for explaining a process. While reading this essay, try to imagine yourself relating such an anecdote to a nine-year-old child to determine whether, in your opinion, the anecdote that Frank Gannon tells to his own child would make sense to another child.*

As a young man, I liked nothing better than playing a game called Rat Patrol. It had nothing to do with rats and little to do with patrols. What it did involve was this: when I was in eighth grade, around 1966, there was on ABC an unpopular program called *The Rat Patrol*. It was canceled very quickly, and I never spent even a single minute actually watching the show. Neither did any of my fellow Rat Patrol players. What we did see (it would have been difficult to miss) was the thirty-second commercial for the show. This commercial ran virtually all day, at perhaps twenty-minute intervals. I sat in front of the television that my dad had gotten cheap because the little square that showed the channel was on sideways, and I watched this commercial, it seemed, all summer. It was always the same. This is how it went.

A deep "announcer" voice:

1

2

THEY PLAYED BY THEIR OWN RULES.

(Shot of jeeps driving very fast through the desert, making hairpin turns, throwing sand all over the camera.) 3

WHAT OTHER MEN CALLED
THE WASTELAND, THEY
CALLED HOME.

(Shot of some grimy-faced guys with bandannas around their necks. They are driving their jeeps very fast and making very abrupt turns that throw sand into the camera.) 4

THIS FALL.
THE RAT PATROL.

(Shot of a really big explosion with a giant wave of sand going all over everything.) 5

I watched it approximately five hundred times. I was not alone. 6
My associates, Andy and Paul, also watched, often in my presence. Although very little was said, I am quite sure that we were all forming the same word in our eighth-grade minds. That word was "cool."

Here is how the game is played. 7
Near my home there is a big sloping hill. Because of some con- 8
struction work done decades ago, one whole side of the hill is composed of sand. Regular beach-type sand. The hill inclines at about a forty-degree angle. So there you have it. Maybe three hundred yards of nothing but sand.
This is the official playing field. 9
Next, you need the equipment. You need at least one full can of 10
lighter fluid or barbecue starter. That's easy to come by. The rest of the equipment gets a bit trickier. You need a whole bunch of aerosol cans. You need to keep your eyes open and your Rat Patrol ears cocked, particularly around the women. The big sisters and the moms are an excellent source of aerosol devices. Hair spray is the most obvious choice, but you have many others. This was, of course,

the days before Sting and Greenpeace, and everybody whacked away at the ozone level on a regular basis. Deodorants. Room fresheners. Furniture polish. Nonstick cooking spray. Bug repellent.

Dads also contributed to the Rat Patrol cause. They all had those 11 cans that they kept in the trunk of the car, canisters that were supposed to come in handy if you had a flat tire. Compressed-air devices. In the weeks of preparation for Rat Patrol, cans disappeared from Dodges and Chevys and Ramblers all over the neighborhood. After a while, we often didn't even know what we were stealing. If it had those magic words WARNING: CONTENTS UNDER PRESSURE, that was good enough for us.

The International Rules of Rat Patrol

1. You must dig a very large hole in the sand. You have to take 12 maybe a half ton of sand out of there. If in doubt, make the hole larger. The hole can't be too big.

2. Throw all of the WARNING: CONTENTS UNDER PRESSURE canisters into 13 the hole. As in the case of the hole, you cannot have too many cans. If you have a hundred cans, that's good. If you have, say, a googolplex cans, that's even better. An infinite number of cans would be infinitely good.

3. You must come up with some kind of fuse. The best kind is one 14 that burns like a sparkler, with lots of little twinkly sparks as it goes along. This is best because (a) it burns slowly enough that you can get the hell out of there before zero hour, and (b) those twinkly sparks are aesthetically pleasing. If Rat Patrol isn't going to be beautiful, then why bother?

4. You have to empty a great deal of lighter fluid into the hole. 15 Again, you can't have too much lighter fluid. Barbecue starter works just as well. A case or two of barbecue starter followed by a case or two of lighter fluid—that would maybe be the ideal formula for the platonically perfect Rat Patrol, the "Rat Patrolness" that exists in the realm of essences.

5. After the fuse has been lit, the lighter of the fuse must run away 16 from the hole for a distance of approximately twenty-five yards. Then he, along with his fellow players, must scream loudly and dive face-down into the sand. All players should remain in said position until the

explosion(s) is (are) over and there are no more flaming can fragments aloft.

    6. This is optional, but the lighter of the fuse may choose to articu-   17
late some words rather than merely screaming. These are some, but not all, of the possibilities:

    A. HIT THE DECK!

    B. THAR SHE BLOWS!

    C. THEY GOT CHARLIE!

    D. EAT LEAD, COPPER!

    I have not played Rat Patrol in almost thirty years. As an adult, I   18
have found that big explosions are no longer very entertaining. I hate action movies. There is no way on earth that anyone could talk me into spending good money to watch Dennis Hopper or somebody blow stuff up.

    The Fourth of July is definitely the most mediocre holiday as far   19
as I'm concerned. Sitting outside at night while mosquitoes attack you, watching stuff explode in the sky, is just about as bad an idea for a holiday as they come. I prefer Labor Day or Columbus Day. You don't get any mail, but nothing blows up.

    Last week, however, I realized that Rat Patrol is still with me. I   20
was watching a movie on TV with my son. The movie was *The Secret Garden*. During a particularly touching moment, I looked over at my son. He appeared to be close to nausea. I asked him whether he liked the movie. He said no, very emphatically. I asked him what he didn't like.

    "Heartfelt moments, Dad," he said.   21

    "What do you like?" I asked.   22

    He looked right at me.   23

    "Explosions," he said. "That's what I like. Lots of explosions."   24

The next day, the boy's mother asks me to have a little talk with my   25
son. He has been showing, she feels, an unhealthy interest in explosives, detonation, carnage, destruction, and other allegedly unhealthy aspects of life. My son is nine years old, and he has the same name—first and last—as I do.

I sit in a chair that makes me look as if I have that thing they call   26
authority. It's a big purple chair with ugly stitching. A chair Goliath
would have picked out at Haverty's if he had had the chance. Now
we are ready to talk.

I clear my throat. Yes, I am the dad. My voice is deeper than his.   27
My tone, when I begin, is somber yet vaguely intense. I tell him the
most appalling stories about explosions that I can devise. After a moment I realize that if I make the stories *too* appalling, they will have
the wrong effect. So I tell stories that are appalling but also a little
boring. I mention grisly details, and occasionally I veer off into narrative. I tell him about the guy in the Ripley's "Believe It or Not"—the
railroad worker. Just another honest workin' man putting in his
time. Maybe looking to qualify for the retirement plan. About ten
o'clock, though, maybe thinking about taking a break for some coffee or something, he pounds a steel railroad spike into the ground
with a sledgehammer. He has done this all day every day for ten
years or fifteen years. Every time, the same thing happens: the spike
goes about four or five inches into the ground. Then it's time to hit it
again. Do this for about five hours and it's time for lunch.

This time, though, it's not like that. This time he hits the spike,   28
just like normal. It goes in about five inches, just like normal. Then
something a little different happens. This time there's a massive, ear-
shattering explosion. The spike flies back at his head at an almost
unimaginable speed. It hits the side of the poor guy's chin with, of
course, the flat end first. The spike, which is about two and a half
inches thick, goes right through the guy's head. It leaves the mother
of all exit wounds. A big, tomato-size exit wound, right on the side
of his head. This poor man, making the post–Civil War equivalent of
$4.25 an hour, has just had a thirty-five-pound spike driven straight
through his post–Civil War head.

As I tell this, my voice gets quieter, more intense, more Clint East-   29
wood. I tell this as intensely as I can, trying with everything I have to
convey the impression that things that explode are things that are bad.
I think, with all due modesty, that I am doing this pretty well. I give
myself at least a B-plus. I'm not Olivier, but I'm not Brad Pitt either.

Nevertheless, I detect in my son's eyes a need for further   30
convincing.

I go to the big well. Vietnam. Northern Ireland. Bosnia. Hir-   31
oshima. Mangled bodies. Severed limbs. Missing eyeballs. Slow de-
capitations. Large pieces of metal flying through tender pieces of human flesh. Fragmentation bombs dropped near elephants. Tiny
babies. Sobbing women. Everywhere anguished wails and unending
human torment.

And why? Why?   32

I'll tell you why, my son. Because of those things that explode,   33
that's why.

I hope I'm clear.   34

Then I realize I can add something very intense and personal   35
and powerful to all this. I pull my hair back from my forehead and
point to a long scar that intersects my left eyebrow.

"See this?" I ask.   36

He leans forward. "Yeah." I can see he's interested.   37

"Let me tell you how I got this." He sits down again. I begin.   38

"When I was in college, one night a bunch of guys and me, we   39
got real bored. So we were looking around for something to do. One
guy had a CO_2 capsule."

"What's that?"   40

"It's a little metal cylinder. CO_2 is carbon dioxide. They use it for   41
scientific stuff. Anyway, he had this empty one. We decided—I forget
whose idea this was—to stuff it full of match heads and make a bomb."

I look at my son's eyes. He's really interested now.   42

"We kept stuffing match heads in it. Finally, we couldn't fit any   43
more in there. That's when we started pounding them in there."

I wince in recollection.   44

"We got a file and pliers and a hammer. We used the pliers to hold   45
the CO_2 capsule while another guy pounded the match heads in. Finally, it got to be like a 'guts' thing. Like who had the nerve to keep
pounding those things in. At the end, a guy named Bob Foundry was
holding the capsule, and I pounded the last match head in."

"Then what happened?"   46

"It exploded. It exploded so loud I really couldn't hear it, just a   47
crazy ringing. I looked over at myself in the mirror, and the whole
left side of my face was covered in blood. They rushed me to the
emergency room and gave me thirty-five stitches. The doctor said

that if I was his son, he would have beaten the hell out of me. There were pieces of the capsule stuck an inch deep in the cinderblock walls of the dorm room. They never did get them out. They were still in the wall when we left at the end of the year. If the capsule had exploded a half inch lower, a fragment would have gone into my eye, and I'd either be blind or, more likely, dead, because the fragment would have just kept going until it entered my brain."

There's a pause. We both just sit there. I finally get up and get a glass of water. My mouth has gotten very dry. 48

About two hours later, my son starts asking me about CO_2 capsule bombs. He wants to make sure he's got the details right. 49

Meaning and Purpose

1. An early part of this essay contains a how-to section—that is, how to make a bomb. How is that information important to Gannon's anecdote?

2. Why does it bother the author that his son does not like the "heartfelt moments" (paragraph 21) in the movie that he and his son watched together?

3. This essay deals with a moral—that which is "good" or "right" in one's conduct. In your opinion, what is the moral of this essay?

4. Why did Gannon entitle his essay "Rat Patrol: A Saga"? Specifically, what does the term *saga* convey to the reader?

Strategy

1. What is significant about Gannon's scar? What does it add to the story that he tells his son?

2. After mentioning a game that he used to play more than thirty years ago, Gannon writes, "Here is how the game is played" (paragraph 7). Why does the author shift to the present tense?

3. Gannon notes that "Dads" helped his friends and him in the "Rat Patrol cause" (paragraph 11). How can you tell by reading the essay

that the "Dads" did not know that they had contributed to that "cause"?

4. Why did Gannon list Vietnam, Northern Ireland, Bosnia, and Hiroshima (paragraph 31)?

Style

1. First, Gannon relates an incident about himself in this essay, and then he relates an incident about himself and his son. In terms of their style, what do the two incidents have in common?

2. When we read on a product's label the words "Warning: Contents Under Pressure," we usually exercise care with that product. Why, then, does Gannon call that warning "those magic words" (paragraph 11)?

3. In the statement "that thing they call authority" (paragraph 26), who are "they"?

4. *Harper's Magazine* has a comparatively educated readership. In your opinion, is the style of this essay a comparatively educated style?

Writing Tasks

1. In our youth, each of us has done something that could have caused us physical or psychological harm. However, at the time we did it, either we did not think about the possibly harmful consequences or we did not care about them. In your essay, describe step by step an incident in your life that could have harmed you or your friends, either physically or psychologically.

2. This essay begins by discussing the television series *Rat Patrol,* a series that began in 1966, ended in 1967, and had a total of 56 episodes, each including a plan on how to attack the enemy or how to resist an attack from the enemy. Write an essay in which you discuss one episode of a current television series that involves its characters in some kind of planning, including the steps in the process involved in that planning.

❦ Donald M. Murray ❦

Donald M. Murray was born in 1924 in Boston. He has had a long and distinguished career as a writer and teacher. Murray has published fiction, nonfiction, and poetry, served as an editor of Time *magazine, and won the Pulitzer Prize for editorial writing in 1959. His teaching career at the University of New Hampshire, Durham, and the textbooks he has published on how to write—A* Writer Teaches Writing, *Write to* Learn, *and* Read to Write—*have established him as one of America's most influential teachers of writing. He sees the writing teacher as a coach and is convinced that a student must want to learn and be willing to exert much effort in order to write well.*

The Maker's Eye
Revising Your Own Manuscripts

Originally published in The Writer, *this essay demonstrates the process professional writers go through to revise their manuscripts. Murray distinguishes the differences in attitudes that student writers and professional writers take to the revising process and cites other professional writers to argue for the essential importance of meticulous revision.*

As you read, note any differences between the methods you use to revise a paper and the methods the professional writer uses. Jot down advice you might find helpful in improving your own writing.

When students complete a first draft, they consider the job of writing done—and their teachers too often agree. When professional writers complete a first draft, they usually feel that they are at the start of the writing process. When a draft is completed, the job of writing can begin.

That difference in attitude is the difference between amateur and professional, inexperience and experience, journeyman and craftsman. Peter F. Drucker, the prolific business writer, calls his first draft "the zero draft"—after that he can start counting. Most writers share the feeling that the first draft, and all of those which follow, are opportunities to discover what they have to say and how best they can say it.

To produce a progression of drafts, each of which says more and says it more clearly, the writer has to develop a special kind of reading skill. In school we are taught to decode what appears on the page as finished writing. Writers, however, face a different category of possibility and responsibility when they read their own drafts. To them the words on the page are never finished. Each can be changed and rearranged, can set off a chain reaction of confusion or clarified meaning. This is a different kind of reading, which is possibly more difficult and certainly more exciting.

Writers must learn to be their own best enemy. They must accept the criticism of others and be suspicious of it; they must accept the praise of others and be even more suspicious of it. Writers cannot depend on others. They must detach themselves from their own pages so that they can apply both their caring and their craft to their own work.

Such detachment is not easy. Science fiction writer Ray Bradbury supposedly puts each manuscript away for a year to the day and then rereads it as a stranger. Not many writers have the discipline or the time to do this. We must read when our judgment may be at its worst, when we are close to the euphoric moment of creation.

Then the writer, counsels novelist Nancy Hale, "should be critical of everything that seems to him most delightful in his style. He should excise what he most admires, because he wouldn't thus admire it if he weren't . . . in a sense protecting it from criticism." John Ciardi, the poet, adds, "The last act of the writing must be to become one's own reader. It is, I suppose, a schizophrenic process, to begin passionately and to end critically, to begin hot and to end cold; and, more important, to be passion-hot and critic-cold at the same time."

Most people think that the principal problem is that writers are too proud of what they have written. Actually, a greater problem for most professional writers is one shared by the majority of students. They are overly critical, think everything is dreadful, tear up page after page, never complete a draft, see the task as hopeless.

The writer must learn to read critically but constructively, to cut what is bad, to reveal what is good. Eleanor Estes, the children's book author, explains: "The writer must survey his work critically, coolly, as though he were a stranger to it. He must be willing to prune, expertly and hard-heartedly. At the end of each revision, a manuscript may look . . . worked over, torn apart, pinned together, added to, deleted from, words changed and words changed back. Yet the book must maintain its original freshness and spontaneity."

Most readers underestimate the amount of rewriting it usually   9
takes to produce spontaneous reading. This is a great disadvantage to the student writer, who sees only a finished product and never watches the craftsman who takes the necessary step back, studies the work carefully, returns to the task, steps back, returns, steps back, again and again. Anthony Burgess, one of the most prolific writers in the English-speaking world, admits, "I might revise a page twenty times." Roald Dahl, the popular children's writer, states, "By the time I'm nearing the end of a story, the first part will have been reread and altered and corrected at least 150 times. . . . Good writing is essentially rewriting. I am positive of this."

Rewriting isn't virtuous. It isn't something that ought to be done.   10
It is simply something that most writers find they have to do to discover what they have to say and how to say it. It is a condition of the writer's life.

There are, however, a few writers who do little formal rewriting,   11
primarily because they have the capacity and experience to create and review a large number of invisible drafts in their minds before they approach the page. And some writers slowly produce finished pages, performing all the tasks of revision simultaneously, page by page, rather than draft by draft. But it is still possible to see the sequence followed by most writers most of the time in rereading their own work.

Most writers scan their drafts first, reading as quickly as possible   12
to catch the larger problems of subject and form, then move in closer and closer as they read and write, reread and rewrite.

The first thing writers look for in their drafts is *information*. They   13
know that a good piece of writing is built from specific, accurate, and interesting information. The writer must have an abundance of information from which to construct a readable piece of writing.

Next writers look for *meaning* in the information. The specifics   14
must build a pattern of significance. Each piece of specific information must carry the reader toward meaning.

Writers reading their own drafts are aware of *audience.* They put themselves in the reader's situation and make sure that they deliver information which a reader wants to know or needs to know in a manner which is easily digested. Writers try to be sure that they anticipate and answer the questions a critical reader will ask when reading the piece of writing. 15

Writers make sure that the *form* is appropriate to the subject and the audience. Form, or genre, is the vehicle which carries meaning to the reader, but form cannot be selected until the writer has adequate information to discover its significance and an audience which needs or wants that meaning. 16

Once writers are sure the form is appropriate, they must then look at the *structure,* the order of what they have written. Good writing is built on a solid framework of logic, argument, narrative, or motivation which runs through the entire piece of writing and holds it together. This is the time when many writers find it most effective to outline as a way of visualizing the hidden spine by which the piece of writing is supported. 17

The element on which writers may spend a majority of their time is *development.* Each section of a piece of writing must be adequately developed. It must give readers enough information so that they are satisfied. How much information is enough? That's as difficult as asking how much garlic belongs in a salad. It must be done to taste, but most beginning writers underdevelop, underestimating the reader's hunger for information. 18

As writers solve development problems, they often have to consider questions of *dimension.* There must be a pleasing and effective proportion among all the parts of the piece of writing. There is a continual process of subtracting and adding to keep the piece of writing in balance. 19

Finally, writers have to listen to their own voices. *Voice* is the force which drives a piece of writing forward. It is an expression of the writer's authority and concern. It is what is between the words on the page, what glues the piece of writing together. A good piece of writing is always marked by a consistent, individual voice. 20

As writers read and reread, write and rewrite, they move closer and closer to the page until they are doing line-by-line editing. Writers read their own pages with infinite care. Each sentence, each line, 21 each clause, each phrase, each word, each mark of punctuation, each section of white space between the type has to contribute to the clarification of meaning.

Slowly the writer moves from word to word, looking through language to see the subject. As a word is changed, cut, or added, as a construction is rearranged, all the words used before that moment and all those that follow that moment must be considered and reconsidered. 22

Writers often read aloud at this stage of the editing process, muttering or whispering to themselves, calling on the ear's experience with language. Does this sound right—or that? Writers edit, shifting back and forth from eye to page to ear to page. I find I must do this careful editing in short runs, no more than fifteen or twenty minutes at a stretch, or I become too kind with myself. I begin to see what I hope is on the page, not what actually is on the page. 23

This sounds tedious if you haven't done it, but actually it is fun. Making something right is immensely satisfying, for writers begin to learn what they are writing about by writing. Language leads them to meaning, and there is the joy of discovery, of understanding, of making meaning clear as the writer employs the technical skills of language. 24

Words have double meanings, even triple and quadruple meanings. Each word has its own potential for connotation and denotation. And when writers rub one word against the other, they are often rewarded with a sudden insight, an unexpected clarification. 25

The maker's eye moves back and forth from word to phrase to sentence to paragraph to sentence to phrase to word. The maker's eye sees the need for variety and balance, for a firmer structure, for a more appropriate form. It peers into the interior of the paragraph, looking for coherence, unity, and emphasis, which make meaning clear. 26

I learned something about this process when my first bifocals were prescribed. I had ordered a larger section of the reading portion of the glass because of my work, but even so, I could not contain my eyes within this new limit of vision. And I still find myself taking off my glasses and bending my nose towards the page, for my eyes unconsciously flick back and forth across the page, back to another page, forward to still another, as I try to see each evolving line in relation to every other line. 27

When does this process end? Most writers agree with the great 28
Russian writer Tolstoy, who said, "I scarcely ever reread my published writings, if by chance I come across a page, it always strikes
me: all this must be rewritten; this is how I should have written it."

The maker's eye is never satisfied, for each word has the poten- 29
tial to ignite new meaning. This article has been twice written all the
way through the writing process, and it was published four years
ago. Now it is to be republished in a book. The editors make a few
small suggestions, and then I read it with my maker's eye. Now it has
been re-edited, re-revised, re-read, re-re-edited, for each piece of
writing to the writer is full of potential and alternatives.

A piece of writing is never finished. It is delivered to a deadline, 30
torn out of the typewriter on demand, sent off with a sense of accomplishment and shame and pride and frustration. If only there were a
couple more days, time for just another run at it, perhaps then . . .

Meaning and Purpose

1. According to Murray, what are the differences in the ways in which
   professional writers and student writers view their first drafts? Do
   his observations ring true? Do both types of writers share any common problems?

2. What two kinds of reading skills does the author distinguish?
   How does the writer's reading skill differ from that of the normal
   readers?

3. What does Murray mean when he says, "Writers must learn to be
   their own best enemy" (paragraph 4)? Explain.

4. In paragraphs 12–30, Murray takes the reader chronologically
   through each of the elements that a writer must consider to revise a
   manuscript. Describe the ways in which a writer must consider
   each of these elements.

5. Murray distinguishes between "information" and "meaning." Explain the difference between the two.

6. Explain Murray's contention that "A piece of writing is never finished" (paragraph 30).

Strategy

1. What is the essay's thesis? Where is it stated?
2. Is the essay an example of directive or informative process analysis (see pp. 396–402)? Explain.
3. Murray cites other writers in his description of the revision process. Why?
4. Explain the author's seemingly odd statement that "most writers share the feeling that the first draft, and all of those which follow, are opportunities to discover what they have to say" (paragraph 2).
5. Murray doesn't actually begin a description of the professional writer's revision process until paragraph 12. What is the purpose of such a long introduction?

Style

1. Murray changes from the third person ("writer," "writers," "the maker") to the first person ("I") in paragraphs 23, 27, and 29. What effect does he create by this change of person?
2. Why does Murray end the essay in midsentence?
3. Use a dictionary to determine the meanings of these words: *journeyman, prolific* (paragraph 2); *euphoric* (5); *schizophrenic* (6); *connotation, denotation* (25).

Writing Tasks

1. Write an essay in which you detail the way in which you revise an essay. In the process, explain why this method might work better for you than the method explained by Murray.
2. If you use a computer to write, explain the advantages of revising on a computer.
3. Write an essay in which you explain to the reader a process that you do regularly and well. Without being moralistic, demonstrate how this might actually benefit the reader.

❦ Responding to Photographs ❦

Process Analysis

Untitled

For some writers the act of writing can be so painful that they go to remarkable lengths to postpone the labor. They travel to the farthest stationery store for the "right" pencil, the one with the exact texture of lead that works best with the amount of pressure they apply to the paper. When they return, they might discover that they are short of the right kind of paper—you know, the yellow pads with the blue lines. Again back to the stationery store. Home once again, all those new pencils must be sharpened to a fine—a very, very fine—point.

What's the solution to this kind of procrastination?

There probably isn't one, for writing is a deeply personal process, one that is full of mystery. Probably no two people go about it exactly the same way. We all use devices to get ourselves started and to keep ourselves at the task. Nevertheless, something must get written. We must get the images and thoughts out of our heads, translate them to words, and put them on paper. Then, of course, a new process begins: the revision process.

Clearly, the untitled photograph here captures a moment in the writing process. For this essay you are to explore the writing process by completing one of the following writing tasks. Before beginning the task, reread the material at the beginning of the chapter to remind yourself of process analysis strategies.

1. Create an appropriate title for the untitled photograph. Then describe its content as capturing part of the writing process. In your essay, account for all the elements in the photograph that relate to the writing process—manuscript, pencils, coffee, calendar, stapler, glasses, desk or table, even the writer's posture.
2. Document your own writing process with photographs of its various stages. Then use the photographs to compose a "photoessay" that concentrates on your own writing process. Use at least five photographs, each one capturing a stage in the process, and explain to your readers what the photographs signify. Keep in mind that writing is a highly personal process, so be sure your photographs and essay embody your personal writing quirks.

❧ *Additional Writing Tasks* ❧
Process Analysis

1. Develop one of these subjects (or one you create for yourself) through *directive process analysis*. Explain the process one step at a time, and be sure to provide your reader with enough detail to make each step clear.

   a. how to prepare a vegetable garden
   b. how to live without an automobile
   c. how to domesticate a wild creature, such as a falcon or rabbit
   d. how to get rid of pests without using poisons
   e. how to prepare for an acting role
   f. how to prepare a canvas for paint
   g. how to show appreciation to others
   h. how to toss a Frisbee, football, baseball, and so on
   i. how to skateboard, roller blade, roller skate
   j. how to bluff at poker
   k. how to survive Muzak
   l. how to complain effectively
   m. how to overcome shyness
   n. how to write an effective essay
   o. how to take effective notes
   p. how to outsmart a video game
   q. how to survive a natural disaster, such as an earthquake or tornado
   r. how to meditate in a crowded setting
   s. how to ride a roller coaster
   t. how to attend a concert
   u. how to run for local elected office
   v. how to win others to your point of view
   w. how to buy a used motorcycle or car

2. Develop one of these subjects (or one you create for yourself) through *informative process analysis*. Remember that this technique does not explain how to do something; it explains how something happens—it informs, often using narrative and descriptive techniques.

   a. how psychoanalysis works
   b. how secret codes are broken

c. how to read detective, espionage, or suspense fiction
d. how to learn from past experience
e. how a stroke damages the brain
f. how Alzheimer's disease develops
g. how dreams work
h. how intuition works
i. how to taste wine
j. how to create a frightening film scene
k. how to create suspense
l. how to collect art, rare books, or something else
m. how to detect lies
n. how to overcome guilt
o. how to change community thinking
p. how to live as an outsider
q. how to become an insider
r. how an idea becomes accepted
s. how voodoo works

11

Classification and Division
Establishing Categories

The Method

Have you ever played Twenty Questions, a parlor game in which one participant selects a person, place, or thing and the other participants try to guess what or who it is? The participants may ask up to twenty yes-or-no questions to find the answer. To discover that answer is a difficult task—unless you understand the principles of **classification.**

The game usually begins with a series of questions that divide the world into three roughly drawn categories: animal, vegetable, or mineral. Once the correct category is determined—"animal," for our purposes—the interrogation begins, the participants moving logically from category to category.

"Does it live in water?" a questioner might ask—a sensible question, for the earth is easily divided into land and water.

"No," the person with the secret responds. But "No" means that the animal lives on land. Of course, birds may fly but may also nest on land. The process of elimination continues.

"Does it have two legs?" Another logical question, because animals can be classified by locomotion.

"No."

"Four legs?" The pace of questions quickens.

"No."

Aha! the questioner has it: "Is this creature an insect?"

"Nope!" Oops . . . must be a snake, right? But what snake? The only two large categories are venomous and nonvenomous. If the answer is venomous, the questions will take one direction, "Does it have rattles?" If the answer is nonvenomous, the questions will move in another direction, "Does it kill by coiling around and crushing its prey?" And so on, until the secret is revealed or the twenty questions are exhausted.

To classify is to divide a large subject into components and sort them into categories with common characteristics, a principle that clearly guides the search in any round of Twenty Questions. Classification is so pervasive that it must be fundamental to the human way of perceiving and understanding experience. Few things, no matter how significant or insignificant, seem to escape classification. Think how chaotic your campus library would be without a clear classification system. Your supermarket trips are probably organized by the manager's way of classifying products—first the vegetables, on to dairy products, rush to meats, march to canned goods, stalled at the register. Television shows, books, actors, restaurants, fun-zone rides—the possibilities for classification are endless because of our desire to understand and organize experience.

Keep in mind, too, that most subjects can be classified in a number of ways, depending on the purpose and who's doing the classifying. Consider the subject *college students.* For statistical purposes, a registrar might classify college students by age, sex, major, grade-point average, or region. An art teacher might classify students by their talent: painters, sculptors, ceramicists, illustrators, and print makers. A political science teacher might classify the same students by their politics: reactionary, conservative, liberal, or radical. Much of this kind of classification is done informally; but in writing, a classification system should be complete and follow consistent principles.

Writers using classification as a pattern of development begin by carefully analyzing their subject—that is, by breaking it into components. They look for qualities that some components share and that others don't share. Using the qualities they've identified, they create categories. They then sort through the various components to group them in the appropriate category. They are careful to be logical, sorting and grouping the parts in a consistent manner. They also keep in mind that their categories must be complete. It would not be complete if they divided voters into Republicans and Democrats, because some voters are registered in the Peace and Freedom and Libertarian parties, among others. But if a writer's subject is limited to elected senators, then the categories might indeed be Republicans and Democrats, because no other party is represented in the Senate. Writers also make sure that their categories do not overlap. To classify a group of congresswomen as Republicans, Democrats, and politicians would not make much sense because all are politicians.

Professional writers distinguish between the terms *division* and *classification,* yet these categories are intellectual companions in the classification procedure. Writers begin by first *dividing* a subject into manageable categories. They then *classify* the components of the subject according to the shared qualities. Consider the subject *movies,* which can be broken down into such categories as mystery, romance, horror, musical, comedy, western, and war. This step is division. Once the categories are established, a writer might evaluate several films, and sort them according to the qualities of each category. This step is classification. Remember, division breaks one subject into categories; classification groups the parts of the subject into the categories. Although this distinction may be important for understanding the intellectual procedure of classification, it is less important in reaching the result, a system that shows the relationship among parts of a subject.

The simplest form of classification is **two-part,** often called binary, classification. This pattern divides a subject in two, usually into positive and negative categories, such as vegetarians and non-vegetarians; smokers and nonsmokers; television viewers and non-television viewers; deaf people and hearing people; or runners and nonrunners. But two-part classification is usually inexact and skirts the edge of comparison and contrast. Most classification systems therefore have at least three categories.

Strategies

Careful writers arrange their classifications in a straightforward division, usually in blocks and according to the order that seems most appropriate. Each block is a subclass and will usually be identified by a name or phrase to keep the reader on track. In the following paragraph, anthropologist Ruth Benedict divides the ceremonial societies of the Zuñi. She clearly identifies each society—the priestly societies, the masked-god societies, and the medicine societies—before describing them.

> This ceremonial life that preoccupies Zuni attention is organized like a series of interlocking wheels. The priesthoods have their sacred objects, their retreats, their dances, their prayers; and their year-long program is annually initiated by the great winter solstice ceremony that makes use of all the dif-

ferent groups and sacred things and focuses all their functions. The tribal masked-god society has similar possessions and calendric observances, and these culminate in the great winter tribal masked god ceremony, the Shalkado. In like fashion the medicine societies, with their special relation to curing, function throughout the year and have their annual culminating ceremony for tribal health. These three major cults of Zuni ceremonial life are not mutually exclusive. A man may be, and often is, for the greater part of his life, a member of all three. They each give him sacred possessions "to live by" and demand of him exacting ceremonial knowledge.

Writers use one of two strategies to identify their categories. They either use ready-made categories or create their own. In the next classification passage, from *Blood and Money,* Thomas Thompson uses subclasses to present his view of the personal characteristics that describe surgeons.

Among those who train students to become doctors, it is said that surgeons find their niche in accordance with their personal characteristics. The orthopedic surgeon is medicine's carpenter—up to his elbows in plaster of Paris—and tradition holds that he is a gruff, slapdash sort of man whose labor is in a very physical area of healing. Away from the hospital, the orthopedists are often hunters, boaters, outdoorsmen.

The neurosurgeon, classically, does not get too involved with his patients. Or, for that matter, with anybody. They are cool men, blunted, rarely gregarious.

Heart surgeons are thundering egotists, star performers in a dazzling operating theater packed with assistants, nurses, paramedics, and a battery of futuristic equipment which could seemingly lift the room into outer space. These are men who relish drama, who live life on the edge of the precipice.

And the plastic surgeon? He is, by nature, a man of art, and temperament, and sensitivity. "We are the artists who deal in beauty lost, or beauty that never was," said one plastic man at a national convention. "Our stitches are hidden, and so are our emotions."

Because Thompson is working with established categories, part of his task is to make his material fresh. Most readers know the professional qualities of surgeons, and so Thompson creates a sense of the person holding the scalpel by including descriptive details of each type's dominant personality trait.

In the next paragraph, Larry McMurtry uses established categories in a slightly different way. He classifies beer bars in the city of Houston according to their location: East side, West side, and North side.

> The poor have beer-bars, hundreds of them, seldom fancy but reliably dim and cool. Most of them are equipped with jukeboxes, shuffleboards, jars of pig's feet and talkative drunks. There are lots of bar burlesques, where from 3 p.m. on girls gyrate at one's elbow with varying degrees of grace. On the East side there are a fair number of open-air bars—those who like to watch the traffic can sit, drink Pearl, observe the wrecks, and listen to "Hello, Vietnam" on the jukebox. Louisiana is just down the road, and a lot of the men wear Cajun sideburns and leave their shirttails out. On the West side cowboys are common. Members of the cross-continental hitch-hiking set congregate on Franklin Street, at places like The Breaking Point Lounge. Symbolic latinos slip over to the Last Concert on the North side; or, if they are especially bold, go all the way to McCarty Street, where one can view the most extraordinary example of Mexican saloon-and-whorehouse architecture north of the border.

McMurtry opens with a general description of Houston beer bars: They are dim and cool with jukeboxes, shuffleboards, jars of pig's feet, and drunks—a watering hole for blue-collar men. After rendering the general qualities of these bars, McMurtry presents the geographic categories, each with a brief description that characterizes it.

Writers often classify a subject that has no ready-made categories. They must, therefore, create their own categories and the labels that identify them. In this paragraph from "Here Is New York," E. B. White divides the population of New York into three categories according to a person's relation to the city.

There are roughly three New Yorks. There is, first, the New York of the man or woman who was born here, who takes the city for granted and accepts its size and its turbulence as natural and inevitable. Second, there is the New York of the commuter—the city that is devoured by locusts each day and spat out each night. Third, there is the New York of the quest of something. Of these three trembling cities the greatest is the last—the city of final destination, the city that is a goal. It is this third city that accounts for New York's high-strung disposition, its poetical deportment, its dedication to the arts, and its incomparable achievements. Commuters give the city its tidal restlessness; natives give it solidarity and continuity; but the settlers give it passion. And whether it is a farmer arriving from Italy to set up a small grocery store in a slum, or a young girl arriving from a small town in Mississippi to escape the indignity of being observed by her neighbors, or a boy arriving from the Corn Belt with a manuscript in his suitcase and a pain in his heart, it makes no difference: each embraces New York with the intense excitement of first love, each absorbs New York with the fresh eyes of an adventurer, each generates heat and light to dwarf the Consolidated Edison Company.

Commuters, natives, and settlers, these are White's three categories. He uses each category to present characteristics of New York City. The commuter gives the city a sense of restlessness; the native gives it solidarity; and the settler, the category he stresses, gives it passion.

Classification and Division in College Writing

The physical sciences, social sciences, and humanities all use classification, which some writers believe is the hardest rhetorical pattern to master. Whether the pattern is difficult or not, you can expect to use it across the academic curriculum.

Guidelines for Writing Classification and Division

1. Select a subject that can be divided into at least three components. Identify the chief characteristics of each component.

Use the characteristics to sort and group the components into categories.

2. Examine the categories with two questions in mind: Are they complete—that is, can all the components of your subject be grouped within them? Are the categories consistent—that is, can any of your component parts be classified in more than one category? If your categories are incomplete or inconsistent, then restructure them or move on to another subject.

3. Compose a thesis that clearly indicates that you will be classifying your subject. If you use ready-made categories or name your categories, include the names as part of the thesis. Naming your categories early will prepare your readers for the shift from one category to another in the discussion.

4. Decide how to arrange your categories effectively, saving the most dramatic for last.

5. Revise your essay, making sure that each category is clearly distinguished and adequately developed.

A Student Essay Developed by Classification

For an assignment in cultural anthropology, Mark Freeman wrote a classification essay on the general topic of people who collect artifacts from popular culture. His assignment was as follows:

> From your own experience and observation, write a 500- to 600-word essay that classifies "collectors," that is, people who collect such popular culture artifacts as baseball cards, garage-sale paintings, bottles, magazines, movie posters, bottle caps, tourist novelties, campaign buttons, and celebrity autographs.
>
> Concentrate on vertical as opposed to horizontal collectors—that is, those who collect one kind of artifact rather than several different kinds.

Freeman selected the general subject "magazines." He quickly narrowed this to the more specific subject "comic books." Since he was once an avid comic book collector, he had plenty of material to work with. First read Freeman's classification and division essay, then reread it and respond to items in Reviewing with a Writer's Eye.

In Search of the Comic

Comic book collectors represent every income level and often fit the stereotype of the computer nerd; that is, whether young or old, they tend to be pale disheveled males who wear glasses and speak a language the uninitiated seldom understand. They can be found rummaging through pile after pile of unsorted, secondhand comics in magazine marts across the country. These collectors, the serious ones, can be classified into four major groups: Antiquarians, Mercenaries, Idolaters, and Compulsive Completers.   1

The Antiquarian searches for classic comics only, subject matter is of no concern. He is looking for a 1933 Funnies on Parade or Famous Funnies, the first publications that are recognizable as comic books and initially used as giveaways in advertising promotions. The Antiquarian, driven by a desire to connect with the past, will travel the country's backroads to find 1933 editions of The Spider, which was reintroduced as the Spiderman series in 1962.   2

The Mercenary searches for value. Certain numbers and titles ring a bell in his cash-register brain and start him checking through a half-dozen price sheets. A pristine first edition of Action Comics (value $12,000) would suit him just fine. He would also hunt down early editions of Marvel Comics, especially the first publications featuring early super heroes, such as Captain America, the Punisher, and the Human Torch. The Mercenary would, no doubt, love to have first editions of <u>Batman</u> and <u>Superman</u> but, being a realist, knows they are locked in vaults.   3

The Idolater has little interest in age or value. He searches for favorites: a <u>Sheena,</u> a <u>Flash Gordon,</u> or an <u>Incredible Hulk</u>. With little money to spend, the Idolater will usually be hiding in the corner of a comic mart, reading the comic books he cannot afford to buy. He will freely announce his dream of creating his own hero figure and is always eager to display his sketches to anyone willing to listen to his heroic tales and future visions. The Idolater will be the last one out of the mart at night and the first one back in the morning.   4

The most frustrated of the group is the Compulsive Completer. This obsessed collector will examine and reject thousands of comics in a search for a badly needed <u>Felix the Cat</u> to complete a year's set. The Completer is usually a specialist,   5 perhaps concentrating on comic books featuring animals, such as Mighty Mouse, a pint-sized superior who became famous when featured in cartoons shown between movies in theaters across America, or Super Rabbit, a long-eared protector of the innocent who became known during W.W. II for fighting Nazis in the pages of Marvel Comics. Compulsive Completers often become so desperate to acquire every issue published in one year they will seek bank loans to cover their costs.

Although driven by different motivations, the Antiquarian, 6
Mercenary, Idolater, and Compulsive Completer share a common trait: They love the thrill of the hunt.

Reviewing with a Writer's Eye

1. What characteristics do all members of Freeman's categories share?
2. Develop your own scratch outline (pp. 42–44) of Mark Freeman's "In Search of the Comic." What do you believe to be Freeman's organizational strategy? Why is the conclusion composed of a single sentence?
3. Should Freeman have created a fifth category named Explorers—that is, people who buy comics, read them, and then toss them aside? Explain.
4. In the first sentence of paragraph 3, Freeman uses the word "searches" for the first time. Where else does he use the word and other words with similar meanings? Why?
5. In a brief note to Freeman, evaluate his essay by the conventions that dominate classification (pp. 433–437). In what ways does his essay succeed? In what ways does it fail?

Peer Review

You may be asked to write an essay about one of the readings that follow. Before you meet with your writing group, review this introduction. As you read the group papers, use these general principles of classification and division to help guide your comments.

1. A classification system should have at least three categories to distinguish it from comparison and contrast.
2. A classification paper should give a reader a fresh way of looking at a subject. Even if the categories used are already established and well known, the content describing each category should be fresh.
3. The categories chosen should not overlap and allow a component to be assigned to more than one class.
4. The categories should be complete, covering the entire subject.

The essays that follow show the variety of ways in which writers divide and classify subjects. Study them closely. Note the categories each writer establishes. Ask yourself whether the categories are complete and consistent, two important tests to determine whether a classification essay is successful.

❧ William Lutz ❧

William Lutz, born in 1940, holds doctorates in both English and law and is a professor and former chair of the Department of English at Rutgers University in New Jersey. He was the editor of the now defunct The Quarterly Review of Doublespeak, *a journal that examines the subject of doublespeak—language that is "carefully designed and constructed to appear to communicate when in fact it doesn't," "language designed not to lead but to mislead," "language designed to distort reality and corrupt thought." He is an expert on the use of the English language who has published numerous articles on language and has authored or coauthored fourteen books. Lutz's* Doublespeak: From Revenue Enhancements to Terminal Living *was a best-seller; its sequel,* Why No One Knows What Anyone's Saying Anymore, *has been equally influential.*

Doublespeak

Language allows us to communicate, and the better we're able to handle language, the more clearly and effectively we can communicate—or so we like to think. But what about language that is deliberately designed to deceive and obfuscate? William Lutz, in this 1989 essay, considers such language.

In reading the essay, keep in mind the things that distinguish each kind of doublespeak from each other, as well as the things they have in common.

There are no potholes in the streets of Tucson, Arizona, just   1
"pavement deficiencies." The Reagan Administration didn't propose any new taxes, just "revenue enhancement" through new "user's fees." Those aren't bums on the street, just "non-goal oriented members of society." There are no more poor people, just "fiscal underachievers." There was no robbery of an automatic teller machine, just an "unauthorized withdrawal." The patient didn't die because of medical malpractice, it was just a "diagnostic misadvanture of a high

magnitude." The U.S. Army doesn't kill the enemy anymore, it just "services the target." And the doublespeak goes on.

Doublespeak is language that pretends to communicate but really doesn't. It is language that makes the bad seem good, the negative appear positive, the unpleasant appear attractive or at least tolerable. Doublespeak is language that avoids or shifts responsibility, language that is at variance with its real or purported meaning. It is language that conceals or prevents thought; rather than extending thought, doublespeak limits it.

How to Spot Doublespeak

How can you spot doublespeak? Most of the time you will recognize doublespeak when you see or hear it. But, if you have any doubts, you can identify doublespeak just by answering these questions: Who is saying what to whom, under what conditions and circumstances, with what intent, and with what results? Answering these questions will usually help you identify as doublespeak language that appears to be legitimate or that at first glance doesn't even appear to be doublespeak.

First Kind of Doublespeak

There are at least four kinds of doublespeak. The first is the euphemism, an inoffensive or positive word or phrase used to avoid a harsh, unpleasant, or distasteful reality. But a euphemism can also be a tactful word or phrase which avoids directly mentioning a painful reality, or it can be an expression used out of concern for the feelings of someone else, or to avoid directly discussing a topic subject to a social or cultural taboo.

When you use a euphemism because of your sensitivity for someone's feelings or out of concern for a recognized social or cultural taboo, it is not doublespeak. For example, you express your condolences that someone has "passed away" because you do not want to say to a grieving person, "I'm sorry your father is dead." When you see the euphemism "passed away," no one is misled. Moreover, the euphemism functions here not just to protect the feelings of another person, but to communicate also your concern for that person's feelings during a period of mourning. When you excuse yourself to go to the "restroom," or you mention that someone is "sleeping with" or "involved with" someone else, you do not mislead anyone about your meaning, but you do respect the social taboos about discussing bodily functions and sex in direct terms. You also indicate your sensitivity to the feelings of your audience, which is usually considered a mark of courtesy and good manners.

However, when a euphemism is used to mislead or deceive, it be- 6 comes doublespeak. For example, in 1984 the U.S. State Department announced that it would no longer use the word "killing" in its annual report on the status of human rights in countries around the world. Instead, it would use the phrase "unlawful or arbitrary deprivation of life," which the department claimed was more accurate. Its real purpose for using this phrase was simply to avoid discussing the embarrassing situation of government-sanctioned killings in countries that are supported by the United States and have been certified by the United States as respecting the human rights of their citizens. This use of a euphemism constitutes doublespeak, since it is designed to mislead, to cover up the unpleasant. Its real intent is at variance with its apparent intent. It is language designed to alter our perception of reality.

The Pentagon, too, avoids discussing unpleasant realities when 7 it refers to bombs and artillery shells that fall on civilian targets as "incontinent ordnance." And in 1977 the Pentagon tried to slip funding for the neutron bomb unnoticed into an appropriations bill by calling it a "radiation enhancement device."

Second Kind of Doublespeak

A second kind of doublespeak is jargon, the specialized lan- 8 guage of a trade, profession, or similar group, such as that used by doctors, lawyers, engineers, educators, or car mechanics. Jargon can serve an important and useful function. Within a group, jargon functions as a kind of verbal shorthand that allows members of the group to communicate with each other clearly, efficiently, and quickly. Indeed, it is a mark of membership in the group to be able to use and understand the group's jargon.

But jargon, like the euphemism, can also be doublespeak. It can 9 be—and often is—pretentious, obscure, and esoteric terminology used to give an air of profundity, authority, and prestige to speakers and their subject matter. Jargon as doublespeak often makes the simple appear complex, the ordinary profound, the obvious insightful. In this sense it is used not to express but impress. With such doublespeak, the act of smelling something becomes "organoleptic analysis," glass becomes "fused silicate," a crack in a metal support beam becomes a "discontinuity," conservative economic policies become "distributionally conservative notions."

Lawyers, for example, speak of an "involuntary conversion" of 10 property when discussing the loss or destruction of property through theft, accident, or condemnation. If your house burns down or if your car is stolen, you have suffered an involuntary conversion of your property. When used by lawyers in a legal situation, such jargon is a legitimate use of language, since lawyers can be expected to understand the term.

However, when a member of a specialized group uses its jargon 11 to communicate with a person outside the group, and uses it knowing that the nonmember does not understand such language, then there is doublespeak. For example, on May 9, 1978, a National Airlines 727 airplane crashed while attempting to land at the Pensacola, Florida, airport. Three of the fifty-two passengers aboard the airplane were killed. As a result of the crash, National made an after-tax insurance benefit of $1.7 million, or an extra 18¢ a share dividend for its stockholders. Now National Airlines had two problems: It did not want to talk about one of its airplanes crashing, and it had to account for the $1.7 million when it issued its annual report to its stockholders. National solved the problem by inserting a footnote in its annual report which explained that the $1.7 million income was due to "the involuntary conversion of a 727." National thus acknowledged the crash of its airplane and the subsequent profit it made from the crash, without once mentioning the accident or the deaths. However, because airline officials knew that most stockholders in the company, and indeed most of the general public, were not familiar with legal jargon, the use of such jargon constituted doublespeak.

Third Kind of Doublespeak

A third kind of doublespeak is gobbledygook or bureaucratese. 12 Basically, such doublespeak is simply a matter of piling on words, of overwhelming the audience with words, the bigger the words and the longer the sentences the better. Alan Greenspan, then chair of President Nixon's Council of Economic Advisors, was quoted in *The Philadelphia Inquirer* in 1974 as having testified before a Senate committee that "It is a tricky problem to find the particular calibration in timing that would be appropriate to stem the acceleration in risk premiums created by falling incomes without prematurely aborting the decline in the inflation-generated risk premiums."

Nor has Mr. Greenspan's language changed since then. Speaking 13 to the meeting of the Economic Club of New York in 1988, Mr. Greenspan, now Federal Reserve chair, said, "I guess I should warn you, if I turn out to be particularly clear, you've probably misunderstood what I've said." Mr. Greenspan's doublespeak doesn't seem to have held back his career.

Sometimes gobbledygook may sound impressive, but when the 14 quote is later examined in print it doesn't even make sense. During the 1988 presidential campaign, vice-presidential candidate Senator Dan Quayle explained the need for a strategic-defense initiative by saying, "Why wouldn't an enhanced deterrent, a more stable peace, a better prospect to denying the ones who enter conflict in the first place to have a reduction of offensive systems and an introduction to defense capability? I believe this is the route the country will eventually go."

The investigation into the Challenger disaster in 1986 revealed 15 the doublespeak of gobbledygook and bureaucratese used by too many involved in the shuttle program. When Jesse Moore, NASA's associate administrator, was asked if the performance of the shuttle program had improved with each launch or if it had remained the same, he answered, "I think our performance in terms of the liftoff performance and in terms of the orbital performance, we knew more about the envelope we were operating under, and we have been pretty accurately staying in that. And so I would say the performance has not by design drastically improved. I think we have been able to characterize the performance more as a function of our launch experience as opposed to it improving as a function of time." While this language may appear to be jargon, a close look will reveal that it is really just gobbledygook laced with jargon. But you really have to wonder if Mr. Moore had any idea what he was saying.

Fourth Kind of Doublespeak

The fourth kind of doublespeak is inflated language that is de-   16
signed to make the ordinary seem extraordinary; to make everyday
things seem impressive; to give an air of importance to people, situations, or things that would not normally be considered important; to
make the simple seem complex. Often this kind of doublespeak isn't
hard to spot, and it is usually pretty funny. While car mechanics may
be called "automotive internists," elevator operators members of the
"vertical transportation corps," used cars "pre-owned" or "experienced," and black-and-white television sets described as having
"non-multicolor capability," you really aren't misled all that much by
such language.

However, you may have trouble figuring out that, when Chrysler   17
"initiates a career alternative enhancement program," it is really laying off five thousand workers; or that "negative patient care outcome" means the patient died; or that "rapid oxidation" means a fire
in a nuclear power plant.

The doublespeak of inflated language can have serious conse-   18
quences. In Pentagon doublespeak, "pre-emptive counterattack"
means that American forces attacked first; "engaged the enemy on all
sides" means American troops were ambushed; "backloading of aug-
mentation personnel" means a retreat by American troops. In the
doublespeak of the military, the 1983 invasion of Grenada was conducted not by the U.S. Army, Navy, Air Force, and Marines, but by
the "Caribbean Peace Keeping Forces." But then, according to the
Pentagon, it wasn't an invasion, it was a "predawn vertical insertion."

The Dangers of Doublespeak

These . . . examples of doublespeak should make it clear that   19
doublespeak is not the product of carelessness or sloppy thinking.
Indeed, most doublespeak is the product of clear thinking and is
carefully designed and constructed to appear to communicate when
in fact it doesn't. It is language designed not to lead but mislead. It is
language designed to distort reality and corrupt thought. . . . When
a fire in a nuclear reactor building is called "rapid oxidation," an explosion in a nuclear power plant is called an "energetic disassembly,"

the illegal overthrow of a legitimate government is termed "destabilizing a government," and lies are seen as "inoperative statements," we are hearing doublespeak that attempts to avoid responsibility and make the bad seem good, the negative appear positive, something unpleasant appear attractive; and which seems to communicate but doesn't. It is language designed to alter our perception of reality and corrupt our thinking. Such language does not provide us with the tools we need to develop, advance, and preserve our culture and our civilization. Such language breeds suspicion, cynicism, distrust, and, ultimately, hostility.

Meaning and Purpose

1. What is Lutz's thesis? Where does he state it?
2. From Lutz's point of view, what distinguishes permissible evasive or esoteric language from doublespeak?
3. What can we do to recognize doublespeak?
4. According to Lutz, what are the dangers of doublespeak?

Strategy

1. By dividing his subject of doublespeak into four different categories, Lutz makes classification and division his primary organizational pattern. What are examples of other organizational patterns in the essay?
2. How do Lutz's first two kinds of doublespeak, euphemism and jargon, differ from his second two, gobbledygook and inflated language?
3. How do paragraphs 2 and 19 reflect each other?

Style

1. Compare the quotes from Alan Greenspan in paragraphs 12 and 13. In what way are the two quotes different? What is the significance of that difference?

2. What is Lutz's tone in this essay? What is his attitude toward his subject? How can you tell?

3. Look up the following words in a dictionary: *variance, purported* (paragraph 2); *tactful* (4); *condolences* (5); *incontinent, ordnance* (7); *pretentious, esoteric, profundity* (9); *dividend* (11); *initiative* (14).

Writing Tasks

1. Find a number of television, magazine, or newspaper advertisements that you think are meant to deceive, and write an essay in which you categorize and explain the types of deception the ads use.

2. Find an example of doublespeak that you find particularly offensive. You might look for examples in television, radio, magazine, or newspaper advertisements or in editorials or articles in newspapers or journals of opinion. Then write an essay in which you analyze the doublespeak and, in doing so, point out why it is dangerous and/or offensive.

❦ Paul Sheehan ❦

A native Australian now living in Sydney, Paul Sheehan has had his work published in The Atlantic Monthly, The New Yorker, *and* The New York Times. *Most of his writing, however, has been for the* Sydney Morning Herald. *After being a Nieman Fellow at Harvard University and having graduated from Columbia University's Graduate School of Journalism, Sheehan spent ten years in New York and Washington as a foreign correspondent.*

My Habit

The essay that follows, first published in a 1996 issue of The New Yorker, *also appears in* The Best American Essays 1997. *As you read it, follow carefully Paul Sheehan's transitions, noting how easily he seems to move from paragraph to paragraph.*

The morning after New York's great January blizzard, I took a 1
long walk to the places where I often explore my arcane little niche of the drug world. I walked up Central Park West from the Nineties to Harlem and Morningside Park, passed under the lee of the Cathedral of St. John the Divine, and crossed over to Riverside Park. All are fertile drug sites for me.

The city looked gloriously serene and cleansed, but I was curi- 2
ous to see if my specialty, the crack trade, had paused during the previous day and night of heavy snow. The crack epidemic still rages quietly, even though it has largely slipped from public concern, and a popular myth has grown that the trade is burning itself out because so many crack addicts became zombies. But the police don't see any burnout among hard-core users. And from my peculiar perch I find that the trade seems as busy as ever. I wanted to see what the snow would reveal.

It revealed that the crack trade had not paused. In two hours, I 3
found a dozen vials newly discarded on the fresh snow. Each had

been used in the narrow space of time since the blizzard had dissipated. Most of the vials had been used outside, but a few had been thrown out of windows and had landed upright in the powdery snow, like little missiles.

Every New Yorker has stepped over empty crack vials, yet most people tell me they don't even know what a crack vial looks like. I look, and so I find. During my walk after the blizzard, I also came upon a man lighting his crack pipe in Morningside Park. It was ten o'clock in the morning, and the park was filled with children and parents playing in the snow. He was clearly, as they say on the street, "thirsty." 4

I waited until he left, then walked to his spot and saw something I had hoped to find. Lying bright on a snowdrift was a small glass tube, not quite an inch long, with a blue plastic cap inserted in the top. The inside surface of the glass was coated with the white residue of crack. I don't know why the man had neatly reinserted the cap before throwing the vial away, but a lot of crack addicts have that fastidious habit. I watched him walking away, then examined the slender vial. I knew I held a totem of the quenchless thirst for crack in my hand, but I did not feel sorry for him, because he had left a type of crack vial I had not seen before. I was thrilled. 5

I write for a living, but I am also the owner and curator of what is almost certainly the world's largest collection of crack vials. The crack vial first turned up in New York and Florida, and was invented specifically as a package for crack cocaine, which comes in a pebble form that must be handled with care. For a decade, the vials have been made illegally in an abundance of styles, and they have been discarded by the tens of thousands on the streets of New York. My collection is a measure of this abundance, and a small monument to it. 6

Inevitably, it has become more difficult to find new vials as the collection has grown into the hundreds, so my search has widened, and the terrain has become more unfamiliar and sometimes dangerous. Last November, I was surrounded by drug dealers in the notorious Cabrini-Green housing project in Chicago. I had gone there looking for Chicago crack vials and had not found any, and so had begun to root around the buildings, until I became an object of inspection for every lookout and enforcer at work in the project that 7 day. They kept asking me, "Wassup, slick boy?" This was an unnecessary risk, an obsessional predicament, and all for something that most people would regard as worthless. I smiled and introduced myself as "Father Sheehan from St. Joseph's," and, with a measured, priestly gait, continued on my way out of Cabrini. (I am not a priest.) And I discovered belatedly that addicts don't use crack vials in Chicago; they use tiny plastic bags.

As I have wandered around rough neighborhoods, talking to addicts and cops and scholars, the underground world of crack has revealed some of itself to me. I learned about "mills," where heroin and cocaine are processed for street distribution. The cocaine powder is cooked into the more potent form of crack cocaine: teams of women, sometimes naked, I was told, fill hundreds of vials a day—an operation known as "bottling up." The idea that naked women are employed to fill crack vials seemed a patently absurd urban myth, but serious people, among them several urban ethnographers, assured me that it was true. Drug dealers are paranoid about pilfering. "A naked woman can't steal it, because she's got nowhere to put it" is how one source explained it.

I learned the street names of many of the vials: bunnies, crazies, supers, skinnies, flavors, bullets, and Taj Mahals. The word "vial" carries the heavy connotation of poison, and it is a term that users avoid, preferring to call the vials "caps." Users in need of the drug are "thirsty" or are "looking for Scotty" (as in "Beam me up, Scotty," from *Star Trek*) or looking for "rock" or "ready rock." New crack vials are usually sold in bags of fifty at grocery stores and bodegas, and the wholesale business appears to be dominated by immigrants from Yemen. "The crack-vial manufacturers have eluded us so far," Inspector William Taylor, of the New York Police Department drug squad, told me. "The information we have is that the vials are brought in from overseas." When I told him I had heard that they are brought in from the Bronx and Queens, he conceded that that may also be true. The police occasionally conduct sweeps against the paraphernalia industry and confiscate display boards, which are kept under shops' counters and used to show drug dealers the available range of vials' colors and designs.

The colors can denote a selling crew or a supplier or a product or a gang territory, or they can simply be random. I have heard dealers on Amsterdam Avenue shouting "We got blue!" or "Blue is up!" to alert buyers that blue-capped crack vials are on the street. Crack is price-driven, and the price is generally three to five dollars per vial, sometimes as low as two. The whole point of crack, which in its most common form is a cooked mixture of cocaine, lidocaine (a synthetic crystalline compound used in anesthetics), and baking soda, is to create more value out of a kilo of cocaine powder by making a drug that can produce an intense high at a very low price, thus vastly expanding the market downward. The more intensely addictive quality of crack is simply a bonus.

Blue caps? I have seventy different ones, blue being the most common color in a collection that at the time of writing contains 562 different crack vials. They are displayed in five Riker Specimen Mounts, thin cases with glass fronts which can be hung on the wall; the cases were designed to hold insects. Each of my cases has a name:

1. The Main Collection. A large case densely overcrowded with plastic vials—no glass vials—representing three quarters of the collection and gathered entirely on the Upper West Side and mostly within a ten-block radius of my apartment building, on West Ninety-eighth Street, off Riverside Drive.

2. The Taj Mahal Annex. A set of fifty-six plastic vials with ornate colored caps. I originally called this collection the Crown Annex, because the caps look like little crowns, but then learned that their street name is Taj Mahals.

3. The Newark Annex. Glass vials collected during two visits to Newark. Everything there was glass, no plastic. Because glass vials break easily and perish quickly once they're discarded, they are much harder to find.

4. The Harlem Annex. A mixture of both glass and plastic vials and caps that are unique to Harlem. They include "jumbo" vials—larger glass vials, developed for the suburban trade.

5. The Gold and Silver Annex. Thirty different vials, either glass or plastic, whose caps are either gold or silver plastic. This is my favorite case.

Among the 562 vials are eighty different cap designs, possibly suggesting eighty different manufacturers, and each cap is usually produced in ten or twelve different colors. The vials themselves have numerous variations—hexagonal, bullet-shaped, long, squat, thin, thick, plastic, glass—totaling more than four dozen different types, but all of them are transparent, so the contents can be seen. Vials produced a frisson of excitement in me last summer when they appeared in tinted versions for the first time: green vials, then blue, then red. Most of the cap and vial designs in the collection are no longer made and will never be on the streets again.

I clean all the vials except those which contain crack residue: I 18 don't touch that. (I also have eight vials with deep teeth indentations, which I keep in a plastic bag, out of sight.)

Why bother? What is the worthiness? Isn't this collection a varia- 19 tion on the parasitism that crack already represents? Similar brutal questions are posed by Geoff Nicholson in *Hunters and Gatherers,* his novel about bizarre and exceptionally useless collections and collectors:

> What was collecting, anyway? You took one thing and you took another thing, you put them next to each other and somehow their proximity was supposed to create a meaning. You put certain artifacts together, drew an artificial boundary around them, and there you were with a collection. So what?
>
> As for the people themselves, I suspected that collectors were deeply inadequate human beings, compensating for a lack of personality, intelligence or love. I pictured them as a bunch of unsocial dullards: shy, oafish, unhip.

I am comfortable with these questions. I asked them myself long 20 ago, and I have the answers.

The collection began as evidence. In 1991, the West 97/98th 21 Street Block Association filed suit to block the reopening, by Volunteers of America, of a residence for homeless people, including some who were mentally ill, at 305 West Ninety-seventh Street. Two years later, the New York State Court of Appeals rejected a "fair share" argument that there were already thirty-eight shelters and treatment centers between West Ninetieth Street and West 110th Street, and almost none on the Upper East Side or on the West Side below Ninetieth Street. Meanwhile, the center reopened in 1992, and neighborhood activists predicted that drug-taking, panhandling, and car break-ins would increase. Whether or not crack users did move

into the building—Volunteers of America always said they did not—
I did notice more crack vials between Ninety-seventh and Ninety-
eighth Streets and began gathering them as tangible evidence that
the block association was right. One of the denizens of West Ninety-
seventh Street, a stick-figure junkie with bleached blond hair who always seemed to be crying, parked herself at the entrance to the
Ninety-sixth Street subway station every day and panhandled. For
the first time, I found vials on the pavement outside the entrance to
my building. I felt that the courts and the city government were
pushing the tide of drugs right to my front door.

Once I started seeing crack vials, I noticed their extraordinary 22
variety. Then the writer Allen Kurzweil came to visit, still basking in
the success of his first novel, *A Case of Curiosities,* and he suggested
that I put the crack vials in a display case—a case of curiosities. He
then brought me a small Riker Specimen Mount from Maxilla &
Mandible, on Columbus Avenue. After we mounted the vials, we discovered that when crack vials are massed in multicolored ranks they
are charismatic. They have something to say. I put them on the wall,
and when people came by they always looked at the crack case before even noticing any of the other art in my living room.

I can't explain why, but collecting became important to me. I 23
stopped worrying about who lived at 305 West Ninety-seventh
Street. Besides, the crying junkie had disappeared, the building had
been cleaned up, and crack vials had become rare on my street. I
felt safe wandering around some of the city's worst neighborhoods,
especially after I noticed that people were calling me "Officer."
Once, in Morningside Heights, a man came out of the bushes with
his hands up when he saw me approaching. In Harlem, while I was
on my knees sifting through a scattering of crack vials under a park
bench, a young woman lolling on the bench, who was high on
something, said to me, "You don't care what people think about
you, do you?"

I have seen the entire panoply of New York's addiction debris: 24
hundreds of discarded butane lighters, hypodermic needles,
"cooker" bottles, tubes of glue, used condoms, empty handbags,
empty bottles of Night Train, baking-soda boxes, rubbing-alcohol
bottles, razor blades, and broken crack pipes.

In a paper that Doug Goldsmith, a New York ethnographer, deliv- 25
ered last year to the Society for Applied Anthropology, he compared
crack vials to the detritus found at archaeological digs. Not long afterward, I spoke with him. "I've been on digs in the Southwest," he told
me, "and I know those indestructible colored tops are the things that
will remain behind, like pottery shards in ancient dwellings."

One day, there will be no more crack vials. And one day, perhaps 26
soon, crack itself will be replaced. When the hard pebbles created by
cooking cocaine were first sold, in the early 1980s, dealers used
small perfume bottles or contact-lens cases to distribute them. Today's small, cheap, transparent, sturdy vials were developed as the
market expanded, and the packaging of crack continues to evolve.
Dealers are increasingly replacing vials with tiny Ziploc plastic bags,
because they are easier to obtain, sell, carry, and, most important,
conceal. When there are no more crack vials, I suppose my collection will have genuine anthropological value.

Artists have tinkered with drug paraphernalia to make aesthetic 27
moral statements. The composer Philip Glass owns a work entitled
Found Dope #2, which was made by a friend of his, and which consists
of crack vials and caps stuck on parchment. The most common reaction to my collection has been that it is beautiful, so I took some of my
cases of vials to a friend, a distinguished art historian, because I
thought he would find layers of meaning that had not occurred to me.
He loved the collection. "It's like looking at a little graveyard, little
tombs," he said. "Except it has these childlike colors from Toys R Us, a
compound of juvenilia and death. It reminds me of the collection of
Dr. Ruysch, a Dutch anatomist who draped fetuses in lace and pre-
served them in jars. Staggeringly horrible oxymorons. But compelling
oxymorons. They ended up in the collection of Peter the Great."

Meaning and Purpose

1. The term *irony* refers to using words to express something different
   from, and often opposite to, a literal meaning. Now that you have
   read the essay, what is ironic about its title?

2. What is ironic about the statement early in the essay, "I look, and so I find" (paragraph 4)?
3. Sheehan speaks of his vial collection as being "a small monument to it" (paragraph 6). To what does the *it* refer in that phrase?
4. Sheehan has five cases filled with crack vials. He has classified them into categories. Do the categories overlap, or are they true categories in that each case contains quite different vials? Support your answer with concrete evidence.
5. Why did Sheehan begin to collect the vials?

Strategy

1. Crack addiction is not only unlawful but also life-destroying. What is Sheehan's opinion of crack users?
2. What evidence in this essay shows that Sheehan is quite serious about collecting crack vials?
3. Why did Sheehan once masquerade as a Catholic priest?
4. In your opinion, why does Sheehan clean all his vials except those that contain crack residue?
5. Some people have said that only a foreigner or a scientist could have written this essay. Why do you think they said that?

Style

1. Sheehan has a "Taj Mahal" collection (paragraph 13). What is the original Taj Mahal?
2. According to Sheehan, crack vials can be "charismatic" (paragraph 22). What does the term *charismatic* mean?
3. Sheehan says that he has seen "the entire panoply of New York's addiction debris" (paragraph 24). What does *panoply* mean? Suggest a synonym.
4. One ethnographer compared crack vials "to the detritus found at archaeological digs" (paragraph 25). What does *detritus* mean in that phrase?
5. What is an "ethnographer" (paragraph 25)? In some sense, could Sheehan be classified as an ethnographer? Why or why not?

Writing Tasks

1. Imagine that we have only three ways to classify: mostly flat, mostly round, and mostly square. Using those three classes, write an essay in which you describe the contents of any room where you live, placing each object in that room in one of the three classes and giving at least one reason for putting each object into a specific class.
2. Visit a restaurant, a cafeteria, or a fast-food franchise. Study its menu carefully, and then write an essay in which you classify each of its items into one of three categories that you yourself invent. Give at least one reason for your having classified each item into one of your categories.

❦ Jim Spring ❦

Jim Spring began his career as a journalist reporting on technology. He then became executive editor of Ski *magazine. Later, in the 1970s, he started SMART (Sports Marketing and Research Technology), a company that pioneered the use of research systems to be used by sports retailers. In 1990, Spring and a colleague formed Leisure Trends, a firm that researches the leisure habits and attitudes of Americans and sells the results of that research to businesses that can benefit from it. Spring also writes a column for several marketing trade magazines and has authored several short books on applying research to marketing.*

Exercising the Brain

The following essay was first published in 1993 in American Demographics, *a magazine designed to appeal to marketers. It focuses on how to judge a market and the changes that are going on in the population. In the essay, Jim Spring offers companies information about consumer attitudes and behaviors so that they can develop effective marketing plans.*

Spring points up the discrepancies between the leisure activities people claim they like to do and those they actually participate in. What accounts for these discrepancies? How does Spring's explanation fit into your own experience?

Norma Puzzle invited Charlie to a concert a month away, and Charlie said he "really wanted to go." Norma considered it a date. But when she showed up to take him, Charlie wasn't home. "Just because I said I wanted to go didn't mean we had a date," he said later. "I want to do lots of things I never do."

Norma wasn't happy. Aside from the costly tickets, she believed he had made a commitment. But Charlie is a typical American, according to Leisure Trends' surveys of leisure activities. Most Americans normally end up doing the things that are easiest to do and not necessarily the things they claim to enjoy the most. The result is a wide gap between the number of people who say they enjoy an activity and the much smaller number who actually do the activity regularly.

To understand this phenomenon, it helps to separate leisure activities into three categories; No-Brainers, Brainers, and Puzzlers. No-Brainer activities are habitual, easy to do, require a low level of decision-making, have few entry barriers, and tend to entertain. Watching television is the best example of a No-Brainer.   3

Brainer activities are less habitual, may involve other people, are more complex because they require some interaction with a person or thing, and have moderate logistical barriers. Hobbies, moviegoing, and socializing at home or on the telephone are good examples of Brainers.   4

Puzzlers tend to break away from habits entirely and include the most difficult activities. The barriers to entry are higher, and the decision-making process is more complex. Puzzlers inspire questions such as "Do I really like Amy?" or "Can I afford it?" Most sports activities, parties, going to the theater, or taking a weekend in the country are examples of Puzzlers. These activities involve thinking and taking inventory. To do them, people must make complex decisions. Before a party for example, many people wrestle with the following puzzler: "Do I have the right clothes, or should I go shopping first?"   5

No-Brainers and Puzzlers

The difference between what people say and what they do shows up clearly in eight activities that fall into the three categories described above. This article compares what people aged 16 or older did the previous day with what they say they "enjoy doing the most."   6

It's no surprise that the most frequent activity reported is the ultimate No-Brainer—watching television. It is simple and can be done alone. While it eats up lots of time and 77 percent of respondents did it the day before the survey, only 14 percent say they enjoy it the most.   7

Television viewing is such a perfect No-Brainer that many people don't remember doing it at all. When asked the open-ended   8 question, "What did you do yesterday in your leisure time?" just 31 percent of respondents spontaneously mention television. We uncovered that 77 percent of the total population actually watched television only by asking this follow-up question: "Did you watch television yesterday?" In this context, the small proportion of Americans who admit that television is their favorite activity starts to look suspicious. Perhaps we don't want to admit we enjoy what is offered on the tube. Or perhaps people don't count the time they spend reading, cooking, or conversing while one eye is on the television. But in any case, the gap between watching, enjoyment, and memorability is so great as to suggest that TV is a low-key form of fun.

Brainer activities such as socializing and going to the movies are 9 done less frequently than No-Brainers. But people claim to enjoy them more, so the gap between saying and doing for Brainers is smaller than for No-Brainers. Shopping for fun and do-it-yourself activities are different. People say they like these activities, and they participate in them frequently. It seems they are sufficiently motivated to overcome the barriers in getting to the store and buying materials. At the other extreme are Puzzler activities, such as fishing. People claim to enjoy them greatly, but don't do them very often.

Attitude clearly does not always predict behavior, and the data 10 offer evidence that most Americans operate on both levels. We are a combination of what we do and what we think, and the two do not necessarily go together. Which form of consumer information best predicts participation or consumption will depend on the product or service being consumed.

Behavioral data are more dependable, because past and present 11 behavior is often the best indicator of future behavior. Yet attitudinal data can indicate new opportunities. Marketers whose products and services fall into the No-Brainer category know that people don't need a great deal of encouragement to participate in them, and that those who do it today will probably do it tomorrow. They can concentrate on broadening their market by enhancing existing products and finding new niches.

For example, snack foods are often consumed during No- 12 Brainer activities such as watching television. Mass media advertising is appropriate for these products. On the other hand, businesses with links to Brainer or Puzzler activities may have to resort to stronger inducements. For activities people say they enjoy but don't do often, marketers can offer incentives such as discount coupons to movies or free transportation to ski areas.

Coaxing Armchair Athletes

The problem with predicting participation in Puzzler and 13 Brainer activities is the large difference between expectation and reality. In a two-part study for the alpine ski industry, we measured the differences between people's intentions to ski and their actual behavior. Over a span of three years, we discovered that in any given year, as few as 65 percent of self-defined skiers actually go skiing.

Many people who consider themselves skiers have not skied at 14 all in the last four to five years. One self-proclaimed skier had not skied since 1947! Yet virtually all self-defined skiers who had not skied in the last several years say they plan to ski again.

Here is a strong positive attitude that defies the facts. Anyone 15 who estimates a market's potential based on intention in this sport will be in for a rude shock. If you're selling a skiing magazine, attitude is as important as behavior. But if you're selling lift tickets, you need a real skier.

Skiing qualifies as a true Puzzler activity because it involves spe- 16 cial equipment, can be quite costly, depends on the weather, and requires special locations and physical skill. Fishing falls into the same category for most of the same reasons. The rule of thumb is that the more difficult something is, the more important behavioral data are in measuring trends in participation.

On the other hand, attitudinal information provides clues about 17 potential markets, because changes in attitudes can signal a potential change in behavior. To understand how attitudes may predict behavior, it is important to understand why people don't do things. People often cite a lack of time or money as the reasons they don't pursue a Puzzler activity. For some, however, excuses disguise the true reason, which is a lack of brain power or energy. People find plenty of time for No-Brainer activities, perhaps because they provide low-energy relaxation. After a long day at work or with the kids, many people don't want to keep co-ordinating and planning. To the time-pressured adult, thinking about a weekend at a local ski area may seem like too much work.

Some people who say they enjoy an activity like skiing are perpet- 18
ual "wannabes." Even given the chance, they will not hit the slopes. But others who say they would enjoy doing something really mean it. To encourage these people, businesses that sell Brainer and Puzzler activities should make it easy for people to translate their positive attitude into behavior. Family ski packages that include bus transportation, rental equipment, lift tickets, and lessons for the children could persuade even weary souls to brave the slopes. For those whose biggest barrier is cost, something as simple as a free trial lift ticket could change a positive attitude into long-term purchasing behavior.

Each Sport is Different

Changes in attitudes and behavior do not always run parallel to 19
each other, so it is important to track both of them. A comparison of attitudes in 1990 and 1992 shows that interest in reading has increased, for example, while interest in watching television and socializing has declined slightly. A look at behavior shows that reading and socializing have increased—but that television viewing has not changed much.

Demographic trends in leisure can be surprising. Reading may 20
be a highly intellectual activity, for example. Yet this study classifies it as a No-Brainer because it is easy to do anywhere and is almost always done alone. More women than men read, and more women consider it their favorite leisure activity. Reported reading is increasing sharply among 16-to-24-year-olds and those aged 45 and older. The attitude of 25-to-34-year-olds toward reading is increasingly positive, but their behavior has not changed much. Adults aged 35 to 44 are showing a decrease in interest in reading, but are reading slightly more.

Movies in theaters, which fall into the Brainer category, are be- 21
coming more appealing to men, according to the 1990 and 1992 surveys. Men are also watching them more often. Americans under age 35 went to more movies in 1992 than they did in 1990, and a greater share considered them a favorite activity.

Do-it-yourself activities are Puzzlers with a twist. In particular,   22
women are more likely to participate in do-it-yourself activities than
to say they enjoy them. But as the share of female do-it-yourselfers
rises, so does their enjoyment level. Perhaps practice does make perfect, as tasks done repeatedly become easier and more fun. It may
also be that people are discovering that do-it-yourself activities are
stress reducers. Baking bread and other activities were once necessi-
ties, but now they are usually done as a way to relax.

Another way to find clues about future trends in leisure behavior is   23
to study the attitudes of people who have just begun a new activity. In
the 1990 interviews, the proportion of people who said they had gar-
dened, camped, hiked, or backpacked for the first time had increased
noticeably over 1988. Two years later, the share of regular participants
in these activities had increased. Similarly, changes in attitudes often
precede changes in behavior. The share of people who enjoy doing
home improvement and yard work grew between 1988 and 1990, and
the share who do these things grew between 1990 and 1992.

What's the leisure forecast for the 1990s? The surveys show that   24
people may be doing more shopping for fun, traveling, walking for exercise, and outside recreational activities such as camping, hiking, and
alpine skiing. Organized religion also seems poised for a comeback,
and interest in working on the home and yard continues to grow.

It is worth noting that all upward trends in attitudes fall into the   25
Puzzler category. Aging baby boomers may be less willing to spend
time on passive activities, but only time will tell if they are ready for
more challenging leisure. By the way, Norma left Charlie's house and
stopped by Lance's house on the way to the concert, and he agreed to
go with her. Two months later, they got married. Now they have a
small Puzzle to ponder, and they don't go to concerts anymore.

Meaning and Purpose

1. What are the common characteristics of "No-Brainer" activities?
2. What are the common characteristics of "Brainer" activities?

3. What are the common characteristics of "Puzzlers"?
4. What seems to account for the discrepancies between what people say they like to do for leisure and what they actually do?
5. Why are behavioral data more dependable in predicting future behavior than data about attitudes?

Strategy

1. Who is Spring's intended audience (see headnotes to the essay)? What is his purpose in the essay? Why does he classify his subject the way he does?
2. Reading is a highly intellectual activity. Why does Spring classify it as a "No-Brainer"?
3. Spring says that "The difference between what people say and what they do shows up clearly in eight activities that fall into . . . three categories . . ." (paragraph 6). What are these eight activities, and into which category does each fall?

Style

1. Why does Spring begin and end his essay with the fictional anecdote about Norma Puzzle? What's the significance of his play on words in the anecdote?
2. Look up the word *wannabe* (paragraph 18). What is its definition? Its derivation? Are its connotations as you've heard the word used positive or negative?
3. Look up the word *demographic*. What are "demographic trends" (paragraph 20), and why is the term pertinent to Spring's presentation?

Writing Tasks

1. Keeping in mind the research data Spring presents about how people spend their free time, as opposed to what they say their favorite activities are, interview at least five people, asking them to list all

the things they did during their leisure time during the past week. Also ask them what things they prefer doing. If the two don't correspond, ask them to explain why they don't. Then write a paper in which you compare the conclusions you draw from your research data to the conclusions Spring draws about his. Make sure to place the activities you discuss into the three different categories Spring has established.

2. List some of your own activities that fall within each of Spring's three categories of leisure activities, making sure those activities meet all the criteria Spring established for each. Then write a paper in which you determine whether your leisure activities fit Spring's conclusion that "Americans normally end up doing the things that are easiest to do and not necessarily the things they claim to enjoy the most" (paragraph 2). Be sure to cite Spring's essay in your discussion.

❦ Responding to Photographs ❦

Classification and Division

Veterans Day

Humans are social beings. We form groups and subgroups for a variety of purposes—social, economic, vocational, political.

Some of these groups are informal and temporary: a study group for the final exam, a tour group to a vacation spot, an ad hoc committee to support a municipal bond issue. Others are more formal and longer lasting, binding together the common interests of large numbers of people across geographic and generational lines. Why do we join groups? What do we expect our membership in the group to accomplish for us or for others? Do groups provide us with a sense of identity? Of self-worth? Undoubtedly, the reasons vary from one individual to another.

The picture "Veterans Day" shows two members of a veterans' group posing in uniform with an American flag unobtrusively in the background. Their stance, legs apart and feet planted firmly, gives a solidity to their figures, which is tempered by the warmth of their smiles. They look content, happy, proud. Clearly, each has found some satisfaction in belonging to this organization.

We might wonder, though, whether the satisfaction of membership or the reason for joining this organization is the same for the woman as for the man. Wearing their uniforms and standing in the noonday sun, they represent the values of the veterans' organization. But as individuals their motivations for being there are personal, a product of their own backgrounds and experiences.

After reviewing the material at the beginning of the chapter, complete one of the following writing tasks.

1. Write a division paper that considers the woman and the man in the photograph separately. Describe the physical appearance of each. For each, determine what you believe are possible motivations for joining the armed services and, later, a veterans' organization. What do you imagine the service experience of each was like? What would the veterans' organization represent to each? What satisfactions would each receive from membership? One caution: Since there are only the two figures prominent in the picture, this will be a binary division. Don't slip into comparison and contrast, but profile the woman and the man separately.

2. Write a classification paper that presents categories of people of similar age: children, youth, young adults, older adults, seniors. Find at least five photographs of people of one age group in social situations. Describe the people in each photograph as representatives of a category of their age group. Discuss the characteristics of each category. Include the pictures when submitting your final draft.

❦ *Additional Writing Tasks* ❦
Classification and Division

1. Choose one of the following subjects and write an essay using division as the dominant pattern. Describe each component in some detail, distinguishing it from the other components. Keep your readers in mind by guiding them carefully from component to component.
   a. A musical performance
   b. A board game, such as chess, Monopoly, Risk, or Clue
   c. The human mind
   d. A ceremonial event, such as a wedding, funeral, campaign rally, banquet, or religious service
   e. A week at a teenage vacation spot
   f. A novel
   g. A police drama, situation comedy, or national news broadcast
   h. Your monthly income
   i. Bargaining in a foreign marketplace
   j. A meal in an expensive restaurant
2. Write an essay using classification as the dominant development method. Sort one of the following subjects into categories. Be sure the basis for your classification is clear. To direct your readers' attention, make up names for each category.
   a. The books, records, and/or videotapes you own
   b. Unusual sports, such as "earth games" or other sports that are seldom televised or reported in newspapers
   c. Talk-show hosts
   d. War toys, family-oriented toys, or intellectual toys
   e. People who like to hunt game
   f. Lies
   g. Ways to read a novel or poem
   h. Ways to watch a horror movie
   i. Kinds of photography
   j. Attitudes revealed by bumper stickers
   k. Trends in dating, marriage, or divorce

l.   Kinds of terror
m.   Responses to a dramatic national or international event
n.   New ways to learn
o.   Kinds of good luck
p.   Kinds of bad luck

12

Definition
Limiting Meaning

The Method

Think of how many words you hear in a day. Tens of thousands? Hundreds of thousands? Millions? Spoken words are plentiful. They are easy to produce: Just open your mouth, activate your larynx, wag your tongue, and words will take flight. Of course, spoken words are often strung together thoughtlessly. If you have any doubts about this description, just turn your television dial to a talk show and listen to the relentless babble.

But written words are different. They require work. Serious writers select them with care. Some words are so technical that only technically trained readers understand them. Some words are so rarely used that few readers know what they mean. Some have meanings so ambiguous that readers understand them differently. That is why definition is indispensable in writing.

Strategies

Professional writers approach definition in three ways: etymological, or lexical, definition; stipulative definition; and extended definition.

Etymological Definition

An etymological definition is a dictionary definition. It defines a word in a narrow way by specifying its class and its distinguishing characteristics. Consider the word *thriller*. A good college dictionary tells you that a thriller is a suspenseful work of fiction—a novel, play, or film—that deals with crime or detection. Sometimes an etymological definition includes synonyms: a thriller might be referred to as a *whodunit*.

Rather than using a ready-made dictionary definition, writers often expand dictionary information to fit the interests of their audience and requirements that suit their purposes. Consider the dictionary definition of *bird*: "a warm-blooded, two-legged, egg-laying vertebrate with a wishbone, feathers, and wings." Now imagine that a writer wishes to define *bird* for a ten-year-old reader. The definition might read something like this:

> A bird is an animal. It has a backbone, is warm-blooded, and walks on two legs, but a human being does, too. It flies, but insects and bats do, too. It lays eggs, but salamanders, some snakes, and turtles do the same.
>
> What then makes birds different from all other animals? Only birds have feathers and a wishbone.

Stipulative Definition

Sometimes a writer uses a common word extensively in a special or limited way. The writer then usually stipulates the meaning of the word—that is, the writer explains how the word is to be understood as it appears throughout the essay. This explanation creates the *stipulative definition.* In this paragraph from *Amusing Ourselves to Death*, educator and communications critic Neil Postman stipulates the meaning of "conversation."

> I use the word "conversation" metaphorically to refer not only to speech but to all techniques and technologies that permit people of a particular culture to exchange messages. In this sense, all culture is a conversation or, more precisely, a corporation of conversations, conducted in a variety of symbolic modes. Our attention here is on how forms of public discourse regulate and even dictate what kind of content can issue from such forms.

Social critic Don Pierstorff stipulates a meaning for "suits" when examining Michael Levine's *Deep Cover*, an exposé of the Drug Enforcement Administration (DEA).

> Who are the "suits"? They are the men and women who crowd the corridors and sit behind the desks of the Drug Enforcement Administration. They are government bureaucrats and managers. According to Michael Levine, they are the people who have no first-hand experience of the drug war and are

unwilling to listen to agents who do. They spend their days shuffling reports and briefing politicians.

Postman's paragraph stipulates the meaning of *conversation* by enlarging it to mean all the methods culture uses to communicate. Pierstorff's paragraph defines the commonly understood word *suits* by presenting its uncommon slang definition, the way in which DEA agents use it. Both authors anticipate that their readers will need to know these special definitions to understand what they are writing about.

Extended Definitions

Etymological and stipulative definitions usually are concisely written for the sole purpose of clarification. Extended definitions are much more detailed and usually employ various patterns of development to fully explain a word or concept. In this paragraph from *Hog on Ice*, C. E. Funk defines *white elephant*. He uses examples to establish its class and a brief narration about the word's origin to differentiate it from others.

> That large portrait of your wealthy Aunt Jane, given by her and which you loathe but do not dare to take down from your wall; that large bookcase, too costly to discard, but which you hope will be more in keeping with your future home; these, and a thousand other like items, are "white elephants"—costly but useless possessions. The allusion takes us to Siam. In that country it was the traditional custom for many centuries that a rare albino elephant was, upon capture, the property of the emperor—who even today bears the title Lord of the White Elephant—and was thereafter sacred to him. He alone might ride or use such an animal, and none might be destroyed without his consent. Because of that latter royal prerogative, it is said that whenever it pleased his gracious majesty to bring about the ruin of a courtier who had displeased him, he would present the poor fellow with an elephant from his stables. The cost of feeding and caring for the huge animal that he might neither use nor destroy—a veritable white elephant—gave the term its present meaning.

In this two-paragraph passage from *Alligators in Sewers and Other Urban Legends*, Jan Harold Brunvand defines *urban legend*. Brunvand first establishes the class to which *urban legend* belongs and then distinguishes it from other members of the class. His definition goes beyond the etymological category because he develops the expression in greater detail, primarily with brief comparison and contrast and examples.

> Urban legends are realistic stories that are said to have happened recently. Like old legends of lost mines, buried treasure, and ghosts, they usually have an ironic or supernatural twist. They belong to a subclass of folk narratives that (unlike fairy tales) are set in the recent past, involving ordinary human beings rather than extraordinary gods and demigods.
>
> Unlike rumors, which are generally fragmentary or vague reports, legends have a specific narrative quality and tend to attach themselves to different local settings. Although they may explain or incorporate current rumors, legends tend to have a longer life and wider acceptance; rumors flourish and then die out rather quickly. Urban legends circulate by word of mouth, among the "folk" of modern society, but the mass media frequently help to disseminate and validate them. While they vary in particular details from one telling to another, they preserve a central core of traditional themes. In some instances these seemingly fresh stories are merely updatings of classic folklore plots, while other urban legends spring directly from recent conditions and then develop their own traditional patterns in repeated retellings. For example, "The Vanishing Hitchhiker," which describes the disappearance of a rider picked up on a highway, has evolved from a 19th-century horse-and-buggy legend into modern variants incorporating freeway travel. A story called "Alligators in the Sewers," on the other hand, goes back no further than the 1930s and seems to be a New York City invention. Often, it begins with people who bring pet baby alligators back from Florida and eventually flush them down the drain.

Both Funk's definition of *white elephant* and Brunvand's definition of *urban legend* involve much more than merely looking up the established meanings; nevertheless, they do make use of a common pattern of definition by placing a term in a class and distinguishing it from other members of the class. Funk and Brunvand can use this pattern because the words they define have been in common use for some time. But the strength of an extended definition is to introduce new terms to readers, or, more accurately, to introduce concepts that those terms represent. This kind of extended definition may be highly personal, embodying a writer's values and independent observation.

In this three-paragraph passage from *Zen and the Art of Motorcycle Maintenance*, Robert M. Pirsig defines "mechanic's feel." Clearly, his definition is based on close observation during personal experience.

> The mechanic's feel comes from a deep inner kinesthetic feeling for the elasticity of materials. Some materials, like ceramics, have very little, so that when you thread a porcelain fitting you're very careful not to apply great pressures. Other materials, like steel, have tremendous elasticity, more than rubber, but in a range in which, unless you're working with large mechanical forces, the elasticity isn't apparent.
>
> With nuts and bolts you're in the range of large mechanical forces and you should understand that within these ranges metals are elastic. When you take up a nut there's a point called "fingertight" where there's contact but no takeup of elasticity. Then there's "snug," in which the easy surface elasticity is taken up. Then there's the range called "tight," in which all the elasticity is taken up. The force required to reach these three points is different for each size of nut and bolt, and different for lubricated bolts and for locknuts. The forces are different for steel and cast iron and brass and aluminum and plastics and ceramics. But a person with mechanic's feel knows when something's tight and stops. A person without it goes right on past and strips the threads or breaks the assembly.
>
> A "mechanic's feel" implies not only an understanding for the elasticity of metal but for its softness. The insides of a motorcycle contain surfaces that are precise in some cases to as little as one ten-thousandth of an inch. If you drop them or get dirt on them or scratch them or bang them with a hammer, they'll lose that precision. It's important to understand that the

metal *behind* the surfaces can normally take a great shock and stress but that the surfaces themselves cannot. When handling precision parts that are stuck or difficult to manipulate, a person with mechanic's feel will avoid damaging the surfaces and work with his tools on the nonprecision surfaces of the same part whenever possible. If he must work on the surfaces themselves, he'll always use softer surfaces to work them with. Brass hammers, plastic hammers, wood hammers, rubber hammers and lead hammers are all available for this work. Use them. Vise jaws can be fitted with plastic and copper and lead faces. Use these too. Handle precision parts gently. You'll never be sorry. If you have a tendency to bang things around, take more time and try to develop a little more respect for the accomplishment that a precision part represents.

Pirsig's definition of "mechanic's feel" is unique. Readers have no resource to consult for a commonly accepted definition of an expression like that. Primarily relying on descriptive techniques, Pirsig carefully delineates the qualities of "mechanic's feel," right down to naming the degrees to which someone might tighten down a bolt: "fingertight," "snug," and "tight." Pirsig points out that metal has elasticity, and that someone with "mechanic's feel" must sense that quality or face the consequences—a broken assembly. Pirsig creates a sense of the soft, delicate surfaces of metal and names the tools someone should use when working on them—hammers of many materials varying in softness, as well as vise jaws fitted with soft faces. Someone with mechanic's feel is precise; in fact, the need for precision seems to be the message beneath the detail.

Definition in College Writing

You will write definitions to clarify important terms or concepts, especially in the social sciences, history, and philosophy. Usually, these will be stipulative definitions that are one or two paragraphs long and serve as part of an essay with another dominant development pattern. But sometimes an entire essay will be devoted to an extended definition. When you write an essay-length extended definition, the basic essay structure does not change: Begin with an introduction that ends with a clear statement of purpose or thesis. Write a discussion that develops the definition in several paragraphs. Write a conclusion that recalls the key points of the definition and restates the central purpose. Usually, a definition will include examples that illustrate the term or concept and comparisons to show the meaning in relation to similar terms or concepts.

Guidelines for Writing a Definition Essay

1. Select a term or concept that is currently being used in a new way or for which there is no clear etymological definition, such as a slang term or a new term from technology.
2. Develop a rough working explanation of what you will be defining. Then use prewriting techniques to generate examples and comparisons to illustrate it for your reader. If you are writing to define a special term, generate information that explains how to use it effectively and how it is misused.
3. Evaluate your prewritten material to see what you can and can't use effectively. Develop a clear purpose for your essay, one that clearly shows you will be writing a definition. Then shape the purpose into a thesis.
4. Write your essay. Organize it by moving from the general to the particular; that is, first create a broad sense of your term or concept, then present particular examples, comparisons, and information to clarify it in more detail.
5. Revise your definition. Be sure your definition is clear, including everything in its category and excluding everything that isn't. Check your examples and comparisons to see that they are integrated effectively into the definition. Polish the entire definition for clarity.

A Student Essay Developed by Definition

For a freshman composition class, Chris Schneider responded to the following writing task:

Use definition to develop any of the following topics in 500 to 600 words. You may use any number of paragraph development patterns, such as description, example, and comparison, to develop your thought.

a. commonsense e. sign
b. code   f. saga
c. myth   g. tale
d. symbol   h. legend

Schneider selected item "c." "Myth" had taken on new significance. She had encountered the new usage in culture studies. First, read Chris Schneider's essay, then reread it and respond to the items in Reviewing with a Writer's Eye, which follows the essay.

Myth Redefined

Do you believe childhood is a time of innocence separated from the emotions and cares of the adult world? Do you count on science to solve the dangers of fossil-fuel shortage, ozone depletion, and toxic pollution? Do you feel that men are rational, and women are intuitive? Men are active; women, passive? Men are ambitious; women, nurturing? If you do, then you have been influenced by common American "myths," as a group of contemporary scholars and social critics known as semiologists would claim.

Semiologists are interested in the study of meaning. They don't limit themselves to the meaning of words. This territory belongs to semanticists, that is, to those scholars who concentrate on linguistic significance. Semiologists may examine words, but they will also explore the ways that advertisements, television programs, films, clothes, toys, and other such things embody meaning, a kind of cultural meaning that semiologists sometimes refer to as "myth."

To most of us, the term "myth" might call to mind marvelous Greek stories of disguised gods cavorting with humans. We might think of heroes wielding swords against dragons or of magicians mesmerizing entire armies. We might recall the story of Johnny Appleseed planting apple trees across the American landscape or of Rip Van Winkle sleeping for twenty years or of John Henry racing against a steam-powered spike driver. These myths are different from legends because they lack historical background and shade into the supernatural. They are also different from fables because they lack an overt moral intent. Like legends and fables they are stories, imaginative stories, that, according to one popular view, embody cultural patterns. Now semiologists are using the term "myth" in a different way.

To semiologists "myth" refers to deeply rooted cultural beliefs, not to ancient stories. These beliefs are held by most members of any given society. Despite whatever evidence there might be to contradict the validity of a myth, semiologists do not judge it as right or wrong. They merely recognize its existence and analyze its social influence. Whether valid or invalid, a myth, therefore, is a psychological and social fact projected onto experience. We never clearly see things as they really are; we only see their reflections in our cultural beliefs. 4

Cultural myths are often used for manipulative purposes. For instance, one myth embedded in cultural conscious is the myth of the rugged individual. Usually a man, the rugged individual is one who can survive on his own in environments that would be hostile to all of us acculturated folks. Advertisers especially associate their products with the image of the rugged individual to manipulate consumers. For example, consider the Marlboro man, the lone cowboy who leads a rugged life herding steers on the open range. He calls to mind the rugged individuals cowboy actors John Wayne and Clint Eastwood play in western films, tough hombres who ride the range alone. Well, not quite alone; he has his cigarette. Of course, not everyone will respond to this myth. That's why advertisers employ many different kinds of cultural myths to sell their products. 5

Myths, as semiologists use the term, pervade every aspect of our cultural experience. Sometimes these belief systems are unrecognized and have a powerful influence on how we view experience. Other times, we become aware of them and through that awareness, change our perception of the world. Remember this myth: The husband is the breadwinner; the wife is the homemaker. The world has changed dramatically since that perception dominated American thinking. 6

Reviewing with a Writer's Eye

1. In "Myth Redefined," Chris Schneider writes an extended definition of the word *myth*. Develop your own scratch outline (pp. 42–44) of Schneider's essay. Begin with the following statement: "Schneider's general purpose is to define a specialized use of the word *myth*." Then write the purpose of each paragraph that follows the introduction and briefly state the strategy she uses to achieve it.

2. Explain how Schneider arranges information from paragraph 2 through paragraph 5.

3. To define *myth*, Schneider uses several paragraph patterns. What is the primary development pattern of paragraph 2? Paragraph 3? Paragraph 5? Why does she use them?

4. Are Schneider's introduction and conclusion effective or ineffective? Why?

5. Do you understand what Schneider means by the word *myth*? Write a note to Schneider that explains your understanding of *myth*. Ask her to clarify any points you don't understand.

Peer Review

You might be asked to write an essay about one of the readings that follow. Before you meet with your writing group, review this introduction. As you read the papers of your group, use these general principles of definition to help guide your comments.

1. A definition paper should go beyond a dictionary definition to give the reader a fuller understanding of the term being defined.

2. A definition paper should have a clear purpose. The reader should be told why the term is important and how it relates to some larger picture.

The essays that follow are developed with definition as their main purpose. Study them. Make note of each writer's strategy. Apply what you learn to your own writing.

❦ Marie Winn ❦

Marie Winn was born in Czechoslovakia in 1936 and, as a child, immigrated with her family to New York City, where she attended public schools. She pursued her education at Radcliffe College and Columbia University, graduating from the latter in 1959. An expert on culture and education, she has had numerous articles published in The New York Times Magazine, The New York Times Book Review, Smithsonian, The Wall Street Journal, *and* The Village Voice. *Her many books include* Children without Childhood, Unplugging the Plug-In Drug, *and* The Secret Life of Central Park. *Winn's most influential book is* The Plug-In Drug: Television, Children and the Family. *The book indicts Americans for their addiction to television and has been translated into French, German, Italian, Spanish, Swedish, and Japanese.*

TV Addiction

This selection from The Plug-In Drug *(orginally published in 1977 and revised in 1985), defines television addiction as a disease that is as severe and crippling as alcohol or drug addiction.*

Notice as you read how carefully Winn defines the terms addiction *and* TV addiction. *Notice, too, how the abundant examples she cites make her points clear.*

Cookies or Heroin?

The word "addiction" is often used loosely and wryly in conversation. People will refer to themselves as "mystery book addicts" or "cookie addicts." E. B. White wrote of his annual surge of interest in gardening: "We are hooked and are making an attempt to kick the habit." Yet nobody really believes that reading mysteries or ordering seeds by catalogue is serious enough to be compared with addictions to heroin or alcohol. The word "addiction" is here used jokingly to denote a tendency to overindulge in some pleasurable activity.

People often refer to being "hooked on TV." Does this, too, fall 2
into the lighthearted category of cookie eating and other pleasures
that people pursue with unusual intensity, or is there a kind of television viewing that falls into the more serious category of destructive
addiction?

When we think about addiction to drugs or alcohol we fre- 3
quently focus on negative aspects, ignoring the pleasures that accompany drinking or drug-taking. And yet the essence of any serious addiction is a pursuit of pleasure, a search for a "high" that
normal life does not supply. It is only the inability to function without the addictive substance that is dismaying, the dependence of the
organism upon a certain experience and an increasing inability to
function normally without it. Thus people will take two or three
drinks at the end of the day not merely for the pleasure drinking
provides, but also because they "don't feel normal" without them.

Real addicts do not merely pursue a pleasurable experience one 4
time in order to function normally. They need to *repeat* it again and
again. Something about that particular experience makes life without
it less than complete. Other potentially pleasurable experiences are
no longer possible, for under the spell of the addictive experience,
their lives are peculiarly distorted. The addict craves an experience
and yet is never really satisfied. The organism may be temporarily
sated, but soon it begins to crave again.

Finally, a serious addiction is distinguished from a harmless pur- 5
suit of pleasure by its distinctly destructive elements. Heroin addicts,
for instance, lead a damaged life: their increasing need for heroin in
increasing doses prevents them from working, from maintaining relationships, from developing in human ways. Similarly alcoholics' lives
are narrowed and dehumanized by their dependence on alcohol.

Let us consider television viewing in the light of the conditions 6
that define serious addictions.

Not unlike drugs or alcohol, the television experience allows the 7
participant to blot out the real world and enter into a pleasurable
and passive mental state. The worries and anxieties of reality are as
effectively deferred by becoming absorbed in a television program as
by going on a "trip" induced by drugs or alcohol. And just as alcoholics are only vaguely aware of their addiction, feeling that they

control their drinking more than they really do ("I can cut it out any time I want—I just like to have three or four drinks before dinner"), people similarly overestimate their control over television watching. Even as they put off other activities to spend hour after hour watching television, they feel they could easily resume living in a different, less passive style. But somehow or other, while the television set is present in their homes, the click doesn't sound. With television pleasures available, those other experiences seem less attractive, more difficult somehow.

A heavy viewer (a college English instructor) observes: 8

"I find television almost irresistible. When the set is on, I cannot   9
ignore it. I can't turn it off. I feel sapped, will-less, enervated. As I reach out to turn off the set, the strength goes out of my arms. So I sit there for hours and hours."

Self-confessed television addicts often feel they "ought" to do   10
other things—but the fact that they don't read and don't plant their garden or sew or crochet or play games or have conversations means that those activities are no longer as desirable as television viewing. In a way the lives of heavy viewers are as imbalanced by their television "habit" as a drug addict's or an alcoholic's. They are living in a holding pattern, as it were, passing up the activities that lead to growth or development or a sense of accomplishment. This is one reason people talk about their television viewing so ruefully, so apologetically. They are aware that it is an unproductive experience, that almost any other endeavor is more worthwhile by any human measure.

Finally it is the adverse effect of television viewing on the lives of   11
so many people that defines it as a serious addiction. The television habit distorts the sense of time. It renders other experiences vague and curiously unreal while taking on a greater reality for itself. It weakens relationships by reducing and sometimes eliminating normal opportunities for talking, for communicating.

And yet television does not satisfy, else why would the viewer   12
continue to watch hour after hour, day after day? "The measure of health," writes Lawrence Kubie, "is flexibility . . . and especially the freedom to cease when sated." But heavy television viewers can never be sated with their television experiences—they do not pro-

vide the true nourishment that satiation requires—and thus they find that they cannot stop watching.

Meaning and Purpose

1. According to Marie Winn, what are the things that are necessary for a habit to add up to an addiction?
2. Why does Winn consider addictions to such things as reading mystery books or gardening harmless, while she views an addiction to television watching as self-destructive?
3. According to the author, what distinguishes alcohol or drug addiction from TV addiction?
4. What is Winn's purpose in writing this essay? Who is her intended audience?

Strategy

1. What is the general movement in this essay, from the specific to the general or from the general to the specific? What is the effect of this movement? Explain.
2. Winn first defines *addiction* (paragraphs 3–5) and then defines *TV addiction* (paragraphs 7–12). How are the two extended definitions organized? How does this organization further the author's purpose (see question 4, above)?
3. What effect does Winn's example of a college English instructor's TV addiction have in her argument?
4. What are some of the rhetorical techniques that Winn uses to develop her definitions?

Style

1. What is the tone of the essay? Explain.
2. Note the diction in the quote from E. B. White (paragraph 1) and some of the words and phrases Winn places in quotation marks:

"high," "don't feel normal" (paragraph 3); "trip" (7); and "habit" (10). What is the significance of this diction? How does it differ from the language in the rest of the essay?

3. Winn begins paragraph 7 with a double negative. How does this reinforce the meaning of what immediately follows?

4. Look up the following words in a dictionary: *wryly, surge* (paragraph 1); *deferred, induced* (7); *sapped, enervated* (9); *ruefully* (10); *adverse* (11); *sated, satiation* (12).

Writing Tasks

1. Write an essay in which you describe and comment on an activity that fits Winn's definition of addiction. The addiction could be your own or somebody else's, and it could be any kind of compulsive behavior, such as collecting antiques, baseball cards, boyfriends, girlfriends, or anything else; hanging out at the local coffee shop; shopping; or surfing the Internet. Treat your subject seriously or humorously, but be consistent.

2. Write an essay in which you analyze the way you most often spend your free time: watching TV, going to movies, reading, hanging out at the mall. Discuss whether or not the behavior is an addiction. Consider both the positive and negative aspects of the behavior.

❦ Francine Prose ❦

Francine Prose, born in 1947, is a novelist and essayist. Her novels include Bigfoot Dreams, Primitive People, *and* Hunters and Gatherers. *Her novel* Household Saints *was made into a critically acclaimed movie in 1993. One critic has compared her recent collection of fiction,* Guided Tours of Hell, *to the work of Mark Twain because of its acerbic social commentary. Her two latest novels,* Blue Angel *and* After, *are written with the same sharp wit. Her essays have appeared in* Mademoiselle, The Atlantic Monthly, The New York Times, *and elsewhere.*

Gossip

In "Gossip," first published in The New York Times *in May 1985, Francine Prose plays the contrarian, defining gossip in unexpected ways by showing that her usually maligned subject serves important social and psychological functions.*

As you read, examine Prose's points with a critical eye to determine whether she really does release gossip from its normally unsavory reputation.

Once I met a woman who grew up in the small North Carolina town to which Chang and Eng, the original Siamese twins, retired after their circus careers. When I asked her how the town reacted to the twins marrying local girls and setting up adjacent households, she laughed and said: "Honey, that was *nothing* compared to what happened *before* the twins got there. Get the good gossip on any little mountain town, scratch the surface and you'll find a snake pit!"

Surely she was exaggerating; one assumes the domestic arrangements of a pair of Siamese twins and their families would cause a few ripples anywhere. And yet the truth of what she said seemed less important than the glee with which she said it, her pride in the snake pit she'd come from, in its history, its scandals, its legacy of "good gossip." Gossip, the juicier the better, was her heritage, her birthright; that town, with its social life freakish enough to make Chang and Eng's seem mundane, was part of who she was.

Gossip must be nearly as old as language itself. It was, I imagine, the earliest recreational use of the spoken word. First the cave man learned to describe the location of the plumpest bison, then he began to report and speculate on the doings of his neighbors in the cave next door. And yet, for all its antiquity, gossip has rarely received its due; its very name connotes idleness, time-wasting, frivolity and worse. Gossip is the unacknowledged poor relative of civilized conversation: Almost everyone does it but hardly anyone will admit to or defend it; and of these only the smallest and most shameless fraction will own up to enjoying it. **3**

My mother and her friends are eloquent on the subject and on the distinction between gossiping and exchanging information: "John got a new job," is, they say, information. "Hey, did you hear John got fired?" is gossip; which is, they agree, predominantly scurrilous, mean-spirited. That's the conventional wisdom on gossip and why it's so tempting to disown. Not long ago I heard myself describe a friend, half-jokingly, as "a much better person than I am, that is, she doesn't gossip so much." I heard my voice distorted by that same false note that sometimes creeps into it when social strain and some misguided notion of amiability make me assent to opinions I don't really share. What in the world was I talking about? **4**

I don't, of course, mean rumor-mongering, outright slander, willful fabrication meant to damage and undermine. But rather, ordinary gossip, incidents from and analyses of the lives of our heroes and heroines, our relatives, acquaintances and friends. The fact is, I love gossip, and beyond that, I believe in it—in its purposes, its human uses. **5**

I'm even fond of the word, its etymology, its origins in the Anglo-Saxon term "godsibbe" for god-parent, relative, its meaning widening by the Renaissance to include friends, cronies and later what one *does* with one's cronies. One gossips. Paring away its less flattering modern connotations, we discover a kind of synonym for connection, for community, and this, it seems to me, is the primary function of gossip. It maps our ties, reminds us of what sort of people we know and what manner of lives they lead, confirms our sense of who we are, how we live and where we have come from. The roots **6** of the grapevine are inextricably entwined with our own. Who knows how much of our sense of the world has reached us on its branches, how often, as babies, we dropped off to sleep to the rhythms of family gossip? I've often thought that gossip's bad name might be cleared by calling it "oral tradition"; for what, after all, is an oral tradition but the stories of other lives, other eras, legends from a time when human traffic with spirits and gods was considered fit material for gossipy speculation?

Older children gossip; adolescents certainly do. Except in the case of those rare toddler-fabulists, enchanting parents and siblings with fairy tales made up on the spot, gossip may be the way that most of us learn to tell stories. And though, as Gertrude Stein is supposed to have told Hemingway, gossip is not literature, some similar criteria may apply to both. Pacing, tone, clarity and authenticity are as essential for the reportage of neighborhood news as they are for well-made fiction.

Perhaps more important is gossip's analytical component. Most people—I'm leaving out writers, psychologists and probably some large proportion of the academic and service professions—are, at least in theory, free to go about their lives without feeling the compulsion to endlessly dissect the minutiae of human motivation. They can indulge in this at their leisure, for pleasure, in their gossip. And while there are those who clearly believe that the sole aim of gossip is to criticize, to condemn (or, frequently, to titillate, to bask in the aura of scandal as if it were one's own), I prefer to see gossip as a tool of understanding. It only takes a moment to tell what someone did. Far more mileage—and more enjoyment—can be extracted from debating why he did it. Such questions, impossible to discuss without touching on matters of choice and consequence, responsibility and will, are, one might argue, the beginnings of moral inquiry, first steps toward a moral education. It has always seemed peculiar that a pastime so conducive to the moral life should be considered faintly immoral.

I don't mean to deny the role of plain nosiness in all this, of unadorned curiosity about our neighbors' secrets. And curiosity (where would we be without it?) has, like gossip, come in for some negative press. Still, it's understandable, everyone wants to gossip, hardly anyone wants to be gossiped about. What rankles is the fear that our secrets will be revealed, some essential privacy stripped away and, of course, the lack of control over what others say. Still, such talk is unavoidable; it's part of human nature, of the human community. When one asks, "What's the gossip?" it's that community that is being affirmed.

So I continue to ask, mostly without apology and especially   10
when I'm talking to friends who still live in places I've moved away from. And when they answer—recalling the personalities, telling the stories, the news—I feel as close as I ever will to the lives we shared, to what we know and remember in common, to those much-missed, familiar and essentially beneficent snake pits I've lived in and left behind.

Meaning and Purpose

1. What is Prose's thesis? Does she state it explicitly or is it implied?
2. Prose broadens the usual negative definition of gossip to include seldom-considered positive connotations of the word. What are those positive connotations? Which aspects of gossip, the negative or the positive, does Prose consider the more important? Explain.
3. In paragraph 8, Prose contends that gossip is "conducive to the moral life." Explain what she means by that.
4. What attributes do literature and gossip share? What does Prose accomplish by comparing the two?

Strategy

1. Why does Prose begin her essay with the anecdote of Chang and Eng, the Siamese twins?
2. The essay is an extended definition of the word *gossip*. What other rhetorical patterns does Prose employ to create that definition?
3. In what way does Prose's description of the etymology of *gossip* further her extended definition of the word?

Style

1. In paragraph 2, Prose uses the third person "one." More commonly throughout the essay, she uses the first person "I." Why?
2. Reread paragraph 6, looking closely at the "roots" metaphor in the fifth sentence. How does the metaphor advance Prose's definition?
3. Look up the etymology of *legend* (paragraph 6). How does the word's history lend meaning to Prose's definition of *gossip*?
4. Look up the following words in a dictionary: *adjacent* (paragraph 1); *legacy, mundane* (2); *speculate, antiquity, connotes, frivolity* (3); *scurrilous, amiability, assent* (4); *slander, fabrication* (5); *etymology, cronies* (6); *fabulists, criteria* (7); *component, compulsion, dissect, minutiae, titillate, bask, aura, conducive* (8); *rankles* (9); *beneficent* (10).

Writing Tasks

1. By giving an extended definition of the term *gossip*, Francine Prose rescues the word from its common, unsavory reputation. Choose some other common activity that has garnered a similar reputation—daydreaming, people watching, nagging, worrying, penny pinching, or the like—and write a paper in which you make a case for its redeeming qualities by giving it an extended definition.
2. Write a paper in which you refute Prose's argument for the human value of gossip. Make sure your thesis is clear, and use an adequate number of specific examples to validate it.

❦ Gloria Naylor ❦

Gloria Naylor was born in 1950 in New York City, where she lived with her family until 1974. After graduating from high school in 1968, she spent the next seven years in part-time jobs as a switchboard operator and fast-food restaurant clerk to support herself while she worked full-time as a Jehovah's Witness minister. She left the Jehovah's Witnesses in 1975, started college, and in 1981 received her B.A. in English from Brooklyn College. In 1982 she was awarded an M.A. in Afro-American Studies from Yale and published her first novel, The Women of Brewster Place, *which received the American Book Award for Best First Novel. Since then she has taught at a number of universities, won numerous awards for her writing, and published three more best-selling novels about the African-American experience:* Linden Hills *(1985),* Mama Day *(1988), and* Bailey's Café *(1992).*

A Word's Meaning Can Often Depend on Who Says It

The following essay was first published in The New York Times *in 1986. It recounts the first time the author was stung by a racist epithet.*

Gloria Naylor uses that occasion as a springboard to examine the word nigger—*because of its ugly history, probably the most emotionally charged word in the American English language. She demonstrates that when the word is used by African Americans it has different shades of meaning that depend on the word's context. Notice as you read how the word she defines has both positive and negative connotations, depending on how it is used by black Americans, while it usually has only one meaning when used by bigoted non-African Americans.*

Language is the subject. It is the written form with which I've 1
managed to keep the wolf away from the door and, in diaries, to

keep my sanity. In spite of this, I consider the written word inferior to the spoken, and much of the frustration experienced by novelists is the awareness that whatever we manage to capture in even the most transcendent passages falls far short of the richness of life. Dialogue achieves its power in the dynamics of a fleeting moment of sight, sound, smell, and touch.

I'm not going to enter the debate here about whether it is language that shapes reality or vice versa. That battle is doomed to be waged whenever we seek intermittent reprieve from the chicken and egg dispute. I will simply take the position that the spoken word, like the written word, amounts to a nonsensical arrangement of sounds or letters without a consensus that assigns "meaning." And building from the meanings of what we hear, we order reality. Words themselves are innocuous; it is the consensus that gives them true power.   2

I remember the first time I heard the word *nigger*. In my third-grade class, our math tests were being passed down the rows, and as I handed the papers to a little boy in back of me, I remarked that once again he had received a much lower mark than I did. He snatched his test from me and spit out that word. Had he called me a nymphomaniac or a necrophiliac, I couldn't have been more puzzled. I didn't know what a nigger was, but I knew whatever it meant, it was something he shouldn't have called me. This was verified when I raised my hand, and in a loud voice repeated what he had said and watched the teacher scold him for using a "bad" word. I was later to go home and ask the inevitable question that every black parent must face—"Mommy, what does *nigger* mean?"   3

And what exactly did it mean? Thinking back, I realize that this could not have been the first time the word was used in my presence. I was part of a large extended family that had migrated from the rural South after World War II and formed a close-knit network that gravitated around my maternal grandparents. Their ground-floor apartment in one of the buildings they owned in Harlem was a weekend mecca for my immediate family, along with countless aunts, uncles, and cousins who brought along assorted friends. It was a bustling and open house with assorted neighbors and tenants   4

popping in and out to exchange bits of gossip, pick up an old quar-
rel, or referee the ongoing checkers game in which my grandmother
cheated shamelessly. They were all there to let down their hair and
put up their feet after a week of labor in the factories, laundries, and
shipyards of New York.

Amid the clamor, which could reach deafening proportions—   5
two or three conversations going on simultaneously, punctuated by
the sound of a baby's crying somewhere in the back rooms or out
on the street—there was still a rigid set of rules about what was
said and how. Older children were sent out of the living room
when it was time to get into the juicy details about "you-know-
who" up on the third floor who had gone and gotten herself "p-r-e-
g-n-a-n-t!" But my parents, knowing that I could spell well beyond
my years, always demanded that I follow the others out to play. Beyond sexual misconduct and death, everything else was considered
harmless for our young ears. And so among the anecdotes of the
triumphs and disappointments in the various workings of their
lives, the word *nigger* was used in my presence, but it was set
within contexts and inflections that caused it to register in my
mind as something else.

In the singular, the word was always applied to a man who had   6
distinguished himself in some situation that brought their approval
for his strength, intelligence, or drive:

"Did Johnny *really* do that?"   7

"I'm telling you, that nigger pulled in $6,000 of overtime last   8
year. Said he got enough for a down payment on a house."

When used with a possessive adjective by a woman—"my   9
nigger"—it became a term of endearment for her husband or
boyfriend. But it could be more than just a term applied to a man. In
their mouths it became the pure essence of manhood—a disembodied
force that channeled their past history of struggle and present survival
against the odds into a victorious statement of being: "Yeah, that old
foreman found out quick enough—you don't mess with a nigger."

In the plural, it became a description of some group within the   10
community that had overstepped the bounds of decency as my family defined it. Parents who neglected their children, a drunken couple who fought in public, people who simply refused to look for

work, those with excessively dirty mouths or unkempt households were all "trifling niggers." This particular circle could forgive hard times, unemployment, the occasional bout of depression—they had gone through all of that themselves—but the unforgivable sin was a lack of self-respect.

A woman could never be a "nigger" in the singular, with its con-   11
notation of confirming worth. The noun *girl* was its closest equivalent in that sense, but only when used in direct address and regardless of the gender doing the addressing. *Girl* was a token of respect for a woman. The one-syllable word was drawn out to sound like three in recognition of the extra ounce of wit, nerve, or daring that the woman had shown in the situation under discussion.

"G-i-r-l, stop. You mean you said that to his face?"

But if the word was used in a third-person reference or short-   12
ened so that it almost snapped out of the mouth, it always involved some element of communal disapproval. And age became an important factor in these exchanges. It was only between individuals of the same generation, or from any older person to a younger (but never the other way around), that *girl* would be considered a compliment.

I don't agree with the argument that use of the word *nigger* at   13
this social stratum of the black community was an internalization of racism. The dynamics were the exact opposite: the people in my grandmother's living room took a word that whites used to signify worthlessness or degradation and rendered it impotent. Gathering there together, they transformed *nigger* to signify the varied and complex human beings they knew themselves to be. If the word was to disappear totally from the mouths of even the most liberal of white society, no one in that room was naive enough to believe it would disappear from white minds. Meeting the word head-on, they proved it had absolutely nothing to do with the way they were determined to live their lives.

So there must have been dozens of times that *nigger* was spoken   14
in front of me before I reached the third grade. But I didn't "hear" it until it was said by a small pair of lips that had already learned it could be a way to humiliate me. That was the word I went home and

asked my mother about. And since she knew that I had to grow up in America, she took me in her lap and explained.

Meaning and Purpose

1. Since Naylor had heard her family use the word *nigger* before, why didn't she recognize it when it was "spit out" at her by her white third-grade classmate (paragraph 3)?
2. How is the white boy's use of the word different from the way Naylor's family uses the word?
3. Summarize Naylor's conclusions about why the black community uses the word *nigger* at all, considering that it is such a hateful and degrading word when used by bigoted non-African Americans.
4. Does Naylor define the various meanings of the word *nigger* in the black community (its denotations), its emotional values (its connotations), or both? Explain.
5. Does Naylor have purposes larger than defining the word *nigger* as used by the black community? What are they? Explain.

Strategy

1. Explain the purpose of paragraphs 1 and 2 in the greater scheme of the essay.
2. Explain the purpose of paragraphs 14 and 15, besides the fact that they conclude the essay.
3. Explain how the organization of each definition of *nigger* is similar.
4. Why does Naylor include the definition of *girl* as it's used in her black community?

Style

1. In paragraph 2, Naylor says that "Words themselves are innocuous; it is the consensus that gives them true power." Explain what she means by this.

2. What does Naylor mean when she says that people came to her family's apartment "to let down their hair" (paragraph 4)? Does she mean this literally?

3. Look up the following words in a dictionary: *transcendent* (paragraph 1); *intermittent, reprieve, innocuous* (2); *nymphomaniac, necrophiliac* (3); *mecca* (4); *clamor, anecdotes, inflections* (5); *unkempt, trifling* (10); *stratum* (14).

Writing Tasks

1. Go about your normal business for a single day, but pay close attention to the way people use labels to describe people and events. Jot down all the labels you encounter, as well as the contexts in which they were used. Arrange the items in your list into categories and write a paper in which you make comment on how labels often oversimplify and diminish the things they describe.

2. Listen carefully to your own language and the language of your friends to determine a word that you all use that has a number of different connotations. Define that word in an essay, using Naylor's essay as your model.

❦ Rose Del Castillo Guilbault ❦

Rose Del Castillo Guilbault was brought up in California's Central Valley farm country, where many of the farm workers are Latino. Since then she has become a prominent figure in the San Francisco Bay Area. She is vice president of Corporation Communication and Public Affairs for the California State Automobile Association and serves on the board of directors for the Latino Issues Forum. She is also the editorial and public affairs director at KGO-TV in San Francisco and is an associate editor at Pacific News Service. She writes a monthly column on issues important to Spanish-speaking Americans for the San Francisco Chronicle.

Americanization Is Tough on "Macho"

The following essay was first published in 1989 as one of Rose Del Castillo Guilbault's monthly columns for the San Francisco Chronicle. *Since then the article has been widely anthologized.*

Guilbault defines the word macho *by comparing the meaning of the word as it is used in Hispanic culture and the way it is used in Anglo culture. As you read, pay attention to the ways a man's behavior can be interpreted in two entirely different ways by the two different cultures.*

What is *macho*? That depends which side of the border you come from. 1

Although it's not unusual for words and expressions to lose their subtlety in translation, the negative connotations of *macho* in this country are troublesome to Hispanics. 2

Take the newspaper descriptions of alleged mass murderer Ramon Salcido. That an insensitive, insanely jealous, hard-drinking, violent Latin male is referred to as *macho* makes Hispanics cringe. 3

"*Es muy macho*," the women in my family nod approvingly, describing a man they respect. But in the United States, when women say, "He's so macho," it's with disdain. 4

The Hispanic *macho* is manly, responsible, hardworking, a man   5
in charge, a patriarch. A man who expresses strength through silence. What the Yiddish language would call a *mensch*.

The American *macho* is a chauvinist, a brute, uncouth, selfish,   6
loud, abrasive, capable of inflicting pain, and sexually promiscuous.

Quintessential *macho* models in this country are Sylvester Stallone,   7
Arnold Schwarzenegger, and Charles Bronson. In their movies, they ex-
ude toughness, independence, masculinity. But a closer look reveals
their machismo is really violence masquerading as courage, sullenness
disguised as silence, and irresponsibility camouflaged as independence.

If the Hispanic ideal of *macho* were translated to American   8
screen roles, they might be Jimmy Stewart, Sean Connery, and Laurence Olivier.

In Spanish, *macho* ennobles Latin males. In English it devalues   9
them. This pattern seems consistent with the conflicts ethnic minority males experience in this country. Typically the cultural traits other
societies value don't translate as desirable characteristics in America.

I watched my own father struggle with these cultural ambigui-   10
ties. He worked on a farm for 20 years. He laid down miles of irriga-
tion pipe, carefully plowed long, neat rows in fields, hacked away at
recalcitrant weeds and drove tractors through whirlpools of dust. He
stoically worked 20-hour days during harvest season, accepting the
long hours as part of agricultural work. When the boss complained
or upbraided him for minor mistakes, he kept quiet, even when it
was obvious the boss had erred.

He handled the most menial tasks with pride. At home he was a   11
good provider, helped out my mother's family in Mexico without
complaint, and was indulgent with me. Arguments between my
mother and him generally had to do with money, or with his stub-
born reluctance to share his troubles. He tried to work them out in
his own silence. He didn't want to trouble my mother—a course that
backfired, because the imagined is always worse than the reality.

Americans regarded my father as decidedly un-*macho*. His char-   12
acter was interpreted as non-assertive, his loyalty non-ambition, and
his quietness, ignorance. I once overheard the boss's son blame him

for plowing crooked rows in a field. My father merely smiled at the lie, knowing the boy had done it, but didn't refute it, confident his good work was well known. But the boss instead ridiculed him for being "stupid" and letting a kid get away with a lie. Seeing my embarrassment, my father dismissed the incident, saying "They're the dumb ones. Imagine, me fighting with a kid."

I tried not to look at him with American eyes because sometimes the reflection hurt. 13

Listening to my aunts' clucks of approval, my vision focused on the qualities America overlooked. "He's such a hard worker. So serious, so responsible," my aunts would secretly compliment my mother. The unspoken comparison was that he was not like some of their husbands, who drank and womanized. My uncles represented the darker side of *macho*. 14

In a patriarchal society, few challenge their roles. If men drink, it's because it's the manly thing to do. If they gamble, it's because it's how men relax. And if they fool around, well, it's because a man simply can't hold back so much man! My aunts didn't exactly meekly sit back, but they put up with these transgressions because Mexican society dictated this was their lot in life. 15

In the United States, I believe it was the feminist movement of the early '70s that changed *macho*'s meaning. Perhaps my generation of Latin women was in part responsible. I recall Chicanas complaining about the chauvinistic nature of Latin men and the notion they wanted their women barefoot, pregnant, and in the kitchen. The generalization that Latin men embodied chauvinistic traits led to this interesting twist of semantics. Suddenly a word that represented something positive in one culture became a negative prototype in another. 16

The problem with the use of *macho* today is that it's become an accepted stereotype of the Latin male. And like all stereotypes, it distorts truth. 17

The impact of language in our society is undeniable. And the misuse of *macho* hints at a deeper cultural misunderstanding that extends beyond mere word definitions. 18

Meaning and Purpose

1. What are the primary characteristics of the Hispanic *macho* man?
2. What are the primary characteristics of the Anglo *macho* man?
3. In what ways did Americans misinterpret Guilbault's father's *macho* qualities?
4. Who, according to Guilbault, is responsible for transforming the qualities associated with *macho* from positive to negative ones?

Strategy

1. Guilbault spends six paragraphs (10–15), a third of her entire essay, describing her father. Why?
2. Reread and compare paragraphs 3 and 17. In what ways are they connected?
3. Look closely at the first nine paragraphs of the essay. What means of development does Guilbault use in this section to begin her definition of *macho*?

Style

1. What does Guilbault mean by "the darker side of *macho*" (paragraph 14)?
2. Find the definition of *macho* in a dictionary. Then look up the meanings of *connotation* and *denotation* in the Glossary of this text. Then answer this question: Is Guilbault defining the denotation or connotation of *macho*? Explain your answer.
3. Look up the following words in a dictionary: *quintessential* (paragraph 7); *ambiguities, recalcitrant, upbraided* (10); *menial, indulgent* (11); *Chicanas, chauvinistic, semantics* (16).

Writing Tasks

1. Write a paper that is an extended definition of the word *masculine*. Before you start writing, make sure to make a list of all the

attributes you consider masculine. If appropriate to your purpose, contrast those attributes you consider masculine with other views. You can look to Guilbault's essay as an organizational model, but be aware that she was writing for a newspaper that typically uses abbreviated paragraphs because of its narrow column format. You will not be writing for a newspaper and will, therefore, mostly have to employ more fully developed paragraphs.

2. Using the same directions as in Writing Task 1, write a paper in which you define *feminine*.

❦ S. I. Hayakawa ❦

S. I. (Samuel Icheye) Hayakawa (1906–1992) was born in Vancouver, British Columbia, Canada, and educated in the public schools of Calgary and Winnipeg, Canada. He received his B.A. from the University of Manitoba in Winnipeg and graduate degrees in English from McGill University, Montreal, and the University of Wisconsin, Madison. He was a world-renowned semanticist who taught at various universities in the United States and served as president of San Francisco State College from 1968 to 1973. He was elected as a Republican to the U.S. Senate, serving one term from 1977 to 1983. He wrote several books, including Through the Communication Barrier: On Speaking, Listening, and Understanding, *in which the following essay was first published.*

What It Means to Be Creative

In this essay, S. I. Hayakawa defines creativity by outlining four personality traits of a creative person. As you read, compare each of the characteristics he describes to yourself and your friends and family. Consider whether or not there might be various degrees of creativity.

What distinguishes the creative person? By creative person I   1
don't mean only the great painter or poet or musician. I also want to include the creative housewife, teacher, warehouseman, sales manager—anyone who is able to break through habitual routines and invent new solutions to old problems, solutions that strike people with their appropriateness as well as originality, so that they say, "Why didn't I think of that?"

A creative person, first, is not limited in his thinking to "what   2
everyone knows." "Everyone knows" that trees are green. The creative artist is able to see that in certain lights some trees look blue or purple or yellow. The creative person looks at the world with his or her own eyes, not with the eyes of others. The creative individual also knows his or her own feelings better than the average person. Most people

don't know the answer to the question, "How are you? How do you feel?" The reason they don't know is that they are so busy feeling what they are supposed to feel, thinking what they are supposed to think, that they never get down to examining their own deepest feelings.

"How did you like the play?" "Oh, it was a fine play. It was well reviewed in *The New Yorker*." 3

With authority figures like drama critics and book reviewers and teachers and professors telling us what to think and how to feel, many of us are busy playing roles, fulfilling other people's expectations. As Republicans, we think what other Republicans think. As Catholics, we think what other Catholics think. And so on. Not many of us ask ourselves, "How do I feel? What do I think?"—and wait for answers. 4

Another characteristic of the creative person is that he is able to entertain and play with ideas that the average person may regard as silly, mistaken, or downright dangerous. All new ideas sound foolish at first, because they are new. (In the early days of the railroad, it was argued that speeds of twenty-five mph or over were impractical because people's brains would burst.) A person who is afraid of being laughed at or disapproved of for having "foolish" or "unsound" ideas will have the satisfaction of having everyone agree with him, but he will never be creative, because creativity means being willing to take a chance—to go out on a limb. 5

The person who would be creative must be able to endure loneliness—even ridicule. If he has a great and original idea that others are not yet ready to accept, there will be long periods of loneliness. There will be times when his friends and relatives think he is crazy, and he'll begin to wonder if they are right. A genuinely creative person, believing in his creation, is able to endure this loneliness—for years if necessary. 6

Another trait of the creative person is idle curiosity. Such a person asks questions, reads books, conducts investigations into matters apparently unrelated to job or profession—just for the fun of knowing. It is from these apparently unrelated sources that brilliant ideas often emerge to enrich one's own field of work. 7

Finally, the creative person plays hunches. "Pure intellect," says Dr. Hans Selye, the great medical researcher at the University of 8

Montreal, "is largely a quality of the middle-class mind. The lowliest hooligan and the greatest creator in the fields of science are activated mainly by imponderable instincts and emotions, especially faith. Curiously, even scientific research, the most intellectual creative effort of which man is capable, is no exception in this respect."

Alfred Korzybski also understood well the role of undefinable   9
emotions in the creative life. He wrote, "Creative scientists know very well from observation of themselves that all creative work starts as a feeling, inclination, suspicion, intuition, hunch, or some other nonverbal affective state, which only at a later date, after a sort of nursing, takes the shape of verbal expression worked out later in a rationalized, coherent . . . theory."

Creativity is the act of bringing something new into the world,   10
whether a symphony, a novel, an improved layout for a supermarket, a new and unexpected casserole dish. It is based first on communication with oneself, then testing that communication with experience and the realities one has to contend with. The result is the highest, most exciting kind of learning.

Meaning and Purpose

1. S. I. Hayakawa defines creativity as "the act of bringing something new into the world" (paragraph 10). What three stages does each creative act go through?
2. How do creative people think differently from ordinary people?
3. According to Hayakawa, why must creative people be able to endure loneliness?
4. From what human capacity do most creative ideas grow?

Strategy

1. Hayakawa uses comparison and contrast in his introductory paragraph. How do the things he contrasts differ? How are the things he compares similar?

2. The author uses the first paragraph as his introduction and the final paragraph as his conclusion. How does he organize the body of his essay (paragraphs 2–9)?
3. How does Hayakawa make clear the way creative people think in paragraphs 2–4?
4. How does citing Dr. Hans Selye (paragraph 8) and Alfred Korzybski (paragraph 9) help bolster Hayakawa's argument?

Style

1. What transitional devices does Hayakawa use to connect paragraphs? Comment on their effectiveness.
2. Hayakawa writes about the rather complex psychological phenomenon of creativity. Does his language fit his subject? Explain.
3. Look up the following words in a dictionary: *imponderable* (paragraph 8); *affective* (9).

Writing Tasks

1. Think of a person you know or are aware of whom you consider creative, and then write an essay in which you demonstrate how and to what degree that person fits Hayakawa's criteria for a creative person. Make sure to use several specific examples to demonstrate your points.
2. Using Hayakawa's essay as a model, write an essay in which you define an ordinary, average, or noncreative person. Use numerous examples to demonstrate your points.

❦ Responding to Photographs ❦

Definition

Touching a Snake

Symbols are visible objects or actions that communicate significance beyond their literal meaning. For example, the American flag might stir our patriotic feelings. A superstitious person might grow anxious if he breaks a mirror, predicting a streak of bad luck for himself. The flag, breaking a mirror—each is a symbol.

Often symbols have conventional meanings; for example, a heart sent on St. Valentine's Day is an emblem of affection. A wedding ring is an emblem of eternal commitment to another person. A Christian cross is an emblem of devotion. Many objects or actions do not have conventional meanings but have significance that is created by their context. For example, imagine that you observe the following scene: A woman in black stands next to a tombstone, which reads:

Harold Ross
1930–1993
May He Rest in Peace

507

Next to the woman, their heads bowed, stand three young children. From a few yards away you watch, believing that this is a widow and her children in mourning. After all, the grave, the tombstone, the black dress, and the bowed heads all suggest this interpretation. But then the woman turns from the grave, and you see her face. She's smiling, joyfully smiling. The children begin to skip and sing, "Who's afraid of the big bad wolf / the big bad wolf / the big bad wolf? Who's afraid. . . ." Suddenly the significance of this symbolic scene has changed. To what? Well, that's open to interpretation, which is characteristic of symbolic experience.

Frequently, a symbolic dimension is at work in photographs. Photographers carefully compose the elements of their images so we sense a symbolic dimension in a photograph. "Touching a Snake" is such a photograph. With definition as the dominant development pattern, complete one of the following writing tasks. Before beginning the task, reread the material at the beginning of the chapter to review the conventions involved in writing a definition.

1. Begin by looking up the definition of *symbol* in an unabridged dictionary or other resource material in the library. From the information you gather and from information you gleaned from the introductory comments to this assignment, develop a full definition of *symbol*, using examples from your experience and reading. Next, interpret the symbolic significance of "Touching a Snake." Consider several elements: the snake itself, which has a rich conventional symbolic history; the teddy bear; the generational difference between the man and the boy; the image on the man's T-shirt. In the process of developing your material, you might decide that there are several ways to interpret the photograph. Try to accommodate them in your essay.

2. Research the symbolic significance of the snake as it has appeared throughout history and in different cultures. Integrating the various symbolic meanings your research has uncovered, define *snake* as a multidimensional symbol, integrating its various interpretations. Finally, using one or more views of the symbolic snake, interpret the meaning of "Touching a Snake."

❦ Additional Writing Tasks ❦
Definition

1. Write an essay that defines one of the following terms. Explore the subject beyond its dictionary meaning, using a variety of methods to develop your definition. As part of this or any extended definition, you can state what the subject *excludes* as a way to clarify your definition.
   a. humanity
   b. education
   c. Armageddon
   d. terror
   e. leadership
   f. honesty
   g. fad
   h. evil
   i. female liberation
   j. male liberation
   k. corruption
   l. intuition
   m. liberation theology
   n. social responsibility
   o. obsession
   p. team player
   q. sociopath
   r. maverick
   s. imagination
   t. tragedy
   u. confidence
   v. luck
   w. glamour
   x. scorched earth
   y. genocide
   z. blindsided
2. From the following list of slang terms, select one and define it in several paragraphs. After you explain the term, create a situation in

which it might apply, using the term in several sample sentences as a speaker might. Also include other slang that has a similar meaning.

   a.   hoodwink
   b.   greenhorn
   c.   whoopee
   d.   scam
   e.   boob
   f.   folknik
   g.   bamboozled
   h.   boodle
   i.   macho
   j.   bonehead

3. As a representative of a student rights organization, you have accepted the responsibility to convince a campus grievance committee composed of students, faculty, and administrators that a sexual harassment policy should be adopted as official college policy. Your first task is to define *sexual harassment* and to illustrate at least three different ways it manifests itself in behavior.

4. a. You are an environmentalist living in a major metropolitan area. You have formed an action group that is committed to protect all the natural landscapes that still exist in your city, even to the point of taking militant action against developers. You have used the phrase "urban environmentalist" to describe people who think and act as you do. In an essay, define *urban environmentalists* and describe what developers can expect from them.

   b. A group of self-designated "urban environmentalists" are disrupting development in the city. They see themselves as saviors of natural settings that exist within the urban landscape, but you regard them as "environmental terrorists." In an essay, define *environmental terrorists*, and predict what city officials can expect from them.

5. Look up the medical explanation of a debilitating ailment such as Alzheimer's disease, Down syndrome, or Hodgkin's disease. Once you understand the medical terminology, write a definition essay that explains the disease to someone who has no background in medicine. Create a case study of a person who has the disease to further explain its debilitating effects.

13

Persuasion and Argument
Convincing a Reader

The Method

An argumentative essay is an attempt to change or reinforce someone's opinion or to move someone to take action. On the one hand, the essay may be emotionally charged, appealing to a reader's feelings with emotional detail and biased language. The writing is then called *persuasion* or *persuasive argument*. On the other hand, an argumentative essay may be highly rational, appealing to a reader's intellect with logical explanation. This writing is called *argument* or *logical argument*. Political writing relies heavily on persuasion, and scientific writing on argument. Rarely, however, does an argumentative essay appeal only to emotion or only to reason. Usually, writers appeal to both, striving to convince their readers that their position is valid.

Imagine that you want to convince your readers of the merits of a vegetarian diet. You might begin by appealing to reason. First, you might contrast the high cost of meat with the low cost of grains that provide comparable protein. Second, you might point out that the grains grown for animal feed would be better used to feed the world's hungry. You might continue by presenting the danger highly marbled meat poses to health. You might then shift the appeal to emotion. You might construct an emotional description of animals being raised in pens, relating examples of force feeding and chemical injections, and describing slaughterhouse procedures. While composing the essay, you would keep an eye on your readers, anticipating their responses to your appeals by asking yourself if you are being too emotional or even too rational.

Throughout an argumentative essay a writer must carefully balance reason and emotion. A writer whose essay is so self-righteous that it ignores reason or so rational that it ignores feelings will alienate most readers. A general rule to follow is that an argumentative essay should be primarily rational or it may fail to convince critical readers. Consequently, writers of effective arguments usually present their opinions persuasively but develop ample and strong evidence throughout their essays.

The ancient Greeks, who formulated the underlying concepts of *logic*, identified three factors that are crucial to the construction of an effective argument:

1. *Logos*, or the quality of arguing soundly, refers to the quality of evidence—that is, examples, facts, statistics, authority statements, and reasonable interpretations.
2. *Pathos*, or the feeling dimension of language, refers to the ability to connect with a reader's emotion—that is, values, attitudes, and psychological needs.
3. *Ethos*, or credibility and honesty, refers to how writers present themselves—that is, as knowledgeable, trustworthy, and logical or as ignorant, shiftless, and erratic.

An effective argument usually blends logos, pathos, and ethos. The exact mixture varies with the audience and your purpose.

An argument is predicated on an *assertion*, that is, an opinion you want a reader to accept or an action you want a reader to take. When stated in a sentence, the assertion is referred to as a **proposition** or **thesis**.

The high-fashion fur industry should be curtailed.
The state should resume capital punishment.
Magazines featuring nudity—such as *Playboy, Penthouse*, and *Playgirl*—should be banned from community magazine stands.

The writer then supports the thesis with *evidence*, which is the proof behind the assertion.

It is the quality of evidence that goes a long way to persuade a reader to agree with a writer and reject an opposing position. Keep in mind that the evidence that writers use to develop an argument is the same as that any of us uses in oral arguments: personal experience, the experience of others, and authoritative sources.

Personal Experience.   Suppose you assert that police are harassing college-age drivers. You have had firsthand experience. Several times, a patrol car has pulled you over while you were driving near campus. Each time, an officer initiated a search of your car. Once one even required you to take a field sobriety test, which you passed. At none of these times did any officer issue a traffic citation. These personal experiences could serve as legitimate evidence to support your position.

Experience of Others. You might narrate a story of a friend who had a similar experience. You might also include observations by a passenger or bystander to corroborate your friend's experience.

When using the experience of others, do all you can to be sure that the information is accurate. You know how accurate a description of your experience is because you lived it, but when you use the experience of others, you are, in effect, vouching for its veracity. It is wise, therefore, to include more than one account of the same event.

Authoritative Sources. An argument gains its strength from the quality of authoritative evidence a writer can marshal. You can develop some authoritative information yourself. Once again, consider the argument supporting the proposition that police are harassing college-age drivers. To support your opinion even more thoroughly, you might research police records. If the research revealed that police stopped and searched a significantly larger number of college-age drivers than older drivers, then you would use the information as evidence.

Sometimes, however, you must rely on other authoritative sources, such as encyclopedias, dictionaries, handbooks, digests, journals, and scientific research as well as people who are recognized as having extensive knowledge about a subject. When citing knowledgeable people to support an argument, be sure that their expertise is in the subject you are discussing. It will not do your argument much good to quote a well-known nuclear physicist's opinion on gun control; your reader won't accept that specialist's word as authoritative.

Facts and statistics from authoritative sources can lend a great deal of credibility to any argument. Facts are irrefutable. No matter what the source, a fact is a fact:

The earth revolves around the sun.
John F. Kennedy, the thirty-fifth President of the United States,
   was assassinated on November 22, 1963.

When facts are corroborated by statistics, they exert a powerful
influence on a reader. For instance:

The United States has more homicides each year than Japan,
Taiwan, and the combined countries of Western Europe.

But what does this statistical fact mean? Should the government execute all convicted murderers? Do we need stricter handgun laws?
Should every citizen arm for self-protection? Answering these questions involves interpretations of fact based on personal feelings and
beliefs; that is, it involves opinions.

Strategies

Writers of argument essays pay particular attention to their readers. Since they can't be all things to all readers, they find it helpful to
lump readers into one of three general categories and then address
them appropriately.

1. *Supportive readers.* They already agree with you. There's no
   need to overload your argument with dry facts and statistics.
   You can emphasize pathos over logos, that is, rely more on
   emotion and less on information. Touch the right emotional
   nerve and this crowd will carry you away on its shoulders.
2. *Wavering readers.* These uncommitted or uninformed readers
   are the ones you want to move through both logos and
   ethos, that is, by presenting solid evidence and by establishing your trustworthiness and honesty. Establish the right image and they will hop on your bandwagon.
3. *Hostile readers.* These readers are apathetic, skeptical, and
   maybe even downright mean. Convincing them of *anything*
   will be like trying to pull an angry bull's tooth with a pair of

pliers. Give them just the facts—simple facts, dramatic facts, any facts that will penetrate their intransigence. Ethos won't help much, since they already see you as a low-down schemer, and pathos will be thrown back in your face. Just keep writing calmly and rely on logos. It's hard to spit in the face of truth.

Argument Essay Structure

Writers frequently structure their arguments in a thesis-evidence-conclusion pattern; that is, they state a thesis with a clear assertion in the introduction, present the evidence in the discussion, and reinforce the assertion in the conclusion. This is similar to the commonly used college essay structure.

Sometimes they will use a generalization-evidence-thesis pattern; that is, they open with a general statement of their position, withholding a succinct thesis statement until the close, develop the evidence, and then state the thesis in the close. Generally, no matter which pattern a writer chooses, an effective argumentative essay will have five elements:

1. A clear representation of the controversial issue and the writer's position on it
2. A clearly stated thesis, in either the opening or the close
3. Ample evidence and an orderly arrangement with a refuting counterargument
4. A reasonable tone with an undercurrent of emotion
5. A compelling close that emphasizes the central assertion

To be convincing, evidence in an argumentative essay must be arranged in logical sequence or risk readers rejecting the writer's conclusion. When composing an argument, writers reason through one of two processes: **induction** or **deduction**.

Argument Paragraph Structure

Like all essays, an argument essay is composed of paragraphs. In fact, a writer will usually employ a variety of paragraph modes, such

as examples, comparison and contrast, cause and effect, and definition. Like all effective discussion paragraphs, these paragraphs will
have a topic sentence and adequate development.

There is another paragraph structure, however, that is unique to
argument: a **refutation** paragraph, which presents an opposing point
and offers the writer's response. For example, in the following passage from "Politics and the English Language," George Orwell recognizes and refutes a point of argument that counters his position.

> I said earlier that the decadence of our language is proba-
> bly curable. Those who deny this would argue, if they pro-
> duced an argument at all, that language merely reflects existing
> social conditions, and that we cannot influence its develop-
> ment by any direct tinkering with words and constructions. So
> far as the general tone or spirit of a language goes, this may be
> true, but it is not true in detail. Silly words and expressions
> have often disappeared, though not through any evolutionary
> process but owing to the conscious actions of a minority.

Orwell's refutation paragraph follows a common structure, or sequence of sentences. He begins by establishing his position. He then
states a counterargument. Next, he writes a sentence that swings the
direction from the counterpoint to his response. He closes with an
interpretation that supports his opinion.

Often writers employ traditional paragraph modes to develop
refutation paragraphs. In the following paragraph from "Scientist: I
Am the Enemy," pediatrician Ron Karpati responds to accusations
made by animal rights activists with stunning brief examples. Notice
how Karpati first summarizes the activists' point before countering it.

> Much is made of the pain inflicted on animals in the name
> of medical science. The animal-rights activists contend that this
> is evidence of our malevolent and sadistic nature. A more rea-
> sonable argument, however, can be advanced in our defense.
> Life is often cruel, both to animals and human beings.
> Teenagers get thrown from the back of a pickup truck and suf-
> fer severe head injuries. Toddlers, barely able to walk, find
> themselves at the bottom of a swimming pool while a parent

checks the mail. Physicians hoping to alleviate the pain and suffering these tragedies cause have but three choices: create an animal model of the injury or disease and use that model to understand the process and test new therapies; experiment on human beings—some experiments will succeed, most will fail—or finally, leave medical knowledge static, hoping that accidental discoveries will lead us to the advances.

In "The Futility of the Death Penalty," Clarence Darrow uses comparison and contrast to refute a counterargument.

> It seems to be a general impression that there are fewer homicides in Great Britain than in America because in England punishment is more certain, more prompt, and more severe. As a matter of fact, the reverse is true. In England the average term for burglary is eighteen months; with us it is probably four or five years. In England, imprisonment for life means twenty years. Prison sentences in the United States are harder than in any country in the world that could be classed as civilized.

In "Letter from Birmingham Jail," Martin Luther King, Jr., uses analogy to refute a public statement made by Alabama clergymen who opposed civil rights demonstrations.

> In your statement you assert that our actions, even though peaceful, must be condemned because they precipitate violence. But is this a logical assertion? Isn't this like condemning a robbed man because his possession of money precipitated the evil act of robbery? Isn't this like condemning Socrates because his unswerving commitment to truth and his philosophical inquiries precipitated the act by the misguided populace in which they made him drink hemlock? Isn't this like condemning Jesus because his unique God-consciousness and never-ceasing devotion to God's will precipitated the evil act of crucifixion? We must come to see that, as federal courts have consistently affirmed, it is wrong to urge an individual to cease his efforts to gain his basic constitutional rights because the

quest may precipitate violence. Society must protect the robbed and punish the robber.

Even process analysis can be effective in refuting a counterpoint. In "Concerning Abortion: An Attempt at a Rational View," Charles Harshrone analyzes the function of a fertilized egg to refute the view that the egg in this early stage is a human being.

> Anti-abortion advocates argue that human life begins at the moment of conception. But this is not accurate.
>
> The fertilized egg is an individual egg, but not an individual human being. For such a being is, in its body, a multicellular organism, a *metazoan*—to use the scientific Greek—and the egg is a single cell. The first thing the egg cell does is to begin dividing into many cells. For some weeks the fetus is not a single individual at all, but a colony of cells. During its first weeks there seems to be no ground for regarding the fetus as comparable to an individual animal. Only in possible or probable destiny is it an individual. Otherwise it is an organized society of single-celled individuals.

Although not all argument writers state an opposing point of argument in order to refute it, it's an effective technique. It shows a reader that a writer has thoroughly considered the issue, thus making an argument all the more convincing.

Inductive Reasoning

Through inductive reasoning, writers accumulate enough specific evidence to justify a general conclusion. In other words, inductive reasoning moves from the **specific** to the **general**. While growing up, we all learned to use induction. A child may bite into a hard green apple and discover that it tastes bitter. When the child tastes a hard green pear, he finds that it, too, is bitter. At another time the child bites into a hard green plum and an apricot. Both are bitter. By induction, he draws the general conclusion that hard green fruit is bitter and should not be eaten.

Argumentative essays written with inductive reasoning follow a similar pattern but with one difference: they usually begin with a *hypothesis* or question that embodies the conclusion the writer wants the reader to accept as valid. To argue that a city named Glenwood is environmentally responsible, a writer will have to present evidence that leads directly to that conclusion.

Hypothesis:	Glenwood is an environmentally responsible city. (or: Is Glenwood an environmentally responsible city?)
Evidence:	Glenwood has instituted these environmental programs: Curbsside recycling for glass, newspaper, aluminum, and plastics; Disposal of household toxic waste; Law prohibiting release of ozone-depleting chlorofluorocarbons from air conditioners; Refuse landfill designed to protect ground water from toxic pollution and to generate methane gas; A wetlands bird habitat preserved as open space.
Conclusion:	Glenwood is environmentally responsible.

Conclusions drawn from the inductive reasoning procedure are usually referred to as *probable conclusions*, or *inferences*, for they are reached with incomplete evidence. The reader's acceptance of a conclusion that follows from inductive reasoning is often referred to as the *inductive leap*. To establish a clear connection between the evidence and the conclusion, you must be sure that the evidence you present is *relevant, sufficient*, and *representative*.

To be relevant, the evidence must support the hypothesis and contribute directly to the conclusion. To be sufficient, the evidence must amply support the conclusion. And to be representative, the evidence must represent the full range of information related to the hypothesis, not just one side or the other. By following these criteria, a writer increases the probability that the conclusion is valid, thus bridging the distance from evidence to conclusion and making the reader's intellectual passage easier.

Deductive Reasoning

Deductive reasoning is the opposite of inductive reasoning. Deductive reasoning moves from general assumptions, called premises, to a specific conclusion that follows from the general *premises*. In formal logic, this deductive pattern is called a *syllogism*, a form of organization that includes a *major premise*, a *minor premise*, and a *necessary conclusion*, one that is the logical result of the two premises. The classic example of syllogistic form comes down to us from Aristotle:

Major premise: All humans are mortal.
Minor premise: Socrates is human.
Conclusion: Therefore, Socrates is mortal.

The conclusion of a syllogism is always drawn from the major and minor premises, both of which must be accurate for the conclusion to be accurate. If the premises are drawn from relevant, sufficient, and representative evidence—the same criteria used to draw sound conclusions in inductive reasoning—the conclusion of a syllogism will probably be accurate. But syllogisms can be illogical. An inaccurate major premise may make the syllogism illogical, as shown below:

Major premise: Professional gamblers carry large quantities of
               cash and drive expensive cars.
Minor premise: John Murphy is a professional gambler.
Conclusion: Therefore, John Murphy must carry large quan-
               tities of cash and drive an expensive car.

The major premise is inaccurate. Ask yourself, Are all professional gamblers successful enough to have large quantities of cash on their person and drive expensive cars? Because the major premise is inaccurate, the conclusion is inaccurate.

Sometimes the language of a syllogism is deceptive. Consider the use of "good American," "accept," and "change" in this flawed syllogism.

Major premise: Every good American accepts the United States
                        Constitution.
Minor premise: Martin Luther King did not accept the United
                        States Constitution because he worked to
                        change it.
Conclusion: Therefore, Martin Luther King was not a good
                        American.

The phrase "good American" is vague, too vague to describe a
class of people accurately. What do "accept" and "change" mean in
this context? The United States Constitution has provisions for
change. In fact, it has been amended many times. Anyone who accepts the Constitution accepts the possibility of changing it. Because language is used deceptively in the premises, the conclusion
is meaningless.

Sometimes a syllogism is illogical because it is constructed improperly. First, examine this properly constructed syllogism:

Major premise: All artists rely on intuition.

In a properly constructed syllogism, the subject of the major
premise, in this example "artists," must appear in the minor
premise and be narrowed.

Minor premise: John is an artist.

The conclusion then follows necessarily from the major and minor
premises.

Conclusion: Therefore, John relies on intuition.

That syllogism is properly constructed and is valid. Now examine
this invalid syllogism:

Major premise: All artists rely on intuition.
Minor premise: All psychics rely on intuition.
Conclusion: Therefore, all psychics are artists.

This syllogism is improperly constructed because the minor premise does not repeat the subject of the major premise. The conclusion, therefore, is invalid.

Like inductive reasoning, deductive reasoning can help to organize an argument. But using deduction is never quite as simple as the skeletal form of syllogisms used to illustrate it.

Imagine that the Sierra Club has established a *representative sample* of environmentally responsible cities. By extensive inductive reasoning, the Sierra Club finds several cities, including Glenwood from our previous example, operating effective environmental programs. On the basis of its analysis of these programs, the Sierra Club defines the environmentally responsible city. A syllogism showing that a city is environmentally responsible might be constructed in this sequence:

Major premise: Cities with ecologically beneficial programs for disposal of waste, conservation of energy, and preservation of open space are environmentally responsible.

Minor premise: San Lorenzo has ecologically beneficial programs for disposal of waste, conservation of energy, and preservation of open space.

Conclusion: Therefore, San Lorenzo is environmentally responsible.

In an argumentative essay, a syllogism seldom appears in such clear form, but often its deductive structure is embedded in the text. If a writer wanted to argue that San Lorenzo is environmentally responsible, he or she might first construct a syllogism such as the one above, analyze the evidence needed to support the proposition, and then arrange the argument, incorporating syllogistic reasoning in the structure.

In the first section of the essay the writer would address the questions raised in the major premise.

1. What is an ecologically beneficial program for disposing of waste?
2. What is an ecologically beneficial program for conserving energy?

3. What is an ecologically beneficial program for preserving open space?

To answer these questions would take several paragraphs, and the writer would have to rely on the authority of the Sierra Club's definition. An ecologically beneficial program for disposing of waste would probably require recycling usable trash, disposing of toxic waste, and stringent restrictions on use of landfills. An ecologically beneficial program for conserving energy would probably mean reducing use of automobiles to save fuel and increasing use of solar energy to save electricity. An ecologically beneficial program for preserving open space would probably include protection for unique land formations and wildlife habitats. This discussion would be rather broad because the definition is based on a representative sample of many cities that may vary dramatically in size and geographic location.

To develop the second section of the essay, the writer would address the questions raised by the minor premise:

1. What specific actions has San Lorenzo taken to implement an ecologically beneficial waste-disposal program?
2. What specific actions has San Lorenzo taken to implement ecologically beneficial programs for conserving energy?
3. What specific actions has San Lorenzo taken to implement an ecologically beneficial program for preserving open space?

The purpose of this section is to present evidence that San Lorenzo does indeed meet the definition of environmentally responsible cities. In this section, which would also require several paragraphs to fully develop, the writer would present as evidence the specific environmental programs San Lorenzo has implemented, thus demonstrating the validity of the syllogism's minor premise.

In the last section of the essay, by far the shortest, the writer would conclude that San Lorenzo is an environmentally responsible city. The writer might choose to summarize the key points of the argument, but here the force of deductive reasoning would be irresistible, making it unnecessary to restate the argument in abbreviated form. But whether to develop a conclusion fully or to leave it implied is the decision of the writer, who is responsible for the argument's coherence and consistency. Risks lie in both strategies.

Examine an Argument

Philosopher Stephen Toulmin developed a simple system to examine the strength of an argument, one that helps writers to check whether they are covering everything they should. It's a simple system to use in ordinary thinking situations and reflects how most people use their minds. It's now called the Toulmin model, and it consists of three main elements:

1. The **claim** is the conclusion you draw from your examination of the information—the thesis.
2. The **grounds** are the pieces of information related to the issue—the evidence.
3. The **warrant** is the principle that links the evidence to the thesis—the assumption.

How does the Toulmin model work? Here's a simplified example: Someone suggests that you and your roommates would have fun camping over the upcoming weekend. You respond by saying, "We can't. We have an examination in freshman composition on Monday."

Claim: We can't go camping.
Ground: We have a midterm exam.
Warrant: Students should stay home and study before a test.

A warrant is often left unstated because it is usually so obvious that the listener will fill it in. *Students should study the weekend before a test* is a warrant that college students would agree with. But suppose someone has a different warrant, one that says *Students should relax before a test.* This person would likely insist that everyone should go camping. You might find this view strange or even unreasonable until you clarified the conflicting assumptions behind each other's thinking.

Notice that a warrant is similar to the generalization used in a syllogism (see pp. 521–525) or the conclusion of an inductive chain. You could easily show the following:

> Students who have a test on Monday shouldn't camp the week-end before.
> All of us have a test on Monday.
> Therefore, we shouldn't go camping Friday, Saturday, and Sunday.

Toulmin's model is especially useful in argument writing. You probably won't write in syllogisms or in pure inductive arrangements. An untrained writer will usually make a claim and offer grounds to support the claim. He or she will not pay much attention to the actual reasoning process that goes into the conclusion and the assumption behind the argument. By using Toulmin's model to identify the warrant, claim, and grounds, you will see that the warrant links the claim and grounds and you can determine whether it should be stated explicitly or left implicit. The model will also help you to clarify or even qualify your claim and help you to determine whether you have enough information to convince a reader that your claim is justified.

Logical Fallacies in Writing

Logical fallacies are common mistakes in reasoning, and an argument tainted by them is ineffective. The word *fallacy* means "deception," or "a fault in reasoning." Fallacies deceive by distorting the truth and making logical conclusions unattainable. Using fallacies consciously signifies dishonesty; using them inadvertently demonstrates muddled thinking.

Study this list of eight most common fallacies. Remember that writers must scrutinize their arguments to avoid slipping into fallacious reasoning.

Overgeneralization. Writers overgeneralize when they draw a conclusion from insufficient or unrepresentative evidence.

> During the last year, three of five award-winning films concentrated on family violence. An examination of family violence was just broadcast on national television. No doubt these events indicate that family violence is on the rise.

A handful of films and a television program do not constitute a trend. The conclusion that family violence is rising could be substantiated with statistics and reports from authorities such as psychologists, sociologists, and law enforcement officers.

Oversimplification. To oversimplify is to ignore essential information from which a conclusion is drawn. Be careful to avoid this fallacy when writing about complicated subjects. You might become too eager to offer a simple explanation to a complicated problem.

> The problems of air pollution, ozone depletion, and global warming are not really problems at all. They are merely manifestations of our educational system. We have too many scientists working in universities with nothing to do but study our environment.

Faulty Either/Or Reasoning. The either/or fallacy is a type of oversimplification in which a writer assumes only two alternatives, black or white, when there are others, including gray. The slogan "America, love it or leave it" implies that love of country must be unqualified, which has the effect of excluding constructive criticism.

> Everyone would agree that America is being severely damaged by the sale and use of illegal drugs. The only two courses of action are these: the country's leaders can ignore the problem, or they can enforce the law to its maximum limits.

Of course, other actions are possible—initiate public education, fund rehabilitation for former drug users, develop agreements with other countries to curtail manufacturing of drugs, and even legalize use of drugs. The choice is not between doing nothing or joining a law-and-order crusade.

Post Hoc Argument.   The complete Latin phrase is *post hoc, ergo propter hoc*, which means "after this, therefore because of this." The assumption in this fallacious argument is that one event causes another event simply because the second follows the first in time.

> For more than a year, I have been meditating nightly for one hour. Although I usually have the flu at least once each year, I didn't have it last year. No doubt the meditation prevented me from catching the flu.

As stated, the only relationship between meditation and catching the flu is that one followed the other. Other explanations could be found: Perhaps that year had no flu epidemic, or perhaps the person was lucky enough to avoid a deadly sneeze. Time sequence alone cannot prove that a cause-and-effect relationship applies.

Non Sequitur.   In Latin, *non sequitur* means "it does not follow." A *non sequitur* is a conclusion that does not logically follow from its premises.

> The city in this county that has the most crime also has the highest-paid police force. The city with the least crime has the lowest-paid police force. It does not make sense for our city to pay higher salaries to our police when doing so will not reduce crime.

The reasons for high crime rates are many, a high incidence of poverty being one of them. But we doubt that high police salaries contribute to a rising crime rate. In fact, dangerous working conditions could lead to higher wages for police.

False Analogy.   Someone using a false analogy assumes that if two things are similar in one or more characteristics, then they are similar in other characteristics.

We should not forget the lessons of Grenada and Panama, when our leaders tried to negotiate settlements and failed. Once we sent in the Marines, peace and a working relationship were restored. The best way to deal with renegade countries who act against our interests is to invade them to show other hostile governments we will not be bullied.

We are not living in the same world we lived in even five years ago. The breakup of Communist bloc countries, the danger of renegade terrorist action, the proliferation of nuclear weapons, all make the international scene too complex for rash action based on a false analogy.

Ad Hominem **Argument.** When a writer attacks a person associated with an issue rather than the argument supporting the issue, then the writer is committing an *ad hominem* fallacy, which in Latin means "to the man."

> Councilman Hunt has made a strong argument against raising the gasoline tax for revenue to build more roads. Why shouldn't he? He takes the bus to work each day, and he has the money to fly to any part of the country where he might want to vacation.

This statement ignores the argument for a tax increase and concentrates instead on the person making the argument.

Association Fallacy. To commit the association fallacy is to claim that an act or belief is worthy or unworthy simply because of the people associated with it.

> Congressman Will is supported by some of Hollywood's leading figures. Because actors, directors, and producers know talent when they see it, you should support Congressman Will too.

Do Hollywood figures know any more about the qualities necessary to serve as an effective congressman than most other voters?

Persuasion and Argument in College Writing

Whether presenting examples, comparing two subjects, explaining a process, or classifying components into distinctive categories, you must think clearly and write logically. One development method, however, holds writers to the highest standard of clear thinking and logical writing: argumentation. At some point in the term, most instructors, especially those in the humanities and social sciences, will require you to take a position in relation to a particular opinion or controversial subject—that is, they will require you to write an argument.

Guidelines for Writing a Persuasion and Argument Essay

1. Once you select a controversial subject and decide on your position, marshal two kinds of evidence: that which supports your position and, if appropriate, that which opposes it.

2. Develop a plan that arranges the evidence in a logical progression. Use inductive arrangement if the presentation of your evidence would best be organized by arguing from specifics to a general conclusion; use deductive arrangement if the presentation of your evidence is best organized by arguing from a general conclusion to the specifics.

3. Determine who your readers are. If you perceive your readers to be committed to your position, then you will not have to establish your credibility, nor will you have to write an argument dense with facts, examples, and statistics. Your goal: to reinforce their support.

   If you perceive your readers to be uncommitted, then you must establish yourself to be a reliable source and offer a detailed presentation of the evidence, one that not only informs them but also stirs their emotion. Your goal: to win their support.

   If you perceive your readers to be hostile, then you must establish your authority, present compelling evidence—that is, indisputable facts and carefully reasoned arguments—and avoid emotional appeals, which they might perceive as an emotional attack on their beliefs. Your goal: to encourage them to question their position.

4. Write the essay. If the arrangement is inductive, begin with a stated or implied hypothesis, and lead your reader through the evidence to a reasonable conclusion.

   If the arrangement is deductive, begin with an introduction that states your position and ends with a thesis that clearly indicates an argument will follow. Develop the evidence, which should address questions your thesis raises, in an orderly, step-by-step fashion. Note, where appropriate, the position that opposes yours. Conclude by restating your thesis and reviewing the evidence to show the reader that your position is valid and should be accepted.

5. Review the essay to catch and correct any errors in reasoning you find. Look for logical fallacies, such as overgeneralization, oversimplification, faulty either/or reasoning, and flawed syllogistic reasoning embedded in your discussion.

A Student Essay Developed by Argument

Rolanda Burris received the following assignment to write an argument essay in a mass communications course.

> In an essay of 1000 to 1250 words, take a position for or against controlling what some social critics perceive to be a detriment to the public welfare that is perpetuated in popular culture. Examples include violence against authority and women in music lyrics; the display and use of weapons in cartoons; and the portrayal of drinking, smoking, drugs, or sexual relations in movies or on television.

Burris decided to convince her readers that films featuring characters who smoke should carry a warning much like the one the law requires cigarette companies to place in magazine advertisements. A movie buff, Burris enjoyed reviewing the history of films to gather evidence of the role that smoking has played. As you read her essay, notice how she uses historical examples to build her case.

Here's Looking at Reality, Kid

Among college students Humphrey Bogart is a cult figure. His films, such as <u>The Maltese Falcon</u>, <u>The Harder They Fall</u>, and <u>To Have and Have Not</u>, are still shown at colleges across America. Just last Saturday our Film Society sponsored a Bogart retrospective. I watched <u>Casablanca</u> again. It becomes more romantic each time I see it. <u>Casablanca</u> is set in an exotic place and time. It features mysterious supporting characters. It concentrates on a dilemma. The beautiful heroine must decide between two men who love her, a political idealist and a world-weary cynic. Bogart, the cynic, is suave. His style dominates the film. During this viewing I saw something I had not noticed before: No actor could handle a cigarette better than Bogart. Hanging from the corner of his mouth as he talks or held between two fingers as he drinks, a smoldering cigarette is clearly associated with the stylish image Bogart will eternally project from the screen. Bogart the actual man, however, was not eternal. At 58 he died from lung cancer after a lifetime of heavy smoking. After the movie, I asked myself how many film buffs smoke because they admired the way Bogart handled a cigarette? If Bogart's style influenced just one filmgoer to smoke, shouldn't <u>Casablanca</u>, in fact all films that feature characters who smoke, carry a warning about the dangers of smoking?

Apparently cigarette manufacturers understand the power of association to influence someone's decision to smoke. In an effort to attract more smokers, Philip Morris, the company that sells Benson and Hedges ("For people who love to smoke") Virginia Slims ("You've come a long way, Baby"), and Merit ("For those who want marital bliss") once paid $350,000 to have secret agent 007 James Bond smoke Larks in <u>License to Kill</u>. Philip Morris seems to believe that many young men are too immature to make the logical connection between smoking and death yet do make the illogical connection between smoking and the adventurous life James Bond leads, even though it is not real life.

A couple of years before <u>License to Kill</u> was released,   3
Philip Morris paid a substantial amount to have Lois Lane
smoke Marlboros in <u>Superman II</u>. One movie critic raised the
question that even if Lois Lane had to smoke, why feature a
particular cigarette brand so prominently? Philip Morris must
have been counting on the power of association even then.
Will every immature young woman who sees Lois Lane lighting up conclude that if she smokes Marlboros, her own Man of
Steel will drop from the sky? Probably not consciously, but the
subconscious might associate smoking with sex appeal.

Recently, cigarette companies have had to pay billions in   4
legal settlements for misleading consumers. A reasonable person might assume they would be chastened after their lies
were exposed publicly. But selling cigarettes has little to do
with reason. The industry seems to be intensifying its effort to
glamorize smoking.

Just the other night on the Movie Channel, I watched <u>Die</u>   5
<u>Hard</u>. There was megastar Bruce Willis smoking Marlboros
and blasting away a band of terrorists. I recently watched the
video of <u>My Best Friend's Wedding</u>. There was the stunning
Julia Roberts nervously puffing on a Newport while trying to
disrupt the wedding plans of a rival. But the most shocking
movie display of smoking came to the public through the cinematic talents of director James Cameron.

In <u>Titanic</u>, the world's largest grossing film to date,   6
Cameron shows every major character smoking. Teen heart-
throb Leonardo di Caprio smokes. His love interest, Kate
Winslet, smokes. At one point, Winslet rebelliously blows
smoke in her social-climbing mother's face. Later, she snatches
a cigarette from a young man's lips in an act of independence.
Cameron portrays smoking as sexy, glamorous, and sophisticated. To smoke, the unstated message suggests, is to have
"style"—maybe not Bogart's style, but style nevertheless.

Movies are rated according to who should be allowed to   7
see them. The National Coalition on Television Violence discovered that cigarette smoking appears in 100 percent of PG-13
films. These movies have been approved for thirteen year olds
who have parental permission to watch. Even if they come
from families who do not smoke, young people may be influenced by powerful images that show smoking as an accepted
behavior. But where is the warning in movies that smoking is
a health hazard?

I can hear opponents now. "One more law designed to con-   8
trol personal freedom," they will charge. "Following this logic,
if government wants to protect people, it also should put
warnings about cars on films with car chases or warnings
about guns on films with shoot-outs." But they would be
wrong. Cars and guns don't kill people, drivers and gun owners kill people. In contrast, cigarettes <u>do</u> kill people, and that's
a well-documented fact. Moreover, the government has already
taken action to control smoking.

Cigarette advertisements have been banned from televi-   9
sion and radio for years. When they appear in magazines, cigarette advertisements must include the Surgeon General's
warning that smoking can result in cancer, heart disease, or
fetal injury in pregnant women. This legal requirement is sensible public-health policy, but where does such a warning appear in films that feature characters who smoke? Clearly cigarette companies believe that by associating cigarettes with
appealing characters they will influence a person's decision to
smoke. Why else would Philip Morris pay movie producers to
feature its products?

The practice of featuring smokers in films is disturbing   10
enough, but when cigarette companies actually pay to have
their brands featured in films, the practice goes beyond being
disturbing to being criminal. It is time government put a stop
to this kind of indirect advertising just as it did with radio and
television advertising. If politicians lack the courage, at the
very least, they should require that films featuring smokers
announce the dangers of smoking before the plot begins. Then
the next time someone watches Humphrey Bogart raise a
glass, squint through a cloud of cigarette smoke at Ingrid
Bergman, and say, "Here's looking at you, Kid," viewers will
not be seduced by the romantic image. Instead, they might be
awakened to the excruciating pain Bogart must have felt while
dying of lung cancer.

Reviewing with a Writer's Eye

1. Explain the irony in Rolanda Burris's title.
2. In your own words, state Burris's thesis—the proposition at the
   heart of her argument.

3. What kinds of evidence does Burris offer to support her thesis? (See pp. 513–515.)
4. In a few sentences, describe Burris's intended reader. What details suggest her reader? (See pp. 515–516.)
5. With a total score of 100, what percentage of Burris's argument relies on logos? On pathos? On ethos? (See p. 513.)
6. Is Burris's essay inductively or deductively arranged? Explain. (See pp. 519–525.)
7. Use the Toulmin model to clarify Burris's argument. Identify the claim, the ground, and the warrant. (See pp. 525–526.)
8. Identify Burris's refutation paragraph. (See pp. 516–519). Is it a successful refutation? Why or why not?
9. In no more than 300 words, write a brief critique of "Here's Looking at Reality, Kid" as if you were writing it to Rolanda Burris. Discuss her success or failure in meeting argument-writing conventions.

Peer Review

You may be asked to write an essay about one of the readings that follow. Before you meet with your writing group, review this introduction. As you read the group papers, use these general principles of persuasion and argument to help guide your comments.

1. As stated on page 516, an argumentation paper should have the following:
   a. a clear statement of the writer's assertion;
   b. an orderly presentation of the evidence;
   c. a clear connection between the evidence and the argument;
   d. a reasonable refutation of evidence that is counter to the writer's assertion;
   e. a conclusion that emphasizes the assertion.
2. An argumentative essay should have an appropriate balance between reason and emotion.
3. An argumentative essay should avoid logical fallacies. See pages 526–529.

❦ Tom Regan ❦

Tom Regan is the University Alumni Distinguished Professor of Philosophy at North Carolina State University. He has won numerous honors and awards, including the Gandhi Award for Outstanding Contributions to the Animal Rights Movement and the Joseph Wood Krutch Medal from the Humane Society of the United States. He is one of the pioneers in the academic movement for animal rights, and his influential and popular book The Case for Human Rights *(1983) established some of the major philosophical principles for that movement. Some of his other books include* Earthbound: Introductory Essays in Environmental Ethics; Animal Rights and Human Obligations, *with Peter Singer;* The Thee Generation: Reflections on the Coming Revolution; *and* Defending Animal Rights.

Animal Rights, Human Wrongs

In this essay, Tom Regan argues the case for animal rights and, in doing so, vividly describes some rather grim cruelties inflicted by humans on other animals. As you read, try to determine whether Regan appeals primarily to emotion or to reason.

At this moment workers on board the mother ship of a whaling fleet are disassembling the carcass of a whale. Though the species is officially protected by agreement of the member nations of the International Whaling Commission, it is not too fanciful to imagine the crew butchering a great blue whale, the largest creature ever to have lived on the earth—larger than thirty elephants, larger even than three of the largest dinosaurs laid end to end. A good catch, this leviathan of the deep. And, increasingly, a rare one. For the great blue, like hundreds of other animal species, is endangered, may, in fact, already be beyond the point of recovery.

But the crew has other things on their mind. It will take hours of hard work to butcher the huge carcass, a process now carried out at sea. Nor is butchering at sea the only thing in whaling that has changed. The fabled days of a real hunt, of an individual Ahab pitted against the treacherous whale, must remain the work of fiction now. Whaling is applied technology, from the use of the most sophisticated sonar to on-board refrigeration, from tracking helicopters to explosive harpoons, the latter a technological advance that expedites a whale's death. Average time to die: sometimes as long as twenty minutes; usually three to five. Here is one man's account of a whale's demise:

> The gun roars. The harpoon hurls through the air and the whale-line follows. There is a momentary silence, and then the muffled explosion as the time fuse functions and fragments the grenade. . . . There is now a fight between the mammal and the crew of the catching vessel—a fight to the death. It is a struggle that can have only one result. . . . Deep in the whale's vast body is the mortal wound, and even if it could shake off the harpoon it would be doomed. . . . A second harpoon buries itself just behind the dorsal fin . . . There is another dull explosion in the whale's vitals. Then comes a series of convulsions—A last despairing struggle. The whale spouts blood, keels slowly over and floats belly upward. It is dead.

For what? To what end? Why is this being done to the last remaining members of an irreplaceable species, certainly until recently, possibly at this very moment, by supposedly civilized men? For candle wax. For soap and oil. For pet food, margarine, fertilizer. For perfume.

In Thailand, at this moment, another sort of hunt, less technologically advanced, is in progress. The Thai hunter has hiked two miles through thick vegetation and now, with his keen vision, spots a female gibbon and her infant, sleeping high in a tree. Jean-Yves Domalain with describes what follows: 3

> Down below, the hunter rams the double charge of gunpowder down the barrel with a thin iron rod, then the lead shot. The spark flashes from two flints, and the gun goes off

in a cloud of white smoke. . . . Overhead there is an uproar. The female gibbon, mortally wounded, clings to life. She still has enough strength to make two gigantic leaps, her baby still clinging to the long hair of her left thigh. At the third leap she misses the branch she was aiming for, and in a final desperate effort manages to grasp a lower one; but her strength is ebbing away and she is unable to pull herself up. Slowly her fingers begin to loosen her grip. Death is there, staining her pale fur. The youngster flattens himself in terror against her bloodstained flank. Then comes the giddy plunge of a hundred feet or more, broken by a terrible rebound off a tree trunk.

The object of this hunt is not to kill the female gibbon, but to capture the baby. Unfortunately, in this case the infant's neck is broken by the fall, so the shots were wasted. The hunter will have to move on, seeking other prospects.

We are not dealing in fantasies when we consider the day's work 4 of the Thai hunter. Domalain makes it clear that both the method of capture (killing the mother to get the infant) and the results just seen (the death of both) are the rule rather than the exception in the case of gibbons. And chimpanzees. And tigers. And orangutans. And lions. Some estimate that for every one animal captured alive, ten have been killed. Domalain further states that for every ten captured only two will live on beyond a few months. The mortality rate stemming from hunts that aim to bring animals back alive thus is considerable.

Nor do we romanticize when we regard the female gibbon's 5 weakening grip, the infant's alarmed clutching, the bonds of surprise and terror that unite them as they begin their final descent. And for what? To what end? Why is this scene played out again and again? So that pet stores might sell "exotic animals." So that the roadside zoos might offer "new attractions." So that the world's scientists may have "subjects" for their experiments.

Not far from here, perhaps this moment, a rabbit makes a futile 6 effort to escape from a restraining device, called a stock, which holds the creature in place by clamping down around its neck. Immediately the reader thinks of trapping in the wild—that the stock must be a sort of trap, like the infamous leg-hold trap—but this is not so. The stock is a handmaiden of science, and the rabbit confined by it is not in the wild but in a research laboratory. If we look closely, we will see that one of the rabbit's eyes is ulcerated. It is badly inflamed, an open, running sore. After some hours the sore increases in size until barely half the eye is visible. In a few days the eye will become permanently blind. Sometimes the eye is literally burned out of its socket.

This rabbit is a research subject in what is known as the 7
Draize test, named after its inventor. This rabbit, and hundreds like it, is being used because rabbits happen not to have tear ducts and so cannot flush irritants from their eyes. Nor can they dilute them. The Draize test proceeds routinely as follows: concentrated solutions of a substance are made to drip into one of the rabbit's eyes; the other eye, a sort of control, is left untroubled. Swelling, redness, destruction of iris or cornea, loss of vision are measured and the substance's eye-irritancy is thereby scientifically established.

What is this substance which in concentrated form invades the 8
rabbit's eye? Probably a cosmetic, a new variety of toothpaste, shampoo, mouthwash, talcum, hand lotion, eye cosmetic, face cream, hair conditioner, perfume, cologne. Why? To what end? In the name of what purpose does this unanesthetized rabbit endure the slow burning destruction of its eye? So that a researcher might establish the eye-irritancy of mouthwash and talc, toothpaste and cologne.

A final individual bids for our attention at this moment. A bob- 9
bie calf is a male calf born in a dairy herd. Since the calf cannot give milk, something must be done with it. A common practice is to sell it as a source of veal, as in veal Parmigiana. To make this commercially profitable the calf must be raised in highly unnatural conditions. Otherwise the youngster would romp and play, as is its wont; equally bad, it would forage and consume roughage. From a businessman's point of view, this is detrimental to the product. The romping produces muscle, which makes for tough meat, and the roughage will contain natural sources of iron, which will turn the calf's flesh red. But studies show that consumers have a decided preference for a pale veal. So the calf is kept permanently indoors, in a stall too narrow for it to turn around, frequently tethered to confine it further, its short life lived mostly in the dark on the floor of wood

slats, its only contact with other living beings coming when it is fed and when, at the end, it is transported to the slaughterhouse.

Envision then the tethered calf, unable to turn around, unable to sit down without hunching up, devoid of companionship, its natural urges to romp and forage denied, fed a wholly liquid diet deliberately deficient in iron so as not to compromise its pale flesh but to keep it anemic. For what? To what end? In the name of what purpose does the calf live so? So that humans might have pale veal! 10

*   *   *

It would be grotesque to suggest that the whale, the rabbit, the gibbon, the bobbie calf, the millions of animals brought so much pain and death at the hands of humans are not harmed, for harm is not restricted to human beings. They are harmed, harmed in a literal, not a metaphorical sense. They are made to endure what is detrimental to their welfare, even death. Those who would harm them, therefore, must justify doing so. Thus, members of the whaling industry, the cosmetics industry, the farming industry, the network of hunters-exporters-importers must justify the harm they bring animals in a way that is consistent with recognizing the animals' right not to be harmed. To pursue such a justification it is not enough to argue that people profit, satisfy their curiosity, or derive pleasure from allowing animals to be treated in these ways. These facts are not the morally relevant ones. Rather, what must be shown is that overriding the right of animals not to be harmed is justified because of further facts. For example, because we have very good reason to believe that overriding the individual's right prevents, and is the only realistic way to prevent, vastly greater harm to other innocent individuals. 11

Let us ask the whaling industry whether they have so justified their trade. Have they made their case in terms of the morally relevant facts? Our answer must be: No! And the cosmetic industry? No! The farmers who raise veal calves? No! The retailer of exotic animals? No! A thousand times we must say: No! I do not say that they cannot possibly justify what they do. The individual's right not to be harmed, we have argued, almost always trumps the interests of the group, but it is possible that such a right must sometimes give way. Possibly the rights of animals must sometimes give way to human interests. It would be a mistake to rule this possibility out. Nevertheless, the onus of justifica- 12 tion must be borne by those who cause the harm to show that they do not violate the rights of the individuals involved.

We allow then that it is *possible* that harming animals might be   13
justified; but we also maintain that those harming animals typically fail to show that the harm caused is *actually* justified. A further question we must ask ourselves is what, morally speaking, we ought to do in such a situation. Reflection on comparable situations involving human beings will help make the answer clear.

Consider racism and sexism. Imagine that slavery is an institu-   14
tion of the day and that it is built on racist or sexist lines. Blacks or women are assigned a rank of slave. Suppose we are told that in extreme circumstances even slavery might conceivably be justified, and that we ought not to object to it or try to bring it down, even though no one has shown that it is actually justified in the present case. Well, I do not believe for a moment that we would accept such an attempt to dissuade us from toppling the institution of slavery. Not for a moment would we accept the general principle involved here, that an institution actually is justified because it might conceivably be justified. We would accept the quite different principle that we are morally obligated to oppose any practice that appears to violate rights unless we are shown that it really does not do so. To be satisfied with anything less is to cheapen the value attributable to the victims of the practice.

Exactly the same line of reasoning applies in the case where ani-   15
mals are regarded as so many dispensable commodities, models, subjects, and the like. We ought not to back away from bringing these industries and related practices to a halt just because it is *possible* that the harm caused to the animals *might* be justified. If we do, we fail to mean it when we say that animals are not mere things, that they are the subjects of a life that is better or worse for them, that they have inherent value. As in the comparable case involving harm to human beings, our duty is to act, to do all that we can to put an end to the harm animals are made to endure. That the animals themselves cannot speak out on their own behalf, that they cannot organize, petition, march, exert political pressure, or raise our level of consciousness—all this does not weaken our obligation to act on their behalf. If anything, their impotence makes our obligation the greater.

We can hear, if we will but listen, the muffled detonation of the   16
explosive harpoon, the sharp crack of the Thai hunter's rifle, the drip
of the liquid as it strikes the rabbit's eye, the bobbie calf's forlorn sigh.
We can see, if we will but look, the last convulsive gasps of the great
blue whale, the dazed terror of the gibbon's eyes, the frenzied activity
of the rabbit's feet, the stark immobility of the bobbie calf. But not at
this moment only. Tomorrow, other whales, other rabbits will be
made to suffer; tomorrow, other gibbons, other calves will be killed,
and others the day after. And others, stretching into the future. All
this we know with certainty. All this and more, incalculably more,
will go on, if we do not act today, as act we must. Our respect for the
value and rights of the animals cannot be satisfied with anything else.

Meaning and Purpose

1. In paragraph 11, Regan claims that those who harm animals "must justify the harm . . . in a way that is consistent with recognizing the animals' right not to be harmed." Summarize Regan's argument about how animal rights are derived and why humans must respect those rights.
2. Does Regan appeal primarily to his readers' emotions (persuasion) or to their reason (argument)? What reasons can you cite to justify your opinion?
3. In paragraphs 14 and 15, Regan uses the examples of racism and sexism to demonstrate why animal rights must be defended. According to the author, in what ways are human rights similar to animal rights? In what ways different?

Strategy

1. In paragraphs 1–10, Regan repeats the same rhetorical pattern four times. Describe that pattern. What is its purpose?
2. Regan cites four separate instances of human cruelty to animals. He employs both typical and specific examples to describe these in-

stances. How do the readers know which is which? For what purposes does he use each?

3. In paragraphs 2, 5, 8, and 10 Regan asks a series of questions. What are the answers to those questions? What common value underlies each answer?

4. Structurally, Regan divides his essay into two parts: paragraphs 1–10 and paragraphs 11–18. What is the rhetorical function of each section?

Style

1. Regan asks a series of questions in paragraph 12 and answers each with an exclamation. What is the purpose of his exclamatory answers?

2. In paragraph 2, Regan quotes an account of a whale's death. Why is the word *keels* in the final sentence of that description particularly appropriate?

3. Look up the following words in a dictionary: *leviathan* (paragraph 1); *expedites, demise* (2); *ebbing, giddy* (3); *ulcerated, literally* (6); *forage, detrimental, tethered* (9); *grotesque* (11); *onus* (12); *detonation, forlorn, convulsive* (16).

Writing Tasks

1. Some animal rights activists cite many forms of animal abuse they argue must be stopped. They protest such things as hunting, the eating of meat, the methods used to raise livestock, the establishment of zoos, the wearing of fur, the use of animals in circuses, and medical experimentation on animals, among others. Choose one such issue and research it in the library and/or over the Internet. Discover the facts surrounding your subject, and read different points of view to determine your own. Then write a paper in which you clearly state and logically defend your point of view. Be sure to admit opposing points of view in your argument.

2. Regan claims that animals have the same basic rights as humans. Write a paper in which you argue for or against that point of view. Make sure to read Stephen Rose's "Proud to be a Speciesist," which follows in this chapter, to get a point of view different from Regan's.

❦ Stephen Rose ❦

Stephen Rose is a professor of biology at Open University in England. He has conducted extensive medical research and experimentation on animals.

Proud to Be a Speciesist

In this essay, first published in 1991, Stephen Rose argues strongly against animal rights "absolutists" who claim that animals have innate rights that must be protected by humans.

As you read, try to determine whether Rose appeals primarily to his readers' emotions or to their reason.

I research on animals. I study the intimate chemical and electrical processes that are the brain's mechanisms for storing information, for learning and memory. To discover those mechanisms, I analyse the cellular changes that occur when young chicks learn and remember simple tasks. An antivivisectionist once asked me whether my research didn't make me feel rather like Dr. Mengele. No, it doesn't, though I can't resist pointing out that the only country ever to have moved to ban animal experimentation was Germany in the Nazi 1930s, showing a sensitivity that certainly didn't extend to those categories of humans regarded as "lives not worth living." 1

I won't cheapen the justification for my work by claiming that it will have *immediate* health benefits in helping children with learning problems or in treating the devastating consequences of Alzheimer's disease, though the fundamental biological mechanisms I am uncovering are certainly of relevance to both. I will insist that what I do is part of that great endeavor to understand human biological nature, and to interpret some of the deepest of philosophical questions about the nature of mind and brain. Of course, science is a social activity, and in a democratic society should be democratically controlled. 2

But the absolutists within the animal rights movement care little 3 for that sort of democratic control. They want to have their argument both ways. On the one hand they claim the *discontinuities* between animals and humans are so great that animal experiments can tell us nothing relevant to the human condition. On the other, they say that because animals are sentient, the *continuities* between animals and humans mean that to privilege the latter over the former is an abuse, for which the pejorative term "speciesism" has been coined. The first statement is plain wrong; the second, the claim that animals have "rights," is sheer cant.

The biological world is a continuum. The basic biochemical 4 mechanisms by which we tick are very similar to those in most other organisms. If they weren't, even the food we eat would poison us. Many human diseases and disorders are found in other mammals— which is why we can learn how to treat them by research on animals. Sure, there are differences, as the thalidomide case so tragically demonstrated. But given the choice between testing the toxicity of a new product on animals and not testing, there is no doubt which would be safer.

Of course, we may ask whether so many new drugs, cosmetics or 5 other products are necessary at all, or whether such proliferation is merely the consequence of the restless innovatory needs of capitalist production. But that is not how the animal activists argue. Instead, they claim that there are alternatives to the use of animals. In some cases this is possible, and research to extend the range of such tests should have a high priority. But for many human diseases, understanding and treatment has demanded the use of animals and will continue to do so for the foreseeable future. There is no way, for instance that the biochemical causes of the lethal disease diabetes, or its treatment with insulin, could have been discovered, without experiments on mammals. And we can't use tissue cultures, or bacteria, or plants, to develop and test the treatments needed to alleviate epilepsy, Parkinsonism or manic depression. Anyone who claims otherwise is either dishonest or ignorant.

Equally, however, no biologist can or should deny the sentience 6 of other large-brained animals. The Cartesian myth—that non-human animals are mere mechanisms, pieces of clockwork whose expressions of pain or suffering are no more than the squeak of a rusty cog—is just that, a myth. It was necessary to the generations of Christian philosophers who, following Descartes, wished to preserve the spiritual uniqueness of "Man" whilst accepting the hegemony of physics and biology over the rest of nature. And it was convenient to some 19th-century physiologists in absolving them from responsibility for the consequences of their experiments. But if I believed for one moment that my chicks were mere clockwork, I might as well stop working with them at all, and go play with computers instead.

Unless, of course. I experimented on humans. And this, the   7
privileging of humans, is the nub of the question. Just because we are humans, any discussion of rights must begin with human rights. How far are those rights to be extended—does it even make sense to talk of extending them—to the "animal kingdom"? The animal kingdom isn't composed only of cats and dogs, mice and monkeys. It includes slugs and lice, wasps and mosquitoes. How far can the concept of right be extended—to not swatting a mosquito that is sucking your blood? To prevent your cat from hunting and killing a rat? Does an ant have as many rights as a gorilla?

Most people would say no—though I have met one activist who   8
argued that even viruses had souls! I think most animal righters are really arguing that the closer animals are to humans, biologically speaking—that is, evolutionarily speaking—the more rights they should have. So where does the cut-off come? Primates? Mammals? Vertebrates? The moment one concedes that question, it is clear that the decision is arbitrary—that it is *we*, as humans, who are conferring rights on animals—not the animals themselves.

Put like this, the spurious nature of the term *speciesism* becomes   9
apparent. It was coined to make the claim that the issue of animal rights is on a par with the struggles for women's rights, or black people's rights, or civil rights. But these human struggles are those in which the oppressed themselves rise up to demand justice and equality, to insist that they are not the objects but the subjects of history.

Non-human animals cannot conceive or make such a claim, and   10
to insist the terms are parallel is profoundly offensive, the lazy thinking of a privileged group.

Indeed, it is sometimes hard to avoid the impression that, for   11
some among the animal rights movement, non-human animals take

precedence over humans. The movement's absolutism and its seeming openness to members of extreme right-wing groups, reinforce the view that, for many of its activists, there is no automatic relationship between a concern for animal rights and one for human rights. Among others, there is an air of sanctimonious hypocrisy. They may, if they wish, refuse insulin if they are diabetic, L-dopa if they have Parkinsonism, antibiotics or surgical procedures that have been validated on animals before being used with humans—but I deny them any right to impose their personal morality on the rest of suffering humanity.

Nonetheless, it is essential to listen to the message that the movement carries. Its strength, despite its inchoate ideology, is, I believe, in part a response to the arrogant claim to the domination of nature that western scientific culture drew from its scriptural roots. The animal rights movement is part of wide-spread romantic reaction to the seemingly cold irrationality of science. Scientists who ignore the strength of this reaction do so at their peril—which is why this week sees the launch, by the British Association for the Advancement of Science of a "Declaration on Animals in Medical Research" signed by more than 800 doctors and scientists, defending the controlled use of animals.   12

The argument about how non-human animals should be treated is at root about how we as humans should behave. It is here that the biological discontinuities between humans and other animals become important. Our concern about how we treat other species springs out of our very humanness, as biologically and socially constructed creatures. We do not expect cats to debate the rights of mice. The issue is not really about animal rights at all, but about the *duties* that we have just because we are human.   13

And I am sure that we do have such duties, to behave kindly to other animals; with the minimum of violence and cruelty, not to damage or take their lives insofar as it can be avoided, just as we have duties to the planet's ecology in general. But those duties are limited by an overriding duty to other humans. I have a much-loved and exceedingly beautiful cat. But if I had to choose between saving her life and that of any human child, I would unhesitatingly choose the child. But I would save my cat at the expense of a fish. And so   14 would the vast majority of people. That is species loyalty—speciesism if you like—and I am proud to be a speciesist.

Meaning and Purpose

1. What does Rose mean by the title of his essay, "Proud to Be a Speciesist"? In what way is the title ironic?
2. Explain Rose's view on the perplexing problem he presents about how and to what extent animal rights can be extended down the animal continuum (paragraph 7).
3. Why does Rose reject the idea of innate animal rights? What idea does he substitute in its place?

Strategy

1. Does Rose appeal primarily to his readers' emotions (persuasion) or to their reason (argument)? Explain.
2. In paragraph 3, Rose asserts that the claim of some animal rights activists that animal experiments can tell us "nothing relevant to the human condition" is "plain wrong" and that their claim that animals have innate rights is "sheer cant." What evidence does Rose present to back up his assertions? Where does he offer that evidence?
3. Rose asks a series of questions in paragraph 7 that should provoke his readers to ask themselves to what extent animal rights can extend down the animal continuum. What conclusions do you draw about these questions? Why do you draw these conclusions?

Style

1. Why is it appropriate for Rose to end his argument with an example?
2. Look up the following words in a dictionary: *antivivisectionist* (paragraph 1); *pejorative, cant* (3); *sentience, clockwork* (6); *nub* (7); *spurious* (9); *inchoate* (12).

Writing Tasks

1. In this essay that defends animal experimentation for medical purposes, Stephen Rose makes references that might be obscure for a casual reader: Joseph Mengele (paragraph 1), the thalidomide case (4), the Cartesian myth (6), and 19th-century physiologists (6). Choose one of those subjects as a topic, research it in the library, and write an essay in which you relate your topic to the arguments for and against animal rights. Make sure to compose a clear thesis that tightly controls your essay's argument.
2. Rose argues that animals have no innate rights, that the only rights they can possibly have are those given to them by humans. Write a paper in which you argue for or against that point of view. Make sure to read Tom Regan's "Animal Rights, Human Wrongs," earlier in this chapter, to get a point of view different from Rose's.

❦ Katha Pollitt ❦

Katha Pollitt is a highly acclaimed columnist for Nation, *a magazine of politics and culture. She has taught at Princeton, Barnard, and the New School University. She has won many prizes and awards for her writing, including a National Magazine Award, a National Book Critics Circle Award, and fellowships from the Guggenheim Foundation, the National Endowment for the Arts, and the Whiting Foundation. She was chosen by the New York City chapter of the National Organization of Women for the 2004 Woman of Power and Influence award for her "extraordinary journalism."*

Adam and Steve—Together at Last

In this essay, Katha Pollitt argues that gays and lesbians should have the right to marry by pointing out flaws in the primary arguments that have been advanced against gay marriage. As you read, notice the evidence she cites to bolster her argument.

Notice, too, where she appeals to reason and where she appeals to emotion. Ask yourself how effectively she blends the two forms of argument.

Will someone please explain to me how permitting gays and lesbians to marry threatens the institution of marriage? Now that the Massachusetts Supreme Court has declared gay marriage a constitutional right, opponents really have to get their arguments in line. The most popular theory, advanced by David Blankenhorn, Jean Bethke Elshtain and other social conservatives is that under the tulle and orange blossom, marriage is all about procreation. There's some truth to this as a practical matter—couples often live together and tie the knot only when baby's on the way. But whether or not marriage is the best framework for child-rearing, having children isn't a marital requirement. As many have pointed out, the law permits marriage to the infertile, the elderly, the impotent and those with no wish to procreate; it allows married couples to use birth control, to get sterilized, to be celibate. There's something creepily authoritarian and insulting about reducing marriage to procreation, as if intimacy mattered less than biological fitness. It's not a view that anyone outside a right-wing think tank, a Catholic marriage tribunal or an ultra-Orthodox rabbi's court is likely to find persuasive.

So scratch procreation. How about: Marriage is the way women   2
domesticate men. This theory, a favorite of right-wing writer George Gilder, has some statistical support—married men are much less likely than singles to kill people, crash the car, take drugs, commit suicide—although it overlooks such husbandly failings as domestic violence, child abuse, infidelity and abandonment. If a man rapes his wife instead of his date, it probably won't show up on a police blotter, but has civilization moved forward? Of course, this view of marriage as a barbarian-adoption program doesn't explain why women should undertake it—as is obvious from the state of the world, they haven't been too successful at it, anyway. (Maybe men should civilize men—bring on the Fab Five!) Nor does it explain why marriage should be restricted to heterosexual couples. The gay men and lesbians who want to marry don't impinge on the male-improvement project one way or the other. Surely not even Gilder believes that a heterosexual pothead with plans for murder and suicide would be reformed by marrying a lesbian?

What about the argument from history? According to this, mar   3
riage has been around forever and has stood the test of time. Actually, though, marriage as we understand it—voluntary, monogamous, legally egalitarian, based on love, involving adults only—is a pretty recent phenomenon. For much of human history, polygyny was the rule—read your Old Testament—and in much of Africa and the Muslim world, it still is. Arranged marriages, forced marriages, child marriages, marriages predicated on the subjugation of women—gay marriage is like a fairy tale romance compared with most chapters of the history of wedlock.

The trouble with these and other arguments against gay mar   4
riage is that they overlook how loose, flexible, individualized and easily dissolved the bonds of marriage already are. Virtually any man

and woman can marry, no matter how ill assorted or little ac-
quainted. An 80-year-old can marry an 18-year-old; a john can
marry a prostitute; two terminally ill patients can marry each other
from their hospital beds. You can get married by proxy, like medieval
royalty, and not see each other in the flesh for years. Whatever may
have been the case in the past, what undergirds marriage in most
people's minds today is not some sociobiological theory about repro-
duction or male socialization. Nor is it the enormous bundle of priv-
ileges society awards to married people. It's love, commitment, stability. Speaking just for myself, I don't like marriage. I prefer the
old-fashioned ideal of monogamous free love, not that it worked out
particularly well in my case. As a social mechanism, moreover, marriage seems to me a deeply unfair way of distributing social goods
like health insurance and retirement checks, things everyone needs.
Why should one's marital status determine how much you pay the
doctor, or whether you eat cat food in old age, or whether a child
gets a government check if a parent dies? It's outrageous that, for example, a working wife who pays Social Security all her life gets no
more back from the system than if she had married a male worker
earning the same amount and stayed home. Still, as long as marriage
is here, how can it be right to deny it to those who want it? In fact,
you would think that, given how many heterosexuals are happy to
live in sin, social conservatives would welcome maritally minded
gays with open arms. Gays already have the baby—they can adopt in
many states, and lesbians can give birth in all of them—so why deprive them of the marital bathwater?

At bottom, the objections to gay marriage are based on religious   5
prejudice: The marriage of man and woman is "sacred" and opening
it to same-sexers violates its sacral nature. That is why so many people can live with civil unions but draw the line at marriage—spiritual
union. In fact, polls show a striking correlation of religiosity, especially evangelical Protestantism, with opposition to gay marriage and
with belief in homosexuality as a choice, the famous "gay lifestyle."
For these people gay marriage is wrong because it lets gays and lesbians avoid turning themselves into the straights God wants them to
be. As a matter of law, however, marriage is not about Adam and Eve

versus Adam and Steve. It's not about what God blesses, it's about what the government permits. People may think "marriage" is a word wholly owned by religion, but actually it's wholly owned by the state. No matter how big your church wedding, you still have to get a marriage license from City Hall. And just as divorced people can marry even if the Catholic Church considers it bigamy, and Muslim and Mormon men can only marry one woman even if their holy books tell them they can wed all the girls in Apartment 3G, two men or two women should be able to marry, even if religions oppose it and it makes some heterosexuals, raised in those religions, uncomfortable.

Gay marriage—it's not about sex, it's about separation of church and state.   6

Meaning and Purpose

1. Briefly summarize Pollitt's objection to the argument that the primary reason for marriage is procreation.
2. What is Pollitt's objection to the idea that "Marriage is the way women domesticate men" (paragraph 2)?
3. How does Pollitt argue against the historical objection to gay marriage?
4. Summarize Pollitt's argument against the religious objections to gay marriage.
5. What does Pollitt think is the primary reason for marriage?
6. Who do you think is Pollitt's intended audience—people who already hold her point of view, people who have not made up their minds about the issue, or people who are already hostile to her point of view? Explain your answer.

Strategy

1. In paragraphs 1, 2, 3, and 5, Pollitt argues against some of the main positions of opponents of gay marriage. Why does she interrupt her attack in paragraph 4? What does she do in that paragraph?

2. Paragraphs 1, 2, 3, and 5, have basically the same structure. Briefly describe that structure. How effectively does that structure advance Pollitt's own argument?
3. The last sentence of paragraph 2 is structured like a declarative sentence but ends in a question mark. What effect does Pollitt seek by doing that?
4. In what ways does Pollitt's argument appeal to emotion? In what ways does it appeal to logic and reason?

Style

1. What is the meaning of the phrase "under the tulle and orange blossom" (paragraph 1)?
2. What is the tone of Pollitt's sentence, "There's some truth to this ["marriage is all about procreation"] as a practical matter—couples often live together and tie the knot only when baby's on the way" (paragraph 1)? Why does she take this tone?
3. What is the tone of the phrase "the male-improvement project" in paragraph 2? Why does she take this tone?
4. Explain the meaning of "so why deprive them of the marital bathwater?" in paragraph 4.

Writing Tasks

1. Write an argumentative essay in which you take a position on a subject and then follow an organizational pattern similar to Pollitt's. That is, line up the main arguments of your opposition and then spend at least one fully developed paragraph showing why each of the arguments doesn't work. Make sure to develop your own counter position in at least one paragraph, as Pollitt does in paragraph 4.
2. Take a position on gay and lesbian marriage—pro, con, or somewhere in the middle—and write an essay in which you incorporate Pollitt's points into your argument. You can agree with her, disagree, or perhaps show how she oversimplifies. Be sure to give her credit by informally referring to her in your text. You can bring others who have written on the subject into your discussion as well—giving them due credit, too, of course.

❦ Michael Edwards ❦

Michael Edwards is a retired college professor who has written several successful college textbooks. He spends a lot of his retirement time playing golf and tennis, reading, writing textbooks, being politically active in his community, and being outspoken in matters of religion and politics.

A Case Against Gay Marriage

In the following essay, Michael Edwards makes his case against same-sex marriage in a contrarian way. He disagrees with the arguments of the people he sides with, and he agrees with the arguments of the people whose conclusions he challenges. Keep a keen eye on how persuasively he makes his own case.

Not long after the Massachusetts Supreme Court ruled in February of 2004 that gays could not be banned from marrying, much of the country went into a frenzy. The Mayor of San Francisco declared the city would issue marriage licenses for gays. Gay couples, both men and women, lined up by the hundreds in the streets of Boston and San Francisco to participate for the first time in legal wedded bliss. 2004 being an election year, national politicians played to their perspective voters. Archconservatives, led by President George W. Bush, all strong states' rights advocates when it suits them, pressed for a federal constitutional amendment to ban gay marriages. They knew such an amendment could never pass Congress, much less gain passage by the necessary two-thirds of the states, but they pressed the issue anyway, pandering to their Christian fundamentalist base to shore them up for the November election. Liberals, normally supporters of both gay rights and a strong central government, evaded the issue by claiming it was a matter for the states and not the federal government, and most certainly not an issue for a constitutional amendment. Would-be pundits of every stripe weighed in on the Internet and in newspapers and magazines. Those supporting gay

1

marriages, mostly liberals and gay rights advocates, advanced arguments that were rational and humane but, for the most part, drew the wrong conclusions. Those who opposed gay marriages, mostly religious fundamentalists, trotted out old homophobic fears and irrelevant biblical admonitions but somehow drew the right conclusions.

The arguments advanced against gay marriage are many, but   2
when one dismisses those that are entirely misinformed or merely silly—such as the notion that homosexuals are by nature more promiscuous than heterosexuals and whose relationships are therefore more inherently unstable—one is left with a short list of arguments, each based on fallacious religious assumptions. The anti–gay marriage advocates tell us, for instance, that the primary reason for marriage is procreation. Why? Because God ordained it so. It's in the Bible. Their ideological opponents have been quick to point out that many people marry who have no intention of having children or who simply can't, the infertile and the elderly, for instance.

Some biblical literalists have also developed a little deductive ar-   3
gument based on the following syllogism: Our Judaic/Christian God has condemned homosexuality. This country was founded on Christian values. Therefore, homosexuality and same-sex marriages must be banned. They justify the validity of their first premise by citing Leviticus 18:22: "You shall not lie with a male as with a woman; it is an abomination." But they have to be a bit choosey using this argument since the Bible prescribes a good many things that are simply absurd to people other than ancient desert nomads reacting to their own peculiar cultural milieu. If the Bible is the literal word of God, then the gay-bashers would also have to approve the selling of their own daughters into slavery, as sanctioned in Exodus 21:7, or the putting to death of their neighbors who work on the Sabbath (Exodus 35:2), or the stoning of blasphemers (Leviticus 24:10–16). If they were intellectually honest, they'd have to conclude that eating shellfish is as grievous a sin as homosexuality since God has declared that act an abomination as well (Leviticus 11:10). No, the argument against gay marriage based on a literal interpretation of the Bible just won't work in a rational world.

Nor does their second premise, that this country is a Christian   4
nation founded on Christian ideals, work either. That idea is a fantasy,

a myth fervently believed by many, perhaps, but an idea entirely divorced from historical fact. Some of the Founding Fathers of this country were indeed Christians, but a breed substantially different from the fundamentalists of today. The majority of the Founding Fathers were, in fact, Deists. Both Christian and Deist Founders were united in expressing Enlightenment rationalism and the ideals of secular government in the Declaration of Independence, the Federalist Papers, and the Constitution. They were all aware, and some had witnessed first hand, the evil that ensues when governments embrace state religions, so they carefully eliminated that danger when they declared in the *Constitution* that there would be a clear separation of church and state. There would be freedom of religion in this country, but there would also be freedom from religion if individuals so chose.

No, the arguments of religious fundamentalists don't hold up under reason or a clear and honest reading of history. But their conclusion that gays should not be allowed to marry is right on target. 5

Some proponents of same-sex marriage have pointed out the shameful history of how homosexuals have been treated in this country. They're right on this score, of course. Homosexuals have been treated with cruelty and brutality, even to the present day. We still have, for instance, the foolish and puerile "Don't ask, don't tell" policy of the U.S. military, a policy based on the hypocritical premise that homosexuals can admirably serve their country only if they hide their private natures from public view. If they are honest and open about themselves before induction, they are denied service. If they are discovered while in service, they are thrown out in disgrace. Soldiers used to be separated into units of different races, and women, when finally allowed to serve, were relegated to menial tasks and not allowed into combat. We have finally eliminated those forms of discrimination because we now recognize it's in our best interest to do so. Now it's about time we grew up and eliminated discrimination against gays in the military. That's in our own self-interest as well— not to mention the simple human decency of treating all men and women equally. And still today there are those so unsure of their own sexuality, so fearful and hateful of homosexuals that they brutalize and murder them. Even today. In 1998, Matthew Shepard, a Wyoming college student, was tortured and murdered 6 simply because he was a homosexual. In 2002, Gwen Araujo, a transgendered teenager from Newark, California, was brutally murdered by three young men in a similar hate crime. These are but two of the more notorious examples of brutal hate crimes against homosexuals to make the news in the last few years. And we'd be dishonest with ourselves if we didn't admit the other myriad and more subtle ways we discriminate against, diminish, and degrade homosexuals in this country. The proponents of same-sex marriage are accurate in these observations, but they need to take a longer and broader perspective of the history of homosexuality to recognize that while homosexuals must be granted all the civil and human rights, all the economic opportunities, and all the respect and dignity due all citizens, they should not be allowed to marry.

Anthropologists tell us that homosexuals have been accepted in   7
one form or another, or to one degree or another, in about two-thirds of all human societies. Some societies have given them special status. In many Native-American societies, for instance, homosexuals, especially transvestites, were accorded respect and attributed with magical powers. Ancient Greece, one of the two primary influences in the development of Western Civilization—the other being ancient Hebrew culture and its offspring Christianity—highly valued homosexuality, especially the homosexual relationships between older men and their younger patrons, and they idealized those relationships in their literature. The ancient Hebrews, on the other hand, condemned homosexuality as an abomination, and there's a cultural explanation for this. There were several competing religions in the Near East as Hebrew culture developed, some with monotheistic beliefs and many with myths and rites similar to those of the Hebrews. Some of these religions made a place for homosexuality, and even bestiality, in those myths and rites. The Hebrews, seeing themselves as unique, the Chosen People, developed other myths and rites to distinguish themselves from their neighbors, thus their condemnation of homosexuality and bestiality as an abomination in Leviticus.

Whether or not cultures have been tolerant or intolerant of homo-   8
sexuality, there have been constants in all of them. First, homosexuals have existed in all human cultures. Up to now there's been no definitive

explanation of why homosexuality occurs, but the universality of its existence strongly suggests it's a natural phenomenon. Secondly, homosexuals have always been a small minority in every culture—estimates vary from two to five percent in any human population. Thirdly, homosexuals have always been excluded from marriage. Even in the most accepting societies—Ancient Greece where male homosexuality was idealized or in Native-American societies where transvestites were given special status and accorded magical powers—marriage was reserved exclusively for members of the opposite sex, men and women.

Same-sex marriage advocates are also correct when they point   9
out that there hasn't been much consistency in the historical forms and practices of marriage. The forms of marriage and family have varied widely among cultures. Polyandry, though practiced, has been rare in human societies. Polygamy has been more common and is still practiced in some contemporary cultures. Monogamy has been the most common form of marriage, especially in modern times. Marriage in its various forms has been employed as a means of transferring property from one generation to another. It has been used to gain political goals—to attain social stability by unifying different families, or tribes, or states, for instance. Women have been treated as chattel in marriage, and for a long time in this country's short history men and women of different races were not allowed to marry. As marriages have taken various forms, so too have families. There have been corporate families organized around a number of important activities, such as hunting within a group's territory, cultivating its land, or trading its products. There have been extended families that include not only the parents and their unwed children but also married children and their wives or husbands and offspring. And, of course, there have been nuclear families consisting only of parents and their children. This type of family has been universal and forms the nucleus of the corporate as well as the extended family. Necessarily, it constitutes the first stage of both.

Such a varied history, however, does not constitute a valid argu-   10
ment for a society to officially authorize the inclusion of same-sex marriage into the marital hodgepodge. In all its various forms and practices, marriage has always had a constant: It has been based on

the union of biological opposites, men and women. From earliest times there seems to have been the universal recognition—more often instinctual than conscious, probably—that the complementary union of opposites, the yin-yang principle applied to individual people, was the most stabilizing force a society could have. As a species, humans have the obligation to perpetuate themselves, not because God told us to do so, but because it is the most basic biological impulse of all living things. Likewise, societies and civilizations are ruled by the same impulse of self-perpetuation, and marriage between the sexes has proven to be the strongest force to counteract the inevitable march to cultural entropy. All civilizations eventually die. Great, visionary poets know this. Percy Bysshe Shelley saw it in terms of the ultimate folly of pride when he looked at the inscription on the ruined monument of Ozymandias, the Greek name for Ramses II of Egypt, 13th century BCE:

> My name is Ozymandias, King of Kings,
> Look on my Works, ye Mighty, and despair!
> Nothing beside remains. Round the decay
> Of that colossal Wreck, boundless and bare
> The lone and level sands stretch far away.
> "Ozymandias," 1818

William Butler Yeats envisioned the end of Western Civilization as a spiral spinning out of control:

> Turning and turning in the widening gyre
> The falcon cannot hear the falconer;
> Things fall apart; the center cannot hold;
> Mere anarchy is loosed upon the world,
> The blood-dimmed tide is loosed, and everywhere
> The ceremony of innocence is drowned;
> The best lack all conviction, while the worst
> Are full of passionate intensity.
> "The Second Coming," 1920

I don't mean to suggest by this that civilization will crumble if gays are given the legal right to marry, or that the traditional institution of marriage will incur a mortal wound, or that long-married couples will suddenly divorce when they discover a pair of married homosexuals live down the street. Of course these things won't happen. What I am suggesting is that government has the responsibility to protect and perpetuate those social institutions that serve as ballast for our always-shaky ship of state. Marriage between the sexes has been that ballast for countless societies for millennia.

Our government, based on Enlightenment values that hold individuals in highest esteem, also has the responsibility to protect and promote the civil and human rights of all individuals. Our Declaration of Independence declares that all men (and women) have the right to "life, liberty, and the pursuit of happiness." Further, the Founding Fathers wrote the Bill of Rights into the Constitution. The civil and human liberties protected by the country's highest law extend to all citizens, no matter what race, religious belief or unbelief, sex, or sexual orientation. This means, in part, that a person's private behavior, as long as it doesn't infringe on the rights of others or do harm to the commonweal, is not the business of the state. What consenting adults do in the privacy of their bedrooms or hotel rooms is their own business and government should not have the right to intrude itself in that private business. Though late in the game, we seem to be moving slowly in that direction. In November of 2004, the U.S. Supreme Court struck down the Texas sodomy laws that made sex between members of the same sex illegal.

If we are to strive to be a fair country as well as one that protects individual liberties, we must level the economic playing field for all people, married and unmarried alike. Tax laws, Social Security and Medicare benefits, health insurance coverage—all those benefits distributed and regulated by the state—must equally apply to all citizens, whether or not they are married or single, whether or not they are heterosexual, homosexual, or asexual. It is simply not fair to give one group of people an economic advantage over another.

Civil and economic equality must be judiciously balanced in a free society with the security and protection of both individuals and the institutions that have proven to be meritorious. Government, therefore, also has the responsibility to enact laws that protect its citizens from harm and its institutions from destabilizing forces. We have laws against theft, burglary, fraud, and murder because those crimes infringe on the rights and freedoms of others and because without those laws anarchy would reign. There is already a large body of marriage laws designed to protect both the institution and the individual members of the family. This is not the infringement of the state into the business of religion because marriage is a social institution as well as a religious one.

Those who oppose same-sex marriage, with their fallacious religious arguments and mephitic homophobia, get the right answers for all the wrong reasons. In their zeal to remedy the social wrongs inflicted on homosexuals, the proponents of gay marriage get the wrong answers for all the right reasons, because they don't take a broad enough view. The crux of the issue of same-sex marriage is fairness to all on the one hand and the protection of stabilizing social institutions on the other. This is the one instance where separate but equal should prevail.

14

Meaning and Purpose

1. What does Michael Edwards think of those who oppose same-sex marriage? How can you determine his attitude?
2. How can those who advocate the legalization of same-sex marriage draw incorrect conclusions if their arguments are both "rational and humane" (paragraph 1), as Edwards claims?
3. Why does Edwards conclude that the argument against gay marriage based on the Bible is invalid?
4. If, as Edwards claims, the government does not generally have the right to intrude itself in the private behavior of individuals, how can he draw the conclusion that same-sex marriage should be banned?

Strategy

1. What is Edwards's thesis? Where does he state it?
2. Why does Edwards's first argue against those whose conclusions he agrees with?

3. What structural function does paragraph 5 serve?
4. Why does Edwards cite the "visionary" poets Percy Bysshe Shelley and William Butler Yeats in paragraph 10?

Style

1. What judgmental words and phrases does Edwards use in the first paragraph to make sure his readers know his attitudes toward the arguments that have been advanced for and against same-sex marriage?
2. What transitional devices does Edwards use to connect one paragraph to another?
3. Why is the word "visionary" important in Edwards's description of the two poets he cites in paragraph 10?
4. Look up the following words: *pandering, pundits, admonitions* (paragraph 1); *promiscuous, inherently, fallacious* (2); *deductive, syllogism, abomination, milieu* (3); *Deists* (4); *puerile, myriad* (6); *transvestites, monotheistic* (7); *polyandry, polygamy, monogamy, chattel* (9); *yin-yang, entropy,* BCE, *incur, ballast, millennia* (10); *commonweal, intrude* (11); *meritorious* (13); *mephitic* (14).

Writing Tasks

1. Write an argumentative essay that uses an analysis of Edwards's essay as the core of your argument. That is, agree or disagree with his conclusion by showing how the evidence he cites and the logic he employs to reach his conclusion are either valid or faulty. Be sure to quote and paraphrase Edwards during your discussion. Be sure, also, to use examples to demonstrate your points.
2. Using Edwards's essay as your structural model, write an argumentative essay in which you first dispose of opposing arguments before you develop your own line of argument.

❦ Gerard Jones ❦

Gerard Jones is a versatile and prolific writer who has published comics, cartoons, and screenplays, including Batman, Spiderman, *and* UltraForce. *He is the author of the newspaper comic strip* Pikachu Meets the Press *and the Web strip* The Haunted Man *(www. hauntedman.com).* Dead Ginny: A Novel Biography of the First Hippie *(www.deadginny.com) is one of his Web books. He is also the author of several conventionally published books, including* Honey, I'm Home! Sitcoms: Selling the American Dream *and* Men of Tomorrow, *a history of the birth of superhero comics.*

Violent Media Is Good for Kids

This essay is an excerpt from the book Killing Monsters. *It was first published in* Mother Jones *(online) in June, 2000.*

The highly esteemed comic-book author Gerard Jones argues that modern kids "grow up too passive, too distrustful of themselves, and too easily manipulated," so that they need media violence as a healthy outlet for their own inner rage and aggression. Read the essay as objectively as you can to determine how convincing his argument is.

At 13 I was alone and afraid. Taught by my well-meaning, pro- 1
gressive, English-teacher parents that violence was wrong, that rage
was something to be overcome and cooperation was always better
than conflict, I suffocated my deepest fears and desires under a nice-
boy persona. Placed in a small, experimental school that was wrong
for me, afraid to join my peers in their bumptious rush into adolescent boyhood, I withdrew into passivity and loneliness. My parents,
not trusting the violent world of the late 1960s, built a wall between
me and the crudest elements of American pop culture.

Then the Incredible Hulk smashed through it. 2

One of my mother's students convinced her that Marvel Comics, 3
despite their apparent juvenility and violence, were in fact devoted
to lofty messages of pacifism and tolerance. My mother borrowed

some, thinking they'd be good for me. And so they were. But not because they preached lofty messages of benevolence. They were good for me because they were juvenile. And violent.

The character who caught me, and freed me, was the Hulk: overgendered and undersocialized, half-naked and half-witted, raging against a frightened world that misunderstood and persecuted him. Suddenly I had a fantasy self to carry my stifled rage and buried desire for power. I had a fantasy self who was a self: unafraid of his desires and the world's disapproval, unhesitating and effective in action. "Puny boy follow Hulk!" roared my fantasy self, and I followed.

I followed him to new friends—other sensitive geeks chasing their own inner brutes—and I followed him to the arrogant, self-exposing, self-assertive, superheroic decision to become a writer. Eventually, I left him behind, followed more sophisticated heroes, and finally my own lead along a twisting path to a career and an identity. In my 30s, I found myself writing action movies and comic books. I wrote some Hulk stories, and met the geek-geniuses who created him. I saw my own creations turned into action figures, cartoons, and computer games. I talked to the kids who read my stories. Across generations, genders, and ethnicities I kept seeing the same story: people pulling themselves out of emotional traps by immersing themselves in violent stories. People integrating the scariest, most fervently denied fragments of their psyches into fuller senses of selfhood through fantasies of superhuman combat and destruction.

I have watched my son living the same story—transforming himself into a bloodthirsty dinosaur to embolden himself for the plunge into preschool, a Power Ranger to muscle through a social competition in kindergarten. In the first grade, his friends started climbing a tree at school. But he was afraid: of falling, of the centipedes crawling on the trunk, of sharp branches, of his friends' derision. I took my cue from his own fantasies and read him old Tarzan comics, rich in combat and bright with flashing knives. For two weeks he lived in them. Then he put them aside. And he climbed the tree.

But all the while, especially in the wake of the recent burst of school shootings, I heard pop psychologists insisting that violent stories are harmful to kids, heard teachers begging parents to keep their kids away from "junk culture," heard a guilt-stricken friend with a son who loved Pokémon lament, "I've turned into the bad mom who lets her kid eat sugary cereal and watch cartoons!"

That's when I started the research.   8

"Fear, greed, power-hunger, rage: these are aspects of our selves   9
that we try not to experience in our lives but often want, even need, to experience vicariously through stories of others," writes Melanie Moore, Ph.D., a psychologist who works with urban teens. "Children need violent entertainment in order to explore the inescapable feelings that they've been taught to deny, and to reintegrate those feelings into a more whole, more complex, more resilient selfhood."

Moore consults to public schools and local governments, and is   10
also raising a daughter. For the past three years she and I have been studying the ways in which children use violent stories to meet their emotional and developmental needs—and the ways in which adults can help them use those stories healthily. With her help I developed Power Play, a program for helping young people improve their self-knowledge and sense of potency through heroic, combative storytelling.

We've found that every aspect of even the trashiest pop-culture   11
story can have its own developmental function. Pretending to have superhuman powers helps children conquer the feelings of powerlessness that inevitably come with being so young and small. The dual-identity concept at the heart of many superhero stories helps kids negotiate the conflicts between the inner self and the public self as they work through the early stages of socialization. Identification with a rebellious, even destructive, hero helps children learn to push back against a modern culture that cultivates fear and teaches dependency.

At its most fundamental level, what we call "creative violence"—   12
head-bonking cartoons, bloody videogames, playground karate, toy guns—gives children a tool to master their rage. Children will feel rage. Even the sweetest and most civilized of them, even those whose parents read the better class of literary magazines, will feel rage. The world is uncontrollable and incomprehensible; mastering it is a terrifying, enraging task. Rage can be an energizing emotion, a shot of courage to push us to resist greater threats, take more control, than we ever thought we could. But rage is also the emotion our culture distrusts the most. Most of us are taught early on to fear our

own. Through immersion in imaginary combat and identification with a violent protagonist, children engage the rage they've stifled, come to fear it less, and become more capable of utilizing it against life's challenges.

I knew one little girl who went around exploding with fantasies 13
so violent that other moms would draw her mother aside to whisper, "I think you should know something about Emily. . . ." Her parents were separating, and she was small, an only child, a tomboy at an age when her classmates were dividing sharply along gender lines. On the playground she acted out *Sailor Moon* fights, and in the classroom she wrote stories about people being stabbed with knives. The more adults tried to control her stories, the more she acted out the roles of her angry heroes: breaking rules, testing limits, roaring threats.

Then her mother and I started helping her tell her stories. She 14
wrote them, performed them, drew them like comics: sometimes bloody, sometimes tender, always blending the images of pop culture with her own most private fantasies. She came out of it just as fiery and strong, but more self-controlled and socially competent: a leader among her peers, the one student in her class who could truly pull boys and girls together.

I worked with an older girl, a middle-class "nice girl," who held 15
herself together through a chaotic family situation and a tumultuous adolescence with gangsta rap. In the mythologized street violence of Ice-T, the rage and strutting of his music and lyrics, she found a theater of the mind in which she could be powerful, ruthless, invulnerable. She avoided the heavy drug use that sank many of her peers, and flowered in college as a writer and political activist.

I'm not going to argue that violent entertainment is harmless. I 16
think it has helped inspire some people to real-life violence. I am going to argue that it's helped hundreds of people for every one it's hurt, and that it can help far more if we learn to use it well. I am going to argue that our fear of "youth violence" isn't well-founded on reality, and that the fear can do more harm than the reality. We act as though our highest priority is to prevent our children from growing up into murderous thugs—but modern kids are far more likely to grow up too passive, too distrustful of themselves, too easily manipulated.

We send the message to our children in a hundred ways that   17
their craving for imaginary gun battles and symbolic killings is
wrong, or at least dangerous. Even when we don't call for censorship or forbid *Mortal Kombat*, we moan to other parents within our
kids' earshot about the "awful violence" in the entertainment they
love. We tell our kids that it isn't nice to play-fight, or we steer them
from some monstrous action figure to a pro-social doll. Even in the
most progressive households, where we make such a point of letting children feel what they feel, we rush to substitute an enlightened discussion for the raw material of rageful fantasy. In the
process, we risk confusing them about their natural aggression in
the same way the Victorians confused their children about their sexuality. When we try to protect our children from their own feelings
and fantasies, we shelter them not against violence but against
power and selfhood.

Meaning and Purpose

1. Why did Jones's mother allow him to read Marvel Comics? In what
    way is her reason for doing so different from Jones's evaluation of
    the comics' value?
2. How did the Hulk liberate the thirteen-year-old Jones? Why did
    Jones then move on to heroes other than the Hulk?
3. Summarize what you think is Jones's main argument of the value of
    media violence for kids.
4. Jones admits that media violence can cause harm (paragraph 16).
    What reasons does he give to justify his advocacy of media violence?

Strategy

1. What functions do the one-sentence paragraphs 2 and 8 serve?
2. How does the story of Jones's son help develop his argument?
3. Describe the function of paragraph 7.

4. In what ways do the personal examples of Jones and his son differ from his examples in paragraphs 13–15?

Style

1. Explain what Jones means by "overgendered and undersocialized" (paragraph 4). Why would a thirteen-year-old boy positively identify with a character with these attributes?
2. At the end of paragraph 6 Jones says his son "climbed the tree." The sentence's literal meaning is clear. Does it have any figurative meaning? What?
3. What does Jones mean by "a theater of the mind" (paragraph 15)? How does this phrasing add dimension to his meaning?

Writing Tasks

1. In paragraph 16, Jones claims that "our fear of 'youth violence' isn't well-founded on reality" but offers no evidence to back his statement up. Research that subject on the Internet and in a library in order to draw your own informed conclusions on the subject, and then write a paper in which you attempt to win your reader to your point of view. Be sure to offer evidence from both sides of the question and, if possible, include points made by Jones and Gregg Easterbrook ("Watch and Learn," which follows in this chapter) in their arguments. Make sure to document your sources clearly.
2. Write an essay in which you argue either for or against Jones's argument about the efficacy of media violence. Include in your argument evidence you gather from the Internet and the library, as well as your own personal observations. Make sure to cite Jones in your argument as well.

❦ Gregg Easterbrook ❦

Born in 1953, Gregg Easterbrook graduated from Colorado College. He has been a contributing editor at Newsweek *and* U.S. News & World Report *and is currently a contributing editor of* The Washington Monthly, The Atlantic Monthly, *and* BeliefNet.com, *a Web site devoted to religious issues. He is also a senior editor of* The New Republic; *a distinguished fellow of the Fulbright Foundation; author of several critically acclaimed books, including* A Moment on the Earth *(1996) and* Beside Still Waters *(1999); and a two-time winner of the Investigative Reporters and Editors Award. He currently lives in Bethesda, Maryland.*

Watch and Learn

The following essay first appeared in the political and cultural journal The New Republic. *It argues that gratuitous media violence has a negative influence on children and inevitably produces real violence.*

As you read, notice what points Gregg Easterbrook chooses to develop his argument, and note, too, the order in which he places them.

Defenders of bloodshed in film, television, and writing often argue that depictions of killing don't incite real violence because no one is really affected by what they see or read; it's all just water off a duck's back. At heart, this is an argument against free expression. The whole reason to have a First Amendment is that people *are* influenced by what they see and hear: words and images do change minds, so there must be free competition among them. If what we say, write, or show has no consequences, why bother to have free speech?

Defenders of Hollywood bloodshed also employ the argument that since millions of people watch screen mayhem and shrug, feigned violence has no causal relation to actual violence. . . . For those on the psychological borderline, the calculus is different. There have, for example, been at least two instances of real-world shootings in which the guilty imitated scenes in *Natural Born Killers*. . . .

Except for the unbalanced, exposure to violence in video "is not   3
so important for adults; adults can watch anything they want," Eron says.* Younger minds are a different story. Children who don't yet understand the difference between illusion and reality may be highly affected by video violence. Between the ages of two and eight, hours of viewing violent TV programs and movies correlates closely to felonies later in life; the child comes to see hitting, stabbing, and shooting as normative acts. The link between watching violence and engaging in violence continues up to about the age of nineteen, Eron finds, after which most people's characters have been formed, and video mayhem no longer correlates to destructive behavior.

Trends in gun availability do not appear to explain the murder   4
rise that has coincided with television and violent films. Research by John Lott Jr., of the University of Chicago Law School, shows that the percentage of homes with guns has changed little throughout the postwar era. What appears to have changed is the willingness of people to fire their guns at one another. Are adolescents now willing to use guns because violent images make killing seem acceptable or even cool? Following the Colorado slaughter, *The New York Times* ran a recounting of other postwar mass murders staged by the young, such as the 1966 Texas tower killings, and noted that they all happened before the advent of the Internet or shock rock, which seemed to the *Times* to absolve the modern media. But all the mass killings by the young occurred after 1950—after it became common to watch violence on television.

When horrific murders occur, the film and television industries   5
routinely attempt to transfer criticism to the weapons used. Just after the Colorado shootings, for instance, TV talk-show host Rosie O'Donnell called for a constitutional amendment banning all firearms. How strange that O'Donnell didn't call instead for a boycott of Sony or its production company, Columbia Tristar—a film studio from which she

*Leonard Eron, a research psychologist, studies correlations of video and actual violence [*The New Republic* Editor's note.]

has received generous paychecks and whose current offerings include *8MM*, which glamorizes the sexual murder of young women, and *The Replacement Killers*, whose hero is a hit man and which depicts dozens of gun murders. Handguns should be licensed, but that hardly excuses the convenient sanctimony of blaming the crime on the weapon, rather than on what resides in the human mind.

And, when it comes to promoting adoration of guns, Hollywood might as well be the NRA's marketing arm. An ever-increasing share of film and television depicts the firearm as something the virile must have and use, if not an outright sexual aid. Check the theater section of any newspaper, and you will find an ever-higher percentage of movie ads in which the stars are prominently holding guns. Keanu Reeves, Uma Thurman, Laurence Fishburne, Geena Davis, Woody Harrelson, and Mark Wahlberg are just a few of the hip stars who have posed with guns for movie advertising. Hollywood endlessly congratulates itself for reducing the depiction of cigarettes in movies and movie ads. Cigarettes had to go, the film industry admitted, because glamorizing them gives the wrong idea to kids. But the glamorization of firearms, which is far more dangerous, continues. Today, even female stars who otherwise consider themselves politically aware will model in sexualized poses with guns. Ads for the new movie *Goodbye Lover* show star Patricia Arquette nearly nude, with very little between her and the viewer but her handgun.

But doesn't video violence merely depict a stark reality against which the young need be warned? American society is far too violent, yet the forms of brutality highlighted in the movies and on television—predominantly "thrill" killings and serial murders—are pure distortion. Nearly 99 percent of real murders result from robberies, drug deals, and domestic disputes; figures from research affiliated with the FBI's behavioral sciences division show an average of only about thirty serial or "thrill" murders nationally per year. Thirty is plenty horrifying enough, but, at this point, each of the major networks and movie studios alone depicts more "thrill" and serial murders annually than that. By endlessly exploiting the notion of the "thrill" murder, Hollywood and television present to the young an entirely imaginary image of a society in which killing for pleasure is a common event. The publishing industry, including some TNR [*The New Republic*] advertisers, also distorts for profit the frequency of "thrill" murders.

The profitability of violent cinema is broadly dependent on the "down-rating" of films—movies containing extreme violence being rated only R instead of NC-17 (the new name for X)—and the lax enforcement of age restrictions regarding movies. Teens are the best market segment for Hollywood: when moviemakers claim their violent movies are not meant to appeal to teens, they are simply lying. The millionaire status of actors, directors, and studio heads—and the returns of the mutual funds that invest in movie companies—depends on not restricting teen access to theaters or film rentals. Studios in effect control the movie ratings board and endlessly lobby it not to label extreme violence with an NC-17, the only form of rating that is actually enforced. *Natural Born Killers*, for example, received an R following Time-Warner lobbying, despite its repeated close-up murders and one charming scene in which the stars kidnap a high school girl and argue about whether it would be more fun to kill her before or after raping her. Since its inception, the movie ratings board has put its most restrictive rating on any realistic representation of lovemaking, while sanctioning ever-more-graphic depictions of murder and torture. In economic terms, the board's pro-violence bias gives studios an incentive to present more death and mayhem, confident that ratings officials will smile with approval.

8

When R-and-X battles were first fought, intellectual sentiment regarded the ratings system as a way of blocking the young from seeing films with political content, such as *Easy Rider*, or discouraging depictions of sexuality; ratings were perceived as the rubes' counterattack against cinematic sophistication. But, in the 1960s, murder after murder after murder was not standard cinema fare. The most controversial violent film of that era, *A Clockwork Orange*, depicted a total of one killing, which was heard but not on-camera. (*Clockwork Orange* also had genuine political content, unlike most of today's big-studio movies.) In an era of runaway screen violence, the '60s ideal that the young should be allowed to see what they want has been corrupted. In this, trends in video mirror the misuse of liberal ideals generally.

9

Anti-censorship battles of this century were fought on firm   10
ground, advocating the right of films to tackle social and sexual issues (the 1930s Hays office forbade among other things cinematic
mention of cohabitation) and free access to works of literature such
as *Ulysses, Story of O*, and the original version of Norman Mailer's *The
Naked and the Dead*. Struggles against censors established that sup-
pression of film or writing is wrong.

But to say that nothing should be censored is very different   11
from saying that everything should be shown. Today, Hollywood
and television have twisted the First Amendment concept that occasional repulsive or worthless expression must be protected, so as
to guarantee freedom for works of genuine political content or
artistic merit, into a new standard in which constitutional freedoms are employed mainly to safeguard works that make no pre-
tense of merit. In the new standard, the bulk of what's being protected is repulsive or worthless, with the meritorious work the rare
exception.

Not only is there profit for the performers, producers, manage-   12
ment, and shareholders of films that glorify violence, so, too, is there
profit for politicians. Many conservative or Republican politicians
who denounce Hollywood eagerly accept its lucre. Bob Dole's 1995
anti-Hollywood speech was not followed up by any anti-Hollywood
legislation or campaign-funds strategy. After the Colorado murders,
President Clinton declared, "Parents should take this moment to ask
what else they can do to shield children from violent images and experiences that warp young perceptions." But Clinton was careful to
avoid criticizing Hollywood, one of the top sources of public back-
ing and campaign contributions for him and his would-be successor,
Vice President Al Gore. The president had nothing specific to propose on film violence—only that parents should try to figure out
what to do.

When television producers say it is the parents' obligation to   13
keep children away from the tube, they reach the self-satire point of
warning that their own product is unsuitable for consumption. The
situation will improve somewhat beginning in 2000, by which time
all new TVs must be sold with the "V chip"—supported by Clinton

and Gore—which will allow parents to block violent shows. But it will be at least a decade before the majority of the nation's sets include the chip, and who knows how adept young minds will prove at defeating it? Rather than relying on a technical fix that will take many years to achieve an effect, TV producers could simply stop churning out the gratuitous violence. Television could dramatically reduce its output of scenes of killing and still depict violence in news broadcasts, documentaries, and the occasional show in which the horrible is genuinely relevant. Reduction in violence is not censorship; it is placing social responsibility before profit.

The movie industry could practice the same kind of restraint   14 without sacrificing profitability. In this regard, the big Hollywood studios, including Disney, look craven and exploitative compared to, of all things, the porn-video industry. Repulsive material occurs in underground porn, but, in the products sold by the mainstream triple-X distributors such as Vivid Video (the MGM of the erotica business), violence is never, ever, ever depicted—because that would be irresponsible. Women and men perform every conceivable explicit act in today's mainstream porn, but what is shown is always consensual and almost sunnily friendly. Scenes of rape or sexual menace never occur, and scenes of sexual murder are an absolute taboo.

It is beyond irony that today Sony and Time-Warner eagerly   15 market explicit depictions of women being raped, sexually assaulted, and sexually murdered, while the mainstream porn industry would never dream of doing so. But, if money is all that matters, the point here is that mainstream porn is violence-free and yet risqué and highly profitable. Surely this shows that Hollywood could voluntarily step back from the abyss of glorifying violence and still retain its edge and its income. . . .

Meaning and Purpose

1. According to Easterbrook, why does media violence negatively affect children and not normal adults?

2. How does the author counter the contention of *The New York Times* that the media cannot be blamed for post–World War II mass killings by the young (paragraph 4)? How effective is his counter-assertion?
3. In paragraph 12, Easterbrook implies that politicians do little or nothing about Hollywood violence because they accept money from the movie industry. What might be some other reasons nothing is done?
4. Easterbrook says the TV and movie industries would be more socially responsible if they would reduce the amount of violence in their programs and films (paragraphs 13 and 14). What solutions does he offer for the problem he presents?
5. According to Easterbrook, in what way is the video pornography industry morally superior to the regular movie industry?

Strategy

1. In what specific ways do the first two paragraphs contribute to Easterbrook's argument?
2. In what ways does the citing of Leonard Eron (paragraph 3) and John Lott Jr. (paragraph 4) bolster Easterbrook's argument?
3. What does Easterbrook imply is the underlying reason that movie ratings give more leeway to extreme violence than to explicit sex (paragraph 8)? How do his points here connect to his later points about sex and violence?
4. Why were the battles against earlier media censorship worthwhile, whereas those now aren't?

Style

1. Why does Easterbrook use the word "normative" rather than "normal" in paragraph 3?
2. Look up the following in a dictionary: *calculus* (paragraph 2); *correlates, felonies, normative* (3); *advent* (4); *sanctimony* (5); *virile* (6); *meritorious* (11); *lucre* (12); *adept, gratuitous* (13); *craven* (14).

Writing Tasks

1. Easterbrook's point of view about media violence is diametrically opposed to Gerard Jones's in "Violent Media Is Good for Kids (preceding this essay). Write a paper in which you argue for Easterbrook's point of view, for Jones's point of view, or for a point of view somewhere in the middle. In whatever approach you take, be sure to cite both authors in your essay.

2. In his argument against media violence, Easterbrook offers no practical solutions on how to deal with the problems he presents. Write an essay in which you either offer some solutions for the problems or argue that nothing should be done. Be sure to cite outside sources in your argument from both the library and the Internet, as well as from Easterbrook's essay itself.

❦ Responding to Photographs ❦

Persuasion and Argument

Saturday Morning—USA

What is the impact of television violence on children? Does television violence cause aggressive behavior? Research has not conclusively proven that it does or does not teach children to use force or violence in their relationships with other children. But most researchers agree that when children watch hours of television they participate in "imitative learning" or "modeling." In simple terms, watching television creates a "monkey-see, monkey-do" effect.

Research has even shown that one-time exposure to televised aggressive behavior can be repeated in children's play by as many as 88 percent of the children who have seen it. Moreover, a single experience viewing a dramatic aggressive act can be recalled and reenacted by children six months after the viewing. Earlier studies indicate that the average child between 5 and 15 will witness during this ten-year period the violent deaths of more than 13,400 humans. Surely the accumulated impact of television violence must influence monkey-see, monkey-do behavior. Or does it?

"Saturday Morning—USA" captures a moment when television generates "imitative learning." Drawing on details from the photograph and from the discussion here, compose an argument based on one of the following assignments. Before beginning your first draft, reread the material at the beginning of the chapter to review the conventions of a sound argument.

1. Compose an inductive or deductive argument that leads your reader to conclude that children should be prevented from watching television violence. Here are a few suggestions to get you started. Include a description of "Saturday Morning—USA" that leads to the conclusion that television has a powerful modeling effect. You might also include some of your own observations of children modeling violent television behavior. You might then point out what research suggests about the effect of television violence on play, thus leading your reader to an obvious conclusion.

2. Compose an inductive or deductive essay that takes the opposing position called for in option 1; that is, the viewing of television violence should not be curtailed because it, like all television viewing, stimulates creative play. Here are a few suggestions to get you started. In this approach, you will describe the contents of "Saturday Morning—USA" but interpret the photograph as an indication that television stimulates imaginative play, not actual violent behavior. You might also draw on your own experience modeling television violence during play, but point out that you and your friends are not criminals or violent people. You might state and agree with the research alluded to in the opening discussion of the writing task, but you would interpret it in a way that supports your point; that is, modeling is a powerful teacher, but children have the ability to separate television behavior from reality.

❦ Additional Writing Tasks ❦
Persuasion and Argument

1. Write an argument in which you express one of your own deeply felt opinions. If the subject you select has undergone extensive public discussion, assume that your reader is familiar with the general elements of the debate, and develop specific evidence based on your own observations, reading, and experience. Use the following list to stimulate your thinking, but do not feel bound by the subjects.
    a. Fraternities
    b. Sororities
    c. Hiring quotas
    d. Euthanasia
    e. Prayer in schools
    f. Giving birth control advice to teenagers
    g. Sex education
    h. Legalized drugs
    i. Capital punishment
    j. Smoking in public buildings
    k. Public profanity
    l. Disruptive behavior in public places
    m. Requiring people on public assistance to work for the city
    n. Animal rights
    o. Student code of conduct
    p. Violence on television
    q. Movie ratings
    r. Subliminal messages in music
    s. Emotional advertising in political campaigns
    t. Censorship

2. Plastic disposable diapers are becoming a significant problem. Each year Americans toss approximately eighteen billion diapers—containing an estimated 2.8 million tons of excrement and urine—in the trash. Every one of these disposable diapers takes up to five hundred years to decompose. Aside from the solid waste issue, there are also growing concerns about infectious material seeping into our soil and ground water, wasted natural resources, the rising

costs of diaper production, "disposal," and increasing risks of severe rashes and toxic shock syndrome in children.

Write an argument essay in opposition to disposable diapers. Direct your essay to new parents.

3. Many people find junk mail entertaining, something to thumb through during a leisure moment. You, however, believe that junk mail is not only a nuisance but also a hazard. For example, all the junk mail you receive this year will have consumed the equivalent of one and a half trees. One year's junk mail sent in the United States amounts to a hundred million trees.

   Write an essay arguing against junk mail. Here are some commonly known facts you might want to use:
   a. Almost two million tons of junk mail are sent each year.
   b. Over 40 percent of all junk mail is never opened.
   c. Junk mail receives special postage rates—currently 10.1 cents per piece if arranged in presorted batches.
   d. The average American will spend eight months of his or her life just opening junk mail.
   e. The junk mail sent to a million people means the destruction of 1.5 million trees.

4. A radical counterculture has emerged in Germany's inner cities. They are the *autonomen*, a term that means the same as "autonomous" in English. The *autonomen*, who wear masks at demonstrations, are composed of squatters and street people. They see themselves as the last hope of revolutionary activism. The group refuses to participate in any political or social system, and its brand of activism is usually spontaneous, unorganized, and often violent.

   The *autonomen* have no counterpart on the American social scene, but some social psychologists predict that our government's failure to solve the problems of homelessness, drug abuse, and street gangs will lead to the formation of groups like the *autonomen* to express the anger and alienation the inner-city underclass already feels.

   Write an essay in which you argue that inner-city life must be improved or city governments will soon be dealing with groups like Germany's *autonomen*. You might begin by using the *Readers' Guide to Periodical Literature* to find background information on these groups.

14

The Reflective Essay

Combining the Modes to Explore Personal Experience

As we've indicated throughout the text, not all essays fall into neat patterns—that is, they are not always arranged in a thesis-support pattern, and they cannot be easily classified as description, narration, examples, comparison and contrast, cause and effect, and so on. In actual practice, most writers employ a mixture of development patterns, depending on what they need to accomplish in a particular passage. If you, for example, were critiquing a novel, your essay would probably include narration, as you would have to represent the plot; description, to create a feel for the characters; cause and effect, to show the relationship among events; comparison, to relate the work to other works; and argument, to convince your reader of the novel's merit. You would therefore be mixing development patterns.

Do you recall what else we wrote when defining the essay? That essays can also do more than convey information. Essays can be impressionistic or exploratory and they can express personal feelings or attitudes based on a writer's experience. Such essays usually, though not necessarily, abandon a subject-thesis structure. Moreover, they are often distinguished from other essays because they have stood the test of time. That is, they've come to be appreciated as works of the imagination, not because they are fictions—they are not—but because they open the world for readers, much as poetry opens the world. We choose to call such essays *reflective essays*. If you like to lean on definitions, you can think of the reflective essay as a short nonfiction composition that explores from a subjective perspective a topic that shapes itself out of deep personal experience.

Let us be a little more specific. Here are some common characteristics of reflective essays.

Meaning and Purpose

Reflective essays often grow out of a writer's curiosity. Writers use their loose structure to explore subjects that mystify them. The reflective essay allows them to probe their own knowledge and to reflect on various aspects of whatever makes them curious. As a result of this process, reflective essays tend to be open-ended—that is, writers will not necessarily clarify what an issue means. It is up to the reader to interpret the essay. So there is meaning and there is purpose, but they are never packaged in a neatly phrased sentence.

Strategy

Given the personal character of the reflective essay, writers tend to place themselves in the foreground. They want it to be very clear that their essays are written by living, breathing human beings. They also tend, but not always, to write as if they are casually conversing with their readers. Often a reflective essay follows the twists and turns of a casual conversation, the writer's thought unspooling onto the page.

This tendency to present the mind at work, or perhaps at play, affects the structure of most reflective essays. Indeed, they may march straight ahead from beginning to end—many of them do—but more frequently, they find their own way, that is, they have their own unique structure. Memory is the fuel for reflection, and memory fuels many reflective essays, too. While our lives move to the relentless tick-tock-tick-tock of the clock, our minds graze in the meadows of the past and transcend time by projecting into the future. Reflective essays, then, do not fall neatly into formulaic structures. Each essay requires a new strategy.

Style

It is style that truly distinguishes reflective essays. Style—we all know what it is when we see it, but to explain it is another matter. This is where you as a reader need to develop an ear for writing. Odd, isn't it, to develop an inner ear that *hears* words on the page?

Style involves a distinctive use of words, sentences, and figurative language. But perhaps the single characteristic that reflective essays share is a unique tone, or voice. Each writer has a unique voice, a quality that speaks in your mind, that whispers beneath the page, an aural signature that, once identified, will never be mistaken for any other voice.

Many of the essays in the earlier chapters are distinguished by voice and embody exceptional imaginative qualities, such as Maxine Hong Kingston's "Photographs of My Parents" and Amy Tan's "Mother Tongue." Review them and others, listen to their voices, and figure out how the writers are able to create a distinctive tone.

Essayists must develop a voice. It does not come naturally, but only with desire, effort, and experience. To begin, the writers must have the burning desire to learn about themselves by recasting their experience into written language. Few of us come willingly to writing, but those who do come to it with a passion, as if an irresistible force draws them to paper, pen in hand. Then they must write—and write a lot. Writing is somewhat like playing a musical instrument. Maybe the novice can play a few notes in sequence, but that's not *real* playing. Real playing takes years of practice for no other purpose but to play well and distinctively.

To give you a taste of reflective essays, we've selected several writers who are generally considered to be accomplished at the essay form. Read them with care, keeping in mind the loose characteristics of the reflective essay.

❦ George Orwell ❦

George Orwell, whose real name was Eric Arthur Blair, was born in India in 1903 and died in England in 1950. While attending Eton, a famous English preparatory school, he published his first writings in college periodicals. Instead of accepting a scholarship to a university, he followed his family's tradition by going to Burma (now Myanmar), where he served in the Indian Imperial Police. Orwell recounted his experiences in Burma and his unfavorable opinions of imperial rule in two famous autobiographical essays, "Shooting an Elephant" and "A Hanging," later reprinted in Orwell's collection, Shooting an Elephant and Other Essays *(1950). Both are recognized as prose classics. In 1927, Orwell decided to live in England, noting that the barriers of race and caste had kept him from mingling with the Burmese. Orwell's first novel,* Burmese Days, *portrays a sensitive person who is emotionally isolated and at odds with an oppressive or dishonest political atmosphere. Orwell was a democratic socialist all his life, but in 1937, after having fought in the Spanish Civil War with the communists against the fascist forces, he returned to England with a lifelong dread of totalitarianism. Orwell's* Animal Farm, *a fierce satire of totalitarianism, made him famous and, for the first time in his life, prosperous. His essay "Politics and the English Language" explores the ways that language is used to conceal political realities. His last novel,* 1984, *which warns about the great dangers of totalitarianism, is Orwell's best-known work.*

A Hanging

This essay seems simple on the surface; however, it deals deeply with the complexities of George Orwell's personal involvement in the British occupation of India in the early part of the last century. A straightforward chronological narrative, "A Hanging" illustrates Orwell's deep sympathy for the oppressed in society.

Notice how Orwell uses simple, understated language to convey the political and social contrasts between the natives and the imperialists.

Notice also how the essay's presentation is calm, a seeming combination of newspaper reportage and objective commentary, a strategy that emphasizes the horror of the event.

Notice the ways in which the essay's narrator gradually comes to see the hideousness of what is occurring.

It was in Burma, a sodden morning of the rains. A sickly light, like yellow tinfoil, was slanting over the high walls into the jail yard. We were waiting outside the condemned cells, a row of sheds fronted with double bars, like small animal cages. Each cell measured about ten feet by ten and was quite bare within except for a plank bed and a pot for drinking water. In some of them brown, silent men were squatting at the inner bars, with their blankets draped round them. These were the condemned men, due to be hanged within the next week or two.

One prisoner had been brought out of his cell. He was a Hindu, a puny wisp of a man, with a shaven head and vague liquid eyes. He had a thick, sprouting mustache, absurdly too big for his body, rather like the mustache of a comic man on the films. Six tall Indian warders were guarding him and getting him ready for the gallows. Two of them stood by with rifles and fixed bayonets, while the others handcuffed him, passed a chain through his handcuffs and fixed it to their belts, and lashed his arms tight to his sides. They crowded very close about him, with their hands always on him in a careful, caressing grip, as though all the while feeling him to make sure he was there. It was like men handling a fish which is still alive and may jump back into the water. But he stood quite unresisting, yielding his arms limply to the ropes, as though he hardly noticed what was happening.

Eight o'clock struck and a bugle call, desolately thin in the wet air, floated from the distant barracks. The superintendent of the jail, who was standing apart from the rest of us, moodily prodding the gravel with his stick, raised his head at the sound. He was an army doctor, with a grey toothbrush mustache and a gruff voice. "For

God's sake, hurry up, Francis," he said irritably. "The man ought to have been dead by this time. Aren't you ready yet?"

Francis, the head jailer, a fat Dravidian in a white drill suit and gold   4
spectacles, waved his black hand. "Yes sir, yes sir," he bubbled. "All iss satisfactorily prepared. The hangman iss waiting. We shall proceed."

"Well, quick march, then. The prisoners can't get their breakfast   5
till this job's over."

We set out for the gallows. Two warders marched on either side   6
of the prisoner, with their rifles at the slope; two others marched close against him, gripping him by arm and shoulder, as though at once pushing and supporting him. The rest of us, magistrates and the like, followed behind. Suddenly, when we had gone ten yards, the procession stopped short without any order or warning. A dreadful thing had happened—a dog, come goodness knows whence, had appeared in the yard. It came bounding among us with a loud volley of barks and leapt around us wagging its whole body, wild with glee at finding so many human beings together. It was a large woolly dog, half Airedale, half pariah. For a moment it pranced around us, and then, before anyone could stop it, it had made a dash for the prisoner, and jumping up tried to lick his face. Everybody stood aghast, too taken aback even to grab the dog.

"Who let that bloody brute in here?" said the superintendent an-   7
grily. "Catch it, someone!"

A warder detached from the escort, charged clumsily after the   8
dog, but it danced and gambolled just out of his reach, taking everything as part of the game. A young Eurasian jailer picked up a handful of gravel and tried to stone the dog away, but it dodged the stones and came after us again. Its yaps echoed from the jail walls. The prisoner, in the grasp of the two warders, looked on incuriously, as though this was another formality of the hanging. It was several minutes before someone managed to catch the dog. Then we put my handkerchief through its collar and moved off once more, with the dog still straining and whimpering.

It was about forty yards to the gallows. I watched the bare   9
brown back of the prisoner marching in front of me. He walked clumsily with his bound arms, but quite steadily, with that bobbing

gait of the Indian who never straightens his knees. At each step his muscles slid neatly into place, the lock of hair on his scalp danced up and down, his feet printed themselves on the wet gravel. And once, in spite of the men who gripped him by each shoulder, he stepped lightly aside to avoid a puddle on the path.

It is curious; but till that moment I had never realized what it   10
means to destroy a healthy, conscious man. When I saw the prisoner step aside to avoid the puddle, I saw the mystery, the unspeakable wrongness, of cutting a life short when it is in full tide. This man was not dying, he was alive just as we are alive. All the organs of his body were working—bowels digesting food, skin renewing itself, nails growing, tissues forming—all toiling away in solemn foolery. His nails would still be growing when he stood on the drop, when he was falling through the air with a tenth-of-a-second to live. His eyes saw the yellow gravel and the grey walls, and his brain still remembered, foresaw, reasoned—even about puddles. He and we were a party of men walking together, seeing, hearing, feeling, understanding the same world; and in two minutes, with a sudden snap, one of us would be gone—one mind less, one world less.

The gallows stood in a small yard, separate from the main   11
grounds of the prison, and overgrown with tall prickly weeds. It was a brick erection like three sides of a shed, with planking on top, and above that two beams and a crossbar with the rope dangling. The hangman, a greyhaired convict in the white uniform of the prison, was waiting beside his machine. He greeted us with a servile crouch as we entered. At a word from Francis the two warders, gripping the prisoner more closely than ever, half led, half pushed him to the gallows and helped him clumsily up the ladder. Then the hangman climbed up and fixed the rope around the prisoner's neck.

We stood waiting, five yards away. The warders had formed in a   12
rough circle round the gallows. And then, when the noose was fixed, the prisoner began crying out to his god. It was a high, reiterated cry of "Ram! Ram! Ram! Ram!" not urgent and fearful like a prayer or cry for help, but steady, rhythmical, almost like the tolling of a bell. The dog answered the sound with a whine. The hangman, still standing on the gallows, produced a small cotton bag like a flour bag and drew it down over the prisoner's face. But the sound, muffled by the

cloth, still persisted, over and over again: "Ram! Ram! Ram! Ram! Ram!"

The hangman climbed down and stood ready, holding the lever. 13 Minutes seemed to pass. The steady, muffled crying from the prisoner went on and on, "Ram! Ram! Ram!" never faltering for an instant. The superintendent, his head on his chest, was slowly poking the ground with his stick; perhaps he was counting the cries, allowing the prisoner a fixed number—fifty, perhaps, or a hundred. Everyone had changed colour. The Indians had gone grey like bad coffee, and one or two of the bayonets were wavering. We looked at the lashed, hooded man on the drop, and listened to his cries—each cry another second of life; the same thought was in all our minds; oh, kill him quickly, get it over, stop that abominable noise!

Suddenly the superintendent made up his mind. Throwing up 14 his head he made a swift motion with his stick. "Chalo!" he shouted almost fiercely.

There was a clanking noise, and then dead silence. The prisoner 15 had vanished, and the rope was twisting on itself. I let go of the dog, and it galloped immediately to the back of the gallows; but when it got there it stopped short, barked, and then retreated into a corner of the yard, where it stood among the weeds, looking timorously out at us. We went round the gallows to inspect the prisoner's body. He was dangling with his toes pointed straight downwards, very slowly revolving, as dead as a stone.

The superintendent reached out with his stick and poked the 16 bare brown body; it oscillated slightly. "*He's* all right," said the superintendent. He backed out from under the gallows, and blew out a deep breath. The moody look had gone out of his face quite suddenly. He glanced at his wrist-watch. "Eight minutes past eight. Well, that's all for this morning, thank God."

The warders unfixed bayonets and marched away. The dog, 17 sobered and conscious of having misbehaved itself, slipped after them. We walked out of the gallows yard, past the condemned cells with their waiting prisoners, into the big central yard of the prison. The convicts, under the command of warders armed with lathis, were already receiving their breakfast. They squatted in long rows, each man holding a tin pannikin, while two warders with buckets marched around ladling out rice; it seemed quite a homely, jolly scene, after the hanging. An enormous relief had come upon us now that the job was done. One felt an impulse to sing, to break into a run, to snigger. All at once everyone began chattering gaily.

The Eurasian boy walking beside me nodded towards the way   18
we had come, with a knowing smile: "Do you know, sir, our friend (he meant the dead man) when he heard his appeal had been dismissed, he pissed on the floor of his cell. From fright. Kindly take one of my cigarettes, sir. Do you not admire my new silver case, sir? From the boxwallah, two rupees eight annas. Classy European style."

Several people laughed—at what, nobody seemed certain.   19

Francis was walking by the superintendent, talking garrulously: 20
"Well, sir, all has passed off with the utmost satisfactoriness. It was all finished—flick! Like that. It iss not always so—oah, no! I have known cases where the doctor was obliged to go beneath the gallows and pull the prissoner's legs to ensure decease. Most disagreeable!"

"Wriggling about, eh? That's bad," said the superintendent.   21

"Ach, sir, it iss worse when they become refractory! One man, I   22
recall, clung to the bars of hiss cage when we went to take him out. You will scarcely credit, sir, that it took six warders to dislodge him, three pulling at each leg. We reasoned with him, 'My dear fellow,' we said, 'think of all the pain and trouble you are causing to us!' But no, he would not listen! Ach, he wass very troublesome!"

I found that I was laughing quite loudly. Everyone was laughing.   23
Even the superintendent grinned in a tolerant way. "You'd better all come out and have a drink," he said quite genially. "I've got a bottle of whisky in the car. We could do with it."

We went through the big double gates of the prison into the   24
road. "Pulling at his legs!" exclaimed a Burmese magistrate suddenly, and burst into a loud chuckling. We all began laughing again. At that moment Francis' anecdote seemed extraordinarily funny. We all had a drink together, native and European alike, quite amicably. The dead man was a hundred yards away.

❦ E. B. White ❦

Known to nearly all readers as simply "E. B. White," Elway Brooks White (1899–1985) was one of America's greatest essayists. After being graduated from Cornell University in 1921, E. B. White was a reporter and freelance writer before joining The New Yorker *magazine in 1927 as a writer and contributing editor. His three books for children,* Stuart Little, Charlotte's Web, *and* The Trumpet of the Swan, *are considered classics. Among professional writers, however, he may be best known for having revised and published* The Elements of Style, *a text originally written by William Strunk, Jr., under whom White had studied at Cornell. That small work has become a standard style manual for writing in the English language. If a manual on style can be said to have a thesis, the thesis of* The Elements of Style *is that no one-to-one relationship exists between big words and good writing. On the contrary, the best words are those that combine in sentences to convey their messages to the readers, while they themselves do not intrude. Good writers write to inform, not to impress; good writers are not theatrically serious. In his foreword to* Essays of E. B. White, *White wrote that the essayist "can pull on any sort of shirt, be any sort of person, according to his mood or his subject matter—philosopher, scold, jester, raconteur, confidant, pundit, devil's advocate, enthusiast." At one time or another in White's writing career, he was each of these.*

Once More to the Lake

This essay was first published in Harper's *in 1941 and collected in* One Man's Meat *(1944). In the essay, E. B. White uses the force of reminiscence to add grace and vitality to the meticulous description of a recent event, which to most readers is common enough: a fishing trip to a lake by a father and his young son.*

However, as you read this essay, notice that the details meld in time: What is recorded of the trip blends with White's memories of his own boyhood experiences at the same lake.

Also notice how White eases naturally from time present to time past, and then forward to time present, and then back to time past. Once readers are made aware of these time shifts, they seem

*self-evident. But most hurried readers are apt to miss them, so well
does White deal with transitions.*

    *Notice, too, how the essay eases from a reminiscence about tak-
ing his young son on a fishing trip to the shock of recognition that the
essayist is growing old.*

August 1941

    One summer, along about 1904, my father rented a camp on a   1
lake in Maine and took us all there for the month of August. We all
got ringworm from some kittens and had to rub Pond's Extract on
our arms and legs night and morning, and my father rolled over in a
canoe with all his clothes on; but outside of that the vacation was a
success and from then on none of us ever thought there was any
place in the world like that lake in Maine. We returned summer after
summer—always on August 1 for one month. I have since become a
salt-water man, but sometimes in summer there are days when the
restlessness of the tides and the fearful cold of the sea water and the
incessant wind that blows across the afternoon and into the evening
make me wish for the placidity of a lake in the woods. A few weeks
ago this feeling got so strong I bought myself a couple of bass hooks
and a spinner and returned to the lake where we used to go, for a
week's fishing and to revisit old haunts.

    I took along my son, who had never had any fresh water up his   2
nose and who had seen lily pads only from train windows. On the
journey over to the lake I began to wonder what it would be like. I
wondered how time would have marred this unique, this holy
spot—the coves and streams, the hills that the sun set behind, the
camps and the paths behind the camps. I was sure that the tarred
road would have found it out, and I wondered in what other ways it
would be desolated. It is strange how much you can remember
about places like that once you allow your mind to return into the
grooves that lead back. You remember one thing, and that suddenly
reminds you of another thing. I guess I remembered clearest of all
the early mornings, when the lake was cool and motionless, remembered how the bedroom smelled of the lumber it was made of and

of the wet woods whose scent entered through the screen. The partitions in the camp were thin and did not extend clear to the top of the rooms, and as I was always the first up I would dress softly so as not to wake the others, and sneak out into the sweet outdoors and start out in the canoe, keeping close along the shore in the long shadows of the pines. I remembered being very careful never to rub my paddle against the gunwale for fear of disturbing the stillness of the cathedral.

The lake had never been what you would call a wild lake. There   3
were cottages sprinkled around the shores, and it was in farming country although the shores of the lake were quite heavily wooded. Some of the cottages were owned by nearby farmers, and you would live at the shore and eat your meals at the farmhouse. That's what our family did. But although it wasn't wild, it was a fairly large and undisturbed lake and there were places in it that, to a child at least, seemed infinitely remote and primeval.

I was right about the tar; it led to within half a mile of the shore.   4
But when I got back there, with my boy, and we settled into a camp near a farmhouse and into the kind of summertime I had known, I could tell that it was going to be pretty much the same as it had been before—I knew it, lying in bed the first morning, smelling the bedroom and hearing the boy sneak quietly out and go off along the shore in a boat. I began to sustain the illusion that he was I, and therefore, by simple transposition, that I was my father. This sensation persisted, kept cropping up all the time we were there. It was not an entirely new feeling, but in this setting it grew much stronger. I seemed to be living a dual existence. I would be in the middle of some simple act, I would be picking up a bait box or laying down a table fork, or I would be saying something, and suddenly it would be not I but my father who was saying the words or making the gesture. It gave me a creepy sensation.

We went fishing the first morning. I felt the same damp moss   5
covering the worms in the bait can, and saw the dragonfly alight on the tip of my rod as it hovered a few inches from the surface of the water. It was the arrival of this fly that convinced me beyond any doubt that everything was as it always had been, that the years were a mirage and that there had been no years. The small waves were the same, chucking the rowboat under the chin as we fished at anchor,

and the boat was the same boat, the same color green and the ribs broken in the same places, and under the floorboards the same fresh-water leavings and débris—the dead hellgrammite, the wisps of moss, the rusty discarded fishhook, the dried blood from yesterday's catch. We stared silently at the tips of our rods, at the dragonflies that came and went. I lowered the tip of mine into the water, tentatively, pensively dislodging the fly, which darted two feet away, poised, darted two feet back, and came to rest again a little farther up the rod. There had been no years between the ducking of this dragonfly and the other one—the one that was part of memory. I looked at the boy, who was silently watching his fly, and it was my hands that held his rod, my eyes watching. I felt dizzy and didn't know which rod I was at the end of.

We caught two bass, hauling them in briskly as though they were mackerel, pulling them over the side of the boat in a businesslike manner without any landing net, and stunning them with a blow on the back of the head. When we got back for a swim before lunch, the lake was exactly where we had left it, the same number of inches from the dock, and there was only the merest suggestion of a breeze. This seemed an utterly enchanted sea, this lake you could leave to its own devices for a few hours and come back to, and find it had not stirred, this constant and trustworthy body of water. In the shallows, the dark, water-soaked sticks and twigs, smooth and old, were undulating in clusters on the bottom against the clean ribbed sand, and the track of the mussel was plain. A school of minnows swam by, each minnow with its small individual shadow, doubling the attendance, so clear and sharp in the sunlight. Some of the other campers were in swimming, along the shore, one of them with a cake of soap, and the water felt thin and clear and unsubstantial. Over the years there had been this person with the cake of soap, this cultist, and here he was. There had been no years.

Up to the farmhouse to dinner through the teeming, dusty field, the road under our sneakers was only a two-track road. The middle track was missing, the one with the marks of the hooves and the splotches of dried, flaky manure. There had always been three tracks to choose from in choosing which track to walk in; now the choice was narrowed down to two. For a moment I missed terribly the

middle alternative. But the way led past the tennis court, and something about the way it lay there in the sun reassured me; the tape had
loosened along the backline, the alleys were green with plantains
and other weeds, and the net (installed in June and removed in September) sagged in the dry noon, and the whole place steamed with
midday heat and hunger and emptiness. There was a choice of pie
for dessert, and one was blueberry and one was apple, and the waitresses were the same country girls, there having been no passage of
time, only the illusion of it as in a dropped curtain—the waitresses
were still fifteen; their hair had been washed, that was the only
difference—they had been to the movies and seen the pretty girls
with the clean hair.

Summertime, oh summertime, pattern of life indelible, the fade-   8
proof lake, the woods unshatterable, the pasture with the sweetfern
and the juniper forever and ever, summer without end; this was the
background, and the life along the shore was the design, their tiny
docks with the flagpole and the American flag floating against the
white clouds in the blue sky, the little paths over the roots of
the trees leading from camp to camp and the paths leading back to
the outhouses and the can of lime for sprinkling, and at the souvenir
counters at the store the miniature birch-bark canoes and the post-
cards that showed things looking a little better than they looked.
This was the American family at play, escaping the city heat, wondering whether the newcomers in the camp at the head of the cove were
"common" or "nice," wondering whether it was true that the people
who drove up for Sunday dinner at the farmhouse were turned away
because there wasn't enough chicken.

It seemed to me, as I kept remembering all this, that those times   9
and those summers had been infinitely precious and worth saving.
There had been jollity and peace and goodness. The arriving (at the
beginning of August) had been so big a business in itself, at the rail-
way station the farm wagon drawn up, the first smell of the pine-
laden air, the first glimpse of the smiling farmer, and the great importance of the trunks and your father's enormous authority in such
matters, and the feel of the wagon under you for the long ten-mile
haul, and at the top of the last long hill catching the first view of the
lake after eleven months of not seeing this cherished body of water.

The shouts and cries of the other campers when they saw you, and the trunks to be unpacked, to give up their rich burden. (Arriving was less exciting nowadays, when you sneaked up in your car and parked it under a tree near the camp and took out the bags and in five minutes it was all over, no fuss, no loud wonderful fuss about trunks.)

Peace and goodness and jollity. The only thing that was wrong now, really, was the sound of the place, an unfamiliar nervous sound of the outboard motors. This was the note that jarred, the one thing that would sometimes break the illusion and set the years moving. In those other summertimes all the motors were inboard; and when they were at a little distance, the noise they made was a sedative, an ingredient of summer sleep. They were one-cylinder and two-cylinder engines, and some were make-and-break and some were jump-spark, but they all made a sleepy sound across the lake. The one-lungers throbbed and fluttered, and the twin-cylinder ones purred and purred, and that was a quiet sound, too. But now the campers all had outboards. In the daytime, in the hot mornings, these motors made a petulant, irritable sound; at night, in the still evening when the afterglow lit the water, they whined about one's ears like mosquitoes. My boy loved our rented outboard, and his great desire was to achieve single-handed mastery over it, and authority, and he soon learned the trick of choking it a little (but not too much), and the adjustment of the needle valve. Watching him I would remember the things you could do with the old one-cylinder engine with the heavy flywheel, how you could have it eating out of your hand if you got really close to it spiritually. Motorboats in those days didn't have clutches, and you would make a landing by shutting off the motor at the proper time and coasting in with a dead rudder. But there was a way of reversing them, if you learned the trick, by cutting the switch and putting it on again exactly on the final dying revolution of the fly-wheel, so that it would kick back against the compression and begin reversing. Approaching a dock in a strong following breeze, it was difficult to slow up sufficiently by the ordinary coasting method, and if a boy felt he had complete mastery over his motor, he was tempted to keep it running beyond its time and then reverse it a few feet from the dock. It took a cool nerve, because if you threw the switch a twentieth of a second too soon you would catch the flywheel when it still had speed enough to go up past center, and the boat would leap ahead, charging bull-fashion at the dock.

We had a good week at camp. The bass were biting well and the sun shown endlessly, day after day. We would be tired at night and lie down in the accumulated heat of the little bedrooms after the long hot day and the breeze would stir almost imperceptibly outside and the smell of the swamp drift in through the rusty screens. Sleep would come easily and in the morning the red squirrel would be on the roof, tapping out his gay routine. I kept remembering everything, lying in bed in the mornings—the small steamboat that had a long rounded stern like the lip of a Ubangi, and how quietly she ran on the moonlight sails, when the older boys played their mandolins and the girls sang and we ate doughnuts dipped in sugar, and how sweet the music was on the water in the shining night, and what it had felt like to think about girls then. After breakfast we would go up to the store and the things were in the same place—the minnows in a bottle, the plugs and spinners disarranged and pawed over by the youngsters from the boys' camp, the Fig Newtons and the Beeman's gum. Outside, the road was tarred and cars stood in front of the store. Inside, all was just as it had always been, except there was more Coca-Cola and not so much Moxie and root beer and birch beer and sarsaparilla. We would walk out with the bottle of pop apiece and sometimes the pop would backfire up our noses and hurt. We explored the streams, quietly, where the turtles slid off the sunny logs and dug their way into the soft bottom; and we lay on the town wharf and fed worms to the tame bass. Everywhere we went I had trouble making out which I was, the one walking at my side, the one walking in my pants.

One afternoon while we were there at that lake a thunderstorm came up. It was like the revival of an old melodrama that I had seen long ago with childish awe. The second-act climax of the drama of the electrical disturbance over a lake in America had not changed in any important respect. This was the big scene, still the big scene. The whole thing was so familiar, the first feeling of oppression and heat and a general air around camp of not wanting to go very far away. In mid-afternoon (it was all the same) a curious darkening of the sky,

11

12

and a lull in everything that had made life tick; and then the way the boats suddenly swung the other way at their moorings with the coming of a breeze out of the new quarter, and the premonitory rumble. Then the kettle drum, then the snare, then the bass drum and cymbals, then crackling light against the dark, and the gods grinning and licking their chops in the hills. Afterward the calm, the rain steadily rustling in the calm lake, the return of light and hope and spirits, and the campers running out in joy and relief to go swimming in the rain, their bright cries perpetuating the deathless joke about how they were getting simply drenched, and the children screaming with delight at the new sensation of bathing in the rain, and the joke about getting drenched linking the generations in a strong indestructible chain. And the comedian who waded in carrying an umbrella.

When the others went swimming, my son said he was going in, 13 too. He pulled his dripping trunks from the line where they had hung all through the shower and wrung them out. Languidly, and with no thought of going in, I watched him, his hard little body, skinny and bare, saw him wince slightly as he pulled up around his vitals the small, soggy, icy garment. As he buckled the swollen belt, suddenly my groin felt the chill of death.

❦ Lewis Thomas ❦

Lewis Thomas (1913–1994) studied at Princeton University and Harvard Medical School. He had a distinguished career as a research pathologist, medical doctor, biologist, professor, and writer but is best known for his collections of essays, many of which first appeared in the New England Journal of Medicine. *He was professor of pathology and medicine at the Cornell University Medical School and served as both president and executive officer of the Memorial Sloan-Kettering Cancer Center in New York City. His first collection,* The Lives of a Cell: Notes of a Biology Watcher, *won the National Book Award and was followed by* The Medusa and the Snail: More Notes of a Biology Watcher, *and by his memoir,* The Youngest Science. *This he followed with three more essay collections:* Late Night Thoughts on Listening to Mahler's Ninth Symphony; Et Cetera, Et Cetera; *and* The Fragile Species.

On Natural Death

In this short essay from The Medusa and the Snail *(1979), Lewis Thomas invites the reader to consider a new way of thinking about death. His examples are taken from his own observations and from medical research, from the professional realm as well as the personal, from the extraordinary and the mundane.*

Keep in mind the essay's title as you read. Apply the title to each paragraph to determine exactly how convincing Thomas's contentions about death are.

Pay close attention to the examples Thomas uses to support his ideas. How effective are they?

Consider as you read why Thomas devotes four paragraphs to his thoughts about the details of a mouse's death and only one to the death of two soldiers.

There are so many new books about dying that there are now 1
special shelves set aside for them in bookshops, along with the
health-diet and home-repair paperbacks and the sex manuals. Some

of them are so packed with detailed information and step-by-step instructions for performing the function that you'd think this was a
new sort of skill which all of us are now required to learn. The
strongest impression the casual reader gets, leafing through, is that
proper dying has become an extraordinary, even an exotic experience, something only the specially trained get to do.

Also, you could be led to believe that we are the only creatures   2
capable of the awareness of death, that when all the rest of nature is
being cycled through dying, one generation after another, it is a different kind of process, done automatically and trivially, more "natural," as we say.

An elm in our backyard caught the blight this summer and   3
dropped stone dead, leafless, almost overnight. One weekend it was
a normal-looking elm, maybe a little bare in spots but nothing
alarming, and the next weekend it was gone, passed over, departed,
taken. Taken is right, for the tree surgeon came by yesterday with his
crew of young helpers and their cherry picker, and took it down
branch by branch and carted it off in the back of a red truck, everyone singing.

The dying of a field mouse, at the jaws of an amiable household   4
cat, is a spectacle I have beheld many times. It used to make me
wince. Early in life I gave up throwing sticks at the cat to make him
drop the mouse, because the dropped mouse regularly went ahead
and died anyway, but I always shouted unaffections at the cat to let
him know the sort of animal he had become. Nature, I thought, was
an abomination.

Recently I've done some thinking about that mouse, and I won-   5
der if his dying is necessarily all that different from the passing of our
elm. The main difference, if there is one, would be in the matter of
pain. I do not believe that an elm tree has pain receptors, and even
so, the blight seems to me a relatively painless way to go even if there
were nerve endings in a tree, which there are not. But the mouse
dangling tail-down from the teeth of a gray cat is something else
again, with pain beyond bearing, you'd think, all over his small
body.

There are now some plausible reasons for thinking it is not like   6
that at all, and you can make up an entirely different story about the

mouse and his dying if you like. At the instant of being trapped and penetrated by teeth, peptide hormones are released by cells in the hypothalamus and the pituitary gland; instantly these substances, called endorphins, are attached to the surface of other cells responsible for pain perception; the hormones have the pharmacologic properties of opium; there is no pain. Thus it is that the mouse seems always to dangle so languidly from the jaws, lies there so quietly when dropped, dies of his injuries without a struggle. If a mouse could shrug, he'd shrug.

I do not know if this is true or not, nor do I know how to prove 7 it if it is true. Maybe if you could get in there quickly enough and administer naloxone, a specific morphine antagonist, you could turn off the endorphins and observe the restoration of pain, but this is not something I would care to do or see. I think I will leave it there, as a good guess about the dying of a cat-chewed mouse, perhaps about dying in general.

Montaigne had a hunch about dying, based on his own close call 8 in a riding accident. He was so badly injured as to be believed dead by his companions, and was carried home with lamentations, "all bloody, stained all over with the blood I had thrown up." He remembers the entire episode, despite having been "dead, for two full hours," with wonderment:

> It seemed to me that my life was hanging only by the tip of my lips. I closed my eyes in order, it seemed to me, to help push it out, and took pleasure in growing languid and letting myself go. It was an idea that was only floating on the surface of my soul, as delicate and feeble as all the rest, but in truth not only free from distress but mingled with that sweet feeling that people have who have let themselves slide into sleep. I believe that this is the same state in which people find themselves whom we see fainting in the agony of death, and I maintain that we pity them without cause. . . . In order to get used to the idea of death, I find there is nothing like coming close to it.

Later, in another essay, Montaigne returns to it:

> If you know not how to die, never trouble yourself: Nature
> will in a moment fully and sufficiently instruct you; she will
> exactly do that business for you; take you no care for it.

The worst accident I've ever seen was on Okinawa, in the early   9
days of the invasion, when a jeep ran into a troop carrier and was
crushed nearly flat. Inside were two young MPs, trapped in bent
steel, both mortally hurt, with only their hands and shoulders visible. We had a conversation while people with the right tools were
prying them free. Sorry about the accident, they said. No, they said,
they felt fine. Is everyone else okay, one of them said. Well, the other
one said, no hurry now. And then they died.

Pain is useful for avoidance, for getting away when there's time   10
to get away, but when it is end game, and no way back, pain is likely
to be turned off, and the mechanisms for this are wonderfully precise
and quick. If I had to design an ecosystem in which creatures had to
live off each other and in which dying was an indispensable part of
living, I could not think of a better way to manage.

❦ Richard Selzer ❦

Richard Selzer is a surgeon who writes essays and stories, aimed at a general audience, about the practice of medicine. Born in the state of New York in 1928, he studied at Union College and Albany Medical School and later at Yale University. He subsequently taught writing at Yale and both taught and practiced surgery at the Yale University Medical School. His articles, for which he received the National Magazine Award in 1975 and an American Medical Writer's Award in 1985, have appeared in Harper's, Esquire, *and* Redbook. *He has published a book of short stories,* Rituals of Surgery, *and several collections of essays, including* Mortal Lessons: Notes on the Art of Surgery, *and* Raising the Dead: A Doctor's Encounter with His Own Mortality.

The Masked Marvel's Last Toehold

Told in the first person, this narrative reveals the anguish of a patient through the eyes of his doctor, Richard Selzer. Selzer finds himself treating a man he had seen fight in a wrestling match many years earlier, when he was a boy. The author's perspective changes as he moves from the present to the childhood memory and back again to the present. The essay is from Selzer's The Confessions of a Knife, *published in 1979.*

On the fifth floor of the hospital, in the west wing, I know that a   1
man is sitting up in his bed, waiting for me. Elihu Koontz is seventy-five, and he is diabetic. It is two weeks since I amputated his left leg just below the knee. I walk down the corridor, but I do not go straight into his room. Instead, I pause in the doorway. He is not yet aware of my presence, but gazes down at the place in the bed where his leg used to be, and where now there is the collapsed leg of his pajamas. He is totally absorbed, like an athlete appraising the details of his body. What is he thinking? I wonder. Is he dreaming the outline of his toes? Does he see there his foot's incandescent ghost? Could he be angry? Feel that I have taken from him something for which he

yearns now with all his heart? Has he forgotten so soon the pain? It was a pain so great as to set him apart from all other men, in a red-hot place where he had no kith or kin. What of those black gorilla toes and the soupy mess that was his heel? I watch him from the doorway. It is a kind of spying, I know.

Save for a white fringe open at the front, Elihu Koontz is bald.   2
The hair has grown too long and is wilted. He wears it as one would wear a day-old laurel wreath. He is naked to the waist, so that I can see his breasts. They are the breasts of Buddha, inverted triangles from which the nipples swing, dark as garnets.

I have seen enough. I step into the room, and he sees that I am   3
there.

"How did the night go, Elihu?"   4

He looks at me for a long moment. "Shut the door," he says.   5

I do, and move to the side of the bed. He takes my left hand in   6
both of his, gazes at it, turns it over, then back, fondling, at last hold-ing it up to his cheek. I do not withdraw from this loving. After a while he relinquishes my hand, and looks up at me.

"How is the pain?" I ask.   7

He does not answer, but continues to look at me in silence.   8
I know at once that he has made a decision.

"Ever hear of The Masked Marvel?" He says this in a low voice,   9
almost a whisper.

"What?"   10

"The Masked Marvel," he says. "You never heard of him?"   11

"No."   12

He clucks his tongue. He is exasperated.   13

All at once there is a recollection. It is dim, distant, but com-   14
ing near.

"Do you mean the wrestler?"   15

Eagerly, he nods, and the breasts bob. How gnomish he looks,   16
oval as the huge helpless egg of some outlandish lizard. He has very long arms, which, now and then, he unfurls to reach for things—a carafe of water, a get-well card. He gazes up at me, urging. He wants me to remember.

"Well, . . . yes," I say. I am straining backward in time. "I saw   17
him wrestle in Toronto long ago."

"Ha!" He smiles. "You saw *me*." And his index finger, held rigid   18
and upright, bounces in the air.

The man has said something shocking, unacceptable. It must be   19
challenged.

"You?" I am trying to smile.   20

Again that jab of the finger. "You saw *me*."   21

"No," I say. But even then, something about Elihu Koontz, those   22
prolonged arms, the shape of his head, the sudden agility with
which he leans from his bed to get a large brown envelope from his
nightstand, something is forcing me toward a memory. He rum-
mages through his papers, old newspaper clippings, photographs,
and I remember . . .

It is almost forty years ago. I am ten years old. I have been sent to   23
Toronto to spend the summer with relatives. Uncle Max has bought
two tickets to the wrestling match. He is taking me that night.

"He isn't allowed," says Aunt Sarah to me. Uncle Max has angina.   24

"He gets too excited," she says.   25

"I wish you wouldn't go, Max," she says.   26

"You mind your own business," he says.   27

And we go. Out into the warm Canadian evening. I am not only   28
abroad, I am abroad in the *evening!* I have never been taken out in
the evening. I am terribly excited. The trolleys, the lights, the horns.
It is a bazaar. At the Maple Leaf Gardens, we sit high and near the center. The vast arena is dark except for the brilliance of the ring at the
bottom.

It begins.   29

The wrestlers circle. They grapple. They are all haunch and   30
paunch. I am shocked by their ugliness, but I do not show it. Uncle
Max is exhilarated. He leans forward, his eyes unblinking, on his
face a look of enormous happiness. One after the other, a pair of
wrestlers enter the ring. The two men join, twist, jerk, tug, bend,
yank, and throw. Then they leave and are replaced by another pair.
At last it is the main event. "The Angel vs. The Masked Marvel."

On the cover of the program notes, there is a picture of The An-   31
gel hanging from the limb of a tree, a noose of thick rope around his
neck. The Angel hangs just so for an hour every day, it is explained,

to strengthen his neck. The Masked Marvel's trademark is a black stocking cap with holes for the eyes and mouth. He is never seen without it, states the program. No one knows who The Masked Marvel really is!

"Good," says Uncle Max. "Now you'll see something." He is fidg-   32
eting, waiting for them to appear. They come down separate aisles, climb into the ring from opposite sides. I have never seen anything like them. It is The Angel's neck that first captures the eye. The shaved nape rises in twin columns to puff into the white hood of a sloped and bosselated skull that is too small. As though strangled by the sinews of that neck, the skull had long since withered and shrunk. The thing about The Angel is the absence of any mystery in his body. It is simply there. A monosyllabic announcement. A grunt. One looks and knows everything at once, the fat thighs, the gigantic buttocks, the great spine from which hang knotted ropes and pale aprons of beef. And that prehistoric head. He is all of a single hideous piece, The Angel is. No detachables.

The Masked Marvel seems dwarfish. His fingers dangle knee-   33
ward. His short legs are slightly bowed as if under the weight of the cask they are forced to heft about. He has breasts that swing when he moves! I have never seen such breasts on a man before.

There is a sudden ungraceful movement, and they close upon   34
one another. The Angel stoops and hugs The Marvel about the waist, locking his hands behind The Marvel's back. Now he straightens and lifts The Marvel as though he were uprooting a tree. Thus he holds him, then stoops again, thrusts one hand through The Marvel's crotch, and with the other grabs him by the neck. He rears and . . . The Marvel is aloft! For a long moment, The Angel stands as though deciding where to make the toss. Then throws. Was that board or bone that splintered there? Again and again, The Angel hurls himself upon the body of The Masked Marvel.

Now The Angel rises over the fallen Marvel, picks up one foot in   35
both of his hands, and twists the toes downward. It is far beyond the tensile strength of mere ligament, mere cartilage. The Masked Marvel does not hide his agony, but pounds and slaps the floor with his hand, now and then reaching up toward The Angel in an attitude of

supplication. I have never seen such suffering. And all the while his black mask rolls from side to side, the mouth pulled to a tight slit through which issues an endless hiss that I can hear from where I sit. All at once, I hear a shouting close by.

"Break it off! Tear off a leg and throw it up here!"   36

It is Uncle Max. Even in the darkness I can see that he is gray. A   37
band of sweat stands upon his upper lip. He is on his feet now, panting, one fist pressed at his chest, the other raised warlike toward the ring. For the first time I begin to think that something terrible might happen here. Aunt Sarah was right.

"Sit down, Uncle Max," I say. "Take a pill, please."   38

He reaches for the pillbox, gropes, and swallows without taking   39
his gaze from the wrestlers. I wait for him to sit down.

"That's not fair," I say, "twisting his toes like that."   40

"It's the toehold," he explains.   41

"But it's not *fair*," I say again. The whole of the evil is laid open   42
for me to perceive. I am trembling.

And now The Angel does something unspeakable. Holding the   43
foot of The Marvel at full twist with one hand, he bends and grasps the mask where it clings to the back of The Marvel's head. And he pulls. He is going to strip it off! Lay bare an ultimate carnal mystery! Suddenly it is beyond mere physical violence. Now I am on my feet, shouting into the Maple Leaf Gardens.

"Watch out," I scream. "Stop him. Please, somebody, stop him."   44

Next to me, Uncle Max is chuckling.   45

Yet The Masked Marvel hears me, I know it. And rallies from his   46
bed of pain. Thrusting with his free heel, he strikes The Angel at the back of the knee. The Angel falls. The Masked Marvel is on top of him, pinning his shoulders to the mat. One! Two! Three! And it is over. Uncle Max is strangely still. I am gasping for breath. All this I remember as I stand at the bedside of Elihu Koontz.

Once again, I am in the operating room. It is two years since I   47
amputated the left leg of Elihu Koontz. Now it is his right leg which is gangrenous. I have already scrubbed. I stand to one side wearing my gown and gloves. And . . . *I am masked*. Upon the table lies

Elihu Koontz, pinned in a fierce white light. Spinal anesthesia has been administered. One of his arms is taped to a board placed at a right angle to his body. Into this arm, a needle has been placed. Fluid drips here from a bottle overhead. With his other hand, Elihu Koontz beats feebly at the side of the operating table. His head rolls from side to side. His mouth is pulled into weeping. It seems to me that I have never seen such misery.

An orderly stands at the foot of the table, holding Elihu Koontz's   48
leg aloft by the toes so that the intern can scrub the limb with anti-septic solutions. The intern paints the foot, ankle, leg, and thigh, both front and back, three times. From a corner of the room where I wait, I look down as from an amphitheater. Then I think of Uncle Max yelling, "Tear off a leg. Throw it up here." And I think that forty years later I am making the catch.

"It's not fair," I say aloud. But no one hears me. I step forward to   49
break The Masked Marvel's last toehold.

❦ Phyllis Rose ❦

Phyllis Rose, Professor of English at Wesleyan University, received her B.A., summa cum laude, from Radcliffe College in 1964, her M.A. from Yale in 1965, and her Ph.D. from Harvard in 1970. She is the author of three biographical works: Woman of Letters: A Life of Virginia Woolf, Parallel Lives: Five Victorian Marriages, *and* Jazz Cleopatra: Josephine Baker in Her Time, *as well as two collections of essays and reviews. She also edited* The Norton Book of Women's Lives. *Her memoir,* A Year of Reading Proust, *was published in 1997. She writes frequently for national publications including* The New York Times Book Review, The Sophisticated Traveler, *and* Civilization *magazine. She is also on the editorial board of* The American Scholar.

Tools of Torture

In this work, first published in The Atlantic Monthly *in 1986, Phyllis Rose takes an uncompromising look at the social and psychological sources of and rationalizations for torture. She uses specific examples from an exhibit in Paris of torture instruments to draw conclusions about the relation of pleasure to pain.*

Determine, as precisely as you can, the answers to these questions: Why are there so many torture devices? Why were they invented in the first place? What are the justifications for institutionalized torture? What is the relationship of pleasure to pain?

In a gallery off the rue Dauphine, near the *parfumerie* where I get my massage, I happened upon an exhibit of medieval torture instruments. It made me think that pain must be as great a challenge to the human imagination as pleasure. Otherwise there's no accounting for the number of torture instruments. One would be quite enough. The simple pincer, let's say, which rips out flesh. Or the head crusher, which breaks first your tooth sockets, then your skull. But in addition I saw tongs, thumbscrews, a rack, a ladder, ropes and pulleys, a grill, a garrote, a Spanish horse, a Judas cradle, an iron maiden, a cage, a gag, a strappado, a stretching table, a saw, a wheel, a twisting stork, an inquisitor's chair, a breast breaker, and a scourge. You don't need complicated machinery to cause incredible pain. If you want to saw your victim down the middle, for example, all you need is a slightly bigger than usual saw. If you hold the victim upside down so the blood stays in his head, hold his legs apart, and start sawing at the groin, you can get as far as the navel before he loses consciousness.

Even in the Middle Ages, before electricity, there were many   2
things you could do to torment a person. You could tie him up in an iron belt that held the arms and legs up to the chest and left no point of rest, so that all his muscles went into spasm within minutes and he was driven mad within hours. This was the twisting stork, a benign-looking object. You could stretch him out backward over a thin piece of wood so that his whole body weight rested on his spine, which pressed against the sharp wood. Then you could stop up his nostrils and force water into his stomach through his mouth. Then, if you wanted to finish him off, you and your helper could jump on his stomach, causing internal hemorrhage. This torture was called the rack. If you wanted to burn someone to death without hearing him scream, you could use a tongue lock, a metal rod between the jaw and collarbone that prevented him from opening his mouth. You could put a person in a chair with spikes on the seat and arms, tie him down against the spikes, and beat him, so that every time he flinched from the beating he drove his own flesh deeper onto the spikes. This was the inquisitor's chair. If you wanted to make it worse, you could heat the spikes. You could suspend a person over a pointed wooden pyramid and whenever he started to fall asleep, you could drop him onto the point. If you were Ippolito Marsili, the inventor of this torture, known as the Judas cradle, you could tell yourself you had invented something humane, a torture that worked without burning flesh or breaking bones. For the torture here was supposed to be sleep deprivation.

The secret of torture, like the secret of French cuisine, is that   3
nothing is unthinkable. The human body is like a foodstuff, to be grilled, pounded, filleted. Every opening exists to be stuffed, all flesh to be carved off the bone. You take an ordinary wheel, a heavy

wooden wheel with spokes. You lay the victim on the ground with blocks of wood at strategic points under his shoulders, legs, and arms. You use the wheel to break every bone in his body. Next you tie his body onto the wheel. With all its bones broken, it will be pliable. However, the victim will not be dead. If you want to kill him, you hoist the wheel aloft on the end of a pole and leave him to starve. Who would have thought to do this with a man and a wheel? But, then, who would have thought to take the disgusting snail, force it to render its ooze, stuff it in its own shell with garlic butter, bake it, and eat it?

Not long ago I had a facial—only in part because I thought I   4
needed one. It was research into the nature and function of pleasure. In a dark booth at the back of the beauty salon, the aesthetician put me on a table and applied a series of ointments to my face, some cool, some warmed. After a while she put something into my hand, cold and metallic. "Don't be afraid, madame," she said. "It is an electrode. It will not hurt you. The other end is attached to two metal cylinders, which I roll over your face. They break down the electricity barrier on your skin and allow the moisturizers to penetrate deeply." I didn't believe this hocus-pocus. I didn't believe in the electricity barrier or in the ability of these rollers to break it down. But it all felt very good. The cold metal on my face was a pleasant change from the soft warmth of the aesthetician's fingers. Still, since Algeria it's hard to hear the word "electrode" without fear. So when she left me for a few minutes with a moist, refreshing cheesecloth over my face, I thought, What if the goal of her expertise had been pain, not moisture? What if the electrodes had been electrodes in the Algerian sense? What if the cheesecloth mask were dipped in acid?

In Paris, where the body is so pampered, torture seems particu-   5
larly sinister, not because it's hard to understand but because—as the dark side of sensuality—it seems so easy. Beauty care is among the glories of Paris. *Soins esthétiques* include makeup, facials, massages (both relaxing and reducing), depilatations (partial and complete), manicures, pedicures, and tanning, in addition to the usual run of *soins* for the hair: cutting, brushing, setting, waving, styling, blowing, coloring, and streaking. In Paris the state of your skin,

hair, and nerves is taken seriously, and there is little of the puritani-
cal thinking that tries to persuade us that beauty comes from
within. Nor do the French think, as Americans do, that beauty
should be offhand and low-maintenance. Spending time and money
on *soins esthétiques* is appropriate and necessary, not self-indulgent.
Should that loving attention to the body turn malevolent, you have
torture. You have the procedure—the aesthetic, as it were—of torture, the explanation for the rich diversity of torture instruments,
but you do not have the cause.

Historically torture has been a tool of legal systems, used to get   6
information needed for a trial or, more directly, to determine guilt or
innocence. In the Middle Ages confession was considered the best of
all proofs, and torture was the way to produce a confession. In other
words, torture didn't come into existence to give vent to human
sadism. It is not always private and perverse but sometimes social
and institutional, vetted by the government and, of course, the
Church. (There have been few bigger fans of torture than Christianity and Islam.) Righteousness, as much as viciousness, produces torture. There aren't squads of sadists beating down the doors to the
torture chambers begging for jobs. Rather, as a recent book on torture by Edward Peters says, the institution of torture creates sadists:
the weight of a culture, Peters suggests, is necessary to recruit tortur-
ers. You have to convince people that they are working for a great
goal in order to get them to overcome their repugnance to the task of
causing physical pain to another person. Usually the great goal is the
preservation of society, and the victim is presented to the torturer as
being in some way out to destroy it.

From another point of view, what's horrifying is how easily you   7
can persuade someone that he is working for the common good. Perhaps the most appalling psychological experiment of modern times,
by Stanley Milgram, showed that ordinary, decent people in New
Haven, Connecticut, could be brought to the point of inflicting (as
they thought) severe electric shocks on other people in obedience to
an authority and in pursuit of a goal, the advancement of knowledge, of which they approved. Milgram used—some would say
abused—the prestige of science and the university to make his point,

but his point is chilling nonetheless. We can cluck over torture, but the evidence at least suggests that with intelligent handling most of us could be brought to do it ourselves.

In the Middle Ages, Milgram's experiment would have had no   8 point. It would have shocked no one that people were capable of cruelty in the interest of something they believed in. That was as it should be. Only recently in the history of human thought has the avoidance of cruelty moved to the forefront of ethics. "Putting cruelty first," as Judith Shklar says in *Ordinary Vices*, is comparatively new. The belief that the "pursuit of happiness" is one of man's inalienable rights, the idea that "cruel and unusual punishment" is an evil in itself, the Benthamite notion that behavior should be guided by what will produce the greatest happiness for the greatest number—all these principles are only two centuries old. They were born with the eighteenth-century democratic revolutions. And in two hundred years they have not been universally accepted. Wherever people believe strongly in some cause, they will justify torture— not just the Nazis, but the French in Algeria.

Many people who wouldn't hurt a fly have annexed to fashion   9 the imagery of torture—the thongs and spikes and metal studs— hence reducing it to the frivolous and transitory. Because torture has been in the mainstream and not on the margins of history, nothing could be healthier. For torture to be merely kinky would be a big advance. Exhibitions like the one I saw in Paris, which presented itself as educational, may be guilty of pandering to the tastes they deplore. Solemnity may be the wrong tone. If taking one's goals too seriously is the danger, the best discouragement of torture may be a radical hedonism that denies that any goal is worth the means, that refuses to allow the nobly abstract to seduce us from the sweetness of the concrete. Give people a good croissant and a good cup of coffee in the morning. Give them an occasional facial and a plate of escargots. Marie Antoinette picked a bad moment to say "Let them eat cake," but I've often thought she was on the right track.

All of which brings me back to Paris, for Paris exists in the   10 imagination of much of the world as the capital of pleasure—of fun, food, art, folly, seduction, gallantry, and beauty. Paris is civilization's reminder to itself that nothing leads you less wrong than your awareness of your own pleasure and a genial desire to spread it around. In that sense the myth of Paris constitutes a moral touchstone, standing for the selfish frivolity that helps keep priorities straight.

❦ Mary McNamara ❦

Mary McNamara was born in Baltimore in 1963, grew up in Westminster, Maryland, and attended the University of Missouri–Columbia, where she majored in journalism and women's studies. She has been a staff writer for the Los Angeles Times *since 1990. Before that she wrote for* Ms. *magazine and Whittle Communications. Her work has appeared throughout the various sections of the* Los Angeles Times, *as well as in* Mademoiselle, Glamour, The New York Times Book Review, *and* Ms.

A Gentle Man and His Love of Guns

The following is a gracefully constructed, multilayered essay. It is a thoughtful exposition of a current social issue, the debate over gun ownership and gun control, a sensitive examination of the author's relationship with her father, who holds views on guns diametrically opposed to her own, and an insightful reflection on how intense, personal relationships can affect intellectual commitments. It is also a love letter from a daughter to her father. Mary McNamara accomplishes all of this in about a thousand words.

Read the essay with care to see how McNamara is able to weave all these elements together in such a seamless and succinct way.

My father has always wanted me to have a gun. The adult me, 1
that is.

When I moved to New York after graduating from college, he of- 2
fered to buy me a handgun. A small one, ladylike, to keep in my
nightstand. I told him I did not have a nightstand, and he offered to
buy me one of those as well.

I sighed and said I did not want a gun because I did not know 3
how to shoot, and should I encounter a member of the criminally in-
clined, I would no doubt shoot myself in the foot.

My father said he would pay for marksmanship lessons. 4

You see what it is like in my family.   5

So I had to resort to clarion honesty. I did not want a gun be-   6
cause I did not like guns. I did not think they were cool or comforting or necessary. I thought owning a gun was part of the problem,
not the solution.

This was hard to say because my father loves his guns and I love   7
my father. But when I read about the debate over gun control in this
country, I can't even take sides, I can't even breathe properly, because
with children dying all around us I cannot believe we are even having a debate. I would like to believe that anyone who has the least little interest in owning a gun is criminal, testosterone-challenged, or
an ill-educated redneck. But then there is my father.

He is a gentle man, scholarly and religious, a Yellow Dog demo-   8
crat who can quote whole passages of the ballad of "Sam McGee"
and hardly ever yells. He never goes anywhere without a book. I remember him sitting in the bleachers at my basketball practices, looking out from behind thick glasses and a Barbara Tuchman tome.
When he was young, he had wanted to be a priest but didn't think
he was good enough.

He grew up on the South Side of Chicago during the Depres-   9
sion; his father had guns. Just because. During the Cold War, father
lounged around the base on Okinawa and learned how to shoot.
Very well.

When he and my mother married, he bowed to her judgment on   10
all things, save one. There was always at least a handgun tucked, un-
loaded, somewhere we kids never discovered.

When we went camping, he would bring a gun with us, for pro-   11
tection and also to teach us to shoot. At tin cans. It was loud and I
never hit a thing and the kick almost threw me off my feet, but my
mother refused to participate so it felt enough like rebellion to make
it worth my while.

Then I got older, and I didn't have so much truck with the war-   12
rior ideal. Who were they warring with? Tin cans? Teenage boys?
Children?

My father got older too and retired to New Mexico, where he   13
bought even more guns, finally convinced my mother to join him at
the firing range, bought her a gun.

I did not understand it. Guns did not fit the meaning of my fa-   14
ther as I knew him. They sat like an occupying army in the consciousness of a quietly socialist, Catholic humanitarian. I remember
when I was a teenager, begging my father to let me see Bonnie and
Clyde's touring "Death Car." After an ominous silence, he spoke.

"Bonnie and Clyde were self-centered cowards," he said, with   15
quiet fury that turned the food in my mouth to wax. "They shot people just for money. People with families, with children, people just
like your mother and me. If someone shot us, would you want people paying to look at their car?"

How could this man enjoy owning and shooting a gun?   16

I do not believe that guns alone kill people. But I do believe that   17
Bonnie and Clyde and Lee Harvey Oswald and Son of Sam and the
two kids in Littleton would not have been capable of killing anyone
if they had not had guns. I believe that guns are made for the sole
purpose of killing things; for handguns and assault rifles, those
things would be people.

My father does not believe this. He believes in gun control—he   18
is more than willing to register and limit and wait. But he also believes in his guns; they give him a feeling of security and safety.
Once, when he and my mother were living alone in our house in rural Maryland, a man—probably drunk—came pounding on the
door, shouting, swearing, demanding to use the phone in the middle
of the night. My father says he opened the door just enough for the
man to see my father's gun, "and suddenly this guy found his manners: 'Could he please' and 'Sorry to disturb' and 'Thank you, sir.' "

I know there are violent people out there; I want my parents,   19
who live far away, to have protection as they grow older. But I don't
consider having a gun protection.

And maybe that is the difference between my father and me. For   20
him, a gun is what you used to prepare yourself for battle, to protect
your wife and children, the desperate measure you hide in the closet.

For me, a gun is what teenagers use to "accidentally" shoot a   21
3-year-old and each other; what a man uses to "save" his wife and
children after he is made despondent by unemployment. To me, a
gun is what enters a situation made volatile by basic human emotions and makes it tragically and irrevocably worse.

But maybe we are not so far apart, my father and I. 22

A few summers ago, I offered to go with him to the shooting 23 range in the hopes it would cheer him up. He practically skipped as he set out the aluminum pie plates we would use as targets. I took the gun out of the holster; it was a different gun than the one I had handled so many years ago, heavier, sleeker. There was a beauty about it, and recognizing that made the blood sing in my head. My father began loading it, explaining the rudiments, but his voice sounded strange, thick and dry. I looked at him, and his hand was shaking.

"I just realized that here is a gun," he said, "and here is my little 24 girl. And it makes me feel afraid." He peered at me through those schoolteacher glasses. "Isn't that strange?" I smiled and shook my head. Then I aimed the gun and blew a hole in the center of the first pie plate, and was unforgivably proud.

Writing Task: The Reflective Essay

To give you a taste of what it's like to reflect on your experience in writing, we've created a five-week sequence of informal notebook entries that will prepare you to write a reflective essay based on personal experience. We hope that completing the sequence will awaken your curiosity about the possibilities of self-exploration through writing. We also hope that you will become engaged in a creative process many writers experience while they pursue the reflective essay.

Reflecting on Experience

Many writers keep a writer's notebook. It is generally a sketchbook of some kind or a looseleaf binder. They use the writer's notebook as a way to collect material for their writing projects. Of course not every entry will be used, but the process of recording details from their lives seems to connect them to their work. But sustaining a writer's notebook is often difficult for beginning writers. They make the mistake of concentrating on what is happening in their immediate experience. Soon the process bogs down in repetition. To avoid getting bogged down, we suggest that you complete the following five weeks of notebook-keeping exercises. They are designed to plunge you into your life in ways you might not have thought of and to help you collect a body of informal writing that can be used in writing reflective essays.

Guidelines for Notebook Entries

1. Think of your entries as freewriting. No one but you will read them. Don't revise them. The goal is to merely collect experience.
2. Write for at least thirty minutes, five days a week.
3. Don't stop to correct your grammar or punctuation. Just write, and write in concrete detail.
4. Date your entries, and leave space between them so that they are clearly delineated.
5. Think of your notebook as an artist thinks of a sketchbook. It will be filled with fragments, random images, and scribbles.

    As part of your notebook writing experience, you might also keep a dream log. There, you can record any dreams you remember.

Five Weeks of Notebook Entries

Week 1: Current Life

Begin by concentrating on your current life. In the words of Henry David Thoreau, you will begin a "simple and sincere account" of your life. He writes:

> I, on my side, require of every writer, first and last, a simple and sincere account of his own life, and not merely what he has heard of other men's lives; some such account as he would send to his kindred from a distant land; for if he has lived sincerely, it must have been in a distant land to me.

The distant land to which Thoreau alludes is the land of the mind. None of us sees, smells, touches, or hears the world as anyone else does. This is what makes each mind a unique landscape.

Day 1.   This entry is to capture where you are in your life. It might be a good idea to begin with a comment on your general situation as you sense it. Begin with a broad comment, then let your mind sweep through your recent life. Record specifics, bits of dialogue, frustrations, pleasures, questions, fantasies—everything that comes to you.

Day 2.   In the previous entry you described where you are in your current life. Today you are going to record impressions of where you live. Try to capture fleeting impressions and details. Let your mind loose, recording the associations it makes. Perhaps your mind will connect with other places where you have lived; work those details into your entry, but always come back to your immediate surroundings. Remember, be specific. Never let your mind linger for long in general statements such as this:

> I live in a pretty white house with a big lawn and some palm trees near the center of town. I like it here. The neighbors are. . . .

Instead, get to the details and the associations they bring:

> My front lawn has gone brown from the drought, but it still has two fat palms about two stories high with drooping limbs. I used to swing on them I was a kid: Ahhhhhh—Tarzan. People could hear my scream all over town (at least my mom said they could). Ahhhhhhh, ahhh, ahhhhhhhh! But now things are different. I've gotten older and the house. . . .

Be specific. Capture the details.

Day 3.   List personal items in your possession. Don't just name individual items; include brief descriptions and associations you have with them. Start by emptying the contents of your wallet or purse. Arrange the items in whatever way suits you, then study them. Hold them. Read the writing on the ones that have writing. Smell the ones that have smells. In your own time, make the list.

As an alternative, go to the medicine cabinet, cosmetic drawer, or refrigerator. List jars, bottles, cans, and individual items. List your associations with these items.

Day 4.   List activities you do: attend classes, read, write papers, take tests; drive, walk, bike, or ride a bus or subway to school; sleep and roll out of bed in the morning; talk with friends, teachers, parents; hold a job or play sports.

Begin by drawing up a list of your activities. Then from the list, select one or two to write about. Record everything that comes to you: how it feels to do them, why you like doing them, how long you've been doing them. Record the associations you have with them. Use specific language.

For example, this student entry about jogging starts off fuzzy, a way many writers begin, then goes past the general comments to the particulars of the experience:

> I like jogging because it makes me feel good. After I finish jogging, I relax. My body is limber—limber, reminds me of lumber. That's how I start in the mornings, my legs like pieces of lumber—I lumber along. But after I run for a while, I feel limber, like a birch tree in the wind. I like the sound of my feet slapping the asphalt and the sound of breathing deep in my chest. I like to jog on cold mornings. Once there was frost on the grass. I ran across the park. Crunch, crunch, crunch.

Day 5.   Write about special places in your current life. Randomly list places that come to mind. These special places need not be your favorite spots, ones that you associate with pleasure; they may also be places you associate with discomfort, such as a doctor's or dentist's office. Perhaps one or two places on your list will be secret places, spots you may visit for a moment or two when the world seems to be coming down around your shoulders, such as a rock overlooking a field, a window looking out to a yard or street, or a couch in a quiet place in your home.

For example, here is a part of one student's list of special places:

- Mountains: love the cool breezes that hum through the pines.
- Beach: but not with people—people everywhere, an anthill.
- Restaurants: Salernos—ummmmm! El Torito, but only on Fridays between four and six. El Tapito: carnitas, jalapenos, flautas.

I like

- My shower
- The park in early morning
- Sitting in the quad
- My granddad's garage—cans of old paint, rusted tools, pipes, bicycle parts, at least a dozen alarm clocks—all waiting to be fixed.

Notice the phrases that follow some of the items. They add the concrete details; often they are lists themselves.

Take a few minutes to draw up your list of special places and record some associations with them. Then select one or two to write about more completely.

Week 2: Life Experiences

You will continue with the exploration of your experience, but this week you will concentrate on the past.

Make a series of brief entries in the form of an extended list that spontaneously captures memories from your past. The key word is spontaneously; the goal here is not to capture only the most important events in your life—although they may be on your list—but to let the memories and images from your past come uncalled. Here is a list of notebook entries by a student who has returned to college to earn a second degree in psychology. They might seem fragmented, as if written in a personalized code:

- I remember walking to school on a cold morning. It had rained—puddles covered with thin ice. Mountains with snow. Graduating from high school. The speech seemed like hours. Fear. Thought I could never do it.

- Running on the mountain trail. A trip with dad. A cabin. Fishing. Hated the smell on my hands.
- Living in the city. Once a man stopped me on the way to school. "Got a quarter, missy? Give me your lunch money." I ran.
- My first real date. Must have taken three hours to get ready. Spilled a Coke in my lap.
- Flunked geometry—the end of the world. Thought all hell would break loose. Mom shrugged her shoulders. Dad said to take it over.
- Mom and dad divorced. Took me a year before I could say the word.
- Away to school. Mixed feelings. Couldn't wait to get out of the house. Yet scared.

This writer dips deeply into her past. In fact, the list appears to stretch from early memories to more recent ones. The list also includes the ups and downs of experience. Often when making life history lists of this sort, writers tend to consciously exclude difficult times. But if the mind finds its own course, the list will include both good and bad memories.

Day 1.   For the first half-hour session, develop a list of memories from your past. Begin by sitting quietly and reflecting on the past. Then record in two or three lines a half dozen to a dozen of the strongest memories that come to you. They may not be big events in your life, but for the moment they will hold your interest. Be sure to write legibly enough to reread your entries, and leave plenty of space around them. Finally, after you finish the list, reread it and write the approximate dates when the events took place.

Days 2–5.   During the rest of this week's writing sessions, expand four entries from your list. In a way, each memory you've listed is like a doorway to your past. To write a brief entry is to open the door just a crack. To expand the entry is to swing the door open wide. Behind it will be a story or interesting detail that you might have forgotten.

Week Three: Portraits

Day 1. Spend your practice time today developing a list of people to use for possible portraits. You can go about doing this in two ways. First, you might draw together a memory list by sitting quietly and allowing your mind to roam throughout your life history. As the names of people come to you, jot them down.

Another way to draw up a list is by browsing through your previous entries to find references to others who might be important to you. Put these people on your list. Remember to add brief comments about the relationship and the experiences you've shared with them. In other words, this is to be an extended list, full of detail and observations.

- Martha K: See her often. Sometimes we walk down University where the sycamores drop their leaves. No real commitment, just comfortable with her. We sometimes have lunch—introduced me to lox and cream cheese on bagels.
- Old Ben: Vietnam. Playing with blocks, Lego blocks. Fishing at the jetty. Taught me about death.
- John C: Three years together on the football team—left and right halfbacks. Everyone called us Heckle and Jeckle. "He's Jeckle," we both once said, while pointing at each other.

Notice that this partial list includes specific detail. The writer does not merely record a few general comments on the page and leave it at that.

Days 2–5. Each day, select one person from your list. Spend your practice time describing the person and the relationship you've shared with the person. Remember to include more than physical details. Include all that comes to you about the relationship. Try to develop a specific event that embodies some aspect of the person's character. Create some tension in the portrait.

Week Four: Paintings and Photographs

Days 1–5. Use paintings and photographs to prompt notebook entries. Select several images of paintings from art books or personal photographs that span your life, and write about them. We suggest that you paste the image, or a photocopy of the image, into your notebook. If that isn't possible, write brief descriptions of the images as part of your entries.

What follows is part of a philosophical response to a photographic slide of Salvador Dali's "Persistence of Memory":

> This morning in art history I saw a slide of a Dali painting. A crazy thing. It was filled with melting pocket watches—pocket watches that looked more real than real watches. These watches were melting in a desert wasteland with some strange trees in the background. One watch had thousands of ants crawling out of it. Another was melting over a strange amoeba-shaped object covered with hair and with a tongue hanging out of an opening.
>
> The painting reminded me of words from an old song: "Time, time, time—what's to become of me. . . ." And I began to wonder about how time worked in my life. Time is a funny thing to be thinking about, but I can't get the thought out of my mind. I wonder how time works. I know I live in time that moves forward, that is, I was born, I went to grammar school, junior high school, and high school. I know all this education has led to college, but in my mind I can be in all these places at once. Time in my mind seems to melt together.

Whereas this writer chose to write about a well-known painting, the following writer chose to record his responses to a series of childhood photographs. His response to a photograph of himself as a baby being held by his father starts like this:

> When I look at this picture, I feel very strange. I know the man standing next to the birch tree is my father and I know the

baby he holds wrapped in a blanket is me. But for some reason I can't emotionally accept the thought. My father seems so young, not any older than I am now, and I find imagining him at my age is difficult.

Did he feel at 22 what I feel?

At that age he had a child—me. It makes me feel he had his life under control. But here I am at 22 without an idea of what I'll be doing four years from now.

My father now, compared to the picture, seems so much older. So changed. Once he was thin, athletic. Now he has a paunch and looks as if he never sees the sun. His hair, once full and wavy, is now thin. His face was smooth, now wrinkled.

At this moment I wonder if somewhere there exists a photograph of him and his father. I wonder if he has ever compared himself to his dad's image. Where does this lead, this photographing, this photographing of fathers and sons?

Where?

Back, back, back. And forward—into the future. The never-ending future. But somehow I feel there's knowledge to be gained from studying these images.

The key to responding to images, whether paintings or personal photographs, is to avoid trying to figure out what you are going to write before you write it. Instead, concentrate on the image and just write.

Week 5: Self-Reflection

For several weeks you have been exploring a subject that is close to you: your life. We hope you are beginning to sense the scope of self-exploration. People, places, memories, feelings, objects, events, books, films, music, dreams, even unharnessed thoughts—all fall into the vast, partially charted territory of your life. We also hope that you have made some discoveries.

We want to lead you a few steps down the path of self-examination, or, as we prefer to call it, self-reflection.

Instead of making a direct assault on yourself, you'll follow a gentler course by merely rereading your entries and recording any responses or insights you have. Novelist Anaïs Nin, after years of keeping diaries, reflected on her recorded experiences:

> In the early diaries I speak of my feeling that I am playing many roles demanded of woman, which I have been programmed to play. But I know also that there is a part of myself that stands apart from that and wants some other kind of life, some other kinds of authenticity. R. D. Laing [a contemporary psychiatrist] describes this authenticity as a process of constantly peeling off the false selves. You can do this in many ways but you can also do it by looking at it, for there is so much that we don't want to look at.

Reflecting on notebook entries need not always lead to deep insights. Often a thought will come that's related to your current life. Or you might feel as if you have reexperienced what you've already described. You might then want to extend it. After rereading a dream that she recalled while recording her past, one student wrote:

> Returned to the cave dream. The whole experience came back to me, almost as if I were in the dream again. When I finished I felt I was still standing at the cave's mouth. Afraid, unable to move, just staring into the darkness. This is crazy, I thought, why am I scared of going in there. Then I began to imagine I went in. I told myself there was no reason to be afraid of the unknown. Unknown! The word sounded in my mind like a scream. Unknown! That's what the cave was. So I imagined I walked into the darkness. I had to put my hands in front of my face the cave was so black. I felt my way around a turn and there was a blue light ahead—a soft hazy glow. In a moment I was at the edge of an underground pond—more the size of a lake than a pond. It was beautiful. It seemed to glow. It was worth the journey through the dark. This entire imaginary journey took only a second, but I saw some truth in it. It told me that I'm often too timid when I face something I don't know or understand. Thinking the word "unknown" made me realize I'm frightened of it, but if I move ahead with some caution, it will be okay.

The sequence of this entry is simple. The writer reflects on the dream, which led her to again face the dream dilemma: to enter or not enter the cave. She suddenly realizes what the dream suggests to her—the unknown—and then does in fantasy what she was unable to do while dreaming. She finally gains the insight that facing unknowns in her life needn't frighten her.

Whether or not her insight will have any lasting significance is not the point. What's important is that she looked at a part of her life and came away with a message. She's been engaged in self-reflection.

Days 1–5.   During this final week of directed notebook entries, spend each day's session both rereading previous entries and recording your responses to them. You might reread several entries before you have a response. That's fine. The appropriate way to do this task is the way that works best for you. Think in terms of what you have learned. Ask yourself whether the lesson could be passed on to someone else in writing.

Writing a Reflective Essay

To write a reflective essay requires a more creative touch than writing a typical college essay. The reflective essay follows no clear pattern; therefore, we can't give you hard-and-fast rules. What we can do is give you some general guidelines.

First, turn to your writer's notebook. Your entries represent the initial phase of a prewriting process. They are probably unedited fragments, that is, bits and pieces of experiences that passed swiftly from your memory to the page. Although some fragments will be nothing more than fleeting thoughts, others will capsulize significant events in your life, events from which you can gain some meaning. Such events might trigger deep emotions. They might hold some mystery. Perhaps one event will represent a milestone in your life. Or perhaps an event that seemed insignificant when it took place has become meaningful over time. Notebook entries that capture such events can launch a reflective essay.

Begin by browsing through your notebook. Look for entries that remind you of previous events that you can now see from a new perspective. Find an event that is meaningful. Such events don't have to be earth-shattering. Often an event that might appear ordinary to others might hold tremendous significance for you. These are "symbolic" events, ones that will reveal some personal insight if you explore them.

Second, after you've identified a meaningful event, make a list of memories you associate with it. Some might already be recorded in your notebook; others will need to be sketched out in new entries. In this prewriting phase, you shouldn't waste time evaluating the associations; you should only identify them without judgment.

Third, after collecting the raw material, you need to shape the whole essay. Like all essays, a reflective essay will have a beginning, a middle, and an end. But unlike a basic college essay, a reflective essay will seldom be organized by a thesis. Instead, the beginning of a reflective essay will usually set the stage for what will follow. It will typically suggest where the writer is headed. It will also include background information, much like the information a fiction writer includes in the opening of a story.

The middle of a reflective essay often weaves together memories of past experiences connected with the central event. The paragraphs, though less rigidly structured than traditional patterns, should begin with sentences that give readers a sense of order. Never let readers stumble in disordered associations, but guide them each step of the way.

The end of the essay reveals the insight you've gained from the experience. This revelation, however, should be suggested, not flatly stated, as the meaningful result of your experience.

Such suggestion is often hard to achieve. To make writing the conclusion easier, we suggest you use an image or thought that leads a reader to reflect on a detail in the essay, one that resonates with significance.

A Student Essay Developed by Reflection

By way of illustration, we offer the following reflective essay. While a freshman student in the 1980s, Larry Swanson, currently a practicing psychotherapist in Southern California, relates an experience he had returning to the home and neighborhood where he was born and raised. His parents were moving to a new house, and his former home was to be destroyed.

Swanson uses the experience to indirectly communicate his feelings about change and to share an insight that comes to him through the encounter. As you read, notice that Swanson never flatly states the purpose behind his essay. Instead, he suggests his feelings by describing early memories he associates with growing up in the old neighborhood. The use of suggestion creates subtle suspense and prepares readers for the final insight.

Before reading Swanson's essay, read his opening comment on the piece; then read the entire piece.

My goal for this essay was very clear—I wanted to communicate what "home" and "change" mean to me. By "home" I mean all those deep feelings, often confused feelings, that seem to be located just below consciousness. By "change" I mean a sense of loss and separation.

I recall developing the essay from various notebook entries. Of course, the entries were incomplete in themselves; I had to polish and add information to make everything fit.

One detail I developed while doing the final draft was the use of "Allie, Allie Oxen Free" in the closing section. In children's games of hide and seek, the phrase means the players can come "home" safely, but in the essay I wanted these words to suggest that childhood was over, symbolized by the fact that I would have no childhood home to return to.

Allie, Allie Oxen Free

In the middle of my freshman year in college I returned to   1
my hometown to visit the old neighborhood. It was the last
time I could go home. Home—the word has a deep meaning
for me.

Driven out by a severe drought, my parents came from   2
the cornfields of Nebraska to the house where they lived for

thirty-five years. I was born in the back bedroom because, as my mother said, "there just wasn't enough time to get to a hospital." My earliest memories center on playing in that house: pushing trucks over the hardwood floors, my pajama knees mopping up the morning dust; rummaging through my mother's pan drawers and banging them on the linoleum; and hiding behind the overstuffed couch whenever I was called for lunch. The backyard seemed to stretch the length of a football field and was the place I would chase my older brother and sisters until I fell down, breathless and sweating. Before I started grammar school, I knew all the neighborhood's marvelous places: the avocado tree where my friends and I used to climb to an ancient treehouse that had been built by children before us, the park where the old-timers would sit on benches and laugh at our wild games, the abandoned garage where we used to spy at the neighborhood through knotholes.

All that came back to me as I drove to pick up my parents for a final visit. You see, my home and the surrounding two blocks were to be destroyed. The City Council, those faceless champions of change, had condemned the neighborhood and planned to replace it with a civic center.   3

As I turned onto the street where my parents had bought a tract home, I saw my father, a little stooped since retiring after years of hard labor, standing before the recently seeded lawn that was beginning to sprout slivers of grass. In work boots, khaki trousers, and plaid shirt, which had become faded and thin from too much sun and too many washings, he didn't seem to belong to the stucco house packed with all the modern conveniences I knew my parents had avoided most of their lives. I pulled to the curb and he climbed in.   4

"Where's Mom?" I asked.   5

"Not coming," he said. "Let's go."   6

That was all he had to say to make me understand that Mom didn't want to make a final visit to the old place and to make me realize I didn't either.   7

As we drove, he filled his pipe, lit it, and began puffing— the smoke carrying the smell of Sugar Barrel, a smell I will always associate with him. We chatted about nothing important. "How're classes?" he asked and I answered routinely, knowing that neither of us wanted to say much about losing our home. Then we were on the old street, and the memories seemed to rise in my blood.   8

I first saw the store the Hungarian couple used to run. 　9
The advertisements were peeling off the walls, the windows
had been boarded up, and the screen door dangled stiffly from
one hinge—empty, abandoned. But I remembered how I once
spent summer afternoons sitting in front of it and playing Monopoly with my friends or chess with old man Jefferson, a retired sailor. The car seats we used to lounge on were still
there, but the stuffing had been torn out and only the springs
remained.

Then we passed Mr. Salling's house. Tall and bony, Salling 　10
was the neighborhood's mysterious figure. The few times I saw
him in the sunlight he wore a gray suit and had gray hair and
skin. But more often I saw him moving behind the curtains
where he paced the darkened parlor or rocked in a creaky
chair. I was told he had been "that way" since "losing his
wife." He wanted only to be left alone. One morning I learned
that he had "left" the night before. I never heard of him
again.

We drove past the vacant lot that had been the scene of 　11
many of my childhood joys. Each Independence Day the neighborhood fathers would set up a fireworks display and thrill us
kids for hours. In the spring we held war games there. Cos-
tumed in makeshift army uniforms and wearing plastic hel-
mets and carrying plastic rifles, we dodged through the tall
grass and dove into foxholes, shouting "TATATATATA, Gotcha!
C'mon you're dead!" During the summer, the lot served as the
center for our nightly game of hide-and-seek. As my father
and I drove past, I imagined hearing Billy Kieler's voice, the
loudest and most melodic among us, echoing throughout the
neighborhood, "ALLIE, ALLIE OXEN FREE! ALLIE, ALLIE OXEN
FREE!" Billy was the first of my childhood friends to move
away. How much had his life changed, I wondered. Yes, how
much?

Then we were in front of our old wood-frame home. My fa- 　12
ther climbed from the car. I looked straight ahead. "Coming?"
he said. But before I knew I had made a decision, I said no. I
turned in time to see him walk the five steps up to the front
porch, unlock the door, and step inside. No, I just could not
bring myself to see the house empty, abandoned.

I sat staring at the front lawn and recalled how I had 　13
spent hundreds of Saturday mornings mowing the grass, trim-
ming the hedges, and hoeing around the rose bushes. I had

hated to spend my Saturday mornings in such labor since I hadn't inherited my dad's love of growing and caring for things. Now the grass was brown and the hedges and rose bushes were dying and I missed the unvarying routine those secure Saturday mornings brought.

In a few moments Dad was returning, lugging a heavy   14
toolbox in each hand. I saw he breathed a little heavy. I went to help him.

"Hard going?" I asked.   15

"It's the last time for me," he said as we hefted the boxes   16
into the car.

At first I didn't make the connection between his words   17
and mine. I had referred to the difficulty he had carrying the boxes. He referred to much more. He referred to the illusion I wished to keep. I glanced up the street to the vacant lot and wished I could hear those comforting words that meant everything was okay, that the game was over and I could return home: ALLIE, ALLIE OXEN FREE!

Did you notice how muted Swanson's essay seems, yet how it still communicates a great deal of emotion? He steadily develops the scene and memories through description that suggests a deeper meaning than he reveals overtly. When he does comment it is done in a quiet way.

Guidelines for Writing a Reflective Essay

The primary methods of development for a reflective essay are narration and description, so you might want to review Chapters 5 and 6. You will also need to work in some background information and responses, but the main intent is to suggest the meaning of the experience, not to explain it.

Even though reflective essays are developed by the unique requirements of their subjects, we do recommend that you use the following procedure:

1. Select an event that means a great deal to you and that brought you some personal insight.
2. Use your writer's notebook to trigger memories you associate with the experience. Collect the raw material in extended lists.
3. Decide what you wish to communicate to readers. Use it as the essay's guiding purpose.
4. Write the essay by beginning with the main experience. Follow with a development of the experience while weaving in the associations you've collected.
5. Round off the essay by stating or implying how you feel or what you've learned from the experience.

Glossary

Abridgment   A shortened version of a work, but one in which the compiler attempts to include all pertinent parts of the longer work.

Abstract   Abstract words or terms describe ideas, concepts, or qualities, as opposed to **concrete** entities. Sample abstract words and expressions are *philosophy, remorse, happiness, beauty, honor, peace, organizational climate, achievement motive,* and *burden of proof* (*see* **concrete**).

Acronym   A word formed by combining the first letters or syllables of words, to form a new word. An example is BASIC, the word that names a computer language; it is an acronym meaning "Beginner's All-purpose Symbolic Instruction Code."

Ad hominem argument   *See* **Logical fallacies**.

Allusion   An allusion briefly and often casually refers to something the writer believes is common knowledge. If you write that your neighbor's fence "looks like the Berlin Wall," you allude to the state of the Berlin Wall, which is in ruins. A Robert Frost poem about the sudden death of a boy is titled " 'Out, Out—,' " an allusion to lines from Shakespeare's *Macbeth*:

> Out, out, brief candle!
> Life's but a walking shadow, a poor player
> That struts and frets his hour upon the stage,
> And then is heard no more. (V,v,23)

Analogy   An analogy is an imaginative comparison between two things, one less familiar than the other, usually intended to clarify a description of the less familiar one. In his novel *The Red and the Black*, the French author Stendhal (Marie Henri Beyle) wrote, "A novel is a mirror that strolls along a highway. Now it reflects the blue of the skies, now the mud puddles underfoot," clarifying his

637

concept of the novel by imaginatively comparing it to a common, familiar item.

Analysis   In an analysis, a writer examines a piece of writing by paying special attention to its elements of thought. An analysis is based on the premise that some ideas or concepts are actually combinations formed of other ideas or concepts. An analysis of an idea or concept as incorporated in an extended piece of writing often shows that many smaller thoughts have been combined into larger thoughts. Analyzing the Pledge of Allegiance to the Flag shows that it includes a definition of an ideal republic, which has its roots in classical Greek philosophy.

Anecdote   An anecdote is an incident, or **narration**, which reveals a facet of character, most often about a well-known person.

Argument   An argument is meant to persuade an audience to accept the qualities of a proposition (a statement to be supported), so that the audience will be convinced of the proposition's truth or falsity. In his commentary on rhetoric, Aristotle spoke of "artistic proofs," so called because they are invented in the sense of being thought up or devised for the specific purpose of swaying an audience to an orator's point of view.

Aristotelian proofs as they are used when writing arguments appeal to the audience in one of three ways: rationally, emotionally, or ethically. A rational appeal (*logos*) appeals to the audience's reason: an emotional appeal (*pathos*) appeals to the audience's emotions or passions; an ethical appeal (*ethos*) appeals to the audience's confidence in the writer's character or credentials. Today, an argument commonly includes more than one of these proofs, and may also embody such nonartistic proofs as statistics, results of polls, scientific data, and other scientifically verifiable statements.

Association fallacy   *See* **Logical fallacies**.

Audience   An audience is a reader or a class of readers whom writers keep in mind while they write and particularly while they revise their writing. Writers determine as much as they can about their audiences, including their expertise, their education, their biases, their political and cultural background, their assumptions, and their interests. Writers deal with many kinds of audiences, including those who already share the writer's convictions. Each audience affects the writer's way of casting the writing.

Knowing as much as they can about their audiences helps writers determine which **strategies** to use, such as sentence structure, reasoning, **definition, emphasis**, organization, and **style**.

Audiences also affect writers' **diction**. A writer aiming at an audience of experienced amateur sailors would use words such as *pulpit* and *roach*, but for an audience knowing nothing of nautical terminology, the writer would use "the platform on the forward part of the ship from which sailors handle and change sails," instead of *pulpit*, and "the curved portion of a sail closest to the rear end of the ship," instead of *roach*.

Body   The main part of a piece of writing is its body. Here, events are dramatized, dialogue is sustained, **conflicts** are developed, and other **strategies** are applied to sustain the reader's involvement.

Categories   Classes or divisions in an organized **classification**. Under the classification *general education requirements*, a writer could list the categories humanities, foreign languages, and sciences. Further, the writer could subcategorize by listing *foreign languages* such as French, Latin, German, and Japanese.

Cause and effect   A cause is that which came before an effect, the effect being the result of that cause. Combined, *cause and effect* is a useful way of analyzing reasons for actions and for the results of those actions. In the sentence, "Because Gwen did not study, she failed the calculus examination," one can see the immediate cause and the immediate effect. But what ultimate cause was behind Gwen's not studying? Not even Gwen can be absolutely sure, because most causes in our daily lives are probable, not certain. Aware of this uncertainty, writers use with caution the cause-and-effect strategy.

Chronological time   In narration chronological time refers to a related sequence of events as they unfold step by step.

Circumlocution   Circumlocution in writing fails to make a point clearly or evades a point because many words are used where fewer would have sufficed. The sentence, "What is the cause of the source of his pain cannot be other than his appendix, which seems to be less than healthy," illustrates circumlocution. The sentence could have been recast as, "His pain is probably caused by appendicitis."

Claim   The philosopher and rhetorician Stephen Toulmin devised a model of reasoning similar to the **syllogism**. One of the Toulmin model's primary elements is *claim*, which is the conclusion. The other two elements are *data*, which form the evidence, and *warrant*, which is the supporting argument. This sentence briefly illustrates the Toulmin model: Jasmah is a physicist (*data*); therefore, Jasmah is intelligent (*claim*) because all physicists are intelligent (*warrant*).

Classification   Classification is a system for sorting things into distinct categories, or classes. A music lover might want to organize her CDs. After sorting them, she sees that she can classify them into these categories, according to types of music: jazz, classical, and country and western. Later, perhaps when she wants to write a paper about her jazz CDs, she can classify them into categories according to the musical styles of the featured artists, making sure that each category is described clearly so that it is distinct from other categories.

Cliché   In French the *cliché* is an outmoded system for making metal printing plates with which to print the same thing again and again. In English the name describes words and phrases that have been used again and again so that they have become worn out, tired. Examples abound: A person can be "as old as the hills." A night can be "as black as coal." We can be "afraid of our own shadow." Someone can have "an ax to grind." A child can be "a chip off the old block." A trend can be "here today; gone tomorrow." An employee can be "a square peg in a round hole." A project can "start from scratch." When revising, writers "keep an eye peeled" for clichés so that they can replace them with fresh, colorful expressions of their own **invention**.

Climax   In a **narration** essay the climax is the conclusion, the highest point of interest. In other kinds of writing the climax, or peak of interest, marks the turning point in the action.

Coherence   Coherence clearly, consistently, and logically connects the parts in a piece of writing. It is the glue that holds together all vigorous, effective writing. Among other techniques, coherence invokes **transitions** to show introductory relationships among ideas, paragraphing to signal shifts in thought, sentences that follow reasonably from those which came before them, and **diction** appropriate to the **audience**.

Colloquial expressions   Colloquial expressions, such as "Don't even try to psych out Professor Sherman" and "Ralph crammed all his stuff into his closet" characterize informal (and often playful) speaking and writing. Therefore they have limited use in formal writing because their very casualness can distract readers.

Comparison and contrast   A comparison involves similarities; a contrast involves differences. Combining these two ways of judging qualities can lead to discoveries about two things formerly thought to be ordinarily alike or unalike. A writer who compares and contrasts an electric typewriter and a computer discovers that whatever an electric typewriter can do, a computer with a word-processing program and printer can do more efficiently (a comparison). The writer will also discover the many things that a computer, equipped with various programs, can do that a typewriter cannot possibly do, such as maintaining a continuous record of household expenditures (a contrast). On the other hand, the writer will discover that both machines can be used for writing brief informal notes, but a computer can also retain easily correctable copies of those notes on a disk (comparison and contrast).

Conclusions   Conclusions are ways of ending essays. The way in which an essay is concluded depends in great part on the content of the essay itself. An essay arguing for or against gun control is likely to end by restating the reasons for taking one position or another. An essay explaining one of the complex relation-ships between human beings and nature might conclude by warning the reader that the relationship is endangered. An essay with several examples of how the world's economies are intertwined might end with one sterling example of an economy that is vitally connected to our own. An essayist offering information about an inexpensive medicine for a common disease might conclude by recommending that readers consult their personal physicians for more information.

Conclusions do not drift into other topics, nor do they shift an essay's emphasis away from its own topic. A writer would not end an essay taking a firm stand against showing pornographic movies on television by writing something like, "It all depends on each person's tastes."

So-called cute conclusions suggest to the audience that the writer was not deeply involved in thinking about the essay's content. They should be avoided.

Conclusions grow logically and sufficiently from the essay, and they should bring an essay to a satisfying close.

Concrete   Concrete words or expressions refer to things experienced by the senses, as opposed to **abstractions**. These words and expressions are concrete: *chair, perfume, music, automobile, bitter, cardboard box, dictionary, window*, and *refrigerator*.

Conflict   In writing, a conflict is a struggle that grows from two opposing beliefs, values, characters, and so on, which are developed in the **body** of the piece.

Connotation   The word *connotation* describes the implied meanings that become attached to words. *Skinny* and *slender* both mean thin or slight, but the first has negative connotations (emaciation and perhaps ill health), and the latter implies grace, even elegance.

The descriptive phrase *cheap furniture* carries connotations of shoddy workmanship and poor quality. The phrase *inexpensive furniture*, however, implies only the furniture's low cost. Although *cheap* and *inexpensive* are dictionary synonyms, the meaning implied in *cheap* sets it apart from *inexpensive*. Careful writers keep in mind what words mean according to dictionaries and what those same words may imply beyond their dictionary definitions.

Data   The proofs in Stephen Toulmin's model of reasoning are *data*. They are the evidence that supports the model's **claim,** or conclusion.

Data are also nonartistic proofs (see **argument**) used in other models of reasoning. These kinds of data come from scientific observations, record keeping, or statistics—facts or figures from which conclusions can be inferred, and information from credible, reliable sources.

Deduction　A deduction is the result of reasoning from a general statement to a specific instance. If your college requires that all prospective students be tested in a foreign language before they are enrolled, then you can reason that Pat, who sits next to you in English class, has taken a test in a foreign language. Deductions are not always that clear-cut, though.

One might think that all small cars get good gas mileage and then buy a small car to save money on fuel, only to find that this car gets poor mileage. The original assumption, then, was false.

Definition　A definition outlines, limits, or states the meaning of a word, term, phrase, or concept.

A formal definition puts a term into a class and then shows how it differs from other members of the same class. A trumpet (term) is a brass musical wind instrument (class) consisting of a tube in an oblong loop or loops, with a flared bell at one end, a curved mouthpiece at the other, and three valves for making tonal changes (difference).

An extended definition, a form of **exposition**, not only defines in the senses above but also explains issues by employing rhetorical strategies, such as **narration, description, example**, and **classification**.

Denotation　The term *denotation* applies to the literal, lexical meaning of a word—that which is explained in a good dictionary.

Description　The technique of making pictures with words is *description*. An effective description includes clear evidence that appeals to one or more of the senses—sight, touch, taste, smell, or hearing—as well as **explanation**. A sentence from Henry David Thoreau's "The Battle of the Ants," demonstrates this combination of description and explanation: "his own breast was all torn away, exposing what vitals he had there to the jaws of the black warrior, whose breastplate was apparently too thick for him to pierce; and the dark carbuncles of the sufferer's eyes shone with ferocity such as only war could excite."

Diction   Diction is deliberate choice of words. Writers conscientiously choose words and the ways in which they use them, being guided by their audience and their purpose. Writers make their selections from various levels of usage, including **standard English, slang**, conversational expressions, regionalisms (choosing among "spigot," "tap," and "faucet"), and scientific and technical **jargon**.

Consider these sentences:

1. "Christine resigned her position."
2. "Chris quit her job."
3. "Chris told him he could take his job and shove it!"

What determines which of these sentences is correct? The audience and the purpose.

Sentence 1 is appropriate for a formal audience and a formal purpose. Perhaps the writer's audience was college-level readers and the purpose was to describe her best friend's employment difficulties.

Sentence 2 might have been for a semiformal audience and a semiformal purpose, such as writing an essay for the readers of a college alumnae newsletter to help graduates keep track of their classmates.

Sentence 3 might have been for an informal audience and purpose, such as writing an essay for other members of a composition class to explain how one of them had reacted to being treated poorly by the manager of a local pizza parlor.

Whoever the audience and whatever the purpose, writers are guided by their own sense of propriety and by dictionaries and a thesaurus. They rarely use a thesaurus, however, without also consulting a dictionary to be sure that the words they have chosen from the thesaurus are in fact appropriate for their audience and purpose.

Direct quotation   The presentation of the precise words of a source is a direct quotation. Direct quotations should be set off by quotation marks, but if a quotation is more than four lines long in a typewritten paper, it should be set off by putting it in block form—that is, by indenting the entire passage ten spaces (or one inch) and double spacing before and after the passage. Do not use quotation marks in block quotations unless they appear in the passage being quoted.

Directive process analysis   A directive process analysis tells how to do something. It is a sequence of directions to guide a reader who wants to complete a specific task. Such an analysis tells how to plant a tree, but *not* how a tree grows, the latter topic being an **informative process analysis**.

Division   Division is a subclass of **classification**. Writers divide a classification into logical parts, usually for description or explanation. Let's say that a writer wanted to describe a personal computer. First, you would classify it, telling how it differs from mainframe computers, from large industrial computers, and from laptop computers. Then you would divide the home computer into its logical parts: the keyboard, the central processing unit, and the video monitor. After making that division, you would describe each of these components. By your division you help the reader to see one component at a time, rather than try to imagine an entire home computer all at once.

Dominant impression   The dominant impression is the main sensation or conception that the author strives to fix in the reader's mind, by carefully shaping the details of a **description**.

Effect   It is part of **cause and effect**, the result or outcome of an occurrence or action, but the word *effect* also refers to the impression that writing—whether a word, sentence, paragraph, essay, or larger work—makes on its audience.

Emphasis   With emphasis, writers emphasize or highlight the things they want their readers to see as most important in their writing. Writers use such **strategies** as **diction**, sentence structure, position, active voice, repetition, and mechanics to emphasize their main points.

Diction: A writer who wanted to emphasize a negative opinion of a newly opened restaurant could write, "This restaurant has food fit to eat only if you are starving."

Sentence structure: If you wanted to emphasize your opinion of the food itself, you could write a periodic sentence, which moves from supporting details to the main idea. "With lukewarm coffee, half-cooked cold chicken, salty mashed potatoes, and burned vegetables, my meal was barely edible." You could emphasize your description of the food by writing a loose sentence, in which the supporting details follow the main idea: "I had a barely edible meal of lukewarm coffee, half-cooked cold chicken, salty mashed potatoes, and burned vegetables."

Position: That which we read last, we remember longest, whether chapters in a book, groups of words in a sentence, or paragraphs in an essay. Commenting on an unsavory experience in a restaurant, you might begin a paper by describing how you had read about the restaurant in a respectable tourist guide, where it had been awarded three stars. Then you might devote a short paragraph to the small problem you had in finding the place because it was in a part of the city unfamiliar to the taxicab driver, who had been profusely apologetic. You then might describe the restaurant's décor, a delightful amalgam of French Provincial and Early American, and your waitress, a pleasant young lady dressed in a peasant frock, who was also attending law school at the nearby university. Finally, because you had been shocked at the poor quality of the food, in utter contrast to the treat you had been expecting, you might conclude the essay with a paragraph meant to shock your readers as well, thus emphasizing the most important point in your experience by putting it last.

Active voice: Verbs in active voice—"This restaurant serves poorly prepared food"—are more emphatic than those in passive voice: "Poorly prepared food is served by this restaurant."

Repetition: "I spent a valuable hour of my vacation sipping the lukewarm coffee at Harry's Restaurant, chewing Harry's half-cooked chicken, tasting the salty mashed potatoes at Harry's, and staring at the vegetables Harry burned. Never again will I eat in Harry's Restaurant."

Mechanics: Usually, the least appropriate way to emphasize formal writing, mechanics include underlining, quotation marks, and exclamation points: "When I was served the 'food' I had ordered in this 'restaurant,' I was *shocked* to see how *poorly* it had been prepared!" Such devices must be used sparingly. Your emphasis will be more successfully communicated with diction, sentence structure, position, active voice, and repetition.

Essay   The word *essay* is from the French *essai,* meaning "attempt" or "experiment." In English, an essay is a relatively short piece of nonfiction prose on a specified topic. It is an attempt by a writer to persuade, inform, explain, argue, describe, narrate, expose, or in some other way organize and develop a topic to interest an **audience**.

Essays are occasionally defined as informal or formal, although the definitions admittedly are vague. Generally, however, a formal essay includes **diction** appropriate to a serious audience, has a serious **tone**, and is focused on a serious topic. An informal essay, on the other hand, often has a light, perhaps humorous tone and informal language, and is focused on a personal, perhaps frivolous topic.

Evaluation   An evaluation determines the worth or quality of a work. If you are revising your own work or reading someone else's, you try to evaluate it objectively, to see how well it fulfills its purpose. Usually, those who evaluate a work look to see how well its thesis is stated and supported, how strongly its proofs support its claims, how clearly it is organized, whether or not its language is clear, and whether or not it is appropriately written for its intended audience.

Evidence   Evidence is support for a theory, claim, or **thesis**. The commonest kinds of evidence are obvious evidence, manifest evidence, and clear evidence. Obvious evidence, usually scientific, is readily perceived or easily inferred. If $6 + 2 + x = 9$, then the evidence is obvious that $x = 1$. Manifest evidence is immediately clear to the understanding, often by intuition. If you see water in its solid state, then you know almost without thinking that it is frozen. Clear evidence, the kind essayists use most often, supports and clarifies a reader's understanding of the writer's thesis. If the writer's thesis is that marriage vows are hopelessly outmoded, then you must offer clear evidence to support that thesis. You must examine and clarify the vows, compare them with the spousal responsibilities in modern marriages, illustrate how those vows conflict with reality, and so on.

Examples   An example is an instance that follows and illustrates the assertion in a statement. Among the more usual are specific examples, typical examples, and hypothetical examples. Specific examples amplify one experience, event, incident, or fact. They clarify in detail your earlier statement. Typical examples illustrate many experiences, events, incidents, or facts. They clarify generally your earlier statement, so that they will be representative. Hypothetical examples are imagined or supposed representations. They clarify the probability of your earlier statement.

Exposition   An exposition is a detailed explanation of the content of an idea, an object, an attitude, or a position. An exposition exposes, makes something accessible to a reader, by using any of a number of **strategies**, including examples, comparisons and contrasts, analogies, and classifications. Most essays in this book are expository, as are most essays written in college.

False analogy   *See* **Logical fallacies**.

Faulty either/or reasoning   *See* **Logical fallacies**.

Figures of speech   Tropes, or figures of speech, make a clear style vivid by adding **connotations** to statements, which appeal to the reader's imagination. The most used figures of speech are metaphor, simile, personification, hyperbole (overstatement), litotes (understatement), synecdoche, metonymy, and paradox.

A *metaphor* is an implied comparison between two dissimilar things: "Jamie is the tiger on the team." Tigers are noted for their speed, intelligence, and strength—the attributes that this metaphor gives to Jamie.

A *simile* is an explicit comparison between two dissimilar things, using the word *as* or *like*: "Jamie is as southern as Georgia."

Personification gives human qualities to inanimate objects or abstract ideas: "Six tall, menacing pine trees guard our campus at night."

Hyperbole (overstatement) is deliberate exaggeration used for emphasis: "It was raining so hard that I almost drowned while driving to school."

Litotes (understatement) is deliberate understatement used for emphasis: "Getting a D on my history test was not my greatest birthday present."

Synecdoche substitutes part of something for the whole: "Two hands left the ship just before it sailed." In this example, *hands* substitutes for "sailors."

Metonymy substitutes the whole for a part of something: "The Pentagon said today that, except for Near Eastern flareups, fewer troops will be needed in the next decade." In this example, *The Pentagon* substitutes for "a spokesperson for the army."

A *paradox* appears to be contradictory, but in fact carries some truth: "The wealthier you are, the poorer you may be." Wealth is not always measured by money. It is also measured by wisdom, knowledge, morality, love, and other qualities.

Focus   In photography a subject that is in focus is sharply defined. That is also true in writing. Writers who focus on their subject bring it into sharp detail. They begin by thinking about a large unfocused topic, such as "crime in the streets." Then they may decide to focus on some part of crime in the streets—"street crime in our city." After they have found their focus, they may narrow it even more—to "street crime in my neighborhood." How sharply they focus on a subject often depends on their **audience** and **purpose**.

General and specific   General words are names for broad classes of things, from which you can move to words that designate members of those classes. One broad class is *automobiles*. A term that designates a member of that class is *sports car*. A designation for a more specific member of the sports-car class is *Alfa Romeo*. Writers are guided by their **audience** and by their **purpose** when they choose among general and specific names.

Generalization   A generalization is a broad statement that rests on personal observation or acquired information. The sentence "Children usually follow their parents' advice" suggests that its writer has experience with raising children and from that experience has written a generalization that includes all children.

Writers sometimes begin with generalizations and then move toward conclusions based on their generalizations. But to avoid hasty generalizations, they often use qualifiers in their conclusions: "She has a degree in English, and so she *probably* knows a lot about

Shakespeare." Or "She has a degree in English, and so she *might* know *something* about Shakespeare." *See also* **induction**.

Grounds   The data that serve as proof in Stephen Toulmin's reasoning model. The grounds are the evidence that supports the model's **claim** or conclusion.

Hyperbole   *See* **Figures of speech.**

Hypothetical examples   *See* **Examples.**

Image   An image appeals to the imagination through the senses. It is a **strategy** many writers apply to help readers "see" what they are reading. The sentence, "Her ancient face was a sheaf of small etched road maps to nowhere," is an image that describes an old and wrinkled countenance. The sentence, "He sings the songs of an old man's childhood, the golden past that never was," describes a person who reminisces about former times, which seem far more attractive now ("the golden past") than they were then.

Induction   An induction is the result of reasoning that interprets limited evidence to arrive at a general truth. A person who has owned three or four friendly and alert cocker spaniels over the years may reason that all cocker spaniels are friendly and alert.

Inductive reasoning is useful in writing because it is a powerful persuader. Writers who want to persuade readers of a general truth use enough sound evidence to make their claims reasonably acceptable. If you wanted to persuade readers of the benefits in jogging, you might offer as evidence all your healthy friends who jog, newspaper articles that endorse jogging as a healthy activity, well-known athletes who jog, your doctor's saying that jogging promotes health, and so on. The more sound evidence you present, the more apt the reader is to accept your persuasive **argument**.

Informative process analysis   With an informative process analysis, you tell how something is done. You describe sequentially the steps in a natural procedure that does not involve intervention. An informative process analysis might tell how a tree grows, but *not* how to plant a tree, the latter topic being a **directive process analysis**.

Introduction   An introduction begins a piece of writing. An effective introduction establishes the essay's topic, tone, and territory. It leads directly into the main idea or issue discussed in the **body** of the paper. Its purpose is to engender readers' interest. To achieve that purpose, writers include such **strategies** as **rhetorical questions**, unusual facts, **anecdotes**, and personal comments.

The length of an introduction depends on the essay's **purpose** and its intended **audience**.

Invention   Writers use invention to develop their subjects. It includes planning the piece of writing, thinking of ways of organizing material, of presenting material, and of deciding how to handle questions that you anticipate readers will raise.

Irony   A difference between appearance and reality creates irony. When it compliments, it is ironically condemning. When it condemns, it is ironically complimenting. The sentence "What a magnificent car," when used to describe a rusting hulk sitting in a junkyard, is ironic. The sentence "It's not a bad paint job," when used to describe Michelangelo's Sistine Chapel ceiling, is ironic. When the irony is not subtle but is intended to cause deliberate offense, it is called **sarcasm**. If someone says, "Thank you. It's just what I've always wanted," when reacting to the ketchup stain you accidentally put on her new blouse, she is using sarcasm.

When they are contrary to our anticipation, situations can also be ironic. You might discover that you were not hired for a job because you failed a company's mandatory typing test, only to learn that the job for which you applied required no typing at all.

Jargon   Jargon is technical vocabulary that is appropriate only among experts in a field. As a kind of shorthand, it saves time in their communication. Among themselves lawyers use such expressions as "caveat," "entrapment," "estoppel," "the M'Naghten Rule," and "mens rea," knowing that they all understand legal jargon. To a lay listener, however, the words mean little. For lay audiences, writers use jargon sparingly, and when they do use it, they include definitions.

Another kind of jargon, sometimes called bureaucratese, is nothing more than pompous **diction** used more to impress readers than to inform them. The sentence "Our consumer demand analysis precludes our implementation of the proposed planning stage"—which means, by the way, "We don't need to plan to produce something that no one wants to buy"—typifies the jargon of pomposity.

Litotes *See* **Figures of speech.**

Logical fallacies Mistakes in reasoning that lead to faulty conclusions are logical fallacies or fallacious reasoning.

An *ad hominem argument* attacks a person rather than the issue that is being considered.

The *association fallacy* suggests that an act or belief is worthy or unworthy merely because of the people who are associated with it.

A writer falls into *false analogy* by presuming that if two things are alike in one or more ways, then they must be alike in other ways as well.

The *either/or fallacy* is a type of oversimplification in which a writer assumes only two alternatives are possible when in fact many others should be considered.

A *non sequitur* is a conclusion that does not follow from the premise.

A writer making an *overgeneralization* draws a conclusion from insufficient or unrepresentative evidence.

With an *oversimplification*, we draw a conclusion while ignoring information essential to the subject.

Someone who accepts the *post hoc* argument assumes that if one event occurred before another, then the second event was caused by the first.

Metaphor *See* **Figures of speech.**

Metonymy *See* **Figures of speech.**

Narration A narration tells a story and often includes extensive **description**. Narrations, usually chronological, include among their purposes entertaining, informing, and instructing. Some narrations have a plot, a story line that moves toward an insight about the principal character in the narration.

Narrative effect   The main **effect** from reading a **narration** is named the *narrative effect*. Each narration incorporates a reason for being. Writers decide the main effect that their narrative should have on their readers, and then form the narrative so as not to depart from their decision.

Non sequitur   *See* **Logical fallacies.**

Nonstandard English   Words and expressions that are often spoken but rarely written except when the writer has a clear reason for using them sometimes include nonstandard English. Some examples are *ain't, nohow, irregardless, theirselves, hisself, we'uns, could care less* (for "could not care less"), and *them* (instead of *those*), as in *Them people ain't got no smarts*, instead of "Those people do not seem intelligent."

Objective and subjective   Objective writing is designed to be a distanced, factual account presented in language that is plain, direct, and free of value judgments. Pure objectivity is hard to achieve because people's perceptions are almost always colored by their experiences, their values, and their biases. But in writing such as scientific papers and technical reports, authors strive for objectivity. Subjective writing is more personal, more indicative of the writer's thoughts, feelings, and attitudes. The emphasis here is on the writer's relationship to the topic rather than the topic itself. Very few essays are exclusively objective or subjective. Most often, writings combine the two.

Opening   An opening is the first part of a three-part narrative essay. The other two parts are the body and the climax. The beginning sentences usually capture the reader's attention without giving away the outcome. The opening may hint at the purpose of the story about to unfold, but may not actually reveal it.

Order of ideas   Ideas can be arranged in various ways, but all are derived from the subject and the writer's purpose. The order may be spatial, moving from top to bottom, side to side, or background to foreground. Or the order may simply be chronological, as in a narrative. The writer may work from least important to most important. The sequence of ideas should always be well thought out, chosen for its greatest effect.

Overgeneralization   *See* **Logical fallacies**.

Oversimplification   *See* **Logical fallacies**.

Paradox   *See* **Figures of speech**.

Paragraph   The paragraph is the basic unit in an essay. It is composed of a group of closely related sentences that together develop one of the essay's main ideas. The main or unifying idea of a paragraph is usually stated in a topic sentence, often found at the beginning of the paragraph. All other sentences in the paragraph relate directly to the topic sentence, thus establishing unity and coherence. But occasionally, a unified and coherent paragraph has no topic sentence. The paragraph then undoubtedly has a leading idea that is strongly implied in every sentence. Paragraphs also work visually in an essay, graphically demonstrating the progress of ideas and also providing visual relief to the reader.

Parallel structure   The repetition of similar grammatical elements within or between sentences makes a parallel structure. Logic dictates that grammatical elements with equal value in a sentence be constructed in the same grammatical form. Thus "I prefer running, jumping, and to swim" does not exhibit parallelism, but does have awkwardness. "I prefer running, jumping, and swimming" demonstrates parallelism and logic. Parallel structure is also a stylistic technique that is often used to create emphasis and drama. The long fourth sentence in paragraph 14 of Martin Luther King, Jr.'s "Letter from Birmingham Jail" (Chapter 13) is a particularly effective example of parallel structure.

Paraphrase   A paraphrase is a restatement of another person's words in your own words. This technique is particularly necessary in writing any essay in which you use others' ideas or words as evidence supporting your own argument. Often, you paraphrase instead of using a direct quotation in order to more easily mold the idea to fit your argument. The sense of the original, as well as the tone and order of ideas, remains the same. In either a paraphrase or a direct quotation you must give credit to your source. In a more informal paper you incorporate the credit into your text: "According to Charles Neerland, being a Minneapolitan means being cold much of the year." In more formal writing, such as a research paper, footnoting is required.

Person The grammatical distinction between the speaker (first person: I, we); the person spoken to (second person: you, singular and plural); and the subject spoken about (third person: he, she, it, or they) is labeled *person*.

Persona A fictional speaker in an essay or the fictional narrator of a story is its persona. The character, attitudes, and ideas of the persona are often different from those of the author. In fact, it is often the persona's character, attitudes, and ideas that are held up for criticism.

Personification *See* **Figures of speech**.

Persuasion or persuasive argument Persuasive writing is an attempt to win readers to a point of view and, often, move them to action. It appeals primarily to the emotions, as opposed to *argument*, which is meant to win the reader by reason and logic. Most often, the two are used together.

Plagiarism Presenting someone else's words or ideas as if they were your own is plagiarism. It is a serious offense in the academic world and can lead to consequences such as failure and expulsion from school. Whenever you use someone else's words or ideas you must give that person credit in your own text or by citation (*see* **paraphrase**).

Point-by-point and subject-by-subject development These are the two basic methods for developing a comparison-and-contrast essay. Point-by-point development alternately presents each point being considered. Subject-by-subject development presents all the details about one side of the argument first and follows with all the details about the other side.

Point of view In an argumentative essay the point of view is the author's opinion or the thesis the writer hopes to advance. In expository essays it is the physical or mental vantage point from which the author views the subject. An essay on professional football told from a player's firsthand experience would be approached differently from that of the team's owner (whose interest may be exclusively financial) or from that of a newspaper reporter. Each would approach the subject with a different kind of authority. And that authority would mean a difference in vocabulary, style, and tone. The player might use first **person** to capture immediacy. The owner might want to involve the reader in experiencing her financial woes and so use second person. Or, to create a mood of objectivity, the reporter might use the third person. The point of view in an essay must remain consistent. An inconsistent point of view can leave the reader confused and disconcerted.

Post hoc argument   *See* **Logical fallacies**.

Premise   A deductive **syllogism** is composed of two premises and a conclusion. The first or major premise is an assumption, and the second or minor premise is a fact or another assumption based on evidence: All mammals are animals (first premise is an assumption). Raccoons are mammals (second premise is a fact). Therefore, all raccoons are animals (conclusion is logically deduced from the two premises).

Prewriting   All the activities a writer goes through before actually beginning to write are part of *prewriting*. These might consist of brainstorming for a subject, doing background reading, narrowing the subject, devising a thesis, planning the essay—everything, in other words, that leads to the actual writing.

Probable conclusions   Conclusions arrived at by inductive reasoning and from incomplete evidence are *probable conclusions*. The reader's acceptance of a conclusion that follows from inductive reasoning is often referred to as the *inductive leap*. To establish a clear connection between the evidence and the conclusion, the writer must be sure to present **relevant evidence, sufficient evidence**, and **representative evidence**.

Process Analysis   In process analysis a writer examines the way in which something works. Though somewhat similar to narration and cause and effect, process analysis concentrates on how something happens, whereas narration concentrates on what happened and cause and effect concentrates on why it happened. Process analysis comes in two forms: **directive process analysis** and **informative process analysis**.

Proposition or **thesis**   In argument the proposition or thesis is a written assertion, the opinion the writer wants a reader to accept, or an action the writer wants a reader to take.

Psychological time   Arranging events in a narrative so as to show how they are connected in memory, shifting back and forth in time while keeping a sense of forward movement, creates *psychological time*.

Purpose   The goal the writer wants to achieve is the *purpose*. The clearer the writer's purpose, the more clarity, coherence, and unity the essay will have. If the writer's purpose is muddled, the essay too will be muddled. All kinds of purposes are possible: to entertain with an amusing story; to inform; to convince readers of a point of view and move them to action. These purposes can be achieved by using the rhetorical modes: narration, description, exposition, and argument. In an essay you may use them alone or in combination.

Qualification   Tempering broad statements to make them more logically acceptable is the technique called *qualification*. In qualifying a statement, the writer admits that exceptions to that assertion are possible or probable, thereby indicating that the statement is not oversimplified. In these days with much emphasis on physical fitness, the statement "Physical exercise is good" might, at first blush, seem valid. But exercise may, in fact, be detrimental to some people. Therefore the statement needs qualifying. "Exercise is good for most people" might be a more acceptable statement.

Reason and result   Another way of saying **cause and effect**.

Refutation   The attempt to counter an opposing argument by revealing its weaknesses is called *refutation*. You must refute the opposition's argument if it is obvious and is strong or logical enough to be a real alternative to your own. The refutation usually is done early in an argumentative essay to get it out of the way so that you can proceed with your own argument. The three most usual strategies are pointing out weaknesses in the opposition's evidence, questioning the argument's relevance, and pointing out errors in logic. Refutation indicates that the writer is aware the issue is complex and is willing to consider opposing opinions. To be effective, refutation must always be done in a moderate tone and must always be accurate in representing the opposing argument. To do otherwise is to risk being judged harshly by the reader for sounding intemperate and for treating the opposition unfairly.

Relevant evidence   You can directly support the essay's thesis and contribute directly to its conclusion with relevant evidence (*see* **representative evidence** and **sufficient evidence**).

Representative evidence   Representative evidence covers the full range of information related to an essay's thesis, not just one side or the other. An argument cannot be convincing unless evidence from every point of view is admitted (*see* **relevant evidence** and **sufficient evidence**).

Representative sample   A representative sample is a typical example chosen from examples that exhibit similar characteristics.

Rhetoric   Rhetoric is the study and art of using prose effectively. The various methods of prose discourse described and exemplified in this textbook—narration, description, exposition, and argument—are rhetorical forms.

Rhetorical question   A rhetorical question is posed for effect and no answer is expected. It is a question meant to provoke thought or to launch the writer into the subject to be discussed in the writing.

Satire   The form of writing using wit, irony, and ridicule to attack foolish and vicious human behavior and the institutions and customs that promote such behavior is *satire*. Two main types of satire are at the writer's disposal: social satire, which is used to attack foolish but not dangerous behavior and does it by invoking laughter and sympathy and ethical satire, which is far sharper and points with anger and indignation at social corruption and evil.

Scene and summary   Events in a narrative essay are presented in two methods—**scene** and **summary**. Scene directly portrays the details of an event on the page, as if a reader were watching the event unfold moment by moment. In narrative essay writing, summary (which should not be confused with a brief recapitulation of previously stated information) refers to a synopsis on an event. Whereas scene relates an event's specific details, summary leaves out the detail and relates an event's high points.

Sentimentality   Sentimental writing overemotionalizes its subject and thus becomes ineffective. Sentimentality is often emotion displayed for the sake of emotion, losing connection with the actuality of the thing that supposedly caused the emotion. Sentimental writers risk readers' ridicule because they don't fully acquaint the reader with that actuality and thus appear to overreact.

Simile   *See* **Figures of speech.**

Slang   Colorful and humorous expressions, mostly short-lived and often peculiar to a group of people, are called *slang*. Almost always informal, slang is unacceptable in formal writing except in quotations and for creating special effects.

Specific examples   *See* **Examples.**

Standard English   The English language in its most widely accepted form, written and spoken by educated people in both formal and informal contexts, and having universal currency though it incorporates regional differences, is *standard English*.

Strategy   The means by which writers effectively accomplish their purpose is *strategy*, which involves evaluating the audience, narrowing the subject, choosing a dominant rhetorical pattern such as narration, description, examples, comparison and contrast, and definition, among others.

Style   The distinctive way in which a writer writes creates an individual *style*. Choice of words, structure of sentences, use or nonuse of figurative language—all contribute to a writer's style. Two writers may write about the same subject, have the same attitude toward the subject (see **tone**), and yet "sound" distinctly different. Style is a writer's writing personality and can be developed with practice.

Subject-by-subject development   *See* **Point-by-point development.**

Sufficient evidence   In an argumentative paper you must supply ample evidence to convincingly support your conclusion (*see* **relevant evidence** and **representative evidence**).

Summary   A summary is a comprehensive and usually brief recapitulation of previously stated facts or statements. Summarizing your main points is one way of concluding a paper.

Suspense   The pleasurable uncertainty or excitement we feel when anticipating what will happen next as we read a story is *suspense*. This tactic is most evident in mystery or detective stories but is less dramatically present in much narration.

Syllogism   A form of deductive reasoning composed of two premises and a conclusion is the *syllogism*. The first premise (major premise) is an assumption and the second (minor premise) is a fact or another assumption based on **evidence**. The conclusion is logically deduced from the two premises: All human beings are animals (major premise is an assumption). Ephraim is a human (minor premise is a fact). Therefore, Ephraim is an animal (conclusion is logically deduced from the two premises).

Symbol   A symbol is any concrete thing that means something beyond itself. Many symbols are, on the surface, clear-cut and readily acceptable. The flag, of course, represents country and elicits patriotic feeling. But ideas and attitudes differ about what constitutes patriotism and what things conjure patriotic feelings. Some people become proud when their country asserts itself militarily. Others find their patriotic values in freedom, tolerance, fairness, and compassion. The flag, a rather simple symbol as symbols go, therefore has a complex of powerful meanings beyond itself. Symbols are employed most in fiction and poetry, less in exposition and argument. But they can be used in the latter to express meaning concisely and palpably.

Synecdoche   *See* **Figures of speech.**

Thesis   The thesis is the main point in expository writing, an idea that all the other ideas and facts in an essay should point to and support. A thesis can be either clearly stated or implied. It is most commonly found at the end of an early paragraph. A thesis cannot be a statement of fact, because facts do not need proving. A thesis, therefore, must have an argumentative edge, a point of view that will be proven or demonstrated in some way somewhere in the paper.

Tone   Diction, sentence variety, figurative language, and anything else that establishes the writer's attitude toward the subject forms the tone, which can vary extensively. A writer's tone can be amused, angry, exasperated, approving, surprised, sarcastic. It can, in other words, run the gamut of human emotions. But tone should be consistent, for it must inform the entire essay and lead the reader to the response the writer desires.

Topic sentence   A topic sentence states the main idea of a paragraph. All other sentences in the paragraph support the topic sentence. Most often, it appears at the beginning but can be placed anywhere in the paragraph.

Transitions   Transitions are words, phrases, sentences, and paragraphs that link ideas. Because a reader cannot get into the writer's head, it is the writer's responsibility to make sure that the ideas are clearly stated and that relationships between the ideas are clear. The first way to ensure that clarity is to organize ideas so that they flow logically from one to another. But even sturdier bridges are needed to carry the reader from sentence to sentence and from paragraph to paragraph. For this continuity you will need to use transitional devices such as these:

1. In the first sentence of a paragraph, repeat some words or phrases from the last sentences in the preceding paragraph.
2. Use pronouns to refer to nouns in the preceding paragraph. You must be careful here to make precisely clear which words the pronouns refer to.
3. Use transitional expressions to carry the reader.

Addition: also, in addition, too, moreover, and besides, further, furthermore, equally important, next, then, finally.

Example: for example, for instance, thus, as an illustration, namely, specifically.

Contrast: but, yet, however, on the other hand, nevertheless, conversely, in contrast, on the contrary, still, at the same time.

Comparison: similarly, likewise, in like manner, in the same way, in comparison.

Concession: of course, to be sure, certainly, naturally, granted.

Result: therefore, thus, consequently, so, accordingly.

Summary: as a result, hence, in short, in brief, in summary, in conclusion, finally, on the whole.

Time sequence: first, second, third, fourth, next, then, finally, afterward, before, soon, later, during, meanwhile, subsequently, immediately, at length, eventually, in the future, currently.

Place: at the front, in the foreground, at the back, in the back-ground, at the side, adjacent, nearby, in the distance, here, there.

Two-part classification   Often called *binary*, two-part classification is the simplest way of breaking a subject down. This pattern divides the subject in two, usually into positive and negative categories, such as vegetarians and nonvegetarians; smokers and nonsmokers; television viewers and nonviewers of television, and so on. But two-part classification is usually inexact and skirts the edge of comparison and contrast. Most classification systems therefore have at least three categories.

Typical examples   *See* **Examples.**

Understatement (Litotes)   *See* **Figures of speech.**

Unity   In a paragraph, every idea and every sentence relates directly to and helps support the main idea, usually stated in the topic sentence. Likewise, in the essay as a whole, every unified paragraph points to and supports the essay's main idea expressed in the thesis.

Warrant   Warrant is the supporting argument in Toulmin's model of reasoning (*see* **Claim**).

Writing process   The various tasks a writer must perform to produce a piece of writing are called the writing process. **Prewriting** entails a series of activities that pave the way for the actual writing. Only after this stage can the writer make the first draft, revise it into a number of subsequent drafts, and then polish it to achieve the final product.

Text Credits

Chapter 1

"In Defense of Talk Shows" by Barbara Ehrenreich from *Time,* December 4, 1995. Copyright © 1995 by Barbara Ehrenreich. Reprinted by permission of International Creative Management, Inc.

Chapter 5

From *The Woman Warrior* by Maxine Hong Kingston, copyright © 1975, 1976 by Maxine Hong Kingston. Used by permission of Alfred A. Knopf, a division of Random House, Inc.

"Hyena" Joanna Greenfield. First published in *The New Yorker,* Nov. 11, 1996. Reprinted by permission of International Creative Management, Inc. Copyright © 1996 Joanna Greenfield.

Excerpt from "Cop Diary" by Marcus Laffey. Adapted from an article originally published by *The New Yorker,* November 10, 1997. Copyright © 1997 by Marcus Laffey. Reprinted by permission of William Morris Agency, Inc. on behalf of the Author.

"The War Room at Bellevue" by George Simpson. Originally published by *New York Magazine,* 1983. Reprinted by permission of the author.

From *A Match to the Heart* by Gretel Ehrlich, copyright © 1994 by Gretel Ehrlich. Used by permission of Pantheon Books, a division of Random House, Inc.

Chapter 6

"Lady of the Ring" Rene Denfeld from *The New York Times Magazine,* August 24, 1997, Section 6. Reprinted by permission of the author. Rene Denfeld is the author of *The New Victorians* and *Kill the Body, the Head Will Fall.*

"Watching My Back" by Jeff Z. Klein from *The New York Times,* July 29, 2001. Copyright © 2001 by The New York Times Co. Reprinted with permission.

May Akabogu-Collins, "Coming to America." Reprinted by permission of the author.

Ryan Boudinot, "The Littlest Hitler." Copyright © 2002 by Ryan Boudinot; originally printed in *Mississippi* Review. Reprinted by permission of Melanie Jackson Agency, L.L.C.

Chapter 7

Chapter 8

Chapter 9

"Why We Crave Horror Movies" by Stephen King. Originally appeared in *Playboy*, 1982. Copyright © Stephen King. Reprinted with permission. All rights reserved.

"How Urban Myths reveal Society's Fears" by Neal Babler. Originally published by *The Los Angeles Times*, November 12, 1995. Reprinted by permission of the author. Neal Gabler is the author of *An Empire of Their Own: How the Jews Invented Hollywood*; *Winchell: Gossip, Power, and the Culture of Celebrity*; and *Life the Movie: How Entertainment Conquered Reality*.

Gina Greenlee, "No Tears for Frankie," from *The New York Times Magazine*, June 10, 2001. Copyright © 2001 by Gina Greenlee. Reprinted by permission of the author.

Michael Moore, "Why Doesn't GM Sell Crack? from *Downsize This*. Copyright © 1996 by Michael Moore. Used by permission of Crown Publishers, a division of Random House, Inc.

Marshall Brain, "Relax, Wage Slaves—Robots Promise You an Endless Vacation" from *The Los Angeles Times*, Oct. 15, 2003. Reprinted with permission.

Chapter 10

"Anatomy of a Joke" by Gary Trudeau *The New York Times*, August 1, 1993. Copyright © 1993 by The New York Times Co. Reprinted by permission.

Headline from *The Washington Post*, Friday, July 23, 1993. Copyright © 1993 by *The Washington Post*. Reprinted with permission.

"Rat Patrol: A Saga" by Frank Gannon from *Harper's* magazine. Copyright © 1996 by *Harper's* magazine. All rights reserved. Reproduced from the magazine by special permission.

"The Maker's Eye: Revising Your Own Manuscripts" by Donald M. Murray from *The Writer*, October, 1973.

Chapter 11

"The World of Doublespeak" from *Doublespeak* by William Lutz. Copyright © 1989 by Blonde Bear, Inc. Reprinted by permission of the Jean V. Naggar Literary Agency.

"My Habit" by Paul Sheehan. First published by *The New Yorker* magazine. Copyright © 1996 by Paul Sheehan. Reprinted by permission of the author

"Exercising the Brain" by Jim Spring from *American Demographics*, October 1993. Copyright, Crain Communications, Inc. 2004. Reprinted with permission.

Photo Credits